# ALERTING AMERICA

# Pergamon Titles of Related Interest

**Borisov et al** MODERN DIPLOMACY OF CAPITALIST POWERS
**Hart** THE PRESIDENTIAL BRANCH
**Kanet** SOVIET FOREIGN POLICY AND EAST-WEST RELATIONS
**Kronenberg** PLANNING U.S. SECURITY
**Nogee & Donaldson** SOVIET FOREIGN POLICY SINCE WORLD WAR II,
Second Edition
**Shultz & Godson** DEZINFORMATSIA: Active Measures In Soviet Strategy

# Database

Brassey's Naval Record

# Related Journals *

DEFENSE ANALYSIS

*Free specimen copies available upon request.

# ALERTING AMERICA

## The Papers of the Committee on
## THE PRESENT DANGER

Edited by Charles Tyroler, II
Introduction by Max M. Kampelman

Published in cooperation with the
Committee on the Present Danger

**PERGAMON·BRASSEY'S**
International Defense Publishers

Washington New York Oxford Toronto Sydney Paris Frankfurt

Pergamon Press Offices:

**U.S.A.**     Pergamon-Brassey's International Defense Publishers,
1340 Old Chain Bridge Road, McLean, Virginia, 22101, U.S.A

Pergamon Press Inc., Maxwell House, Fairview Park,
Elmsford, New York 10523, U.S.A.

**U.K.**     Pergamon Press Ltd., Headington Hill Hall,
Oxford OX3 0BW, England

**CANADA**     Pergamon Press Canada Ltd., Suite 104, 150 Consumers Road,
Willowdale, Ontario M2J 1P9, Canada

**AUSTRALIA**     Pergamon Press (Aust.) Pty. Ltd., P.O. Box 544,
Potts Point, NSW 2011, Australia

**FRANCE**     Pergamon Press SARL, 24 rue des Ecoles,
75240 Paris, Cedex 05, France

**FEDERAL REPUBLIC**
**OF GERMANY**     Pergamon Press GmbH, Hammerweg 6,
D-6242 Kronberg-Taunus, Federal Republic of Germany

Library of Congress Cataloging in Publication Data
Main entry under title:

Alerting America.

"Published in cooperation with the Committee on
the Present Danger."
1. Committee on the Present Danger (U.S.)--History--
Sources. 2. United States--Foreign relations--1977-
1981--Sources. 3. United States--Foreign relations--
1981-   --Sources. 4. United States--Foreign
relations--Soviet Union--Sources. 5. Soviet Union--
Foreign relations--United States--Sources. I. Tyroler.
Charles. II. Committee on the Present Danger (U.S.)
E840.A59  1984   327.73047   88—1113
ISBN 0-08-031926-2
ISBN 0-08-031925-4 (pbk.)

*None of the Committee's policy statements or research studies is
copyrighted. Thus, any of them may be reproduced and distributed in
whole, or in representative part, provided that due attribution to the
Committee is made. The Committee approves and welcomes such
distribution. However, the name—Committee on the Present Danger® —is
registered with the U.S. Patent Office and may not be used by any other
organization or group for any purpose.*

**Printed in the United States of America**

# CONTENTS

## COMMITTEE ON THE PRESENT DANGER
### Members of the Board of Directors Appointed to the Reagan Administration

| Name | Title | Service |
|---|---|---|
| Ronald Reagan | President of the United States | January 20, 1981 |
| Kenneth L. Adelman | Deputy United States Representative, to the United Nations<br>Director, Arms Control and Disarmament Agency | August 4, 1981–April 14, 1983<br>April 22, 1983— |
| Richard V. Allen | Assistant to the President for National Security Affairs<br>Chairman, President's Commission on the German-American Tricentennial | January 20, 1981–January 4, 1982<br><br>November 1982–April 1983 |
| Martin Anderson | Assistant to the President for Policy Development<br>Member, President's Foreign Intelligence Advisory Board<br>Member, President's Economic Policy Advisory Board | January 20, 1981–February 4, 1982<br><br>February 4, 1982—<br><br>February 4, 1982— |
| James L. Buckley | Under Secretary for Security Assistance, Science and Technology<br>Counselor, Department of State<br>President, Radio Free Europe/Radio Liberty | February 7, 1981–August 1982<br>August 20, 1982–October 31, 1982<br>November 1, 1982— |
| W. Glenn Campbell | Chairman, President's Intelligence Oversight Board<br>Member, President's Foreign Intelligence Advisory Board | October 20, 1981—<br><br>October 20, 1981— |
| William J. Casey | Director, Central Intelligence Agency | January 1981— |
| William P. Clements, Jr. | Member, President's Commission on Strategic Forces<br>Member, National Bipartisan Commission on Central America | January 7, 1983—<br><br>August 10, 1983— |
| John B. Connally | Member, President's Foreign Intelligence Advisory Board | October 20, 1981–February 1, 1983 |
| Midge Decter | Member, Task Force on Food Assistance | September 8, 1983— |
| John S. Foster, Jr. | Member, President's Foreign Intelligence Advisory Board | October 20, 1981— |
| J. Peter Grace | Chairman, President's Private Sector Survey on Cost Control | March 3, 1982— |
| William R. Graham | Chairman, General Advisory Committee on Arms Control and Disarmament | September 22, 1982— |
| Colin S. Gray | Member, General Advisory Committee on Arms Control and Disarmament | September 22, 1982— |
| Amoretta M. Hoeber | Deputy Assistant Secretary of the Army for Research and Development | March 30, 1981— |
| Francis P. Hoeber | Member, General Advisory Committee on Arms Control and Disarmament | September 22, 1982— |
| Fred Charles Iklé | Under Secretary of Defense for Policy | April 2, 1981— |
| Eli S. Jacobs | Member, General Advisory Committee on Arms Control and Disarmament | September 22, 1982— |
| David C. Jordan | Ambassador to Peru | February 29, 1984— |
| Max M. Kampelman | Chairman, U.S. Delegation to Conference on Security and Cooperation in Europe | September 1980— |
| Geoffrey Kemp | Director for Near East and South Asian Affairs, National Security Council<br>Senior Director of Near East and South Asian Affairs, and Special Assistant to the President, National Security Council | February 1981–May 1983<br><br><br>May 1983— |
| Lane Kirkland | Commissioner, National Commission on Social Security Reform<br>Member, National Bipartisan Commission on Central America | February 24, 1982–February 19, 1983<br><br>August 10, 1983— |
| Jeane J. Kirkpatrick | U.S. Representative to the United Nations | January 22, 1981— |

ix

## COMMITTEE ON THE PRESENT DANGER
### Members of the Board of Directors Appointed to the Reagan Administration

| Name | Title | Service |
| --- | --- | --- |
| John F. Lehman, Jr. | Secretary of the Navy | February 5, 1981— |
| Clare Boothe Luce | Member, President's Foreign Intelligence Advisory Board | October 20, 1981— |
| John H. Lyons | Member, President's Commission On Strategic Forces | January 7, 1983— |
| Leonard H. Marks | Chairman, U.S. Delegation to the International Telecommunication Union Conference on High Frequency Broadcasting | September 1, 1983— |
| Charles Burton Marshall | Member, General Advisory Committee on Arms Control and Disarmament | September 22, 1982— |
| Edward A. McCabe | Chairman, Board of Directors, Student Loan Marketing Association | December 1981— |
| Paul W. McCracken | Member, President's Economic Policy Advisory Board | March 1981— |
| Paul H. Nitze | Chief Negotiator to Intermediate Range Nuclear Forces Talks | November 20, 1981–March 30, 1984 |
| | Special Representative for Arms Control and Disarmament Negotiations | March 30, 1984— |
| Edward F. Noble | Chairman, U.S. Synthetic Fuels Corporation | May 14, 1981— |
| Michael Novak | U.S. Representative to the United Nations Commission on Human Rights | 1981–1982 |
| | Member, Board for International Broadcasting | October 3, 1983 |
| Jaime Oaxaca | Member, General Advisory Committee on Arms Control and Disarmament | September 1982— |
| Peter O'Donnell, Jr. | Member, President's Foreign Intelligence Advisory Board | October 20, 1981— |
| David Packard | Member, White House Science Council | March 9, 1982— (Board term expired 2/28/83) |
| Richard N. Perle | Assistant Secretary of Defense for International Security Policy | August 4, 1981— |
| Richard Pipes | Director of Soviet Affairs, National Security Council | February 9, 1981–December 17, 1982 |
| John P. Roche | Member, General Advisory Committee on Arms Control and Disarmament | September 1982— |
| Eugene V. Rostow | Director, Arms Control and Disarmament Agency | May 7, 1981–January 12, 1983 |
| | Member, President's Foreign Intelligence Advisory Board | January 14, 1983— |
| Donald H. Rumsfeld | Member, General Advisory Committee on Arms Control and Disarmament | September 1982— |
| | Personal Representative of the President in the Middle East | November 3, 1983–May 17, 1984 |
| Richard M. Scaife | Member, President's Commission on Broadcasting to Cuba | September 22, 1981–September 30, 1982 |
| | Member, U.S. Advisory Commission on Public Diplomacy | March 1, 1984— |
| Richard Schifter | U.S. Representative to The United Nations | January 28, 1983 |
| | Deputy U.S. Representative in The Security Council of the United Nations | June 11, 1984 |
| Paul Seabury | Member, President's Foreign Intelligence Advisory Board | October 20, 1981— |
| Frank Shakespeare | Chairman, Board for International Broadcasting | January 5, 1982— |
| George P. Shultz | Secretary of State | July 16, 1982— |
| John R. Silber | Member, National Bipartisan Commission on Central America | August 10, 1983— |

## COMMITTEE ON THE PRESENT DANGER
### Members of the Board of Directors Appointed to the Reagan Administration

| Name | Title | Service |
|------|-------|---------|
| Laurence H. Silberman | Member, General Advisory Committee on Arms Control and Disarmament | September 1982— |
| Herbert Stein | Member, President's Economic Policy Advisory Board | March 20, 1981— |
| R. G. Stilwell | Deputy Under Secretary of Defense for Policy | February 1981— |
| Richard B. Stone | Member, President's Commission on Broadcasting to Cuba<br>Ambassador-at-large to Central America | November 1981–January 1, 1983<br>June 2, 1983–March 1, 1984 |
| Robert Strausz-Hupe̅ | Ambassador to Turkey | July 24, 1981— |
| Edward Teller | Member, White House Science Council | February 1982— |
| W. Scott Thompson | Associate Director, Bureau of Programs, U.S. Information Agency | May 5, 1982–February 1, 1984 |
| Charles Tyroler, II | Member, President's Intelligence Oversight Board | October 20, 1981— |
| Joe D. Waggonner | Commissioner, National Commission on Social Security Reform | December 16, 1981–January 20, 1983 |
| Charls E. Walker | Member, President's Economic Policy Advisory Board | March 20, 1981— |
| W. Allen Wallis | Under Secretary of State for Economic Affairs | September 22, 1982— |
| Seymour Weiss | Member, President's Foreign Intelligence Advisory Board | October 20, 1981— |
| Edward Bennett Williams | Member, President's Foreign Intelligence Advisory Board | October 20, 1981— |

# EDITOR'S PREFACE

This volume contains all of the publications of the Committee on the Present Danger from its inception on 11 November 1976 to this writing. All, that is, with one exception—only one of Paul Nitze's influential 18-paper series on SALT II is included. Not only are the papers lengthy but much of the material is necessarily duplicative.

The Appendix contains two significant exchanges of private letters on arms control between Charls Walker, CPD Executive Committee Chairman, and President Reagan. The White House has cleared these for publication and this marks the first time they have been publicly available.

Chapters 19 and 20 contain the full results and related materials of the nationwide scientific surveys conducted for the Committee between 31 March and 2 April 1984 on the U.S. Defense Effort and Nuclear Arms. We believe that these are the most comprehensive and revealing opinion surveys ever conducted on these subjects. They are here published for the first time.

Finally, let me point out that this volume has not been edited in the usual sense. The papers appear exactly as they did originally. Not a word has been changed; not a word added or deleted.

From the first, the Committee has made available to scholars and other interested parties the research materials on which our papers are based and our positions taken. This policy continues and our office welcomes inquiries and visits.

With the exception of the papers signed by Messrs. Marshall, Nitze, and Pipes, all of the material in this volume is multiauthored, a joint product of drafting groups of up to 18 members of the Executive Committee. This may seem a wasteful process and goodness knows it *was* time-consuming. But out of it came, we like to think, a better product—most certainly a product to which each of us felt intimately attached and one commanding our pride, enthusiastic support and defense.

Charles Tyroler, II
*Washington, D.C.*
*October 1984*

# INTRODUCTION

"Success has many fathers . . ." the saying goes. With the Committee on the Present Danger this is literally true.

The Committee was an instance of parallel invention and development over a period of two years, ending in the public announcement of its formation on 11 November 1976.

Eugene V. Rostow[1] had been thinking and talking about such an effort since early 1975. So had Charls E. Walker,[2] Paul H. Nitze,[3] Richard V. Allen,[4] Lane Kirkland,[5] Henry H. Fowler,[6] and Admiral Elmo R. Zumwalt.[7] They had talked with each other and some of them had consulted James R. Schlesinger, who was then serving as Secretary of Defense and who offered strong encouragement to the proposed effort.

After much discussion and correspondence and many telephone calls, an organizing meeting was held on 12 March 1976 at the Metropolitan Club in Washington. It was chaired by Rostow (just as all meetings were for the next five years) with Walker, Nitze, Fowler, Zumwalt, Allen, Kirkland, Schlesinger, and me present along with David Packard,[8] Charles Burton Marshall,[9] Edmund A. Gullion,[10] and Charles Tyroler, II.[11] Tyroler was known to almost all of those in attendance and was, unknown to him, the consensus choice to take on the day-to-day operations of the Committee. Tyroler declined that designation after the meeting but agreed to participate on a volunteer basis.

At the Metropolitan Club that day, one of 13 Rostow drafts of our first policy statement, which was to become "Common Sense and the Common Danger," our manifesto, was considered line-by-line—really word-by-word. Subsequent drafts were to be considered over the next eight months, first at Walker's office and then at Tyroler's. The latter was to become the headquarters and meeting place of the Committee for the next four years.

The organizing group met ten more times between that day, 12 March, and 11 November 1976 and conferred by telephone or in smaller meetings many more times. The agenda of each meeting was the same:

1. The latest draft of the Rostow statement;
2. Proposed members of the Committee;
3. Finances;
4. D-day—when to "go public" with the Committee.

The intellectual basis for the Committee grew out of the work of the now-famous Team B which presented its view that the CIA had consistently underestimated the massive Soviet military effort.

Richard Pipes[12] chaired Team B, which also included Nitze and William R. Van Cleave.[13] All three became key members of the CPD Executive Committee.

The purpose of the Committee was simple and straightforward—to alert American policy makers and opinion leaders and the public at large to the ominous Soviet military buildup and its implications, and to the unfavorable trends in the U.S.-Soviet military balance. We were all convinced that international stability and peace with freedom required a strong America—one that could and would deter Soviet adventurism and aggression.

None of us thought that the Committee would be in business for more than a year or two. Rostow's early drafts always referred to an "emergency committee," implying a relatively short lifespan.

The prospective membership of the Committee consumed considerable time at each session but, as the discussions wore on, a clear pattern emerged. The Committee would be bipartisan, with liberals and conservatives, but the principal qualification for membership would be expertise and experience in the areas of foreign and defense policy. Thus, we would concentrate on inviting persons who had held top posts in State, Defense, and Treasury, as well as senior figures in appropriate departments at leading universities around the country. What we were striving for was credibility—the essential ingredient in the process of persuasion.

During the formative months, there was much talk about finances and most estimates of need were considerably more than what turned out to be the case. Curiously, Tyroler was almost alone in presenting the view that only modest financing would be required, that the real strength of a citizens committee lies in volunteer effort of a quality that cannot be purchased on the open market. In its eight years the Committee's entire staff has never exceeded four full-time and two part-time employees.

But even modest financing was elusive. There was much talk of large pledges and commitments, but none materialized in hard cash or, for that matter, in anything else.

Charly Walker listened to all this with growing impatience and finally, without advance notice to his fellow organizers, let alone promises, took himself off to Texas in August. In Houston, he and former Governor John B. Connally hosted a small luncheon and raised $37,000 over coffee. That was the first money raised for the Committee and it was the only money contributed until shortly before we went public in November. In that first year—1976—a total of $79,608 was all that the Committee received. We started in business on the proverbial shoestring.

The question of the Committee's name was considered inconclusively at many sessions and finally "Committee on the Present Danger" was adopted, borrowing from a distinguished citizens group headed by James B. Conant, President of Harvard, in the early '50s with which Tyroler and Nitze had worked. Curiously, it was almost five years before anyone publicly made the name connection between the two groups.

While Rostow was struggling with successive drafts of our manifesto, Tyroler took on the task of drafting a plan of operations—"How the Committee on the Present Danger Will Operate—What It Will Do, and What It Will Not Do." It was approved virtually without change. There were important points in that paper which were to shape the Committee's activities in the next eight years:

1. Membership would be limited to private citizens;
2. The Committee would have no organizational affiliates;
3. Individual contributions to our annual operating budget would be limited to $10,000;
4. Under no circumstances would we solicit or accept contributions from companies or persons who derive a substantial portion of their income from the defense industry;
5. The members of the Committee would be "free and independent citizens recognizing no ties or obligations to any Administration, to political parties, or to their individual or corporate pocketbooks";

6. The Committee would concern itself with broad principles and policy objectives, not with short-range tactics or maneuvers;

7. Finally, the Committee would not urge the election or defeat of individual candidates for office at any level of government, nor would it support or oppose nominees for appointive office.

All of these points turned out to be important:

No. 1 made it clear that we were a private citizen organization.

No. 2 kept our identity free of contamination by similar but far from identical efforts.

No. 3 kept us free of the charge that anyone exerted an undue influence on our positions and activities.

No. 4 kept us free—and uniquely so—of the charge that we were the voice of defense contractors who profit from large Pentagon budgets.

No. 5 emphasized the Committee's true bipartisan membership and nonpartisan attitude.

No. 6 made it possible for the Committee to concentrate on the big issues and to avoid getting embroiled in every controversy, thus diluting our effectiveness.

No. 7 reinforced No. 5 and together, they were at the heart of the Committee's effectiveness.

Simultaneously, I was developing the Articles and Bylaws for the Committee. There were two highly significant features—one provided that the Committee not be a broad membership organization, thus avoiding the conflicts and control problems presented by local chapters and the like. The only members were to be the members of the Board of Directors, limited to 100. (This limitation of 100 had to be raised even before we announced the Committee's formation on 11 November 1976, because the response to our invitations to membership far outstripped our expectations. We had hoped for 50 initial Directors and would have been delighted with 75. To our astonishment we received 141 acceptances in a period of five days.)

The second significant feature was of at least equal importance. We decided to become a nonprofit research and educational organization rather than a lobbying group. Thus, under IRS regulations, contributions to the Committee could be deducted for Federal Income Tax purposes. Throughout its existence, the Committee has scrupulously observed the limitation on lobbying. We have never testified before the Congress except on rare occasion by invitation and at no time have we requested that we be invited to testify. We have never even sent our materials to members of Congress (or their offices) except on their request.

Additionally, although this was not covered in our bylaws or plan of operations, we have not purchased or developed mailing lists for the distribution of our materials or for soliciting funds. Our mailing list, with the exception of our media list, is now composed of more than 14,000 individuals and organizations who have requested to be placed on it and of those that they, in turn, have suggested be added. Finally, we decided not to engage in paid advertising of any kind and we have adhered to this policy despite frequent pressures to abandon it.

The question of D-day—when to "go public" with the Committee—turned out to be complex and controversial. There were both Republicans and Democrats in the organizing group and although all but one of the Republicans—Dick Allen—favored President Ford over Governor Reagan, the Democrats were divided among several candidates. None wanted our launching to appear to favor one candidate over another, particularly over one's own! So first it was decided to wait until after the Democratic Convention, then until after the Republican Convention and, finally, until after the Presidential election itself. The invitations to membership on the Board of Directors were dispatched on the weekend before the election and the press conference announcing the Committee was set for Thursday, 11 November, two days after the election.

The conference was held at the National Press Club in Washington, D.C. and the room was jammed with well over a hundred media representatives, including all networks, all the wire services and top correspondents from almost every major newspaper in the country, as well as a good representation from overseas.

"Common Sense and the Common Danger" was divided into three sections and read in turn by the Committee's three Co-Chairmen, Henry H. Fowler, Lane Kirkland, and David Packard. All of the organizers sat at a long table facing the media. The press conference, including extensive and intensive questioning, lasted more than 90 minutes. Virtually all of it was recorded by the networks. We anxiously awaited the results.

That night not a word appeared on TV or radio. Not a line appeared in the Washington *Evening Star*. The next morning, not a line appeared in the *Washington Post* or *The New York Times*. All of us found it hard to conceal our disappointment. Associated Press, United Press International and other wire services sent out substantial stories, versions of which appeared in scores of newspapers across the country, but, taking their lead from the top Eastern papers, they did not accord it prominent or substantial space.

Thus, the Committee's message was slow in reaching the public. It wasn't until two months later that a brief excerpt from our initial policy statement appeared in *The New York Times*.

But the Committee's message did not go unheeded by the U.S. press. Within days, editorials started trickling in and soon they became a rivulet—the *Washington Star*, the *Richmond Times-Dispatch*, the *Denver Post*, and other papers in twenty states. Columnists then started to pick up the story. Most of the attention was favorable and almost all accepted the credibility of our founding members.

And the Committee did not go unnoticed abroad. The *London Times* and the *Economist* picked up the story at once and in Moscow a virtual torrent of criticism appeared with cartoons to match. To *TASS* and *Izvestia*, we were a "Flock of Hawks" and "Firebrands," but, from that day to this, they have never failed to give close and prominent attention to our efforts. The Soviet press and leading Moscow journals never underestimated the importance of the Committee. One said: "Since the organization's members include extremely influential 'liberal' politicians and military figures and it is backed by strong business groups, it cannot be regarded as one of the usual anti-Soviet and anti-Communist groups which spring up with such frequency in the United States."

So by January 1977, the Committee was on its way, still primarily concerned with the unfavorable trends in the U.S.-Soviet military balance.

We immediately began work on a major assessment of the U.S.-Soviet military balance. This, the first of a series, and entitled, "Is America Becoming Number 2? Current Trends in the U.S.-Soviet Military Balance," was published on 5 October 1978. Our answer to the question was "Yes." Our second study in the military balance series was titled, "Has America Become Number 2? The U.S.-Soviet Military Balance and American Defense Policies and Programs" and appeared on 29 June 1982. Again our answer to the question was "Yes." The third study in the series is at the printer's as these words are being written. It is titled, "Can America Catch Up? The U.S.-Soviet Military Balance." And the answer to that question is "Yes, we can catch up, but not at the present and projected rate of increase in the overall defense effort."

We had thought that these studies were to be the major, in a sense the only, contribution of the Committee.

But this was not to be.

At the first meeting of the Executive Committee following the announcement of the Committee it was decided to prepare a paper analyzing the Soviet Union—the principles on which it is organized, the motives by which it is driven, and the "Grand Strategy" which it pursues. We strove to contrast the radical differences between our two societies and to illustrate the danger that the Soviets constitute to the United States and to other democracies.

This paper became "What Is the Soviet Union Up To?" and had very considerable influence here and abroad. It also was tangentially to have a profound impact on the next four years of the Committee's life. One day when Tyroler was discussing the paper with Dean Rusk,[14] one of the early members of our Executive Committee, Rusk dictated a sentence which was to start the Committee on the production of twenty-six studies and policy statements on arms control. The paragraph follows (the italicized sentence is Rusk's):

> We live in an age in which there is no alternative to vigilance and credible deterrence at the significant levels of potential conflict. *Indeed, this is the prerequisite to the pursuit of genuine detente and the negotiation of prudent and verifiable arms control agreements that effectively serve to reduce the danger of war.*

"Where We Stand on SALT" appeared in July '77 and from that time on, until President Carter withdrew the SALT II Treaty in the fall of '79 when it was clear that the Senate would not ratify it, the SALT II negotiations and the emerging treaty became the principal preoccupation of the Committee.

There was in the general public very little understanding of the issues raised by the treaty negotiations and, more dangerously, considerable misunderstanding of the provisions being negotiated.

The Committee tried to correct this situation by its publications and by sending leading CPD spokesmen—Nitze, Rostow, Pipes, and Zumwalt—to meet with editorial boards across the country. These meetings were to have a profound and demonstrable effect. The editorials following these sessions were carefully monitored and in almost every instance a change in tone was noticeable. These CPD leaders and others made themselves available for numerous debates and other appearances on TV and radio as well as before private groups.

Our purpose, as exemplified in the landmark series of 18 studies by Paul Nitze titled, "Current SALT II Negotiating Posture," from 1 November 1977 to 8 November 1979, was educational. We were attempting to evaluate the emerging treaty on its merits and to have others evaluate it the same way.

Asking simplistic polling questions such as, "Do you favor or oppose a new agreement between the United States and Russia which would limit nuclear weapons?" fostered the impression that there was widespread support for a specific treaty—in this case, SALT II. It certainly wasn't suprising that 81% said "Yes" to the above question. The only wonder is that there wasn't 100% affirmative response.

The Committee therefore decided to conduct its own nationwide scientific poll and found that less than one out of five Americans supported SALT II, either strongly or reluctantly. But of at least equal importance was the finding that the public was not merely uninformed about the emerging treaty but was actually misinformed. This was demonstrated in the answers to True-False questions where flipping a coin would come up with the correct answer half of the time. Yet the public picked the wrong answer an average of more than two-thirds of the time.* After the Committee's poll, the other pollsters changed their method of operation in this area.

During endless discussions in the Executive Committee we were never free of the big question: "Can America Afford the Defense It Needs?" The result—and the answer— was in the work for the Committee of Herbert Stein.[15]**

What has the Committee accomplished? Perhaps the answer to that question is better left to outsiders and to history. Nevertheless, a tentative conclusion may be ventured.

From 1977 to 1981, as reported by public opinion polls, there was a steady increase in public perception of growing Soviet military strength and the threat that this posed to the United States and its allies. At the same time, there was a simultaneous surge in popular support for an increased defense effort and a corresponding sharp drop in sentiment for a decreased effort. To what extent this was due to the efforts of the Committee is impossible to gauge. It could be merely a coincidence but our presumption is that it is not.

It is always difficult to apportion credit properly for the success of an enterprise. Gene Rostow and Paul Nitze (Chairman of the Executive Committee and Chairman of Policy Studies, respectively) played central roles in CPD from the first, and their monumental contributions have been recognized by the media here and abroad. Others have not generally received adequate recognition for their contributions. Charly Walker was a key figure from the first day to this writing—first as Treasurer and then succeeding Rostow as Chairman of the Executive Committee. Richard V. Allen has been an enthusiastic and unselfish supporter of the Committee throughout its life. He not only made major inputs to our important statements but was the Committee's most productive fundraiser. Charles Burton Marshall worked long, hard and effectively for our full eight-year period. Richard Pipes made a major contribution from 1977 on. So did Admiral Zumwalt and General Richard Stilwell.[16] David Acheson[17] has been a tower of strength, particularly in recent years. William R. Van Cleave has furnished generous and effective leadership in preparing and assigning policy statements during Paul Nitze's leave of absence in government service.

Our first balance sheet statement, "Is America Becoming Number 2? Current Trends in the U.S.-Soviet Military Balance," might never have seen the light of day without the painstaking and patient work over a two-year period of Francis P. Hoeber.[18] Albert Shanker[19] has on numerous occasions brought the Committee's message to a nationwide audience in his widely published and eloquent column on public affairs. John P. Roche[20] did the same in his nationally syndicated column and in his other writings. Adda Bozeman[21] and Valerie Earle[22] have spoken eloquently for the Committee and have carried our message across the country.

Henry H. Fowler, Co-Chairman of the Committee from the beginning, gave sage counsel at many critical points in the Committee's existence and on at least one occasion took the lead in preventing a fatal misstep that had been proposed. In eight years, Fowler has hardly missed a meeting.

Fred Iklé,[23] Edward Rowny,[24] and Richard Perle[25] have been valued friends and workers both in and out of government. Lane Kirland and David Packard gave freely of

*See Chapter 10
**See Appendix to Chapter 17

their time and tangible support. So did Lloyd H. Smith[26] and Douglas Dillon.[27] Richard Scaife[28] helped throughout with his self-effacing support. Hobart Taylor,[29] before his untimely death, and Bernard T. Renzy,[30] gave us wise guidance on more than a few occasions. So have Hugh Scott,[31] William Graham,[32] Richard Whalen, Kenneth Adelman, and Charles M. Kupperman. Bayard Rustin[33] furnished us with the support of his distinctive and symbolic career as a champion of liberty. And there are dozens and dozens of others.

And who can put a value on the inspiration that has been brought to the Committee by the energy, vision, and support of America's greatest living soldier—CPD founding member, General Matthew Ridgway.[34]

Finally, one must recognize and applaud the pivotal role played by our Director, Charles Tyroler, and his tiny, dedicated staff.

To all those who have helped the Committee over the past eight years, may this volume act as a partial repayment.

Max M. Kampelman
*Washington, D.C.*
*October 1984*

# NOTES

*Note:* The principal past affiliations given are as of 11 November 1976. Subsequent government posts are given on pages ix–xi.

1. Sterling Professor of Law, and former Dean, Yale Law School; Under Secretary of State for Political Affairs under President Johnson.
2. Deputy Secretary of the Treasury under President Nixon.
3. Deputy Secretary of Defense under President Johnson; Secretary of the Navy under Presidents Kennedy and Johnson.
4. Deputy Assistant to President Nixon for International Economic Affairs.
5. Secretary-Treasurer, AFL-CIO.
6. Secretary of the Treasury under President Johnson.
7. Former Chief of Naval Operations.
8. Deputy Secretary of Defense under President Nixon.
9. Member, Policy Planning Staff, Department of State under Secretary Dean Acheson and President Truman.
10. Dean, Fletcher School of Law and Diplomacy.
11. Director, Manpower Supply, Department of Defense under Secretary Marshall and President Truman.
12. Frank B. Baird, Jr. Professor of History and former Director, Russian Research Center, Harvard University.
13. Professor of International Relations, University of Southern California.
14. Secretary of State under Presidents Kennedy and Johnson.
15. Chairman, Council of Economic Advisers under President Nixon.
16. Former Commander, U.N. Forces in Korea.
17. District Attorney for D.C. under Presidents Kennedy and Johnson.
18. Defense Analyst and Author.
19. President, American Federation of Teachers.
20. Professor, Fletcher School of Law and Diplomacy; Special Consultant to President Johnson; Former National Chairman, Americans for Democratic Action.
21. Professor of International Relations, Sarah Lawrence College.
22. Professor of Government, Georgetown University.
23. Director, U.S. Arms Control and Disarmament Agency under Presidents Nixon and Ford.
24. Lieutenant General, United States Army; Joint Chiefs of Staff Representative to the SALT II Delegation.
25. Key Assistant to Senator Henry M. Jackson.
26. President, Paraffine Oil Corporation.
27. Under Secretary of State under President Eisenhower; Secretary of the Treasury under Presidents Kennedy and Johnson.
28. Publishers, *Tribune-Review.*
29. Director, Export-Import Bank under President Johnson.
30. Partner, Hamel, Park, McCabe & Saunders, Attorneys at Law.
31. Minority Leader, U.S. Senate.
32. Physicist and Electrical Engineer; authority on nuclear weapons systems and military systems survivability.
33. President, A. Philip Randolph Institute.
34. General, United States Army, Retired; Supreme Commander, Korea; Supreme Commander, SHAPE; Former Army Chief of Staff.

# ALERTING AMERICA

# HOW THE COMMITTEE ON THE PRESENT DANGER WILL OPERATE—

## What It Will Do, and What It Will Not Do

### I

Our Committee is wholly independent and nonpartisan, with no political axe to grind. We welcome the participation and support of Democrats, Republicans and Independents.

We are incorporated as a nonprofit organization. Our membership is limited to those in private life and therefore does not include elected or appointed full-time Federal or State officials, or active candidates for public office.

The Committee has no organizational affiliates. All members serve in their individual capacities and not as official representatives of any other group or organization.

The Committee's activities are to be wholly financed by voluntary contributions.

We are limiting annual contributions from a single source to $10,000. Our objective is a broad base of public support. For special projects, particularly those appropriate for foundation support and not contained in our regular budget, we may accept larger amounts.

Under no circumstances, will we solicit or accept contributions from companies or persons who derive a substantial portion of their income from the Defense Industry.

### II

Our basic purpose is to facilitate a national discussion of the foreign and national security policies of the United States directed toward a secure peace with freedom. Our primary views are contained in our declaration of principles, "Common Sense and the Common Danger," and all future statements of the Committee will be clearly consistent with it.

Our effort is not a one-shot affair. We shall stay in business until we are no longer needed.

Our principal activity will be educational. Although we will not refrain from expressing our own viewpoint and will not prevent persons affiliated with us from expressing or advocating their own viewpoints, we will seek to assure that our judgments are based upon a full, fair and objective factual foundation and that this foundation is made known to the audiences whom we will be addressing.

We are all free and independent citizens on this Committee. We recognize no ties or obligations to this or any Administration, to political parties, or to our individual or corporate pocketbooks.

Many of us have worked with one or more of the last seven Presidents in formulating and executing foreign and national security policy. Others, as private citizens, at home and abroad, in business, labor, academic life or the professions, have taken a keen interest in these critical matters. Our membership is being drawn from every section of the country and every major walk of life.

# III

We recognize that the responsibility of the United States in today's changing world cannot be easily or cheaply met. We may be involved for a long time in expensive, painful and frustrating situations—and the solutions of yesterday will not suffice for today and tomorrow. That is the price we must pay for freedom and for avoiding a third World War. Peace is not a cut-rate commodity. We must be wary of oversimplified and easy solutions to complex international problems.

Our organization will concern itself with broad principles and policy objectives. It is not within our purview or our competence to comment on the intricacies and complexities of short-range tactics or maneuvers. Our concern is with strategies and goals, with the broad thrust and direction of policy, not with all the ramifications and details of its day-to-day implementation.

Our organization will not urge the election or defeat of individual candidates for office at any level of government. Neither will we support or oppose nominees for appointive office. On occasion, we may be obliged to express support for or opposition to specific legislative proposals, but we do not view it as our mandate to take a position on all legislation which affects foreign and national security policy. We will concern ourselves with the relatively few major proposals that are unmistakably critical to our basic objective.

Our basic operational task is to further the two-way process of communications here at home on foreign and national security policy matters. To this end, we will encourage, conduct, and participate in conferences and seminars across the nation, involving as many sectors of society as our resources permit. We shall strive to provide occasions, speakers and materials for the rational exchange of views based upon facts and history. We will make our findings available to the public through pamphlets and articles and possibly through advertising in the media.

We will avail ourselves, to the maximum extent consistent with our time and resources, of all media of communication for the exposition and consideration of our findings.

# IV

The Committee on the Present Danger has set a big task for itself. We are fully aware how difficult it will be to accomplish. But, as concerned citizens, we feel an obligation to speak out in support of our convictions and in reflection of the lessons that we have learned together. For us there is no higher priority than peace with freedom and security for our country.

*8 September 1976*

2

# COMMON SENSE AND THE COMMON DANGER

## Policy Statement of the Committee on The Present Danger

### I

Our country is in a period of danger, and the danger is increasing. Unless decisive steps are taken to alert the nation, and to change the course of its policy, our economic and military capacity will become inadequate to assure peace with security.

The threats we face are more subtle and indirect than was once the case. As a result, awareness of danger has diminished in the United States, in the democratic countries with which we are naturally and necessarily allied, and in the developing world.

There is still time for effective action to ensure the security and prosperity of the nation in peace, through peaceful deterence and concerted alliance diplomacy. A conscious effort of political will is needed to restore the strength and coherence of our foreign policy; to revive the solidarity of our alliances; to build constructive relations of cooperation with other nations whose interests parallel our own—and on that sound basis to seek reliable conditions of peace with the Soviet Union, rather than an illusory detente.

Only on such a footing can we and the other democratic industrialized nations, acting together, work with the developing nations to create a just and progressive world economy—the necessary condition of our own prosperity and that of the developing nations and Communist nations as well. In that framework, we shall be better able to promote human rights, and to help deal with the great and emerging problems of food, energy, population, and the environment.

### II

The principal threat to our nation, to world peace, and to the cause of human freedom is the Soviet drive for dominance based upon an unparalleled military buildup.

The Soviet Union has not altered its long-held goal of a world dominated from a single center—Moscow. It continues, with notable persistence, to take advantage of every opportunity to expand its political and military influence throughout the world: in Europe; in the Middle East and Africa; in Asia; even in Latin America; in all the seas.

The scope and sophistication of the Soviet campaign have been increased in recent years, and its tempo quickened. It encourages every divisive tendency within and among the developed states and between the developed and the underdeveloped world. Simultaneously, the Soviet Union has been acquiring a network of positions including naval and air bases in the Southern Hemisphere which support its drive for dominance in the Middle East, the Indian Ocean, Africa, and the South Atlantic.

For more than a decade, the Soviet Union has been enlarging and improving both its strategic and its conventional military forces far more rapidly than the United States and its allies. Soviet military power and its rate of growth cannot be explained or justified by considerations of self-defense. The Soviet Union is consciously seeking what its spokesmen call "visible preponderance" for the Soviet sphere. Such preponderance, they explain, will permit the Soviet Union "to transform the conditions of world politics" and determine the direction of its development.

The process of Soviet expansion and the worldwide deployment of its military power threaten our interest in the political independence of our friends and allies, their and our fair access to raw materials, the freedom of the seas, and in avoiding a preponderance of adversary power.

These interests can be threatened not only by direct attack, but also by envelopment and indirect aggression. The defense of the Middle East, for example, is vital to the defense of Western Europe and Japan. In the Middle East the Soviet Union opposes those just settlements between Israel and its Arab neighbors which are critical to the future of the area. Similarly, we and much of the rest of the world are threatened by renewed coercion through a second round of Soviet-encouraged oil embargoes.

## III

Soviet expansionism threatens to destroy the world balance of forces on which the survival of freedom depends. If we see the world as it is, and restore our will, our strength and our self-confidence, we shall find resources and friends enough to counter that threat. There is a crucial moral difference between the two superpowers in their character and objectives. The United States—imperfect as it is—is essential to the hopes of those countries which desire to develop their societies in their own ways, free of coercion.

To sustain an effective foreign policy, economic strength, military strength, and a commitment to leadership are essential. We must restore an allied defense posture capable of deterrence at each significant level and in those theaters vital to our interests. The goal of our strategic forces should be to prevent the use of, or the credible threat to use, strategic weapons in world politics; that of our conventional forces, to prevent other forms of aggression directed against our interests. Without a stable balance of forces in the world and policies of collective defense based upon it, no other objective of our foreign policy is attainable.

As a percentage of Gross National Product, U.S. defense spending is lower than at any time in twenty-five years. For the United States to be free, secure and influential, higher levels of spending are now required for our ready land, sea, and air forces, our strategic deterrent, and, above all, the continuing modernization of those forces through research and development. The increased level of spending required is well within our means so long as we insist on all feasible efficiency in our defense spending. We must also expect our allies to bear their fair share of the burden of defense.

From a strong foundation, we can pursue a positive and confident diplomacy, addressed to the full array of our economic, political and social interests in world politics. It is only on this basis that we can expect successfully to negotiate hardheaded and verifiable agreements to control and reduce armaments.

If we continue to drift, we shall become second best to the Soviet Union in overall military strength; our alliances will weaken; our promising rapprochement with China could be reversed. Then we could find ourselves isolated in a hostile world, facing the unremitting pressures of Soviet policy backed by an overwhelming preponderance of power. Our national survival itself would be in peril, and we should face, one after another, bitter choices between war and acquiescence under pressure.

## IV

We are Independents, Republicans and Democrats who share the belief that foreign and national security policies should be based upon fundamental considerations of the nation's future well being, not that of any one faction or party.

We have faith in the maturity, good sense and fortitude of our people. But public opinion must be informed before it can reach considered judgments and make them effective in our democratic system. Time, weariness, and the tragic experience of Vietnam have weakened the bipartisan consensus which sustained our foreign policy between 1940 and the mid-60's. We must build a fresh consensus to expand the opportunities and diminish the dangers of a world in flux.

We have therefore established the Committee on the Present Danger to help promote a better understanding of the main problems confronting our foreign policy, based on a disciplined effort to gather the facts and a sustained discussion of their significance for our national security and survival.

*11 November 1976*

## FOUNDING BOARD MEMBERS—NOVEMBER, 1976

## Board of Directors

ACHILLES, THEODORE C. Vice Chairman, Atlantic Council of the U.S.; former Counselor of the Department of State

ALLEN, RICHARD V. President, Potomac International Corp.; former Deputy Assistant to the President for International Economic Affairs

ALLISON, JOHN M. Former Ambassador to Japan, Indonesia and Czechoslovakia

ANDERSON, EUGENIE. Former Ambassador to Denmark

BARDACH, EUGENE. Associate Professor of Public Policy, University of California

BARNETT, FRANK R. President, National Strategy Information Center, Inc.

BAROODY, JOSEPH D. Public Affairs Consultant

BEAM, JACOB D. Former Ambassador to Poland, Czechoslovakia and the Soviet Union

BELLOW, SAUL. Author (Nobel Prize 1976 in Literature)

BENDETSEN, KARL R. Former Under Secretary of the Army

BISHOP, JOSEPH W., JR. Professor of Law, Yale Law School

BOZEMAN, ADDA B. Professor of International Relations, Sarah Lawrence College

BRENNAN, DONALD G. Director of National Security Studies, Hudson Institute

BROWNE, VINCENT J. Professor of Political Science, Howard University

BURGESS, W. RANDOLPH. Former Under Secretary of the Treasury and Ambassador to NATO

CABOT, JOHN M. Former Ambassador to Sudan, Colombia, Brazil and Poland

CAMPBELL, W. GLENN. Director, Hoover Institution on War, Revolution and Peace, Stanford University

CASEY, WILLIAM J. Former Chairman, SEC, Under Secretary of State, and President, Export-Import Bank

CHAIKIN, SOL C. President, International Ladies' Garment Workers' Union

CLARK, PETER B. President, The Evening News Association

CLINE, RAY S. Director of Studies, Georgetown University Center for Strategic and International Studies

COHEN, EDWIN S. Former Under Secretary of the Treasury

COLBY, WILLIAM E. Former Director of Central Intelligence

CONNALLY, JOHN B. Former Secretary of the Treasury

CONNELL, WILLIAM. President, Concept Associates, Inc.; Executive Assistant to Vice President Humphrey

CONNOR, JOHN T. President, Allied Chemical Corp.; former Secretary of Commerce

DARDEN, COLGATE W., JR. President Emeritus, University of Virginia

DEAN, ARTHUR H. Former Chairman, U.S. Delegations on Nuclear Test Ban and Disarmament

DILLON, C. DOUGLAS. Former Secretary of the Treasury

DOGOLE, S. HARRISON. Chairman, Globe Security Systems Inc.

DOMINICK, PETER H. Former U.S. Senator

DOWLING, WALTER. Former Ambassador to Germany

DuBROW, EVELYN. Legislative Director, International Ladies' Garment Workers' Union

DuCHESSI, WILLIAM. Executive Vice President, Amalgamated Clothing and Textile Workers' Union

EARLE, VALERIE. Professor of Government, Georgetown University

FARRELL, JAMES T. Author

FELLMAN, DAVID. Vilas Professor of Political Science, University of Wisconsin

FOWLER, HENRY H. Partner, Goldman, Sachs & Co.; former Secretary of the Treasury

FRANKLIN, WILLIAM H. Chairman of the Board (Ret.), Caterpillar Tractor Co.

FRELINGHUYSEN, PETER H. B. Former Member of Congress

FRIEDMAN, MARTIN L. Assistant to President Truman

GINSBURGH, ROBERT N. Major General, USAF (Ret.); Editor, Strategic Review

GLAZER, NATHAN. Professor of Education and Sociology, Harvard University

GOODPASTER, ANDREW J. General, U.S. Army (Ret.); former NATO Supreme Allied Commander, Europe

GRACE, J. PETER. President, W. R. Grace & Co.

GRAY, GORDON. Former President, University of North Carolina, and Secretary of the Army

GULLION, EDMUND A. Dean, Fletcher School of Law and Diplomacy

GUNDERSON, BARBARA BATES. Former Civil Service Commissioner

HANDLIN, OSCAR. University Professor, Harvard University

HANNAH, JOHN A. Executive Director, United Nations World Food Council; former Chairman, U.S. Commission on Civil Rights, and Administrator, Agency for International Development

HARPER, DAVID B. Gateway National Bank of St. Louis

HARRIS, HUNTINGTON. Trustee, The Brookings Institution

HAUSER, RITA E. Attorney, Stroock & Stroock & Lavan; former Representative to the Human Rights Commission of the United Nations

HELLMANN, DONALD C. Professor of Political Science and Asian Studies, University of Washington

**HERRERA, ALFRED C.** Research Associate, Johns Hopkins University, Washington Center of Foreign Policy Research

**HOROWITZ, RACHELLE.** Director, Committee on Political Education, American Federation of Teachers

**HUREWITZ, J. C.** Director, The Middle East Institute, Columbia University

**JOHNSON, BELTON K.** Chairman, Chaparrosa Agri-Services, Inc.

**JOHNSON, CHALMERS.** Professor & Chairman, Department of Political Science, University of California

**JOHNSTON, WHITTLE.** Professor of Government and Foreign Affairs, University of Virginia

**JORDAN, DAVID C.** Professor & Chairman, Woodrow Wilson Department of Government and Foreign Affairs, University of Virginia

**KAMPELMAN, MAX M.** Attorney, Fried, Frank, Harris, Shriver & Kampelman

**KEMP, GEOFFREY.** Professor of International Politics, Fletcher School of Law and Diplomacy

**KEYSERLING, LEON H.** President, Conference on Economic Progress; Chairman, Council of Economic Advisers under President Truman

**KIRKLAND, LANE.** Secretary-Treasurer, AFL-CIO

**KIRKPATRICK, JEANE J.** Professor of Government, Georgetown University

**KOHLER, FOY D.** Professor of International Studies, University of Miami (Florida); former Ambassador to the Soviet Union

**KROGH, PETER.** Dean, School of Foreign Service, Georgetown University

**LEFEVER, ERNEST W.** Professor of International Relations and Director, Ethics and Public Policy Program, Georgetown University

**LEMNITZER, LYMAN L.** General, U.S. Army (Ret.); former Chairman, Joint Chiefs of Staff, NATO Supreme Allied Commander Europe

**LEWIS, HOBART.** Chairman, Reader's Digest

**LIBBY, W. F.** Former AEC Commissioner (Nobel Prize 1960 in Chemistry)

**LIEBLER, SARASON D.** President, Digital Recording Corp.

**LINEN, JAMES A.** Director and former President, Time Inc.

**LIPSET, SEYMOUR MARTIN.** Professor of Political Science and Sociology, Stanford University

**LORD, MARY P.** Former Representative to the Human Rights Commission of the United Nations

**LOVESTONE, JAY.** Consultant to AFL-CIO and ILGWU on International Affairs

**LUCE, CLARE BOOTHE.** Author; former Member of Congress, Ambassador to Italy

**LYONS, JOHN H.** General President, Ironworkers International Union

**MacNAUGHTON, DONALD S.** Chairman and Chief Executive Officer, The Prudential Insurance Company of America

**MARKS, LEONARD H.** Former Director, United States Information Agency

**MARSHALL, CHARLES BURTON.** School of Advanced International Studies, Johns Hopkins University; former Member, Policy Planning Staff, Department of State

**MARTIN, WILLIAM McCHESNEY, JR.** Former Chairman, Federal Reserve Board

**McCABE, EDWARD A.** Counsel to President Eisenhower

**McCRACKEN, SAMUEL.** Author

**McGHEE, GEORGE C.** Former Under Secretary of State for Political Affairs, Ambassador to Turkey and Germany

**McNAIR, ROBERT E.** Former Governor of South Carolina

(l. to r.) William R. Van Cleave, Paul H. Nitze, Ronald Reagan, Eugene V. Rostow, Charles Tyroler,II
(Back to camera) Edwin Meese

(l. to r.) William R. Van Cleave, Charles M. Kupperman, Paul H. Nitze, James L. Buckley, Joseph D. Douglass, Jr., Max M. Kampelman, Eugene V. Rostow, Edward L. Rowny

(l. to r.) Max M. Kampelman, Charles Tyroler, II, Richard V. Allen, Eugene V. Rostow, Henry H. Fowler, Charles Burton Marshall, Charls E. Walker
(Backs to camera) Paul H. Nitze (l.) Edward Bennett Williams (r.)

(l. to r.) Richard G. Stilwell, John F. Lehman, Jr., Amoretta M. Hoeber, Fred C. Iklé

---

(Note: All members serve in their individual capacities and not as official representatives of any other group or organization. Affiliations are listed solely for identification.)

# 3

# WHAT IS THE
# SOVIET UNION UP TO?

A rich, democratic and seemingly secure country such as the United States tends to conceive its national aspirations in domestic terms: full employment, less inflation, better health care, a higher standard of living and improved opportunities. International objectives are defined primarily in broad terms, such as enduring peace, preservation of human rights and a freer flow of people and goods. Both at home and abroad, our open, democratic society, with its many centers of decision-making and limited constitutional government, is committed to these objectives.

## A DIFFERENT SOCIETY

The Soviet Union is radically different from our society. It is organized on different principles and driven by different motives. Failure to understand these differences and to take them seriously constitutes a grave danger to the democratic societies. We tend to think of others as being like ourselves and likely to behave as we would under similar circumstances. This habit of "mirror-imaging" leads many Americans to ignore, to rationalize or to underestimate the Soviet challenge.

There are many reasons why the Soviet Union is different from the United States, but the most important are rooted in its history and geography, its economic conditions and structure, and its political system and ideology.

Notwithstanding its vast territory and rich mineral resources, the Soviet Union can only with difficulty support its population. Its extreme northern latitude makes for a short agricultural season, a situation aggravated by the shortage of rain in areas with the best soil. Its mineral resources, often located in areas difficult to reach, are costly to extract. Its transportation network is still inadequate. These factors have historically been among those impelling Russia—Tsarist and Soviet alike—toward the conquest or domination of neighboring lands. No empire in history has expanded so persistently as the Russian. The Soviet Union is the only great power to have emerged from World War II larger than it was in 1939.

Soviet economic deficiencies and their effects are aggravated by the character of the regime and the lengths to which it goes to maintain its hold. Except for brief periods in its history, Russia has been governed by small elites unresponsive to the needs and desires of the population at large. After the Bolshevik Revolution of 1917, power became even more concentrated than under the Tsars.

## A RULING ELITE

Soviet Russia today is a country in which a ruling elite and those whom it designates live comfortably, while the remaining 250 million citizens not only have few material advantages but are deprived of basic human liberties. This elite can enjoy its monopoly of advantages only so long as it is able to keep the deprived population under effective control—a significant relaxation of that control could spell the end of its favored status and advantages. The elite, however, is not guided merely by self-serving motives. The Soviet leadership asserts that it is the vanguard of a revolutionary society which has discovered the fundamental laws of history. The openly stated ultimate Soviet objective is the worldwide triumph of Communism. This triumph would give the Soviet elite ready access to the world's resources, both human and material; it would also do away with all external challenges to its privileged position by eliminating once and for all alternative political and social systems.

Through its highly authoritarian regime, the Soviet ruling elite is able to coordinate and pursue its international objectives in a relatively coherent manner. This is not to say that it has set "time-tables" or drawn up specific "blueprints" for conquest or domination. Such precise schedules are simply not possible in an unpredictable world. It does mean, however, that the Soviet elite, as directed by the Politburo, can exercise total control of the country's political institutions, economic resources and media and set for itself short-term as well as long-term objectives, disregarding the wishes of its own population. By varying its tactics to suit changing circumstances, it can pursue these objectives in an organized and decisive manner, taking advantage of every opportunity to enhance its power in the world.

Because Russia was the first country to experience a Communist revolution and because it is likely to remain the most powerful Communist state, the Soviet elite believes that in a Communist world it should lead and dominate. However, the Soviet elite now indicates, perhaps for tactical reasons, that it is prepared to accept less. Some outside observers believe that it may have no choice but to acquiesce in the compromise ideal of a polycentric global Communist community in which the Soviet Union is not so much the directing center as the first among equals. In any event, the notion of a stable world order in which nations based on differing political principles cooperate rather than contend is alien to Soviet psychology and doctrine. According to Soviet theory, "peaceful coexistence" is not a concept involving a stable world order, but a strategy that adapts the methods of waging international conflict to the era of nuclear weapons, an era which, because of its inherent dangers, more than ever before calls for the patient and prudent pursuit of global objectives.

## THE SOVIET "GRAND STRATEGY"

The attainment of the ultimate Soviet objective—a Communist world order—requires the reduction of the power, influence and prestige of the United States, the country which the Soviet leaders perceive as the central bastion of the "capitalist" or enemy camp. They see the global conflict as a drawn-out process with the Soviet Union and America the two principal contenders. In that contest they see their task as isolating America and, despite temporary reverses for their side, reducing it to impotence.

In its global activities the Soviet Union pursues a "grand strategy" involving the use of a great variety of means to attain the ultimate end: the reduction of any potential opponent's ability to resist. These means include economic, diplomatic, political and ideological strategies against a background of military strength, to be used separately or together as instrumentalities of power. The Soviet eagerness to increase its trade with the Western world or to participate in arms limitation negotiations does not preclude politico-military campaigns to outflank and envelop centers of non-Communist influence, such as the long and patient Soviet efforts to penetrate and dominate the Middle

East, and now the drive, supported by client states, to establish regimes friendly to Soviet domination in Africa.

It would be incorrect to see the U.S.-USSR rivalry exclusively in terms of the military balance. The conflict extends across the spectrum of political, cultural and economic relations. Propaganda is a weapon. Trade is a weapon. In theory and in practice, Soviet "grand strategy" conceives military power as only one weapon (albeit a central and indispensable one) in a large arsenal of means of persuasion and coercion.

The peoples of the Soviet Union have suffered enormously in past world wars. Their rulers would doubtless prefer to gain their objectives without another. But they believe they can survive and win a war if it comes and therefore are not unwilling to risk confrontation in order to attain their objectives.

## MEDIUM-TERM OBJECTIVES

The principal medium-term objectives of Soviet grand strategy include:

1. *Strengthening the Soviet economy through a process of intensive modernization as an essential prerequisite to the improvement of the country's military capacity.* This aim is to be achieved in part by heavy borrowing of capital and technology in the advanced "capitalist" countries, and in part by accelerating the integration of the economies of the Communist countries. The desire for access to foreign capital, credit and know-how has been an important factor in the support by the Soviet elite of Western emphasis on "détente."

2. *Multiplying and tightening the links connecting Western Europe to the Soviet Union and its dependencies, and concurrently cutting it adrift from the United States.* The partial or total integration of West European economies into an expanding Communist economy would give the Soviet bloc that level of productive and technological capacity which it requires to be able to deal with the United States from a position of potentially intimidating strength. With this vital objective in mind, the USSR has acquiesced in the adoption by the leading West European Communist parties of more flexible programs and tactics. The experiences of Chile and Portugal show that only through such an approach can Communist parties have a chance of coming to power and paving the way for Soviet hegemony in Western Europe. They hope to profit from a growing perception in Western Europe of a decline in United States will and power and a concurrent illusion that the Soviet threat has ended. This would bring about the fatal weakening of NATO and help ease the United States out of Europe.

3. *Undercutting the economic links connecting the "capitalist" world, and especially the United States, with the countries of the Third World, on the assumption that lack of access to the raw materials, labor and markets available in these countries would throw the industrialized democracies into a series of fatal convulsions.* Particular attention is paid to energy resources, especially oil. The USSR wishes both to make oil more costly (in part to profit from its own oil exports) and more importantly to be in a position to control oil supplies necessary to the West and thus to be able to exert political and economic pressure.

4. *Containing and isolating China, which the USSR presently does not fear as a military power but about which it has profound, almost atavistic anxieties as a long-term threat.* Although Moscow still hopes to mend relations with the post-Mao regime, the Soviet leadership fears that unless China is dismembered through the separation of border regions (such as Manchuria and Tibet) and the creation of buffer states, it will pose a

growing long-term threat. The USSR still maintains an estimated 45 divisions in Siberia along the border with China.

## THE ULTIMATE INSTRUMENT—MILITARY POWER

Although the pursuit of these four aims calls principally for the use of economic and political measures, the ultimate instrument—and the backbone of Soviet strategy—is military power. The principal instrument at its disposal with which it can realistically expect to surpass the United States, its allies and friends in overall strength is military power.

To be sure, at present the Soviet Union lags behind the United States in both productive capacity and many areas of weapons technology, but our lead in these particulars may not last forever. Moreover, the USSR can compensate for current deficiencies with other advantages. Its leadership is not restrained by democratic dissent, legislative limitations or public opinion in expending the country's resources on the military, and it can and does commit a disproportionately high share of its limited resources to its objectives. It can also mobilize its population at will, whether to undergo compulsory military training or to participate in civil defense. Nor is it inhibited internally in the way it disposes of these forces; it can send military aid or dispatch its military forces to any part of the world where opportunity beckons. It can also influence client states to take similar action. These inherent advantages cause the Soviet leadership to rely heavily on military policy as an instrument of grand strategy not only in the strictly military sense of subduing and conquering, but also in the political sense of intimidating potential opponents.

## THE SOVIET BUILDUP

The Soviet military buildup of all its armed forces over the past quarter century is, in part, reminiscent of Nazi Germany's rearmament in the 1930s. The Soviet buildup affects all branches of the military: the army, the air force and the navy. In addition Soviet nuclear offensive and defensive forces are designed to enable the USSR to fight, survive and win an all-out nuclear war should it occur.

*The SALT I arms limitation agreements have had no visible effect on the Soviet buildup.* Indeed, their principal effect so far has been to restrain the United States in the development of those weapons in which it enjoys an advantage. Nor has the self-imposed restraint by the United States in the past decade in the development and deployment of its strategic nuclear forces evoked similar restraint on the part of the USSR. On the contrary: the Soviet Union has shown a determination to forge ahead with the development and deployment of all weapons which promise to enhance its global military posture. Neither Soviet military power nor its rate of growth can be explained or justified on grounds of self-defense.

By its continuing strategic nuclear buildup, the Soviet Union demonstrates that it does not subscribe to American notions of nuclear sufficiency and mutually assured deterrence, which postulate that once a certain quantity and quality of strategic nuclear weapons is attained, both sides will understand that further accumulation or improvement becomes pointless, and act accordingly. Soviet strategists regard the possession of more and better strategic weapons as a definite military and political asset, and potentially the ultimate instrument of coercion. The intensive programs of civil defense and hardening of command and control posts against nuclear attack undertaken in the Soviet Union in recent years suggest that they take seriously the possibility of nuclear war and believe that, were it to occur, they will be more likely to survive and to recover more rapidly than we.

## STRATEGIC SUPERIORITY

In recent years, the Soviet Union has been increasing its military expenditures at an annual rate of at least 3 to 4% while the United States has until recently been decreasing its military expenditures at a rate of 3%, taking inflation into account in both cases. The experts disagree as to whether the Soviet Union is already ahead of the United States in military strength, either overall or in particular theaters. However, we are convinced, and there is widespread agreement among knowledgeable experts, that *if past trends continue, the USSR will within several years achieve strategic superiority over the United States*. The USSR already enjoys conventional superiority in several important theaters.

Superiority in both strategic and conventional weapons could enable the Soviet Union to apply decisive pressure on the United States in conflict situations. The USSR might then compel the United States to retreat, much as the USSR itself was forced to retreat in 1962 during the Cuban missile crisis. As an example, one could conceive of another war in the Middle East in which the USSR, having acquired local conventional superiority and overall nuclear superiority, could compel the United States to withdraw its influence from that area.

Soviet pressure, when supported by strategic and conventional military superiority, would be aimed at forcing our general withdrawal from a leading role in world affairs, and isolating us from other democratic societies, which could not then long survive.

Thus conceived, Soviet superiority would serve basically offensive aims, enabling the USSR to project its power in various parts of the globe without necessarily establishing a major physical presence in any single country. Soviet strategic superiority could lead the USSR to believe that should it eventually succeed in isolating the United States from its allies and the Third World, the United States would be less likely, in a major crisis, to lash out with strategic nuclear weapons, in a desperate attempt to escape subjugation.

## THE SOVIET DRIVE

The Soviet doctrine calls for ambitious goals; Soviet actions confirm that it continues persistently to pursue those goals. Its resources are limited, it confronts major internal difficulties, and its forays into world politics often experience setbacks. Nevertheless, it is driven by internal, historical and ideological pressures toward an expansionist policy which, given its enormous military might, makes it a uniquely dangerous adversary. There is no evidence that SALT, expanded economic and cultural relations, the Helsinki agreement, or any of the other features of "détente" have weakened the Soviet drive. Its objectives are global, its instrumentalities varied, and its ability to pursue long-term objectives while exploiting short-term opportunities remains unchanged.

## THE CHALLENGE TO AMERICA

To ignore declared Soviet intentions and demonstrated Soviet capabilities in an erroneous conviction that we have "enough" to defend ourselves and that there is always "time" to strengthen ourselves could prove to be fatal shortsightedness. In the nuclear age "enough" may not be enough, and "time" may run out unless our efforts keep pace.

We live in an age in which there is no alternative to vigilance and credible deterrence at the significant levels of potential conflict. Indeed, this is the prerequisite to the pursuit of genuine détente and the negotiation of prudent and verifiable arms control agreements that effectively serve to reduce the danger of war.

Weakness invites aggression, strength deters it. Thus, American strength holds the key to our quest for peace and to our survival as a free society in a world friendly to our hopes and ideals.

*4 April 1977*

# Where We Stand on SALT

In our Committee's initial policy statement, "Common Sense and the Common Danger," we said:

"The goal of our strategic forces should be to prevent the use of, or the credible threat to use, strategic weapons in world politics; that of our conventional forces, to prevent other forms of aggression directed against our interests. Without a stable balance of forces in the world and policies of collective defense based upon it, no other objective of our foreign policy is attainable.

"From a strong foundation, we can pursue a positive and confident diplomacy, addressed to the full array of our economic, political, and social interests in world politics. It is only on this basis that we can expect successfully to negotiate hardheaded and verifiable agreements to control and reduce armaments."

For nearly ten years the United States and the Soviet Union have been engaged in sporadic negotiations concerning strategic arms, a dialogue that has come to be known as SALT—an acronym for Strategic Arms Limitation Talks.

We are engaged in such talks because of a justified desire to achieve sensible limitations upon weapons of mass destruction and thus to restrain the costly and dangerous competition in strategic arms. Three successive administrations in Washington have supported the SALT process and important U.S.-USSR agreements have been signed.

## DOUBT AND CONFUSION

Nevertheless, there is a lingering sense of unease about the prudence of the U.S. posture in these protracted negotiations. The ambiguous consequences of the first SALT agreement in 1972 and the complex nature of the current negotiations have tended to generate doubt and confusion in public and Congressional opinion.

The subject matter, at once formidable and forbidding, imposes novel strains on our democratic system of political communication, debate and decision-making. Consideration of the technical aspects of SALT and serious analysis of the negotiating process have become the concern of a small number of specialists. Journalists and commentators, sometimes unfamiliar with the complex issues, have borne the principal burden of interpreting SALT to the public at large and to most members of the Congress who must ultimately accept or reject an arms control treaty with the Soviets. Hence the question, echoing the concern of uneasy citizens: Where do we stand on SALT?

The U.S. negotiating posture should be analyzed in the light of SALT's basic premise and its future prospects.

## DIFFERING OBJECTIVES

From the U.S. point of view, the main objective of SALT has been to reduce the weight of nuclear arms in the relationship between the U.S. and the Soviet Union as a factor in world politics. Agreement has been sought on measures designed to assure 1) that both sides have essential equivalence in nuclear capabilities and 2) that neither side could hope to gain more than it would lose by striking first. Thus assured, both the U.S. and the USSR could progressively reduce the proportion of resources devoted to nuclear weapons, releasing them for other pressing needs and priorities.

The U.S. hoped to slow down the brutal momentum of the massive Soviet strategic arms buildup—a buildup without precedent in history. To demonstrate its own sincerity of purpose, the U.S. has restrained its research, development and weapons deployment programs as well as its public statements. The U.S. has hoped to encourage a matching Soviet response.

Yet the "parallelism" assumed in this approach, has not been evident in the Soviet Union's bargaining stance and tactics. From the beginning of SALT at Helsinki in 1969, the Soviet objective has been to extend its gains in relative posture while encouraging maximum restraint upon U.S. programs. In the classic Soviet fashion, negotiations have been regarded as a means of stalling and impeding the adversary's momentum while maintaining its own.

Far from heeding the American example of restraint, the Soviets have used to advantage the mounting pressure of their high rate of technical developments and weapons deployments relative to our own. To the extent that these trends appeared likely to continue, the U.S. was encouraged to conclude that time was running against its position. This increased the pressure on the U.S. to move prematurely—and perhaps unwisely—toward partial agreements of limited usefulness. There has been no similar time pressure on the Soviets.

Simultaneously, the Soviets have sought to use public opinion and Congressional pressure to induce Washington to agree to unequal compromises unfavorable to the United States. Meanwhile, the Soviet Union was under no such pressure and could blame the U.S. when negotiations faltered or threatened to collapse.

A third factor of some value to the Soviet Union is the unrealistic level of expectations stirred by the optimistic statements of successive U.S. administrations. Inevitably, SALT has become enmeshed in domestic politics and popular hopes for détente, and "progress" has seemed a political imperative.

In implementing the SALT I agreements, the Soviet side ignored the U.S. interpretation of their ambiguities and stretched the agreed language to its full limits or beyond.

## A NEW U.S. APPROACH

The arrival of the Carter Administration in Washington brought changes in the U.S. approach. A new team of policy makers, diplomats and specialists undertook a fundamental review of the U.S. SALT posture.

In March 1977, President Carter instructed Secretary of State Cyrus Vance to present at Moscow:

1) a comprehensive proposal involving substantial mutual force reductions coupled with significant limitations designed to restrain improvements in intercontinental ballistic missiles (ICBMs) and, as an alternative,

2) a modest approach designed to continue earlier progress toward implementing the Vladivostok Accord while deferring for future negotiations two highly controversial items, the Soviet Backfire bomber and the U.S. cruise missile.

The main provisions of the March comprehensive proposal were:

• Reduction of the Vladivostok limit of 2,400 strategic offensive launch vehicles by

about 20 percent to 1,800/2,000;
- Reduction of the Vladivostok limits of 1,320 MIRVed (multiple independent reentry vehicle) missile launchers by about 15 percent to 1,100/1,200;
- A sublimit of 550 MIRVed ICBM launchers;
- Inclusion of all Soviet SS-17s, SS-18s and SS-19s within the 550 subceiling;
- A limit of 150 on Soviet SS-9 and SS-18 modern large ballistic missiles (MLBMs) within the 550 subceiling, with zero MLBMs permitted to the U.S.;
- A ban on the testing or deployment of all new or mobile ICBMs and prohibition of modification of existing ICBMs;
- A limitation to six flight tests per year for all ICBMs and an equal limit on all submarine-launched ballistic missile (SLBM) flight tests;
- A ban on armed cruise missiles with range greater than 2,500 kilometers.

## THE BASIC QUESTIONS

Given this background, it is crucial to pose four questions:

1. Would an agreement based on the March comprehensive proposal significantly improve mutual deterrence, enhance stability in crisis and thereby reduce the risk of war?

2. Would the probable situation resulting from the implementation of such an agreement favor the U.S., favor the USSR, or would it be reasonably equal?

3. Would implementation of such an agreement require the U.S. or the USSR to make greater changes from present and planned deployments?

4. Could the Soviet Union be expected to agree to the proposal? In other words, is it negotiable?

The terms of the comprehensive March 1977 proposal would effectively bar the U.S. from improving the destructive power of its ICBMs, thus assuring the survival of Soviet ICBM silos in the event of either an initial or a retaliatory U.S. strike. America's MIRVed ICBMs would be restricted to the 550 Minuteman IIIs presently deployed, with an aggregate throw-weight[1] of 1.25 million pounds. The Soviet Union's MIRVed ICBMs—SS-17s, SS-18s and SS-19s—would also be limited in number to 550 but, because of their much larger size, would have a throw-weight of approximately 5.2 million pounds—*more than four times* that allowed the U.S.

The number of Soviet MIRVed ICBM reentry vehicles would be more than twice as large as ours, and the yield of each reentry vehicle would be some *five times* the yield of ours. Moreover, the U.S. cannot be assured that we possess, and will continue to possess, a sufficient margin of qualitative superiority to offset these Soviet quantitative advantages.

## SOVIET ADVANTAGES

It has become the conventional wisdom to maintain that such Soviet advantages do not really matter. Yet detailed calculations, covering the range of reasonable assumptions, demonstrate that under any of the SALT agreements now being considered, and assuming current programs continue, regardless of whether the U.S. or the USSR strikes first, the Soviets would destroy more strategic targets and damage more people and industry in a nuclear war. Moreover, their destructive potential and strategic advantage are growing.

The March comprehensive proposal, while halting improvements in U.S. ICBMs, would merely delay Soviet improvements to some degree; the question is how much and for how long?

## THE ANSWERS

Thus, in response to the first two questions, it appears that the March 1977 comprehensive proposal is potentially unfavorable for the United States. Agreement on the basis of this proposal would not assure crisis stability and mutual deterrence; and its terms would disproportionately favor the USSR as against the U.S.

As to the third question, under the U.S. comprehensive proposal, the USSR would be forced to make significant changes in their present and planned programs, while relatively fewer would have to be made in our own. We would have to forgo the yet to be approved new mobile ICBM (MX) engineering development program, but the Soviets would have to cut their SS-18 deployment program by more than half, and would be forced to realign their SS-17 and SS-19 programs. Finally, they would have to give up the large effort already invested in follow-on missile programs.

The Soviets have astutely used the fact that they would have to make more and greater changes in their programs to charge the U.S. with making unfair proposals. We, on the other hand, have not sufficiently emphasized that, even after the called for reductions in their planned forces, the Soviets would still retain significant advantages over the U.S.

As President Carter has made clear, however, the test for the fairness of SALT agreements is not how much each side has to give up, but whether the resulting agreement gives solid assurance of mutual deterrence against the use or the credible threat to use nuclear weapons in world politics. The relatively greater Soviet reductions required by our March proposals simply reflect the fact that we have allowed the Soviet Union to gain a potentially destabilizing lead in this field.

It was, of course, unlikely that the Soviets would wish to accept a freeze on technology. They have made it an important part of their doctrine to equal or surpass the U.S. in every phase of military technology.

In any case, Chairman Brezhnev and Foreign Minister Gromyko lost no time in forcefully making it clear that the Soviet side had no intention of even discussing our comprehensive proposal. They insisted that we negotiate an agreement to include those terms most favorable to the Soviet Union discussed during negotiations with the last Administration pursuant to the Vladivostok Accord.

## THE MAY PROPOSAL

In May, Secretary Vance put forward a proposal for a new negotiating framework. He suggested that it was designed to arrive at the same general results as the March comprehensive proposal but over a somewhat longer period of time.

The new framework would have three tiers. The first tier would be an eight-year treaty, presumably similar to Mr. Vance's March alternate deferral proposal. The second tier would be a protocol to the treaty to last for only three years. The third tier would be an agreed statement of principles to guide the continuing negotiations on an agreement which it is hoped would come into effect upon the termination of the three-year protocol.

It appears that the suggested three-year protocol would ban the testing or deployment of new ICBMs, specifically including mobile ICBMs, and ground- and sea-launched, but not air-launched, intermediate range cruise missiles. It would limit the deployment of the very large Soviet SS-18 ICBMs to a number significantly higher than the March proposal. It would have no separate limit covering the aggregate number of SS-17s, SS-18s and SS-19s, other than the overall limit on MIRVed launchers in the treaty. It further appears that there might be an equal but separate limit on the numbers of Backfire bombers and heavy bombers equipped with intermediate range cruise missiles to be produced and deployed during the period.

According to press reports, the U.S. suggested in May 1977 that the guidelines for future negotiations call for a SALT III agreement to provide deep reductions in the number of ICBMs, particularly in large MIRVed ICBMs, and that the Soviet side suggested that so-called "forward based systems" be taken into consideration, including tactical aircraft based in Europe and aboard carriers, but not their SS-20 IRBMs or Backfire bombers.

## THE FALL BACK

It is noteworthy that Mr. Vance's May proposal appears to have raised the limit of 150 on SS-18s, abandoned the limit of 550 on MIRVed ICBMs and dropped the limit on the number of ICBM and of SLBM flight tests. Thus, almost all of those elements of the March proposal designed to delay the Soviet threat to the future survival of U.S. land-based ICBMs have been given up. On the other hand, the May proposal would appear to contain provisions which would make impossible, or at least delay, a U.S. response to that threat, such as deployment of mobile launchers for our ICBMs, the MX missile and the Mark-12A warhead.

The Soviet reaction to Washington's prompt and substantial retreat from the March proposals was brazenly to announce that "the U.S. has not yet ceased to seek unilateral advantages."

There can no longer be any reason to doubt the firmness and one-sidedness of the Soviet Union's SALT negotiating position. The Soviets evidently believe that their position is so strong, and that the U.S. is so eager to achieve an agreement, that they have merely to say "No" to our proposals, and we will come forward with modifications progressively more advantageous to their side.

## A STRATEGY FOR THE UNITED STATES

How should the U.S. deal with this situation?

In the short run, it is unlikely that a comprehensive and safe SALT agreement can be negotiated. In the longer run, our March proposal, adjusted to remove its more obvious inequities to the U.S., might constitute a framework for mutually productive negotiations—provided that we meanwhile demonstrate in action our determination, agreement or no agreement, to maintain forces fully adequate to deter attack against the U.S. and our allies. This course would require us to move forward promptly on several pending and projected strategic systems to restore the credibility of our second-strike deterrent.

We must demonstrate that we are firmly committed to a course of action designed to safeguard our strategic interests. Therein lies our only hope of persuading the Soviets that it is in their interest to negotiate within the general provisions of a modified U.S. comprehensive approach.

## THE PROGRAM

There are a number of elements essential to achieving this posture. A critical one is the development of the MX mobile missile. Deployment of the MX system in a mobile multiple aim-point mode will yield great bargaining leverage. The MX so deployed should be highly survivable in the face of a Soviet first strike, and the surviving MX missiles should be capable of neutralizing a large number of those Soviet missiles not utilized in an initial strike.

MX, therefore, could significantly reverse the unfavorable trends in the U.S.-Soviet nuclear balance which would otherwise continue unchecked.

To proceed with the MX requires that we not ban new or mobile ICBMs or the testing of new ICBMs. We should also not accept limitations which would affect our ability to take other measures, including the development and deployment of those cruise missiles which may be deemed necessary to cover the period before the MX can be deployed in adequate numbers.

In other words, the essentials of the U.S. comprehensive proposal would have to be withdrawn until the Soviet Union demonstrated a willingness to negotiate with an equal desire to reduce the dangers to both sides from the existence of powerful fixed ICBMs and forces able to destroy them.

## ASSURING U.S. SECURITY

To be effective, agreements must serve the interests of the parties professing to adhere to them. When circumstances or perceptions change, the chance of serious miscalculation increases. Our deterrent strength serves to minimize the inherent risks of a Soviet miscalculation, and reinforces our political will to resist Soviet aggression.

The Soviet view is that the best deterrent is the capability to fight and win a nuclear war—and to survive in the process. It is our task to deny them that capability.

SALT agreements can contribute to U.S. national security by establishing agreed limits on Soviet nuclear deployments, just as they can increase Soviet security by agreed limits on our nuclear deployments. But such limits can make only a partial contribution to U.S. security. The essential deterrent function must still be provided by U.S. strategic forces.

Thus, before the United States accepts any SALT agreements, we should assure ourselves that the verifiable limitations on Soviet deployments, coupled with the military potential of the weapons the U.S. actually intends to develop and deploy within the framework of the agreement, are truly adequate to assure U.S. security. We must satisfy ourselves that, at all times, we will be in a position to deny the Soviets any rational grounds for testing deterrence.

If we face up to the disturbing state of our strategic forces, make use of the potential of our technology and productive capacity, and demonstrate our determination to maintain an adequate deterrent force, the Soviets should, in time, respond positively to our hopes for peace and stability in the world.

It is disappointing that arms control agreements cannot in themselves assure a nuclear standoff and permit a smaller U.S. effort. At best, such agreements can set some rules limiting the nature of the competition—similar to agreeing on the size of a football field and the number of players on each side. Such agreement, however, does not assure a season of tie games. One of the teams might think it important to win, whatever the agreed rules. If the rules were to allow their side thirteen men and ours only ten, they might be even more eager to try.

*6 July 1977*

## NOTES

1. Throw-weight is the power of a missile's boosters to propel useful payload into an intercontinental trajectory.

# 5

# Peace With Freedom

## A Discussion by the Committee on
## The Present Danger Before the Foreign
## Policy Association
## 14 March 1978

## What Is the Soviet Union Up To? The Status
## of SALT II; U.S. Posture In the World

Responding to an invitation from the Foreign Policy Association, the Committee on the Present Danger presented a distinguished panel of Board members to address a special luncheon meeting of the Association in the Grand Ballroom Suite of the New York Hilton on Tuesday, 14 March 1978.

The Foreign Policy Association is a national educational organization. Ever since its founding in 1918, the Association has worked to help Americans gain a better understanding of significant issues in United States foreign policy and to stimulate a wide and constructive citizen participation in world affairs.

### PROGRAM

**Introduction:**
CARTER BURGESS
President, Foreign Policy Association

**Presiding:**
HENRY H. FOWLER
Co-Chairman, CPD

**Moderator:**
DAVID PACKARD
Co-Chairman, CPD

**The Panel**
RICHARD E. PIPES
Member, Executive Committee, CPD
"What Is the Soviet Union Up To?"

PAUL H. NITZE
Chairman, Policy Studies, CPD
"The Status of SALT II"

EUGENE V. ROSTOW
Chairman, Executive Committee, CPD
"U.S. Posture In the World"


## INTRODUCTORY REMARKS

**MR. BURGESS:** It is my great pleasure to present Henry H. Fowler, Co-Chairman of the Committee on the Present Danger, who will introduce the program and tell you what's to come. Mr. Fowler?

(Applause.)

**MR. FOWLER:**[1] Thank you very much, Carter Burgess. As Co-Chairman of the Committee on the Present Danger, may I express on behalf of the Executive Committee our sincere appreciation to the Foreign Policy Association for this opportunity to be heard by this distinguished group. What better or more fitting forum for such a discussion could be found than this luncheon sponsored by the Foreign Policy Association as a part of its continuing program of national education on significant issues of American foreign policy?

The basic purpose of our Committee, which was established on November 11, 1976, is to facilitate a national discussion of the foreign and national security policies of the United States directed toward a secure peace with freedom. The Committee is a non-profit, nonpartisan educational organization, wholly independent in character, with no political axes to grind. We welcome the support of Democrats, Republicans and Independents, and our membership amply reflects all of these categories.

The 141 men and women who are the founding members have unanimously endorsed the policy statement entitled, "Common Sense and the Common Danger." They believe that, to follow the bipartisan consensus which sustained our foreign policy between 1940 and the mid-'60s, we must build a fresh consensus to expand the opportunities and diminish the dangers of a world in flux. They believe further that the principal threat to our nation, to world peace, and to the cause of human freedom is the Soviet drive for dominance based upon an unparalleled military buildup.

I invite your careful attention to our policy statement, to its analysis of the present danger and the nature of the military and the political threat facing our country from Soviet expansionism, which threatens to destroy the world balance of forces on which the survival of freedom and our national security depend.

I invite you to examine the list of founding members which is contained in our policy statement. You will find that they make up a broad cross-section of private citizenry, serving no personal or official interest other than their country's peace with freedom and security. Their objectivity and their experienced judgment cannot be denied.

I invite your attention to a full reading of the brief brochure entitled, "How the Committee on the Present Danger Will Operate—What It Will Do, and What It Will Not Do," dealing with affiliations, financing, political activity and operations generally.

Finally, I welcome your presence here today to the panel discussion which my Co-Chairman, David Packard, will lead, and to the presentations of three distinguished members of our Executive Committee who will offer their substantive views on the pressing foreign policy issues which emerge from the present danger we all face.

Thank you very much.

(Applause.)

MR. PACKARD:[2] Ladies and gentlemen, I'm very pleased to be here with my Co-Chairman, Mr. Fowler. I want to add my words of appreciation to the Foreign Policy Association for allowing us to be with you.

Each of the three members of the panel will have a statement of about ten minutes. They promised me they would not be too long, so that then we will have some time for questions. Now for the introductions:

At the far end of the table is Professor Eugene V. Rostow, the Chairman of the Executive Committee of the Committee on the Present Danger. He is as much as anyone else responsible for the formation of this Committee, because he began talking about it with a number of us many months before the Committee was formed. He is Sterling Professor of Law and Public Affairs at Yale Law School and formerly was the Dean. He served as Under Secretary of State under President Lyndon Johnson. Mr. Rostow has published widely on international affairs and is considered to be one of the outstanding experts in this country on American foreign policy.

Next to him is Dr. Richard E. Pipes, a member of the Executive Committee of our Committee. Dr. Pipes is Frank B. Baird, Jr. Professor of History at Harvard University. He was Director of the Russian Research Institute at Harvard from 1968 to 1973. In 1976, he served as the Chairman of the now famous Team B Competitive National Estimate Committee which surveyed U.S.-Soviet defense capabilites. Paul Nitze also served on Team B.

Dr. Pipes has published a number of distinguished papers on various aspects of Soviet relations. Last year, his paper on why the Soviet Union thinks it could fight and win a nuclear war attracted widespread attention. He is recognized, without any question, as one of the outstanding American authorities on Russian history and the present relationship between the two countries.

Our third panel member is Mr. Paul H. Nitze, the Chairman of Policy Studies of the Committee on the Present Danger. Mr. Nitze has had very long experience in Washington. He was the Vice Chairman of the United States Strategic Bombing Survey from 1944 to 1946. Subsequently, he was Director of the Policy Planning Staff of the State Department under President Truman. Then he became Assistant Secretary of Defense for International Security Affairs under President Kennedy. He then went on to become Secretary of the Navy and was my predecessor as Deputy Secretary of Defense. I had the opportunity to become acquainted with Paul in 1969 and he was very helpful to us at that time in the various studies that were being undertaken in preparation for the SALT negotiations. As you know, he was a member of the United States Delegation to the Strategic Arms Limitation Talks under President Nixon.

Mr. Nitze is now the Chairman of the Advisory Council of the School of Advanced International Studies at Johns Hopkins University. He is one of the few people in Washington with long and intensive experience in the field of arms control.

We will begin with a statement from Dr. Pipes.

## Panel Discussion

DR. PIPES: Thank you, Mr. Chairman. As you are no doubt aware, the Committee on the Present Danger does not hold a monopoly on the discussion of American-Soviet relations or on the military balance. We have competition in the form of the American

Committee on East-West Accord, which consists of eminent, honorable and knowledge-able people, who nevertheless hold views which are diametrically opposed to ours. To me, both as a concerned citizen and as a historian, it always seems very interesting to find out why people who start from basically the same premises and hold the same values can disagree so violently on what to do and how to go about doing it.

It seems to me that the difference between us and them boils down to two fundamental differences of perception of the Soviet Union and specifically, what is presently happen-ing in the Soviet Union, i.e., how it is evolving, and, secondly, what are Soviet intentions?

The ideological leaders of the other committee, Professor George Kennan, for exam-ple, believe that the Soviet Union, in the past 25 years, has undergone a very fundamen-tal change which makes our (and his own) old view of the Soviet Union no longer realistic. From a country which indeed was totally despotic and bent on world aggres-sion, they believe that it has become a more or less normal society, which shares the same objectives as we.

I think this assessment is wrong, because, as a historian, I believe that changes, to be meaningful, have to be institutional changes. They have to be changes in existing institutions—political, judicial and economic—if they are to have meaning and be effective. No such constitutional changes have occurred in the Soviet Union since the death of Stalin. In looking at the Soviet Union today, compared to 25 years ago, we see changed policies but we do not see a changed structure. The mechanism of repression, which Stalin left on his death, remains intact. When Brezhnev passes from the scene, it would be entirely possible to reactivate the Stalinist policy, for which reason we are opposed to mortgaging our security and our future to hopes of fundamental change in the Soviet Union.

The second disagreement between us concerns Soviet intentions and specifically, Soviet military intentions. There is not a great deal of difference between what one may call the Team A and the Team B view of the Soviet military buildup. The basic difference is in the significance one attaches to it and the way one explains the reasons behind it. The Team A point of view (I'm using this phrase in a figurative sense) is that the Soviet Union fundamentally reacts to United States initiatives, that it is the United States that engages and has been engaging since World War II in a massive military buildup which the Soviet Union perceives as threatening, and that the most significant Soviet military moves are best explained as responses.

We do not look at it this way. We see an internal logic to the Soviet military buildup, which proceeds largely independently of what we do. We see that, for example, over the past ten years during which we have frozen our ICBM forces in the hope of inducing the Russians, after they've caught up with us, to slow down their pace of ICBM buildup as well, that this self-restraint has not been reciprocated.

So we have here a very fundamental difference of perceptions. From it flow also different views of what Soviet policy is and what we ought to do about it. Speaking for myself, because Committee members don't necessarily agree on all details, my view is that the primary Soviet priorities, as of now, are two-fold. One is to build up a significant preponderance in strategic weapons, which will have the effect of neutralizing the American strategic deterrent as well as of making the Soviet Union absorb an American first strike and then retaliate with an overwhelming force. I can't see how one can explain otherwise a great variety of moves which the Russians are making in the strategic field, both of an offensive and a defensive nature, and their unwillingness to make meaningful concessions in SALT in particular, their unwillingness to cut down on the number of SS-18 missiles, which, as I see it, are primarily a first-strike weapon. This is for the Soviet Union priority number one.

Closely linked to it—I can call it priority one-B—is the severance of the ties between the United States and its allies primarily in Western Europe. The way the Soviet Union intends to accomplish this is with a variety of means of which perhaps an across-the-frontier invasion is the least likely.

The most effective form which this threat takes is first, an enormous military buildup on the European frontier, which has the psychological effect of intimidating European public opinion and creating a sense of helplessness; and, secondly, through a flanking movement, via the Middle East and Africa, which endangers European oil supplies and a large proportion of European mineral supplies from South Africa. These measures can bring Europe to its knees without any shots necessarily being fired.

I think this is Soviet strategy and I must say that some of the conversations I have had with Chinese military experts confirmed that they see things exactly the same way. This agreement does not necessarily mean we're both right. We may both be wrong, but the coincidence is rather striking to me, at least, and reassuring.

Finally, what needs to be done? It is my opinion, and I think it's the opinion of most of my colleagues on the Committee, that we must seriously improve the quality and the credibility of our strategic deterrent, which is deteriorating due to aging and technological obsolescence, but which is also deteriorating in view of the pronounced unwillingness of the present Administration to engage in the buildup of two of the three legs of our Triad. We are really left only with one leg: if nothing is done, our main strategic deterrent will be the submarine.

Europe too needs to be beefed up. It is essential that we manufacture and deploy the so-called, unfortunately called, "neutron bomb," despite Russian threats, because it is of great importance in balancing the vast Soviet preponderance in tanks and other armored fighting vehicles, both in quantity and quality. We should apply all the pressure we can on our European allies to join us in this effort, openly, because after all, we have at stake the lives of 300,000 American troops there. Finally, we should draw closer to China politically and, if need be, also militarily.

Unless these things are done, we will suffer the fate of becoming an impotent giant, unable to protect his interests. We can, of course, retreat to a fortress America. This, however, would have profoundly adverse consequences not only on the standard of living of America but also on the quality of its life.

We are already in danger of this happening to us. The Russians, if I may interpret their actions, already begin to treat us as inferiors; I judge by the way they refuse to make any concessions in SALT II or in their African policy. They are already treating us as a power that is potentially still dangerous but fundamentally no longer in a position systematically to defend its interests abroad. This is a very dangerous situation because the Russian leadership, by virtue of its traditions, and by virtue of its collective political psyche, is inclined to take advantage of such situations. Our Committee is trying very hard to prevent them from so doing.

Thank you.

(Applause.)

**MR. NITZE:** I propose to say a few words about the SALT negotiations. It is my view that one should look at SALT II not just as an arms control agreement; one should also look at SALT in the context of, and as it bears on, our evolving strategic nuclear defense posture relative to the USSR. Furthermore, one should look at our strategic nuclear defence posture as it bears on our general defense posture and at our general defense posture as it bears on our foreign policy and the future of this country.

For many reasons and going back for about a decade to the last year of the Johnson administration, the United States hasn't really been addressing itself in a serious and consequent way to how our strategic nuclear posture has been, and would be, developing relative to that of the Soviet Union. It was thought that a SALT agreement would be the best solution to that growing problem. It was hoped that an equitable and effective SALT deal could be negotiated. Therefore, we didn't need to worry too much about correcting adverse trends in our relative strategic nuclear posture.

By 1972 we had worked out an ABM Treaty which was equal in its terms; it had a number of bugs in it, but, by and large, it was a balanced and, I believe, useful Treaty. It proved impossible, however, to work out a comparably equitable and useful treaty limiting offensive nuclear armaments. The Interim Agreement was a mere stopgap; the hope was that it would provide time to negotiate a more meaningful agreement.

By 1974 there was clear evidence that there was no longer much chance of negotiating an equitable and useful SALT II treaty. At that time, some of us recommended to President Nixon that we again address ourselves to assuring, through our own programs, that we always have a strategic nuclear posture of rough equality with, and able to counter, the expanding Soviet programs. But President Nixon became so engrossed in Watergate that he ceased to pay serious attention to much else.

Subsequently President Ford, relying on Dr. Kissinger, negotiated the Vladivostok Accord. It didn't accomplish much, but didn't need to hurt us if we didn't go beyond Vladivostok, didn't further tie our hands, and took those actions permitted under Vladivostok which it was wise for our side to take.

Today it is even clearer that it is no longer possible to accomplish anything significant through SALT II toward assuring against the growing vulnerability of our ICBMs, a large percentage of our bombers, our SLBMs in port and perhaps even some of our SLBMs at sea, and certainly not our industry or population, no matter how successful our negotiators are in resolving the still disagreed issues. There now appears to be little we can do, SALT or no SALT, to avoid having a situation arise during the next three to eight years of significant strategic nuclear inferiority to the Soviet Union.

But does this make any difference? Paul Warnke still argues that we are much stronger than the Soviet Union and that we will continue to be so almost regardless of what we do. However, almost no one, except Warnke, any longer accepts that argument.

To my mind, one of the most important measures of the relative strategic positions of the two sides is the prompt countermilitary potential of each side. It is hard to see how the U.S., even if it carries out all currently approved programs without unanticipated delays, is going to avoid being at an eight to one—maybe twelve to one—disadvantage as measured by that index in 1985.

Similarly, by 1985 we are likely to be at more than a three-fold disadvantage in megatonnage, the best index of population vulnerability to fallout. It is only in the number of warheads in the peacetime inventory that we can expect to remain somewhat ahead; but that index wrongly implies that weapons which differ more than 500-fold in their yield are equivalent in effectiveness.

The President, a few months ago, made the decision to increase that portion of our defense expenditures related to the NATO central front by three percent per annum in real terms, but to take at least part of the money out of funds that had been programmed for the Navy, and from those that had been programmed for strengthening our nuclear deterrent. Strategically, I believe he has his priorities wrong. In the short run, politically and cosmetically, I can see why he made such a decision. But if we don't get at correcting the upcoming deficiencies in our central nuclear posture, it would be fool-hardy actually to fight in defense of Europe as opposed to merely posturing. And if we don't correct our naval deficiencies, we will not be able to sustain a military effort for any length of time at any distance beyond our own shores.

Some Executive Branch proponents, rather than taking exception to the main thrust of the preceding analysis, argue a different series of points along the following line:

1. The President's March 1977 comprehensive SALT II proposal leaned over backward in attempting to be fair to the Soviet Union. It offered them complete assurance against any significant counterforce threat from the United States while not assuring comparable protection for the United States.
2. That proposal was wholly unacceptable to the USSR, and any proposal which would in fact assure stability and rough equivalence at lower levels of nuclear armaments would be even more unnegotiable.
3. To insist on such an equitable agreement would assure that there would be no success, at least in the next few years, in negotiating a SALT II set of agreements. Such a delay would risk a breakdown of détente.
4. Rather than risk such a breakdown, it is wiser to negotiate the best deal that is now reachable, preserve at least the outward forms of détente, and open the way to follow-on negotiations for a better deal in the future.
5. And, in any case, a deterioration in the state of the strategic nuclear balance will have no adverse political or diplomatic consequences.

To those who lived through the Berlin crisis in 1961, the Cuban crisis in 1962, or the Middle East crisis in 1973, the last and key judgment in this chain of reasoning—that an adverse shift in the strategic nuclear balance will have no political or diplomatic consequences—comes as a shock. In the Berlin crisis of 1961 our tactical theater position was clearly unfavorable; we relied entirely on our strategic nuclear superiority to face down Chairman Khrushchev's ultimatum. In the Cuban crisis the Soviet Union faced a position of both theater inferiority and strategic inferiority; they withdrew the missiles they were deploying. In the 1973 Middle East crisis, the theater and the strategic nuclear balances were roughly equal; both sides compromised.

It is hard to see what factors in the future are apt to disconnect international politics and diplomacy from a consideration of the underlying balance in the real factors of power. The nuclear balance is, of course, only one element in the overall power balance. But in the Soviet view, it is the fulcrum upon which all other levers of influence—military, economic, or political—rest. Can we be confident that there is not at least a measure of validity to that viewpoint?

In summary, I believe the issue is not so much whether a SALT II Treaty can be negotiated and ratified, but rather what the United States should be doing to correct the currently adverse trends in our strategic posture.

Thank you.

(Applause.)

MR. PACKARD: And now, Mr. Rostow.

MR. ROSTOW: Allen Nevins started his great book, *The Ordeal of the Union*, shortly after World War II, and in its shadow. As most of you will recall, his theme is that the Civil War was a reproach to a generation of weak and inadequate leaders who failed to prevent it, as two generations of weak and inadequate British leaders failed to prevent both World Wars. You will recall as well the title of the first volume of Churchill's memoir of the Second World War: *The Unnecessary War.*

It need not have been.

This is the conviction which led us to form the Committee on the Present Danger in 1975 and 1976—the conviction that the conditions of world politics today are strikingly like those of the decades before 1914 and 1939. Since the final bitter phases of the Vietnam War, our governments have been reacting with the same fear, passivity, and inadequacy which characterized British and American policy so fatally in the Thirties, and British policy before 1914.

A second reason led us to come forward. The bipartisan consensus about foreign policy which President Truman and Secretary of State Acheson achieved in the late Forties has been gravely weakened by the passage of time and the shocks of the final period of the war in Indo-China. A new generation has emerged—a generation which knew not Pharaoh.

A third aspect of our situation stirred us to form the Committee. This time we must arrest the slide toward chaos before it explodes into war. Both world wars were appalling and destructive events. We are still living with many of their consequences. The evil of totalitarianism is the worst, but there are others. The risks of a third general war in a nuclear environment are terrible to contemplate. Yet war may come if we feel ourselves threatened and coerced; if we sense that the last vestige of our power to govern our own destiny is slipping out of our hands; if the Soviet Union takes control of one strong point after another, and achieves domination in Western Europe or Japan, or in a number of places whose power in combination spells hegemony. We can never recall too often Thucydides' comment that the real cause of the Pelopennesian War was not the episodes of friction and conflict which preceded it, but the rise in the power of Athens, and the fear this caused in Sparta.

We therefore resolved to do everything we could while there was still time to promote a serious and disciplined discussion among our people about how to protect our national interests in world politics in peace.

There is no longer any real doubt or even debate about what is happening, although there is still some disagreement about what these trends mean, and what we should do about them. One after another, those who have been defending and explaining Soviet behavior as no more than "defensive" or "suspicious" have been falling silent, or confessing error. The pressures of Soviet imperial ambition, backed by a military buildup without parallel in modern history, are threatening the world balance of power on which our ultimate safety as a nation depends. It is touching nerves to which we are immensely sensitive as a maritime power—an island, really:—the freedom of the seas, access to raw materials, our free alliances with the great industrialized democracies of Europe and the Pacific Basin, and our promising rapprochement with Communist China.

In a recent White Paper, the British government concluded, just as our Committee did eighteen months ago, that the Soviet military posture and building program are offensive in character, and cannot be explained by considerations of defense. President Carter used almost the same words last May about the Soviet military position in Europe. Secretary of Defense Brown estimates that after fifteen years of steady growth, the Soviet military budget is 20%-40% higher than our own—the higher figure excludes military pensions from the comparison. In pensions we are well "ahead."

Other estimates conclude that the Soviet military budget today is between 60% and 80% higher than our own. Secretary Brown believes that the Soviet military budget is growing at a rate between 3% and 4% a year in real terms. Others put the rate of growth at 5% a year. President Carter has just proposed a rate of increase in our own budget of 1.8% a year in real terms. On this basis, we will fall further behind.

In presenting the budget, Secretary Brown used the metaphor of the tortoise and the hare. It is an appropriate one. Unfortunately, however, the hare is still asleep.

Meanwhile, using, threatening, and deploying its military power, the Soviet Union has moved forward since 1970 with increasing boldness in Asia, Africa, and the Middle East. The massive Soviet threat to China persuaded the Chinese to turn to us as the only force on earth that could deter Soviet pressure. The rapprochement between China and the United States is one of the most important and constructive developments of recent years.

What, if anything, should the United States do about the growing danger of Soviet expansionism?

Some, of course, suggest that we relax, and let it happen. The nightmare of totalitarianism will pass in a century or two, they say. And that in the meantime the discipline will do us good. Needless to say, the members of the Committee on the Present Danger are not of this persuasion.

Another branch of this school advises accommodation to the point of appeasement. We must choose, they say, between policies they label as being those of "cold war," and those of "détente"; between "war fighting" and "deterrence"; between the complete militarization of policy and making peaceful agreements with the Soviet Union.

These are misleading and indeed unworthy ways of talking about the problem. Except for a small band of genuine sympathizers with the Soviet cause and their gulls, all Americans favor policies of true détente with the Soviet Union. Certainly that is the policy of the Committee on the Present Danger. But true détente requires that both sides, not just one, recognize the need for effective, mutual, peaceful deterrence. Certainly that is the position of our Committee.

In nearly forty years of exposure to the problem, I have never met a responsible American official or writer, military or civilian, who favored a preventative war or any other kind of war, cold or hot, with the Soviet Union. Everyone strongly favors fair and useful agreements with the Soviet Union. We certainly do. But military strength is not an alternative to such agreements: it is their predicate and necessary condition. We should have learned from our long experience in negotiating with the Russians that it is impossible to reach such agreements with them except from a position of strength.

There is a strange mood in the country of resistance to bad news. The pressures of Soviet policy have been greater since 1970 or so than ever before. The agreements for peace in Indo-China were torn up and disregarded. The Soviets supported aggressive and large-scale war in Bangladesh, in the Middle East, and in Africa. There has been an alarming slide toward chaos.

Yet as things got worse, some writers and politicians told us that they were getting better. The cold war was over, they said. We were living in an age of détente, in which negotiation had replaced confrontation.

This is pure or rather impure public relations, alas. Détente has not been a reality but an aspiration. The notion that there has been a change for the better in Soviet-American relations since 1972 is persiflage, or worse—a figment of political imagination.

The question, then, is how we restore deterrence, and a sense of order and stability to the world political system. The Committee on the Present Danger has stated its position in these terms:

> "There is still time for effective action to ensure the security and prosperity of the nation in peace, through peaceful deterrence and concerted alliance diplomacy. A conscious effort of political will is needed to restore the strength and coherence of our foreign policy; to revive the solidarity of our alliances; to build constructive relations of cooperation with other

nations whose interests parallel our own—and on that sound basis to seek reliable conditions of peace with the Soviet Union, rather than an illusory détente.

"Only on such a footing can we and the other democratic industrialized nations, acting together, work with the developing nations to create a just and progressive world economy—the necessary condition of our own prosperity and that of the developing nations and communist nations as well. In that framework, we shall be better able to promote human rights, and to help deal with the great and emerging problems of food, energy, population, and the environment."

Secretary of Defense Brown has recently given the first systematic statement of the Administration's foreign policy. In its broad approach, it is similar to our own. We have stated our support for his position, although we have criticized the Administration's defense budget as insufficient to carry out these goals.

The approach the Committee on the Present Danger has put forward will require energy, and specifically some increases in the defense budget. It means achieving deterrent strength in the sphere of strategic weapons, both for its own sake and for the sake of deterrence at the level of conventional forces in every theater important to our interests. Unless the ultimate strategic deterrent is there—that is, unless the adequacy of our second-strike nuclear capability is clear—our position in every lesser conflict is in peril. That is one of the ultimate lessons of Vietnam.

We, the Europeans, the Japanese, our other allies, and China together have more than enough power to achieve these ends in peace, if we understand the problem, and do what is necessary to deal with it. To accomplish that end, we need to clear our minds of cant, illusion, and wishful thinking—to face the world as it is, and to act with our normal energy, optimism, and imagination.

In his book on the decline of British power, Corelli Barnett asks why Britain failed to prevent World War II—*why* men like Baldwin, MacDonald, Chamberlain, and Simon held sway in Britain between the wars; *why* opinion was so pacifist; *why* appeasement was so congenial; and *why* the governments of the day handled crises in the feeble and nerveless way they did.

We share many of the impulses and yearnings of the British view of world politics. Our educational system suffers similar defects. But we are not as well off as Britain was in 1913 or 1938. No matter how badly Britain conducted its affairs, the American giant always loomed in the wings, able to protect Britain against the ultimate consequences of its folly. If we persist in our present course, there is no similar sleeping giant to save *us* from our folly.

(Applause)

## QUESTION AND ANSWER SESSION

**MR. PACKARD:** Thank you very much. The panel will be very pleased to respond to some questions which have been sent up to the podium from the audience.

There are several questions relating to the Soviet military buildup and I think they deserve a little further discussion. Let me read one of them.

"There is a widespread conviction that the Soviet Union's arms buildup in recent years requires the United States to spend more to catch up, and that's the general Administration policy, but will that really buy security or will it merely spark a new arms race in which the Russians will increase their spending still higher?"

Paul Nitze, you might begin with a response to that.

**MR. NITZE:** The Soviet Union is already putting a very high percentage of its GNP into defense. They're also putting a much higher percentage of their skilled manpower, their technicians and scientists and those who are expert producers of high quality goods, into the defense business. One cannot guarantee that they wouldn't spend more on defense if we did, but I believe that an increment to the U.S. defense expenditures would have a much greater pay-off toward righting the balance than any increment to Soviet defense expenditures.

The final point is that most people believe that in recent years there has been, in fact, a race between the Soviet Union and ourselves. Let's take just the strategic nuclear expenditures. Today, we are spending in real dollars, corrected for inflation, one-third as much as during the six years from 1958 to 1964. When we cut our expenditures by two-thirds, that is hardly a race. The Soviet expenditures, of course, have gone up during this entire period. I don't think that it's fair to say that it's a race when only one side has been racing.

**MR. PACKARD:** Paul, I'd just like to add emphasis to the last part of your response. I recall very clearly, when the Defense Department began looking at this problem in 1969, there had been over most of the previous decade a belief that the Soviets, who were behind us at that time, would merely catch up with us and then level off. We began seeing the continued buildup in their strategic forces and we had a very difficult time convincing people who had been taken in with the earlier belief that the Soviets were only going to catch up. We have, as Paul pointed out, made rather substantial reductions in our forces, both nuclear forces and conventional forces, and there's no evidence whatsoever that the Soviets are following suit. On the contrary, they're going in the other direction.

Here's a question for Professor Pipes.

"To what extent would the economic changes and the desire for freedoms now in process in Eastern European countries bear upon the Soviet arms buildup? Is it possible this buildup has more defensive elements than your brief remarks might allow?"

**PROFESSOR PIPES:** I'm afraid I don't see the connection between the first and second half of this question. As concerns the economic changes and quest for freedoms in Eastern Europe: there is some tolerance on the part of the Soviet Union for a certain amount of free enterprise in countries like Poland and Hungary, but these pockets of free enterprise hardly affect the defense budget.

The questioner asks whether it is possible that the Soviet buildup is more defensive than my brief remarks might allow. My remarks may be brief, but they are based on not inconsiderable study. There are defensive elements in the Soviet military buildup, but, according to Soviet military theory, and indeed according to Soviet military practice, there is no sharp distinction between defensive and offensive. That is, even if you pursue an offensive strategy, you still have to defend yourself. The boxer who is out to knock out his opponent must also protect his own jaw, but his left arm shielding his face does not signify that he is merely defending himself. All indications are that the Soviet posture is overwhelmingly offensive-minded and the defensive element, whether you're speaking about air defenses or civil defenses, represents an aspect of an offensive strategy.

**MR. PACKARD:** There are several questions here relating to the situation in the Far East and I might take two of them together.

"Somebody called China the 16th member of NATO, because it is tying down some 42 Soviet divisions in Asia. Do you think there's any significant connection between our posture in the European theater and our relations with China? If so, how would you describe that connection?"

Very much along the same line is this one.

"What is the thrust of Soviet Russia in the Far East, where the United States has been a dominant and traditional power, both militarily and commercially?"

Paul, would you like to start on that? You were in China a few weeks ago.

MR. NITZE: The Chinese have a very clear theory of strategy and tactics as it applies to the current world. The first point in their appraisal is that the Soviet Union has fundamentally changed its nature from being a Communist country to being a class country, what they call a "state capitalist fascist country," and that it does aspire to world domination and will, in fact, try to achieve it even if that means war. The Chinese believe the Soviet Union does not want to have a war on two fronts, that their focus is upon Europe and that they look upon China as a secondary theater, a theater where they want to be on the defensive, that they consider China to be a much tougher nut to crack, because you've got 950 million people opposed to them there, and that Europe is their immediate target. They think that, for Russia to achieve hegemony over Europe, the best way to do that is to outflank Europe through the Middle East and the best way to achieve hegemony in the Middle East is to outflank the Middle East through Africa. When some of us recently were in Peking, we said that we agreed with them that the Soviet Union appeared to be determined upon world hegemony, but we thought it was not only the Chinese who needed peace; Europe needed peace, the Middle East needed peace, Africa needed peace, we needed peace; and peace could only be achieved by a close collaboration by everybody who was threatened. In particular, we said that we did not think it was possible to predict the tactics of the Soviet Union; we could not be sure that they wouldn't attack China but were dedicated only to attacking Europe.

They finally agreed with that. They said, "We're not members of the Soviet general staff and we're not sure that they won't attack us, rather than Europe or you, but we think the chances are that they're more likely to attack Europe than they are the Far East."

The Russians are devoting an enormous amount of effort to the 42 divisions on the Chinese borders and they have all kinds of other forces in the Pacific areas of their country, but they've put those forces there without withdrawing any forces from the European theater.

MR. ROSTOW: May I add a word to that? If we look at the problem in terms of political decisions, certainly the centerpiece of the Soviet strategic view of world politics has always been that if Russia could control Western Europe and bring it under its dominion, and the areas upon which Western Europe is dependent in the Middle East and Africa, that it would thereby control the world. There can be no question that Soviet reduction of Western Europe or equally of China, but more emphatically Western Europe, either envelopment or through direct attack, or through coercion and political influence, would be read in Japan and in China and in many other parts of the world as a clear political signal that the balance of power had shifted disastrously against the United States, that American guarantees were no longer effective or credible and that China and Japan would correspondingly make the best deal they could with the Soviet Union.

That's one of the reasons why we think the problem is so urgent and requires preventive action very quickly at the political level, because without credible deterrents, both strategic and conventional, our promising and constructive relation with China could evaporate. Our alliances could erode. Then we would face the world alone and isolated in a position of total military inferiority. The situation to which we are accustomed, to which I referred in my opening remarks, a situation of strength, or at least of potential strength, need not last indefinitely. Any fundamental change in that balance, either in Asia or in Europe, could produce political consequences disastrous for us in

Japan, in China and in Europe.

MR. PACKARD: This is a question which I hope we've already largely answered, but since it has been asked, I thought we might have another try at it.

"Under the present Administration, Dr. Brzezinski has stated that the primary threat to world peace is no longer the Soviet Union, but unrest in the Third World. The latter, meaning unrest in the Third World, then should be our primary concern as reflected in American foreign policy."

Paul?

MR. NITZE: The interaction between what are called "East-West problems," in other words, the relationship between the USSR and its allies and the United States and its allies, is sometimes said to be totally distinct from the North-South problems, in other words, the Third World and its issues and those of Europe and the United States.

It is the view of our Committee that those issues are interrelated. You can't make a total distinction between what happens on the North-South issues and what happens on the East-West issues. In fact, the point of Russia's interest in Africa is to do what the Chinese say, and that is to create positions there which will outflank the Middle East. Why are they interested in the Middle East? Because that will create positions which will outflank Europe and Japan and that, in turn, is of great strategic interest to the United States.

Therefore, we do have to address ourselves to the North-South issues, because if not attended to, those will be exploited by the Soviet Union on strategic grounds. The essence of what I'm trying to say is that we should try to look at the world from a strategic approach. That causes one to see the interrelationship between the economic problems, the political problems and the military problems and between the North-South problems and Third World problems and the East-West problems.

MR. ROSTOW: I entirely agree with what Paul Nitze said. I'd only add that I suspect that Mr. Brzezinski has changed his mind since making that celebrated remark. Secretary Brown has just said for the Administration that the central problem of our foreign policy and defense policy is our relationship with the Soviet Union. I fully agree that we have no chance of addressing the North-South issues constructively and effectively unless we first stabilize the East-West relationship.

MR. PACKARD: Here's a very simple question, but I think it's important to our subject today. It's addressed to Dr. Pipes.

"Can the USA win a nuclear war against the USSR? Please define 'win.' "

If you can give us a good answer to that question, Dr. Pipes, we'll adjourn the meeting.

DR. PIPES: I believe the question is unanswerable, because it would all depend on the scenario. Undoubtedly, if the United States were mad enough out of the blue to launch its entire force of strategic weapons against the Soviet Union, against its strategic forces as well as against population and industrial centers, we could destroy that country and, of course, be destroyed in turn, leaving no victors. But this is not a realistic scenario at all. Under more realistic circumstances, in crisis situations, each side would be more likely to employ a part of its strategic forces against selected targets—and here victory is quite feasible exactly as it is in any military conflict, i.e., one side disables the other and inflicts its will upon it.

What can be said is that unless the United States in the next few years undertakes programs which will strengthen its land-based as well as airborne missile forces, the Soviet Union will be in a position, sometime in the '80s, to unfold such an array of forces that we will not only be unable to win any strategic conflict but might not be able even to retaliate meaningfully and we would, therefore, be inclined to capitulate. That is the danger and that is the real issue, as I see it.

**MR. PACKARD:** Thank you very much. Ladies and gentlemen, we've reached an end of this program. I want to thank you all very, very much for giving us the opportunity to appear before you.

**MR. BURGESS:** Thank you, David Packard. We thank Mr. Packard and Mr. Fowler and this distinguished panel for spending this lunchtime with us on this very important subject.

Thank you so much.

The preceding transcript has been edited by the participants for purposes of clarity but nothing substantive has been changed, added or deleted.

*14 March 1978*

## NOTES

1. Mr. Fowler is a general partner with Goldman, Sachs & Company. He served as Secretary of the Treasury 1965–1968.
2. Mr. Packard is the Chairman of the Board, Hewlett-Packard Company. He served as Deputy Secretary of Defense, 1969–1971.

# 6

# AN EVALUATION OF "U.S. AND SOVIET STRATEGIC CAPABILITY THROUGH THE MID-1980s: A COMPARATIVE ANALYSIS"*

This statement is a brief evaluation of a paper entitled "U.S. and Soviet Strategic Capability through the Mid-1980s: A Comparative Analysis." The paper in question was prepared at the behest of a group formed in the Executive Branch to promote acceptance, over the country and specifically at the Capitol, for the package of SALT II agreements now reportedly in final stages of negotiation. The Arms Control and Disarmament Agency published the paper in August of this year [1978], apparently without the concurrence of the Department of Defense and the Joint Chiefs of Staff.

The importance of the topic indicated in the title is manifest. Taken at face value, the conclusions seem eminently reassuring. The paper professes to see an indisputable present lead for the U.S. in strategic destruction capability. It predicts increments of such capability for both superpowers in the interval ahead and essential parity between them in the mid-1980s, with the U.S. retaining retaliatory capability exceeding the present level, even after a hypothetical Soviet first strike. A series of graphs purports to authenticate the findings. Certain inferences would logically flow from the conclusions: Neither side would be in position to achieve a determinative advantage by striking first. Mutual deterrence would be intact. The American people could not be placed in disproportionate hazard: Strategic stability would persist under SALT II and vindicate the Administration's policies.

Unfortunately, the ACDA paper does not hold up under analysis. In a basic misconception, the paper construes strategic capability as mere destructive capability unrelated to actual targets in a real world. The paper compares the respective countries' pertinent capabilities now and later by assessing the theoretical impacts of attacks against 6,500 point targets. Of those, 1,500 are assumed to be "hard" or heavily-protected military assets (such as missile silos, launch-control and nuclear-storage facilities, and command and communication bunkers), and 5,000 to be "soft" or highly vulnerable targets (such as industrial plants, barracks, airfields, and cities).

The method—pitting the forces of the two sides against an abstraction rather than against each other—enables the ACDA paper to arrive at the desired answers by steering around an array of important disparities basic to the superpower strategic relationship. By this method, the disparities do not have to be discounted or explained away. They are simply ignored.

---

*"U.S. and Soviet Strategic Capability Through the Mid-1980s: A Comparative Analysis," U.S. Arms Control and Disarmament Agency, Washington, D.C. August 1978.

Consider, for example, the matter of hard targets in the two countries. In numbers and hardness of protected militarily important targets, the Soviet Union already surpasses the U.S. Furthermore, the Soviet Union is increasing its advantage, while the United States remains at a standstill. Under current trends, by the mid-1980s such targets within the Soviet Union will be double those within the United States both in number and in hardness and therefore far more difficult to destroy. The ACDA paper skips over these asymmetries. As a related matter the ACDA paper takes no account of the vulnerability of this country's command, control, and communications facilities—again a serious point of disparity between the superpower military establishments.

Consider asymmetries in respect to soft targets. Besides assuming parity in soft targets, the ACDA paper reflects an assumption that all soft targets are point targets and therefore destructible by one weapon, without regard to its yield. In reality, soft targets within the Soviet Union and those in the U.S. are not numerically equal as in the ACDA supposition. To the contrary, those in the Soviet Union are two to three times as numerous as the ones here. In reality, moreover, most soft targets are area targets. The distinction is important. Destructive power against soft area targets is a function of the yield, not simply the number, of the weapons employed. Against soft area targets the Soviet megaton-range warheads are some eight times as effective as the warheads on which the United States would principally rely for a retaliatory strike (i.e., predominantly POSEIDON warheads of 40 kilotons).

As a related matter, the ACDA method takes no account of fallout—a nuclear effect basically proportionate to the aggregate fission yield of warheads exploded close to the ground rather than of the number of such warheads. The most worrisome and difficult nuclear effect from the standpoint of protecting one's population is fallout. The Soviet Union's civil defense program, designed to shelter population and industry against blast and fallout, is notably active and extensive. The United States' attention to this aspect is virtually nil. The ACDA paper ignores the implications of the contrast.

Besides ignoring real differences between the target bases of the two countries, the ACDA paper has other evident defects.

Factors of time and timing in a nuclear exchange are important for strategic calculations. Flight times for intercontinental and submarine-launched ballistic missiles are measured in minutes, and their arrival on target can be coordinated to the second. In contrast, bombers whether with bombs or cruise missiles take from six to eight hours to reach their strategic targets.

For retaliation against hard targets after a strategic nuclear attack the United States relies principally on B-52 bombers now carrying gravity bombs and, according to the ACDA assumptions, cruise missiles later on toward the mid-1980s. The ACDA calculations of United States retaliatory capabilities assume that the United States forces have been "fully generated"—that is, have received a day or more of warning of an impending attack employing ballistic missiles and thus have on alert more than double the usual number of B-52s. In the current period almost all of United States retaliatory capability to destroy hard targets, as reflected in the ACDA's computations, comes from the assumed capability of each penetrating B-52 to survive Soviet air defenses of progressive density and sophistication and then to drop at least one gravity bomb with high accuracy against each of a series of such targets, which apparently lack terminal defenses. For the mid-1980s, the ACDA paper similarly appears to assume almost perfect performance for B-52s with their cruise missiles.

The significance of the Soviet BACKFIRE bomber is also ignored—a critical omission. With the BACKFIRE included in the calculations, the destructive potential of U.S.

bombers against soft targets would be approximately equalled by the Soviet Union's capability and therefore would not be an offset to the large advantage that the Soviet Union will possess in the destructive capability of their missile forces against those of the United States.

Finally, the ACDA paper ignores the fact and the significance of the cold-launch method for launching a considerable portion of Soviet intercontinental ballistic missiles. That Soviet method leaves silos relatively undamaged and available for prompt reloading and thus presents an obvious potential for the Soviet Union to offset limitations and reductions in the number of missile launchers resulting from SALT agreements.

Here we have cited a representative list, not an exhaustive list, of deficiencies in the ACDA paper. In their combined effect, the deficiencies are enough to invalidate the conclusions.

*29 September 1978*

# 7

# IS AMERICA BECOMING NUMBER 2?

## Current Trends In the U.S.-Soviet Military Balance

### FOREWORD

In our initial statement on 11 November 1976, "Common Sense and the Common Danger," we identified "the Soviet drive for dominance based upon an unparalleled military buildup" as the "principal threat to our nation, to world peace, and to the cause of human freedom." In our subsequent statements, "What Is the Soviet Union Up To?" and "Where We Stand on SALT," we offered a more detailed analysis of Soviet goals in world affairs, and the nuclear weapons component of Soviet strategy for attaining those goals.

In this study, we bring together the facts about the conventional and nuclear Soviet military buildup and the evolving Soviet-American military balance, insofar as those facts are publicly available, and we assess their political meaning.

The study consists of six parts:
    I. Facing Basic Facts
   II. The Changing Strategic Balance
  III. The Imbalance of General Purpose Forces
  IV. The Decade Ahead
   V. Implications for U.S. Defense Policy
  VI. Summary and Conclusions

### I. FACING BASIC FACTS

It is an unwelcome novelty for Americans to have to pay sustained attention to military factors as the ultimate basis of national security. Many of us still cling to the outlook of the century before 1917, when, behind the screen of the British fleet, we enjoyed something close to immunity from the fact or the threat of external attack. This state of affairs came about for two reasons: our remoteness from the centers of military competition; and Britain's success in maintaining the European balance of power and in guiding the Concert of Europe based upon it. There was a brief period of peril during the Civil War, when France and Britain were tempted to recognize the Confederacy and permanently weaken The United States. But otherwise, America was aptly said to "sail upon a summer sea."

We have now lost that uniquely fortunate privilege and the sense of security it inspired. The two great wars of the twentieth century and the political upheavals stemming from them, have made the United States and the Soviet Union the leading forces in world politics. Individually and collectively, the nations of Western Europe no longer play predominant roles in world politics—their greatest influence is as allies and partners of the United States or as satellites of the Soviet Union. Because of the logic of nuclear power, this is largely the case for Japan as well.

The two superpowers have utterly opposing conceptions of world order. The United States, true to its traditions and ideals, sees a world moving toward peaceful unity and cooperation within a regime of law. The Soviet Union, for ideological as well as geopolitical reasons, sees a world riven by conflict and destined to be ruled exclusively by Marxism-Leninism. The U.S. and the USSR are now alone in possessing the military capacity to challenge each other. In the decades since World War II, the adversary relationship between the Soviet Union and the United States has therefore been the paramount consideration in the security of the United States and of those countries linked to us. The Soviet-American conflict also deeply affects the relationship between the industrialized democracies as a group and the developing nations of the southern hemisphere. The Soviet Union has sought to exploit difficulties among the developing nations, and between them and the industrialized nations, in order to gain positions of strategic importance in its drive for global dominance.

The Soviet Union, driven both by deep-rooted Russian imperial impulses and by Communist ideology, insists on pursuing an expansionist course. In its endless, probing quest, it attempts to take advantage of every opportunity to enlarge its influence. And military strength is more than ever the foundation underlying its policy. In order to maintain and increase the momentum of its expansion, the Soviet Union seeks to outstrip the United States and its allies in every category of military power, both in numbers and in technological sophistication. The strategists and political planners of the Soviet Union are trained to understand that military power is the essential guarantor to expanding political influence. It is the first object of their policy to assure that guarantee.

Thus, it would be irrational as well as imprudent to ignore the military element in the Soviet-American relationship. Although the political, economic, and human aspects are each important, the military dimension is fundamental and potentially decisive.

Cycles of technological change are transforming the military art far more rapidly than at any earlier period of history, and both superpowers and many other nations are caught up in this dynamic process. In thinking about national security, we must now take into account the explosive potential of nuclear warheads; the use of outer space as an environment for warfare; and the instant operational readiness of rockets and advanced aircraft for missions over enormous ranges. These factors make the globe itself a single strategic theater and bring within the sphere of plausible calculation the idea of settling the military outcome of a great intercontinental war by a few powerful but integrated strokes.

The shadow of that possibility has a profound impact on politics, and on the political will of adversaries. Any party to a possible war would of course prefer to have its way on the issues of the conflict without the risks and costs of actual combat. And any rational government would strive to avoid a war it believes in advance it could not win at all, or could win only at unbearable cost. If the balance of forces is so unfavorable to a state that it would be forced to view its prospects in these terms, its diplomatic positions in dealing with crisis situations will inevitably be weakened.

These two postulates, fundamental to the avoidance of war in any era, have become increasingly important during the past three decades. They have been at the heart of the process of challenge, deterrence, and conciliation that has marked the course of Soviet-American relations since 1947.

The Soviet goal in the drive for what its spokesmen call "a visible preponderance of military power" is not to wage a nuclear war but to win political predominance without having to fight. For reasons we consider in Part II, the primary issue in the field of strategic weapons is the continued adequacy of our second-strike capability and therefore of our deterrence posture. If we should allow the Soviet Union to achieve visible strategic superiority, the ultimate force on which we have relied since 1945 to deter attacks against our vital national interests—notably the independence of Western Europe and Japan— would cease to exist. Suppose that the Soviet Union possessed so numerous a force of powerful and accurate nuclear weapons that it could attack our intercontinental ballistic missiles (ICBMs) and other military installations and still have greater numbers of more powerful weapons left than we had, would it then be wise for any American President to plan to launch a retaliatory attack on Russian cities and industries, knowing they could respond in kind and much more powerfully? Or would it be wiser for him to seek a political settlement, even if it were unfavorable to our interests, before the threat of a first strike which could escalate to such a holocaust? Under such circumstances, we would be vulnerable to the scenario of a Cuban Missile Crisis in reverse—a confrontation in which we should have to yield in the face of overwhelming force. A clearly superior Soviet *third*-strike capability, under the assumption of clear Soviet strategic nuclear superiority, would undermine the credibility of our second-strike capacity, and could lead us, either to accommodation without fighting or to the acceptance of unmanageable risks.

Uncertainty on such critical choices could lead to profoundly demoralizing crises. It should be the first object of our policy to expand our leaders' range of prudent options. American security policy should aim to prevent the President of the United States from being confronted with a choice between retreat or a nuclear war under grossly unfavorable circumstances and thus likely to end in both devastation and defeat.

The United States must be able to deter military aggression throughout the spectrum of armed conflict with forces appropriate to the threat. Even when we had a nuclear monopoly, and then a position of overwhelming nuclear superiority, we were not immune from Soviet pressures for expansion, as we saw in Eastern Europe, Iran, Greece and Turkey; in Berlin; in Korea; and later in Cuba. As our nuclear superiority has eroded, these tests and probes have become more and more difficult to contain. A doubtful U.S. strategic nuclear posture can be of little practical use to us and our allies in deterring Soviet expansion behind the Red Army or proxy forces (such as the Cubans in Africa), or the credible threat to use them, in areas important to our security.

The analysis in Part III of this paper is therefore devoted to the present and prospective balance between the non-nuclear forces of the Soviet Union and its Warsaw Pact allies on the one hand, and those of the United States and its allies on the other. It takes into account the differing strategic and tactical missions of the NATO and Warsaw Pact forces and of the U.S. and Soviet naval forces. It also deals to some extent with the force balance in other areas of the world.

Our evaluation of the military balance deals primarily with the 1980s, the period in which the effects of present programs can be reasonably foreseen and also the earliest time at which defense program changes made in the near future could influence the balance. Section IV considers long-term technological and economic trends that might affect the ability of either side to maintain military preparedness programs beyond the 1980s.

## Soviet Military Doctrine

The implications of the facts about the military balance cannot be fully understood without some consideration of Soviet military doctrine and the statements of Soviet political leaders.[1]

This Soviet literature—not propaganda written for the West but Russians talking to Russians—tells us that the Soviets do *not* agree with the Americans that nuclear war is unthinkable and unwinnable and that the only objective of strategic doctrine must be mutual deterrence. On the contrary, it tells us that they look at the world quite differently; that war is an extension of diplomacy; that nuclear superiority is politically usable and that the Soviets must prepare for war-fighting, war-surviving and war-winning. The goal of their strategic nuclear program is not necessarily to start a war, but to attain a position of such nuclear superiority as to be able to coerce our policy through a credible array of unacceptable risks. Yet they also believe that the United States and its allies may well turn and fight when they are driven into the ultimate corner. The Soviets therefore plan on the assumption that war is quite possible even though not desirable or inevitable. They believe the best deterrent is the capability to win and survive were deterrence to fail.

If war is started by the "imperialists," Soviet spokesmen say, "victory will go to the side that is best prepared in equipment, doctrine and morale." If Soviet intelligence reveals that the "imperialists" are preparing a nuclear attack, it is incumbent on the Soviet forces to conduct a preemptive strike on enemy forces, command-control centers, nuclear and conventional reserves, and military-support industries. This attack must be well coordinated to achieve surprise and destroy enemy capabilities. It must be rapidly exploited by attack on the ground (the Soviets do not always distinguish in their literature between strategic and theater arenas of conflict).

Soviet literature does warn of the destructiveness of nuclear war and of the risk of nuclear escalation in a major conflict. When the Soviets acquired nuclear weapons, they came to recognize their potential for deterrence of the West. In 1956 Khrushchev said: "War is not fatalistically inevitable. Today there are mighty social and political forces possessing formidable means to prevent the imperialists from unleashing war and, if they actually try to start it, to give a smashing rebuff to the aggressors and frustrate their adventurist plans."[2] In the late 1950s and early 1960s, Khrushchev sought to deter us with exaggerated claims about Soviet nuclear forces, even though the Soviets were not to achieve actual parity until the 1970s.

Nevertheless, the doctrine described above is that of a nation that does not rely solely upon the theory of deterrence. The crucial difference from a common U.S. approach lies in the Soviet recognition that deterrence might not succeed and that the Soviet Union must be prepared to fight, survive and win, even in nuclear conflict.

Soviet doctrine affirms the utility of defense in the nuclear age. The Soviets espouse and implement both active defense and passive civil defense measures, whereas many Americans tend to believe that such defenses are futile and can be "destabilizing." The Soviets believe in the importance of air defense of their homeland, whereas the United States has abandoned air defense on the premise that it is not useful in the absence of ballistic missile defense. The Soviets also believe in ballistic missile defense. They signed the ABM Treaty in 1972 because the United States had a long technological lead, not because we had converted them to the concept of Mutual Assured Destruction (MAD), the mutual-hostage theory.

While we have deactivated and partially dismantled our sole permitted ABM site, and have cut back our ABM research and development program, the Soviets have maintained their Moscow site and are vigorously pursuing ABM research and development, with apparent emphasis on systems that would be rapidly deployable should they, or we, decide to abrogate the ABM Treaty. Moreover, they are moving toward a counterforce damage-limiting capability: that is, sufficient accuracy for their large MIRVed (Multiple Independently-Targetable Reentry Vehicle) warheads to permit high confidence in "hard-target kills" against U.S. ICBM silos.

Consistent with their doctrine, the Soviets have long maintained non-nuclear, or conventional, superiority in the European theater and may well be more willing to use that superiority either for war or for coercive diplomacy in the event they achieve significant strategic nuclear superiority.

The Soviets are moving toward a capability, if diplomacy fails, to prevail in Europe without destroying it, using more accurate weapons of lower nuclear yields. Moreover, Soviet doctrine embraces conventional, chemical, and nuclear weapons, and the Soviets have large chemical warfare capabilities, including defenses—again, a potential means of winning battles and taking territory without destroying its assets. The United States, in contrast, neglects chemical defenses for its troops, vehicles, ships and airfields, and pursues unenforceable agreements to outlaw chemical warfare.

In sum, Soviet doctrine, as shown in its literature, forces and practices, reflects a determined opponent whose strategy seeks global objectives and backs that strategy with the appropriate and necessary means—while the United States appears to be retreating for both policy and budgetary reasons to a posture of "finite deterrence," perhaps even to a "fortress America."

## Soviet Concerns and Motives

While Soviet strategic nuclear forces are deployed primarily against the United States, Soviet interests, and the forces to support them, are worldwide in scope. Soviet theory holds that the Soviet Union is the vanguard of the "progressive" socialist forces of the world.

The Soviets explain their formidable standing array of forces against Western Europe and China in these terms:

- They must stand guard against Western Europe, they say, because it is geographically proximate, because West Germany is potentially aggressive, and because it has been the source of threats and invasion during the past two centuries. Therefore, they contend, they must maintain nuclear forces that hold Europe "hostage," plus conventional forces that could defend against (or deter) the only large potential conventional threat to the Soviet Union. The Warsaw Pact array of force against the Central Front and both the northern and southern flanks of Europe constitutes a clear and present danger to the political independence and indeed to the territorial integrity of Western Europe. As President Carter has said, the Soviet military posture in Europe cannot be explained on defensive considerations. For many years, the principal strategic goal of Soviet policy has been to bring Western Europe under its control. If that could be done, they believe, China and Japan would draw obvious conclusions. The global balance of power would be transformed to Soviet advantage, and the United States would be left isolated in a hostile world.

- Similarly, the Soviets explain their military posture vis-a-vis China as necessary because China is traditionally antagonistic and currently revisionist in Soviet eyes. The Soviet Union claims its huge deployment of forces against China is essentially defensive. To the Chinese, of course the Soviet deployment is threatening.
- The Eastern European countries are regarded by the Soviets as in their "sphere of influence" and properly under Soviet hegemony. Remembering Hungary in 1956 and Czechoslovakia in 1968, they insist on maintaining large conventional forces in the area to assure control and maintenance of their hegemonic system, described as the "Socialist Commonwealth."
- The Soviets regard the Middle East as a most important geopolitical target. They believe that control over the space, the waterways, and the oil of the region would be a major and even decisive weapon in permitting them to dominate Europe, Africa, and large parts of Asia. They are tempted by the oil they expect to need in the 1980s and by the pressure that denial or the threat of denial of oil to the West can put on Europe, Japan, and the United States.
- In the Third World, the Soviet Union aspires to socialist leadership and supports "wars of national liberation." The Soviets therefore require capabilities to project power throughout the Southern Hemisphere, as well as resources for the support of "sub-conventional" or guerrilla warfare. They are particularly interested in positions which out-flank the Middle East or China.

Some or all of these needs may have to be met simultaneously. For example, while in a land conflict in Western Europe, the Soviets might also face Chinese pressure in the East, and even Eastern European unrest or opposition. These pressures may, indeed, appear to the Soviets to impose cumulative requirements that are insupportable with conventional weapons alone and therefore constitute an important motive behind the Soviet drive for nuclear superiority, with its potential for achieving quick and irreversible American retreats from Europe, the Mediterranean and other areas. Some say that we need not be disturbed by the Soviet military buildup, because in their opinion Soviet leadership is now more conservative and cautious than it was in Stalin's time. The Soviet Union, men of this persuasion assure us, is governed by elderly bureaucrats concerned only with the safety of the Soviet Empire in Eastern Europe. The conclusive demonstration of the falsity of this view is the pattern of Soviet behavior. In recent years, the elderly bureaucrats of the Kremlin have undertaken programs of expansion far beyond Stalin's dreams. Stalin probed toward Turkey, Greece, Berlin, and Korea, and pulled back when the risks became serious. His successors have sponsored wars of far greater magnitude — the breach of the 1973 agreement for peace in Indo-China, for example; the Arab aggression in the Middle East of October 1973; and the current campaign in Africa. It is an illusion to suppose that the Soviets do not mean what they say. It is folly to ignore how they act.

We believe that the United States cannot afford to minimize or to ignore the fundamental threat to its security posed by the Soviet Union. The USSR has declared its basic differences with the United States; has manifested its intent to acquire superior military strength; and has clearly stated its doctrinal belief in the political influence of military power and tried many times to apply that doctrine in diplomacy. Most important, the USSR bases its foreign policy on the premise that nuclear war can be waged rationally and can be won by the side better prepared for it. Because we believe the nation's security and survival are in jeopardy, we present to the American people the following evaluation of the military balance and its implications.

## II. THE CHANGING STRATEGIC BALANCE

The task of evaluating the strategic balance between the Soviet Union and the United States poses formidable problems of measurement and comparison. However, in our considered judgment, the essential criterion for judging either the present or the future situation is whether we have and can expect to continue to have an adequate second-strike capability. Since the essence of United States' policy is deterrence, both in terms of strategic weapons and theater forces, it is essential that our second-strike capacities be convincing and visible beyond the shadow of a doubt.

Technological developments make it increasingly difficult, however, to be certain that we have and will continue to have a clear and effective second-strike capability. The primary justification for the SALT I Interim Agreement in 1972 was that, while it allowed the Soviet Union more missiles than the United States, we were ahead in the technology of MIRVing and thus had more warheads and more accurate ones. Today, the Soviets have an advanced MIRV technology. They also use more thrust in their larger missiles, which have a greater capability (throw-weight) to put useful payloads into an intercontinental trajectory than ours. With greater throw-weight, they can put heavier and more numerous MIRVed warheads on a single missile than we.

Taking full account of these and other critical variables, the analysis which follows will attempt to bring out the facts needed for a rational answer to basic questions—Do we now have a clear and adequate second-strike capacity? Will we have a clear and adequate second-strike capability if present trends continue? And finally, what will be the effects of alternative SALT agreements on our second-strike capability?

In 1969, at the start of the Strategic Arms Limitation Talks (SALT), Secretary of State William Rogers said that the Soviets had achieved strategic parity and that this fact made SALT possible. In 1972, President Nixon reported that the Soviet missile forces had approximately doubled in numbers since 1969. (U.S. deployments of launchers had not increased but we had MIRVed a number of our ICBMs and SLBMs.) Despite the change

Table 1. Interim Agreement Limits
on Strategic Offensive Arms[a]

|  | USSR | US |
|---|---|---|
| ICBM Silos | 1,618[b] | 1,054 |
| Including Modern Large Ballistic Missiles (MLBMs) | 313[b,c] | 0 |
| SLBM Launchers | 740/950[d] | 656/710[d] |
| Modern Nuclear Powered Submarines (SSBNs) | 62[d] | 44 |

[a]The Agreement signed May 26, 1972 and entered into force October 3, 1972, covered ballistic missiles only. Bombers and cruise missiles were not covered.
[b]U.S. estimates; the Soviets did not offer numbers. The limits included launchers "deployed or under construction at the time of signing" (specified as July 1, although actually May 26, 1972). The United States had no silos or missile submarines under construction at the time.
[c]MLBMs meant the Soviet SS-9s, of which 288 were believed to be deployed and some 25, later reduced to 20, believed to be under construction. Operational MLBM launchers (as opposed to launchers used for testing purposes) at the Soviet test ranges were not included in these numbers.
[d]These figures were given to a Protocol accompanying the Agreement. The numbers in parentheses referred to higher ceiling permitted if equivalent numbers of pre-1964 type missiles were retired: in the Soviet case, up to 210 SS-7s and SS-8s; for the United States, 54 Titan IIs.

Table 2. Characteristics of SALT I Missile Forces
(ICBMs)[a]

A. USSR

| TYPE | SS-7, SS-8 | SS-11 | SS-13 | SS-9 | TOTAL |
|---|---|---|---|---|---|
| Aggregate Warheads/Missile (no.) | 1 | 1[b] | 1 | 1 | |
| Yield/Warhead (megatons)[c] | 5 | 1 | 1 | 18-25 | |
| Throw-weight/Missile (lbs.)[d] | 8,000 | 2,000 | 2,000 | 10,000 | |
| Deployment (no.) | 209 | 1,012 | 60 | 288-313 | 1,600 |
| Aggregate Throw-weight (millions of lbs.) | 1.7 | 2.0 | 0.1 | 2.9-3.1 | 6.7-6.9 |
| Warheads (no.) | 209 | 1,012 | 60 | 288-313 | 1,600 |

B. UNITED STATES

| TYPE | TITAN II | MINUTEMAN II | MINUTEMAN III | TOTAL |
|---|---|---|---|---|
| Warheads/Missile | 1 | 1 | 3 | |
| Yield/Warheads (megatons) | 5-10 | 1-2 | .170 | |
| Throw-weight/Missile (lbs.) | 8,000 | 2,500 | 2,500 | |
| Deployment (no.) | 54 | 450 | 550 | 1,054 |
| Aggregate Throw-weight (millions of lbs.) | 0.4 | 1.1 | 1.4 | 2.9 |
| Aggregate Warheads | 54 | 450 | 1,650 | 2,154 |

SLBMs

A. USSR

| TYPE | SS-N-4 | SS-N-5 | SS-N-6 | SS-N-8 | TOTAL |
|---|---|---|---|---|---|
| Range (nautical miles) | 300 | 650 | 1,500 | 4,300 | |
| Warheads/Missile (no.) | 1 | 1 | 1 | 1 | |
| Yield/Warhead (megatons) | 1+ | 1+ | 1+ | 1+ | |
| Deployment (no.) | | | | | |
| Aggregate Warheads (no.) | 27 | 54 | 544 | 220 | 845[e] |
| Aggregate (no.) | 27 | 54 | 544 | 220 | 845[a] |

B. UNITED STATES

| TYPE | POLARIS A-3 | POSEIDON C-3 | TOTAL |
|---|---|---|---|
| Range (nautical miles) | 2,500 | 2,500 | |
| Warheads/Missile (no.) | 3 | 10 | |
| Yield/Warhead (megatons) | .200 | .050 | |
| Deployment (no.) | 160 | 496 | 656 |
| Aggregate Warheads (no.) | 480 | 4,960 | 5,440 |

[a]Figures reflect deployments in early 1975, when the United States had completed the deployment of the MIRVed Minuteman III, and just before the USSR had started the deployment of the SS-17, SS-18, and SS-19, or the dismantling of the SS-7s and SS-8s. The Soviet deployments projected in Table Three, below, were started in 1975 and are continuing today; at mid-1976, about 150 SS-17s, SS-18s, and SS-19s had been deployed. The SS-7s and SS-8s have now been dismantled (to permit the current SLBM deployments).
[b]Some SS-11s are understood to have been deployed with "triplet" multiple re-entry vehicles (MRVs). Since these are not independently targeted (that is, are not MIRVs), they are not shown as separate warheads here.
[c]Yields are highly approximate. Megatons (MT) are millions of tons of TNT-equivalent. Thousandths of MT are kilotons (KT); for example, .170MT = 170 kilotons.
[d]Throw-weight estimates are highly approximate. They may vary for a given missile, as there is a trade-off between throw-weight and range, and some may be given less throw-weight (for example, by off-loading MIRVs) in order to reach more distant targets. Estimates for ICBMs are for the maximum useful load propelled in tests to intercontinental ranges; for SLBMs, estimates are for the maximum tested throw-weight.
[e]Soviet SLBM deployments may be exceeding the limit of 950.

in the balance since 1969, the SALT I Interim Agreement on Strategic Offensive Arms, signed May 26, 1972, was justified as "codifying strategic parity." The principal terms of this Agreement are shown in Table 1 and the characteristics of the 1972 forces are given in Table 2.

It was immediately noted that the Agreement permitted the Soviets 50 percent more ICBM launchers and from 13 to 45 percent more submarine ballistic missile launchers than the United States. Moreover, the useful payload or "throw-weight," of the then-deployed Soviet ICBMs was more than double that of the U.S. ICBMs.

Henry Kissinger said at the time that these Soviet advantages were more than offset by certain U.S. advantages. First, he contended, because of our superior MIRV technology, the U.S. missiles had twice as many warheads as those of the Soviets. This advantage would increase to 3 to 1 during the five-year life of the Interim Agreement (assuming the completion of the U.S. programs for MIRVed Minuteman III and Poseidon missiles, and no Soviet MIRV deployments during that period). In addition, the U.S. was said to have about a 3 to 1 advantage in heavy bombers, which were not covered in the Agreement. There was no mention, however, of the large numbers of Soviet medium bombers assigned to naval missions but usable, with aerial refueling or in one-and-a-quarter-way missions, against the United States; nor was there mention of the high level of Soviet air defenses against our bombers (the light U.S. air defenses were already being phased out). SALT I also ignored the several hundred submarine-launched cruise missiles (SLCMs), which the Soviet Union had deployed even then. There was an allusion to the U.S. "forward-based systems" (FBS), mainly fighter-bomber aircraft on carriers and forward bases, which can reach the Soviet Union; these are not covered by the Agreement, but neither are the Soviet medium- and intermediate-range missiles plus aircraft that can both attack our FBS and devastate our Western European allies. Finally, Kissinger said that the Agreement stopped large ongoing Soviet programs at a time when we had no such programs and no prospect of getting new programs through Congress.

In the following years, the assumptions underlying Henry Kissinger's rationale for SALT I turned out to be incorrect. The Soviets deployed a MIRV capacity. They have deployed mobile ICBMs, according to President Carter, have deployed long-range Backfire bombers and are developing larger bombers, submarines and submarine missiles. It is not at all clear that any Soviet programs were in fact stopped by the Interim Agreement. Meanwhile, we have closed our Minuteman III production line, delayed the development of the presumably mobile MX, and cancelled the B-1.

## The Soviet Drive for Superiority Under SALT

True to the diplomatic axiom that the Soviets "push on every unlocked door," Brezhnev told President Nixon the USSR would pursue all avenues open to it under the Interim Agreement. In the year following the effective date of that Agreement (October 3, 1972, the date of the Congressional Joint Resolution of Concurrence), the Soviets tested a new family of ICBMs, the SS-16, SS-17, SS-18, and SS-19 series, all but the SS-16 with MIRVed payloads. These systems, we now know, were under development throughout the SALT I negotiations. The Soviet catch-up in MIRV technology started years before the date predicted by our intelligence estimates. Once again, the Department of Defense and the CIA underestimated Soviet capabilities.

Deployment of the SS-17, SS-18, and SS-19 started in 1975. These missiles were designed to take advantage of the greater throw-weight of Soviet ICBMs. The size of each of these missiles is greater than that of those they are replacing. In addition, the Soviets adopted "cold-launch" for the SS-17 and SS-18 (that is, the missile is lifted out of its silo by a gas generator before the booster motors are ignited, thus permitting a greater throw-weight with a given missile size as well as more rapid reloading than in a silo which is damaged by hot gases when the motors are ignited inside it).

With these steps, plus improvements in the fuels used, the Soviets are almost doubling the throw-weight of the present generation of ICBMs over the generation deployed in 1972. With greater throw-weight, it is possible to have more or heavier warheads on a single MIRVed missile. When deployment is completed in the early 1980s, the number of warheads will have been multiplied by 4 or 5 or more. The resulting Soviet forces, conservatively estimated, are shown in Table 3.[3]

The United States, in contrast, will by the early 1980s have deployed no additional ICBM throw-weight since 1972. With the Minuteman III program completed, the only modernization of the American ICBM force will consist of the possible deployment of the Mark 12A warheads on the Minuteman III in the early 1980s, roughly doubling the 170-kiloton yield of the present Mark 12 warheads and possibly increasing accuracy. The Soviets will have deployed more and much larger yield MIRVs and will probably have caught up with the United States in accuracy. And, as Secretary of Defense Brown announced on September 15, 1977, the Soviets have still another generation of four new missiles under development. These may be expected to have heavier throw-weights, greater accuracy and probably more reentry vehicles. The Soviets will have an impressive hard-target kill capability with the family of missiles currently being deployed, and a still greater capability with the follow-on generation that could be deployed in the early 1980s. The SS-18 force alone, because of its very large throw-weight and high-yield warheads, has a formidable silo-kill capability.

It is often argued that this hard-target capability cannot be used against U.S. silos because these missiles could be launched on warning—that is, launched after verification

Table 3. Soviet Missile Forces, 1980–83
ICBMs[a]

| TYPE | SS-16 | SS-17 | SS-19 | SS-18 | TOTAL |
|---|---|---|---|---|---|
| Warheads/Missile (no.) | 1 | 4 | 6 | 8 | |
| Yield/Warhead (megatons) | 1 | .9 | .5-1 | 2 | |
| Throw-weight/Missile (lbs.) | 2,000 | 6,000 | 7,000 | 15-18,000 | |
| Deployment (no.) | 0-60 | 100-500 | 600-1,000 | 308-313 | 1,400 |
| Aggregate Throw-weight (millions of lbs.) | 0-1.2 | .5-2.5 | 4.2-7.0 | 4.6-5.6 | 11-13 |
| Aggregate Warheads (no.) | 0-60 | 400-2,000 | 3,600-6,000 | 2,400-3,100 | 6,500-9,200 |

SLBMs

| TYPE | SS-N-6 | SS-N-8 | SS-N-18 | TOTAL |
|---|---|---|---|---|
| Range | 1,500 | 4,800 | 5,600 | |
| Warheads[b] | 1 | 1 | 3[d] | |
| Yield (megatons) | 1+ | 1+ | 1+ | |
| Deployment[c] | 416+ | 406 | 128+ | 950? |
| Aggregate Warheads | 416+ | 406 | 384+ | 1,206? |

[a]Development of the SS-16-19 series started in the early 1960s and was completed during the 1969–72 SALT I negotiations. The table does not attempt to forecast the rate of substitution of the next generation of Soviet ICBMs, due for initial deployment around 1980. These are the SFO (small follow-on) to replace the SS-17 and SS-19, and the LFO (large follow-on), to replace the SS-18.
[b]The Soviets could MIRV their SLBMs. The Secretary of Defense has said that over 800 Soviet SLBMs will be fully modernized with multiple warheads by the late 1980s. MIRVs are being deployed on the SS-N-18.
[c]It is assumed that the old G-class (9 nuclear, 11 diesel) and H-class (7 nuclear), which carry only 3 missiles (SS-N-4s and SS-N-5s) per boat, will be phased out by the early 1980s. The future mix of missiles is highly uncertain; we have assumed all new deployments (after 1976) to be SS-N-8s, although the arithmetic does not work out exactly: 186 additional missiles cannot be deployed in any combination of full-loaded boats that hold 12 (Delta-I) or 16 (Delta-II) missiles per boat.
[d]The Zumwalt/Bagley Report of 30 July 1978 says that, according to new intelligence, each Soviet SS-N-18 SLBM is capable of carrying 7 MIRVs. N.B. SLBM throw-weights are not available.

that enemy missiles had been fired at U.S. targets but before those warheads arrived. In theory, this possibility may preserve deterrence but launch-on warning is an extremely dangerous doctrine. It would reduce policy making to the spasm of conditioned reflex. There would be no time for diplomatic maneuvers or intelligent presidential decision-making during the scant 30-minute flight of an enemy ICBM, or more likely in the 10 to 15 minutes after confirmation of the enemy launching and calculation of the trajectories. Who indeed would want the President to make such a world-shaking decision in 10 or 15 minutes? And what could the President decide? Against what targets would it be wise to launch U.S. missiles? Against Soviet silos? The Soviets might also have a launch-on-warning doctrine, so that the U.S. counterattack would insure that they fired their remaining missiles against other U.S. targets, all of our ICBM silos already having been targeted.

Alternatively, the President might launch our missiles against Soviet cities, carrying out the deterrent threat. In either case, the decision to launch would be a decision to escalate the war to the holocaust of all-out nuclear exchange.

A third and perhaps wiser option might be to attack Soviet military bases and facilities other than ICBMs, in an attempt to deprive the Soviet Union of the means to project power, and perhaps even to defend themselves, in a post-nuclear-exchange world. This would still be a risky move, since one can never be sure what the Soviet response might be. In any case, how could the President almost instantaneously decide on a course that might well be suicidal, ignoring the possibility that the warning was in error and foreclosing all opportunities for a negotiated end to the war while we still have significant strategic reserves in being and the cities of each side are still left standing?

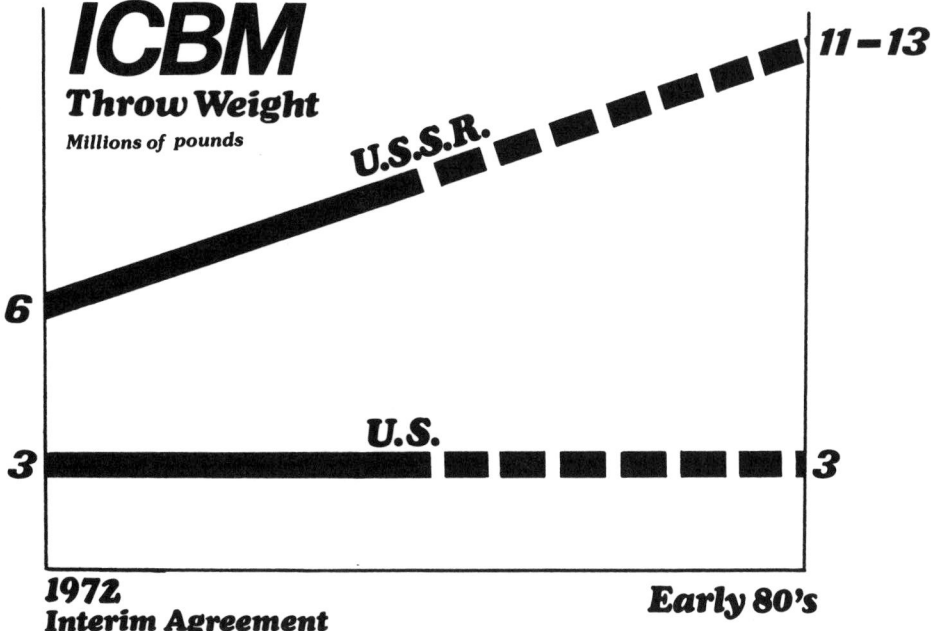

FIGURE 1. ICBM Throw Weight

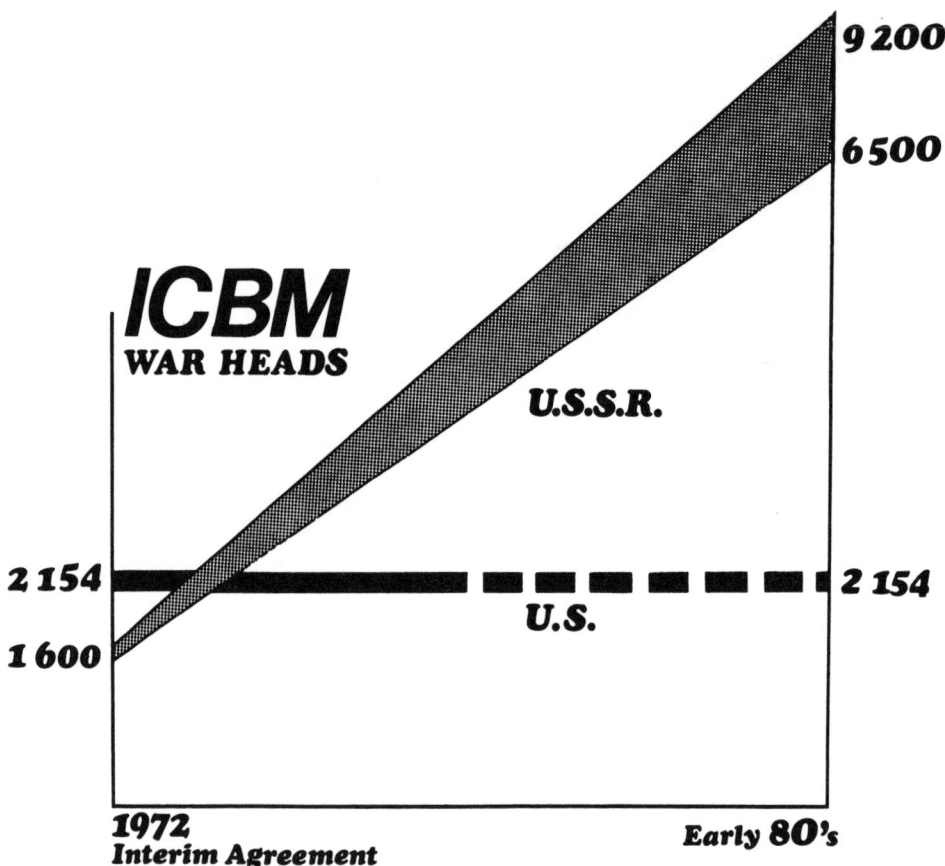

FIGURE 2. ICBM Warheads

## Why the Soviet Missile Advantages May Be Understated

Before leaving this disquieting comparison of U.S. and Soviet ICBM forces, it must be added that the figures given may understate the adverse trends, for two reasons. First, SALT limitations have covered launchers only, not ballistic missiles. Both sides, indeed, manufacture additional missiles for research and development, operational testing and training purposes. The Minuteman III line kept open during the past year for that purpose was ordered closed down before July 1978. It has been alleged that the Soviets have produced large numbers of extra missiles for the purpose of having a capability, in the event of war, to reload silos from which missiles have already been fired. In point of fact, silos are not necessary for the launching of missiles; it is perfectly feasible to use stationary or mobile "soft" launchers deployed anywhere. One can conceive of launch directly from the missile factories or warehouses through openings in the roof. Neither of these alternatives would be a violation of the present or prospective SALT agreements.

But the existence or non-existence of back-up missiles is difficult to verify by unilateral observation, and their numbers cannot be accurately counted. Mobile launchers presumably will be detected in both testing and deployment. As noted, President Carter has said that the Soviets have deployed mobile missiles, but, again, their numbers cannot accu-

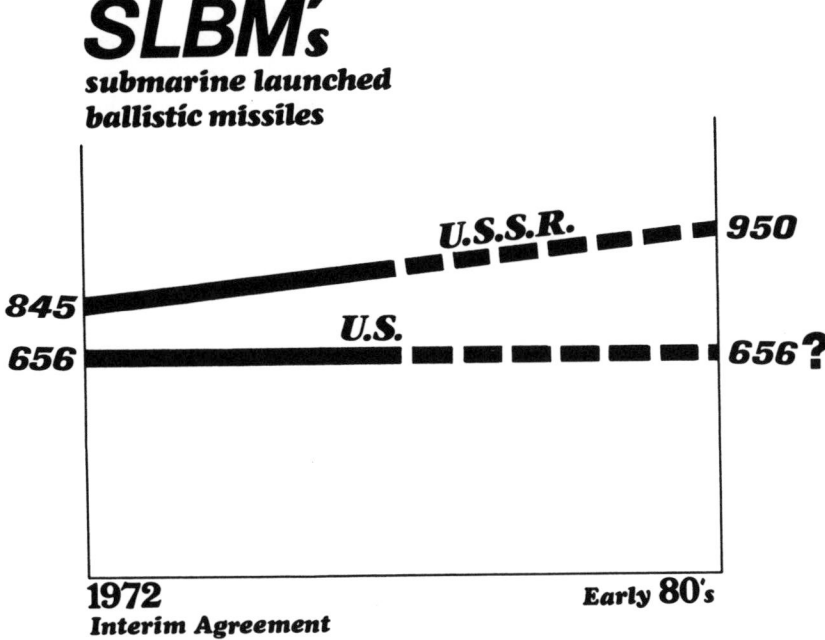

FIGURE 3. SLBM's

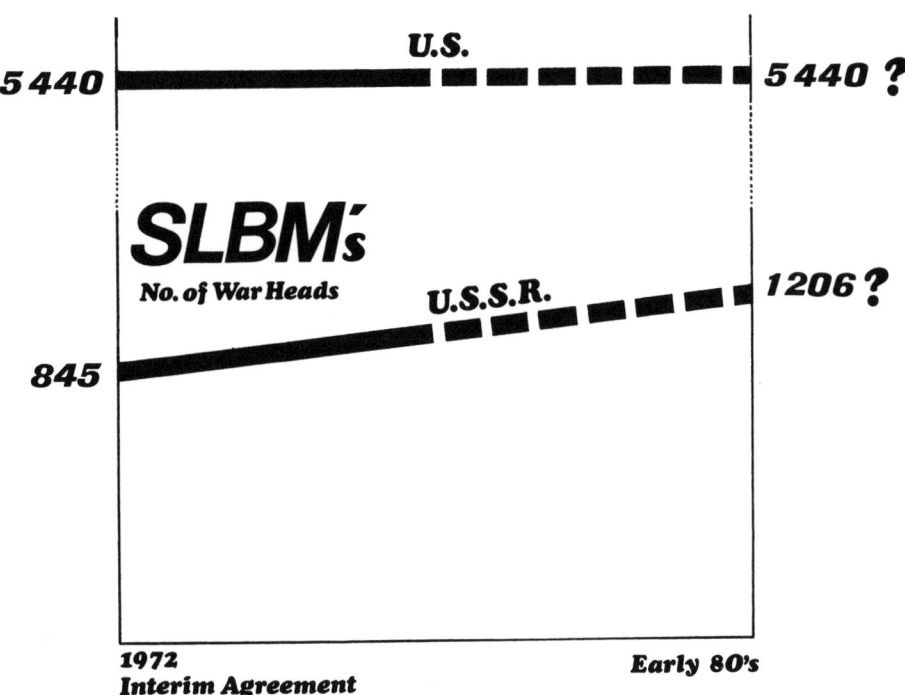

FIGURE 4. SLBM's Warheads

rately be counted. On the other hand, mobile launchers or "multiple-aim-point-systems" are difficult and costly to attack and thus decrease the threat of counterforce attacks. Although the Soviets have mobile missiles, and the United States does not (the first tests of mobile launchers for a possible future MX deployment are just now being planned), the Soviets have a far larger proportion of their strategic forces in fixed silos either because they do not believe the United States is yet approaching a hard-target kill capability or because they do not yet have the desired accuracy and command control capabilities for their mobile systems (including SLBMs), or for both reasons. A further uncertainty with respect to the adequacy of our second-strike capability is the durability of our command, control, surveillance and communications networks against the initial Soviet counterforce strike on these facilities that their doctrine calls for.

The emerging Soviet strategic superiority may be further understated because of what have become known in SALT parlance as "gray area systems." These are "non-central systems" (central systems being those treated directly in SALT) that may constitute strategic threats. The system of particular concern at this time is the SS-20. This is an intermediate range (3,100-mile) missile that has been tested in both fixed and mobile modes with three MIRV warheads. It has been reported that some 1,200 of these Soviet missiles are being produced.[4] It is assumed that the first mission of the SS-20 is to replace the old SS-4 and SS-5 missiles deployed in western Russia against western Europe. With three smaller MIRVed warheads each and an accuracy reported to be an order of magnitude greater than that of the crude first generation missiles, the SS-20 will greatly increase the threat to our NATO allies and our forces overseas, and support an apparent Soviet doctrine of attempting to take European territory relatively intact in the event of conflict. There could be missiles left over for deployment against China.

There is an additional potential use for these missiles. The SS-20 consists of the two lower stages of the ICBM known as the SS-16. With SS-16 third stages added (or offloading RVs, or deploying SS-20s to northern launch points), there could be a sudden proliferation of ICBMs that would raise the Soviet strategic missile force far beyond present or future agreed SALT launcher limits.

When we turn to strategic naval forces, we find Soviet submarine-launched ballistic missile (SLBM) forces also continuing to grow, both quantitatively and qualitatively. Not long after the signing of the Interim Agreement in 1972, the Soviets tested their SS-N-8 SLBM at a range of 4,200-4,500 nautical miles, and they are now estimated to have more than 250 of these deployed on Delta-class submarines.

This missile, coming on line several years before the 4,000 mile U.S. Trident I, would permit Soviet submarines to attack all U.S. targets from near their home ports near Murmansk, in the north and Petropavlovsk, in the east. In 1972, the Soviet Union argued that it needed more strategic submarines and SLBMs than we did in order to offset U.S. forward bases at Holy Loch, Scotland and Rota, Spain. It is now obvious that this claim was made with tongue in cheek, to put it most charitably, since the Soviets had tested and would soon deploy the long-range SS-N-8. (Note also that the United States signed a new base agreement with Spain in January 1976 that provides for the phasing out of nuclear missile submarines from the Rota base in the first six months of 1979, to coincide with the planned initial deployment of Trident I—now delayed until 1980 at the earliest.)

Nevertheless, the Soviets are expected to reach their permitted 950 SLBM level in 1978. The SS-N-8 has now been tested at 5,600 nautical miles—close to the projected 6,000-mile range of the Trident II missile planned for the U.S. forces in the late 1980s. And a new class of submarine, the Typhoon, carrying 20-24 ballistic missiles and "in the Trident class" is now reported.[5]

The Soviets have extensively tested both multiple reentry vehicles (MRVs) and multiple independently-targetable reentry vehicles (MIRVs) on SLBMs, and they have two MIRV-capable SLBMs, the SS-NX-17 and SS-NX-18. Soviet SS-NX-18 SLBMs are in the process of being deployed on Delta III submarines. As long as the Vladivostok limitation of 1,320 MIRVed delivery vehicles is tacitly observed, or if a SALT II Agreement at this or a lower level is reached, the Soviets may choose to reserve their MIRVed missile quota for the presently more accurate land-based missiles.

The United States will not begin the modernization of its SALT I Polaris/Poseidon SLBM force until 1980. At that time the Trident I missile is expected to start replacing the MIRVed Poseidon missile. Deployment of the new Ohio-class Trident submarine, which will have 24 missiles per boat and is designed ultimately to carry the 6,000-mile Trident II missile, has been further delayed. By the end of 1985, ten Ohio-class submarines are scheduled to be deployed. These in part, are scheduled to replace the ten old Polaris boats carrying 16 Polaris A-3 missiles with three warheads each (MRV, not independently-targetable).

## The Decline of U.S. Bomber Superiority

We turn now to airborne systems—manned bombers and cruise missiles, which were not covered by the 1972 Interim Agreement. Strategic bombers were included in the strategic nuclear delivery vehicle limits of the 1974 Vladivostok Accords, or "Guidelines" for a comprehensive "SALT II" Agreement to replace the Interim Agreement. Those guidelines were announced at the time of President Ford's visit, then withdrawn for clarification. It has not been possible in three years to reach Soviet-American agreement on exactly what was decided at Vladivostok.

In 1972, as we have noted, the United States had more heavy bombers than the Soviets, roughly 450 to 140 at that time; currently the ratio is about 300 to 135. But in 1972 the Soviet Union also had some 1,100 medium bombers assigned to "tactical" missions. Their deployment against Europe or Japan directly threatens most vital interests of the United States. These aircraft are also potentially available for strategic employment against the United States. There is no comparable American equivalent to these medium bombers. The fighter-bombers in the so-called forward-based systems in Europe and the Mediterranean can reach the Soviet Union, but they are committed to the defense of NATO and are offset in any event by Soviet theater systems.

In addition to the old Soviet medium bombers, the Soviets are now deploying the Backfire. This is a supersonic swing-wing bomber similar in many respects to the B-1, whose production was cancelled by President Carter on June 30, 1977. It is about 30 percent lighter, considerably smaller in dimensions and carries about one-fourth of the payload (which need not, however, include defense suppression weapons and other penetration aids, as a U.S. bomber payload must against sophisticated Soviet air defenses). The Soviets have insisted that it has a limited range and is designed only for naval and European theater missions. Published estimates in the U.S. however, have given one version a range of up to 6,000 nautical miles. With considerably less range, it would reach many U.S. targets, starting from Soviet Arctic bases and landing, say, in Cuba; with aerial refueling, for which the current model, the Backfire-B, is equipped, it could fly full two-way missions.

Even if the Soviet explanation were factually correct, however, the capability of the Backfire cannot be ignored. It constitutes a major threat to the security of Europe, the Middle East, Japan, and to major strategically important areas of the seas and oceans.

The United States, in contrast, has cancelled the B-1. The announced substitution of the cruise missile is misleading. If the cruise missile lives up to its promise during the 1980s, it will modernize the aging, and obsolescent B-52 to some extent. But it could have been an effective armament for the far more survivable B-1.

An effective bomber force is essential to the overall effectiveness of the American strategic deterrent. Given the implacable arithmetic of the present and prospective balance, a new bomber should be promptly built in order to restore stability quickly. The air breathing force should be a mix, including modern bombers that can penetrate Soviet airspace carrying shorter range cruise missiles and older bombers carrying cruise missiles with sufficient range to permit launching from "stand-off" positions outside the range of Soviet air defenses. (The vulnerability of a pure cruise missile/stand-off aircraft to Soviet air defenses, and the advantages of a "mix" in stressing those defenses, are discussed below.)

The bomber is complementary to the ICBMs and SLBMs. It provides insurance against surprise attack and technological surprise. It also provides a unique advantage in crisis management. Unlike missiles, the bomber can be safely launched on warning. Since it is under positive control until it reaches the enemy's airspace, it can be recalled (it is, indeed, automatically recalled if it does not receive a "go order"). It thus provides 6 to 8 hours or more—not the 10 to 15 minutes of computer-controlled missiles—for thought and negotiation, hours in which to seek crisis or war termination "while something is left standing." It would give the President the controlled strength to allow him to be "slow to take offense."

Because this cautious slowness could mean the difference between success and failure in ending a confrontation with the Soviet Union, we disagree with the cancellation of production of the B-1 simply because there is a cruise missile on the horizon. It has been claimed that that cancellation does not mean the end of the airborne leg of the strategic Triad, since cruise missiles can be mounted on old B-52s or new, still undesigned carriers.

It is doubtful whether the cruise missile alone can adequately modernize the bomber leg of the Triad and contribute to redressing the strategic balance. In 1972, at the time of SALT I, the Soviets had already deployed several hundred Shaddock submarine-launched cruise missiles. (That was the principal stimulus for the renewed U.S. interest in cruise missiles, starting in 1972, after the SALT I agreements were signed.) The Shaddock has a 250 to 350 mile range that can reach an estimated 50 percent of U.S. targets, since U.S. assets are concentrated on and near the seaboard and are essentially undefended. The range of these missiles could also be doubled relatively easily.

It is often asserted that the Soviet Union lags significantly behind the United States in cruise missile technology, notably in guidance and in efficient small engines, but we should by now be suspicious of such self-serving claims. Like the Japanese a generation ago, Soviet science has often surprised our experts by the speed of its development when a priority effort is made. This was the case recently in the field of MIRV technology. There are many other instances. Policy should prudently assume that Soviet cruise missile technology, as applicable to their needs, will soon at least equal our own. Furthermore, we note that their more primitive cruise missiles can accomplish their missions today.

The U.S. need for more sophisticated technology stems from two causes. First, the targets are much deeper in the huge Soviet landmass. Second, as we have already noted, the Soviets maintain large-scale air defenses.

There are also serious SALT problems raised by the cruise missile. First, the current expectation in SALT is that each aircraft carrying long-range cruise missiles will be counted as equivalent to a MIRVed ballistic missile. This means that we will be forced to phase out some of our Minuteman III or Poseidon ballistic missiles, even though as we approach our planned deployment of 10 Trident submarines we deploy cruise missiles on no more than 120 of our B-52s.

Second, the Administration's proposal for a three-year moratorium on the deployment of U.S. sea-launched and ground-launched cruise missiles of greater than 600-kilometer (324 nautical mile) range raises other problems. It adds a further element of uncertainty and delay to the catch-up program we should be pursuing with the utmost urgency.

The American position has opened a door which our policy has kept locked during the entire period of Soviet-American arms discussion and negotiation—the door of alliance solidarity. Sea or ground-based cruise missiles with more than 600-kilometer range could be enormously useful in the defense of Europe. Therefore, both in the United States and Western Europe there is entirely justifiable concern that this feature of the forthcoming SALT II agreement would put Europe at risk by jeopardizing its defenses.

Range limitations on cruise missiles have not been precisely defined and are not verifiable. Cruise missiles do not have to be tested at maximum range; they can be tested on closed courses and their testing may not even be observed. It has been argued that this is a Soviet, not a U.S. problem since we are ahead in cruise missile technology and it is we who perceive requirements for long-range cruise missiles. But, again, technological leads can vanish and perceived mission requirements can change.

## The Role of Strategic Defense

Reliance on "pure deterrence" has long been embodied in the American concept of "Mutual Assured Destruction." Under this theory, both parties cooperate in assuring that each side can inflict "unacceptable damage" on the other; each side is thus assured of holding in "hostage" the peoples, the cities, the industry of the other side; neither side can gain by starting a nuclear war—each can only commit suicide.

For this situation to remain stable, the hostages must remain naked—they must not be defended. Yet we have already noted that the Soviets do not believe in cooperating with us to assure that *they* are deterred; they do believe that it is to their interest that *we* be deterred from striking them, first or second. They therefore reject Mutual Assured Destruction. However plausible the Mutual Assured Destruction theory may have been more than a decade ago, a doctrine of Mutual Assured Destruction that is not reciprocal is a dubious basis for American policy.

## Present and Potential Asymmetries in ABM

Nowhere has the mutual-hostage theory been more evident than in the matter of antiballistic missile (ABM) defenses. When the ABM Treaty was signed in 1972, it was argued that the Soviet signature was evidence of Soviet acceptance of MAD. We would contend, on the contrary, that the Soviets were simply trying to neutralize, and gain time to overcome, our significant lead in ABM technology. The system the Soviets had started deploying around Moscow was not technologically sophisticated, and tests were not going well. The Treaty nullified the U.S. advantage, cut our ABM technology programs to a small fraction of what they had been, and gave the Soviets a breather in which to catch up and then take the lead.

The ABM Treaty limited each side to two ABM sites, with 100 interceptor missiles at each site. One site could defend an ICBM field and one the "National Command

Authority" (Washington and Moscow). The Soviet Union had already built a site at Moscow and the United States built one at Grand Forks, North Dakota. Under a Protocol agreed to in 1974, each side is limited to one site with 100 interceptor missiles. In 1975 the United States deactivated and partially dismantled its one site. The Soviets maintain the Moscow site with 64 launchers but with an impressive array of radars.

The Soviet Union is reported to have stepped up its technology program and has emphasized the development of movable ABM radars and high acceleration interceptors.

There is a significant risk that at some time in the future the Soviets will believe their ABM technology has reached a point at which it might be useful for them to "break out" of the Treaty by deploying ABM radars and missiles (including perhaps the upgrading of new, high-technology air defense missiles to an ABM capability) so rapidly that the United States would not be able to match their move.

## The Asymmetry in Air Defense

In the three years following ratification of the ABM Treaty in 1972, the United States phased out the bulk of its continental air defenses. The Defense Department stated that with limited ABM deployment, especially, after the 1975 Protocol, "the utility of air defense in a major attack on the United States is . . . restricted."[6] All the surface-to-air missile (SAM) defenses were deactivated and only a token force of six squadrons of obsolescent F-106 interceptors has been retained "to ensure the sovereignty of our air space in peacetime."[7]

The limited number of Soviet heavy bombers and the much larger numbers of medium bombers, including Backfire, must therefore be reckoned a serious potential threat to the United States (as well as to Europe, to Japan, to China and to the U.S. Navy). They would be essentially unopposed in the United States unless and until the Airborne Warning and Control System (AWACS—a converted Boeing 707 aircraft with a large "look-down" radar and on-board computers) plus interceptors with a look-down-shoot-down missile (e.g., the F-14 with Phoenix) were deployed in adequate numbers to protect the country.

In contrast, there are some 12,000 surface-to-air missile launchers and 2,700 interceptor aircraft deployed in the Soviet Union. These air defenses are continually being modernized.

The effectiveness of the U.S. bomber threat to the USSR depends upon how it is designed to penetrate these defenses. Because the B-52 has a declining expectancy of penetrating the Soviet air defenses, the B-1 was specifically designed for this mission in the 1980s and beyond. It can fly much lower, with terrain-following equipment for "treetop" flight at 50% more speed than the B-52—Mach .85-.90 vs. Mach .55-.60. It has a radar cross-section (or equivalent radar reflective area) far smaller than that of the B-52, carries much larger capabilities for electronic countermeasures (ECM) to hide from and confuse enemy radars, has a much larger capacity to carry defense suppression weapons (the supersonic SRAM, or short-range attack missile) and has equipment to detect mobile air defense radars, which it can then attack or avoid by maneuver.

The B-52/cruise missile combination that is now to be substituted for the B-1 has far less bomber prelaunch survivability and the B-52 itself may be vulnerable before it launches its cruise missiles. In addition, the cruise missiles after launching are vulnerable to air defense, both in flight and as they approach their targets. It is proposed to launch the cruise missiles from 500 miles outside the Soviet Union, which is 200 miles outside estimated Soviet-defended air space. Clearly the Soviets could in the 1980s extend the range of over-water radar coverage by using airborne and shipborne radars and radars in satellite territories and bases in the Middle East and Africa. Since the current cruise missile must be launched from an altitude of several thousand feet, the B-52s would be high-value targets for long-range interceptors (even the present generation SU-19 Fencers or MIG-23 Floggers). If we eventually select wide-bodied transports, or Boeing 747-type carriers for the missiles, they would offer even fatter sitting ducks. Such a makeshift system would risk catastrophic failure.

This risk has apparently received increased recognition from the Administration since the B-1 decision, for one of the reported recent U.S. proposals in SALT is to extend, after the expiration of the Protocol, the permitted cruise missile range from 1,500 to 1,800 miles or more (or from 2,500 to 3,000-3,500 kilometers), allowing the missiles to be launched from 800 miles away (and perhaps also increasing target coverage). Whether this change would allow the offense to stay ahead of the defense for long is not clear. Moreover, there are size and weight penalties for increasing cruise missile range that will increase the cost of the system as a whole.

Consideration is now also being given to building a new cruise missile carrier, with a low radar cross-section and greater speed and hardness against nuclear attack, but this will increase the cost of the system without necessarily assuring penetration.

"Stretching" the FB-111 and converting it to the more powerful engines developed for the B-1, in an attempt to make an FB-111H penetrating bomber, has also been proposed by the Department of Defense (though not funded in FY 1977 or FY 1978). This scheme merely casts further doubt on the wisdom of the decision to cancel the B-1.

Although the cruise missile has a small head-on radar cross-section, from the side it has a much larger radar image; it can readily be detected by today's radars; it is vulnerable to surface-to-air missile defenses as well as interceptors, to "local" as well as "area" defenses. While the cruise missile can, like the B-1, fly low in a terrain-following mode, like the B-1, the Soviets can, as has already been reported, mount air defense radars on high towers to increase their line of sight. The cruise missile at low altitude flies more slowly than the B-1—about as fast as the B-52—and it does not carry electronic countermeasures. It does not carry equipment to detect mobile air defenses or have a capacity for unprogrammed maneuver if it did detect such defenses.

## Anti-submarine and Anti-satellite Defenses

Other areas of active strategic defense are not neglected by the Soviets. They are known to have a large anti-submarine warfare (ASW) program. We have, we think, maintained a lead in the quieting of submarines, to reduce their vulnerability to detection. The advent of long-range SLBMs also, as noted above, tends to decrease the vulnerability of strategic submarines.

Nevertheless, the potential vulnerabilities of the American SLBM forces continue to be of concern. First, the new Ohio-class Trident submarine, though quieter than any previous submarine, is also much larger. With its 24 missiles, it is a high-value target. It may also become more vulnerable to detection by semi-active, or bistatic, systems that can potentially operate at great distances under the sea, generating noise signals by underwater explosions or other means. Reflections of these explosions by large underwater objects may be detected by two or more receivers in order to locate the object by triangulation.

Second, the communications systems needed to maintain command control of a submerged submarine must be by means of very low-frequency (VLF) long wave radio signals which can penetrate seawater. To generate these signals requires large powerful transmitters. The transmitters are more vulnerable to attack than the submarines themselves. An airborne backup system, "Tacamo," also has its risks and limitations. A highly survivable, extremely low frequency (ELF) transmitter using buried cables covering thousands of square miles has been proposed in recent years. Environmental concerns have generated local opposition in the few areas which are geologically suitable, and there is at present only limited funding ($15 million) for the development and testing of an ELF system called Seafarer.

The Soviet preoccupation with defense has also led them to extensive testing of anti-satellite techniques. Both sides place increasing reliance on satellites for many strategic purposes. Satellites carry photographic and other sensors for intelligence, including SALT verification, detection of missile launches, and monitoring of a wide variety of electronic and other events. They can also be used to transmit or relay signals for many purposes, including navigational and guidance aids. Soviet exercises in the interception and destruction of satellites imply a threat that could seriously degrade our capabilities in crisis or wartime. Reported intensive Soviet developmental efforts in high-energy lasers and directed-energy charged-particle beams may also threaten satellites if not the primary kill mechanisms for a Soviet anti-satellite satellite, and pose exotic ABM threats in the years ahead.

## Soviet Civil Defense

Finally, there is passive defense, a subject of increasing importance and justified concern, which directly affects the basic arithmetic of deterrence. The Soviet Union is known to have a massive civil defense program including shelter, training, and evacuation program for the population, and dispersal and hardening of industrial facilities. These programs emphasize the protection of civil authorities and their communication facilities, and of key workers, plus the maintenance of essential production in wartime.[8]

There is no equivalent U.S. counterpart of these programs and perhaps there cannot be, given the unattractiveness of civil defense to an open society. But the potential effect of such a war-survival program on our deterrent could be so great as to nearly nullify it — some calculations indicate that Soviet civil defense and industrial dispersal programs would reduce Soviet casualties during a full nuclear exchange to *one-tenth* those of the United States.

It is widely argued that the Soviet civil defense programs would not be efficiently carried out in time of crisis, and in particular, that evacuation during a crisis would be economically and socially disruptive and could not be sustained.[9] Such arguments seem to us not to be fully responsive. If the programs are only half as effective as claimed, the Soviet losses in an all-out nuclear exchange still would be but a fraction of those of the United States, which has no civil defense. If the Soviets expected this outcome, they might well perceive circumstances in which such losses would be risked, especially if they judged that our perception of the imbalance of risks would be such as to create opportunities for self-serving diplomacy.

## The Approaching Soviet Strategic Superiority

Drawing conclusions from this mass of variables requires us to focus again on the clear-cut issue with which we started this analysis: do we now have an adequate and effective deterrent second-strike capability? What would be the effect of possible SALT agreements on the adequacy of our second-strike capability?

In answering these questions we must consider the number and vulnerability of missiles and warheads, their accuracy, their ability to reach key targets, and the effects of active and passive defense programs on the vulnerability of Soviet targets of all kinds.

We know that the Soviet Union is continuing to build and modernize its strategic nuclear missile force at an alarming rate—150-200 ICBMs a year, as compared to a rate of zero for the United States; 6 ballistic missile submarines a year, as compared to zero for the United States (1½ a year in the 1980s); and 30-50 intermediate to long-range bombers a year as compared to zero for the United States. The Soviet Union builds missiles of far greater throw-weight than ours, and can therefore put more or larger MIRVed warheads on each missile than we can so that even under the proposals we made in March, 1977, it could have twice as many ICBM warheads of five times the individual yield of ours.[10] They have made rapid advances in catching up on our previous technological advantage in MIRVing, accuracy, and smaller RVs.

Those facts alone raise doubt as to whether we possess an adequate second-strike capability today. They leave no doubt whatever that we shall have to reverse these trends decisively and soon in order to maintain that capability in the 1980s.

During that fateful decade, the Soviets will have, as they do now, more ICBMs, heavier throw-weight, larger warheads and greater megatonnage. They will have overcome our present advantage in the number of MIRVed ICBM warheads, and probably in accuracy. They will have a counterforce capability (that is, a combination of numbers, accuracy and yield in their warheads) that would permit them to attack our Minuteman and Titan forces and to destroy all but a small fraction of them, thus shifting the strategic balance further in their favor.

At sea, they will have more nuclear missile submarines and SLBMs. They will have more long-range SLBMs at least for a time. They will have MIRVed a portion of these SLBMs—what portion will depend on SALT and on Soviet policy.

In the air, they will have overtaken our advantage in bombers. Their bombers will have a substantial "free ride" against our negligible defenses, while our bombers and cruise missiles will face increasingly formidable air defenses.

Even if the ABM Treaty continues in effect, we will face an increasing possibility of a rapid surprise deployment of ballistic missile defenses. All of our strategic forces will face the possibility of the blinding of our satellite eyes and the destruction or jamming of much of our communications network. And these forces will have their retaliatory capabilities against urban industrial targets further reduced—perhaps radically so—by the Soviet civil defense of its leadership, population and industry.

It is often argued that fear of a Soviet preponderance in numbers of strategic delivery vehicles, throw-weight, and megatonnage is misguided, at least while the United States has more warheads than the Soviets. The corollary argument is that against "soft" targets such as cities, damage is less than proportional to warhead yield—that is, more, smaller weapons can produce nuclear weapons effects that kill more people and damage more buildings than fewer, larger yield weapons. These effects are taken into account in a measure called "equivalent megatonnage (EMT)."[11]

It is also argued that if B-52s armed with ALCMs are included and Soviet Backfires and medium bombers (although both are quite capable of flying intercontinental missions) are excluded, the United States will maintain a significant advantage in warheads and some margin in delayed hard-target kill potential (see Figure 5). Several points implicit in these arguments require discussion.

First, the U.S. advantage in numbers of warheads is a transient one. The inherent

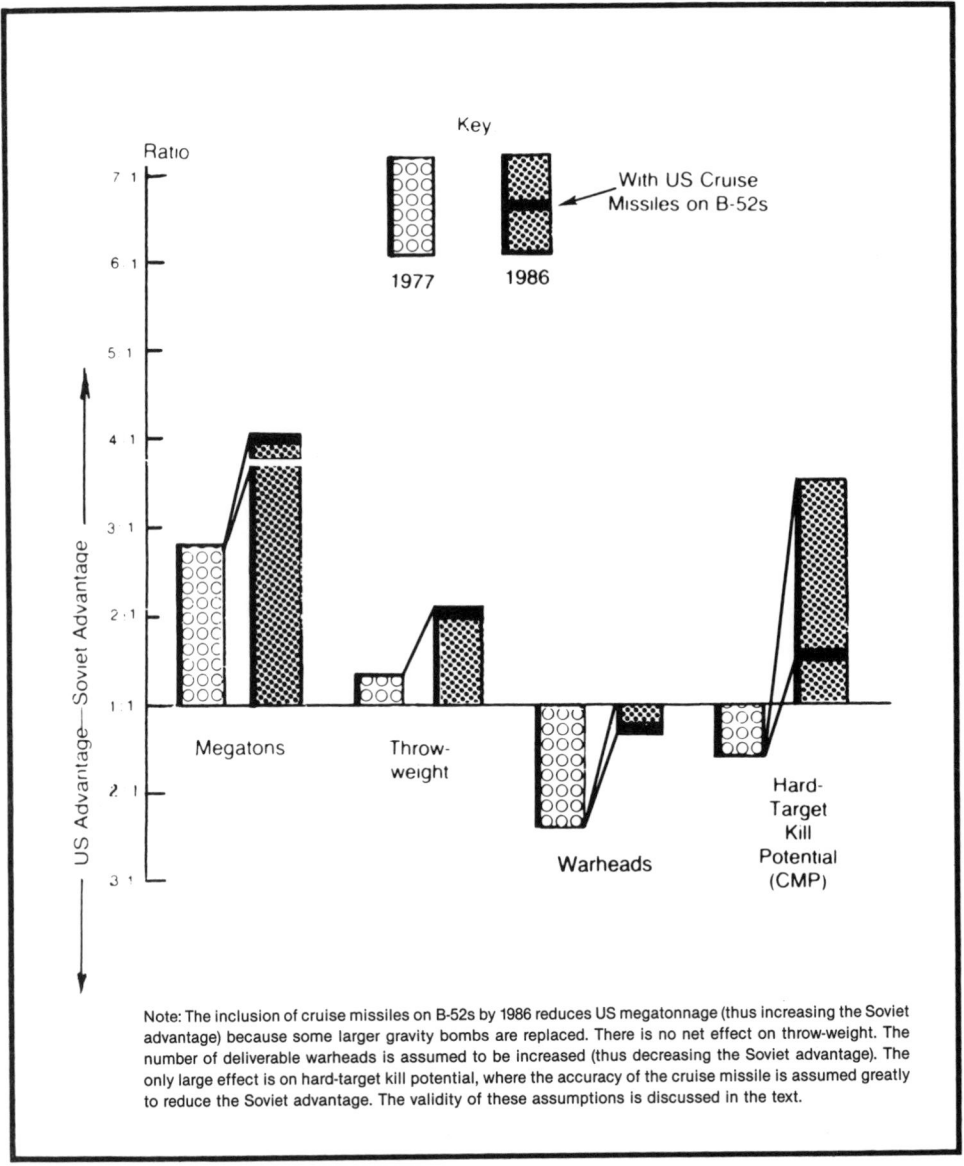

*Source:* Francis P. Hoeber, David B. Kassing, William Schneider, Jr., *Arms, Men, and Military Budgets Issues for Fiscal Year 1979.* New York: Crane, Russak & Company, Inc., 1978, p. 31.

FIGURE 5. Static Measures of Strategic Balance ("Political Sufficiency")

flexibility afforded by large throw-weight Soviet ICBMs and the present momentum of the Soviet MIRV program will erase the U.S. advantage in numbers of warheads. Second, if U.S. and Soviet strategic capabilities are measured in EMT rather than MT, the ratios and trends are still negative for the U.S. Third, using "equivalent megatonnage" as the principal criterion of warhead effectiveness is unduly narrow. The U.S. must address the entire Soviet target spectrum and this strategic requirement cannot be met efficiently with only low-yield weapons, even if targeted in salvos. Soviet strategy is designed to exploit large numbers of large-yield warheads. This capability provides the Soviet Union additional strategic targeting flexibility and efficient coverage of the U.S. target spectrum—from soft to hard targets. Possession of this capability also provides the Soviet Union additional insurance against serious degradation in operational missile accuracy. And this capability also confers on the Soviet Union a useable political-diplomatic instrument to be wielded in superpower diplomacy.

Fourth, by 1986 the Soviet position will have improved in every measure and the Soviets will then possess a strategically significant advantage in *prompt* counterforce and in particular, *prompt* hard-target counterforce[12] potential. This advantage could be exploited politically—in the deliberate instigation of U.S.-Soviet crises, in the conduct of such crises, and as the ultimate factor in their resolution. And if necessary, this Soviet advantage could be exploited in the conduct of various strategic nuclear war-fighting operations—as the dynamic U.S.-Soviet force exchange ratios are more meaningful than static peacetime force comparisons. Given these conditions, U.S. "equivalent megatons" would then reside between the megaton and warhead lines. Soviet strategic doctrine, with its emphasis on first-strike (hard-target) counterforce/damage-limitation combined with impressive and growing civil defense/war-survival programs, could reduce significantly the effectiveness of residual U.S. strategic forces.

The dashed lines in Figure 5 reflect the inclusion of cruise missiles to be carried on B-52s. The only trend that is strongly affected is that of hard-target kill potential, reflecting

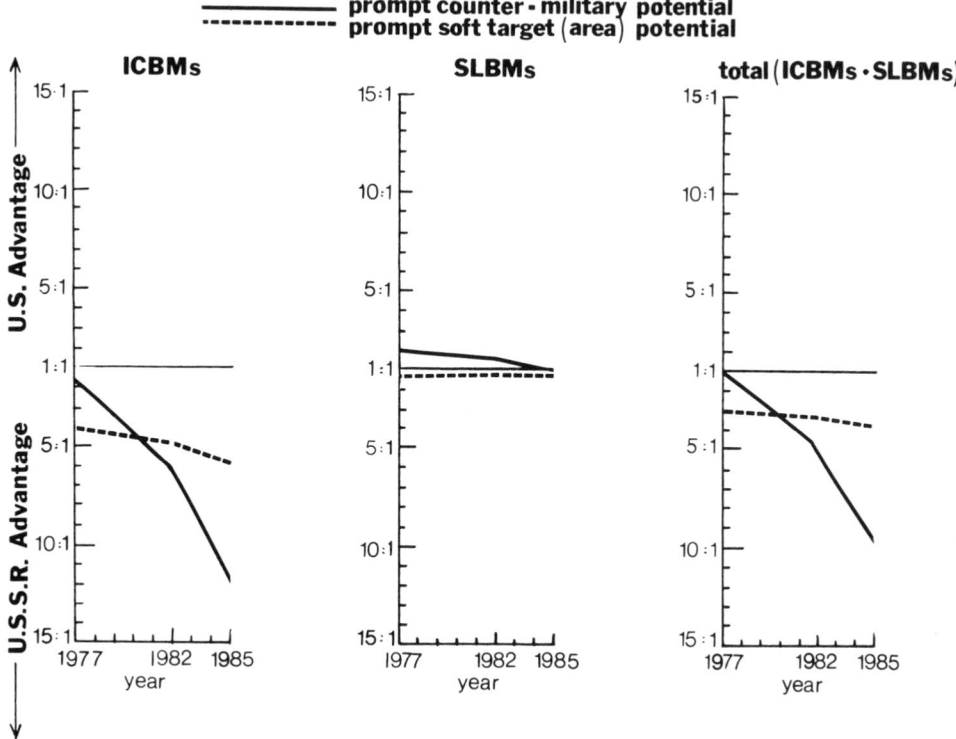

FIGURE 6A. The Balance - Consequences of Current SALT Proposals: *Time Urgent* Counter-Military and Soft Target Destruction Potential

the expected high operational accuracy of the cruise missile. The chart is based on the unclassified "back-up" for the testimony of Secretary of Defense Harold Brown before the House Armed Services Committee on August 2, 1977.

It is important to again distinguish between *prompt* (*hard-target*) counterforce and *delayed* (hard-target) counterforce potential (see Figure 6A and 6B). Each has unique strategic and political implications for political sufficiency, crisis stability, and nuclear war-fighting. U.S. cruise missiles cannot offset the emerging asymmetry in U.S.-Soviet prompt (hard-target) counterforce potential because of the inherent slowness of the

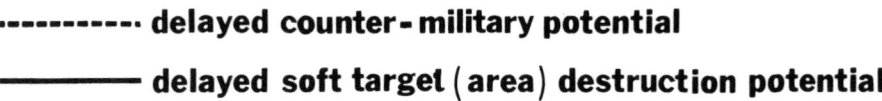

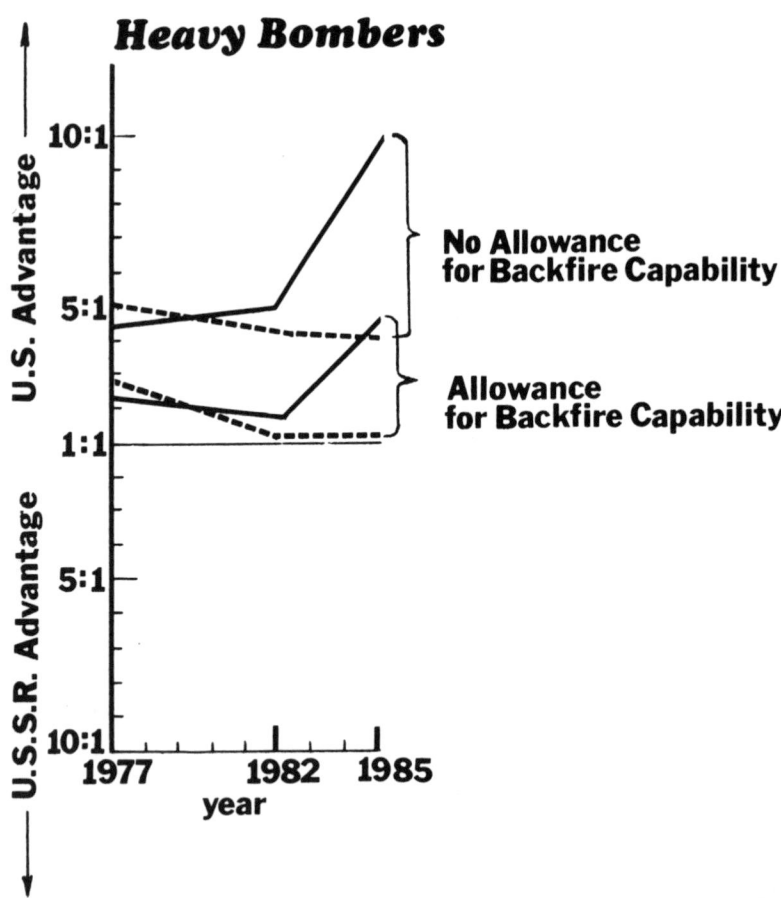

THIS FIGURE ASSUMES THE U.S. PROGRESSIVELY EQUIPS 120 B·52s EACH WITH 20 ALCMs OF HIGH ACCURACY. IT INCLUDES NO ALLOWANCE FOR THE POTENTIAL OF AIR DEFENSES.

FIGURE 6B. Delayed Counter-Military and Soft Target Destruction Potential bomber-cruise missile combination. Furthermore, the B-52/cruise missile combination could prove to have less-than-expected prelaunch survivability. A well-executed Soviet counterforce strike could destroy a substantial fraction of this force on the ground or during its escape. The B-52/cruise combination could also prove to be more vulnerable to extended Soviet air defenses, on alert and poised to intercept U.S. B-52s prior to launching their cruise missiles. The demands on Soviet air defenses are reduced significantly by a Soviet first-strike and their ability to concentrate air defense assets in the limited number of East-West and Arctic flight corridors (windows) that approach the periphery of the Soviet Union.

## If the Soviets Strike First. . . . .

Weapons inventory, by whatever measure, is a static indicator of balance. It is considered relevant to "political sufficiency," in Secretary Brown's presentation. However, conflict situations by definition are dynamic and extremely volatile. If deterrence were to fail, the stability of the relationship—and of the world—would be sensitive to the opportunities open to the antagonists quickly to alter the balance. With its growing MIRV capabilities and increasing hard-target kill potential, the Soviet Union could greatly change the initial strategic balance (as measured by static indicators) in its own favor.

Figure 7 presents Secretary Brown's estimates of the degree to which a Soviet first strike against U.S. strategic forces—particularly our fixed ICBMs—could alter that balance. While the Soviet ability to do this today is limited, it is increasing rapidly; by 1986 the Soviets could roughly double their relative advantage, by every measure.

While we do not have the assumptions and the detailed calculations on which the Secretary's conclusions are based, we believe that they understate the growing Soviet advantage. No credit is given the Soviets for potential strategic use of their several hundred medium bombers (including the long-range Backfire) or their several hundred Shaddock submarine-launched cruise missiles. No discount is applied for the greater Soviet efforts in passive defense of people, industry and military targets. Nor does the potential degradation of a B-52/cruise missile force by Soviet offshore and local air defenses appear to be adequately taken into account.

We do not have to assume that the Soviet Union will actually attack U.S. strategic forces. The point is that they will have the capability to *increase their advantage* with a counterforce first strike. After such a first strike, the United States would still have a capability for a second-strike retaliation against Soviet economic and political targets— in plain words, against their "hostage" cities and industrial centers. If Soviet civil defense failed, we could do "unacceptable damage" to them, but their forces held in reserve would still be greater than ours, and we have no effective civil (or air) defense. Their third-strike potential would make our second-strike less credible. It would leave the U.S. with a dangerously inadequate deterrent.

If, then, we permit these clear trends to materialize, we may expect to lose the "battle of perceived capabilities." The horrors of nuclear war may continue to deter its actual occurrence. But the political effects of such a shift, and its effects on the feasibility of conventional war or proxy war, is very great. We should recall that even the American nuclear monopoly did not deter conventional force aggression against important American security interests such as Korea, Greece, and Iran, and that aggressions of that kind can be expected to become worse, and more difficult to control, as our nuclear capability declines. Would the end of United States strategic adequacy make it impossible for us to

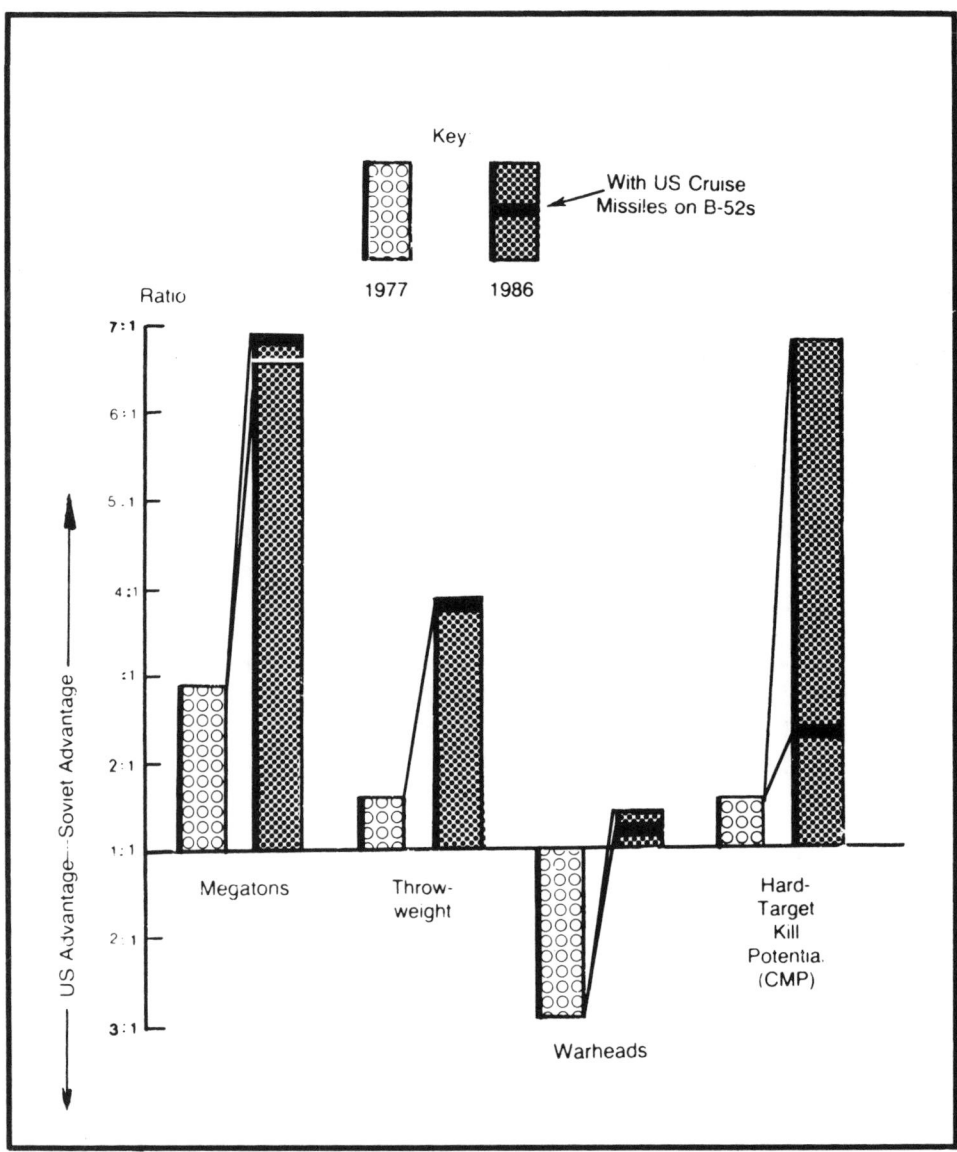

Source: Francis P. Hoeber, David B. Kassing, William Schneider, Jr., *Arms, Men, and Military Budgets Issues for Fiscal Year 1979*. New York: Crane, Russak & Company, Inc., 1978, p. 33.

FIGURE 7. Measures of Strategic Balance After Soviet First Strike ("Crisis Stability")

deter conventional force aggression, even against vital American interests like Europe or the Middle East or Japan? Our waning capabilities might not continue to inspire the confidence, allegiance and cooperation of our allies and our General Purpose Forces might not be sufficient to deter aggression at lower levels. We believe the risks of such a situation are unacceptable.

Prudence, therefore, requires that prompt corrective actions be taken to restore both real and perceived strategic adequacy for the 1980s. We recommend:

1.) Urgent attention to the survivability and endurance of our information, communications, and command and control systems;

2.) Rapid deployment of an alternate basing mode for our ICBMs;

3.) Development of a more capable follow-on missile to replace our MINUTEMAN IIIs;

4.) Procurement of a high quality strategic bomber and cruise missile-tanker system with high prelaunch survivability and penetrability;

5.) Acceleration of the TRIDENT I SLBM deployment program, TRIDENT II development, and, if possible, TRIDENT submarine construction, and renewed study and development of a smaller SLBM submarine;

6.) Rehabilitation of the air defense program with AWACS, F-14/Phoenix, and new surface-to-air missiles;

7.) Reexamination of the token U.S. civil defense program;

8.) Reinvigoration of ABM research and development programs.

## III. THE IMBALANCE OF GENERAL PURPOSE FORCES

Ever since 1946–47, when the United States hastened to "bring the boys home" and demobilize its World War II forces, while the Soviet Union did not, the Soviets have enjoyed a preponderance of military power in the areas close to their borders. This country watched unhappily while they used their power to acquire and consolidate control of the "buffer state" satellites of Eastern Europe. But, beginning with the Truman Doctrine in 1947, we said, in effect: "Thus far, and no farther!"

The threat of our nuclear power, naval strength, and mobilization potential were sufficient to uphold this position in the late 1940s. We did partially mobilize to wage the Korean War in the early fifties, and we called up reserve divisions during the Berlin Crisis of the early sixties. Thereafter, our strategic nuclear dominance combined with our forward-deployed ground forces and our naval capacity to project power, continued to deter major aggression, as the Cuban Missile Crisis demonstrated; but this kind of deterrence did not work in secondary theaters like the Middle East and Indo-China. Even as nuclear parity became a reality in the late sixties and early seventies, our "second-strike" capability and the enormity of nuclear conflict made it tolerable, if imprudent, for a time to run the risks associated with an active foreign policy despite our conventional inferiority in areas close to the Soviet perimeter.

But as we have seen, the early 1980s threaten to be a period of Soviet strategic nuclear superiority. It will be difficult to prevent the emergence of such a gap altogether, even through crash programs. An awakened American concern could lead to programs that would restore strategic adequacy and cause the era of Soviet superiority to be brief, even as Soviet determination is now making nuclear parity only a transient condition. But it is also possible that the first political use of Soviet strategic superiority will be to back coercive pressures designed to prevent our catching up.

Moreover, if we wait for a period in which Soviet strategic superiority becomes an unambiguous reality, we may experience conventional threats and outright aggression on a much larger scale. The major expansive thrusts the Soviet Union supported during the early seventies in Indo-China, the Indian subcontinent and the Middle East, and the campaigns it has been conducting in many parts of Africa since that time, could well seem minor skirmishes in comparison. Mobilization potential, the traditional basis of American strength, cannot deter superior Soviet General Purpose Forces that are backed by nuclear preponderance, nor could it stem the tide in the early—and perhaps decisive—stages of a major conventional conflict. As the 1973 Arab-Israeli conflict demonstrated, future wars are likely to be of unparalleled intensity, due to the increased destructiveness of weapon systems and the increased mobility of forces.

The Soviets recognize the usefulness of strategic nuclear superiority in enabling them to use superior General Purpose Forces with far diminished risks of escalation. As an article in one of their military journals put it, "Superiority in the relationship of forces of the higher (strategic) level creates favorable conditions for the successful military actions of lower (tactical-conventional) levels."[13]

What are the missions of our general purpose forces and theater nuclear forces? The United States has a vital national interest in the political independence and territorial integrity of Western Europe, Canada, Japan, and a number of other countries around the world to whose security we are committed for reasons of geopolitics, history, or political association—Israel, Egypt, the major oil producing states of the Persian Gulf, Taiwan, South Korea, Australia and New Zealand, the nations of Latin America and others. If any of these nations fell under the control of the Soviet Union, it could threaten the security of the United States in a fundamental way. It is greatly to our advantage to assist a number of other nations to retain their independence. China, for example, whose turn against the USSR and therefore toward the West since 1971 has been one of the most significant recent developments in world politics.

The significance of other events to our security would emerge only in context, as a regional crisis developed in one pattern or another. If the Soviet Union gained control of a small country in Africa, that fact might be a matter of concern to us, but not in itself a threat. If Soviet control spread throughout a large part of Africa, however, and began to outflank the Middle East and raise questions about our capacity to control sea lanes leading to the Persian Gulf, to obtain access to raw materials, and to project power where necessary, our security problem would greatly magnify.

It is apparent therefore that no part of the world can be excluded in advance from our security concerns. The globe itself is the strategic theater of the central conflict of our time.

It follows that we and our allies need forces in being at all times capable of deterring attack and, if necessary, defending the nations to whose security we are committed. Especially needed are mobile forces capable of dealing with local situations affecting our interests. Specifically, this force planning guideline requires us to have land, naval, air forces, and tactical nuclear forces which would, if necessary, control simultaneously both oceans, and deal with potential threats to those nations whose security is linked with our own. The implications of such preparedness can only be determined with reference to the size, sophistication, and rate of growth of the forces of the Soviet Union and its allies.

One conclusion that flows from our analysis, therefore, is that it is urgent to reexamine the General Purpose Force balance, current trends in this balance, and the implications of these trends for the United States and its allies. Strategic balance would not reduce the need for approximate balance also at each theater level vital to our interests.

The present disequilibrium between Warsaw Pact and NATO forces and rates of military production in Europe, and between Soviet and American forces and rates of military buildup relevant to other theaters vital to our security, is very great indeed, as Tables 4, 5, and 6 on pages 68, 70, and 71, demonstrate. We were therefore surprised to read President Carter's statement in July 1977 that the limited improvements underway in NATO forces would be sufficient to redress the balance of forces in Europe, and we were dismayed at the contradictory revelation that discussions of PRM-10 considered options for conceding one-third of West Germany in a European war because the costs of an adequate defense would be provocative to the American public, and a *significant increase* in forces would be provocative to the Soviets.[14] Present NATO policy requires force improvements at the rate of "at least 3 percent a year in real terms." It is difficult to see how the President's policy could overcome the present gap, and keep up with a Soviet rate of approximately 5 percent a year. Moreover, the Fiscal Year 1979 budget announced in January 1978 called for an increase of only 2 percent—and of zero for procurement in constant dollars. (The Office of Management and Budget argued that the NATO agreement applies only to spending for forces committed to NATO.)

The General Purpose Force balance is more complex than the strategic nuclear balance. Conventional, or "general-purpose" forces are more heterogeneous; as the term "general-purpose" implies, they must be prepared for a broad spectrum of contingencies in many parts of the world; their usefulness is greatly affected by the adherence or opposition, the aid or drain, of allies on both sides; their success in combat is highly dependent on the intangible factors—generalship, morale, tactical skill, intelligence, staying power—that make the performance of armies vary so widely among nations, in different wars and at different times. Nevertheless, in conventional (not guerrilla) wars large armies comparably equipped tend to deter or defeat small armies, and when forces are of comparable size, well-equipped forces tend to deter or defeat ill-equipped forces. Superior strategy can compensate for inferior numbers of weapons, but only to a degree.

In the comparison of U.S. and Soviet forces, we are to be concerned in particular with: (1) overall strengths, on land and in the air; (2) the European theater; and (3) the navies—all in their largely disparate missions and strategies. We shall first make quantitative comparisons and then consider qualitative differences, where determinable, taking account of differences in geography and in missions. We shall comment on the relevance of nonmilitary strengths and constraints. Finally, we shall consider both levels and trends.

## The Overall Soviet Lead

In simplest terms, the Soviets have armed forces of some 4.9 million men; the U.S., forces of 2.1 million. We are outnumbered by more than two-to-one (Table 4). However, the simplest terms may also be simplistic.

It has been argued that a number of items should be deducted from the Soviet side of the ledger. For example, over half-a-million Soviet soldiers are tied up in air defense, an activity which the United States has abandoned. But we have already pointed out that the Soviet air defenses are a vital factor in judging the effectiveness of our second-strike capability as a deterrent and create an important asymmetry in favor of their strategic forces. The most that may be properly said is that Soviet air defenses are manpower-intensive. It can be asked whether that means they are inefficient. In evaluating such arguments, we should note that the Soviets commit three times as many men as we do to the strategic offensive forces, which are relatively symmetrical in numbers, and in which the U.S. state of peacetime alert, or readiness, is said to be higher.

It is also pointed out that half a million Soviet personnel are committed to frontier and internal security, where the Soviets have problems quite different from our own. But if we take only the General Purpose Forces, the Soviet ratio of superiority is more than 3:2, backed by reserves in a ratio of 5:1. And U.S. reserves appear to be dwindling under the impact of the Volunteer Army. And if we look at land combat forces (Army and Marines), for which numbers of men are a reliable measure of strength, the Soviet ratio is 2½:1, backed by reserves of 4:1 (not shown separately in Table 4).

But, it is pointed out, the Soviets keep at least half-a-million men on the Chinese

Table 4. The Military Manpower Balance 1977

REGULAR FORCES, RESERVES, CIVILIAN EMPLOYEES (THOUSANDS)

|  | UNITED STATES | SOVIET UNION |
|---|---|---|
| Regular Forces | | |
| Strategic Nuclear | | |
| Offensive | 109 | 365 |
| Defensive | 37 | 640 |
| Total Strategic Nuclear | 146 | 1,005 |
| M/IRBM Forces | 0 | 125 |
| General Purpose Forces | | |
| Army | 781 | 2,467 |
| Navy | 507 | 398 |
| Air Force | 447 | 430 |
| Marines | 192 | 12 |
| Total General Purpose | 1,927 | 3,307 |
| Total Regular Forces | 2,073 | 4,437 |
| Paramilitary—Frontier & Internal Security | 0 | 460 |
| Civilian Employees | 957 | 732 |
| Reserves | 1,189 | 6,800 |
| GRAND TOTAL | 4,219 | 12,429 |

Source: *American and Soviet Military Trends Since the Cuban Missile Crisis.* John M. Collins. The Center for Strategic and International Studies, Georgetown University, Washington, D.C., 1978, pp. 52–57.

border. We have already noted that both sides have conventional forces for many purposes besides opposition to each other. Such forces are nevertheless usable against each other under some circumstances. We also note that during the years of buildup in the East, the Soviets have also increased their forces stationed in Europe. More could be shifted westward in a European conflict. But the forces now stationed in Europe are believed to be maintained in a high state of readiness and capable of launching an attack on NATO with very few days' warning.

The major factors bearing on a NATO-Warsaw Pact confrontation in Europe are considered below. Here we simply note that, by any measure, the Soviets maintain significantly more men than the United States in, and mobilizable for, military forces.

In addition to the comparison of numbers of men, we examine the equipment available to the armed forces of each side. Table 5 shows major items of land and air equipment at the disposal of these forces (excluding the strategic arms discussed above).

Two facts stand out: first, the Soviets have larger inventories of all but two categories of equipment—helicopters and anti-tank missiles—and in many categories their superiority in numbers is overwhelming; second, they are producing military equipment at a much greater annual rate than we are, except for anti-tank missiles. They are, therefore, widening the gap and appear likely to continue to do so.

There is one notable exception. On land, the massive Soviet force of tanks is opposed by considerable numbers of U.S. anti-tank missiles. *If* the U.S. infantry can survive (against artillery, air power, and tank guns) and deploy to use these weapons effectively, they may prove to be one key element in defeating armored thrusts, especially if there should be greatly increased emphasis on complementary support with the new technology of "scatterable" (air-, missile-, or artillery-delivered) mines. Greater numbers may be needed; most certainly there must be great improvement in protecting the anti-tank missile operators and in giving the missiles "all-weather" capability.

It has been widely assumed and often asserted that American technology gives us a qualitative offset to Soviet quantitative advantages. It is characteristic of the American outlook to assume that American science and technology is always the best in the world. This view is not necessarily valid across the board.

The Soviets are catching up in many areas and forging ahead in some. The Soviet T-72 main battle tank (MBT), now being deployed is highly rated; the new U.S. MBT is expected to be more than a match for the T-72—but it is still in development. The Soviet armored personnel vehicle, the BMP, is unmatched by any U.S. vehicle. It is designed to permit their infantry to fight without the necessity of dismounting. The T-72 and BMP are equipped to survive on a nuclear battlefield with compressors to create positive internal air pressure to keep out radioactive particles and chemical gases. American combat vehicles have no such equipment, nor is any planned.

The Soviets apparently devote considerable effort to preparation—in both training and equipment—for chemical warfare, both defensive and offensive. The United States does not. There are persistent U.S. arguments about the political acceptability and military usefulness of chemical agents, but the very limited U.S./NATO capabilities for defense against chemical attack may prove to be a Western Achilles heel.

U.S. tactical airpower has long been considered qualitatively superior. A new generation of U.S. tactical aircraft—A-10, F-14, F-15, F-16—is currently being built and deployed.

But new Soviet tactical aircraft are being deployed at a faster rate. These include the MIG-23S (Flogger B), MIG-23B (Flogger D), SU-19 (Fencer-A), SU-19C (Fitter C), MIG-25 (Foxbat B), and MIG-21SMT (Fishbed). These third generation aircraft account for an exponential growth, starting in 1969, in the payload, range and low-altitude capabilities of the Soviet tactical air forces.

Unless we move rapidly to redress present imbalances (certain armaments have a long leadtime even if we do) U.S. quality cannot be expected to offset Soviet quantity, or "mass," in the 1980s.

## The European Theater Balance

The primary Soviet concern with Western Europe is tempered by interests and perceived threats in many other parts of the world. Similarly, the United States has many security interests in the world other than its concern for Western Europe. But for both the Soviet Union and the United States, Western Europe is of central concern. If the Soviet Union could gain control of Western Europe with its territory, its population, its skills and its capital, the world balance of power would be altered drastically in the Soviets' favor. Such an event would immediately alter the expectations of China, Japan, and many other nations, which might well feel impelled to accommodate their policies to those of the Soviet Union as best they could, leaving us isolated in a hostile world.

It follows that the national security interest of the United States in the territorial integrity and political independence of Western Europe is fundamental. Europe must be protected not only against direct attack, but also against envelopment from the North or from the Middle East and Africa, as well as against political subversion.

In considerable part, therefore, the General Purpose Force structures and contingency plans of both the United States and the Soviet Union are geared to the possibility of conflict over Europe. The U.S. heritage and traditional ties are European, and only Western Europe and Japan, have both the Western orientation and the economic strength to stand between the United States and isolation—and alienation—from the world.

Table 5. U.S. vs Soviet Strength

SELECTED LAND AND AIR WEAPONS: INVENTORIES & PRODUCTION RATES

|  | 1976 INVENTORY | | RECENT ANNUAL PRODUCTION | |
| --- | --- | --- | --- | --- |
|  | U.S. | SOVIET | U.S. | SOVIET |
| TANKS |  |  |  |  |
| Heavy and Medium | 6,400 | 42,000 | 450 | 2,600 |
| COMBAT VEHICLES[a] | 13,500 | 41,900 | 1,400 | 3,700 |
| ARTILLERY | 5,200 | 19,000 | 200 | 1,400 |
| ANTI-TANK GUIDED MISSILES | 72,000 | 6,000 | 48,000 | 27,000 |
| COMBAT AIRCRAFT—all types | 7,300 | 9,400 | 5,700 | 2,000 |
| Bombers, fighters, bomber fighters, Excl Naval | 2,000 | 3,300 | 500 | 1,100 |
| Helicopters | 9,400 | 7,800 | 200 | 900 |

[a]Includes armored personnel carriers, armored fighting vehicles, and amphibious vehicles.

Sources: American and Soviet Military Strength, Contemporary Trends Compared, 1970–1976, John M. Collins, in Congressional Record, August 5, 1977, p. S14064ff.; Hoeber, Schneider op. cit.; Annual Defense Department Report, FY 1978.

In modern times, the main security threats to Russia and the Soviet Union have come from the West, not the East. Today the Soviets' perceived threat is aggravated by their stated fear of facing China in a two-front war.

For many years the basic aim of Soviet strategy against the United States has been to gain control of Western Europe. Despite Soviet concerns with the East, which never abate, they have long given primacy to Europe. It was with an eye on Western Europe— primarily West Germany—after World War II that they took control of the satellites as buffer states in Eastern Europe. It was against Europe that they first deployed the nuclear-armed medium and intermediate-range ballistic missiles (M/IRBMs) that preceded Soviet intercontinental ICBMs and constituted the genuine "missile gap" of the late fifties and the early sixties. While they built up their forces on the Chinese border in the late 1960s and early 1970s, they simultaneously strengthened their forces in the West.

It is, therefore, important to consider the U.S.-Soviet balance first in the context of the European theater. We will examine this theater in terms of the static NATO-Warsaw Pact balance of forces and of the match (or mismatch) of tactical doctrines and what they may portend for the probable outcome of a war.

Table 6 presents estimates of some elements of the NATO-Warsaw Pact forces. All of these measures require qualification, but some generalizations may be drawn.

In Northern and Central Europe, NATO is heavily outnumbered by the Warsaw Pact in every one of the selected categories. Even if only Soviet forces are counted, the imbalance persists in every category except manpower (in which inclusion of the French troops stationed in Germany gives NATO a slight edge).

One important item omitted from the table is precision anti-tank weapons, in which Table 5 shows a large U.S. advantage. There are no adequate data available for the European theater, and the numbers are presumably changing fast. One authority states that Warsaw Pact deployment of anti-tank missile launchers had exceeded the NATO deployment by 1975.[15] Since the NATO forces are configured (in the West) for the defensive, there may be a tendency to understate NATO capabilities. However, the principal threat to anti-tank weapons is artillery, in which the Warsaw Pact has a two-to-one advantage. Moreover, the NATO forces also have the mission of counterattacking to regain any ground lost to an initial invasion. In such efforts, a deficiency in tanks,

Table 6. The European Theater Balance
NATO vs. Warsaw Pact (WP)
(thousands)

| | NORTHERN & CENTRAL EUROPE | | | | SOUTHERN EUROPE | | | |
|---|---|---|---|---|---|---|---|---|
| | NATO | (U.S.) | WP | (USSR) | NATO | (U.S.) | WP | (USSR) |
| Troops—Combat & Direct Support | 680* | (193) | 945 | (640) | 560 | (5) | 390 | (145) |
| Division Equivalents** | | | | | | | | |
| Armored | 10 | (2) | 31 | (22) | 4 | (NA) | 6 | (2) |
| Infantry, Mechanized, & Airborne | 17 | (4) | 38 | (23) | 33 | (NA) | 27 | (9) |
| Tanks (peacetime operational, medium & heavy) | 7,000 | (3,000) | 20,500 | (13,500) | 4,000 | (NA) | 6,700 | (2,500) |
| Artillery | 2,700 | (NA) | 5,600 | | 3,500 | (NA) | 2,700 | |
| Aircraft (operational) | 2,085 | (492) | 4,230 | (2,500) | 475 | (NA) | 1,100 | (400) |
| Light Bombers | 150 | (NA) | 125 | (125) | – – | | 50 | (50) |
| Fighter Bombers | 1,500 | (NA) | 1,375 | (925) | 625 | (NA) | 325 | (125) |
| Interceptors | 400 | (NA) | 2,050 | (900) | 200 | (NA) | 1,000 | (425) |
| Reconnaissance | 300 | (NA) | 550 | (350) | 125 | (NA) | 200 | (150) |

*Includes 50,000 French troops stationed in Germany but not assigned to NATO.
**Divisions, brigades and similar formations aggregated on the basis of three brigades to a division.

*Sources: The Military Balance, 1976–1977; and 1977–1978, London: The International Institute for Strategic Studies, 1976 and 1977; Karber, op. cit.*

armored fighting vehicles, and artillery appears more important than numerical superiority in anti-tank weapons.

The data also conceal a particular weakness on the Northern Flank. Northern Norway is remote and vulnerable, and Norwegian policy does not permit the stationing of foreign troops within its borders. One Norwegian brigade group is stationed in the north, facing two Soviet divisions and a brigade on the Kola Peninsula. Moreover, the area is also vulnerable to Soviet naval forces, which now regularly patrol to the west of Northern Norway—that is, between Norway and Scotland. As Norwegians often remark, "We are behind the Iron Curtain, too." The potential invasion route, unless by air, is narrow and runs along a natural escarpment, but prospects for an extended Norwegian holding action do not seem bright.

Only on the Southern Flank do the numbers favor the West. However, the NATO forces in that area are widely dispersed from Italy to Turkey, with a large share in Italy, far from the likely site of any southern attack. Moreover, the NATO position on the Southern Flank has been weakened by the unresolved quarrel between Greece and Turkey.

## The Soviet Buildup in Europe

The figures in Table 6 do not reflect the continuing, major Soviet program of modernizing and strengthening their forces without increasing the number of units deployed. The Soviet Order of Battle has not been altered since 1968, when the five divisions used in the invasion of Czechoslovakia were left in place, but recent improvements in the Soviet posture include:[16]

(1.) Addition of a fourth tank battalion (31 tanks) to the tank regiment of the motorized rifle divisions, and 1,500 men; tank divisions now include 375 heavy tanks.[17]

(2.) Doubling of the number of artillery pieces since 1968. Multiple rocket launchers have contributed to a nine-fold increase in the single-salvo capability of each division since the end of World War II. Moreover, self-propelled artillery is being introduced. In the past, the Soviets have relied on towed artillery, used for bombardment prior to armored attack. Self-propelled artillery that can keep pace with armored units will enhance their capability to maintain the momentum of advance in a "blitzkrieg."

(3.) Introduction of a high-performance attack helicopter, heretofore not part of the Soviet forces (although transport helicopters have long been emphasized).

(4.) Forward deployment (near the East German border) of new river-crossing equipment to enhance overland mobility (essential to rapid advance in Western Europe, where there are major north-south rivers every 90-100 kilometers, medium ones every 25-30 km, and small rivers every 5-10 km). This equipment includes heavy amphibious vehicles and heavy bridging equipment capable of spanning a 600-meter water obstacle.

(5.) A 25 percent increase in aircraft per air regiment, and continued upgrading of aircraft performance, as already noted.

(6.) Continued improvement in air defenses, including low-altitude capabilities. Soviet air defenses are superior to those of NATO, both qualitatively and quantitatively.

(7.) Expansion and modernization of airlift capabilities for both logistics support and paratroop drops. In combination with widespread prepositioning of heavy equipment and combat consumables (ammunition, fuel and food), this airlift capability permits more rapid concentration and thus reduces required warning time.

(8.) Electronic Warfare—Soviet capabilities to disrupt NATO C3 while maintaining secure Soviet C3 are significant.

## Reinforcements

The figures in Table 6 depict peacetime deployments. NATO has always assumed it would have substantial warning time to reinforce its defenses, both from in-theater reserves and from Great Britain and the United States. This assumption is no longer valid. The Soviets can mobilize for attack rapidly and in considerable secrecy (under cover of maneuvers, among other measures), as was shown in Czechoslovakia in 1968. Their doctrine is based on the concept of the "standing start"—the notion of permanent readiness to attack with forces already in forward positions. The Arab attack in the Middle Eastern War of October 1973 illustrates that doctrine in action. Moreover, the West is always reluctant to respond to ambiguous signs of threat. While a hair trigger is dangerous, inability to act to counter reinforcement would undermine the whole idea of the utility of warning time.

Mobilization of reserves in Europe could be quite rapid, but the numbers available are limited, except for the half-million-man German Territorial Army, lightly armed and trained for home defense. In the event of attack, NATO's principal reliance for fast reinforcement in Central Europe would therefore be on deployments from the United States. Such deployments can only be rapidly accomplished by air. But the United States has not developed a large-scale airlift capability. In the fall of 1976 NATO exercises, 12,560 persons and 348 helicopters were airlifted to Europe.[18] The number in wartime would have to be far larger. It is hardly encouraging to note that the USSR airlifted 125,000 troops in 14 days during their 1976 annual rotation of forces in the Warsaw Pact countries. In 1973, the Soviets prepared to airlift 5-7 divisions into the Sinai. Those preparations precipitated an American nuclear alert, and led to the cease-fire. The Soviets have the advantage of "interior lines of communication," with no ocean to cross, and they have made institutional arrangements for prompt utilization of civilian transport.

Movement of materiel, however, is a much greater problem than movement of personnel. For support of the initial deployment augmentation, the United States plans on the utilization of stocks prepositioned in Europe. Current programs for prepositioned equipment are supposed to support 2-2/3 divisions, and there are plans to provide for at least two more. However, as of September 1975,[19] former Secretary of Defense Donald Rumsfeld reported shortfalls of 36 to 68 percent below requirements for the prepositioning program (called POMCUS, for Prepositioning of Materiel Configured to Unit Sets). These shortfalls were the result of inadequate funding of the General Purpose Forces, which has never been sufficient to rebuild the supplies drawn down in the massive air and sea lifts to Israel in the October 1973 War. Despite restocking of 20 to 30 percent since 1975, the POMCUS shortfalls were still serious in 1977; moreover, the requirements have not been increased to reflect the high attrition and consumption rates experienced in the October War.

Massive reinforcement and resupply for a long war in Europe would require sea lift across the Atlantic. In a present-day Battle of the Atlantic, we would face a Soviet submarine force far more numerous, modern and effective than that of Germany in World War II. To be sure, allied antisubmarine warfare (ASW) capabilities are far greater than in World War II, although recent rumors of Soviet advances in ASW, are not reassuring. The Soviet air threat to the U.S. Navy is also formidable. The consensus of experts appears to be that the United States could, after a number of weeks and heavy initial losses, win such a battle, although it is not at all clear that this will remain true in the 1980s if the Soviet naval buildup—particularly of attack submarines and land-based naval air—continues and the U.S. naval forces continue to shrink.

In any event, the expert consensus is that it would take two or more months to reduce the Soviet submarine and naval air forces sufficiently to ensure the Atlantic supply line. During these months, losses of supplies can be expected to be very large. With the present level of logistic support in NATO, and the tremendous rate of consumption of materiel in modern warfare, as demonstrated in the October 1973 war, victory in a protracted battle for the sea-lanes is an essential but not a sufficient condition to a favorable decision in a European conflict, even if nuclear weapons are *not* used.

The maintenance of strong NATO ASW and counter naval air capabilities for control of the Atlantic is based on the need to sustain both NATO morale and the deterrence of Soviet attack on Western Europe by denying to the Soviets the capability of isolating Europe and ensuring a quick victory. NATO requires the means to resupply and reinforce for counterattack, when and if ways are found to counter and delay a Soviet invasion.

This raises the question of the likely nature of warfare that can be expected in the European theater, and its implications for the duration of conflict. Soviet doctrine calls for "blitzkrieg" and Soviet forces are deployed for "blitzkrieg" tactics. These tactics prescribe the utilization of armor, supported by massive firepower (artillery and air), for shock action, penetration and envelopment. The essence is rapid advance along multiple axes. U.S. and NATO doctrine is one of forward defense of the Federal Republic of Germany, giving ground reluctantly if at all to trade territory for time. It assumes eventual counterattack (hence the shock in Europe when it was said that those discussing PRM-10 even considered the possibility of foregoing the capability for prompt counterattack).

This NATO doctrine reflects a philosophy of war that seeks to defeat the enemy head on. It is in essence a war of attrition, not maneuver, until there may be opportunity for counterattack to recapture NATO territory. We do not at present have adequate stocks in place to wage such a campaign nor adequate reinforcement and resupply possibilities, nor is a Soviet attack likely to allow us time to correct these deficiencies.

We have noted that the Soviet Union may not have the full support of its satellites in an offensive war. The risk runs from lack of cooperation to direct opposition from one or more of its Warsaw Pact allies. But it would be unwise to bank heavily on this possibility, and it should be remembered that the Warsaw Pact has a unified command, integrated doctrine and standard materiel. NATO, in contrast, is a coalition, with only a nominal supreme command except in grave emergency. (France does not even participate.) Doctrine is not fully agreed upon and weapons are not standardized. The Common Market is more efficient than Comecon—its Soviet-East European counterpart—for commercial purposes, but Soviet dominance of the Warsaw Pact is more efficient in making weapon choices and procurement decisions than the Western alliance of competitive sovereign states.

While there is wide disagreement on the likelihood of war in Europe and on the degree of surprise the Warsaw Pact could achieve, there is a near consensus on the inadequacy of present NATO forces and preparations to contain a Soviet offensive, should it occur, to defend Western Europe successfully with conventional arms, and above all to counterattack effectively. One recent estimate suggested a cost of $46 billion, over five years, to make such a defense possible.[20] The Department of Defense rejoined that the cost would be $30 billion—but only because some of the programs were already planned.[21] The remedial measures involve primarily increased prepositioning of war materiel in West Germany (but dispersed, concealed and protected—and one hopes, not overrun) and increased airlift capacity, to permit the deployment of six additional U.S. divisions within two weeks, plus substantial increases in firepower and in-force readiness and protection.

Nine billion dollars a year (one-half of one percent of the GNP)—if it will do the job—does not seem to us to be a high price for the ability to defend Europe, and to deter attack, especially in a period of nuclear parity or inferiority.

## The Nuclear Equation

No assessment of the NATO/Warsaw Pact military balance would be meaningful without consideration of the theater nuclear postures of the two Alliances. Although there is a tendency in some quarters to view these capabilities as separate from the non-nuclear balance, they are integral to the continuum of force which enters into the calculus of political ledgers and military commanders in peace, crisis management and war itself.

The nuclear weapons systems (delivery vehicles and associated warheads) committed to NATO play a key role in the Alliance's declaratory strategy of flexible response. That strategy envisages NATO's first use of nuclear weapons against the invading force whenever and wherever necessary to reinforce the conventional defense, halt the momentum of the Soviet offensive and force the aggressor to weigh the consequences of continued military action. In the NATO concept, its nuclear arsenal has two major deterrent roles—one general and one specific. The general role performed in conjunction with the non-nuclear posture is to make any aggression against NATO an unattractive option. The specific role is to deter the Soviets from first use of nuclear capability should aggression occur.

As noted earlier, Soviet doctrine (in essence, a declaratory strategy, too) stresses the utility—indeed decisiveness—of nuclear strikes in speeding the advance of attacking ground forces. That doctrine provides scope for withholding of nuclear weapons at the outset of an offensive but it is clear that pre-emptive strikes would be launched against NATO's nuclear arsenal if it were determined that NATO was preparing a nuclear riposte to Soviet conventional attack. This is clearly the Soviet gambit for deterring NATO's first use of nuclear weapons and blunting such a riposte if it were executed.

Formidable capabilities give substance to the declaratory strategies of both sides. More than a decade ago, Secretary of Defense Robert McNamara gave a figure of 7,000 as the approximate number of U.S. tactical nuclear weapons—aerial bombs, short-range missiles, and nuclear artillery shells—deployed in Europe. Against these there were then said to be arrayed 3,500 Soviet tactical nuclear weapons. There have been no new U.S. deployments since that time, but the Soviets have increased their deployments, probably catching up with the United States, as in so many other areas.[22] In addition, since 1960 the Soviets have had 600–700 medium and intermediate-range ballistic missiles (M/IRBMs) targeted on Europe from Western Russia, as well as hundreds of bombers that can reach Western Europe. The planned 1,200 SS-20 IRBMs reported in 1976,[23] and initially deployed in 1977,[24] with three MIRVs each, will multiply the Soviet M/IRBM number if most or all are deployed against Europe. Hence, NATO may soon be vastly inferior in theater nuclear forces.

The crucial question remains, if the Soviets have strategic nuclear superiority in the 1980s, can NATO theater nuclear weapons deter the Soviets, and be prudently used if deterrence fails? When the United States had strategic superiority, the NATO declaratory policy of linking the conventional, tactical nuclear, and strategic nuclear forces appeared viable. With the strategic and tactical situations reversed, this may no longer be either prudent or credible. Even if the strategic balance can be restored in the 1980s, numerous other problems will have to be resolved, in order to assure this viability.

First, a tactical nuclear war would start, and perhaps largely remain, on Western European territory. Most European countries are no better prepared than the United States in passive civil (or military) defense for war-survival and war-fighting, even with the apparent Soviet trend toward the deployment of discrete nuclear weapons.[25]

Other asymmetries also put NATO at a disadvantage, notably the structure of alliance command and control. Since the weapons in question are American, they cannot be used without American approval. And since the consequences of their use are so grave, their use by American commanders is not authorized without the consent of NATO host countries and without specific approval, or release, by the American Commander-in-Chief, the President.

Studies and exercises of the command, control, and communications system are understood to have suggested that it might take many hours to gain the agreement of NATO chiefs of state and a U.S. presidential weapons release after the need was perceived by NATO commanders and the request was made by the Supreme Allied Commander Europe (SACEUR). In contrast, Soviet central command control is much more direct, and Soviet doctrine explicitly calls for nuclear pre-emption "when the enemy is preparing to use nuclear weapons." The doctrine also calls for surprise and for massive attack, with the first targets on the list being enemy (U.S.) nuclear weapons and storage sites.[26] The U.S. nuclear storage sites are concentrated, not greatly hardened, and presumably are known to the Soviets. With warning, the weapons might be dispersed, reducing but not eliminating their vulnerability. Moreover, NATO communications themselves are highly vulnerable, whereas Soviet communications centers and lines are hardened and redundant.

Much would have to be done to make U.S. use of nuclear weapons feasible. And even if NATO conceivably could and would fire first, the Soviet reply could be devastating. We cannot pre-empt in the sense that the Soviets can. Even if we could make more rapid decisions, if we knew the location of the Soviet nuclear storage sites (which is doubtful), if they were not hardened (which they probably are), and if we could pinpoint the enemy nuclear weapons (they are attacking, and thus moving, against at least partially static defenses), — if all this were true, we still would be faced with the enormous peril of starting nuclear war on East European territory, giving up the appearance of strictly defensive use and greatly increasing the probability of escalation to intercontinental nuclear war.

Finally, the U.S. tactical nuclear arsenal in Europe has not been modernized since it was first deployed, despite the opportunities provided by new technology for making nuclear weapons more capable of more discrete application, with greatly reduced civilian, or "collateral damage." One partial answer proposed for the modernization problem — the "neutron," or "enhanced radiation," or "reduced blast" warhead — is the subject of current debate. In concept, the neutron warhead is designed for use against enemy personnel, primarily those in tanks and other armored vehicles, on NATO territory. The warhead has a greatly enhanced proportion of its energy in prompt neutron radiation that would affect only personnel. For equal anti-personnel effects it can therefore be of much smaller yield, thus sharply limiting the area around the target in which blast and heat would destroy buildings and equipment. In an air-burst mode, the neutron warhead would not create radioactive fallout. With the increasing accuracy of present and prospective delivery means, the neutron warhead would reduce collateral damage by several orders of magnitude.

Public debate on the neutron warhead has been highly emotional and generally uninformed. The prompt nuclear radiation effects on people have been stressed ignoring the fact that these effects strengthen the NATO deterrent. There is little or no continuing radiation from their use. (Soviet SS-4 and SS-5 warheads, if ground-burst would contaminate hundreds of square miles). Opposition to this new weapon appears also to be based on recognition that its military effectiveness would make its use more probable, thus making nuclear war more "thinkable" and therefore more probable. We believe that the final evaluation of this weapon should take account of the other side of the coin: because it is more usable it serves as a more credible and effective deterrent for NATO and it is long-term fallout, rather than prompt radiation which is the greater threat.

President Carter last year indicated that he would approve production of the neutron warhead. He then backed off, putting the burden on our allies to "request" the weapon. When, with considerable political courage, the West Germans did so, Carter announced "deferral" of the decision. We believe that this uncertain policy has been damaging to our relations with our NATO allies and that the President should end the uncertainty with a prompt announcement that production of this defensive weapon will proceed.

We do not know if the Soviets are working on a neutron warhead, but one cannot assume that the Soviets do not care about collateral damage to the West. On the contrary, there is much evidence to suggest that in such a conflict, the Soviets would not want to devastate territory they propose to take.[27] We have already noted that the SS-20, far more accurate and with much lower warhead yield than the early SS-4 and SS-5 missiles deployed against Europe, suggests a desire to be able to hit military targets with less collateral civilian damage than was heretofore feasible. And we have noted that Soviet emphasis on chemical warfare has a similar direction. Chemicals are in fact in many respects similar to the neutron warhead—and could be used without incurring quite the same onus as nuclear use.

## What Needs to be Done

In sum, given present trends, NATO in the 1980s will not be as reliably sheltered under the American strategic nuclear umbrella as in the past. Nor will it have a favorable General Purpose Force or tactical nuclear balance to give it deterrent credibility.

To reverse these trends will require the urgent acquisition of more ready reserves, more arms, and more appropriate tactics, but especially these measures:

- Greater mobility of forces.
- Increased stockpiles of forward prepositioned equipment, to permit more rapid reinforcement.
- Increased airlift capacity to carry out such reinforcements.
- War reserve materiel (WRM) stocks based on realistic rates of consumption in modern warfare. These reserves should be better dispersed and concealed against enemy preemptive attack.
- More survivable and reliable information sensors and command, control and communications facilities and arrangements.
- Increased levels of modernized artillery.
- Increased and improved stocks of anti-tank missiles, including an all-weather capability.
- Mounting of anti-tank missiles on armored personnel carriers, with provision for firing without exposure of personnel.
- Expedited procurement and deployment of the new main battle tank.
- Improvement of the tactical nuclear weapons, with respect to: survivability (dispersal and mobility); ability to reduce collateral damage (neutron warhead discreteness, accuracy); command control.
- Increased levels of air defense and improved systems.
- Greater standardization of arms and equipment, to the extent politically achievable— and interoperability of the equipment of NATO members as a *sine qua non*.

Finally, we must note that, if the U.S. were to be engaged against superior forces across the Atlantic in Europe, it would be hard pressed to handle contingencies that might occur elsewhere in the world—the so-called one-and-a-half war capability, established as a goal for our military capabilities during the Nixon Administration and still in effect. This is a concern not dissimilar to the Soviet concern about a two-front war, but perhaps more likely in the sense that the Soviets have a capacity for starting "proxy wars" in the Third World. "One-and-a-half" wars might become two or two-and-a-half, if the U.S. allies were threatened. Until we have adequate capabilities for the most demanding contingency, we can hardly have assurance of deterring aggression or winning on additional fronts.

## The Naval Balance

The naval balance should be evaluated in the light of the missions of the respective national navies, and general global strategic objectives, which are discussed in subsequent sections. First, we will present important statistics and trends as a basis for thinking about the adequacy of the resources for carrying out the missions to be discussed.

Tables 7A and 7B show that the Soviet Union has more naval ships than the United States in every category except aircraft carriers and destroyers, that they have more shore-based naval aircraft, and that they have ship-based anti-ship cruise missiles, with both nuclear and non-nuclear warheads, while the United States has none. The U.S. has greater ship tonnage, more aircraft in the aggregate and more naval personnel manning our fewer but larger ships. (Table 4, page 68).

The number of U.S. ships has declined precipitously in the past decade, as the useful life of the great World War II generation of ships came to an end. Tonnage has also declined, but not quite proportionately. The number of ships is slated to increase slowly in the next few years. As retirements have slowed, some 18 new ships have been authorized to start in FY 1978, and the Navy has plans for 102 more in the following five years. But the recent record has been one of consistent delays in ship construction (See "The Case of the Phantom Ships: A Comparison of U.S. Navy Fleet Plan with Reality," Congressman Les Aspin, August 1977), and the FY 1979 budget eliminated three planned new layings.

Soviet ship numbers have also been declining, at a slower proportional rate, but their tonnage and overall capability have been growing steadily as they shift from coastal to ocean-going ships.

The U.S. Navy still "outweighs" the Soviet Navy almost two-to-one, by the traditional measure of aggregate tonnage (4.9 to 2.8 million tons). In a Trafalgar type fleet battle, the larger ships of the U.S. might be assumed to prevail. But our limited fleet (half the number of only ten years ago) cannot be everywhere, and small ships with the modern fire power of guided missiles and torpedoes may be the equals of larger ones in single encounters.

Before we can assess the meaning of these numbers, we should ask: What must these navies do? What are their respective missions? The answers are quite different for the two nations. (We will defer for the moment the strategic mission of the missile-launching submarines, which were treated in the section on the strategic balance.)

## The U.S. Naval Missions

The missions of the naval forces of the United States, an "island power" are:

(1.) Control of the Seas.

In addition to protection of the strategic missile submarines and the projection-of-power forces, this primary mission involves the capability to defeat Soviet forces which challenge U.S. naval forces. Second, it involves the protection of the sea lines of communication (SLOCs) i.e., protection of the commerce of the United States and its allies—especially, for the foreseeable future, the transport of oil from the Persian Gulf to Europe, Japan, and the United States and, in wartime, protection of the supply routes for military forces of the United States and/or its allies. We have already discussed the importance of the SLOC to Western Europe. No less important may prove to be the SLOC to the Middle East, for the support of Israel and conceivably U.S. forces. The sea control mission includes antisubmarine warfare (ASW)—of a conventional, or tactical, nature and also, the conceivable scenarios, strategic ASW (against the ballistic missile launching submarines of the Soviet Union). The mission may also include at times the denial of Soviet LOCs in third-area conflicts.

Table 7

| A. 1978 U.S.-SOVIET NAVAL COMBATANT FORCE LEVELS* | | | B. AIRCRAFT ON CARRIERS, LAND-BASED NAVAL AIRCRAFT, & CRUISE MISSILES ON SHIPS* | | |
|---|---|---|---|---|---|
| | U.S. | USSR | | U.S. | USSR |
| Warship Classification | | | Aircraft on Carriers | | |
| Aircraft Carrier Type | 13 | 1** | Fighters | 600 | 15 |
| Cruisers | 27 | 37 | ASW Aircraft | 78 | 0 |
| Destroyers | 64 | 90 | Helicopters | 112 | 180 |
| Frigates | 65 | 105 | Land-Based Naval Aircraft | | |
| Surface Combatant Total | 156 | 232 | Bombers | 0 | 430 |
| Submarine Type | | | ASW Aircraft | 203 | 245 |
| Attack Nuclear (SSN, SSGN) | 68 | 80 | Cruise Missiles on Ships** | | |
| Attack Diesel (SSG, SS) | 9 | 180 | Nuclear | 0 | 575 |
| Auxiliary | 2 | – – | Non-Nuclear*** | 0 | 480 |
| Submarine Total | 79 | 260 | | | |
| Warship Classification Total | 289 | 584 | | | |
| Other Combatant Classification | | | | | |
| Patrol Combatant | 3 | 50 | | | |
| Amphibious Helo/Landing Craft Carriers | 23 | 0 | | | |
| Landing Craft Carrier | 38 | 82 | | | |
| Miscellaneous | 2 | 0 | | | |
| Amphibious Warfare Total | 63 | 82 | | | |
| Mine Warfare Total | 3 | 265 | | | |
| Other Combatant Classification Total | 69 | 397 | | | |
| Auxiliary Classification | | | | | |
| Underway Replenishment | 39 | 58 | | | |
| Material Support | 25 | 47 | | | |
| Mobile Logistics Total | 64 | 105 | | | |
| Fleet Support | 30 | 158 | | | |
| Other Auxiliaries | 7 | 517 | | | |
| Support Total | 37 | 675 | | | |
| Auxiliary Classification Total | 101 | 780 | | | |
| FORCE LEVEL TOTAL | 418 | 1670 | | | |

*U.S. Congress, House, Hearings Before A Subcommittee of the Committee on Appropriations, "Department of Defense Appropriations for 1979," 95th Congress, 2nd Session, Washington D.C.: GPO, 1978, p. 559.
**Two additional Soviet carriers are undergoing sea trials but have not been commissioned.

*American and Soviet Military Strengths, Contemporary Trends Compared, 1970–1976. John M. Collins. Congressional Research Service, in Congressional Record, August 5, 1977, p. S 14064ff.; Arms, Men, and Military Budgets Issues for Fiscal Year 1978, Francis P. Hoeber and William Schneider, Jr., editors, New York: Crane, Russak & Company, Inc., 1977; Norman Polmar, U.S. Editor, Jane's Fighting Ships, personal communication; Annual Defense Department Report Fiscal Year 1978.
**Deployed on ships.
***U.S. total will increase as HARPOON is deployed.

(2.) The projection of power.

The projection-of-power mission ranges from "showing the flag," in places where U.S. interests may be in jeopardy to foreign actions that could be deterred by a U.S. show of force, to the actual use of power by landing troops for peacekeeping or combat and the provision of air power in locations beyond the reach of land-based aircraft.

## The Soviet Naval Missions

The Soviet Naval missions have historically reflected geopolitical realities of the central landmass of Russia: coastal defense and tactical support of land forces. But since World War II the Soviet Union has built a "blue water" navy, capable of operating anywhere in the world oceans. The Soviet Navy is acquiring the capability, and apparently now has the mission, of power projection for political and military purposes, as seen in the support of military action in Lebanon, Egypt, Syria, Libya, Angola, the Horn and elsewhere in Africa.

The Soviet Navy also has an important control-of-the-sea mission, essentially to deny U.S. control and use of the sea. The Soviet Navy is configured primarily for reduction and defeat of its adversaries' naval forces, both strategic and general purpose and the interdiction of enemy sea-lanes.

These missions are reflected in the principal characteristics of the Soviet naval forces. Although Soviet naval ships are on the average smaller than those of the United States, they emphasize speed and have greater fire-power. In particular, the Soviets have exploited the technology of submarines and of cruise missiles for the development of an attack capability that could quickly decimate the U.S. surface forces in a preemptive attack. Soviet naval forces depend importantly on long-range land-based aviation. Half of their Backfires are currently assigned naval missions.

One of the early-model Soviet anti-ship missiles, the Styx, has already sunk the Israeli destroyer Eilat in the 1967 war although it was not effective in the October War in 1973. Newer cruise missiles and ship-launched ballistic missiles are threats to our aircraft carriers as well as other ships, particularly in a concerted attack involving submarine torpedoes and air-to-surface missiles from land-based aircraft, as well as ship-launched surface-to-surface cruise missiles. U.S. aircraft carriers and power projection forces face a severe Soviet cruise missile threat.

## Ship Defense Against Cruise Missiles

American ships, especially aircraft carriers, are not without some defense against Soviet cruise missiles. These defenses include air attack of the Soviet ships beyond missile range and some point defense against the cruise missiles themselves. However, the U.S. does not yet have ship-borne air defense systems that have a high capability against multiple attacks by such missiles. Defense against simultaneous multiple cruise missile attacks is an expensive and technically-demanding task. The Aegis system is designed for fleet air defense, but the planned refitting of the nuclear cruiser Long Beach with the Aegis system was taken out of the budget this year because of its cost.

The United States is just starting deployment of an anti-ship cruise missile, the Harpoon, to attack Soviet ship-launched cruise missile platforms. The longer-range Tomahawk remains in engineering development. The Navy plans to deploy large numbers of anti-ship cruise missiles in the 1980s (although we will have fewer naval platforms for them and will present the Soviets with fewer targets than they present to us).

## The Role of U.S. Endurance at Sea

There is a clear American advantage in the at-sea endurance of its ships, achieved through larger reload reserves and a considerable capability for and experience in underway replenishment of fuel and supplies. This capability is important in crisis management, enabling the United States to project and sustain forces in sensitive areas, independent of overseas bases, thus contributing to deterrence. Endurance would also have considerable weight in a long war at sea (as in World War II). It has little relevance to countering a Soviet fleet designed for a one-shot all-out attack on our surface fleet or hit-and-run tactics over a longer period. The one-shot "shoot-out" scenario is consistent with the Soviet doctrine we have already discussed—a short, high-intensity war involving surprise and shock.

Endurance might have great significance in a limited nuclear war. Since it must be presumed that naval bases, port facilities and airfields would have been targeted by both sides, surviving naval forces would be dependent on their ability to remain at sea and to reach and utilize allied and neutral ports. Because it has greater endurance as well as more allies (especially allies with major port facilities), the U.S. Navy could have an important advantage in its ability to support post-war recovery and Alliance maintenance.

## Defense of the Sea-Lanes

A recent study by the Congressional Budget Office,[28] focuses on the defense of the sea-lanes to Europe as the most demanding U.S. sea-control task. It finds serious deficiencies in the U.S. posture, against both Soviet land-based air and submarines.

Protection against bombers from northwest Soviet bases requires land-based defenses in Norway, Britain and/or Iceland for both early warning and interdiction. Carrier-based forces would be vulnerable and would require reinforcement. A few days warning time, if available and acted upon immediately, would permit the redeployment of existing carrier forces to the vicinity of Iceland if they were not needed elsewhere. Norwegian bases are vulnerable because of their proximity to the Soviet Union. U.S. early warning and interceptor forces in Iceland (and, British forces in the U.K.) are obsolescent and provide little real capability against modern Soviet aircraft.

The Congressional study therefore found an urgent need for the procurement of E-3A AWACS (Airborne Warning and Control System) aircraft and interceptors sufficient for 30-day continuous on-station coverage, at a 15-year procurement and operating cost of about $1.2 billion. (The somewhat cheaper E-2C might be used.) The best interceptor would be the F-14 with Phoenix air-to-air missiles. The F-4E could be used as stopgap. The F-15, with the Sparrow missile, would be cheaper but less effective. Availability should be the first basis of choice, it was found.

The Congressional study said that a "longer-term, more sustained threat" to the Atlantic sea-lanes comes from the formidable Soviet nuclear attack submarine force, which can stay at sea almost indefinitely and can be surged to the Atlantic from worldwide deployments. The primary threat would be from the Soviet Northern (Barents Sea) Fleet that must traverse the Norwegian Sea through the Greenland-Iceland-United Kingdom (GIUK) gap into the North Atlantic.

A GUIK barrier of U.S. nuclear attack submarines (SSNs), in addition to SSN escorts for the carrier task forces, would require building up the SSN force to over 100 boats by the mid-1980s. This means increasing construction from two to five boats per year (which may require a new and efficient shipyard), and authorizing an additional $6 billion (1978 dollars) in the next five years.

In addition, there would be a need for more surface escort ships for convoys. This would mean building twelve guided missile frigates (FFGs) per year (nine have been requested to be authorized for FY 1978), at $0.5 billion a year more for the next five years than next year's $1.4 billion.

Other theaters would impose additional burdens. As long ago as the 1973 October War in the Middle East, the Chief of Naval Operations, Admiral Elmo Zumwalt, found that the survival of the Sixth Fleet in the Mediterranean could not be guaranteed primarily because of the proximity of Soviet land-based air and the Soviets' ability to surge naval forces into the theater. Again, in crisis and wartime there would be need for continuous AWACS/interceptor coverage, as there would be in the Persian Gulf and Indian Ocean areas—a tremendous area—to protect the tanker sea-lanes. Adequate coverage of the Pacific would also be a difficult and expensive undertaking.

## U.S. Naval Deficiency in the 1980s

To summarize, the United States' postwar dominance of the seas is now uncertain. Our Navy's capability for supporting U.S. objectives—maintaining capabilities to project power, to protect U.S. interests offshore, and to control the seas, to ensure both the peacetime flow of commerce and wartime lines of communication of the United States and its allies—can be questioned. This uncertainty will continue for a time, simply because naval forces have very long lead-times for decision-making, design, procurement, construction and deployment. Ships authorized today for construction cannot be deployed until the late 1980s. The number of keels to be laid under the FY 1979 budget was cut from 19 to 15. Thus, the United States is bound to continue to fall behind what has been deemed to be its requirements in the 1980s and cannot hope to catch up at least until the 1990s.[29]

Furthermore, ships have a service life, with modifications, of about 30 years—any vessels that are started now should be in use well into the twenty-first century. The sensors, aircraft, missiles, torpedoes and mines deployed on these ship "platforms" have, however, much shorter life cycles. Platforms must be designed to incorporate future modernization and technological improvements. Nevertheless, choices made today will bear upon capabilities many years into the future. There will always be pressures not to commit ourselves today because next year more information and technology might be available, presumably permitting a better decision then. There must, therefore, be consistency and continuity in the decision-making process for ship construction.

While this principle applies to force planning in general, it is particularly vital for the navy. A "rolling" program—like that of the Soviets—is required.

## IV. THE DECADE AHEAD

## The Emerging Technology Gap—In Whose Favor?

The superiority of U.S. technology has been assumed for many decades. It is disturbing that the heading of this section must now be put in the form of a question. The Soviets are now ahead in some areas, and as we have already noted, they are substantially outspending us in research and development. Table 8 is from testimony by Under Secretary of Defense, William J. Perry, a recent authoritative evaluation of the areas in which each side is superior and where there is uncertainty.

There is no way of assigning relative weights to the various categories and adding them up to arrive at an overall assessment, but two factors dominate. First, the day is past when one could say that the United States had clear overall technological superiority and could count on a technological, or qualitative, advantage to offset substantial Soviet numerical advantage in weapons. Second, the very fact that the Soviets have overtaken us in so many areas demonstrates that the trends are running in their favor.

Moreover, it is important to note two omissions from the Perry list. One is anti-satellite technology. From the eight Soviet tests of satellite interception reported by the press in the past two years, it is clear that the Soviet Union's operational ASAT capability places it well ahead of the United States. The significance of this development cannot be exaggerated. We now depend on satellites to a remarkable extent for intelligence of all kinds and for communications and control. A successful attack on satellites could be completely paralyzing. The second category is that of Soviet experimentation with high-powered lasers and charged-particle beams. This has also been reported by the U.S. press during the past year. Whether their considerable efforts in this area are yielding a militarily useful payoff is not yet clear, but there can be no dispute that they are allocating substantial resources and presumably believe the possibility of payoff justifies the investment.

That the Soviets are succeeding in closing the military technology gap (as are the West Europeans and Japanese in other, nonmilitary areas) is not surprising in view of the evidence on the efforts they have made. Soviet expenditures on military research and development have been increasing at 6 to 8 percent a year for many years, and are scheduled to continue to do so under the present Five-Year Plan. U.S. RDT&E (Research, Development, Test and Evaluation) expenditures, after rising by 45 percent (in constant dollars) in the five years following Sputnik, leveled off until 1967; thereafter, these expenditures declined for eight years until, in 1976, they were less than 10 percent above the pre-Sputnik level. In the past two years the downtrend has been reversed. But today we spend only about 14 percent of our total defense effort on RDT&E (adjusted to include NASA and the defense component of the Energy Department, for comparability with the Soviet data); the Soviets spend over 20 percent.

Since the total Soviet military effort is now considerably above ours (see below), the Soviet level of R&D effort is probably currently *double* ours. The Soviet purpose in continued greater spending is to produce advantages of strategic significance.

The Soviets maintain impressive continuity in their development programs, as well as a surprising degree of competition among their design teams, and they demonstrate willingness to commit new developments to production. The U.S. may handicap itself by its lack of continuity, its tendency to push to the limits of the state of the art on new developments, and subsequent tendency to produce very expensive equipment that sharply limits the numbers than can be procured. In areas of mature technology, operating near the limits means diminishing marginal returns and increases the prospect of a Soviet catch-up.

The Soviets channel most of their total R&D effort into military areas, and continue to import Western technology to the maximum extent possible, which releases additional resources for military programs. This strategy saves valuable time and resources in the pursuit of their objectives. Moreover, the Soviets are deploying new technology faster than the U.S. as they pursue more rapid force modernization.

We cannot determine the point in time at which the Soviet Union may achieve technological superiority over the United States in military equipment, but it is clear that unless present trends are reversed they will achieve superiority. The continued decline in the U.S. technological advantage contributes significantly to the present danger in the evolving military balance. Moreover, the consistently high Soviet level of effort increases

Table 8. Some Performance Comparisons Between Deployed U.S. and USSR Systems Technology

**Strategic Forces** (Deployed Systems)

**ICBM**

| Accuracy: | The U.S. leads, but the Soviets are rapidly improving and narrowing the gap. |
|---|---|
| Throw-weight/Propulsion: | The USSR has achieved a greater throw-weight capability than the U.S.; basic U.S. solid propellant technology is more advanced. |
| MIRV Technology: | We are not certain. The U.S. appears to lead, but the Soviets are rapidly improving and closing the gap. |
| Silo Hardness: | The Soviets have emphasized achieving greater hardness than the U.S. |

**SLBM**

| Accuracy: | We are not certain. The U.S. appears to lead. |
|---|---|
| Throw-weight/Propulsion: | The Soviets deploy larger missiles than the U.S. The U.S. leads in solid-propellant technology, but the USSR has successfully employed liquid propellants to achieve greater ranges. |
| MIRV Technology: | The U.S. leads. |

**Heavy Bombers**

| Payload: | The U.S. leads, unless BACKFIRE is converted. |
|---|---|
| Range: | The U.S. leads. |

**Defensive Systems**

USSR leads in mobile SAMs, diversity.

U.S. leads in look-down/shoot-down interceptor technology.

USSR is making a substantial effort to advance ABM technology.

**Tactical Forces** (Deployed Systems)

**Land Forces**

| Tanks: | Soviet tanks being deployed are less vulnerable than U.S./NATO tanks and fire a more lethal round at higher rates of fire. |
|---|---|
| Artillery: | The U.S./NATO lead in accuracy and lethality, but USSR artillery leads in range. |
| Infantry Combat Vehicles: | Soviets/Pact lead in survivability, firepower, and chemical warfare defense equipment. |
| Battlefield Air Defense: | Soviets/Pact lead in diversity, mobility, salvo capability and crew protection. The U.S. leads in lethality and in engagement envelope. |
| Anti-tank Guided Munitions: | The U.S. leads, but Soviets are improving. |
| Helicopters: | Soviets have a slight overall lead in firepower. |
| Chemical Warfare: | Soviets lead; U.S. effort only in defensive capability. |

**Tactical Air Forces**

| Air to Air Combat: | U.S. leads, but MIG-25 is the fastest operational fighter in the world. |
|---|---|

Table 8. (Continued)

| | |
|---|---|
| **Tactical Air Forces (continued)** | |
| Weapons Payload/Range: | U.S. leads, but the Soviets have focused on improving this capability. |
| Surveillance and Reconnaissance: | U.S. has a strong lead. |
| Accuracy of Air to Surface Munitions: | The U.S. leads, but the USSR has major effort underway to improve their capability. |
| **Naval Forces** | |
| Anti-ship Cruise Missiles: | The USSR leads, but the U.S. has some capability in Harpoon. |
| Surface Ships: | Soviets lead in speed, sea-keeping properties and armament. The U.S. leads in ship range and size, and has a substantial advantage in sea-based tactical air. |
| ASW: | The U.S. appears to have an overall lead, but the Soviets appear to be striving to achieve substantial capabilities. |
| Mine Warfare: | The USSR leads. |
| **Command, Control, and Communications** (Deployed Systems) | |
| Survivability: | Soviets have an advantage in the survivability of $C^3$ systems and installations against physical and jamming attack. |
| Information Collection Systems: | U.S. leads, but the USSR has unique ocean surveillance and targeting capability. |
| Data Communication Links: | U.S. leads in this technology. |
| Satellite Based Systems: | U.S. satellites are superior in performance, but some Soviet systems have no U.S. counterparts. |
| Automated Control of Combat Forces: | U.S. leads, but the Soviets are placing emphasis on this area. |

*The FY 1979 Department of Defense Program for Research, Development, and Acquisition.* Washington, D.C.: GPO, 1978.

their chances of producing a strategically significant "breakthrough," e.g., in ASW, AAW, ABM, or charged-particle beams, that could give them, overnight as it were, a decisive military advantage.

## Economic Strength vs. Political Constraints

It is a truism that a nation's power is not derived from its military potential alone. Economic power also plays a major role in world affairs. In gross economic terms of production, it should be possible to maintain U.S. preeminence.

While economic comparisons are imprecise, the United States has more than twice the Soviet GNP and at least three times the Soviet standard of living. Theoretically, we should also have a greater mobilization capacity. We have already noted, however, that modern war, conventional or nuclear, may not afford time for bringing industrial mobilization to bear in the pattern of World Wars I and II, or even Korea. Moreover, there is persuasive evidence that the Soviet goal is political coercion without war.

The question must be asked, therefore, what is being done with the economic strengths of the superpowers? On the Soviet side, simply put, how have they paid for all the armaments described above? For years, the U.S. (CIA) grossly underestimated Soviet military expenditures. But in 1976, the CIA, citing new information, doubled its published estimates of the Soviet military expenditures in 1970, roughly from 6 to 12 percent of Soviet GNP. Independent analyses have suggested that the CIA still understates current Soviet military expenditures because it estimates 3 to 5 percent growth in these expenditures during the 1970s, whereas for 1970–75 the figure should be 8 percent or more.[30] Thus estimated, military effort is allocated at least 13 to 15 percent of Soviet GNP. This is, in peacetime terms, the allocation pattern of a partially mobilized economy. *It means that the Soviets are operating, on a sustained and increasing basis, above the U.S. peak allocation of 13 percent during the Korean War.*

In contrast, U.S. military expenditures are below 5.1 percent of GNP, the lowest level since before Korea. This comparison is not intended to suggest that the United States should spend more simply because the Soviet Union does. U.S. defense expenditures should be based on the nation's true defense needs—hence the foregoing review of the major areas of military threat and defense.

The implied comparison of military budgets is conservative. Since U.S. military salaries were raised to achieve comparability with civilians, a process which began even before the advent of the Volunteer Army, U.S. manpower expenditures have soared to 56 percent of the military budget, compared with under 35 percent for the Soviets. This is true despite the fact that Soviet military manpower is more than double that of the United States.

The remainder of the budgets is of particular interest here—the 44 percent of the U.S. budget and 65-plus percent of the Soviet budget that buys military hardware, construction, and R&D. The Defense Department now estimates that the Soviets outspend the United States overall in dollar equivalents by 45 percent and in military hardware and R&D, by 75 percent. Such comparisons are imprecise because the exchange rate between the dollar and the ruble is artificial, and because the cost structures in the two countries are radically different, but they appear to be conservative in relation to estimates of the forces the Soviets are fielding.

A recent CIA study projects severe strain on the Soviet economy in the next decade.[31] Soviet growth is expected to slow because of a decline in the growth rate of the Soviet labor force and of capital productivity, the inefficiency of Soviet agriculture, aggravated by "a return of the harsher—but probably more normal—climatic patterns that prevailed in the 1960s," and a limited capacity to earn hard currency to pay for needed technology imports and intermittent massive grain purchases. The last point reflects in large part the assumed Soviet shift from net exporter to net importer of oil and petroleum products.

Nevertheless, the current Soviet Five-Year Plan indicates planned continued growth of military expenditures as a percentage of GNP; and the CIA expects Soviet military spending in the first years of the next decade to increase by 4 to 5 percent annually, continuing the present trend.[32]

We cannot fully assess the prospects and effects of:

- Soviet efforts to obtain Western capital and technology; to meet Western hard currency debt owed by the Warsaw Pact countries (roughly a third by the Soviet Union), and to overcome the financial and political obstacles facing large Soviet capital requirements, especially for the exploitation of the Eastern Siberian gas and oil reserves.
- Soviet moves to solve oil problems that may arise in the bloc countries, including continued pressures on the Middle East.

- Soviet willingness and power to slow or halt improvement in consumption standards and to rationalize agriculture production.

But those uncertainties are fairly long-term. The risks of the shifting military balance threaten the position of the United States in international diplomacy now and in the 1980s. Economic trends that might significantly weaken Soviet military power in the next two decades would mean little for the United States if during the 1980s, the Soviets had exploited their advantage in the international balance of power against the United States and its allies.

Whatever the future economic constraints on the Soviets, the decisive limitations on U.S. efforts to compete are political. The United States has dramatically shifted its priorities in the past decade. Military expenditures have declined from 44 percent of federal expenditures in FY 1970 to 23 percent in FY 1977. The U.S. economy is operating well below capacity—unemployment is above 6 percent and plant utilization approximately 82 percent. Inadequate U.S. efforts to correct its defense deficiencies reflect political will, not economic constraints.

## V. IMPLICATIONS FOR U.S. DEFENSE POLICY

The facts of the shifting military balance and current trends are alarming. The United States cannot continue to base its security on optimistic assessments of the balance, on prideful claims of inherent American superiority, on fanciful prospective accomplishments in SALT and other arms control negotiations, on the prospects for a Soviet economic depression, on the presumed benign intent of the Soviet Union, or on the impossibility of war. Strength is the only reliable guarantor of national security.

As the analysis in Part II of this statement demonstrates, Soviet strategic superiority soon will become a visible and unacceptable reality unless we move promptly to increase the survivability and effectiveness of our strategic forces. All three legs of the nuclear Triad—intercontinental ballistic missiles, submarine-launched ballistic missiles, air-delivered nuclear weapons—remain of basic importance in view of their special capabilities and the rate at which the Soviet Union is increasing and improving its nuclear arsenal, its air defenses and its program of fallout shelters and other aspects of civil defense. Our capacity to deliver nuclear weapons from the air, with sophisticated and effective bombers as well as with cruise missiles, has a special political importance in crisis management, since a modern bomber force could be launched and still provide the President with 6 to 8 hours of time for maneuver and negotiation, an opportunity not available if we rely solely on ballistic missiles.

Only prompt and prudent strategic initiatives can restore the adequacy and credibility of our fading second-strike deterrent capability. Only such action could demonstrate to the Soviet Union that the United States is determined to maintain forces and alliances fully adequate to deter attack or coercion by any rational group in the Kremlin against the United States, its allies and its important national interests. And only such action could persuade the Soviet Union to negotiate and accept a fair, balanced and verifiable SALT II agreement.

Without the maintenance of strategic nuclear balance, perceptions of friends, allies, and adversaries would surely become increasingly adverse to the United States' security interests. The maintenance of such a strategic balance is essential. Theater deterrence must also be maintained because continued Soviet encroachment could isolate the United States from the political and military affairs of a Soviet-dominated Eurasian landmass.

Our conclusions on the magnitude and momentum of the Soviet strategic and general purpose force buildup fully reaffirm the judgment of President Carter, stated in his speech before the North Atlantic Council on May 10, 1977:

> The threat facing the Alliance has grown steadily in recent years. The Soviet Union has achieved essential strategic nuclear equivalence. Its theater nuclear forces have been strengthened. The Warsaw Pact's conventional forces in Europe emphasize an offensive posture. These forces are much stronger than needed for any defense purpose.

The President's words could be applied equally to Soviet military dispositions in Siberia and naval deployments in the North and South Atlantic, the North Sea, the Baltic, the Mediterranean, the Red Sea, the Indian Ocean, and the Sea of Japan.

Indeed, public opinion throughout the West in the past few years has become increasingly concerned about the Soviet military buildup, and the implications for our security of Soviet policies throughout the world. Although some in the West continue to dismiss these trends, the informed consensus today would agree with this Committee's earlier statement:

> To ignore declared Soviet intentions and demonstrated Soviet capabilities in an erroneous conviction that we have 'enough' to defend ourselves and that there is always 'time' to strengthen ourselves could prove to be fatal shortsightedness. In the nuclear age 'enough' may not be enough, and 'time' may run out unless our efforts keep pace.
>
> We live in an age in which there is no alternative to vigilance and credible deterrence at the significant levels of potential conflict. Indeed, this is the prerequisite to the pursuit of genuine détente and the negotiation of prudent and verifiable arms control agreements that effectively serve to reduce the danger of war.
>
> Weakness invites aggression, strength deters it. Thus, American strength holds the key to our quest for peace and to our survival as a free society in a world friendly to our hopes and ideals.[33]

We believe that when the facts of the shifting military balance and the potential Soviet political uses of military superiority in the nuclear age are made clear to the American people in a searching national debate, their political response will be prompt and general approval of those programs and sacrifices necessary to meet this clear and present danger.

## VI. SUMMARY AND CONCLUSIONS

The Soviet Union is "our principal national security problem," declares Secretary of Defense Harold Brown in the *Department of Defense Annual Report Fiscal Year 1979*, and "the main objective of our collective security system must be the maintenance of an overall military balance with the Soviet Union."

The debate on the state of the U.S.-Soviet military balance has already produced a consensus judgment that, if present trends continue, the U.S. will soon be in a situation of military inferiority. This judgment was reached by our Committee almost two years ago. Further, it is now widely agreed that such a position of U.S. inferiority would increase instability in international politics by making it possible for the Soviet Union to attempt political coercion backed by the credible threat of superior conventional and nuclear force, and allow Soviet exploitation of "targets of opportunity." The foregoing overall assessment is our Committee's latest analysis of the current trends in the U.S.-Soviet military balance and our view of their implications.

However, the debate has not produced a comprehensive examination of Soviet doctrine, strategy, and concepts as they relate to Soviet military power. This Committee study presents the Soviet strategic doctrinal framework as it relates to Soviet forces and the U.S.-Soviet military balance.

The Soviet Union is seeking positions of dominance in Europe, the Middle East and Africa—positions from which it believes it could in time bring Japan and China into its sphere of influence, and isolate the United States.

The Soviet Union approaches these strategic objectives with the open-ended and firm conviction that strength and military superiority over the U.S. wherever attainable is highly desirable and usable, directly or indirectly. It is the heart of Soviet doctrine to seek such strength.

The actions of the Soviet leaders over the last 15 years leave no doubt that they consider the shift in the U.S.-Soviet balance favorable to them and the growth of the Soviet military power—specifically, of Soviet nuclear power—to be basic to all else that has happened, or may happen, in the evolution of world politics.

In order to achieve their global objective, the Soviets emphasize the need to expand and enhance their military power, the combat readiness of their forces, the morale and vigilance of the Soviet citizenry, and the vigilance of their "allied forces of Socialism." They expect U.S. resistance to the expansion of Soviet influence to be deterred principally by Soviet military power. They view the state of the U.S.-Soviet military balance as basic to the evolution of political and psychological relations in the significant areas of the world.

U.S. accommodation to the Soviet drive for strategic superiority would confer on the Soviet Union the ability to intimidate and coerce the West into accepting unfavorable bargains. Soviet strategic superiority would give the Soviets dominance in crisis situations; the U.S. would then have to recognize that, if a crisis were to escalate to a strategic nuclear war, the Soviet Union would expect, at a high but perhaps not intolerable cost, to prevail while maintaining a post-war preponderance of global military power.

The Soviet military buildup has been steady, impressive in scale and quality, and dramatic in breadth and depth. It has gone on for more than fifteen years and continues steadily at a rate reliably estimated to be between at least 4% to 5% a year. The Soviet military budget today is far greater than our own—between 40% and 60% greater. Some estimates go as high as 80%. No aspect of military power has been ignored by the Soviets. They have concentrated a national effort behind their military expansion and have invested great resources in it.

In the critical area of strategic nuclear strength, Soviet programs confirm beyond any reasonable doubt the rejection of our notions of nuclear stability and sufficiency, and of mutual deterrence. The Soviet buildup reflects the basic doctrinal precepts of Soviet strategy—that strategic nuclear offensive and defensive programs are designed to enable the Soviet Union to fight, survive, and win a nuclear war, should it occur.

The Soviet Union continues to invest heavily in its fixed land-based ICBM force. The fourth generation of ICBMs is now being deployed and the fifth generation is being developed. These systems have substantially greater throw-weight, improved accuracy, and high-yield MIRV warheads. They are designed for a preemptive strike against U.S. forces, while reserving sufficient forces to hold the U.S. population and industry hostage. It is a formidable threat.[34]

In the area of submarine forces, the Soviet Union has developed and deployed improved versions of the modern DELTA-class submarine, carrying a new generation of more accurate missiles of intercontinental range. Two new MIRVed SLBMs, also intercontinental in range, have been developed, with one being deployed. Another new follow-on SLBM is under development and the Soviets are readying a newer, more capable modern submarine, the TYPHOON, that is equivalent in many respects to our future TRIDENT submarine.

Soviet deployment of the BACKFIRE bomber and the mobile MIRVed SS-20 missile continues. These systems threaten our allies, our forces overseas, and the United States itself.

In strategic defense, the Soviet Union, in sharp contrast to the United States, maintains vast air defenses while the U.S. has merely token air defense forces. The Soviets have pursued a vigorous ABM R&D program, one that could provide them with a strategically significant, rapidly deployable "breakout" capability for the aerospace defense of the Soviet Union. They have repeatedly tested an operational anti-satellite system, another capability unmatched by the United States. The Soviets also continue to explore many advanced technologies for strategic defense, and Soviet efforts in the area of anti-submarine warfare (ASW) are no less significant.

In conjunction with these activities, the Soviet Union has been engaged for some time in a comprehensive national civil defense program designed to ensure Soviet nuclear war-survival, recovery, and emergence as the dominant post-war global power.

An extensive network of blast shelters and evacuation procedures exists to protect the Soviet leadership, "key" industrial workers, and the civilian population. The Soviets continue to harden and disperse their industrial and economic assets, further reducing their vulnerability to U.S. strategic forces. These programs not only undercut the potential political and military effectiveness of our deterrent, but also can undermine our will to prudently confront the Soviet Union in crisis situations throughout the world.

Against this specter of rapidly expanding Soviet strategic nuclear offensive and defensive capabilities is a U.S. strategic program that is struggling with production and development problems in the TRIDENT program, design and decision problems with basing for a new ICBM, and that has placed enormous faith in the cruise missile program which is still only in development.

In Europe, Soviet forces are designed for surprise attack and the *offensive*. The West is outnumbered in military manpower, reserves, tanks, artillery, and tactical aircraft. Soviet forces are trained and equipped to fight and survive on the nuclear and chemical battlefield and are deployed for a nuclear and chemical blitzkrieg. The Soviets are modernizing their ground, air and naval forces. Large quantities of new and improved heavy tanks, nuclear-capable self-propelled artillery, and other armored fighting vehicles are being deployed. And the Soviet Union continues to out-produce the U.S. in these major categories of weapons. Present Soviet force modernization programs will be completed well before effective NATO initiatives are fielded. The trends are clearly running in the wrong direction for us and, without an adequate strategy for European defense, the common argument that NATO quality compensates for Soviet-Warsaw Pact quantity is specious.

There has been significant growth in the offensive capability of Soviet tactical air-power. Deployment of fourth generation aircraft with greater range, payload, and sophisticated weaponry continues. These aircraft can strike all types of targets throughout the European theater and the Middle East.

The Soviet Union is a continental power with secure interior lines of communications and an autarkic economic system. The Soviet Navy is designed for offensive political and military operations against our naval forces, our vital sea lines of communication to NATO and our allies in the Pacific, and our access to supplies of raw materials.

The Soviet Navy continues to refine its offensive combat capability and global reach. Soviet ships are heavily armed with cruise missiles, air defense weapons, and ASW sensors and weapons. Soviet naval strategy seeks the immediate destruction of the West's navies, at the outset of a war. Soviet land-based airpower supports this strategy by adding another means to attack U.S. surface forces, defend the Soviet fleet and support the ASW mission. The Soviet navy has developed into a major threat to vital sea-lanes and as an important diplomatic instrument to expand and consolidate Soviet power.

The size, sophistication, and rate of growth of Soviet military power far exceeds Soviet requirements for defense. The Soviet military buildup reflects the offensive nature of the Soviet political and military challenge and the Soviet belief that the use of force remains a viable instrument of foreign policy.

While we welcome President Carter's recent strong statements reaffirming our commitment to maintain a balance of power with the Soviet Union, the Defense Budget for the 1979 fiscal year is inadequate to meet this objective and will not reverse the adverse trends. As our Committee pointed out in our basic policy statement of 11 November, 1976:

> Unless decisive steps are taken to alert the nation, and to change the course of its policy, our economic and military capacity will become inadequate to assure peace with security. . . . We must restore an allied defense posture capable of deterrence at each significant level and in those theaters vital to our interests. The goal of our strategic forces should be to prevent the use of, or the credible threat to use, strategic weapons in world politics; that of our conventional forces, to prevent other forms of aggression directed against our interests. Without a stable balance of forces in the world and policies of collective defense based upon it, no other objective of our foreign policy is attainable.[35]

*5 October 1978*


# NOTES

1. On strategic nuclear doctrine, see especially A. A. Grechko, *On Guard Over Peace and the Building of Communism* (Moscow: 1971), JPRS 54602, National Technical Information Service, U.S. Department of Commerce, Springfield, Virginia 22151; N. A. Lomov, ed., *Scientific-Technical Progress and the Revolution in Military Affairs (A Soviet View)* (Moscow: 1973), translated by The U.S. Air Force in *Soviet Military Thought*, no. 3 (Washington: U.S. Government Printing Office, 1974); V. D. Sokolovskiy, *Soviet Military Strategy*, third edition, edited by Harriet Fast Scott (New York: Crane Russak, 1975); and V. D. Sokolovskiy and M. I. Cherednichenko, "On Contemporary Military Strategy," in *The Nuclear Revolution in Soviet Military Affairs*; translated and edited by William R. Kintner and Harriet Fast Scott (Norman, Oklahoma: University of Oklahoma Press, 1968). Also useful for its relating of strategic and tactical doctrine and its extensive bibliography is Joseph D. Douglass, Jr. *The Soviet Theater Nuclear Offensive*, Studies in Communist Affairs, Vol. 1 (Washington, D.C.: U.S. Government Printing Office, under the auspices of the U.S. Air Force, 1976). On naval matters, Sergei G. Gorshkov, *Red Star Rising at Sea* (Annapolis: U.S. Naval Institute, 1974); see also discussion by R. G. Weinland, R. W. Herrick, M. McGuire, and J. M. McConnell, in *Survival*, vol. 17, No. 2 (March-April 1975).
2. N. Khrushchev, "CC-CPSU Accountability Report to the 20th CPSU Congress," *Pravda*, February 15, 1956.

3. On September 15, 1977, Secretary of Defense Brown indicated that the Soviet Union is increasing its ICBM force at a rate of "100 to 150" a year. Some estimates range as high as 200 for 1978.

4. William Beecher, "Soviet Mobile Missile Worries US," *Boston Globe*, September 5, 1976.

5. *Aviation Week and Space Technology*, April 3, 1978, p. 17.

6. *Annual Defense Department Report, FY 1976* and *FY 1977*, p. II–41.

7. *Ibid.*

8. See the extensive description of the Soviet civil defense program by Leon Goure in *War Survival in Soviet Strategy, USSR Civil Defense* (Miami: Center for Advanced International Studies, University of Miami, 1976). See also Chuikov, *Civil Defense* (Grazhdanskaya Oborona) (Moscow: 1969), translated from the Russian and edited by Oak Ridge National Laboratory, April 1971, and T. K. Jones' testimony to House Armed Services Committee, Subcommittee on Investigations, Civil Defense Panel, February 26, 1976.

9. See, for example, Representative Les Aspin, "Soviet Civil Defense: Myth and Reality," *Arms Control Today*, September 1976.

10. See Committee on the Present Danger Statement, "Where We Stand on SALT," Chapter 4.

11. The equivalent megatonnage (EMT) of a weapon of given yield, Y, in megatons (MT is $Y^{2/3}$ for Y greater than 1 MT and $Y^{1/2}$ for Y less than 1 MT).

12. CMP takes account of both yield and accuracy. It is based on the formula, $Y^{2/3}$ (CEP)$^2$, where CEP is "circular error probable," or the radius within which half of the warheads are expected to land. Some adjustments are made in the first term for small-yield weapons. Other formulas have been proposed; all give rather similar results. For very low CEPs, an adjusted formula called ECMP is necessary to avoid significant anomalies.

13. *Methodological Problems of Military Theory and Practice*, (Moscow: 1969), Air Force translation FTD-MT-24-S7-71; Springfield, Virginia: National Technical Information Service, 1971 (AD 738–734), p. 339.

14. It was reported on August 26, 1977 (*New York Times*, page 1) that the President had signed a secret strategic directive which rejected these alleged PRM-10 options, possibly because of considerable public reaction against them. We welcome his decision and his suggestion in the same article that increases in the General Purpose Force preparations "should increase defense spending by about 3 percent each year in real terms, with inflation discounted, in conjunction with similar action by the other members of NATO." However, we do not believe these changes are sufficiently far-reaching to redress the growing imbalance described here.

15. Philip A. Karber, *Evolution of the Central European Military Balance*, Washington, D.C.: The BDM Corporation, June 1977.

16. The principal source of this list is William Schneider, Jr., Hoeber and Schneider, *op. cit.*

17. *Aviation Week & Space Technology*, August 15, 1977, quoted General Haig, Supreme Allied Commander, Europe, as citing increases in the past ten years of 2–3,000 men and 40 percent in tanks, per Soviet division.

18. *Aviation Week & Space Technology*, August 15, 1977.

19. Secretary of Defense D. H. Rumsfeld, *Annual Defense Department Report, FY 1977*, pp. 263–264.

20. Representative Les Aspin, *Congressional Record*, March 15, 1977, H2211–16.

21. Harold J. Logan, *Washington Post*, August 18, 1976, p. A-2.

22. John Erickson estimates that the Soviets had 7,000 tactical nuclear weapons in Europe in 1975, "Soviet Military Capabilities in Europe," Royal United Services Institute/Royal Military Academy—Sandhurst Research Center *Bulletin*, March 1975.

23. William Beecher, *Boston Globe*, September 5, 1976.

24. Department of Defense Press Conference, December 27, 1977.

25. Joseph D. Douglass, Jr., "Soviet Nuclear Strategy in Europe: A Selective Targeting Doctrine?" *Strategic Review*, Fall 1977.

26. Joseph D. Douglass, Jr., *The Soviet Theater Nuclear Offensive*, Studies in Communist Affairs, Vol. 1 (Washington, D.C.: U.S. Government Printing Office under the auspices of the U.S. Air Force, 1976).

27. See Joseph D. Douglass, Jr., "Soviet Nuclear Strategy in Europe: A Selective Targeting Doctrine?" *Strategic Review*, Fall 1977.

28. *The U.S. Sea Control Mission: Forces, Capabilities, and Requirements*, Congressional Budget Office, U.S. Congress, Government Printing Office, Washington, D.C., June 1977.

29. It cannot have in the 1980s the "three ocean Navy" it should have to meet its responsibilities in the Atlantic, Pacific, and the Mediterranean, Red Sea, and Indian Ocean.

30. See William T. Lee, "Intelligence: Some Issues of Performance," in Hoeber and Schneider, *op. cit.*

31. U.S. Congress, Joint Economic Committee, "Soviet Economic Problems and Prospects," 95th Congress, 1st Session, Washington, D.C.: GPO, August 8, 1977.

32. Drew Middleton, "CIA Expects a Rise in Soviet Military Outlays," *New York Times*, June 30, 1978.

33. "What Is The Soviet Union Up To?" Committee on the Present Danger, Chapter 3.

34. The one and only new U.S. ICBM since 1970 is now planned for initial deployment in 1986 or 1987.

35. "Common Sense and The Common Danger," November 11, 1976, Chapter 3.

8

# LOOKING FOR EGGS
# IN A CUCKOO CLOCK

## Observations on SALT II

*Charles Burton Marshall*

Notwithstanding the contretemps at the Vance-Gromyko meeting in Geneva last month, reports of a SALT II accord just around the corner are becoming credible. So the next phase—it is under way already—will center on trying to stir up support over the country generally and within the Senate in particular. Executive branch salesmanship—I refer to the so-called SALT Sellers—is pressing the case along the following lines:

- The asserted value of preserving the SALT process.
- The alleged preferability of the terms, whatever they are, over having no pact.
- Hints of plans to bolster our strategic nuclear deterrent in ways compatible with the SALT II terms.

Junctures like the one now looming make me wish I were a Senator. Were I one, I should judge the case rigorously in light of the constitutionally imposed duty to provide for the common defense.

## LOOKING AHEAD

The root meaning of "to provide" is to see ahead. Yet in such matters prevision is not within our capabilities. The future is not foreseeable. So one is reduced to what is required for navigating in thick weather—looking ahead because of the impossibility of seeing ahead. The present obligation is to make provident resource allocations so as to ensure for those to be responsible for national security later on in face of events not now foreseeable adequate means to protect the territorial base, to fend off forcible intimidation from without, and to assure access to external sources of materials necessary for national well-being.

With that obligation in mind, let us now turn to appraising the value of the SALT process not as something abstract and hypothetical but as a palpable part of experience.

The author, Charles Burton Marshall, is a member of the Executive Committee of the Committee on the Present Danger. He was formerly Professor, School of Advanced International Studies, Johns Hopkins University, and a member of the Policy Planning Staff of the U.S. Department of State.

Our government's aims at the outset of SALT II more than six years ago provide a frame of reference. The aspiration then was to bridle offensive nuclear power in ways counterpart to the controls on defensive nuclear weapons agreed to in the then newly ratified ABM treaty. Subject to constraints pertinent to verifiability and to the need to protect our allies' particular security needs, the aims, in more specific terms, were—

- Equality in offensive nuclear capabilities between the two sides at levels affordable to the U.S.
- Prevention of either side from gaining a putative advantage by a first strike, thus relieving them both from temptations ever to strike preemptively—the short term for all that being crisis stability.
- Reductions in offensive nuclear armaments and related expenditures, in the risk of nuclear war, and in the overhang of nuclear armaments on world politics.

Examining the SALT II terms, one does find a color of equality in the even limits of 2400 and later on 2250 prescribed for intercontinental missile launchers and of 820 for launchers for land-based intercontinental ballistic missiles (ICBMs) fitted to carry multiple independently-targeted reentry vehicles (MIRVs).

## DANGEROUS DISPARITIES

The evenness, however, is offset by three disparities. One is a difference in permitted numbers of launchers for the largest and latest type of MIRVed ICBMs—none for us as against some 300 for the Soviet Union. A second disparity concerns numbers of warheads on MIRVed ICBMs—three each on ours in contrast to four, six, and ten each on varying Soviet types. The terms do authorize our side to test a 10-warhead missile, but none will become operational within the interval covered by the treaty. The third disparity applies to prospective deployments of MIRVed ICBMs. Whether for want of money or of will, our side will fall short of the authorized 820 by about a third—so much for the criterion of affordability! In contrast, the Soviet side will surely fulfill its quota. One notes also the exemption of certain bomber types with intercontinental potential from being counted as strategic launchers. The two sides agree in effect to pretend to regard Soviet Backfire bombers—there will be 300 to 400 of them or perhaps even more—as not being what they obviously are. In a formalistic tradeoff, our far less formidable and less numerous FB-111s—they number under 100—also will not be counted.

The disparities bear on a most critical aspect—crisis stability. Here is the prospect. In the early 1980s the Soviet Union will be in position to knock out some 90 percent of our ICBMs by an expenditure of about a third of its MIRVed ICBMs. The residual strategic nuclear forces at our command—mostly surviving bombers and nuclear-armed submarines—would be enormously outmatched by the Soviet Union's retained strategic nuclear war-fighting capability. For all the theoretically possible retaliatory damage, the sequel to a retaliatory blow would find our side strategically defenseless. Therein is the basis for a determinative strategic imbalance. Our country and its people and interests would be at disproportionate hazard in the calculations of interacting effects central to strategy. That implicit imbalance—both sides will know it—will be sure to count at every highly charged juncture involving a clash of purposes. The burden to scramble for terms of accommodation so as to avoid a ruinous war must fall disproportionately on our side.

## SPECIOUS SECURITY

I do not mean to discount risk of war. The pact is already being portrayed—the portrayal will be intensified—as representing deliverance from danger, a significant advance toward the goal of peace and security. Such it is not. To anticipate any such effect one has to have the kind of optimism that looks for eggs in a cuckoo clock. The specious sense of security engendered by that portrayal is all too likely to aggravate the very risks that SALT II is purported to alleviate. As for reducing the nuclear strategic burden on world politics, it is hard to see any such effect from the prospective pact. The overhang of nuclear factors on world politics will be more severe than ever in the period covered by this upcoming pact.

As for reductions in nuclear armaments and expenditures, the answer depends on whether one is content merely to count launchers. During the span of the treaty, numbers of nuclear warheads can be expected to go up threefold for the Soviet side, 50 percent or so for ours. Nuclear strategic power calculated in terms of capability for area destruction will double on the Soviet side and rise by about an eighth on ours. Capability to knock out hard targets—missile silos, command and communication centers, and the like—will go up 1000 percent or so on the Soviet side and perhaps 400 percent on ours, depending on progress in cruise missile developments. A reduction on expenditures for nuclear forces on either side is not in prospect.

The considerations noted provide a basis for evaluating the SALT process—so crucially important to save, according to devotees.

Devoted to producing agreement as a good *per se*, our policy makers entertain extravagant expectations. The SALT process can no more abolish strategic competition than regulating the spatial and temporal dimensions of the game of football can cause every contest to end in a tie.

## THE BASIC ANTITHESIS

The facade of agreement scarcely conceals the fundamental antithesis. The respective sides' goals do not mesh. One side strives to neutralize nuclear strategic factors in world politics. The other side presses to ensconce itself in strategic primacy so as to be in position to determine the direction of world politics. One side wants a maypole dance, as it were, while the other engages in tug-o'-war.

Has the SALT process, now in progress more than nine years, actually restrained either or both sides in respect of channeling resources into military uses? That is the first of two very practical questions pertinent to the proposition concerning the inherent worthiness of the SALT process.

On our side, the apparent answer is yes. A tendency to subordinate security policies to wishes for advancing arms control instead of shaping arms control policies to security needs is surely evident—evident, moreover, not merely in successive administrations' solicitousness in the SALT negotiations but also in the slippage in the mobile-missile and Trident submarine programs, the B-1 bomber cancellation, and the sidetracking of neutron weapon technology.

That approach goes unreciprocated. By every sign, the Soviet Union is intent to go about as far as it can go in its drive for strategic ascendancy. The Kremlin means business. The diversion of Soviet gross national product into military uses is at the level of 14 to 15 percent and heading toward an estimated 18 percent by 1980. Such a level is hardly surpassable under conditions short of actual belligerency.

SALT II has scarcely altered attitudes or endeavors. The tradeoffs have been confined to marginal matters. Mainly the terms settled on do no more than register formally what the two sides have wanted to do anyway. SALT II is properly describable as much ado about not so much after all—a protracted pseudo-event.

## A BETTER PROSPECT?

The second practical question—is there a prospect for something better in the successive phase, SALT III? We heard from President Carter, speaking in Memphis the other day, about his tentative belief concerning a sharing of pertinent aspirations with Leonid Brezhnev—a basis for hopes for more significant concord later on. I cannot imagine where on earth the President could find information supporting that belief. Instead of the treaty of unlimited duration sought by the U.S., the SALT II pact will expire in 1985. That will be a time of serious strategic disadvantage for our side. The Soviet Union will be in position to squeeze even harder then—or in anticipation of that situation. To suppose otherwise is fanciful.

I turn now to the better-this-than-nothing argument—recounting its elements insofar as I have heard them and adding my own evaluations. Debating points of the better-this-than-nothing sort will undoubtedly proliferate with the prolongation of deliberations through the winter, into the spring, and maybe until summer. Perhaps they will pick up in persuasiveness. Up to now the quality has not been good.

## PHANTOM RESTRAINTS

Not to ratify, according to the SALT Sellers, would mean to forego a genuine arms control aspect in the limitation of intercontinental launchers, with its corollary requirement of a 10 percent cut in the Soviet Union's present aggregate of about 2500. That requirement would be unilateral, because our side falls far short of the prescribed maximum. Canceling the limitation would leave the Soviet Union free to add to existing panoply some 400 intercontinental launchers to be produced in ongoing programs—still more weight to the nuclear threat. Such is the substance of the case.

The offsetting considerations are these. Launchers slated for retirement to meet the prescribed cut are approaching obsolescence anyway. Whether keeping them on would enhance the Soviet threat is subject to doubt. If, however, the Soviet Union should perceive advantage in yet further increasing its nuclear capabilities, the effect would be achievable by transferring surplus missiles from launchers to reserve inventory to be available for soft-pad launching or for silo reloads—something completely permissible under SALT terms, which cap the numbers of launchers only.

## IF SALT II FAILS . . .

Not to ratify—so goes a companion contention—would leave the Soviet Union free to go all-out in multiplying the nuclear threat to the United States and thus to place this country in still deeper danger. The counter consideration is the level of military effort present and prospective. Within its economic limitations, the Soviet Union is already pushing at the limit of military aggrandizement—about as near to all-out as imaginable. The feasibility of significantly more ominous increments of military effort and production short of war is highly doubtful.

In another version, withholding ratification of SALT II would impair or even wreck détente, with all its purported boons. More specifically, not to ratify SALT II would endanger further United States-Soviet cooperation in halting nuclear proliferation. In answer—the Soviet Union has solid reasons for opposing nuclear proliferation. That opposition, based on self-interest, is not likely to be renounced in pique over a stillborn SALT II pact. Anyway, the argument is topsy-turvy, because the basic stimulus to nuclear proliferation is anxiety traceable to the palpable erosion of our relative strategic strength as discerned by the nations directly or indirectly protected by it in the past.

Rejection of SALT II would seriously reduce the President's authority for conducting external affairs—thereby weakening the country's position—and at the same time aggravate acerbity and dangers in the world situation. These are weighty considerations. Such risks are not to be gainsaid—all the more reason for deploring the failure to bring off a treaty supportable for intrinsic merits. The point in question would be more persuasive if there were grounds for believing SALT II, ratified, to mark an avenue to safety and improvements in the climate of international politics.

## PRESERVING OUR DETERRENT

The centerpiece in the better-this-than-nothing issue is likely to focus on the looming vulnerability of the land-based component of our strategic missile force. That problem links in turn to the Administration's professed intention to bolster our endangered side of the nuclear strategic balance.

The logical method is, while keeping within the prescribed limits, to preserve deterrence by multiplying the number of targets which the other side would feel compelled to hit in undertaking a preemptive strike. One such scheme, called MAPS for "multiple aim point system," would rely on rotating our ICBMs among a multiplicity of structures outwardly indistinguishable from missile silos—subject to sufficient inspection to assure the other side against cheating. Among several schemes, MAPS is the only one to stand up under hard technical study. Our negotiators have broached a question regarding the compatibility of MAPS with SALT II provisions already agreed and have drawn an unsurprising negative from the other side. The Executive branch is now reportedly trying to find a plausible alternative system.

Whether the Administration has a workable plan to offer for preserving the land-based component of our strategic nuclear deterrent—a plan compatible with the SALT II terms—is the core of the question whether SALT II is consistent with the obligation to provide for the common defense.

Assurance on that point—indispensable as it is—will not redeem the SALT II agreement. The emerging pact is a bad one for U.S. interests. Better a bad treaty than no treaty—one hears even that argument—does not persuade me. Making agreement an end in itself can only foreclose us from reaching a good one.

*22 January 1979*

# 9

# DOES THE OFFICIAL CASE FOR THE SALT II TREATY HOLD UP UNDER ANALYSIS?

## An Evaluation of "SALT and American Security" as issued by the Department of State and the Arms Control and Disarmament Agency

This statement comments on a 2600-word brochure with the title of "SALT and American Security."[1] The brochure was recently produced and is now being widely distributed by the Department of State and the Arms Control and Disarmament Agency. The professed purpose of the brochure is to advance public understanding of the strategic arms treaty between the United States and the Soviet Union. The brochure begins with a summary of the rationale, procedures, and course of the negotiation and follows with answers to thirteen questions that "Americans are asking" about the results.

The need to set straight some of the more significant among many questionable assertions in the brochure prompts this statement. The endeavor is in keeping with a basic purpose of the Committee on the Present Danger, "to help promote a better understanding of the main problems confronting our foreign policy, based on a disciplined effort to gather the facts and a sustained discussion of their significance for our national security and survival."[2]

The comments correspond to the order of topics in the brochure.

## THE POLITICAL AND STRATEGIC SETTING

According to the introductory synopsis in the State-ACDA brochure, "the SALT process" represents a joint quest for "equitable and adequately verifiable limitations on strategic arms to enhance the national security for both sides." The process came into being because the superpowers shied away from "an unlimited arms race." Its initial success was a treaty to end competition in defensive strategic systems coupled with a five-year interim agreement to regulate certain aspects of superpower rivalry in offensive strategic systems. Some "six years of tough bargaining" have brought the superpowers to the verge of a follow-on interim agreement, SALT II. Without that agreement, according to the brochure, "we could face the possibility of an escalating arms race, increasing tension between this nation and the Soviet Union, and a greater risk of the catastrophe of nuclear war."

**Comment:** An observation quoted from one of the late Dr. Merle Fainsod's authoritative writings on the character of the Soviet polity is pertinent:

> Perhaps the greatest single source of distortion in foreign affairs derives from the image of "the enemy" which is deeply imbedded in Marxist-Leninist patterns of thought. The politics of Communism are built around the concept of the implacable capitalist adversary who has to be disarmed and defeated lest he in turn annihilate Communism. The Leninist dialectic which the leadership has been trained to apply is essentially a vision of progress and triumph through conflict and struggle. Such a Weltanschauung reduces any accommodation to a negative virtue. Compromise becomes at best a disagreeable necessity rather than a creative achievement . . . The essence of politics remains the clash with the capitalist enemy . . .
>
> Since . . . even the temporary ally of today represents a potential political enemy tomorrow, the information that filters through to the ruling group tends to be perceived, arranged, and analyzed in categories which take such hostility for granted. Expressions of antagonism to the Soviet Union constitute verification of the profundity of the Communist perception of reality; professions of friendship tend to be discounted as wily or naive stratagems designed to lull the vigilance of the Soviet leadership . . . .[3]

The interplay between armaments and character in such a society standing within the first rank among nations is central to contemporary security problems. An analytic statement by the Committee on the Present Danger titled "What Is the Soviet Union Up To?"[4] examines the relevance of the Soviet Union's political character to an appraisal of the SALT II treaty terms. Without taking into consideration the antithesis between the meliorative policies of the United States and the revolutionary purposes underlying the Soviet Union's role in world affairs, it is virtually impossible to understand how the treaty terms have been arrived at or what they portend for this country's interests, including preeminently its security.

The portrayal in the State-ACDA brochure, however, plays down that antithesis as if nonexistent or inconsequential. Instead, the aura there conveyed reflects symmetry of situations and complementarity of purposes between the negotiating sides. Empathy prevails. The spirit is that of being in the same boat.

A proper basis for evaluating that portrayal requires a brief but searching review of pertinent events beginning with the United States' initiative soon after the end of World War II to bring about a solution to the security problems posed by nuclear technology as a novel and hugely destructive instrument of warfare.

The plan then offered called for the United States to cede its nuclear monopoly— inevitably temporary as it was destined to be—to an international authority to be vested with ownership of and control over nuclear resources and facilities wherever located, thereby neutralizing nuclear power as a strategic factor. The idea was stillborn—thanks in essential part to Soviet opposition. Besides being already well along with nuclear plans of its own, the Soviet Union at that juncture also had a headstart in developing rocketry as a means, prodigious in speed and reach, for delivering nuclear destruction on enemy targets. As is now apparent in retrospect, foundations for a steady progression, combining increments of nuclear military power and continuous improvements in rocketry in phase with advances in other aspects of military capability, were firmly established by the Soviet Union during the 1950s.

For the time being, however, military preeminence on balance remained with the United States. The components included naval primacy in the principal waterways, supremacy in military aviation, and an army attuned to victory. The basis of American preeminence during the early post-war period was a continuing edge in nuclear capabilities—coupled in due course with superiority in rocket technology as a means of delivery additional to bombers.

The United States' comprehensive strategic strength provided the underpinning for such successful undertakings as resistance to the Berlin blockade, repulsion of the Soviet-abetted attack on South Korea, an array of alliances shielding important positions in Europe and the Orient otherwise subject to threat from the Soviet Union, and the forced retraction of Soviet surface-to-surface missiles from Cuba.

The last episode deserves particular attention. The Soviet dispatch of such missiles to Cuba appears in retrospect to have been a miscalculated bid to hurry along the future by a stealthy, sudden redress of the strategic nuclear balance—a somewhat uncharacteristic gamble probably induced by a misguess of the likely U.S. response. While compelled to scrub the experiment, the Soviet Union in the aftermath perserved with the longer-range task of improving and enlarging stage by stage its strategic capabilities.

According to an interpretation then widely accepted among Americans, the lesson from the Cuban missile crisis was the inapplicability of strategic nuclear weaponry as an instrumentality of war and as a factor in the reckonings of international political competition short of war. However wishful and unsubstantiated it may be, that thought achieved a degree of acceptance within governing circles as well as among the public. One effect was to stimulate efforts to register that idea in a negotiated contract with the Soviet Union.

The unfolding purpose was to establish a sure basis for mutual deterrence and crisis stability between the superpowers. Under the conditions to be agreed on, neither of them would be in position to make a first strike on the other with strategic nuclear weapons without incurring unacceptable damage in retaliation. Thus neither superpower could gain strategic advantage by getting in the first blow. Each side would be confident of the other side's reciprocal perception. Temptations toward a preemptive strike at junctures of heightened clash would be forestalled. The strategic nuclear factor overhanging international politics would thereby be neutralized. The effect in this respect would be akin to the earlier proposal for an international nuclear monopoly, but the means in this new version would be reciprocal controls on weapons, assuring stability in a crisis.

Such a design hinges on a sharing of goals. Thus pertinent U.S. policy has banked on a reciprocal outlook on the part of the Soviet Union. It is now obvious, fifteen years later, that our belief, founded on a wish rather than on reality, has been reflected in a succession of versions. In an interview given in the mid-1960s, the U.S. Secretary of Defense then in office went so far as to postulate the Soviet Union's relinquishment of any design to match the U.S. in strategic nuclear strength. When ascertained facts about Soviet production and deployments overturned that happy assumption, a succeeding theory was developed: the Soviet Union was only trying to catch up strategically. As that idea in turn has been rendered implausible by the volume and variety of the Soviet progression in nuclear weaponry, a substitute conceptual reassurance has emerged—called nuclear sufficiency or essential equivalence. That concept is preoccupied with avoidance of nuclear war. It regards the probability of retaining a capacity to deliver an appreciably damaging second strike to be sufficient for forestalling a preemptive attack. The concept discounts the import of disparity between the superpowers' nuclear armories. As a corollary to denying the idea of strategic superiority, the theory writes off the intimidatory potential of strategic nuclear preponderance as a fulcrum for political leverage in conditions short of war.

Whatever the passing rationale—by whatever name—the United States' strategic nuclear resources have been kept under unilateral restraint since the middle 1960s, with certain qualitative improvements balanced against a considerable concurrent numerical reduction in launchers. In contrast, over the same fifteen years the Soviet Union has carried out successive enlargements and improvements of its nuclear strategic armory, each stage a steppingstone to the next advance. The contraposition, with one side marking time while the other forges onward and upward, is what unconditionally committed devotees to arms control call the "arms race."

With the above background, it becomes feasible to see the SALT setting in a proper perspective. The picture painted in the brochure of the two sides in the bargaining earnestly striving for terms, to "preserve the security of both nations," does not wash. That concept of mutual security is entertained unilaterally rather than shared. The phrases associated with the concept—mutual deterrence, nuclear sufficiency, essential equivalence, and the like—are terms of art used within the United States' arms control community, but they are extraneous to the SALT dialogue because the concept reflected in them is no part of Soviet thought.

There is, however, a facade of concord: both sides in SALT II do want an agreement—though for divergent reasons. The discrepancy is linked to the antithesis between the superpowers' purposes in world affairs. In contradistinction to the United States' design for neutralizing strategic nuclear factors in international politics, the Soviet Union strives to firm up and validate a strategic foundation for what Soviet Foreign Minister Andrei Gromyko, in Communist forums, refers to as "increasingly visible preponderance" on the basis of which to control the direction of world politics.

The U.S. approach puts a premium on arriving at a pact. The Soviet approach puts a premium on avoiding any impingement on Soviet ambitions. Issue by issue in the negotiation, the typical sequence is: presentation of a formulation by the U.S. side, Soviet rejection of elements counter to the Soviet Union's ambitious strategic goals, and then revision to accommodate the Soviet position. The "tough bargaining" referred to in the brochure, rather than characterizing the bilateral negotiation, has occurred among concerned U.S. agencies over how far to go in eroding U.S. positions in order to accommodate to Soviet demands.

The reference in the introductory portion of the brochure to the dire consequences of a failure of the agreement is echoed in its final portion. A comment on the idea is made in that connection below.

A strategic standoff between the superpowers has become a built-in circumstance. The reference to inherent "economic and technological strength" as our hedge against any sinister surprise implicitly waves aside as immaterial the Soviet Union's continuing investment in military research and production at a rate 70 percent above ours.

"Is America Becoming Number 2?"[5]—a study of current trends in the U.S.-Soviet military balance issued by the Committee on the Present Danger—is recommended as a realistic antidote to the complacency reflected in the brochure. Brief quotations from the Committee's comprehensive study must suffice here:

> In the critical area of strategic nuclear strength, Soviet programs confirm beyond any reasonable doubt the rejection of our notions of nuclear stability and sufficiency, and of mutual deterrence. The Soviet buildup reflects the basic doctrinal precepts of Soviet strategy—that strategic nuclear offensive and defensive programs are designed to enable the Soviet Union to fight, survive, and win a nuclear war, should it occur.
>
> . . . The Soviet military buildup reflects the offensive nature of the Soviet political and military challenge and the Soviet belief that the use of force remains a viable instrument of foreign policy.

# THE CONTENTS OF THE TREATY

In answer to a question, "What will be in the SALT TWO agreement?" the brochure sums up the provisions thus far agreed and allocates them among the basic agreement to run to 1985, a protocol "which will expire well before that date," and a set of guidelines for negotiating a successor to the basic agreement. It enumerates the limits on numbers prescribed for strategic nuclear launchers: a comprehensive ceiling for each side of 2400 to be reduced to 2250 during the life of the agreement; within that ceiling, a limit of 1320 on the aggregate of launchers of land-based intercontinental ballistic missiles (ICBMs) equipped with multiple independently-targeted reentry vehicles (MIRVs), launchers of MIRVed submarine-launched ballistic missiles (SLBMs), and airplanes equipped for long-range cruise missiles (ALCMs); within that 1320, a further limit of 1200 on launchers of MIRVed ICBMs and SLBMs; and within that 1200 a still further limit of 820 on launchers of MIRVed ICBMs.

**Comment:** Except for a reference to benefits from the sublimit on launchers of MIRVed ballistic missiles, this segment of the brochure avoids appraisals and conclusions. It omits mention of the unequal allocation of launchers of MIRVed ICBMs of the latest and largest type, 308 for the Soviet Union in contrast to none for the United States. The omission is important. These formidable and accurate Soviet heavy weapons, alone, could destroy our ICBM force and much besides—airfields, submarine bases, and other military and industrial targets. Its allusion to "equal" prescribed totals for strategic nuclear launchers may be faulted also for failing to note the exemption of Soviet Backfire bombers, but the point is discussed elsewhere in the brochure. The status and effects of the protocol, matters of considerable importance, are dealt with in the comments below on the cruise missile and mobile intercontinental ballistic missile.

# THE MEANING FOR U.S. SECURITY

In answer to a question, "What will the SALT TWO agreement mean for American security?" the brochure finds much to rejoice about. The specifics include imposed "equal limits on the overall U.S. and Soviet strategic forces" and a prospective Soviet dismantling or destruction of "up to 300 strategic systems" (compared to none of ours) so as to comply, and a limitation on "Soviet strategic forces . . . well below what they could deploy in the absence of an agreement." There are vague references to a reduction in "uncertainty in our own strategic planning," to "important provisions to help us determine that the Soviets are living up to their obligations," to "flexibility . . . to continue the strategic programs we require," and to "essential equivalence."

**Comment:** The reference to "equal numerical limits on . . . strategic forces" is unsubstantiated and unsustainable. Measurement of such forces in relation to each other embraces a wide array of considerations such as (to name a few) quantities and qualities of warheads deployed and in inventory, numbers of missiles deployed and in inventory, numbers of launchers, their facility for reloading, throw-weight (meaning gross capacity to project payloads to adversary targets), accuracy of delivery systems, gross power to knock out hardened sites such as missile silos and command-and-control and communication centers, relative hardening or vulnerability of such vital strategic centers, gross area-destruction capabilities, and relative protection or vulnerability of populations and industry. Among all the relevant dimensions, SALT is preoccupied with gross numbers of intercontinental strategic nuclear launchers. Even with respect to them, one must take "equal numerical limits" with a grain of salt. As noted in the London *Economist's* appraisal, "On the surface the proposed new treaty is neatly balanced; but it conceals, just under the surface, a large imbalance in Russia's favor."

One offsetting disparity applies to permitted numbers of launchers for the largest and newest types of MIRVed ICBM's—308 for the Soviet Union in contrast to none for the U.S. The treaty terms likewise confirm a Soviet advantage in permissible numbers of warheads on MIRVed ICBMs. As a result of progress in MIRVing and accuracy, the Soviet Union's warheads will, within the life span of the treaty, surpass ours in gross numbers, destructive power, and versatility. Another disparity concerns prospective deployments of MIRVed ICBMs within the span of the treaty—a full quota of 820 for the Soviet Union, in contrast to a shortfall by about one-third for the U.S. Moreover, the Soviet Union is excused from having to count its Backfire bombers against the prescribed limits, notwithstanding their capability to reach targets in the United States.

There is less than meets the eye in the prospective Soviet reduction of "up to 300 strategic systems." The launchers to be retired are nearing obsolescence and are becoming superfluous with the progressive deployment of increasingly capable new Soviet launchers and missiles. The scheduled retirement is in phase with Soviet military plans developed and carried out without reference to SALT. There is no basis for assuming the contemplated reduction in launcher numbers to represent a net cutback in Soviet strategic capability. To the contrary, Soviet strategic capability is due to rise concomitantly with the reduction. In any event, nothing in the treaty would prevent the Soviet Union from putting into inventory—as standbys for reloading or soft-pad launching—any missiles left over from the prospective reductions.

The description of Soviet strategic forces as "well below what they could deploy in the absence of an agreement" is too vague for much disputation. By implication, the Soviet Union is portrayed as having renounced even more formidable increments of strategic power in deference to its desire for a pact. No one can demonstrate or refute the implication, for no one ever knows how different things might be if things were different. The present and prospective levels of Soviet military endeavors, however, are enormous by any measure—and especially so when measured against the Soviet gross national product. The notion that the Soviet Union is holding unused in reserve a large potential for additional strategic efforts is dubious at best.

## VERIFICATION

"How can we be sure that the Russians will live up to the agreement?" In answer to that question, the brochure declares, "In SALT, we do not rely on trust or Soviet good faith." It then names and briefly explains three continuing elements already provided under SALT I: primary reliance on "national technical means"—that is to say, detection devices within each side's possession and operational control—for checking on compliance; a mutual prohibition against interference and concealment designed to obstruct the operation of such means; and a joint Standing Consultative Commission to handle questions regarding alleged violations of SALT obligations. The brochure commends the effectiveness of the latter institution: "In each case the United States has raised, the activity in question has either ceased or additional information has allayed our concern." Without giving specifics, the brochure predicts in SALT II "additional detailed provisions to increase our confidence." The brochure affirms U.S. intentions, known to the Soviets, "to call them to account for any questionable activities" and "to expect satisfactory resolution."

**Comment:** It is important to put the question of verification in perspective. In general, the importance of verifiability of performance varies in direct proportion to the desirability of an agreement. Thus, while beneficial terms are susceptible of being nullified by malperformance, a bad contract is not redeemable even by absolute assurance regarding compliance. The salient question regarding SALT II is whether it represents a provident contract from the standpoint of United States security, even with impeccable performance on the Soviet side. The brochure omits the most plausible premise for confidence in Soviet fidelity to SALT II obligations: the temptation to cheat on a contract so palpably favorable to Soviet interests and ambitions should be minimal.

Those points aside, the case as stated in the brochure is questionable. Consider the assertion that "we do not rely on trust or Soviet good faith." Belief in Soviet intentions, consonant with those of the United States, to bring an end to the overhang of nuclear power on international politics is integral to the agreement. A color of that belief runs through the entire rationalization for SALT II and the prospectus for SALT III as given in the brochure.

As a specific, furthermore, the United States relies on trust and Soviet good faith in accepting as sufficient the Soviet Union's assurances on numbers, deployments, and missions for the Backfire bomber. Reliance on trust and good faith rather than verification applies also to Soviet performance respecting restrictions under the protocol on the operating span of land-based and sea-based cruise missiles permitted to be flight tested and deployed. A case also eminently pertinent, unmentioned in the brochure, is the United States' retreat on an issue growing out of Soviet encrypting of telemetric signals in missile tests. U.S. acquiescence—registered in the SALT II negotiation—is in response to a Soviet pledge not to encrypt signals significant, in Soviet judgment, for U.S. monitoring of compliance with SALT obligations. The formula makes the Soviet Union judge in its own cause. A clearer instance of relying on trust and Soviet good faith for compliance would be hard to imagine.

Unfortunately, the record scarcely warrants the affirmativeness expressed in the brochure regarding the effectiveness of the Standing Consultative Commission for enforcing compliance. Whether cessation of a "questionable activity" after the lodging of a protest provides reassurance may hinge on a question of time. As an illustration—Soviet desistance from testing of an air defense interceptor in violation of the SALT I treaty did follow a U.S. protest, but only after the completion of a lengthy series of tests ample for producing all the information sought.

## VULNERABILITY OF THE UNITED STATES' FIXED-SITE ICBMs

"Under the SALT agreement, won't our Minuteman missiles be vulnerable to Soviet attack?" The answer to that question in the brochure is: yes, but do not blame the SALT process. The brochure identifies as the cause the Soviet Union's advances in accuracy and numbers of ICBMs. For long-run reassurance, the brochure cites an eventual possibility of "alternative, more survivable methods for basing ICBMs." For reassurance during an indefinite interim, the brochure refers to "substantial uncertainties" considered likely to dissuade Soviet authorities from attacking this country's vulnerable land-based ICBMs. The dissuasive doubts are expressed in the following words: ". . . how reliable and accurate will their missiles really be; can they avoid having the explosion of one attacking warhead damage the effectiveness of subsequent attacking warheads; can they be certain of the hardness of our missile silos; and would the United States launch its own ICBMs once it was determined that a massive ICBM attack was underway, thus leaving only empty holes for the Soviet missiles to hit?" The brochure quotes advice from the incumbent Secretary of Defense against regarding vulnerability of our ICBMs as "synonymous with the vulnerability of the United States, or even of the strategic deterrent." The brochure adds, "Any Soviet planner must realize that even a successful attack on the Minuteman would still leave the Soviet Union vulnerable to massive response by our ballistic missile-firing submarines and heavy bombers. The damage these remaining forces could do would be devastating."

**Comment:** No item in any contract ever arrived at in the strategic arms limitation talks stipulates vulnerability for the ICBM component of U.S. strategic forces. In that sense true enough, the increasing threat to that mainstay of U.S. strategic security "is not the result of SALT." What is true: steady increments in Soviet offensive strategic nuclear power have occurred while the SALT I interim agreement has been in effect and will continue during the contemplated span of the SALT II treaty. The concern over Minuteman vulnerability voiced at the Capitol during consideration of the interim agreement, and the call in Congress for more efficacious limitations on Soviet offensive forces in SALT II, have proved unavailing. Vigorous research and development programs as a hedge against the expanding Soviet threat to Minuteman—such programs were pledged in Executive assurances given during consideration of the interim agreement—have not materialized. Thus the spirit underlying the U.S. approach to SALT—shaping security policies in hope to advance arms control rather than shaping arms control policies to serve U.S. security—has contributed in a basic way to the worsening problem of ICBM vulnerability.

To comprehend the prospective predicament for U.S. security, one must take realistic account of the contingency of war and also look beyond that contingency to effects under conditions short of war. The reassurances attempted in the brochure are unpersuasive because they fail to come to grips with the extent of the emerging danger whether on a hypothesis of war or of conditions short of war.

Under existing trends, by the early 1980s the strategic ratios will be such as to put the Soviet Union in position to knock out about 90 percent of U.S. ICBMs with a preemptive strike using only about a third of its MIRVed ICBMs. Of U.S. submarines fitted as strategic missile launchers, about half—the portion usually in port for overhaul at anytime—would probably be destroyed in such an attack. As much as 60 percent of the strategic bomber force—the portion usually not on alert at any moment—might well be lost also.

Even after such a damaging attack—provided that command-and-control points and communications networks were sufficiently undamaged to be able to marshal a retaliatory attack—the remnant U.S. strategic nuclear forces would be theoretically sufficient to inflict enormous damage on portions of Soviet population not dispersed from major cities and on Soviet industrial facilities without appropriate protection. Against hardened targets—such as Soviet missile silos, command centers, and strategic communication facilities—the residual forces would be substantially ineffective. By any reasonable calculation, the surviving portion of the U.S. strategic nuclear force would be hugely outmatched by the Soviet Union's retained war-fighting capability. Under such conditions, a retaliatory strike, even if technically feasible, would be a vain gesture of revenge. In its aftermath, the United States would be left strategically defenseless against an adversary still in command of enormous strategic nuclear resources capable of inflicting pervasive ruin on this country. In such a situation, those in authority here would be confronted with a choice whether to submit before or after a devastating Soviet strategic counterblow.

The Committee on the Present Danger takes no satisfaction from offering so foreboding an analysis. It adduces the analysis only to indicate the flimsiness of the foundations for the sort of optimism, reflected in the brochure, that discounts the import of the prospective strategic eclipse of Minuteman. Like other rationalizations under the rubric of essential equivalence, the outlook in the brochure—preoccupied with avoidance of war—neglects the importance of strategic strength in preserving acceptable conditions of peace and the penalties of being second in a showdown short of war. This contrasting analysis in this statement is not a prediction of a chain of events necessarily culminating in nuclear war. The aim, rather, is to stress the effects of the looming strategic disparity on superpower relationships short of war.

Under the conditions now in prospect, the idea of a U.S. retaliatory strike would lose plausibility. That would surely be the case insofar as the outlook of those in authority here is concerned. It would surely be beyond bounds of responsible calculation to attribute to Soviet decision-makers a higher degree of belief in the hypothetical probability of a U.S. second strike than entertained here. In sum, mutual deterrence would have eroded. This country and its people would be placed at disporportionate hazard. That circumstance—and the shared awareness of that circumstance—would be borne in upon the minds of those in charge of strategic-political affairs in both superpower capitals. Those in charge here would be the ones under compulsion to scramble for terms of propitiation in any juncture charged with high controversy.

The suppositions in the brochure regarding doubts likely to beset Soviet decision-makers and stay any launching of a strategic attack are scarcely substantial enough to be counted on to restore strategic equilibrium in face of such palpable disparity.

One item in the list of hypothetical restraining doubts deserves special note. It is the one concerning a Soviet misgiving lest "the United States launch its own ICBMs once it was determined that a massive ICBM attack was underway." The term of art for such an instant riposte is launch-on-warning. The concept involves a paradox amounting to a contradiction: it posits the success of deterrence on a hypothetical recklessly self-defeating reaction to its failure. Anyway, the feasibility of launch-on-warning is subject to serious doubts on technical grounds. That point aside, the concept, if ever put into operation, would require the making of the most fateful choice imaginable—on notice of five minutes or less. For lack of time, launch-on-warning would probably have to be geared up as an automatized response to electronic stimuli. The President's discretionary function would be reduced to the possibility of interposing an instant decision—in the nick of time—to call off a counterattack likely to induce ruinous consequences for the United States. A situation compelling reliance on launch-on-warning must be regarded as highly unstable and dangerous. A strategic ratio which lends any relevance to the concept is surely to be avoided. The allusion to the idea in a brochure with the title "SALT and American Security" is incongruous.

## THE SIGNIFICANCE OF SOVIET CIVIL DEFENSE EFFORTS

"What about Soviet civil defense?" The answer to that question in the brochure acknowledges the Soviet civil defense effort to be "substantially larger than ours" but discounts it, nevertheless, on grounds that "Soviet civil defense cannot change the current strategic weapons balance or the fundamentally disastrous nature of a major nuclear exchange between the United States and the Soviet Union," involving for the Soviets "the deaths of tens of millions of their citizens and the destruction of most of their industrial resources and urban areas." The brochure cites from a CIA source an expression of disbelief "that the Soviets' present civil defenses would embolden them deliberately to expose the U.S.S.R. to a higher risk of nuclear attack."

**Comment:** On the one hand there is a preconception, reflected many times in the brochure, of parallelism and complementarity between the Soviet strategic outlook and that of the United States. On the other hand there is manifold evidence concerning the magnitude and elaborateness of the Soviet civil defense effort and the significance manifestly attributed to it by the Soviet regime. It is difficult to a point of impossibility to get the preconception and the evidence to jibe. Contradiction between a preconception and phenomena presents a necessity either to revise the preconception or to explain away the import of the phenomena. The brochure tries the latter course by posing an imprecise question and supplying an evasive answer. To bolster the answer with a show of authenticity the brochure quotes selectively from a now outdated CIA report—significantly omitting portions of the context at variance with the desired conclusion.

A properly thought-out question would be: in view of changes in the strategic weapons balance already achieved or looming ahead, how much importance, if any, should we attach to the Soviet civil defense program? A proper answer would be along the following lines.

Occurring apart from other large-scale Soviet strategic efforts, the Soviet civil defense program might be of only marginal significance for the United States. Considered in conjunction with the ongoing Soviet buildup in strategic nuclear weapons, the expanding Soviet civil defense effort takes on considerable strategic importance.

Strategic nuclear war is not unthinkable to the Soviet Union. There the idea represents a plausible part of futurity. Notions that neither side can win—that both sides must lose—in such a war are no part of Soviet thinking. The Soviet view calls for being the winning side. Protection of essential portions and elements of the population, along with industrial assets, is regarded as a fundamental requirement for successful waging of nuclear war and the attainment of victory. Civil defense is thus an integral part of Soviet war-fighting capability.

To cite the strategic significance of Soviet civil defense—demonstrated by the impressive scope and elaborateness of the ongoing program—does not necessarily prefigure a Soviet preemptive strike. Civil defense, nevertheless, is definitely a factor in efforts to place the Soviet Union observably in better position than this country to cope with the eventuality of nuclear war. The pertinent program contributes to establishing a position of visible preponderance. It is thus an element in efforts to establish a strategic ratio placing the United States and its population at disproportionate hazard so that this country's policy-makers will be the ones under pressure to come forth with terms of accommodation in future contests of purpose under the shadow of war.

To express disbelief "that the Soviets' present civil defenses would embolden them deliberately to expose the U.S.S.R. to a higher risk of nuclear attack"—in the words of the brochure, cited from a CIA report—misses the main point. What counts is the effect of the civil defense effort in reducing the Soviet regime's estimates of risk entailed in ambitious ventures. A Soviet civil defense program capable of reducing Soviet fatalities resulting from a hypothetical U.S. retaliatory strike from 95 million to 10 million or less—those figures are reflected in authoritative U.S. estimates—is indeed a strategic factor to be reckoned with when considered with other aspects of Soviet strategic endeavors. Portions of the CIA report not quoted in the brochure affirm the potential of the Soviet civil defense program as a factor in a strategically significant shift in the nuclear balance.

## THE BACKFIRE BOMBER ISSUE

"What about the Soviet 'Backfire' bomber?" In answer, the brochure acknowledges the Soviet Backfire bomber to be capable of reaching "a significant number of targets in the United States on one-way, high-altitude, unrefueled missions." The brochure takes note of this government's stated reluctance about exempting the Backfire from being counted as an intercontinental launcher within the prescribed numerical limits, and alludes to U.S. urgency to have Backfire deployments and production rates placed under contractual restraints. Here is the pertinent language in the brochure: "The United States has indicated to the Soviets that the Backfire can be excluded from the permitted overall SALT totals if, and only if, the Soviets undertake commitments which will inhibit the Backfire from assuming an intercontinental role in the future, as well as impose limits on its production rate. These commitments would have the same status as the SALT agreement, binding the Soviets to the commitments contained therein. Although there are no assurances that the Backfire would not be used against the United States in time of conflict, these commitments by the Soviet Union are designed to inhibit the Backfire from being given an operational intercontinental role and to limit its overall strategic potential."

**Comment:** The quick transition from "no assurances" to "commitments" is baffling. So is the attribution to something omitted from a contract "the same status" as if it were included.

There are important omissions from the presentation in the brochure. A one-way mission for the Soviet Backfire, landing in Cuba after operating against targets in the United States, could be accomplished without refueling. Such a mission would be counterpart to the kind of mission allotted to the United States' B-52 bomber. A B-52, however, on such a mission would have to be refueled. The target coverage and operational flexibility of Backfire for intercontinental strike missions, moreover, are susceptible of being significantly increased by refueling in flight. Every Backfire is fitted for such refueling. U.S. air defenses against penetration by Backfire are notably lacking. Yet the Backfire is exempted from being counted against the permissible launcher totals in SALT II. The B-52 is not exempted. The difference in treatment is one of the more prominent paradoxes in SALT II.

What the Soviet Union tenders in response to U.S. anxieties is a non-contractual statement of intentions not to regard the Backfire bomber as being what it actually is and not to use it in ways for which it is indisputably fitted. This country's acquiescence will not relieve policy-makers and strategic planners from having to count the Backfire as an intercontinental factor in the calculation of risks. The numbers involved, already appreciable, will go on steadily expanding during the time-span of the SALT II treaty.

## EFFECTS ON THE CRUISE MISSILE PROGRAM

In answer to the pertinent question—"Won't SALT TWO constrain the United States' cruise missile program?"—the brochure makes a point concerning the care taken "to preserve those cruise missile options most important to our defense needs." The terms give a green light for deploying long-range cruise missiles on heavy bombers and for flight-testing other types of cruise missiles. A ban on deploying ground-launched and sea-launched cruise missiles with operating spans over 600 kilometers is portrayed as due to lapse with the protocol. The brochure anticipates cruise missile limitations among the agenda for negotiating a contract to succeed the main agreement due to expire about three years after the protocol.

**Comment:** It is pertinent to revert to an assurance expressed in the brochure in connection with outlining the contents of the treaty: that the protocol, imposing limitations of operating ranges for sea-based and land-based cruise missiles, "will expire well before" the basic portion does.

In evaluating that assurance, one should note the scheduling of a SALT III negotiation to follow immediately on ratification of the SALT II treaty and the sure prospect for including cruise missile questions in the SALT III agenda. What is certain is not the lapse of constraints on deployments of cruise missiles; it is that the question of continuing or abandoning those constraints will be subsumed into SALT III.

That consideration puts a different light on a supporting argument implicit in the brochure—to wit, that deployments of cruise missiles with the proscribed characteristics within the specified interval are no part of United States plans anyway, so that the sacrifice is akin to giving up watermelon for Lent.

That argument prompts a question: if only that gratuitous sacrifice is involved, then why bother to include the proscription? The question suggests an answer. The protocol is included not for inconsequentiality but for enduring and important intended effects. The prudent approach in appraising the provisions in the protocol must be to consider them as important constraints designed to the shape of things to come rather than transient gestures. The brochure omits several important considerations that help explain the significance of the cruise missile constraints.

The permitted maximum range—600 kilometers, or about 372 miles—is a minor fraction of the minimum operating range considered strategic in the sense of the SALT purview. Verification of the adherence to the restriction, moreover, is impracticable. The anomalous inclusion of the restriction in a treaty supposed to focus on strategic matters and to be governed by the principle of verification is due to Soviet insistence. (*Pravda*, in an editorial on 11 February 1978, has put the argument in strongest terms: to oppose the limits is "to wreck the agreement as a whole.") The subject matter must be important to the Soviet Union.

The permitted operating range—applicable to cruise missiles carrying non-nuclear charges and those bearing nuclear warheads—represents a drastic constriction on the uses of cruise missiles for tactical missions and regional defense. Accordingly, the implications apply especially to Western European security. SALT II, meanwhile, leaves the Soviet Union free to deploy the Backfire bomber and the SS-20 ballistic missile (with a range nine times greater than the cruise missiles concerned) as additions to its striking power against Western Europe.

According to an argument frequently heard from SALT advocates, SALT II is an essential steppingstone to the opportunity in SALT III to straighten out inequities such as the hobbling of cruise missiles as instrumentalities for European defense while leaving reciprocal threats untrammeled. By the line of reasoning presented, U.S. freedom to increase the operating range of sea-based and land-based cruise missiles after the expiration of the protocol can be traded for Backfire and SS-20s reductions. The better-luck-next-time argument suggests a counter question: in view of U.S. negotiators' inability to have Backfire (let alone the SS-20) included in the SALT II treaty in return for accepting the cruise missile restriction, why expect a better package deal later on after the deployment of considerable numbers of Soviet Backfire and SS-20 missiles? Trading off something contingent for something else already in hand is likely to entail more intrepidity in bargaining than yet shown by U.S. SALT negotiators.

# EFFECTS ON MOBILE LAUNCHERS

The brochure answers "no" to the question, "Will SALT TWO stop us from developing mobile intercontinental ballistic missiles?" The question pertains to a prohibition against deploying mobile ICBM launchers and flight-testing ICBMs from mobile launchers, but not pertinent research and development programs, during the three-year interval covered by the protocol. The brochure refers briefly to versions of mobile ICBM-basing concepts under study, "including some involving alternate launch points for each missile." It adds in reassurance, "The current and projected capabilities of our strategic forces give us time to study thoroughly questions of technical feasibility, military effectiveness, and cost prior to making decisions about deploying mobile ICBMs. The parts of the draft text . . . already . . . agreed upon allow deployment of mobile ICBM systems of the types we are considering. The draft agreement explicitly permits deployment of mobile ICBM launchers during its term, after the expiration of an interim protocol period which would end well before mobile ICBM systems would be ready for deployment." In connection with such systems, as yet hypothetical, the brochure stresses the necessity of conformity "with all provisions—including the verification provisions—of a strategic arms limitation agreement."

**Comment:** The cognizance of mobility as a characteristic for special attention in SALT in connection with regulating intercontinental launchers stems from a U.S. initiative growing out of concern for verification. The importance of the questions at hand relates to problems now looming as a result of the growing vulnerability of the fixed-site land-based components of U.S. strategic nuclear forces, discussed earlier in this statement.

The allegation in the brochure about preassured permissibility for deploying mobile ICBM launchers after the protocol period lapses needs to be recast. All that one is entitled to be sure about in this connection is this: issues about mobile launchers for ICBMs are bound to be on the agenda for SALT III, if there is one. Besides focusing on permissibility, the issues subject to negotiation will include matters of definition, for there is no present agreement between the superpowers on what characteristics are covered by the term "mobile."

One should be wary also about the assurance of there being plenty of time—thanks to "current and projected capabilities of our strategic forces." The looming threat to U.S. security growing out of Minuteman vulnerability will have become an established circumstance during the time-span of the SALT II treaty and indeed during the shorter interval covered by the protocol. The problem is one calling for solution by 1982 or thereabouts—not one for the 1990s.

A pertinent matter of utmost importance concerns the status, in relation to the restraints in question, of methods for preserving deterrence—while keeping within the prescribed launcher limits—by multiplying the number of targets which the other side would feel compelled to hit in undertaking a preemptive strike. In that connection, the reference in the brochure to the United States' study of "a number of mobile ICBM basing concepts, including some involving alternate launch points for each missile" is significant in implying that whatever systems are under study—being "mobile"—therefore comes within the category embraced by the restrictions in the protocol against deployment and flight-testing.

The description is wholly in line with a recent United States demarche in SALT II identifying several possible systems of that general character as "mobile" and indicating the United States' reservation of the right to deploy some such system after the expiration of the protocol. A matter deserving special note is the specific mention in that demarche of one system—a multiple vertical protective structure system. That system would add no ICBMs beyond the number permitted by SALT, could be made readily comformable to the verification requirement, and would not involve "mobile" launchers within any meaning of the term in common usage. In the Air Force's judgment, moreover, that system, among the several conceivable systems, is the only one practicable in the sense of being feasible to build at reasonable cost and, when made operational, capable of preserving the survivability and endurance of our ICBMs.

By logical inference from the U.S. demarche, the Soviet Union is in position to exercise a gratuitous veto, at least for the term covered by the protocol, over a preferred method for alleviating the danger to Minuteman and to crisis stability. By further logical inference from the U.S. demarche, the Soviet Union is permitted, under the treaty, to deploy such a system whether we do or do not do so.

## EFFECTS ON ALLIES

"How will SALT TWO affect our NATO allies?" As pointed out by the brochure in answer to that question, such matters as the following are not within the SALT II purview: France's and the United Kingdom's nuclear forces, U.S. nuclear and other forces stationed in Europe, and U.S. efforts in cooperation with allies to strengthen NATO conventional forces. "There will be no ban on the transfer of cruise missile and other sophisticated technology," the brochure adds. It stresses the United States' attentiveness to consultation with its allies and to their security concerns.

**Comment:** The United States is the mainstay of the alliance on which their security hinges. Any weakening of the United States' strategic position vis-a-vis the Soviet Union must inevitably undercut the North Atlantic Alliance. That is the main consideration affecting the country's European allies.

After taking account of disparities in the SALT II terms, a recent editorial in the London *Economist*[6] speculates on broad implications for the alliance and goes on to consider aspects of narrower though still important concern. The portion quoted below serves as a commentary on the brochure:

> . . . The allies of the United States have got into the habit of measuring its ability to protect them against Russia by totting up the units of American nuclear power. That is the "nuclear umbrella." If that power is seen to be getting smaller than Russia's, one spoke of the umbrella after another, public opinion in these allies will grow more nervous about the value of American protection; and nervousness could crack the alliance.
>
> . . . The most dangerous place for such mistrust to grow is western Europe. The second major criticism of SALT-2 is that it has managed to increase Europeans' doubts about America most of all.
>
> The planned treaty, while setting limits on the number of missiles Russia can aim at America, says nothing about the growing number of missiles it points at western Europe, especially the powerful new SS-20; and the only reference to Russia's Backfire bomber will apparently be some sort of Soviet "assurance" (outside the treaty itself) that this Europe-busting nuclear-bombing aircraft will not be used to bust America too. This hardly encourages the Europeans. They are not reassured by the fact that the American-designed cruise missile, which could be one way of equalising things, may be denied to them under the SALT-2 clause which says that neither side may do anything to "circumvent" the treaty. The Americans say this should not prevent them providing the Europeans with the knowhow, and

maybe some of the parts, to make the cruise missile; but Russia says flatly it will prevent just that.

The Europeans also find it worrying that the kinds of cruise missiles most useful to them— the ones launched from ships or from the ground—will be limited to a feeble 375-mile range by the protocol which will regulate a few particularly tricky problems during the first two or three years of the general treaty. They suspect that when those two or three years are over Russia will try to bully Mr. Carter or his successor into prolonging the protocol, and with it the range restriction, and they are not confident of Mr. Carter's ability to defy Russia . . .

## COLLATERAL ISSUES IN NATIONAL DEFENSE

In the phrasing found in the brochure, "How do cancellation of the B-1 bomber and the decision to defer production of the 'neutron bomb' relate to SALT?" According to the answer given, the connection is nil, for the matters involved in both decisions—choices concerning strategic bomber types and tactical weapons—come within the United States' autonomous discretion, and neutron weapon technology is not within the SALT purview at all. The brochure depicts the B-1 cancellation as a creditable decision "made . . . in the interest of providing the United States with a strong, efficient, and cost-effective national defense." The brochure describes the sidetracking of the neutron warhead as an initiative taken in hope to induce "appropriate, meaningful restraint by the Soviet Union" in response.

**Comment:** The brochure overlooks a significant relationship. The B-1 bomber cancellation and the sidetracking of neutron weapon technology—and this observation applies also to deliberate slippage in the mobile missile and Trident submarine programs—reflect a subordination of national security policies to wishes for promoting arms control instead of shaping arms control to security needs. The same inclination dominates the U.S. approach to SALT.

The stated rationale for canceling the B-1 bomber program and trying to make do with the B-52 instead is not convincing. As instrumentalities for advancing cruise missiles to transoceanic targets, B-1 bombers are demonstrably superior to the B-52s in efficiency, cost-effectiveness, and capability to escape from an attack and therefore to survive.

The decision on neutron weapon technology constitutes a recission *sine die*, rather than a contingent deferment as portrayed in the brochure. Significant aspects are ignored in the brochure. For example, nothing is said about the Soviet Union's pervasive and energetic propaganda campaign to head off neutron weapons, about the unanimous recommendations from the President's defense advisors overriden by the President's decision, or about the resulting consternation among the United States' European allies. The most important potential of neutron warheads pertains to their utility for countering attacks by tanks and similar armored tactical vehicles without doing enormous damage to the physical surroundings in the manner of existing types of tactical nuclear weaponry. Neutron technology thus would be a basis for a more cogent defense for the central front against the threat from the East posed by a heavy preponderance of Soviet armor in the European theater. Hence the sidetracking of neutron weapon technology is an act of renunciation with special impact on the security of the United States' transatlantic allies.

The nature of the Soviet forbearance looked for in reciprocity to the U.S. decision remains as vague in the brochure as it was in the President's announcement. The sole sign of response from the Soviet side so far has been a not surprising disavowal of any plan to develop its own neutron weapons. The logic chain from the U.S. rescission to the Soviet

Union's renunciation has an analog in a fabled householder's decision to forego acquiring a tomcat pending more evidence on what the mice planned to do—whereupon the mice announced their reciprocal intention to make do for the time being without acquiring a tomcat of their own.

## LINKAGE TO SOVIET CONDUCT

The pertinent question as phrased in the brochure is: "Why should we sign an agreement with the Soviet Union when that country promotes instability in Africa and other parts of the world?" The answer takes abstract cognizance of U.S. opposition to "Soviet policies where they conflict with ours," advises against regarding SALT as "a reward that we are giving the Soviet Union for good behavior," calls SALT justifiable "only if, by itself, it promotes our national security," and then asserts the worthiness by that criterion of SALT as a support to "continued nuclear stability" and a reducer of the risk of nuclear war.

**Comment:** The brochure thus takes only passing note of the antithesis between U.S. and Soviet purposes in world affairs—and does so only to wave it aside as marginal, notwithstanding its central importance to the security issues in SALT. It is appropriate here to cite a more apt appraisal of the salient realities from "What Is the Soviet Union Up To?"[7]

> The attainment of the ultimate Soviet objective—a Communist world order—requires the reduction of the power, influence and prestige of the United States, the country which the Soviet leaders perceive as the central bastion of the "capitalist" or enemy camp. They see the global conflict as a drawn-out process with the Soviet Union and America the two principal contenders. In that contest they see their task as isolating America and, despite temporary reverses for their side, reducing it to impotence.
>
> In its global activities the Soviet Union pursues a "grand strategy" involving the use of a great variety of means to attain the ultimate end: the reduction of any potential opponent's ability to resist. These means include economic, diplomatic, political and ideological strategies against a background of military strength, to be used separately or together as instrumentalities of power. The Soviet eagerness to increase its trade with the Western world or to participate in arms limitation negotiations does not preclude politico-military campaigns to outflank and envelop centers of non-Communist influence, such as the long and patient Soviet efforts to penetrate and dominate the Middle East, and now the drive, supported by client states, to establish regimes friendly to Soviet domination in Africa.

The import of Soviet designs in such regions is by no means marginal. The steady purpose of Soviet endeavors there is to impinge on sources of materials and lines of supply essential to the security of the United States and its allies. That purpose is wholly consonant with the Soviet approach to SALT—the two being coordinated parts of the drive for visible preponderance.

The advice in the brochure against regarding SALT as "a reward" to the Soviet Union "for good behavior" is salutary if, taken alone, it is construed as a rebuttal of those who say their misgivings about the SALT II treaty might be assuaged by an interval of Soviet forbearance in external affairs. The brochure is correct in asserting the touchstone for judging the SALT II treaty to be the effect of its provisions on national security. The description of the SALT II treaty as beneficial to United States security, however, is left as uncorroborated in this context as it is elsewhere in the brochure. Under logical and informed analysis, the SALT II treaty is seen as the inverse of that portrayal. The assertion concerning continued strategic stability reflects nothing more substantial than preoccupation with counting permissible numbers of intercontinental missile launchers. As for the declaratory reduction in risks of nuclear war—a spurious sense of security is, among all moods, the one most likely to propel the nation toward the predicament of having to choose between capitulation and a doomed belligerency.

## EFFECTS ON STRATEGIC COMPETITION

The short answer given in the brochure to the final question—"Will SALT TWO really slow the arms race?"—is yes. The brochure continues, ". . . the SALT process has already slowed the arms race." The supporting argument recalls accomplishments in SALT I—namely, the treaty to end competition in certain strategic defensive systems and the interim agreement on offensive strategic nuclear weapons—as a precedent to justify optimism. Turning to the SALT II treaty, the brochure discerns contributions to stability and security in the prescribed "equal aggregate ceilings for strategic nuclear vehicles . . . and common subceilings on launchers for missiles carrying MIRVs," corollary requirements for the Soviet Union "to reduce a considerable number of strategic systems," and—as an item mentioned for the first time—expected "constraints on the introduction of new types of ballistic missiles." The argument emphasizes the importance of the SALT II treaty as a steppingstone to SALT III, from which it anticipates "further progress in reducing the nuclear arsenals on both sides . . . and further restrictions in qualitative improvements." Concerning "the price of not reaching agreement," the brochure warns, "An expansion of the strategic arms competition, at significant monetary cost, could follow, with an increasing danger that future weapons systems could increase the incentives to resort to nuclear weapons in time of crisis."

**Comment:** The metaphoric phrase "arms race" means different things to different people at different times and in some contexts becomes almost impossible of definition. For example, if "arms race" is taken to characterize the superpower strategic interplay preceding the SALT I accords, then the phrase must denote a relationship between one side under unilateral restraint and in the course of reducing strategic deployments and another side pressing ahead with utmost will and vigor in diverting resources to strategic uses. "Arms race" in that sense, however, can scarcely be taken to include something "slowed" by SALT I—as alleged in the brochure—for the effect of SALT I has been to register and extend the increasingly disparate strategic relationship as it had been developing.

Certainly the SALT I interim agreement has not—as alleged in the brochure—served to "stop the Soviet buildup of ICBM launchers." The Soviet Union has persevered in that buildup at rates projected in long antecedent plans. A statement in the brochure hailing the SALT I treaty on defensive strategic nuclear arms for having "curtailed an expensive competition" that "could have stimulated the expansion of offensive strategic forces to offset them" must also be examined warily. A principal effect of that treaty—by which the United States shelved a program that was making sound headway in return for Soviet abandonment of a counterpart program that was faltering badly—has been to free resources for diversion into helping sustain the Soviet offensive buildup designed for gaining ascendency over the U.S. strategic forces which the ballistic missile defense system was designed to protect.

The important present questions, however, relate to the portrayal of the SALT II treaty. As already noted in the discussion on "The Meaning for U.S. Security," the prospective cutback on Soviet launchers, far from signaling a reduction of offensive strength, fits in with the Soviet schedule of steady increments in offensive nuclear striking power. The interpretation of the cutback in the brochure only reflects the engrossment with launcher-counting, characteristic of the U.S. approach to SALT.

To turn from counting launches to measuring other dimensions may help put the SALT II treaty in better perspective as a reputed arms control venture. During the span of the agreement numbers of nuclear warheads can be expected to rise by 300 percent on the Soviet side, in comparison to about 50 percent for the U.S. In the same period, strategic nuclear power represented in capability for area destruction will double on the Soviet side and rise by approximately an eighth for the U.S. —a disparity between growth rates in a ratio of 16 to 1. Capability for destroying hard targets such as missile silos and command-and-control and communication centers will rise by 1000 percent on the Soviet side and—depending on the degree of progress in cruise missile developments— perhaps 400 percent for the U.S.

Another key to evaluating the SALT II treaty is to measure its provisions against the United States' hopes and aims at the outset of the negotiation in 1972. One aspiration then was to limit offensive nuclear power in ways counterpart to the permanent controls on defensive nuclear weapons in the SALT I treaty. That design was abandoned early in deference to Soviet insistence on having instead another interim agreement to expire at a time—1985—when the ratio of Soviet strategic power to that of the United States will be signally to the United States' disadvantage.

As a related goal, the hoped-for treaty should provide for equality in offensive nuclear capabilities between the two superpowers at levels politically and economically affordable for the United States. The equality actually obtained is a superficial one applied only to numbers of intercontinental launchers irrespective of important qualitative differences—and subject to the critical exemption of Soviet Backfire bombers. As for affordability—whether for want of will or of money, the United States will prospectively fall short of its allotted share of MIRVed ICBMs by one-third in contrast to a full complement for the Soviet Union.

Yet another earlier hope was that of bringing about reductions in offensive nuclear armaments and related expenditures. The SALT II treaty, as is now apparent, will not fulfill that hope. The limits to be imposed under its terms—reflecting an absorption with counting launchers to the exclusion of centrally important considerations such as numbers, power, and accuracy of missiles and warheads—affect the wrong things and are so high as to be at variance with any valid version of arms control. The prospective cutback in Soviet launchers, made much of in the brochure, will be devoid of substantive significance. As for the "constraints on the introduction of new types of ballistic missiles" mentioned in the brochure, U.S. proposals for rigorous specifics to give the idea true effect have been put aside in favor of a weakened formulation in deference to Soviet insistence.

The terms originally envisioned were to be constrained by the verification principle and by the need to take account of the security interests of the United States' allies. The terms as actualized are wanting in both respects.

An essential effect envisioned at the outset was prevention of either side from being able to gain advantage by a first nuclear strike. Thereby both sides were to be relieved from temptation to strike preemptively. The nuclear threat would be neutralized. Thus the condition of crisis stability would be established. The shadow of war would be lifted from junctures of heightened adversariness. That cluster of aims, too, is going by the board with the expansion of the Soviet threat to Minuteman. The SALT II treaty will not check the threat to this country, its population, and its military forces in any significant way.

All the goals recalled above may be summed up as the hope of reducing the risk of nuclear war and the weight of nuclear armaments overhanging international politics. The SALT II treaty contributes nothing to that hope as it pertains to the world at large and to the United States in particular. The period ahead coterminous with the SALT II treaty appears charged with troubles. Surely it would exceed the bounds of reason to attribute them all to SALT. The shortcoming in SALT, pronounced in the upcoming treaty, pertains to the failure to redress the unfavorable strategic trends all too likely to place the United States in a situation, unprecedented in its experience, of having to fend for its interests and survival from a position of palpable disadvantage.

In light of that prospect, one may evaluate assurances in the brochure concerning "further progress" for SALT III in achieving the kind of benefits alleged to be accomplished in the SALT II treaty. The troublesome prospect for SALT III is precisely in the likelihood of furtherance of the unfavorable momentum which SALT II, far from arresting, seeks to register as part of the supreme law of the land.

In weighing the question whether to authenticate the inequitable SALT II provisions in a ratified treaty—rightly tagged by the brochure as "this most serious of issues"—one may well heed Shakespeare's wise words:

> . . . To persist
> In doing wrong extenuates not wrong,
> But makes it much more heavy . . .

The United States' approach in SALT, with its premium on agreement to the disparagement of our own true interests and security, is wrong. Its results put the country in a perplexity from which it is far easier to extricate now than it will be in 1985.

The argument in the brochure concerning a putative "significant money cost" as part of "the price of not reaching agreement" is to be regarded skeptically. No data support it. With or without an approved SALT II treaty, great expenses are now imperative for correcting the unfolding deficiencies in our strategic defenses. To invoke the cost argument, with its false hint of potential savings, can only serve to impede acceptance of the indispensable. Contrary to the monition in the brochure, the SALT II treaty, carried out in the spirit exemplified by the Administration, would all too probably foreclose more economical and efficacious options and compel recourse to costlier but less effective means on behalf of the common defense. The point is illustrated in the question how to shore up Minuteman: by the timely and relatively economical method which the Administration is maneuvering to put aside in deference to the Soviet attitude, or by some system—hugely more expensive and yet impossible to complete in time to fill the bill—along the lines now being contemplated by the Administration as possible alternatives?

The warning in the brochure of "increasing danger" in consequence of a rejection of the SALT II treaty must be weighed against a candid appraisal of the dangers inherent in going ahead with it. There is nothing inappropriate in this country's deciding to stand instead for a solidly based treaty consonant with the purposes in mind at the time of undertaking the negotiations—one manifestly equitable and free of the serious liabilities of the current proposal, including especially its inherent conduciveness to a strategically unstable environment.

* * * * * * * *

The answer to the question posed in the title of this memorandum, "Does the Official Case for the SALT II Treaty Hold Up Under Analysis?" is: no. The emerging terms of SALT II, against a backdrop of the unfavorable trends in the U.S.-Soviet military balance, do not square with the security of the United States. The arguments advanced in the brochure "SALT and American Security" ignore this ominous prospect.

*14 March 1979*

## NOTES

1. "SALT and American Security," issued by the Department of State and the Arms Control and Disarmament Agency, U.S. Government Printing Office, Washington, D.C., November 1978.
2. "Common Sense and The Common Danger," Committee on the Present Danger, November 11, 1976, Chapter 2.
3. Merle Fainsod, *How Russia Is Ruled*, Cambridge: Harvard University Press, 1963, pp. 341–342.
4. "What Is The Soviet Union Up To?" Committee on the Present Danger, April 4, 1977, Chapter 3.
5. "Is America Becoming Number 2? Current Trends in the U.S.-Soviet Military Balance," Committee on the Present Danger, October 5, 1978, Chapter 7.
6. "Seven Lean Years," *The Economist*, London, December 30, 1978, pp. 7–9.
7. "What Is The Soviet Union Up To?" Committee on the Present Danger, April 4, 1977, Chapter 3.

# 10

# PUBLIC ATTITUDES ON SALT II

## The Results of a Nationwide
## Scientific Poll of American Opinion

### THE POLL

WHY WE HAD IT DONE
WHEN IT WAS DONE
WHO DID IT FOR US
HOW IT WAS CONDUCTED

The Committee has been increasingly puzzled by the reported results of national polls, commissioned by networks and newspapers, which assert that American public opinion is overwhelming in support of SALT II. We have been especially puzzled, and even disbelieving, in the face of the other published data showing that the American public is deeply and increasingly suspicious of Soviet good faith and intentions and also increasingly concerned that the United States is declining in military strength relative to the Soviet Union.

Inspection of the actual polling questions, which were not usually carried in the news, revealed that the respondents were being asked whether they favored the concept of arms limitation without reference to any of the specific provisions of the actual treaty under negotiation. For example, here is the question asked by CBS and *The New York Times*:

Do you think the U.S. should or should not negotiate a treaty with the Russians to limit strategic military weapons?

It is not surprising that 63% responded "Yes." And here is the question asked by NBC and the Associated Press:

Do you favor or oppose a new agreement between the United States and Russia which would limit nuclear weapons?

Again, the expected happened—81% said "Yes."

The only wonder is that there wasn't 100% affirmative response.

Both questions dealt with a hypothetical treaty—a treaty that, by implication, would place equal limits on both sides and would be enforceable and verifiable.

Highly generalized, hypothetical and simplistic questions with no effort to measure gradations of response provide data which furnish little insight into relevant public attitudes and are apt to be completely misleading.

If you ask the wrong questions, you get the wrong answers.

Therefore, in accord with our basic purpose of achieving a national discussion of the foreign and national security policies of the United States and with our continuing research and educational activities directed toward that objective, the Committee on the Present Danger last month commissioned a nationwide scientific poll of American attitudes toward SALT II and related issues, providing highly specific questions and a range of highly specific responses.

The poll was made by telephone during the period beginning 23 February and ending 3 March 1979. The polling was conducted for the Committee by George Fine Research, Inc. of New York City, a highly respected and experienced independent polling organization which has conducted previous polls on other subjects for media companies such as *The New York Times*, *The Washington Post* and the Columbia Broadcasting System (CBS), for AT&T and its operating companies, for universities such as Harvard, Syracuse and Penn State, and for manufacturing companies and advertising agencies.

The poll encompassed 1211 respondents and secured responses to 12 substantive questions (7 multiple choice and 5 true/false). The respondents represented a scientifically developed sample of the American people above 18 years of age. The margin of error in polls of this nature and size is generally recognized to be at plus or minus 3%.

Here are all the questions which were asked in the poll, and the results.

## THE POLL QUESTIONS AND THE RESULTS

1. The United States is now negotiating a strategic arms agreement with the Soviet Union in what is known as "SALT TWO." Which *ONE* of the following statements is closest to your opinion on these negotiations:

| | |
|---|---|
| • I strongly support SALT II | 8.3% |
| • SALT II is somewhat disappointing, but on balance, I would have to support it | 11.7% |
| • I would like to see more protection for the United States before I would be ready to support SALT II | 41.7% |
| • I strongly oppose the SALT II arms agreement with the Russians | 8.6% |
| • I don't know enough about the SALT II Treaty to have an opinion yet | 29.6% |

2. I am going to mention several U.S. aims in foreign policy. Please tell me which one *YOU* think is *most* important:

| | |
|---|---|
| • A Strategic Arms Agreement with Russia | 18.1% |
| • A peace treaty between Egypt and Israel | 29.9% |
| • Strengthening ties with Communist China | 9.1% |
| • Strengthening NATO's ability to defend Europe against possible Russian attack | 15.4% |
| • A stable government in Iran friendly to the U.S. | 17.0% |
| • Don't Know/Refused | 10.6% |

3. What percentage of this country's total economic output do you think now goes to national defense? Would you say that it is:

| | |
|---|---|
| • 5% or Less | 9.8% |
| • 15% | 25.9% |

- 25%                                              26.3%
- 35% or More                                      26.6%
- Don't Know                                       11.3%

4. I am going to read you several statements about the proposed SALT II Treaty. Please tell me whether you think each statement is true or false.

|  | TRUE | FALSE | DON'T KNOW |
|---|---|---|---|
| a. The Treaty would require the U.S. and Russia to reduce military spending | 47.5% | 37.5% | 15.0% |
| b. The Treaty would restrict the explosive power of nuclear warheads on both sides | 65.2% | 21.8% | 13.0% |
| c. The SALT II Treaty would require each side to reduce its capabilities for making a nuclear attack on the other | 58.1% | 28.6% | 13.3% |
| d. All arms restrictions in the Treaty will be subject to full verification regarding compliance | 57.6% | 23.8% | 18.7% |
| e. The Treaty would not regulate the number of strategic nuclear missiles or warheads to be retained or manufactured by each side | 27.1% | 57.1% | 15.9% |

5. The Soviet Union has a modern bomber called the "Backfire" which is capable of attacking the U.S. with nuclear weapons. If the proposed SALT Treaty does not count the "Backfire" bomber as a Soviet strategic nuclear delivery system, would you then be:

- definitely opposed to the Treaty                    42.4%
- somewhat inclined to oppose the Treaty               30.7%
- in support of the Treaty, nevertheless              16.4%
- Don't Know/No Opinion                               10.5%

6. By the end of the proposed SALT Treaty, that is—by 1985, the ability of Soviet ballistic missiles to destroy American missile sites and other protected military targets is expected to be ten times that of U.S. ballistic missiles' ability to destroy similar targets in Russia. In view of this information, which of the following statements comes closest to your feelings about the SALT Treaty:

- I am much more inclined to *oppose* the Treaty        26.5%
- I am somewhat more inclined to *oppose* the Treaty    21.1%
- I am somewhat more inclined to *support* the Treaty   10.7%
- I am much more inclined to *support* the Treaty        7.1%
- It does not change my position                        24.9%
- Don't Know/No Opinion                                  9.7%

7. If you were convinced that there was no adequate way for the United States to check on whether or not the Russians were living up to one or more parts of the agreement, how would this affect your position on the SALT Treaty? Would you then:

- definitely oppose the agreement                       45.4%
- be more inclined to oppose the agreement              31.6%

- still support the agreement                                                    14.7%
- Don't Know/No Opinion                                                          8.3%

8. With what you now know about the proposed Strategic Arms Agreement, if one of your Senators voted against the Treaty, which of the following would be your reaction:

- I would definitely oppose him for reelection                                   7.9%
- I would be more inclined to oppose him than now                                9.7%
- I would be more inclined to support him than now                               8.0%
- I would definitely support him                                                 6.1%
- It wouldn't make that much difference; I would make up my mind on his overall record    60.9%
- Don't Know/Refused                                                             7.3%

## MAJOR CONCLUSIONS OF THE COMMITTEE

1. The American people are skeptical about SALT II, don't know much about it and, clearly, are not prepared to support the treaty without additional safeguards.

   We have been reading and hearing from the Administration and the media that a large majority of Americans back the new SALT treaty and that support for it is at the highest level in three years. To the contrary, this current poll demonstrates that only 8.3% of those polled strongly support SALT II—almost precisely matched by those (8.6%) who strongly oppose the treaty. Another 11.7% support it "on balance" despite their feeling that the treaty is "somewhat disappointing." So the total of those who now support it, strongly or reluctantly, is only 20%—1 out of 5. On the other hand, 41.7% would like to see more protection for the United States before they would be ready to support SALT II and 29.6% say that they don't know enough about the treaty to have an opinion yet. Thus, a total of 79.9% oppose SALT II, are not ready to support it without additional safeguards for the U.S., or say that they do not yet know enough to have an opinion. Further, 71% of those who do have an opinion on SALT II are either opposed to it or want more protection in the treaty for the United States. (See Question 1.)

2. A large amount of Americans do not have sufficient information on SALT II to reach a considered judgment. This is demonstrated not only by the 29.6% who state it in Question 1 but also by the answers given to the true and false statements about the proposed SALT II treaty in Question 4. A substantial majority of those answering true or false to each of these statements gave the wrong answer. The correct answers to A, B, C, D, and E are False, False, False, False and True. Yet, with the "Don't Knows" excluded, 56% said A was True, 75% said B was True, 67% said C was True, 71% said D was True and 68% said E was False. The majority was wrong every time—and by a huge margin.

   The public is not merely *uninformed* about SALT II (then they could be expected to give the right answer 50% of the time)—they are actually *misinformed* about the treaty and its provisions.

3. When Americans become aware of important elements of the emerging SALT II treaty that are causing concern to many experts, definite opposition to, and doubts about, the treaty increase dramatically. For example, the information about BACKFIRE increases the percentage of those definitely opposed to the treaty from 8.6% to

42.4%. Similarly, when asked if they would support a treaty that was not wholly verifiable, the definite opposition increased from 8.6% to 45.4%. (See Questions 5, 6 and 7.)

4. As our Committee has long pointed out (see "Where We Stand on SALT," 6 July 1977) a national decision on SALT II should not be reached except in full awareness of the state of the U.S.-Soviet military balance and, even more importantly, the adverse trends in the balance. In this connection, the responses to multiple choice Question 3 are particularly disturbing although not wholly surprising. The correct answer was given by only 9.8% of those polled. The correct answer to how much of the country's total economic output goes to national defense is "5% or less." Yet 78.8% of those polled thought that we spent 3 to more than 7 times as much as we actually do.

5. Finally, the poll results demonstrate beyond doubt that an open and searching national debate is essential on the critical matter of SALT II. This means that the Administration should give the American people the unvarnished facts about the treaty—what it will do and what it will not do. The Administration has an obligation to explain the actual provisions of the treaty so that it can be judged on its merits and not in a climate of insufficient information or, even worse, actual misinformation.

*15 March 1979*

# 11

# CURRENT [1979] SALT II NEGOTIATING POSTURE

*Paul H. Nitze*

The negotiations are intended to produce a SALT II Treaty, a Protocol, and a Statement of Principles.

## 1. THE SALT II TREATY

The Treaty is to run to December 31, 1985. Significant points regarding its contents follow:

a.  The aggregate number of strategic nuclear launch vehicles (SNLVs)[1]—i.e., launchers for intercontinental ballistic missiles (ICBMs), plus launchers for submarine-launched ballistic missiles (SLBMs), plus "heavy bombers," plus launchers for air-to-surface ballistic missiles with a range greater than 600 kilometers (ASBMs)—is to be limited initially to 2,400 each for the United States and the Soviet Union. By December 31, 1981, the initially authorized limit of 2,400 SNLVs is to be reduced to 2,250.

b.  Within the permitted aggregate number of SNLVs a sublimit of 1,320 will be placed on the number of launchers for ICBMs carrying multiple independently-targeted reentry vehicles (MIRVs), plus launchers for MIRVed SLBMs, plus aircraft equipped to carry armed air-launched cruise missiles (ALCMs) with a range greater than 600 kilometers (which are also to be counted under the SNLV ceiling as "heavy bombers").

c.  A sublimit of 1,200 is to be placed on the number of MIRVed ICBM launchers plus MIRVed SLBM launchers.

d.  A sublimit of 820 is to be placed on the number of MIRVed ICBM launchers. Within this 820 limit the Soviet Union will be permitted to have a number of fixed modern heavy ballistic missile (MHBM) launchers equal to their present force level—which is 308 (or 326 if 18 operational MHBM launchers at the Soviet test range are counted). The United States—which has no fixed MHBM launchers—will be permitted none in the future. New ballistic missiles with useful payloads (throw-weight)

This is one of a series of briefings given by Paul H. Nitze on current U.S. SALT II negotiating posture. Mr. Nitze is Chairman, Policy Studies, of the Committee on the Present Danger. He was formerly Secretary of the Navy (1963–67), Deputy Secretary of Defense (1967–69), and a Member of the U.S. SALT Delegation (1969–74).

greater than that of the Soviet SS-19 will be considered to be MHBMs, and ballistic missiles with useful payloads greater than that of the Soviet SS-18 will be banned.

e.  Any missile booster of a type which has been tested with MIRVs is to be considered to be a MIRVed missile booster. Any launcher of a type from which a MIRVed missile booster has been launched will be considered to be a launcher for MIRVed missiles. What is meant by "type" has not been precisely defined.

f.  One of the remaining disagreed provisions concerns limits on the modification of existing types of ICBMs.

It is agreed that any test of an ICBM with more RVs than have previously been tested on that type of ICBM will cause it to be classified as a "new type." The U.S. has tested 7 small RVs on the MINUTEMAN III on two occasions, although none of our deployed MINUTEMAN missiles carries more than 3 RVs. The U.S. will continue to have the option of deploying 7 RVs on MINUTEMAN III without such a variant counting as a "new type." There are, however, no U.S. plans to proceed with the deployment of such a variant. The Soviet Union has tested and will be permitted to deploy 4 RVs on its SS-17, 6 RVs on its SS-19, and 10 RVs on its SS-18 type missiles. It has been reported in the press that the Soviets have demonstrated that the front end of an SS-18 has the capability to release at least 14 RVs, although there is no evidence that more than 10 have actually been carried or released in a test.

There is reported to be disagreement concerning the testing of other modifications of an existing type permissible without causing that type to be classed as a "new type." The disagreement concerns the degree of change permissible in factors such as the power of the missile's boosters to put a useful payload into intercontinental orbit, the missile's dimensions, its launch weight, and the type and total impulse of its fuel. The U.S. position is reported to be that the testing of any change in these factors by an amount exceeding 5 percent up or down would cause that type to be classed as "new." The Soviet Union was reported as insisting on greater flexibility, particularly on the down side, perhaps to 12 percent down. It is now reported that the Soviet Union has accepted the U.S. position.

The sides have agreed that each side will be permitted to flight test and deploy one "new type" ICBM (MIRVed or unMIRVed) during the Treaty period. No "new type" MHBM may be tested. There is no limit on the number of "new type" SLBMs which the sides are permitted to test and deploy during the life of the Treaty.

g.  During the period of the Treaty there will be a ban on the flight testing and deployment of a larger number of RVs on any "new type" ICBM missile than the largest number already flight tested by either side on an ICBM (i.e., 10) and a similar ban on SLBMs (i.e., 14). B-52s, B-1s, BEARS, and BISONS will be limited to 20 ALCMs per bomber. The average number of ALCMs carried on all ALCM-carrying aircraft is to be limited to a number less than 30.

h.  As a general rule, United States' B-52s and B-1s and the USSR's BEARS and BISONS are to be counted as "heavy bombers" and thus counted under the ceiling on SNLVs. Also, all transport aircraft equipped to carry ALCMs with a range greater than 600 kilometers are to be counted as "heavy bombers." If new bombers, such as the B-1 type bomber reported to be under development in the USSR, are deployed, agreement by both sides is required for them to be classed as "heavy bombers."

i.  The Soviet BACKFIRE bomber is not to be counted as a "heavy bomber" (unless equipped to carry ALCMs of range greater than 600 kilometers).

   • The Soviet Union is reported to have agreed to make an informal declaration — outside the contractual forms of the Treaty — of its intention not to raise the production rate of the BACKFIRE above the current rate of about 30 per year. The United States, on its part, will declare its intent to retain the option of producing and deploying a new penetrating bomber of a type similar to BACK-FIRE which also would not be counted against the SNLV limit.

- Soviet "heavy bomber" variants (these include BEARS and BISONS reconfigured to reconnaissance, tanker, and antisubmarine roles but still retaining their bomb bays) are not to be counted as "heavy bombers."
- In addition to "heavy bombers" (currently including BEARS, BISONS, B-52s, and B-1s), only transport aircraft newly constructed for the specific purpose of carrying ALCMs may be equipped to carry ALCMs.

j.  Cruise missile range is defined as the maximum distance the missile can achieve measured by projecting its flight path onto the earth's surface. Thus, the operational range, after allowing for zigs and zags to avoid defense, will be significantly less than the range from launcher to target. With respect to ICBMs, intercontinental range is specified as being 5,500 kilometers or more. No specification has been agreed as to the range cutoff distinguishing SLBMs classed as SNLVs and submarine-launched missiles considered to be for tactical use only.

k.  There are no limits on the number of missiles or warheads which may be produced and stored. The storage near launching sites of ICBMs in excess of those needed for permitted launchers is banned, and storage facilities for such ICBMs are prohibited. The development, testing, and deployment of rapid reload systems for ICBM launchers is also prohibited.

l.  Both sides agree not to take any action which would circumvent the purposes of the agreements and not to transfer to third countries weapons limited by the agreements. The extent to which this would ban the transfer of components or technology associated with such weapons is not clear. The USSR interpretation has been reported to be that the transfer of components, blueprints, and technology directly pertinent to such weapons is precluded by such a ban.

m.  Obligations for reciprocal disclosures of pertinent data have been agreed. The Soviet Union has made certain data available and has agreed that additional information will be made available. The Soviets have insisted that they not be required to provide the numbers of heavy missiles (SS-9 and SS-18).

n.  There is agreement in principle to refrain from interfering with the national technical means unilaterally controlled by the respective sides for verification of compliance with the terms of the agreements by the other side. There is disagreement, however, with respect to the specifics of that agreement in principle, in particular as they bear on the encryption of telemetry. It is reported that the United States proposes that there be no change in practices existing prior to a date ante-dating the date of the first encryption by the Soviet Union of telemetry associated with missile tests. It is reported that the Soviet Union does not agree to that proposal.

o.  The start of additional, and the relocation of existing, fixed ICBM launchers is banned.

## 2. THE PROTOCOL

The Protocol is to cover the period to December 31, 1981, when it will terminate (unless earlier renegotiated).

The only significant restriction in this Protocol, beyond those in the Treaty, concerns mobile ICBMs, ASBMs, and launchers for armed ground- and sea-launched cruise missiles.

a.  The flight testing or deployment of mobile ICBMs and of ASBMs is to be banned during the period of the Protocol. After the expiration of the Protocol, the Treaty language, unless earlier amended, would permit the development, testing, and deployment of mobile ICBMs and ASBMs, but launchers for each missile would have to be counted under the pertinent limits. Testing of mobile launchers for mobile ICBMs during the Protocol is not prohibited, provided that no missile is fired from such launchers.

It has been reported that the Soviets have raised serious concern over a United States' insistence that the deployment of a multiple aimpoint (MAP)[2] system (which is more precisely a transportable, rather than a mobile, system) would be permitted under the terms of the Treaty after the expiration of the Protocol.

b.  During the period of the Protocol the deployment of armed and nuclear-armed ground-and sea-launched cruise missiles with a range greater than 600 kilometers will be prohibited.

c.  The Soviets are reported recently to have demanded that the Protocol ban cruise missiles with multiple warheads and that the limits on armed cruise missiles be extended also to cover remotely controlled unmanned vehicles even if not armed.

## 3. THE STATEMENT OF PRINCIPLES

The negotiations for the next stage in SALT, with the Principles serving as guidelines, are anticipated to follow-on soon after the completion of SALT II.

a.  The United States has proposed the following principles, or targets:
    • A reduction in the aggregate number of SNLVs
    • A reduction in the MIRVed missile launcher limit
    • Provisions further restricting the development, testing, and deployment of new ICBMs and SLBMs
    • Provisions restricting the flight testing of ICBMs and SLBMs
    • Further restrictions on strategic defenses, including air and civil defense
    • Steps to strengthen verification through "cooperative measures," in addition to "national technical means."

b.  The Soviet Union's position is that such a statement of principles should make clear that the United States and allied theater nuclear weapons capable of reaching the Soviet Union must be taken into account in arriving at new ceilings, that the subject of restrictions on strategic defenses beyond those contained in the ABM Treaty is not appropriate for SALT, and that no "cooperative measures" other than in support of "national technical means" should be considered.

*23 April 1979*

## NOTES

1.  The phrase strategic nuclear delivery vehicle (SNDV) is often, but less precisely, used to describe this aggregate.
2.  The U.S. Air Force now prefers the name "multiple protective structure" (MPS) system; see General Lew Allen's letter of December 29, 1978, to the Chairman of the House Armed Services Committee. A more precise acronym for the system he describes is MVPS (multiple vertical protective structure system).

# 12

# CONSIDERATIONS BEARING ON THE MERITS OF THE SALT II AGREEMENTS AS SIGNED AT VIENNA

## Assuming that Currently Projected U.S. and USSR Defense Programs are Continued in a Manner Consistent with SALT II

*Paul H. Nitze*

## 1. U.S. SALT II OBJECTIVES AND THE CONSTRAINTS WITHIN WHICH THOSE OBJECTIVES HAVE HAD TO BE SOUGHT

The SALT II negotiations began seven years ago. The U.S. objective was a treaty of indefinite duration, limiting offensive nuclear forces, to match the treaty limiting ABM defenses which had just been ratified. It was intended that the SALT II treaty should provide equal limitations on the two sides such that essential equivalence in offensive nuclear capabilities would be assured and such that "crisis stability" could and would be maintained. "Crisis stability" was the phrase used to describe a situation in which neither side could hope to gain in relative capabilities from initiating the use of nuclear weapons in a crisis. It was hoped that, if these two objectives had been met, a foundation would have been laid for a reduction in the resources both sides would consider necessary to devote to their offensive nuclear armaments.

It was recognized that there were four constraining considerations which must be taken into account in achieving the primary U.S. objectives. One constraint was that the limitations strategically important to the U.S. should be verifiable. The second was that the legitimate interests of our allies must be taken into account and the terms of the agreement be reasonably acceptable to them. The third constraint was that the limitations be such that it would be economically and politically practicable for the United States to deploy those permitted forces necessary to maintain essential equivalence and crisis stability. The fourth was that the terms of an agreement be negotiable; that is, be acceptable to the Soviet side and also be ratifiable by the Congress.

Early in the SALT II negotiations it was evident that there were potential conflicts among these objectives and constraints, and that difficult choices would have to be made in finding an optimum solution. One such conflict was between the objective of maintaining crisis stability and the constraint of verifiability. It had long been recognized that limiting the number and quality of missiles was much more important than limiting the number of launchers. But it would require cooperative measures to monitor the production and storage of missiles; satellite sensors would be inadequate. The Soviets refused to agree to cooperative measures. ICBM silos, however, could be photographed from satellites, and counted and their size estimated. It was also recognized that it was more important to limit the aggregate throw-weight of a force than the number and size of its launchers. This proved to be impossible to negotiate. Verifiable and negotiable controls over missile accuracy also proved to be unattainable. The basic and primary currency of the negotiations thus became limits on the number of launchers, not limits on missiles or their characteristics. This has proven to be the wrong currency.

During the course of the seven years of the SALT II negotiation, the originally formulated three U.S. primary objectives and the first three of the constraints have been progressively compromised so as to accommodate one aspect of the fourth constraint — that the terms of the agreements be acceptable to the Soviet side, thereby facilitating their negotiability. At the same time, the U.S. side has been inhibited in publicizing Soviet recalcitrance in the negotiations because of the other aspect of the fourth constraint — that the agreements be ratifiable by the Congress.

The first casualty among our original objectives was that of achieving a treaty of indefinite duration. That objective was given up in the summer of 1974 in order to announce a negotiating breakthrough at the Moscow conference which otherwise would have been without result. Instead of a treaty of indefinite duration we settled for the target of an agreement expiring in 1985.

Each negotiating "breakthrough" since the Moscow conference has involved a further retreat from our original objectives.

What we have gained from these concessions has been a series of relatively unimportant adjustments in what otherwise would have been the Soviet program for deployments over the next six years, more than offset by limitations on our programs for future deployments. In essence, most of the negotiating process has been one of trading marginal adjustments to their large strategic program versus more significant adjustments to our much smaller one.

The following sections deal with the principal considerations involved in arriving at a judgment on the merits of the agreements as they appear to be emerging from that process and from the differential strategic nuclear programs of the two sides.

## 2. THE ICBM BALANCE TO BE EXPECTED BY 1985

### a. The MIRVed ICBM Balance

This component of the overall balance is of particular significance. It is likely that if deterrence fails, this component, because of its power and accuracy, its short time of flight, the greater reliability of its command and control, and its known location, would be the key element in an initial strike and any initial counterforce response. This exchange could well determine the military outcome of the war.

(1) The U.S. has closed down the MINUTEMAN III production line and has delayed the initial operating capability (IOC) date of a follow-on missile to 1986 or beyond. Therefore, there is essentially no possibility of the U.S. having any deployed MIRVed ICBM launchers by the expiration date of the treaty in 1985 other than the 550 MINUTEMAN III silos currently deployed. The accuracy of the MINUTEMAN III

has recently been significantly upgraded and it is planned to substitute MARK-12A warheads (with approximately double the yield) for the MARK-12 warheads currently deployed on 300 of the MINUTEMAN III. No other significant changes in MINUTEMAN III are now planned. The useful payload of the MINUTEMAN III is approximately 2,400 pounds. The maximum permitted number of reentry vehicles on the MINUTEMAN III is three RVs. The aggregate useful payload (throw-weight) of the U.S. MIRVed ICBM force in 1985 will therefore not exceed 550 × 2,400 which equals approximately a million three hundred thousand pounds. The aggregate number of MIRVed ICBM warheads in the U.S. force will not exceed 550 × 3, which equals 1,650 RVs.

(2) The USSR is permitted by the proposed terms of the agreement to deploy in excess of 300 SS-18s and approximately 500 SS-19s and -17s. The SS-18s have a useful payload approximating 16,000 pounds, the SS-17s and -19s have a useful payload approximating 7 to 8,000 pounds respectively. The SS-18s have been flight tested with as many as ten RVs, the SS-17s four RVs, the SS-19s six RVs. It can therefore be anticipated that the aggregate throw-weight of the Soviet Union's MIRVed ICBM force will approximate nine million pounds of throw-weight by 1985, and that the number of RVs deployed on those MIRVed missiles will approximate six thousand, each RV having a yield two to four times that of the U.S. RVs. There is no reason to believe that the accuracy of the Soviet MIRVed RVs by 1985 will be significantly less than that of the improved accuracy of the MINUTEMAN III RVs. The U.S. is developing its more radical accuracy improvement, the Advanced Inertial Reference System (AIRS), for incorporation in a new follow-on missile to be deployed after 1985.

(3) If current accuracy is no better than approximately a fifth of a mile, it would be difficult for them to eliminate more than 70 percent of our MINUTEMAN silos in an initial strike, assuming that they target two of their RVs on each silo. If their accuracy approximates fifteen hundredths of a mile, around 90 percent of our silos would be vulnerable to such a two-on-one attack. A two-on-one attack would require less than half of the MIRVed ICBM RVs they are expected to have available by 1985. When their accuracy exceeds an eighth of a mile, more than 80 percent of our silos will become vulnerable to an attack by a single RV against each silo, provided that additional RVs are programmed to substitute for missiles that fail during their launch phase.

(4) If we were to use all our MINUTEMAN III, taking account of their improved accuracy and the substitution of MARK-12A for MARK-12 RVs, it is unlikely we could destroy more than 50 percent of the Soviet ICBM silos.

## b. The UnMIRVed ICBM Balance

The utility of large single RV ICBMs, which can have very high megatonnage and thus very high fallout potential, is largely as terror weapons to deter the other side from using its surviving deterrent in a second strike.

(1) Until 1985 or beyond the U.S. is expected to have 450 MINUTEMAN II, each with a throw-weight of less than 2,000 pounds and carrying a single RV in the megaton range. These would give us approximately 700,000 pounds of throw-weight and 550 megatons of yield in our unMIRVed MINUTEMAN ICBM force. In addition, we

may choose to maintain the 54 TITAN missiles which were deployed prior to 1965. They have an aggregate yield of some 450 megatons.

(2) In coming down to the 2,250 limit, the Soviet side can be expected to retain at least 360 non-MIRVed ICBMs during the life of the treaty. It now being agreed that each side will be allowed to test and deploy one new type of ICBM (MIRVed or non-MIRVed) during the period of the Treaty, it is likely that the Soviet side, having little need for a new MIRVed ICBM, will test and then deploy a new non-MIRVed ICBM with a throw-weight of approximately 8,000 pounds and a warhead yield of 15 to 20 megatons, and substitute it for approximately 360 of the currently deployed SS-11s. The aggregate throw-weight of such an unMIRVed ICBM force could be in excess of two and one-half million pounds, and its megatonnage approximately six thousand megatons.

## 3. THE SLBM BALANCE BY 1985

SLBM forces at-sea are particularly difficult to find and destroy. They can be expected to endure beyond the initial exchanges. They should, therefore, be prime candidates for being held back as strategic reserve forces to influence the later phases of a war or influence the period of war termination and beyond. It is not expected that SLBMs will achieve high accuracy by 1985. The reliability of SLBM communications constitutes a continuing problem.

### a. MIRVed SLBMs

The U.S. is scheduled to have the following MIRVed SLBMs by 1985:

- 21 POSEIDON boats, each with 16 missiles, each missile carrying eight to ten RVs, the yield of each RV being 40 kilotons;
- 10 POSEIDON boats, each "backfitted" with 16 TRIDENT I missiles, each carrying approximately eight RVs, each missile with a substantially longer range (4,000 miles) and each RV with more than double the yield of the 40 kiloton POSEIDON RV;
- 7 TRIDENT boats, each with 24 TRIDENT I missiles.

It was thus expected that we would, by 1985, have 38 nuclear-propelled MIRVed SLBM submarines with some 664 MIRVed missile tubes with a theoretical loading of 5,312 RVs. Some 60 percent of these might be at-sea at any given time, giving us some 3,200 MIRVed RVs at sea. Assuming a reliability rate of 80 percent, this amounts to approximately 2,550 at-sea reliable RVs, representing an aggregate yield of approximately 200 megatons. In the event of a crisis, it should be possible, in a number of days, to increase the at-sea force by some 25 percent.

The Soviet side, if they deploy close to the full 820 MIRVed ICBM launchers permitted under the MIRVed ICBM limit, will be able to deploy close to 380 MIRVed SLBM launchers and still stay within the 1,200 limit on MIRVed missile launchers. It is expected that the new Soviet TYPHOON submarine will be significantly larger than the present Soviet SLBM submarines and will carry 20 to 24 missiles each with up to 14 RVs; their smaller MIRVed SLBMs, the SS-N-18, are expected to have no more than half that number of MIRVs. The TYPHOON missile could have the throw-weight of the projected U.S. TRIDENT II missile, development of which has not yet been authorized. The

TRIDENT II missile is planned to be approximately twice the size (volume) of the TRIDENT I missile, but cannot be deployed prior to 1985.

It is probable, nevertheless, that the U.S. will continue to have a lead in the number of MIRVed SLBM tubes and RVs into the 1985 time period. However, the accuracy and yield of the U.S. SLBM force does not now, and is not expected by 1985, to add significantly to our capability against Soviet hard targets, such as hardened silos.

## b. UnMIRVed SLBMs

The U.S. is expected to phase out at least half of its unMIRVed POLARIS force by about 1985 and thus to have no more than 80 unMIRVed SLBMs by that time.

The Soviet Union, on the other hand, can be expected to retain over 600 unMIRVed SLBM tubes. Some of these may carry multiple, but not independently guided, RVs (MRVs) as our POLARIS missiles do today. Such missiles may be as useful as MIRVed missiles against small area targets that are not very hard, such as airfields.

## 4. THE BOMBER/CRUISE MISSILE BALANCE IN 1985

The essential characteristic of the bomber/cruise missile forces is that while—particularly on the U.S. side—they have great potential power, it is only that portion of the force that is on alert prior to the initial attack that can be expected to survive, and the bulk of even that portion of the force must be used within the initial eight hours of a nuclear war or it too runs the danger of being lost.

The B-1 issue was incorrectly stated by the administration to be a choice between relatively cheap cruise missiles and expensive B-1s. Cruise missiles have to be launched from some kind of survivable platform, preferably one that can endure in a nuclear war environment for more than a few hours. The Executive Branch's position is that this preferably should be an aircraft. Thus, one requires a bomber/cruise missile system consisting of bombers and tankers so based as to give a high probability of prelaunch survivability for those that are on alert, whose take-off is sufficiently rapid and which are so hardened against nuclear effects that it becomes difficult to barrage their escape routes; bombers that are able to penetrate close enough to the target to launch cruise missiles to destroy or suppress defenses; and cruise missiles able to penetrate area and terminal defenses and accurate enough to kill the targets they are aimed at. The cruise missile is thus only part of a multifaceted system. The bomber that launches it and the tankers that refuel the bombers are equally essential parts of the system. The system is greatly improved and the enemy's defensive problem greatly increased, if some of the bombers have the capability for rapid take-off, are hardened against radiation, are more confidently able to penetrate Soviet defenses and thus to launch SRAMs, other types of missiles, or gravity bombs, close to the target.

The B-1 program having been cancelled, the 1985 bomber/cruise missile balance depends critically on whether a Soviet barrier around the northern perimeter, and on the eastern and western flanks, of the Soviet Union against the B-52s is possible, upon the number of cruise missiles that will be able to penetrate new Soviet terminal defenses, upon the number of B-52s equipped with cruise missiles that we deploy, the prelaunch and escape survivability of our B-52s and their tankers, and the extent to which a portion of the bomber force can be reconstituted, after it is flushed on warning, so as to endure in a war environment, protracted for more than a few hours.

Without limitations on air defense systems, including forwardly deployed, area, and terminal defenses, the effectiveness of U.S. cruise missiles may be degraded during the mid to late 1980s. Limitations on air defenses are not to be included as a part of the SALT II agreements and the Soviets do not appear to be willing even to discuss this issue as part of the SALT III negotiations.

The U.S. contemplates deploying some 120 aircraft equipped with intermediate range ALCMs. The majority of these aircraft are planned to be B-52s; however, some type of aircraft carrying a larger number of ALCMs than does a B-52 is also being considered; the average number of ALCMs per ALCM carrier cannot, however, exceed 28.

As it now stands, if we maintain 550 MINUTEMAN III launchers, plus our 496 POSEIDON launch tubes, and deploy the 168 TRIDENT tubes, this would total 1,214 MIRVed missile launchers. This number would exceed the 1,200 limit on MIRVed missile launchers. Therefore, unless there is a further delay in the TRIDENT program, we will, in any case, have to phase out a small number of POSEIDON or MINUTEMAN III launchers. If we propose to deploy more than 120 ALCM-carrying planes, we will have to phase out additional POSEIDON or MINUTEMAN III launchers to stay within the 1,320 limit. It is uncertain that the Navy would recommend phasing out POSEIDONs or the Air Force the MINUTEMAN III.

Even if we assume 120 deployed ALCM-carrying aircraft, it would be unlikely that more than some 50 percent would be on continuous alert or that more than some 90 percent could be brought to readiness under conditions calling for fully generated strategic forces.

The Soviet Union faces a much simpler problem. The U.S. has no substantial air defenses and the Soviet BACKFIRE is not to be counted under any of the proposed limits. Even if BACKFIRE production is limited to 30 per annum, the number deployed will grow to significant numbers, they can be dispersed to a larger number of fields than our B-52s, and their chances of surviving an initial exchange are thus enhanced. In view of our limited defense, BACKFIRE carried cruise missiles would not need to have a range greater than 600 kilometers. If the Soviets exploit their current technology, they could deploy a significant number of such short-range ALCMs on BACKFIREs prior to 1985. The potential of the BACKFIRE to survive the initial exchanges of a nuclear war coupled with its capability to penetrate very limited U.S. defenses contributes significantly to a greater possibility of Soviet domination of the subsequent phases of such a war.

Whether the FB-111H (which is 40 percent the size of the BACKFIRE) can penetrate depends, among other things, on whether U.S. tankers can survive in sufficient numbers for the required multiple inflight refuelings of the FB-111Hs. If the FB-111H were to carry ALCMs with a range greater than 600 kilometers, they would have to be counted under both the 2,250 ceiling and the 1,320 ceiling.

## 5. THE DEFINITION AND VERIFICATION PROBLEM

It is impossible to verify compliance unless what is to be limited and the nature of the limitation have been clearly defined and the definition agreed in depth between the parties.

It is evident that seven years of negotiation failed to produce such clear and agreed definitions. The main provisions of the treaty concern limitation on the number of various types of missile launchers. But the definition of what is a launcher is purely circular; for instance, ICBM launchers are defined as "launchers which have been developed and tested for launching ICBMs" and "if a launcher contains or launches an ICBM that launcher shall be considered to have been developed and tested for launching

ICBMs." We are told by the Executive Branch that the U.S. can deploy the thousands of silos required for the "shell game" ICBM deployment system because the definition of "launcher" is unclear, and we can interpret it to refer to the canister which will contain the MX missile and not the silo which contains the canister. On that interpretation the Soviet Union could claim that none of the modern Soviet missile silos are launchers either; their most modern ICBMs are also canisterized with the device that cold launches them contained within the canister. With such uncertainty as to what the definitions mean, verifiability becomes impossible.

Similarly, we are told that the principal constraint in the treaty is the limitation of "new" ICBMs to one new type. A "new ICBM" is defined as one having a different number of stages, or using a different type of propellant (that is, liquid or solid) than a missile flight tested prior to May 1, 1979, even if it does not differ from such a previously tested missile by five percent in length, largest diameter, throw-weight or launch-weight; as will any missile, even though it does not differ in number of stages or type of propellant, that does differ by more than five percent in length, diameter, throw-weight or launch-weight from any previously tested missile. It is noteworthy that no list of previously tested Soviet missiles and their characteristics is provided and that the above limitations may not fully apply until after the 24th "new type" missile flight test.

In view of the fact the Soviets have tested some 20 types of ICBMs prior to May 1, 1979, with a wide range of weights and dimensions, that in the past we have believed that we could monitor these characteristics to an accuracy no greater than ±15 percent, and that the Soviets have provided no data base as to the characteristics of types tested prior to May 1, 1979, it would be a bold man who would assert we can be certain the Soviets will be effectively limited to one "new" ICBM type.

Even where the limitations appear to be precisely defined, compliance is in many cases difficult to verify. The range of ALCMs in one place in the treaty is related to maximum range tested, in another place to "capability to fuel exhaustion": what happens if it is never tested to "fuel exhaustion?" Different types of ALCMs are to be distinguished on the basis of "externally observable design features," but these do not necessarily bear on the range of the ALCM. Can one be sure of observing ALCM tests in a manner adequate to determine range by any criterion? How do you distinguish an ALCM from a GLCM or SLCM, or assure that an ALCM cannot be launched from a sea- or land-based launcher? How do you determine whether it is armed, and, if so, conventionally armed or nuclear armed? How do you determine that a new missile having the throw-weight of an SS-19 and carrying a bus similar to an SS-19 bus, but with a single RV, is not capable of being deployed as a MIRVed missile? How do you determine that a missile tested both from land-based launchers and SLBM submarines cannot be deployed as an ICBM? How do you determine that retired missiles or missiles taken out of retired launchers or extra, newly produced missiles are not being stockpiled to be available for relatively prompt deployment on soft pads or for reload in surviving launchers?

In many instances unambiguous verification of the SALT II limitations will not be possible. For this reason the arms control community now uses the phrase "adequately verifiable." It is correct that "verifiability" is not an absolute requirement; it is a means toward the end of a good agreement. A wholly verifiable bad agreement is still a bad agreement. If those provisions of an agreement which are strategically significant to us are adequately verifiable, the agreement might be a good agreement, even if its less important provisions are not confidently verifiable. The difficulty, however, rests in determining which provisions are "strategically significant" to us and what is meant by the word "adequate." Both phrases lend themselves to subjective judgments and thus to blatant misuse. If one assumes that no capabilities beyond those required for a city damaging role are significant, then none of the SALT II limitations are "strategically significant": they may assure the Soviet Union strategic nuclear superiority without denying us a city damaging capability.

## 6. THE ACTIVE AND CIVIL DEFENSE ASPECTS OF THE PROBLEM

The United States has, over the last twenty years, phased out most of its continental air defense capabilities. The Congress has forced the virtual deactivation of the U.S. ABM defenses permitted under the ABM treaty. In the mid-sixties the U.S. Navy was told that it was not to ask for equipment, men or funds for the purpose of developing ASW capabilities designed to attack Soviet SLBMs; as far as we know that order has never been rescinded.

The USSR has persistently put relatively more emphasis on active defensive capabilities than has the United States.

The Soviet Union has devoted a truly enormous effort to air defenses. It has deployed 12,000 surface-to-air missiles and approximately 2,700 interceptor fighters. It has deployed thousands of inter-netted air defense radars and ground-control-interceptor centers. It is apparently about ready to deploy a new high capability mobile phased-array radar/missile system called the SAX-10. It has recently been reported that the SAX-10 is being deployed on surface ships, thus affording the Soviets the beginnings of a capability to deploy a forward barrier defense against our bomber aircraft.

The Soviet Union has maintained and somewhat improved those ABM capabilities it had earlier deployed in the Moscow area. It is significantly increasing the capabilities of its phased-array ABM "early warning" radars around the periphery of the USSR. This is permitted under the ABM Treaty on the assumption that, in the event of war, such a network, being close to the periphery, could be destroyed with limited effort. It is also assumed that the even more powerful radars in the Moscow area could, with greater effort, be destroyed. However, the large Soviet phased-array radar deployments, when coupled with the development of a transportable phased-array ABM radar and high acceleration interceptor combination, could give the USSR a reasonably rapid break-out toward an important "damage limiting" ABM capability, particularly against U.S. SLBM RVs.

Even more important are the civil defense aspects of the problem. Many who have carefully studied the problem concur that a well executed civil defense program—to evacuate most of the population of Moscow and Leningrad would take several days—can reduce fatalities by a factor of five to ten as well as substantially reducing industrial damage and the time necessary for economic recovery. There is now little doubt that the Soviet Union is working on civil defense much harder than was realized as recently as two years ago.

It was reported earlier this year that the Executive Branch would request an expansion of the U.S. civil defense program to include work to enable more rapid evacuation of our urban population in the event of a crisis. Approval of such a program could have been of major importance. Later, however, the President reversed his position. It should be noted, however, that, even if that program had been approved, our program would have cost about one-tenth of what the Executive Branch estimates the Soviets are spending on civil defense.

## 7. THE NUMBER AND HARDNESS OF TARGETS PROBLEM

The potential effectiveness of offensive nuclear forces should be judged in the light of the target structure they might be called upon to strike. From the standpoint of the military outcomes of war, were deterrence to fail, the most important targets are hard targets (silos; launch control facilities; command, control, and communication bunkers; nuclear storage facilities; and the like). It is because of their strategic significance that they have been hardened. The list of Soviet hard targets is larger than ours, and the targets are generally harder. Their list is growing while ours is not. The Soviets will, by the mid-1980s, have twice as many hard targets as the United States and on the average they will be twice as hard.

Against soft targets the important criteria are soft target (area) potential, i.e., (EMT), megatonnage, number of warheads, and the relative effectiveness of the civil defense measures on the two sides.

## 8. THE BREAK-OUT PROBLEM

The essential effort in the ABM Treaty negotiation was to assure that neither side could break-out of the agreement and thereafter rapidly deploy a significant ABM defense. That was why the main emphasis was put on preventing the deployment of a widespread ABM-capable radar network, the element requiring the longest leadtime.

In the early SALT II negotiations the break-out problem with respect to offensive systems was given much attention by the U.S. side. This effort was put to one side in the interest of negotiability. This has resulted in provisions that leave rapid break-out by the Soviet Union entirely feasible.

For instance, the proposed provisions designed to limit Soviet ability to reload their silos cannot be counted on to be effective for more than a number of hours.

Those who have actually designed cruise missiles say that any bomber with hard points on its wings can rapidly be converted to carry cruise missiles and that any cruise missile operable from a plane can rapidly be adapted to be launched from ground- or sea-based launchers.

New Soviet transportable air defense systems designed to counter the U.S. SRAM/cruise missiles have a substantial break-out potential in an ABM damage limitation role.

## 9. THE COMMAND, CONTROL, COMMUNICATION AND PRE- AND POST-ATTACK INTELLIGENCE PROBLEM

Second-strike deterrent forces will fail in their purpose if responsible civil authority is not able effectively to command and control them. This requires that responsible civil authority survive an attack, have time for a considered and intelligent decision, and be able to communicate with those in immediate control of the launching of surviving forces. For these decisions to be intelligent and effective, continuing information, both as to the status of our own forces and those of the enemy, is essential.

Neither those in the Executive Branch, nor those outside it, have confidence in the current status of what is called our $C^3+I$. In fact, improving its effectiveness and survivability is given the highest priority by most analysts of our strategic posture. There is little doubt that the Soviet Union has put a vastly greater effort than has the U.S. into providing themselves with redundant and survivable $C^3+I$ systems capable of enduring, if necessary, through a protracted nuclear war. They have also been developing antisatellite and other capabilities which could deny us pre- and post-attack intelligence.

It was hoped that the SALT II provision obligating each side not to interfere with the other side's national technical means of verification would give useful protection to our pre-attack technical intelligence capabilities. With the ambiguous resolution of the test range telemetry encryption problem, much of our technical intelligence capability becomes dependent on unilateral Soviet decisions.

The diminishing survivability and endurance potential of our strategic forces to be expected during the treaty period sharpens the need for improved U.S. post-attack $C^3 + I$.

## 10. THE RELATION OF THE STRATEGIC NUCLEAR BALANCE TO THE THEATER BALANCE, CONVENTIONAL AND NUCLEAR

At all times since World War II the Soviet Union has had superior non-nuclear forces on the European central front and on its northern and southern flanks. This has been due in part to geography, the USSR enjoying the central position and interior lines, and, in part, to the greater effort that has been made by the USSR and the Warsaw Pact than by NATO.

In the years up to the early 1950s this was offset by the U.S. nuclear monopoly. Later the conventional deficiency was in large measure offset by U.S. superiority in theater nuclear weapons. Today that theater nuclear superiority has disappeared and it has proved necessary to assign a number of our POSEIDON submarines to cover targets of interest to NATO, and thus maintain a theater balance. It has been estimated that the Soviet Union has two to three times as many theater nuclear systems, with six times the area destructive potential, ten times the throw-weight, and twenty-five times the megatonnage as we. As the Soviets deploy increasing numbers of SS-20 MIRVed missiles, BACKFIRE and other high performance theater bombers, maintaining a theater nuclear balance will become increasingly difficult. In addition to the theater nuclear imbalance, we must consider the substantial and one-sided Warsaw Pact chemical warfare capabilities. More and more of our surviving strategic nuclear forces will be called upon for assignment to offset theater imbalances. This consideration is rarely taken into account when the strategic nuclear balance is being examined; it should be.

Moreover, the SALT II agreement could have a serious negative effect upon the evolution of the conventional balance. The European NATO countries have hoped to exploit cruise missile technology in its theater conventional weapon applications. Agreement that armed cruise missiles with a range greater than 600 kilometers are to be limited in SALT favors the Soviet side. It supports the erroneous Soviet claim that nuclear ballistic missiles deployed in the Soviet Union for peripheral area missions, with medium or intermediate ranges, which under SALT II can be up to 5,500 kilometers, are not "strategic," while cruise missiles deployed in NATO Europe, if over 600 kilometers in range, whether nuclear or conventionally armed, are "strategic."

In specific terms, the SALT II agreements, particularly now that the Soviet position that conventionally armed cruise missiles, as well as nuclear armed missiles, are to be limited, has been accepted, may prevent the United States from transferring technology important to the conventional defense of Europe as well as prohibiting the deployment by the U.S. of conventionally armed cruise missiles with ranges greater than 600 kilometers.

These limitations will also result in the U.S. Navy being effectively limited to cruise missiles with less than 600 kilometers in range, while countries not party to the agreements will not be so limited, and can then significantly outrange it.

## 11. THE IMPACT OF THE AGREEMENT UPON THE UNITED STATES' ABILITY TO REVERSE CURRENT TRENDS

The Vladivostok Accord did not restrict the USSR from deploying those new weapon systems it planned to deploy, but neither did it restrict us from deploying those weapon systems necessary to maintain stability and rough equivalence, and thus reversing then current trends. It did not restrict the ability of the United States to deploy the B-1, the MINUTEMAN III and the MX missile in a survivable deployment mode, TRIDENT II, ALCMs, GLCMs, and SLCMs of any range, continental air defenses, more durable and reliable command and control, or enhanced civil defense preparations.

U.S. program decisions and delays in making decisions since Vladivostok plus the terms of the probable SALT agreement now make it impossible to maintain crisis stability and rough equivalence, at least during the period of the treaty and probably for many years thereafter.

It is argued by some that the restrictions in the agreements, as they apply to the United States, are of little significance; they do not keep us from doing anything we now should, or would want to, do during the period of the agreements. This depends in large measure on whether or not the agreements permit the deployment of a multiple protective structure system (MPS). Under this concept the U.S. would construct a large number of vertical protective shelters or silos, each capable of holding a canister containing an ICBM (a MINUTEMAN III or a follow-on missile such as the MX) and its launch mechanism; or, alternatively, a canister which would contain no missile or launch mechanism but which would be indistinguishable from those that did. The canisters containing the missile and launch mechanism would, periodically and randomly, be moved and substituted among those that did not. The U.S. is reported to have told the Soviets that it considered that such a system was a mobile system and thus permitted under the treaty. The Soviet side is reported to have told us that deployment of such a system would be in violation of both the letter and spirit of the agreements.

The Executive Branch has for many months been searching for a truly mobile system which would both provide the necessary survivability and durability and be verifiable in place. They have now come up with the so-called Racetrack system. Whether it will be as effective as an MPS system is still very much in doubt. What is not in doubt is that any such system will be considerably more expensive than the MPS system and cannot be operational until after the expiration of the treaty.

Under the provisions of the SALT II agreements, it is difficult, if not impossible, to see how we can reverse recent adverse trends. Beginning in the early to mid-1980s, we would have to rely on an ICBM force useful, if deterrence fails, only if the President decides to launch it from under an attack in the few minutes he may have available to do so, a bomber force largely capable of enduring for no more than a few hours and thus having to be used within that time span or else lost, and an SLBM force at-sea of less than 25 boats, each boat constituting four percent of our "enduring" deterrent power and thus worth enormous Soviet efforts to negate.

## 12. THE SITUATION IN THE ABSENCE OF AN AGREEMENT

The proponents of ratification of the treaty emphasize that whereas the USSR now has some 2,500 strategic launchers, under SALT II they will have to reduce these to 2,400 some months after entry into force of the agreements, and to 2,250 some three years thereafter. They assert that in the absence of an agreement, the Soviet side may not make any such reductions and may well add some 400, or even more, new strategic launchers to those to which they would be limited under SALT II.

Based upon past experience, this is unlikely. The most careful student of Soviet past military budgets and programs, William Lee, tells us that he can identify little, if any, modification in the general magnitude of Soviet military budgets and therefore of military programs in response to international events or changes in U.S. programs. Whereas it is generally said that the increased Soviet emphasis on expanding its intercontinental strategic capabilities was in direct response to the Cuban missile crisis, Lee finds no evidence that this is so. The Soviet five-year planning process is so interrelated and complex that anything beyond marginal adjustments is extremely disruptive and, in the past, has rarely occurred. He also notes the difficulty the Soviets would have in increasing the percentage of their GNP devoted to defense, which he estimates has now risen to approximately 18 percent.

Nevertheless, the possibility cannot be excluded that the Soviet side, in the absence of SALT II, would not decrease the number of its strategic launchers to 2,250 and, instead, would increase them.

It should be noted, however, that the 300 launchers they are expected to phase out to reach 2,250 are obsolescent ICBMs and SLBMs which would add little to their overall capability. Their presently programmed forces, largely composed of new missiles, will provide them with such an excess of MIRVed hard target kill capability, of unMIRVed megatonnage, and of RVs needed for target coverage, that it is hard to see what strategic benefit more of the same would give them. Increased intermediate range systems to cover requirements against European NATO and China are not limited by SALT.

It is now anticipated that, as the Soviet side completes their deployment of new ICBMs and SLBMs, they will concentrate more heavily on adding to their defensive capabilities. This is where the principal gaps in their warmaking potential now lie. In particular, they are expected to add more attack submarines designed for an ASW role, and aircraft with improved look-down/shoot-down radar capabilities, and to deploy improved antiaircraft systems such as their SAX-10 mobile antiaircraft batteries, etc. For the Soviet Union to shift resources back to offensive forces from a contemplated strengthening of their defenses may not be disadvantageous to the United States.

The more important question is what the United States can be expected to do under the SALT II agreements—and in the absence of such agreements—to reverse currently unfavorable strategic nuclear trends.

## 13. THE QUESTION OF STRATEGY

Fundamental to the debate over SALT II and over our strategic nuclear program is the question of what strategy to follow, if deterrence were to fail, and the relationship of strategy to deterrence.

Some start from the assumption that a nuclear war is "unthinkable"; that those who do think about it must be Dr. Strangeloves; that deterrence has nothing to do with the military strategy either side intends to follow in the event deterrence were to fail; that, regardless of strategy and of the probable balance of the initially surviving and then enduring nuclear forces, there could be no meaningful winner or loser in a nuclear war.

On the contrary a nuclear war is thinkable; the United States can best avoid a nuclear war, while preserving its independence and honor, by thinking seriously about nuclear war and taking prudent and timely actions to forestall it. The quality of deterrence is importantly affected by the strategy we intend to follow and could effectively implement, if deterrence were to fail. The wisdom and credibility of a so-called minimum deterrence strategy is questionable. Under such a strategy, deterrence would depend on the United States' ability and will to launch, in response to a Soviet attack, a few hundred missiles, warheads or megatons (they are generally imprecise about which) against Soviet cities and industry protected by extensive active and passive defenses. The fact that the remaining U.S. military forces and U.S. population and industry would then be defenseless against ten thousand megatons or more of a Soviet third and fourth strike capability would be ignored.

Few now overtly support the minimum deterrence approach. They are more apt to describe their position with such phrases as "sufficiency" or "flexibility." This leads to the question of how much of what is enough? That judgment in turn must rest importantly upon the relative emphasis placed on the counterforce aspect of nuclear strategy and on the countervalue aspect. Neither aspect can be ignored. If our counterforce capabilities, survivable after an initial Soviet strike, were sufficient to out-match Soviet residual forces, while our other forces were capable of holding Soviet population and industry in reciprocal danger to our own, the quality of deterrence would be high because the Soviets would know we were in a position to implement a credible military strategy in the event deterrence were to fail.

If our strategy were restricted to a revenge attack on, for instance, the 200 largest Soviet cities, the military forces required to support such a strategy would be relatively small. Such a strategy, however, would be suicidal if implemented, vastly more destructive to us than to the Soviet Union, and militarily hopeless. One could, therefore, have only limited confidence in deterrence based upon an implied determination to execute such a strategy to defend vital U.S. interests.

Those that claim that we are stronger than the Soviet Union now and will continue to be so during our lifetimes, more or less regardless of what we do, must equate forces designed to support such a minimum deterrence strategy with superiority.

## 14. THE CONTINUING NEGOTIATION PROBLEM

It has been characteristic of the SALT negotiation process that the U.S. Executive Branch, in justifying proposed agreements, has stressed its hope that their deficiencies will be corrected in future agreements. This argument characterized the justification of the SALT I Interim Agreement. That agreement specified that its terms were not to prejudice, in any way, the scope or terms of the long-term comprehensive agreement contemplated for its replacement, the negotiation of which both sides had agreed should begin immediately after entry into force of the Interim Agreement. Despite the best efforts of the U.S. side, the terms of the Interim Agreement have, in fact, prejudiced the terms of SALT II. The nature of the continuing programs of the two sides and the political and psychological pressures on the U.S. made it difficult to achieve any other result.

SALT III negotiations are contemplated to begin shortly after SALT II is ratified and enters into force. Two hurdles must be met by the U.S. negotiators during those negotiations. The first is the expiration of the Protocol on December 31, 1981; the second will be the expiration of the treaty at the end of 1985. It is likely that negotiations will concern themselves with both subjects and that the Soviet side will press for the extension of those provisions of the Protocol which they would have preferred to see in the treaty, and link that pressure to the SALT III treaty negotiation. The question of whether the U.S. can expect to prevail with respect to its hopes for SALT III will largely depend on the relative bargaining position of the two sides during the negotiations. The evolution of the relative strength of the two sides in the strategic nuclear arena is almost certain to be negative during the entire period prior to expiration of the SALT II Treaty. If the MX and TRIDENT II are then close to their IOCs, this could have some offsetting bearing on the negotiations. The impending deployment of the MX version could, however, be destabilizing if a basing mode capable of assuring its survivability and endurance were not concurrently available.

If the SALT II Treaty were to approach expiration in 1985 without replacement and without a survivable and durable U.S. ICBM component, the U.S. could face unprecedented dangers. We would then have to take seriously both the then existing degree of Soviet nuclear strategic superiority and Soviet superiority in break-out potential. To avoid the attendant risks, we could well be under pressure to agree to a SALT III far less favorable to the U.S. even than SALT II.

## 15. THE POLITICAL AND DIPLOMATIC CONSEQUENCES OF A SHIFT IN THE STRATEGIC NUCLEAR BALANCE

Some proponents, rather than taking exception to the main thrust of the analysis contained in the preceding sections, argue a different series of points along the following line:

a. The United States' March 1977 comprehensive proposal leaned over backward in attempting to be fair to the Soviet Union. It offered them complete assurance against any significant counterforce threat from the United States while not assuring comparable protection for the United States.

b. The proposal was wholly unacceptable to the USSR, and any proposal which would in fact assure stability and rough equivalence at lower levels of nuclear armaments would be even more unnegotiable.

c. To insist on such an equitable agreement would assure that there would be no success, at least in the next few years, in negotiating a SALT II set of agreements. Such a delay would risk a breakdown of détente.

d. Rather than risk such a breakdown, it is wiser to negotiate the best deal that is now attainable, preserve at least the outward forms of detente, and open the way to follow-on negotiations for a better deal in the future.

e. And in any case, a deterioration in the state of the strategic nuclear balance will have no adverse political or diplomatic consequences.

To some of us who lived through the Berlin crisis in 1961, the Cuban crisis in 1962, or the Middle East crisis in 1973, the last and key judgment in this chain of reasoning—that an adverse shift in the strategic nuclear balance will have no political or diplomatic consequences—comes as a shock. In the Berlin crisis of 1961 our theater position was clearly unfavorable; we relied entirely on our strategic nuclear superiority to face down Chairman Khrushchev's ultimatum. In Cuba, the Soviet Union faced a position of both theater inferiority and strategic inferiority; they withdrew the missiles they were deploying. In the 1973 Middle East crisis, the theater and the strategic nuclear balances were more balanced; both sides compromised.

It is hard to see what factors in the future are apt to disconnect international politics and diplomacy from the underlying real power balances. The nuclear balance is only one element in the overall power balance. But in the Soviet view, it is the fulcrum upon which all other levers of influence—military, economic, or political—rest.

In any international crisis seriously raising the prospect that the military arms of the United States and of the USSR will become engaged in active and direct confrontation, those directing U.S. and Soviet policy would have to give the most serious attention to the relative strategic nuclear capabilities of the two sides.

Unequal accommodation to the Soviet Union would then have resulted not in cooperation and peace but in forced withdrawal or an unequal military disaster.

## 16. CONCLUSIONS

It is clear from the above that the United States faces a perilous situation. It is also clear that there was no need for it to be placed in this position, for it has always had the capability to prevent Soviet military superiority. How, then, has this situation arisen?

The present situation is the result of the American tendency toward self-delusion. Throughout the 1960s and 1970s, American intelligence analysts consistently underestimated Soviet military growth. The SALT process, regrettably, has contributed to this tendency by creating the illusion that a fundamentally new era in the strategic competition had arrived. By confronting the Soviets with the superiority of American strategic thought, of which the Soviets were presumably ignorant, we could convince them that further buildup of their strategic forces would be against their own interests.

At the initial sessions of SALT I in Helsinki, therefore, the U.S. delegation dwelt at length on the distinction between a zero-sum game, in which one side's gains are equal to the other side's losses, and a non-zero sum game, in which both sides can either win or lose. We argued that an agreement which provided essential equivalence, and which maintained or enhanced crisis stability, would add to the security of both sides, reduce the risk of nuclear war, do so at a reduced cost in resources, and thus be of mutual benefit.

The Soviet side did not accept this viewpoint. Soviet doctrine has always placed heavy emphasis upon what they call the "correlation of forces." In this term, they include the aggregate of all the forces bearing upon the situation—including psychological, political, and economic factors. Soviet officials took the view that the correlation of forces had been moving and would continue to move in their favor. They deduced from this the proposition that even though we might, at a given time, believe their proposals to be one-sided and inequitable, realism would eventually bring us to accept at least the substance of them.

This is, in fact, the way things have turned out. The net correlation of forces has been, and is, changing in their favor. Until this trend changes, the prospects for obtaining arms control agreements which would significantly relieve the strain upon the U.S. defense posture are less than good.

For the Soviet side to become persuaded to approach the negotiations from a non-zero-sum approach rather than from a zero-sum approach requires that there be an evident change in their view as to the probable evolution of the correlation of forces in the future. Since SALT II vindicates their approach, it places the United States in an unfavorable position from which to negotiate SALT III. Consequently, in order to provide the preconditions necessary for an agreement that satisfies American interests, ratification of SALT II should be withheld. The United States should first take appropriate steps to correct the problems I have mentioned, which would put it in a better position to negotiate a new and better SALT agreement.

*1 October 1979*

# APPENDIX

The following charts and graphs were prepared by Paul H. Nitze and distributed as appendices to the above statement.

## Appendix to Chapter 12

*Prepared by Paul H. Nitze*
*1 November 1977–8 November 1979*

### THE BALANCE IN NUMBERS OF
### STRATEGIC NUCLEAR LAUNCH VEHICLES (SNLVs)

| | 1977 | | June 18, 1979 | | Consistent with SALT II 1982 | | 1985 | |
|---|---|---|---|---|---|---|---|---|
| | U.S. | S.U. | U.S. | S.U.° | U.S. | S.U. | U.S. | S.U. |
| **ICBMs** | | | | | | | | |
| —MIRV | 550 | 82 | 550 | 608 | 550 | 820 | 536 | 820 |
| —Non-MIRV | 504 | 1,474 | 504 | 790 | 504 | 390 | 504 | 360 |
| TOTAL | 1,054 | 1,556 | 1,054 | 1,398 | 1,054 | 1,210 | 1,040 | 1,180 |
| **SLBMs** | | | | | | | | |
| —MIRV | 496 | 16 | 496 | 144 | 640 | 296 | 664 | 356 |
| —Non-MIRV | 160 | 776 | 160 | 806 | 160 | 680 | 80 | 620 |
| TOTAL | 656 | 792 | 656 | 950 | 800 | 976 | 744 | 976 |
| **HEAVY BOMBERS** | | | | | | | | |
| —Non-ALCM | 346* | 160 | 340* | 156 | 331 | 64 | 226 | 90 |
| —ALCM | | | | | | | | |
| Carriers | 0 | 0 | 3 | 0 | 15 | 0 | 120 | 0 |
| TOTAL | 346* | 160+ | 343* | 156+ | 346 | 64+ | 346 | 90+ |
| TOTAL SNDVs | 2,056* | 2,508+ | 2,053* | 2,504+ | 2,200 | 2,250+ | 2,130 | 2,246+ |

o  Figures are those given by Soviet Union in their data base for that date; not all of these systems are as yet operational.

*  Excludes 230 mothballed B-52s U.S. plans to scrap.

+  Excludes Soviet BACKFIRE bombers and succeeding tables exclude their armaments.

## THE BALANCE IN NUMBERS OF WARHEADS

| | 1977 | | June 18, 1979 | | Consistent with SALT II 1982 | | 1985 | |
|---|---|---|---|---|---|---|---|---|
| | U.S. | S.U. | U.S. | S.U. | U.S. | S.U. | U.S. | S.U. |
| **ICBMs** | | | | | | | | |
| —MIRV | 1,650 | 560 | 1,650 | 4,120 | 1,650 | 5,752 | 1,608 | 5,752 |
| —Non-MIRV | 504 | 2,584 | 504 | 1,700 | 504 | 970 | 504 | 480 |
| TOTAL | 2,154 | 3,144 | 2,154 | 5,820 | 2,154 | 6,722 | 2,112 | 6,232 |
| | | | | | | | | |
| **SLBMs** | | | | | | | | |
| —MIRV | 4,368 | 48 | 4,320 | 432 | 5,456 | 2,912 | 5,648 | 3,752 |
| —Non-MIRV | 480 | 1,320 | 480 | 1,350 | 480 | 1,080 | 240 | 1,324 |
| TOTAL | 4,848 | 1,368 | 4,800 | 1,782 | 5,936 | 3,992 | 5,888 | 5,076 |
| | | | | | | | | |
| **HEAVY BOMBERS (ALCMs, SRAMs, Gravity Bombs)** | | | | | | | | |
| TOTAL | 2,584 | 640 | 2,560 | 624 | 2,824 | 260 | 4,504 | 420 |
| TOTAL WARHEADS | 9,586 | 5,152 | 9,514 | 8,226 | 10,914 | 10,974 | 12,504 | 11,728 |

## THE BALANCE IN AREA DESTRUCTION POTENTIAL—EMT ($nY^{2/3}$)

| | 1977 | | June 18, 1979 | | Consistent with SALT II 1982 | | 1985 | |
|---|---|---|---|---|---|---|---|---|
| | U.S. | S.U. | U.S. | S.U. | U.S. | S.U. | U.S. | S.U. |
| **ICBMs** | | | | | | | | |
| —MIRV | 507 | 462 | 507 | 3,040 | 664 | 4,751 | 651 | 4,751 |
| —Non-MIRV | 741 | 4,115 | 741 | 1,956 | 741 | 1,155 | 741 | 1,934 |
| TOTAL | 1,248 | 4,587 | 1,248 | 4,997 | 1,406 | 5,906 | 1,393 | 6,686 |
| | | | | | | | | |
| **SLBMs** | | | | | | | | |
| —MIRV | 586 | 30 | 645 | 272 | 878 | 995 | 920 | 1,282 |
| —Non-MIRV | 174 | 1,015 | 174 | 997 | 174 | 855 | 87 | 933 |
| TOTAL | 760 | 1,046 | 820 | 1,269 | 1,053 | 1,851 | 1,007 | 2,216 |
| | | | | | | | | |
| **HEAVY BOMBERS (ALCMs, SRAMs, Gravity Bombs)** | | | | | | | | |
| TOTAL | 1,795 | 640 | 1,771 | 624 | 1,837 | 260 | 2,137 | 420 |
| TOTAL AREA DESTRUCTION | 3,370 | 6,160 | 3,839 | 6,890 | 4,297 | 8,018 | 4,538 | 9,322 |

NOTE: Decimal points not rounded off.

## THE BALANCE IN HARD TARGET KILL POTENTIAL—CMP ($nY^{2/3}/CEP^2$)

| | 1977 | | June 18, 1979 | | Consistent with SALT II 1982 | | 1985 | |
|---|---|---|---|---|---|---|---|---|
| | U.S. | S.U. | U.S. | S.U. | U.S. | S.U. | U.S. | S.U. |
| **ICBMs** | | | | | | | | |
| —MIRV | 22,539 | 10,464 | 22,539 | 105,194 | 46,175 | 211,169 | 45,279 | 211,169 |
| —Non-MIRV | 13,188 | 24,036 | 13,188 | 7,182 | 13,188 | 29,170 | 13,188 | 126,912 |
| TOTAL | 35,727 | 34,501 | 35,727 | 112,376 | 59,364 | 240,340 | 58,467 | 338,082 |
| **SLBMs** | | | | | | | | |
| —MIRV | 9,377 | 336 | 9,899 | 3,024 | 14,059 | 13,871 | 14,723 | 18,469 |
| —Non-MIRV | 697 | 3,040 | 697 | 2,968 | 697 | 2,702 | 348 | 2,254 |
| TOTAL | 10,074 | 3,376 | 10,597 | 5,992 | 14,757 | 16,574 | 15,072 | 20,724 |
| **TOTAL PROMPT CMP** | 45,801 | 37,877 | 46,324 | 118,368 | 74,121 | 256,914 | 73,539 | 358,806 |
| **HEAVY BOMBERS (ALCMs, SRAMs, Gravity Bombs)*** | | | | | | | | |
| **TOTAL DELAYED CMP** | 148,675 | 16,000 | 146,275 | 15,600 | 158,729 | 8,000 | 229,112 | 33,000 |
| TOTAL CMP | 194,477 | 53,877 | 192,599 | 133,968 | 232,851 | 264,914 | 302,652 | 391,806 |

* It should be noted that bomber CMP differs from missile CMP in that the former arrives in 6 to 10 hours in comparison to 10 to 40 minutes for the latter.

NOTE: Decimal points not rounded off.

## THE BALANCE IN MEGATONNAGE

| | 1977 | | June 18, 1979 | | Consistent with SALT II 1982 | | 1985 | |
|---|---|---|---|---|---|---|---|---|
| | U.S. | S.U. | U.S. | S.U. | U.S. | S.U. | U.S. | S.U. |
| **ICBMs** | | | | | | | | |
| —MIRV | 280 | 420 | 280 | 2,760 | 430 | 4,314 | 423 | 4,314 |
| —Non-MIRV | 1,026 | 7,326 | 1,026 | 3,297 | 1,026 | 1,935 | 1,026 | 4,590 |
| TOTAL | 1,306 | 7,746 | 1,306 | 6,057 | 1,456 | 6,249 | 1,449 | 8,904 |
| **SLBMs** | | | | | | | | |
| —MIRV | 220 | 24 | 241 | 216 | 364 | 582 | 383 | 750 |
| —Non-MIRV | 105 | 909 | 105 | 939 | 105 | 777 | 80 | 796 |
| TOTAL | 326 | 933 | 347 | 1,155 | 469 | 1,359 | 464 | 1,546 |
| **HEAVY BOMBERS (ALCMs, SRAMs, Gravity Bombs)** | | | | | | | | |
| TOTAL | 1,624 | 640 | 1,600 | 624 | 1,624 | 260 | 1,624 | 420 |
| **TOTAL MEGATONNAGE** | 3,256 | 9,319 | 3,253 | 7,836 | 3,550 | 7,868 | 3,537 | 10,870 |

NOTE: Decimal points not rounded off.

## THE BALANCE IN THROW-WEIGHT (M/lbs)

| | 1977 | | June 18, 1979 | | Consistent with SALT II 1982 | | 1985 | |
|---|---|---|---|---|---|---|---|---|
| | U.S. | S.U. | U.S. | S.U. | U.S. | S.U. | U.S. | S.U. |
| ICBMs | | | | | | | | |
| —MIRV | 1.32 | 2.82 | 1.32 | 6.23 | 1.32 | 8.82 | 1.29 | 8.82 |
| —Non-MIRV | 1.17 | 6.90 | 1.17 | 2.96 | 1.17 | 1.38 | 1.17 | 2.52 |
| TOTAL | 2.49 | 9.72 | 2.49 | 9.19 | 2.49 | 10.20 | 2.46 | 11.34 |
| SLBMs | | | | | | | | |
| —MIRV | 1.60 | 0.04 | 1.58 | 0.36 | 1.99 | 1.04 | 2.06 | 1.34 |
| —Non-MIRV | 0.18 | 1.29 | 0.18 | 1.35 | 0.18 | 1.15 | 0.09 | 1.05 |
| TOTAL | 1.78 | 1.33 | 1.76 | 1.71 | 2.17 | 2.19 | 2.15 | 2.39 |
| HEAVY BOMBERS | 3.32 | 1.23 | 3.26 | 1.25 | 3.32 | 0.51 | 3.32 | 0.72 |
| TOTAL TW (M/lbs) | 7.59 | 12.28 | 7.51 | 12.15 | 7.98 | 12.90 | 7.93 | 14.45 |

## U.S. SYSTEMS

| | MT/Warhead (y) | Nos/Warhead (n) | Total MT (yt) | EMT $(ny^{.666})$ | CEP (nmi) | CMP $(ny^{.666}/CEP^2)$ | TW (K/lbs) |
|---|---|---|---|---|---|---|---|
| Minuteman | 1.2 | 1 | 1.2 | 1.13 | .2 | 28.25 | 1.6 |
| Minuteman III (NS-20/MK12) | .17 | 3 | 0.51 | 0.922 | .15 | 40.98 | 2.4 |
| Minuteman III (INS-20/MK12) | .17 | 3 | 0.51 | 0.922 | .12 | 64.03 | 2.4 |
| Minuteman III (INS-20/MK12A) | .335 | 3 | 1.0 | 1.448 | .12 | 100.56 | 2.4 |
| Titan II | 9.0 | 1 | 9.0 | 4.32 | .7 | 8.82 | 8.3 |
| Polaris A-3 | .22 | 3 | .66 | 1.09 | .5 | 4.36 | 1.1 |
| Poseidon C-3 | .04 | Avg. 9 | .36 | 1.05 | .25 | 16.80 | 3.3 |
| Poseidon C-4 | .1 | 8 | .8 | 1.73 | .25 | 27.68 | 2.9 |
| Trident | .1 | 8 | .8 | 1.73 | .25 | 27.68 | 2.9 |
| B-52 (w/Gravity Bombs) | 1 | 4 | 4 | 4 | .1 | 400 | 9.6 |
| B-52 (w/ALCMs) | .2 | 20 | 4 | 6.85 | .08 | 1,070.31 | 9.6 |
| B-52 (w/SRAM+ Gravity Bombs) | .2+1 | 8+4=12 | 5.6 | 2.74+4=6.74 | .2/.1 | 68.5+400=468.5 | 9.6 |

USSR SYSTEMS

| System | MT/Warhead (y) | Nos/Warhead (n) | Total MT (yt) | EMT (ny.666) | CEP (nmi) | CMP (ny.666/CEP²) | TW (K/lbs) |
|---|---|---|---|---|---|---|---|
| SS-7/SS-8 | 3 | 1 | 3 | 2.08 | 1.0 | 2.08 | 4 |
| SS-9 | 20 | 1 | 20 | 7.35 | .5 | 29.4 | 13.5 |
| SS-9 MRV | 3.5 | 3 | 10.5 | 6.91 | 1 | 6.91 | 13.5 |
| SS-11 | 1.0 | 1 | 1 | 1.0 | 1 | 1.0 | 2 |
| SS-13 | .75 | 1 | .75 | .826 | 1 | .826 | 1 |
| SS-18 Single | 20 | 1 | 20 | 7.35 | .2 | 183.75 | 16 |
| SS-18 (1977) | .75 | 10 | 7.5 | 8.26 | .2 | 206.5 | 16 |
| SS-18 (6/18/79) | .75 | 10 | 7.5 | 8.26 | .17 | 285.81 | 16 |
| SS-18 (1982) | .75 | 10 | 7.5 | 8.26 | .15 | 367.1 | 16 |
| SS-18 (1985) | .75 | 10 | 7.5 | 8.26 | .12 | 573.61 | 16 |
| SS-19 (1977) | .75 | 6 | 4.5 | 4.96 | .2 | 124.0 | 8 |
| SS-19 (6/18/79) | .75 | 6 | 4.5 | 4.96 | .17 | 171.62 | 8 |
| SS-19 (1982) | .75 | 6 | 4.5 | 4.96 | .15 | 220.4 | 8 |
| SS-19 (1985) | .75 | 6 | 4.5 | 4.96 | .12 | 344.4 | 8 |
| SS-19/SS-17 | 15 | 1 | 15 | 6.07 | .2 | 151.75 | 7 |
| SS-17 (1977) | .75 | 4 | 3.0 | 3.3 | .2 | 82.5 | 7 |
| SS-17 (6/18/79) | .75 | 4 | 3.0 | 3.3 | .17 | 114.18 | 7 |
| SS-17 (1982) | .75 | 4 | 3.0 | 3.3 | .15 | 146.67 | 7 |
| SS-17 (1982) | .75 | 4 | 3.0 | 3.3 | .12 | 229.17 | 7 |
| New Missile (1982) | 15 | 1 | 15 | 6.07 | .15 | 269.78 | 8 |
| New Missile (1985) | 15 | 1 | 15 | 6.07 | .12 | 421.53 | 8 |
| SS-N-6 | 1.0 | 1 | 1.0 | 1.0 | .5 | 4.0 | 1.6 |
| SS-N-6 MRV | .5 | 3 | 1.5 | 1.89 | .75 | 3.36 | 1.6 |
| SS-N-8 | 1.0 | 1 | 1.0 | 1.0 | .5 | 4.00 | 1.8 |
| SS-NX-17 | .75 | 1 | .75 | .826 | .25 | 13.22 | 2 |
| SS-N-18 MIRV | .5 | 3 | 1.5 | 1.89 | .3 | 21.0 | 2.5 |
| SS-N-18 MIRV | .2 | 7 | 1.4 | 2.39 | .3 | 26.56 | 2.5 |
| New MIRV | .2 | 14 | 2.8 | 4.79 | .25 | 76.64 | 5 |
| BEAR/BISON | 1 | 4 | 4 | 4 | .2 | 100.00 | 8 |
| New Bomber | 1 | 5 | 5 | 5 | .1 | 500.00 | 8 |

## 1977—U.S./USSR ICBMs

| | NO. LAUNCHERS | NO. WARHEADS | TOTAL MT | EMT | CMP | TW |
|---|---|---|---|---|---|---|
| **U.S. ICBMs** | | | | | | |
| Titan | 54 | 54 | 486 | 233.3 | 476.3 | 448.2 |
| MM II | 450 | 450 | 540 | 508.5 | 12,712.5 | 720 |
| MM III (NS-20/MK12) | 550 | 1,650 | 280.5 | 507.1 | 22,539 | 1,320 |
| MIRV TOTAL | 550 | 1,650 | 280.5 | 507.1 | 22,539 | 1,320 |
| NON-MIRV TOTAL | 504 | 504 | 1,026 | 741.8 | 13,188.8 | 1,168.2 |
| TOTAL | 1,054 | 2,154 | 1,306.5 | 1,248.9 | 35,727.8 | 2,488.2 |
| **USSR ICBMs** | | | | | | |
| SS-7 | 139 | 139 | 417 | 289.12 | 289.12 | 556 |
| SS-8 | 19 | 19 | 57 | 39.52 | 39.52 | 76 |
| SS-9 (Single) | 164 | 164 | 3,280 | 1,205.4 | 4,821.6 | 2,214 |
| SS-9 (MRV) | 100 | 300 | 1,050 | 691 | 691 | 1,350 |
| SS-18 (Single) | 22 | 22 | 440 | 161.7 | 4,042.5 | 352 |
| SS-18 (MIRV) | 22 | 220 | 165 | 181.72 | 4,543 | 352 |
| SS-11 (Single) | 455 | 455 | 455 | 455 | 455 | 910 |
| SS-11 (MRV) | 455 | 1,365 | 682.5 | 859.95 | 3,439.8 | 910 |
| SS-17 (Single) | 10 | 10 | 150 | 60.7 | 1,517.5 | 70 |
| SS-17 (MIRV) | 10 | 40 | 30 | 33 | 825 | 70 |
| SS-19 (Single) | 50 | 50 | 750 | 303.5 | 7,587.5 | 400 |
| SS-19 (MIRV) | 50 | 300 | 225 | 248 | 6,200 | 400 |
| SS-13 | 60 | 60 | 45 | 49.56 | 49.56 | 60 |
| MIRV TOTAL | 82 | 560 | 420 | 462.72 | 10,464.8 | 822 |
| NON-MIRV TOTAL | 1,474 | 2,584 | 7,326.5 | 4,115.45 | 24,036.3 | 6,898 |
| TOTAL | 1,556 | 3,144 | 7,746.5 | 4,578.17 | 34,501.1 | 7,720 |

## 1977—U.S./USSR BOMBERS

| | NO. LAUNCHERS | NO. WARHEADS | TOTAL MT | EMT | CMP | TW |
|---|---|---|---|---|---|---|
| **U.S. BOMBERS** | | | | | | |
| B-52 (SRAMS Gravity Bombs) | 150 | 1,800 | 840 | 1,011 | 70,275 | 1,440 |
| B-52 (Gravity Bombs) | 196 | 784 | 784 | 784 | 78,400 | 1,881.6 |
| TOTAL | 346 | 2,584 | 1,624 | 1,795 | 148,675 | 3,321.6 |
| **USSR BOMBERS** | | | | | | |
| BEAR and BISON | 160 | 640 | 640 | 640 | 16,000 | 1,280 |

## 1977—U.S./USSR SLBMs

| | NO. LAUNCHERS | NO. WARHEADS | TOTAL MT | EMT | CMP | TW |
|---|---|---|---|---|---|---|
| U.S. SLBMs | | | | | | |
| Polaris A-3 | 160 | 480 | 105.6 | 174.4 | 697.6 | 176 |
| Poseidon C-3 | 400 | 3,600 | 144 | 420.8 | 6,720 | 1,320 |
| Poseidon C-4 | 96 | 768 | 76.8 | 166.08 | 2,657.28 | 278.4 |
| MIRV TOTAL | 496 | 4,368 | 220.8 | 586.08 | 9,377.28 | 1,598.4 |
| NON-MIRV TOTAL | 160 | 480 | 105.6 | 174.4 | 697.6 | 176 |
| TOTAL | 656 | 4,848 | 326.4 | 760.48 | 10,074.88 | 1,774.4 |
| USSR SLBMs | | | | | | |
| SS-N-6 (Single) | 272 | 272 | 272 | 272 | 1,088 | 435.2 |
| SS-N-6 (MRV) | 272 | 816 | 408 | 514.08 | 913.92 | 435.2 |
| SS-NX-17 | 12 | 12 | 9 | 9.91 | 158.64 | 24 |
| SS-N-8 | 220 | 220 | 220 | 220 | 880 | 396 |
| SS-N-18 (MIRV) | 16 | 48 | 24 | 30.24 | 336 | 40 |
| MIRV TOTAL | 16 | 48 | 24 | 30.24 | 336 | 40 |
| NON-MIRV TOTAL | 776 | 1,320 | 909 | 1,015.99 | 3,040.56 | 1,290.4 |
| TOTAL | 792 | 1,368 | 933 | 1,046.23 | 3,376.56 | 1,330.4 |

## JUNE 18, 1979—U.S./USSR ICBMs

| | NO. LAUNCHERS | NO. WARHEADS | TOTAL MT | EMT | CMP | TW |
|---|---|---|---|---|---|---|
| U.S. ICBMs | | | | | | |
| Titan | 54 | 54 | 486 | 233.3 | 476.3 | 448.2 |
| MM II | 450 | 450 | 540 | 508.5 | 12,712.5 | 720 |
| MM III (NS-20/MK12) | 550 | 1,650 | 280.5 | 507.1 | 22,539 | 1,320 |
| MIRV TOTAL | 550 | 1,650 | 280.5 | 507.1 | 22,539 | 1,320 |
| NON-MIRV TOTAL | 504 | 504 | 1,026 | 741.8 | 13,188.8 | 1,168.2 |
| TOTAL | 1,054 | 2,154 | 1,306.5 | 1,248.9 | 35,727.8 | 2,488.2 |
| USSR ICBMs | | | | | | |
| SS-9 (Single) | 120 | 120 | 2,400 | 882 | 3,528 | 1,620 |
| SS-18 (MIRV) | 188 | 1,880 | 1,080 | 1,189.44 | 41,155.2 | 3,008 |
| SS-11 (Single) | 215 | 215 | 215 | 215 | 215 | 430 |
| SS-11 (MRV) | 455 | 1,365 | 682.5 | 859.95 | 3,439.8 | 910 |
| SS-17 (MIRV) | 140 | 560 | 420 | 462 | 15,985.2 | 980 |
| SS-19 (MIRV) | 280 | 1,680 | 1,260 | 1,388.8 | 48,053.6 | 2,240 |
| MIRV TOTAL | 608 | 4,120 | 2,760 | 3,040.24 | 105,194 | 6,228 |
| NON-MIRV TOTAL | 790 | 1,700 | 3,297.5 | 1,956.95 | 7,182.8 | 2,960 |
| TOTAL | 1,398 | 5,820 | 6,057.5 | 4,997.19 | 112,376.8 | 9,188 |

## JUNE 18, 1979—U.S./USSR SLBMs

| | NO. LAUNCHERS | NO. WARHEADS | TOTAL MT | EMT | CMP | TW |
|---|---|---|---|---|---|---|
| **U.S. SLBMs** | | | | | | |
| Polaris A-3 | 160 | 480 | 105.6 | 174.4 | 697.6 | 176 |
| Poseidon C-3 | 352 | 3,168 | 126.72 | 396.6 | 5,913.6 | 1,161.6 |
| Poseidon C-4 | 144 | 1,152 | 115.2 | 249.12 | 3,985.92 | 417.6 |
| MIRV TOTAL | 496 | 4,320 | 241.92 | 645.72 | 9,899.52 | 1,579.2 |
| NON-MIRV TOTAL | 160 | 480 | 105.6 | 174.4 | 697.6 | 176 |
| TOTAL | 656 | 4,800 | 347.52 | 820.12 | 10,597.12 | 1,755.2 |
| **USSR SLBMs** | | | | | | |
| SS-N-6 (Single) | 254 | 254 | 254 | 254 | 1,016 | 406.4 |
| SS-N-6 (MRV) | 272 | 816 | 408 | 514.08 | 913.92 | 435.2 |
| SS-NX-17 | 12 | 12 | 9 | 9.91 | 158.64 | 24 |
| SS-N-8 | 268 | 268 | 268 | 220 | 880 | 482.4 |
| SS-N-18 | 144 | 432 | 216 | 272.16 | 3,024 | 360 |
| MIRV TOTAL | 144 | 432 | 216 | 272.16 | 3,024 | 360 |
| NON-MIRV TOTAL | 806 | 1,350 | 939 | 997.99 | 2,968.56 | 1,348 |
| TOTAL | 950 | 1,782 | 1,155 | 1,270.16 | 5,592.56 | 1,708 |

## JUNE 18, 1979—U.S./USSR BOMBERS

| | NO. LAUNCHERS | NO. WARHEADS | TOTAL MT | EMT | CMP | TW |
|---|---|---|---|---|---|---|
| **U.S. BOMBERS** | | | | | | |
| B-52 (SRAMS Gravity Bombs) | 150 | 1,800 | 840 | 1,011 | 70,275 | 1,440 |
| B-52 (Gravity Bombs) | 190 | 760 | 760 | 760 | 76,000 | 1,824 |
| ALCM Carriers | 3 | 0 | 0 | 0 | 0 | 0 |
| TOTAL | 343* | 2,560 | 1,600 | 1,771 | 146,275 | 3,264 |
| **USSR BOMBERS** | | | | | | |
| BEAR and BISON | 156 | 624 | 624 | 624 | 15,600 | 1,248 |

*Excludes 230 mothballed B-52s U.S. plans to scrap.

## 1982—U.S./USSR ICBMs

| | NO. LAUNCHERS | NO. WARHEADS | TOTAL MT | EMT | CMP | TW |
|---|---|---|---|---|---|---|
| U.S. ICBMs | | | | | | |
| Titan | 54 | 54 | 486 | 233.3 | 476.3 | 448.2 |
| MM II | 450 | 450 | 540 | 508.5 | 12,712.5 | 720 |
| MM III (INS-20/MK12A) | 300 | 900 | 303 | 434.4 | 30,168 | 720 |
| MM III (INS-20/MK12) | 250 | 750 | 127.5 | 230.5 | 16,007.5 | 600 |
| MIRV TOTAL | 550 | 1,650 | 430.5 | 664.9 | 46,175.5 | 1,320 |
| NON-MIRV TOTAL | 504 | 504 | 1,026 | 741.8 | 13,188.8 | 1,168.2 |
| TOTAL | 1,054 | 2,154 | 1,456.5 | 1,406.7 | 59,364.3 | 2,488.2 |
| USSR ICBMs | | | | | | |
| SS-11 (MRV) | 290 | 870 | 435 | 548.1 | 2,192.4 | 580 |
| SS-18 (MIRV) | 308 | 3,080 | 2,310 | 2,544.08 | 113,066.8 | 4,928 |
| SS-17 (MIRV) | 200 | 800 | 600 | 660 | 29,334 | 1,400 |
| SS-19 (MIRV) | 312 | 1,872 | 1,404 | 1,547.52 | 68,768.8 | 2,496 |
| New Missile (Single) | 100 | 100 | 1,500 | 607 | 26,978 | 800 |
| MIRV TOTAL | 820 | 5,752 | 4,314 | 4,751.6 | 211,169.6 | 8,824 |
| NON-MIRV TOTAL | 390 | 970 | 1,935 | 1,155.1 | 29,170.4 | 1,380 |
| TOTAL | 1,210 | 6,722 | 6,249 | 5,906.7 | 240,340 | 10,204 |

## 1982—U.S./USSR SLBMs

| | NO. LAUNCHERS | NO. WARHEADS | TOTAL MT | EMT | CMP | TW |
|---|---|---|---|---|---|---|
| U.S. SLBMs | | | | | | |
| Polaris A-3 | 160 | 480 | 105.6 | 174.4 | 697.6 | 176 |
| Poseidon C-3 | 336 | 3,024 | 120.96 | 352.8 | 5,644.8 | 1,108.8 |
| Poseidon C-4 | 160 | 1,280 | 128 | 276.8 | 4,428.8 | 464 |
| Trident C-4 | 144 | 1,152 | 115.2 | 249.12 | 3,985.92 | 417.6 |
| MIRV TOTAL | 640 | 5,456 | 364.16 | 878.72 | 14,059.52 | 1,990.4 |
| NON-MIRV TOTAL | 160 | 480 | 105.6 | 174.4 | 697.6 | 176 |
| TOTAL | 800 | 5,936 | 469.76 | 1,053.12 | 14,757.12 | 2,166.4 |
| USSR SLBMs | | | | | | |
| SS-N-6 (Single) | 200 | 200 | 200 | 200 | 800 | 320 |
| SS-N-6 (MRV) | 200 | 600 | 300 | 378 | 672 | 320 |
| SS-NX-17 | 12 | 12 | 9 | 9.91 | 158.64 | 24 |
| SS-N-8 | 268 | 268 | 268 | 268 | 1,072 | 482.4 |
| SS-N-18 | 176 | 1,232 | 246.4 | 420.64 | 4,674.56 | 440 |
| New MIRV | 120 | 1,680 | 336 | 574.8 | 9,196.8 | 600 |
| MIRV TOTAL | 296 | 2,912 | 582.4 | 995.44 | 13,871.36 | 1,040 |
| NON-MIRV TOTAL | 680 | 1,080 | 777 | 855.91 | 2,702.64 | 1,146.4 |
| TOTAL | 976 | 3,992 | 1,359.4 | 1,851.35 | 16,574 | 2,186.4 |

## 1982—U.S./USSR BOMBERS

| | NO. LAUNCHERS | NO. WARHEADS | TOTAL MT | EMT | CMP | TW |
|---|---|---|---|---|---|---|
| U.S. BOMBERS | | | | | | |
| B-52 (SRAMS | | | | | | |
| Gravity Bombs) | 150 | 1,800 | 840 | 1,011 | 70,275 | 1,440 |
| B-52 (w/ALCMs) | 15 | 300 | 60 | 102.75 | 16,054.65 | 144 |
| B-52 (Gravity | | | | | | |
| Bombs) | 181 | 724 | 724 | 724 | 72,400 | 1,737.6 |
| MIRV TOTAL | 15 | 300 | 60 | 102.75 | 16,054.65 | 144 |
| NON-MIRV TOTAL | 331 | 2,524 | 1,564 | 1,735 | 142,675 | 3,177.6 |
| TOTAL | 346 | 2,824 | 1,624 | 1,837.75 | 158,729.65 | 3,321.6 |
| USSR BOMBERS | | | | | | |
| BEAR | 60 | 240 | 240 | 240 | 6,000 | 480 |
| New Bomber | 4 | 20 | 20 | 20 | 2,000 | 32 |
| TOTAL | 64 | 260 | 260 | 260 | 8,000 | 512 |

## 1985—U.S./USSR ICBMs

| | NO. LAUNCHERS | NO. WARHEADS | TOTAL MT | EMT | CMP | TW |
|---|---|---|---|---|---|---|
| U.S. ICBMs | | | | | | |
| Titan | 54 | 54 | 486 | 233.3 | 476.3 | 448.2 |
| MM II | 450 | 450 | 540 | 508.5 | 12,712.5 | 720 |
| MM III | | | | | | |
| (INS-20/MK12A) | 300 | 900 | 303 | 434.4 | 30,168 | 720 |
| MM III | | | | | | |
| (INS-20/MK12) | 236 | 708 | 120.36 | 217.59 | 15,111.08 | 566.4 |
| MIRV TOTAL | 536 | 1,608 | 423.36 | 651.99 | 45,279.08 | 1,286.4 |
| NON-MIRV TOTAL | 504 | 504 | 1,026 | 741.8 | 13,188.8 | 1,168.2 |
| TOTAL | 1,040 | 2,112 | 1,449.36 | 1,393.79 | 58,467.88 | 2,454.6 |
| USSR ICBMs | | | | | | |
| SS-11 (MRV) | 60 | 180 | 90 | 113.4 | 453.6 | 120 |
| SS-18 (MIRV) | 308 | 3,080 | 2,310 | 2,544.08 | 113,066.8 | 4,928 |
| SS-17 (MIRV) | 200 | 800 | 600 | 660 | 29,334 | 1,400 |
| SS-19 (MIRV) | 312 | 1,872 | 1,404 | 1,547.52 | 68,768.8 | 2,496 |
| New Missile | | | | | | |
| (Single) | 300 | 300 | 4,500 | 1,821 | 126,459 | 2,400 |
| MIRV TOTAL | 820 | 5,752 | 4,314 | 4,751.60 | 211,169.6 | 8,824 |
| NON-MIRV TOTAL | 360 | 480 | 4,590 | 1,934.4 | 126,912.6 | 2,520 |
| TOTAL | 1,180 | 6,232 | 8,904 | 6,686 | 338,082.2 | 11,344 |

## 1985—U.S./USSR SLBMs

|  | NO. LAUNCHERS | NO. WARHEADS | TOTAL MT | EMT | CMP | TW |
|---|---|---|---|---|---|---|
| U.S. SLBMs |  |  |  |  |  |  |
| Polaris A-3 | 80 | 240 | 80.66 | 87.2 | 348.8 | 88 |
| Poseidon C-3 | 336 | 3,024 | 120.96 | 352.8 | 5,644.8 | 1,108.8 |
| Poseidon C-4 | 160 | 1,280 | 128 | 276.8 | 4,428.8 | 464 |
| Trident C-4 | 168 | 1,344 | 134.4 | 290.64 | 4,650.24 | 487.2 |
| MIRV TOTAL | 664 | 5,648 | 383.36 | 920.24 | 14,723.84 | 2,060 |
| NON-MIRV TOTAL | 80 | 240 | 80.66 | 87.2 | 348.8 | 88 |
| TOTAL | 774 | 5,888 | 464.02 | 1,007.44 | 15,072.64 | 2,148 |
| USSR SLBMs |  |  |  |  |  |  |
| SS-N-6 (MRV) | 352 | 1,056 | 528 | 665.28 | 1,182.72 | 563.2 |
| SS-N-8 | 268 | 268 | 268 | 268 | 1,072 | 482.4 |
| SS-N-18 | 176 | 1,232 | 246.4 | 420.64 | 4,674.56 | 440 |
| New MIRV | 180 | 2,520 | 504 | 862.2 | 13,795.2 | 900 |
| MIRV TOTAL | 356 | 3,752 | 750.4 | 1,282.84 | 18,469.76 | 1,340 |
| NON-MIRV TOTAL | 620 | 1,324 | 796 | 933.28 | 2,254.72 | 1,045.6 |
| TOTAL | 976 | 5,076 | 1,546.4 | 2,216.12 | 20,724.48 | 2,385.6 |

## 1985—U.S./USSR BOMBERS

|  | NO. LAUNCHERS | NO. WARHEADS | TOTAL MT | EMT | CMP | TW |
|---|---|---|---|---|---|---|
| U.S. BOMBERS |  |  |  |  |  |  |
| B-52 (SRAM Gravity Bombs) | 150 | 1,800 | 840 | 1,011 | 70,275 | 1,440 |
| B-52 (w/ALCMs) | 120 | 2,400 | 480 | 822 | 128,437.2 | 1,152 |
| B-52 (Gravity Bombs) | 76 | 304 | 304 | 304 | 30,400 | 729.6 |
| MIRV TOTAL | 120 | 2,400 | 480 | 822 | 128,437.2 | 1,152 |
| NON-MIRV TOTAL | 226 | 2,104 | 1,144 | 1,315 | 100,675 | 2,169.6 |
| TOTAL | 346 | 4,504 | 1,624 | 2,137 | 229,112.2 | 3,321.6 |
| USSR BOMBERS |  |  |  |  |  |  |
| BEAR | 30 | 120 | 120 | 120 | 3,000 | 240 |
| New Bomber | 60 | 300 | 300 | 300 | 30,000 | 480 |
| TOTAL | 90 | 420 | 420 | 420 | 33,000 | 720 |

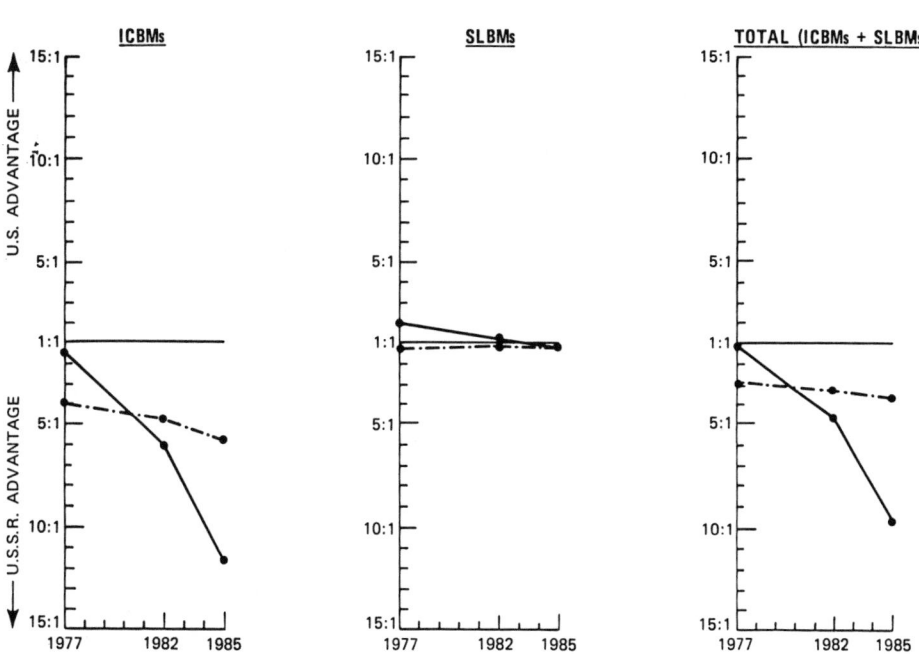

FIGURE 1. The Balance - Consequences of Current SALT Proposals: Time Urgent Counter-Military and Soft Target Destruction Potential

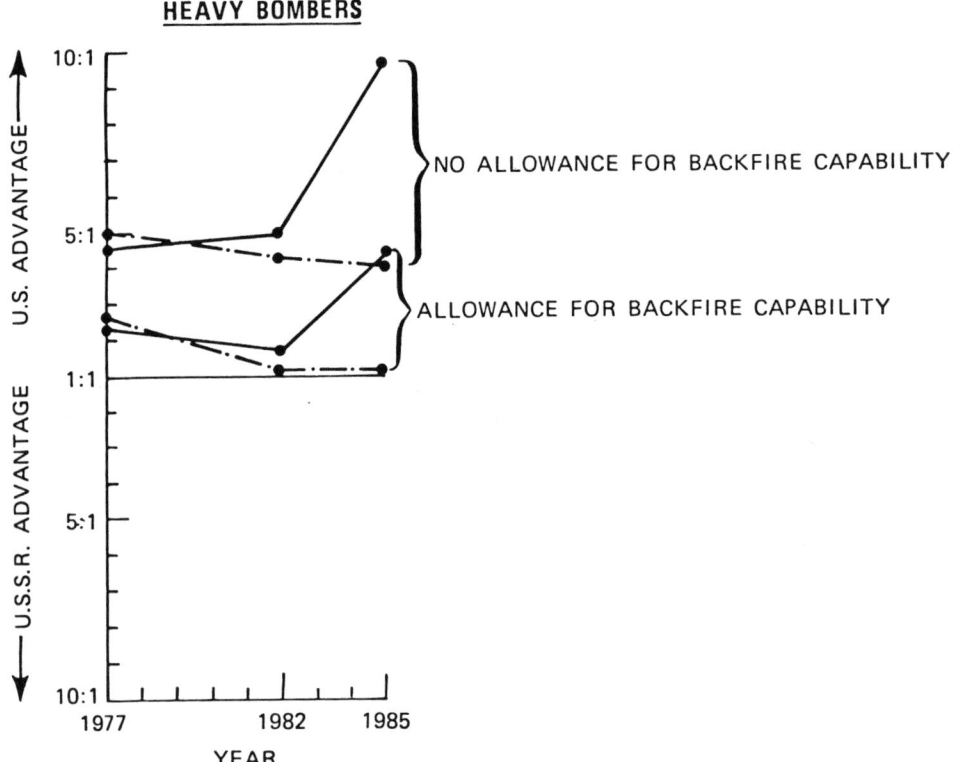

THIS FIGURE ASSUMES THE U.S. PROGRESSIVELY EQUIPS 120 B-52s EACH WITH
20 ALCMs OF HIGH ACCURACY.  IT INCLUDES NO ALLOWANCE FOR THE POTENTIAL
OF AIR DEFENSES.  IT ALSO INCLUDES NO ALLOWANCE FOR THE POSSIBLE DEPLOYMENT
ON BACKFIRE OF CRUISE MISSILES WITH LESS THAN 600 KM RANGE THAT INCORPORATES
THE TECHNOLOGY OF CURRENT SOVIET DEVELOPMENTAL PROGRAMS.

FIGURE 2. The Balance - Consequences of Current SALT Proposals: Delayed Counter-Military and Soft
Target Destruction Potential

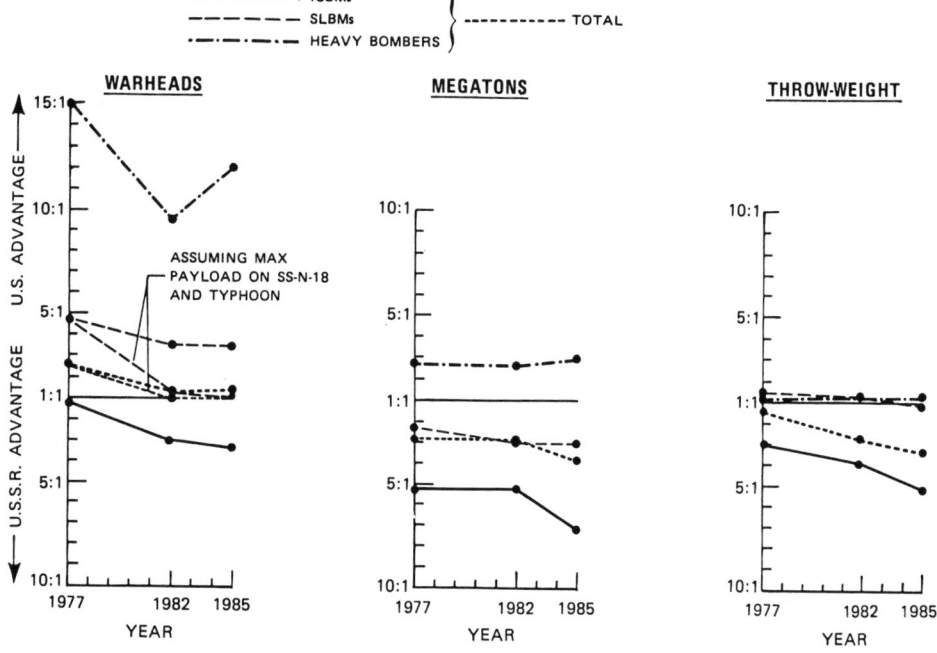

FIGURE 3. The Balance - Consequences of Current SALT Proposals: Warhead, Megatonnage and Throw-Weight

Table 1. Comparison of Calculations in Figures 1, 2, & 3
with Sec Def Brown's Figures in FY 1978 Budget Amendment Testimony, Table 2

| | Static Measures of Strategic Balance (U.S. as % of Soviet) | | | |
|---|---|---|---|---|
| | BROWN'S | | FIGURES 1, 2, & 3 | |
| | 1977 | 1986 (B-52/CM) | 1977 | 1985 (B-52/CM) |
| WARHEADS | 240% | 126% | 249% | 149% |
| MEGATONS | 35% | 25% | 36% | 27% |
| THROW-WEIGHT | 75% | 48% | 68% | 47% |
| COUNTER-MILITARY POTENTIAL | 160% | 67% | 165% | 67% |

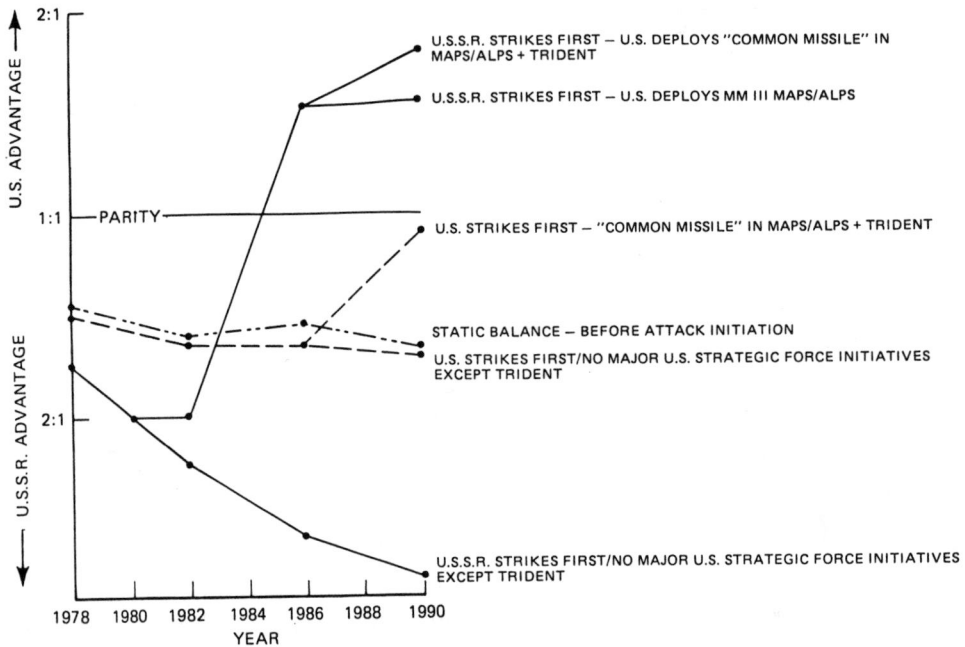

THIS FIGURE DOES NOT INCLUDE ALLOWANCES FOR BACKFIRE CAPABILITY

FIGURE 4. Consequences of Current SALT Proposals: Comparison of Residual Equivalent Megatons After a Counterforce Strike

# 13

# Is SALT II a Fair Deal for the United States?

*Paul H. Nitze*

The President tells us, I believe correctly, that the issues surrounding SALT II are the most important facing this country. Those issues include the basic thrust and direction of our foreign policy, the evolving conventional and nuclear military balance, our defense programs and budgets, and the relationship of SALT II to those issues.

Let me begin with the conventional military balance, the strategic nuclear balance, and SALT II.

## THE CONVENTIONAL AND THE STRATEGIC BALANCE

At all times since World War II the Soviet Union has had superior conventional forces on the European central front and on its northern and southern flanks. This has been due, in part, to geography, the USSR enjoying the central position and interior lines, and, in part, to the greater effort of the Warsaw Pact nations.

In the years up to the early 1950s this Soviet conventional superiority was offset by the U.S. nuclear monopoly. Later NATO's conventional deficiency was in large measure offset by U.S. theater nuclear weapons. Today the U.S. theater nuclear superiority has disappeared, and it has proved necessary to assign a number of our Poseidon submarines to cover targets of interest to European NATO. As the Soviets deploy increasing numbers of SS-20 MIRVed missiles, Backfire, and other high performance theater bombers, more of our surviving strategic nuclear forces will be needed for theater missions.

For most of the post-World War II era the U.S. Navy has enjoyed unchallenged control of the seas. This assured that we could project our power, wherever needed, on the periphery of the Eurasian landmass. The Soviet Union, together with its associates, is on the way to developing such a capability. Even now Soviet intermediate-range nuclear weapons, such as the SS-20s and the Backfires, provide an umbrella arching out some two to three thousand miles from the Soviet borders over Europe, the Middle East, South Asia, China, and the bordering seas.

The prudence, and therefore the likelihood, of either the Soviet Union or the United States using conventional or theater nuclear weapons, even in connection with an issue not directly involving the territory of the other, is importantly affected by the confidence

---

The author, Paul H. Nitze, is Chairman, Policy Studies, of the Committee on the Present Danger.

it has in the quality of its strategic intercontinental nuclear forces relative to those of the other side.

The Soviet ruling group has a full understanding of the potential destructiveness of nuclear weapons. Otherwise, they would not have demanded such enormous sacrifices from their population to create their huge military machine. Nor would they have persisted year after year in a civil defense program twenty times as elaborate and costly as ours. The Soviet rulers do not want nuclear war. They believe the best way to avoid a nuclear war and still achieve their objectives is to have overwhelming superiority. As von Clausewitz, the famous military strategist, put it, the aggressor never wants war; he would prefer to enter your country unopposed.

But the Soviet Union does propose that no important decisions be made in the world without its aims and ambitions being taken fully into account. And beyond that, much of what they say to internal audiences within Russia, and what they do, is consistent with an aspiration to world hegemony.

## SOVIET GLOBAL STRATEGY

For many years the focus of Soviet strategy has been on Western Europe. By achieving dominance over the Middle East, they aim to outflank Europe. They propose to outflank the Middle East by achieving controlling positions in Afghanistan, Iran, and Iraq on one side, South and North Yemen, Eritrea, Ethiopia, and Mozambique on the other, and by achieving the neutrality of Turkey to the north. Concurrently, they are attempting to encircle China by pressure on Pakistan and India, by alliance with Vietnam, and dominance over North Korea. The United States is the only power in a position potentially to frustrate these aims. It is therefore seen as the principal enemy.

In seeking each specific objective within their global policy, the Soviet rulers use the lowest level of pressure or of violence necessary and sufficient to achieve that objective. The purpose of their capabilities at the higher levels of potential violence, all the way up to intercontinental nuclear war, is to deter, and if necessary control, escalation by us to such higher levels.

It is a copybook principle in strategy that, in actual war, advantage tends to go to the side in a better position to raise the stakes by expanding the scope, duration or destructive intensity of the conflict. By the same token, at junctures of high contention short of war, the side better able to cope with the potential consequences of raising the stakes has the advantage. The other side is the one under greater pressure to scramble for a peaceful way out. To have the advantage at the utmost level of violence helps at every lesser level. In the Korean war, the Berlin blockades, and the Cuban missile crisis the United States had the ultimate edge because of our superiority at the strategic nuclear level. That edge has slipped away.

These circumstances form a background for understanding the stakes in SALT II. In broad terms the U.S. aim has been to arrange a standoff so as to neutralize the strategic nuclear threat overhanging superpower rivalry. The Soviet Union's contrasting aim has been and is to take over and nail down the advantage which the U.S. has appeared willing to relinquish.

## WHAT WE WANTED IN SALT II

Our aim, when we began the SALT II negotiations six years ago, was a treaty of indefinite duration, to parallel the ABM Treaty, and with these objectives:

• Limits on offensive nuclear capabilities equal for both sides.

- Terms assuring "crisis stability," that is, a situation where, in a crisis threatening war, there would be no significant advantage to the side striking first, preempting, or launching from under indications of attack.
- Limits calling for, or consistent with, true reduction in offensive nuclear armaments and their capabilities and in related expenditures.
- The limits should be verifiable; they should meet the legitimate concerns of our allies; they should be low enough to be economically and politically feasible for the United States to attain.
- In sum, the agreements should be such as to reduce the risks of nuclear war and the weight of nuclear armaments on world politics.
- Finally, for there to be a valid agreement, the terms must be acceptable both to the Soviet leadership and to two-thirds of the United States Senate—the necessary requirement for a valid agreement.

For reasons to be considered below, the SALT II terms, now all but finally agreed, meet none of these original objectives, except perhaps the last.

## U.S. CASUALTIES IN THE NEGOTIATIONS

The first negotiating casualty, abandoned in 1974, was the hope for a treaty of indefinite duration paralleling the ABM Treaty. We settled in 1974 for a short-term pact to end in 1985—a time when the strategic relationship between the two sides is likely to be far less favorable to the United States than it was in 1974.

The second casualty was equality. Notwithstanding the equal limits of 2,400—and later 2,250—on strategic nuclear delivery vehicles, and of 820 on MIRVed ICBM launchers, neither the actuality of equality nor the appearance, if one takes a second look, is preserved. To illustrate:

- Within the permitted number of ICBM launchers, the Soviet Union is permitted more than 300 very large ICBMs of the latest type. Our side none.
- It will be impossible for the U.S. to have more than 550 MIRVed ICBM launchers at the time the treaty lapses and probably fewer. The Soviet side almost certainly will have deployed its full 820 by 1985—probably by 1982.
- We will have no more than three warheads on each of our MIRVed ICBMs. The Soviet Union is permitted and is expected to have deployed four, six, and ten warheads on each of its SS-17s, -19s, and -18s, respectively. The U.S. will be permitted to test a new ICBM missile with up to ten warheads during the period of the treaty. However, we will almost certainly not be able to deploy such a missile within that time period.
- The Soviet Backfire bombers, and comparable U.S. bombers, will be exempt from the count of strategic launchers. The USSR will have 300 to 400 Backfire bombers by 1985. Our side will have no similar planes by 1985; our FB-111s are less proficient and much less numerous.

The third casualty, and the most worrisome, is "crisis stability." Over the past fifteen years it would not have profited either side to attack first. It would have required the use of more ICBMs by the attacking side than the attack could have destroyed. By the early 1980s that situation will have changed. By that time, the Soviet Union will be in a position to destroy 90 percent of our ICBMs with an expenditure of a fifth to a third of its ICBMs. Even if one assumes the survival of most of our bombers on alert for sufficient time to launch an immediate response, and the survival of our submarines at sea for a much longer time, our remaining forces after a Soviet initial counterforce attack would be strategically outmatched by the Soviet Union's retained war-making capability.

The fourth casualty has been true reductions. Although the number of Soviet launchers will decline from around 2,500 to 2,250 during the term of the treaty, the more significant indices of nuclear power will rise dramatically on the Soviet side, and to a lesser extent on our side as well. From the beginning of 1978 to the end of 1985, the number of Soviet warheads will have doubled; ours will have increased by a half. The area destructive capabilities of Soviet weapons will have increased by a half; ours by a quarter. The capability of their weapons to knock out hardened targets, such as missile silos, will have increased tenfold; even if our cruise missiles, still under development, fulfill present expectations, our capability will have increased fourfold.

By 1985, under the limits of SALT II and taking into account the current programs of the two sides, it will be virtually impossible for the United States to avoid a situation in which our prompt counterforce capability against hardened military targets (silos; command, control, and communications centers; storage depots; and shelters for leadership personnel; etc.) will be an eighth that of the Soviet Union or even less. This will be compounded by the fact that they will have twice as many hard targets as we, and their targets will be, on average, twice as hard as ours.

## SALT II: A BAD BARGAIN

Even the sponsors of SALT II do not anticipate that SALT II will warrant a reduction in our expenditures on nuclear forces, or that the Soviets will reduce theirs.

A bad agreement does not cease to be a bad agreement by being wholly verifiable. But SALT II is not only a bad agreement, it is also far from being verifiable. Even before the loss of our key monitoring facilities in Iran and the compromise of our KH-11 satellite through Soviet espionage, we did not have the ability to verify Soviet compliance with important provisions of the treaty. Now our ability has been significantly weakened. The problem of verification is further confounded by imprecise definitions used in the treaty and by the absence of definition with respect to certain important terms.

I believe SALT II, as now envisaged, will not reduce the risks of war. On the contrary, it can increase the risks of war if it reinforces the judgment that we are militarily stronger than the USSR at a time when we are not. War and defeat can arise from just such gross misjudgments of relative military capabilities by the weaker of two opposing powers.

A more sober evaluation of the balance, at a time when it is too late to reverse trends, could result in forced accommodation to the Soviet Union leading to a situation of global retreat and Finlandization.

Our budgeted direct expenditures on strategic nuclear forces are now about $10 billion a year. In the six years from 1956–1962 they averaged approximately $30 billion a year in today's dollars. We simply cannot reverse present adverse trends with currently projected programs and expenditures.

I hope the upcoming SALT debate will provide a much more solid basis of understanding in the public mind of what is happening to the political-military balance and what is necessary to reverse current trends. Only in light of such an understanding can the public and the Congress wisely judge what to do about SALT II.

## HOW THE ADMINISTRATION WILL TRY TO SELL SALT II

What will be the Executive Branch's main lines of support for ratification of the SALT II agreements by the Senate in that debate?

## 1. Prospects for SALT III, IV, V, etc.

One line may very well go as follows. First they will argue that everyone should be, and almost every one is, in favor of the concept of "arms control." Then they will say that even though the SALT II agreements may be imperfect, they represent a start at controlling the offensive nuclear arms of both sides; that they begin a process of reductions in nuclear arms; that what is important is the process of negotiation. Finally, they will contend that the process opens up a prospect for SALT III, SALT IV, SALT V, and so on. In other words, they will argue that SALT II should not be judged on its intrinsic merit but rather on one's approbation for the concept of arms control and on one's hope for the long-run outcome of negotiations associated with that concept.

The initial point in this line of argument is correct. Almost everyone is, and I believe should be, in favor of the concept of arms control and of negotiations directed to that end. But to be for the concept is not necessarily to be for a specific agreement, in particular to be for SALT II. To favor the institution of marriage is not to wish to be married to the Wicked Witch of the West.

SALT II does make a start at controlling offensive strategic nuclear arms. But is it a good start? It limits the wrong things. The limits are imprecisely defined. They are too high—they are so high as to have nothing to do with effective arms control. Even Senators McGovern, Hatfield, and Proxmire tell us they intend to vote against SALT II because it isn't arms control.

The reductions called for are in the number of deployed launchers, not in missiles or warheads or in their effectiveness. Under SALT II, as pointed out earlier, the capability of Soviet missiles to destroy hardened military targets is expected to rise by 1,000 percent. With such a precedent what should we expect from SALT III?

One of my colleagues tells me that as a young man he bought a suit from the local haberdasher for $29.50. The haberdasher explained that the suit was so cheap because the manufacturer lost money on every suit he sold; he was only able to stay in business because he sold so many. On that theory think of what great shape we should be in as we go on from SALT II to SALT III, SALT IV, and SALT V.

The SALT negotiations have now been going on for ten years. Therefore, it is possible to examine the historical record and have some judgment as to the nature of the process and the factors that drive the outcome.

Several points emerge. The first is a difference of approach to the negotiations. The purposes of the two sides were discrepant from the outset. We wished for equal limitations designed to diminish the impact of nuclear weapons upon world politics. The Soviet side viewed the negotiations as an engagement between adversaries. The Soviet task was to achieve the right to that nuclear predominance which we appeared willing to relinquish.

Again, as my colleague puts it: "Our side yearns for even outcomes. The other side is determined on drawing ahead. Our side thinks it is in a Maypole dance. The Russians are playing tug of war."

Related to our discrepant purposes have been our discrepant programs. We thought it wise to exercise restraint in our nuclear programs, hoping that such restraint would demonstrate our good will and might lead to reciprocal restraint on the other side. Our restraint turned out to be unilateral.

Senator Tower went to Geneva to participate with our delegation in the negotiations for a few days. He arrived shortly after the President had announced his decision to cancel the B-1. Senator Tower asked Academician Shchukin, the most able and distinguished member of the Soviet Delegation, what the Soviet side would do to reciprocate for our cancellation of the B-1. Mr. Shchukin replied: "You misunderstand us. We are not pacifists nor are we philanthropists." I am sure Mr. Shchukin had in mind a third point but was too polite to make it. "Nor are we fools."

The result has been that the United States has only one new missile in engineering development, the Trident I missile. The Soviet Union has progressed with whole families of new ICBMs, SLBMs, and bombers. While our strategic weapons program has been shrinking, theirs has been rapidly expanding. As a result, the pressure has been heavy on the U.S. negotiators to make concessions to get an agreement promptly. Every delay meant a deterioration in our trading position. A delay of a few months or even years did not worry the Soviet side. They were confident that as time passed the strategic balance would move further in their favor and thus improve their underlying trading position. As Henry Kissinger put it, "our negotiating position was hardly brilliant."

These considerations bear upon the prospects for SALT III. Unless we promptly act to reverse current trends, the strategic power realities reflected in the SALT III negotiations will be even more unfavorable to us than those which have been reflected in the SALT II negotiations.

## 2. Phantom U.S. Military Superiority

Another of the Executive Branch's lines of support for ratification of the SALT II agreements will be quite different. The President has asserted, contrary to all the evidence, that the United States is "much stronger militarily than the Soviet Union and will remain so during our lifetimes." He has made that statement without qualification. Sometimes he links it to the statement that we are stronger economically which indeed we are. But each military service was directed not to propose an increase in its expenditures over the next five years of more than 3 percent annually, assuming a 6 percent inflation rate. Since the real inflation rate is at least 9 percent, this would amount to no growth at all, in contrast to the 4 to 5 percent annual growth rate for Soviet expenditures, which are already some 40 percent greater than ours. This is an Alice in Wonderland approach to meeting the Soviet threat.

## 3. False Reading of Public Attitudes

A third line of support for ratification of the SALT II agreement is the claim that a vast majority of the American people favor it. Last February *The Washington Post* published an article with the headline, "81% in U.S. Back New SALT in Poll." Some of us wondered what the question was that evoked that favorable response. When we obtained the actual question, we found that SALT II was not even mentioned; the question asked: "Do you favor or oppose a new agreement between the United States and Russia which would limit nuclear weapons?" Who wouldn't be for that?

Subsequently, the Committee on the Present Danger conducted a poll, the first question of which differed only in being more specific. It asked: "The United States is now negotiating a strategic arms agreement with the Soviet Union in what is known as SALT II. What is your opinion on these negotiations?" Only 8.3 percent strongly supported SALT II and only another 11.7 percent said that although SALT II is somewhat disappointing, on balance they would have to support it. Later the Associated Press asked a similar question in a follow-up poll and got a similar result. Both polls demonstrate that, though most people support the concept of arms control, they do not know enough about SALT II to have any firm opinion about it. When the people are informed as to some of the important provisions and probable consequences of the SALT II treaty, opposition becomes overwhelming. It therefore appears that this third line of support has no more intrinsic merit than the other two.

## 4. The SALT Sellers' Campaign

The final line of support will be to mobilize, centrally direct, and integrate the full power of the Executive Branch in speeches, articles, Congressional testimony, and television appearances in support of the President's position. Each Cabinet member and Agency head will be under orders to explain why SALT II is essential from his Agency's point of view. Even the military will be under pressure to speak in favor of SALT II or to submit their resignations. This effort will find expression in a host of diverse, and often misleading, arguments. We have seen the beginnings of this campaign in the recent efforts of Secretaries Vance and Brown.

The force of this campaign will be great indeed. I believe, however, that the merits of the case are clear and that on an issue of this magnitude the Senate will act with care and with wisdom.

*16 May 1979*

# 14

# WHY THE SOVIET UNION WANTS SALT II

*Richard Pipes*

My purpose is to explain Soviet attitudes on nuclear weapons, the prospect of nuclear war, and arms limitation. My paper bears on several related questions: why do the Russians insist on the right to the exclusive possession of modern heavy missiles? Why do they demand the Protocol and the "non-circumvention" clause? Why do they make so much of all those things which, we are told by the advocates of SALT II, have no military value and, if conceded, would not in the least affect U.S. security?

In dealing with my subject I shall draw on Soviet military literature as well as on what we know of Soviet strategic deployments, reinforcing both sources of information with references to Soviet history and politics. It clearly is essential to try to understand Soviet behavior as a reflection of Soviet traditions, values, and aspirations—matters generally overlooked by the more zealous advocates of the Treaty.

## THE SOVIET MILITARY STATE

From its inception the Soviet regime has placed great reliance on military instrumentalities both to ensure its internal security and advance its external goals. Russia is an inherently poor country, and, by depriving the population of meaningful incentives, the Communist system guarantees that it remains poor. At the same time, however, the Communist system, which places the country's entire human and economic resources in the hands of a self-perpetuating elite of rulers, is excellently adapted for purposes of military mobilization. Such power as the Soviet Union enjoys in the world today is due almost exclusively to its military might. In a world from which all weapons would be banned, the USSR would at once become a second-rate power since it possesses neither the level of civilization nor the material wealth to qualify as a nation of the first rank. Contrary to some of the sentiments expressed in the debate over SALT II, there is no contradiction between Soviet Russia's low living standards and her willingness to commit immense funds for armaments. The Soviet military drive is in fact a natural corollary to

The author, Dr. Richard Pipes, is a member of the Executive Committee of the Committee on the Present Danger. He is Frank B. Baird, Jr., Professor of History at Harvard University and was formerly Director of Harvard's Russian Research Institute (1968–73). In 1976, Dr. Pipes served as the Chairman of the now famous Team B Competitive National Estimate Committee which surveyed Soviet strategic objectives. This current paper was used as the basis for Dr. Pipes' testimony before the Senate Foreign Relations Committee in July 1979.

endemic poverty. These economic factors making for militarism are reinforced by an ideology which views the modern age as the time of a life-or-death struggle between "capitalism" and "socialism." Militarism is the very essence of the Communist mentality. It has aptly been said that Lenin put Clausewitz on his head by transforming politics into the waging of war by other means.

## SOVIET NUCLEAR STRATEGY

When nuclear weapons first made their appearance, the Soviet government found itself in a quandary. It realized their potential importance early enough. As we now know, Stalin had a research program to construct atomic weapons underway at the outbreak of World War II. The United States, however, forged ahead. Hence for some time a tendency prevailed in the Soviet Union to denigrate the effectiveness of these new weapons. Immediately after Stalin's death a keen debate, in which the professional military played a commanding role, developed in Russia on this subject. The conclusion—reached sometime in the late 1950s and signaled by the establishment of the Strategic Rocket Forces as a separate, fourth branch of the armed services—was that nuclear weapons had indeed become the decisive weapons of modern warfare. That conclusion was the very opposite to the one reached more or less concurrently by the United States civilian strategists.

Soviet nuclear strategy, in correlation with Soviet political purposes, is internally consistent and intellectually impressive—at any rate, to anyone who is not **a priori** convinced that the Russian military have nothing to teach us. It rests on several related propositions.

1. The combination of nuclear warheads and intercontinental delivery vehicles has revolutionized warfare in the sense that henceforth the ultimate strategic objective— incapacitating the enemy's military forces—can be attained directly and immediately rather than gradually, by means of many separate operations.
2. The traditional principles of the science of war remain fully intact: the advantages of preemption, of superior quantity and quality, of good defenses, and so forth remain as valid in the nuclear age as they were in the gunpowder era.
3. Even under the most auspicious circumstances, however, the destructive potential of nuclear weapons is so enormous that great-power conflict likely to lead to nuclear war ought to be avoided. Thus, in the nuclear age, the struggle against capitalism must of necessity assume indirect forms such as flanking movements and proxy wars—forms subsumed under the Soviet version of "détente."
4. Nevertheless, "détente" may fail. An all-out war with the United States might break out—such an eventuality could result if some local conflict should get out of control. Alternatively, the United States, isolated and driven against the wall, might lash out in a Samson-like act of universal destruction rather than submit to final defeat. This contingency, however brought on, would require a quick, surgical preemptive strike designed to eliminate the bulk of the United States nuclear arsenal and thereby to reduce greatly the United States' ability to inflict retaliatory damage.

It is sometimes said that the Soviet "war-winning" strategy is "irrational" and need not be taken seriously in view of the strong prospect that a Soviet first strike against the United States would invite a devastating counter-attack on Soviet cities and industrial centers. The idea rests on an assumption that a Soviet first strike would come about as the result of a cold calculation. Such an out-of-the-blue assault is not part of Soviet doctrine, and no responsible specialist considers it likely. A Soviet decision to preempt would come under conditions of extreme crisis, after the Soviet leadership had concluded that general war had become unavoidable. It would not be an act of adventurism; rather, its aim would be to minimize inescapable casualties and material losses. It must be realized in this connection that inasmuch as fractionalization of nuclear warheads allows a single missile to destroy several enemy nuclear systems, under conditions of modern war preemption is even more attractive militarily than it has been in the past.

The Soviet strategic buildup must be understood in the light of these premises and expectations. The Soviet Union has never adopted the United States doctrine of Mutual Assured Destruction. Such concepts as "parity" or "essential equivalence"—integral as they are to American thinking about strategic nuclear relations—are no part of Soviet theory and practice. These are concepts of people who do not believe in the military and political utility of nuclear weapons. Once it had made up its own mind on the issue, the Soviet Union has consistently striven to attain overwhelming strategic superiority that would make allowance for all kinds of unforeseen contingencies as well as the prospect, which it takes seriously, of a protracted nuclear conflict.

## SALT: RESTRAINING THE UNITED STATES

In Soviet calculations, SALT is not a vehicle for general disarmament—as it is with us—but a device to inhibit the United States response to Soviet long-term strategic programs.

In the Soviet view, SALT, on the most elementary level, fixes the number of United States systems and thereby facilitates the task of estimating what is required to render them harmless.

On a higher level, SALT alleviates the Soviet Union's recurrent nightmare that an American technological achievement (such as ABM or the cruise missile have been in the past) should suddenly neutralize the ponderous and incremental Soviet buildup.

Last but not least—in the Soviet outlook—SALT serves to create in the United States a political atmosphere obstructive to defense expenditures. SALT persuades much of the American public that any improvements in strategic forces are "destabilizing." SALT inhibits the U.S. government from funding weapons programs presumptively subject to becoming limited or even prohibited in later negotiations.

All these features of SALT are inherently beneficial to the Soviet Union. It likes to depict SALT as the linchpin of détente, as it depicts détente as the only alternative to nuclear holocaust. It is not so apparent why an American administration would adopt this point of view, unless it believes that SALT can be translated into domestic political benefits at minimum military risk.

## IF SALT II IS REJECTED . . .

What is likely to happen should SALT II, for whatever reason, not come into force?

There is no reason to believe that the Senate's assertion of its constitutional prerogative to advise amendments or reject the terms outright would result in any of the harrowing scenarios being put forth to promote acceptance of the treaty intact as signed. The inability of great powers to agree on the terms of a treaty resolving their differences does not, in and of itself, cause their relationship to deteriorate. For any such result to occur there must be other, more palpable reasons driving them toward hostility. The Soviet ruling elite has entered into SALT negotiations not in order to maintain a favorable climate in U.S.-Soviet relations. Had it desired the latter, it would not have dispatched military advisors and proxy forces to the four corners of the world following the signing of SALT I. It has entered into these negotiations in the hope of securing the distinct military and political advantages enumerated above. Should SALT II fail, the Russians will promptly write it off as a bad investment and try to secure the same results by other means, if necessary, by a more equitable SALT. Their military programs, already operating at or close to peak capacity, are not likely to be accelerated in any significant way as a result.

There is something unreal about the proposition, advanced by both the Soviet ruling group and by the U.S. Administration, that the choice is either to ratify this treaty as written and advance along the road to peace or else risk growing enmity and war. Indeed, such doomsday scenarios place in doubt the very basis of the proposed accord. The viability of international treaties ultimately depends on a combination of self-interest and good will of the signatories. Either such self-interest and good will exist in respect to SALT II, or these qualities are lacking. In the former case the parties will be willing to persevere in negotiating and renegotiating until they arrive at a reciprocally acceptable agreement. If the qualities of self-interest and good will are lacking, the treaty will not hold in any event and ought to be rejected. Realistically, no treaty can be said to advance the cause of peace if its sole alternative is hostility and all-out war.

*17 September 1979*

# 15

# THE 1980 CRISIS AND WHAT WE SHOULD DO ABOUT IT[1]

## I. THE SOVIET CHALLENGE

The Committee on the Present Danger declared in its first Statement, on 11 November 1976:

> "Our country is in a period of danger, and the danger is increasing. Unless decisive steps are taken to alert the nation, and to change the course of its policy, our economic and military capacity will become inadequate to assure peace with security.

> "The principal threat to our nation, to world peace, and to the cause of human freedom is the Soviet drive for dominance based upon an unparalleled military buildup.

> "The Soviet Union has not altered its long-held goal of a world dominated from a single center—Moscow. It continues, with notable persistence, to take advantage of every opportunity to expand its political and military influence throughout the world: in Europe; in the Middle East and Africa; in Asia; even in Latin America; in all the seas."

The Committee recommended increases in conventional and strategic forces, and in research and development efforts, to provide the necessary foundation for a fresh, active and concerted diplomacy of Allied unity to deter Soviet expansion and to preserve the balance of power on which peace with security depends. The Committee concluded:

> "There is still time for effective action to ensure the security and prosperity of the nation in peace, through peaceful deterrence and concerted alliance diplomacy. A conscious effort of political will is needed to restore the strength and coherence of our foreign policy; to revive the solidarity of our alliances; to build constructive relations of cooperation with other nations whose interests parallel our own—and on that sound basis to seek reliable conditions of peace with the Soviet Union, rather than an illusory detente.

> "Only on such a footing can we and the other democratic industrialized nations, acting together, work with the developing nations to create a just and progressive world economy— the necessary condition of our own prosperity and that of the developing nations and communist nations as well. In that framework, we shall be better able to promote human rights, and to help deal with the great and emerging problems of food, energy, population, and the environment."

The analysis offered by the Committee in 1976 has been fully confirmed by subsequent events. The trends in Soviet policy to which the Committee called attention have continued with accelerating momentum. From the Persian Gulf, Africa, and the Middle East to the Caribbean, South East Asia, and the approaches to China and Japan, the

Soviet military presence and the strategic threats it represents are more obvious and more ominous than was the case three years ago.

As the Soviet Union has moved forward, exploiting its growing seapower and airlift capacity, the United States has continued to retreat. In many areas where bases and support facilities were once available to the United States or its Allies they are now at the disposition of Soviet forces. As a result, the Soviet Union can dominate Western economic and military lifelines through the Persian Gulf, the Arabian Sea, and the Indian Ocean, and threaten our use of the South Atlantic, the Caribbean, and the Western Pacific. If the Soviet Union should decide to use proxy forces, or its own forces, in one or several of these areas, we should find ourselves locally outgunned, and in no position to face the risk of potential nuclear escalation as we did in the Cuban Missile Crisis of 1962, when our local forces were clearly superior to those of the Soviet Union and our strategic nuclear capacity was beyond challenge.

Even more important, the Administration refuses to acknowledge that the United States has been becoming Number Two in military power. But the largest segment of the American people—in frustration and anger—believes that our country has already reached that unenviable posture. This country no longer has the capacity to protect its interests and American citizens abroad.

Looking back at our 1976 Statement, the Committee on the Present Danger reaffirms its analysis, and repeats its call for action. The Committee emphasizes that more will be required today than would have been required had action been taken then. During the past three years the United States has reduced its Navy, closed the production line of the Minuteman III missile, cancelled the B-1 bomber and the so-called "neutron bomb," and delayed the Trident submarine and the MX missile, weapons systems which had been planned and scheduled earlier as essential to a balanced military posture.

Following a long series of adverse political and military developments, the United States faces a world crisis—a world crisis caused by the Soviet Union's lunge for dominance, and by our country's inadequate response. During those years the United States turned away from the foreign policy pursued from Truman right up to the collapse in Vietnam. The new United States foreign policy has been characterized by an unwillingness to compete with the Soviet Union and to hold its drive in check.

If the United States rallies a coalition to respond to the Soviet challenge, a system of order may be restored. If not, the non-Communist world faces continuing collapse. It is still true that the NATO Allies, Japan, and other like-minded countries have more than enough actual and potential power to arrest this slide toward anarchy, if our country and the others perceive the crisis for what it is, and act quickly, firmly, calmly, and above all with persistence.

## II. THE PERSIAN GULF PROBLEM

The problems in the Persian Gulf area are among the most urgent confronting United States foreign policy and constitute an appropriate focus for this statement.

Today, in mid-January 1980, United States diplomatic personnel in Iran are still being held under humiliating conditions in open violation of one of the most ancient and essential rules of international law—immunity for diplomats. But the seizure of our diplomats in Iran, outrageous as it is, is only a symptom of a much larger process which will not end if they are released. The anarchy in Iran cannot now be easily reversed. The armed forces of Iran apparently are no longer capable of restoring order and government in that tortured country. The violent movements of social and religious protest of the last few years in Iran were actively promoted by the Soviet Union from the beginning.

A point has now been reached where a Soviet move to seize control of Iran is a distinct possibility. This has been made more likely by the Soviet occupation of Afghanistan, and by the strong positions the Soviet Union has achieved in Ethiopia, North and South Yemen, Iraq, Syria, Lebanon, and Libya. Control of Iran would open the way to Soviet control of Saudi Arabia and the entire Persian Gulf region. This has been one of the major goals of Soviet strategy for many years.

Given the present importance of oil and of well-located air bases and logistic facilities, Soviet control of the Persian Gulf would expose the non-Communist world to the danger of strangulation.

The Persian Gulf problem does not exist in isolation. There are other serious but less dramatic difficulties pressing upon the United States in many parts of the world, from the Far East to the Caribbean. In the Caribbean, for example, the Soviet Union has been steadily improving its position. Soviet planes, submarines, and combat troops are based in Cuba, and military assistance has been given from Cuba to revolutionary movements in Nicaragua, El Salvador, and other countries in the area. A potential is being built up from which the Soviet Union can threaten our Atlantic sea-lanes, our communications with Central and South America, and the territory of the United States itself.

Security problems of this order surely cannot be dealt with on the footing of business as usual.

## III. A FAILED POLICY

The events of 1979 and early 1980 both in the Caribbean and the Persian Gulf make it clear that the Administration's policy is wrong; it must be changed unequivocally and at once.

The United States, particularly in the three years of the Carter presidency, has, by words and acts of restraint, taken one unilateral step after another in the hope that the Soviet Union would accept such a policy of restraint for itself. The results of these efforts have been uniformly negative. The Soviet Union has continued to accelerate its program of worldwide expansion and its rapid military buildup. In these activities, it has undertaken and supported flagrant violations of the Charter of the United Nations, including support of North Vietnam's attack on South Vietnam, the Vietnamese invasion of Cambodia, the Palestine Liberation Organization's attacks on Israel, the use of poison gas against the Meo tribesmen in Laos, and the Soviet direct and inspired attacks on Afghanistan, Angola, Ethiopia, Somalia and North and South Yemen. During the crisis over the capture of the American Embassy and the imprisonment of American diplomatic representatives in Iran, Soviet radio, broadcasting to Iran and to the Islamic world, applauded the lawless acts of the militants masquerading as "students"; falsely charged American involvement in the attacks on the Mosques of Mecca and Medina; and urged other countries to follow the Iranian example.

President Carter in January 1980 announced that he had changed his opinion of what the Soviets' ultimate goals are. That change of opinion has not yet been accompanied by a matching turn in United States policy, and by the adoption of programs adequate to meet the challenges facing the nation. It is the view of our Committee that the USSR will continue its program of expansionism unless and until we are able to confront it with an array of unacceptable risks.

# IV.  UNITED STATES FOREIGN AND DEFENSE POLICY

Before presenting our Committee's program of action, it is appropriate to make clear what we consider to be the necessary and abiding principles of United States foreign and defense policy.

The foreign policy of the United States, like every other aspect of our policy, draws its substance from taproots deep in the American earth, from the principles and ideals which make this nation what it is. America is more than a superpower. The idea of the United States is a living part of Western civilization, with a compelling and altogether special history which belongs to all who cherish human liberty. Washington, Franklin, Jefferson, and Lincoln are revered throughout the world not merely because the United States has been concerned, as every state must be concerned, with the balance of power in world politics as the ultimate assurance of its own safety and that of other nations. What the great American leaders said and did remains a force for freedom.

The ultimate mission of the foreign policy of the United States is not order alone, but justice—not simply a balance of terror, but a world in which this nation can continue to develop as a democracy, a world in which the values and principles embodied in the United Nations Charter are respected by all states and all peoples.

Between President Truman's time immediately after World War II and the revulsion against Vietnam during the last decade, this country had a generally coherent foreign policy, which was supported by a bipartisan majority of the American people. The main features are familiar:

First, there was the network of programs, starting with the Marshall Plan, through which the United States helped to restore the industrialized democracies and knit them and much of the Third World into a dynamic, worldwide, and progressive economy. Between 1947 and the early 1970s, these policies were successful, helping both the industrialized and many of the developing nations to achieve high rates of growth and social progress under reasonably stable conditions.

Second, the United States supported decolonization and initiated programs of economic and technical assistance to the developing nations, most of them newly liberated from imperial rule. Here the record of success was uneven, but many developing nations, from Taiwan, Malaysia, and South Korea to Mexico, Brazil, and, until recently, Iran, made striking advances as integral parts of the world economy.

Third, the United States developed and supported bilateral and multilateral policies of international political cooperation to encourage social and political development, education, cultural improvement and the self-determination of peoples.

Finally, this country conducted a long, patient and thus far largely unsuccessful campaign to bring nuclear weapons and nuclear technology under effective and useful international control.

Shortly after the initiation of this policy under the Truman Administration, it became clear that the Soviet Union was marching to a different drummer—it continued to pursue its expansionist goals in Eastern Europe by moves against Iran, Greece, and Turkey, and rejected the American offers of the Marshall Plan, the Baruch Plan, and proposals to develop the Security Council as an effective peacekeeping institution. Throughout the succeeding period, every American president sought to persuade the Soviet Union to accept the rules of genuine coexistence in this sense, and, when these efforts failed, sought to deter and if necessary repel, by the limited use of force, Soviet-backed expansion. These United States efforts were successful, in the post-war crises over Iran, Berlin,

Yugoslavia, Greece and Turkey, Korea, and the Cuban Missile Crisis, in maintaining a balance of power in world politics.

The commitment of the Western nations to this approach to the problem of peace began to weaken after the frustrations of the Korean War, and weakened a great deal during and after the war in Indo-China. The new policy which emerged was based upon the illusion of moral symmetry—the illusion that the Kremlin shared with the United States the same basic principles and the same desire for a true détente.

The American people were assured that negotiation had been substituted for confrontation in our relationship with the Soviet Union; that the Cold War was over; and that a condition of "détente" with the Soviet Union had been achieved at last. But Soviet foreign policy has not mellowed, as many hoped it would or even claimed it had. Indeed, its pressures are greater and more pervasive than ever, because it can be backed by far more powerful military forces and conducted in a more confident manner.

Pursuing a policy built on illusion, we have been adrift and uncertain while the Soviet Union expanded its power and empire on every continent and on all the seas.

The Committee on the Present Danger was organized in 1976 to address that condition and to encourage an active and disciplined discussion of the main problems of United States foreign and defense policy. The Committee adheres to the view that in a democracy sound policy must have a solid foundation in public understanding and support.

Constructive changes in public opinion on foreign policy questions have occurred since 1976. In the Committee's view, the American people are ready once more, without illusion or wishful thinking, to support an effective foreign policy and the programs necessary to protect American interests.

## V. A COMMON POLICY ON SOVIET AGGRESSION

The slide toward anarchy in international politics must be reversed.

This country's national interest in preserving the political independence of Western Europe, Japan, and a number of other countries is obvious. That interest can be threatened not only by direct attack but by envelopment and indirect aggression as well. The defense of the Middle East, for example, is vital to the defense of Western Europe, and that of South Korea and Taiwan to the defense of both Japan and China. Each problem must be examined in context as it arises. In a world which is becoming smaller every day, the United States cannot protect its interests by drawing an arbitrary line around certain areas and ignoring the rest of the world. That approach was tried once. It resulted in the Korean War.

Attempts of this kind—attempts, that is, to define the national security interests of the United States in terms less comprehensive than those of the United Nations Charter—all fail for the same fundamental reason: The Soviet strategy of imperial expansion, worldwide in scope, is a dynamic process, focusing now on one area, now on another, and is constantly nourished and strengthened by the Soviet perception of its emerging military superiority. No region of the world can be excluded in advance from the agenda of our concern, for each may be used as an instrument of expanding the means of control as Soviet campaigns develop. For example, it is hard to imagine areas of the world more remote from the United States than Afghanistan and the Yemeni states. Yet the United States has rightly asserted an interest in their independence, since they can be used to support pressure on Iran, Saudi Arabia, and the Persian Gulf region generally.

The time has come, we are convinced, for the United States, its Allies, and other nations to reach a common and concerted position on Soviet aggression. United States foreign policy should be based on the principle that this country, its Allies, and other nations should act together in solidarity as partners in the great tasks of peace and progress where our interests are parallel.

The rules of the United Nations Charter were carefully thought through and were approved by the entire international community. They are inherent in the nature of the interstate system, and, ever since 1945, have been interpreted in the same way by United Nations studies, decisions of the International Court of Justice, and the Security Council. Except in cases of individual or collective self-defense, or enforcement action by the Security Council, the Charter prohibits the international use of force against the territorial integrity or political independence of any state, and imposes upon all states absolute responsibility for the international use of force from their territories by irregular forces, guerrillas, mercenaries, or armed bands. The Brezhnev Doctrine and so-called wars of national liberation violate the Charter as categorically as do all other forms of aggression.

There is still time for effective international action to protect the safety and prosperity of the United States through peaceful deterrence and well-conceived Alliance diplomacy, rather than through war itself.

## VI. AN URGENT PROGRAM FOR THE UNITED STATES

To make such a program of active deterrence and Allied solidarity effective, the Committee on the Present Danger proposes a series of steps to be taken by the government and people of the United States with support and reinforcement by their Allies and other friends.

President Carter's 1981 budget and program proposals should provide for a prompt and adequate increase in our military strength—strategic, theater nuclear, and conventional. Areas which merit emphasis include:

(1) Maintaining a clear and credible second-strike strategic capability, by moving promptly to protect our land-based, air-based, and sea-based strategic launchers against the risk implicit in the looming counterforce Soviet nuclear arsenal. Time is now of the essence in achieving this goal. We should proceed urgently with the MX and Trident programs. To cover the period of danger before MX is available in useful numbers in 1989, Minuteman III should be redeployed in the most effective and timely way; that is, in the multiple vertical protective shelter system. We should begin immediately to take steps to preserve the survivability and penetration capability of our air-breathing systems. In that connection, we should get on with the production of a more survivable penetrating bomber and cruise missile carrier. The adequacy of improvements to our command, control and communications systems and of development work on cruise missile technology and ballistic missile defense should be reexamined.

(2) Initiating the long-term process of restoring our all-oceans Navy, capable of protecting our interests against the Soviet fleet in the Atlantic, in the Pacific, in the Mediterranean, and in the Indian Ocean and the Persian Gulf. The budget should also provide adequate funds for our ready forces and reserves and increased funds for research and development.

(3) Modernizing U.S. theater nuclear forces. While we endorse the recent decision to deploy ground-launched cruise missiles and the Pershing II in Europe, this move in itself will not reverse the growing imbalance in theater nuclear systems. Deployment of enhanced radiation weapons remains a basic requirement for defending NATO.

(4) Urgently reviewing our military manpower requirements and policies, in view of the magnitude of the effort which will be necessary to arrest the momentum of the Soviet drive for dominance and of the shortcomings of the volunteer recruitment program. The machinery for manpower registration should be reconstituted at once, so that a democratic and equitable Selective Service system can be instituted as changing circumstances require.

(5) Increasing our long-term military presence in a number of key regions of the world, in order to make it possible promptly to defend, and to make it apparent that this nation is prepared to defend, its interests by military means, should such action become necessary.

In order to make it possible for the United States to sustain support for such a program of increased military strength, the United States must pursue far more effective economic programs both nationally and internationally. It must control inflation and rebuild its position in the world monetary system on a more stable footing. In that perspective, reducing the need for oil imports, both through conservation and through increased production of domestic energy, is key.

On the solid foundation of such a United States policy, others in the world threatened by the spreading Soviet drive for military and political dominance would be given hope and encouragement to increase their own defense effort. This nation and its Allies should then be able to deal with problems in the Persian Gulf and many other parts of the world by firm and prudent diplomacy.

## VII. THE LESSON OF THE 1930s
## AND TWO QUESTIONS FOR THE 1980s

The problems which the United States faces are in some ways similar to those confronted by the Western world before the Second World War.

In the years before 1939, people watched with disbelief as the world political system disintegrated toward anarchy, and anarchy led to war. During those years, the world order, partly restored at Versailles in 1919, fell apart under the hammer blows of Adolph Hitler. Today a similar process is taking place as the Soviet Union pursues a program of expansionism even more ambitious than that of Hitler, claiming the sanction of scientific Socialism for designs in the ancient model of conquest and predation.

In the 1930s, respected public figures understood the dangers and the risks, and called them eloquently to the attention of the Free World. But the British and American authorities were incapable of acting decisively on what they knew to be the facts. For profound reasons rooted in the educational systems and the culture of the Anglo-Saxon nations, they clung to the illusion that things were not so bad as they seemed; that those who warned of the danger of war and called for the restoration of world public order were "alarmists" and "extremists"; and that somehow a compromise would be reached and war averted.

History has judged those men harshly. They were Pollyannas whose good will and good intentions paved the road to disaster. To them, the facade of the familiar peaceful everyday world seemed permanent and immutable. In a moment, however, that facade proved to be as fragile as a stage set.

Even with the experience of 1914 vivid in their memories, the British and American people simply could not bring themselves to imagine in the mid-1930s that world war would come again. For them, the taboo against the political use of military force was a powerful restraint. Therefore they waited until it was too late to save peace and freedom without war.

As we Americans face the problems of foreign and defense policy, we should remind ourselves of that terrible experience. Even towering Western leaders like Churchill and Franklin D. Roosevelt failed to prevent war. President Roosevelt, active as he later was in achieving Lend-Lease, the Destroyer-Bases Agreement, the convoys to Europe, and all the other important actions of the period after World War II had begun, did not join with Britain and France during the middle 1930s when the war might well have been prevented.

The tides are once again rushing the world toward general war. The United States and its Allies still have time to protect their vital national interests by the methods of peace, but that time is growing short.

The American people are ready to answer a call for action and, where necessary, sacrifice. Will their leaders chart an adequate program—and will they do so in time? The answers to those questions will determine whether the 1980 crisis is the forerunner of catastrophe for the non-Communist world or whether it marks a turning point toward restoring peace with security and freedom.

*22 January 1980*

## NOTES

1. This statement was prepared and issued before the 23 January 1980 State of the Union address by President Carter. The President's speech emphasized this country's military commitments to Iran and Pakistan. However, the President's budget proposals presented the following week did not reflect the urgency of the present crisis or the magnitude of the United States commitments which he activated.

# 16

# COUNTERING THE SOVIET THREAT

## U.S. Defense Strategy in the 1980s

### BACKGROUND

Both the military and the economic aspects of the nation's perilous international position require resolute and coordinated action. National security and economic well-being are concurrent, compatible and, indeed, interdependent ends. Given confidence that their leaders have thought through the requirements and have fully explained them, the people of the United States are prepared to do what is necessary to safeguard both the nation's security and its economic strength.

In its 22 January statement, "The 1980 Crisis and What We Should Do About It," the Committee on the Present Danger addressed the world crisis caused by the Soviet Union's lunge for dominance and the inadequate response of the United States. In the Committee's view, the Soviet Union will continue to expand until it is confronted by unacceptable risks. We outlined a six-point program of action calling for an increase in defense funding to restore the nation's capacity to deter and contain Soviet expansion.

The United States must concern itself with economic conditions here and abroad. Working closely with the key industrial nations, the United States must bring the insidious and destructive process of inflation under control. As the Committee on the Present Danger has emphasized since its first Statement on 11 November 1976, a strong, progressive and stable economy is an essential foundation for a sound and adequate program of national security.

For more than ten years this country has neither provided adequately for the common defense nor protected its economic stability. Continuation of such improvidence is unacceptable. The nation must now move decisively to restore its security and to stabilize the economy.

To help clarify the issues involved, the Committee has undertaken an analysis of costs entailed in programs to reverse negative trends in this country's defenses and to enable the nation to look forward with confidence to a more secure and peaceful world. Those programs would provide forces substantially better in quality and generally larger in quantity than those contemplated by the Executive Branch's revised budget requests.

The programs recommended include a quick fix program (1) to preserve our country's second-strike strategic nuclear deterrent — the fulcrum on which its entire defense rests — and (2) to restore the fighting capability of U.S. naval and other general purpose forces. To save precious months, such a quick fix program would be authorized by a supplemental appropriation for the present fiscal year. The Committee programs would also include a start at rebuilding and expanding U.S. forces to meet the challenges of the late 1980s and the 1990s.

In their entirety, these programs would call for increases in expenditures of about $1 billion in fiscal year 1980 and of $23 billion in fiscal year 1981. Over the six-year period (fiscal years 1980–1985), however, they would call for a total increase of about $260 billion in obligational authority, measured in 1981 dollars. That figure approximates the amount by which the Soviets have exceeded the United States in military expenditures over the last decade.

Those increases, representing net additions to the Administration's budget requests, are large. In financing them, care to avoid worsening the rate of inflation would be imperative. During fiscal years 1980 and 1981, the emphasis would be on increasing defense obligational authority, but some increase in actual budgetary outlays would still be required. The Committee on the Present Danger remains confident concerning the American people's willingness in the end—given strong political leadership—to make adjustments necessary to ensure both an adequate defense and a healthy economy.

Here follows a program and budget analysis of the security posture the Committee believes to be required to support a prudent and outward-looking foreign policy. It is certainly possible to refine or modify the details of the programs here suggested; what is essential is that they be considered urgently with a view to action.

## THE U.S. SECURITY PROBLEM

The Administration's defense budget proposals do not begin to correct the dangerous shifts in the world balance of power achieved by the Soviet Union at an accelerating rate in recent years, both through its military buildup and through new power deployments—made feasible by that buildup—in Asia, the Middle East, Africa and the Caribbean. As its defense budget proposals make clear, the Administration is still unwilling to recognize the consequences for the United States of the Soviet push for military superiority and to come forward with programs capable of arresting and containing the Soviet drive.

## U.S. DEFENSE REQUIREMENTS

The nation requires forces, alliances and bases to make feasible the defense of United States interests through political means, backed when necessary by the use of, or the credible threat to use, conventional forces. Our strategic arsenal must be made adequate to prevent the Soviet Union or any other country from using, or threatening to use, nuclear weapons in world politics. If that is accomplished, U.S. conventional forces can again become the effective bulwark of our diplomacy.

What is the essential task of U.S. foreign policy today—the task our armed forces must be organized to support? The Administration conceives the goals of U.S. foreign policy to be the solution of a number of discrete problems or conflicts (the Panama Canal; the Arab-Israeli dispute; the conflict over Rhodesia) on the assumption that these are normal episodes of friction within the framework of a stable state system.

The Committee on the Present Danger, on the other hand, has been calling attention since 1976 to the Soviet Union's efforts to destroy the state system reflected in the Charter of the United Nations and to impose an imperial system dominated by Soviet will. The Soviet Union has made important progress toward that end, especially since the collapse of United States efforts in Indo-China.

The basic task of U.S. foreign policy, therefore, is to bring together a coalition of Allies and other nations to restore a world order based on political cooperation among independent states. Europe, the United States, Japan, China and many smaller nations threatened by Soviet expansionism have the potential to arrest the disintegration of the world political system, and to insist on general—and reciprocal—respect for the rules of world public order. Neither the policies nor the proposed programs of the Administration match the magnitude of the problem.

## THE ADMINISTRATION'S DEFENSE PROGRAM

The Administration's national security policies are still based on the outdated strategies of the 1960s. Its defense programs are inadequate to support even those strategies. Its new budget proposals were in final form months before the Soviet invasion of Afghanistan, and are widely recognized as having been designed to secure key Senate votes for ratification of SALT II. None of the proposed increases would be effected in 1980, and they would be inadequate to reverse the trend of the last decade toward U.S. military inferiority.

\* \* \*

The Committee on the Present Danger's alternative program is based on the following major revisions to current U.S. foreign and defense policy objectives:

## CONVENTIONAL FORCES

Our national strategy should be designed to contain Soviet or proxy aggression against our interests in the Atlantic and Mediterranean, the Pacific and the Persian Gulf and Indian Ocean—simultaneously if necessary—as well as Soviet efforts in the Western Hemisphere through the Caribbean basin. As we commented in our recent statement, "The 1980 Crisis and What We Should Do About It," "No region of the world can be excluded in advance from the agenda of our concern. . . ."

The current one-and-a-half war strategy is clearly inadequate to maintain the NATO deterrent and to head off aggression against American interests in the Pacific, the Indian Ocean or the Caribbean. Indeed, existing U.S. forces cannot support even the present strategy. The Administration's military posture in the Persian Gulf area could be supported only by dangerous reductions in NATO and Pacific naval strength, and by extended overseas deployments of such duration that retention of adequate numbers of experienced enlisted personnel would not be feasible.

## NUCLEAR FORCES

In nuclear weapons, the rapid growth of Soviet strategic and theater capabilities has led to an ominous political and military threat: the threat that beginning in the early 1980s and lasting at least until 1989, when MX is planned to become available in significant quantities, both the survivability and the counter-force capability of U.S. deterrent forces will lack credibility. If this condition is permitted to develop, the use of either conventional or nuclear forces in defense of important U.S. and Allied interests would be rendered imprudent.[1] Preventing such a development requires substantial action and brooks no delay. Simultaneously, the U.S. should proceed steadily over the longer term to reverse the shift toward Soviet nuclear superiority—and to forestall any Soviet notion that it could fight, survive and win a nuclear war.

The Administration's budget would not fund the necessary modernization of the U.S. triad of nuclear forces. Instead of reviving strategic defenses to offset the Soviet Union's formidable offensive lead, that budget would eliminate strategic defenses altogether, and gives only token attention to civil defense requirements. It could not result in the United States regaining strategic parity or in restoring the effectiveness of our second-strike capability until the 1990s—if then.

## FORCE READINESS AND WAR RESERVES

The readiness of existing U.S. military forces should be increased so that they could, if required, resist and overcome military aggression by the Soviets or their client states for a sustained period of time.

Under the defense budgets of the past three years, the operational readiness of U.S. forces has declined. Many components are not combat-ready, and lack the human and material reserves necessary to sustain combat operations for more than a few weeks. A considerable fraction of the fiscal year 1980 supplemental appropriation recommended by the Committee would necessarily be addressed to this problem. The Administration's plan to absorb unanticipated inflation in the current fiscal year 1980 budget will further reduce U.S. operational readiness. Only a 1980 supplemental appropriation can counter this dangerous trend.

## EQUIPMENT MAINTENANCE

The procurement of modern operational military equipment should be increased to overcome current rates of wear and tear and permit a sizable increase in active force levels over the next five years.

Defense procurements have been so restricted in recent years as to assure steady net depreciation in operational equipment. In several force components, both conventional and nuclear, it is almost too late to stave off block obsolescence and the attendant reductions in operational force levels.

## PERSONNEL, SKILLS AND PAY

The present wage ceilings on military pay have forced U.S. uniformed personnel to absorb a disproportionate share of uncontrolled inflation and devalued dollars abroad. A 20 percent disparity between military and civilian pay scales has been condoned. Inadequacy of pay and allowances is a principal reason for the Services' inability to retain adequate numbers of middle-grade commanders, supervisors and skilled technicians. There should be an immediate and substantial pay increase for military personnel to improve the retention rate of skilled people and to attract more capable volunteers.

A democratic and equitable Selective Service system should be instituted as changing circumstances require. The call for simple draft registration, without even classification, will do nothing, by itself, to provide and retain skilled personnel necessary for the armed forces. Nothing short of a program to mobilize the nation's human resources can solve the problem.

## INDUSTRIAL MOBILIZATION

Along with substantially increased defense procurement, the United States should reconstitute its lost capabilities for industrial mobilization, in order to support future military and civil defense requirements.

Over the past three years, reductions in defense procurement have wiped out the last vestiges of U.S. industrial mobilization capabilities. There are no present programs for a civil defense mobilization effort. Meanwhile, Soviet civil defense and industrial mobilization capabilities have improved steadily.

## ARMS TRANSFERS

The U.S. should resume production and stockpiling of arms suitable for rapid transfer to endangered friends and allies. The U.S. cannot afford to draw down its own military inventories as the price for supporting friends.

## STRENGTHENING U.S. CONVENTIONAL FORCES

The Committee's proposal for the period 1980–1986 calls for the expansion of U.S. conventional forces in the particulars indicated below.

*None of these items is provided for in the Administration's budget for the coming year or in its program for the five following years.*

- Five active Army divisions would be added so as to provide rapidly deployable forces without reducing deterrent strength required for the security of NATO, Japan, South Korea and other Allies.
- Nine active tactical air wings (six Air Force, three Navy/Marine) would be added to support ground force increases and to permit the rotational forward deployment of air wings to support stability in the Middle East, the Persian Gulf and other trouble-prone areas.
- Ten additional tactical airlift squadrons would be provided to support in-theater movements of U.S. and Allied forces.
- Current strategic airlift capabilities would be doubled—a considerable increase over the Administration proposal. The use of currently available designs would help accelerate production at minimum cost.
- Additional ships to create a 650-ship navy by 1990—the minimum necessary to provide a three-ocean navy and a permanent Caribbean presence. The Committee recommends that this program be authorized in the 1980 supplemental so that a start can be made on letting contracts. No actual expenditures would be incurred in fiscal year 1980.

| 6-YEAR<br>SHIP CONSTRUCTION | ADMINISTRATION'S<br>PROGRAM | COMMITTEE'S<br>PROGRAM |
|---|---|---|
| Submarines | 21 | 27 |
| Surface Combatants | 49 | 107 |
| Amphibious ships | 3 | 20 |
| Support ships | 33 | 79 |
| TOTAL | 106 | 233 |

- Increases in defense manpower levels would be provided as indicated in the following tabulation—with data for 1964 included for comparison (expressed in thousands):

|          | 1980 | 1981 | 1982 | 1983 | 1984 | 1985 | (1964) |
|----------|------|------|------|------|------|------|--------|
| Army     | 774  | 806  | 836  | 866  | 896  | 926  | (972)  |
| Navy     | 713  | 728  | 743  | 758  | 773  | 788  | (857)  |
| Air Force| 558  | 573  | 588  | 603  | 618  | 633  | (856)  |
| TOTAL    | 2045 | 2107 | 2167 | 2227 | 2287 | 2347 | (2685) |

## STRENGTHENING U.S. NUCLEAR FORCES

For the six-year period, the Committee's program includes strengthening U.S. nuclear forces to overcome near-term and long-term deficiencies. Significant elements provided in the program include:

- Two additional TRIDENT submarines. In an effort to reduce spending, the TRIDENT submarines are currently being built at a rate so slow that block obsolescence of the current POSEIDON fleet is certain to cause a reduction in U.S. sea-based missile platforms.
- The first 100 B-1A long-range combat aircraft capable of penetrating enemy airspace on nuclear or conventional missions. These would subsequently be followed by other B-1 derivatives fitted for carrying cruise missiles, and for other missions (replacements for the aging B-52 fleet are omitted in the current U.S. program).
- Construction of 300 MINUTEMAN IV ICBM missiles—to be used in proliferated vertical launching silos. The more expensive MX missile program would be continued at a more modest pace.
- Additional air-launched, ground-launched and sea-launched cruise missiles and PERSHING I and PERSHING II tactical ballistic missiles in an overall aggregate of 1300.
- The production and deployment of enhanced radiation warheads to enhance the U.S. nuclear posture at strategic and theater levels.
- Expanded civil defense planning and preparations. The current U.S. civil defense program is virtually nonexistent. It is predicated on a fundamental belief that nuclear war is too horrible to justify attempts to survive it—a view not shared by the rulers of the Soviet Union.
- Various quick fixes to rectify the rapidly shifting strategic balance within the next few years. These measures include modernization and rebasing of MINUTEMAN III in multiple vertical shelters, improving B-52 survivability by rebasing the bomber force inland and hardening, and re-engining the B-52 bomber for better performance or possibly producing the improved FB-111 bomber recommended by the Strategic Air Command.

*9 May 1980*

## NOTES

1. The Committee on the Present Danger has documented those trends in "Is America Becoming Number 2? Current Trends in the U.S.-Soviet Military Balance." The strategic nuclear balance has been analyzed in a series of papers by Paul H. Nitze prepared for and distributed by the Committee (see Chapters 11, 12).

# 17

# IS THE REAGAN DEFENSE
# PROGRAM ADEQUATE?

## I. BACKGROUND

In our 9 May 1980 statement[1] the Committee on the Present Danger highlighted the expanding Soviet military threat to U.S. national security interests and the role of U.S. nuclear weapons, especially strategic nuclear weapons, in preserving deterrence and insuring strategic stability:

> In nuclear weapons, the rapid growth of Soviet strategic and theater capabilities has led to an ominous political and military threat: the threat that beginning in the early 1980s and lasting at least until 1989, when MX is planned to become available in significant quantities, both the survivability and the counter-force capability of U.S. deterrent forces will lack credibility. If this condition is permitted to develop, the use of either conventional or nuclear forces in defense of important U.S. and Allied interests would be rendered imprudent. Preventing such a development requires substantial action and brooks no delay. Simultaneously, the U.S. should proceed steadily over the longer term to reverse the shift toward Soviet nuclear superiority—and to forestall any Soviet notion that it could fight, survive and win a nuclear war.

It is this situation which the Committee addressed in its defense blueprint for the early 1980s—the most critical period of U.S. strategic force vulnerability.

The survivability of U.S. strategic nuclear forces is the bedrock of a prudent and credible foreign policy. A survivable strategic arsenal serves as a deterrent against Soviet use of nuclear weapons or the threat to use those weapons, and it bolsters the deterrent capacity of U.S. conventional forces.

The program recommended by the Committee on the Present Danger in May 1980 was built around (1) a "quick fix" program to preserve the U.S. strategic nuclear deterrent and (2) a restoration of the fighting capability of U.S. naval and other general purpose forces.

While refinements or modifications to parts of the Committee's program may well be desirable because of factors that bear upon current conditions—production capacity, lead-times, and so forth—a comparison of the Reagan Administration's defense program with the defense plan recommended earlier by the Committee on the Present Danger helps determine the degree to which the Administration has a strategy adequate to defend the United States.

## II. METHODOLOGY

The Committee's current analysis weighs the adequacy of the Administration's defense program by comparing the recently approved defense plan for FY '82 (including Administration revisions and Congressional action) plus the Administration's proposals for

FY '83-FY '87 with the program proposed in 1980 by the Committee on the Present Danger. While Congress is likely to propose revisions to the Administration's FY '83 defense plan (as was the case in FY '82), the Administration's FY '83 proposal is its blueprint for addressing the national security problems facing the United States.

## III. THE ECONOMICS OF DEFENSE

The Committee on the Present Danger recognizes that national security and economic well-being are interdependent objectives. The Committee has emphasized since its initial Statement on 11 November 1976 that a strong, progressive and stable economy is an essential foundation for a sound and adequate program of national security. In funding the levels of defense effort which we believe are necessary to redress the U.S.-Soviet military imbalance, care to avoid exacerbating current economic difficulties is taken into account but is not and should not be determinative. The requirements of national security should be determinative of the levels of defense spending—not some contrived or artificial budgetary formula, involving non-defense spending, taxes and borrowing. There is no question that the American economy is capable of supporting an increased defense effort.

The most important thing to note about the economics of defense is also the simplest. Defending the country is not free. It has its costs. But so do all other good things. To say that defense, like other good things, has its costs, does not imply that those costs are not worthwhile.

The argument is often advanced that there is something special about expenditures for defense in that they yield no product. But of course there is a product. The product is the national security. That is an extremely valuable product. Without it, most of the other products would not last long or be worth very much.

The Committee recognizes that it is possible to spend too much or too little on national defense, just as it is possible to spend too much or too little on anything else. Even if it is agreed that more spending for defense yields more national security there is a point beyond which the addition to the national security is too small to be worthwhile. Likewise, there is some point beyond which reducing spending for defense is obviously too risky. The problem is to find the right point.

During World War II the United States devoted about 50 percent of its national output to the war effort. No one thought that was too much. No one now thinks anything like that is needed today. In the 1920s we spent less than one-half of one percent of our national output for defense. Hardly anyone thinks that would be adequate today.

Numerous misconceptions exist regarding the economic effects of increased defense spending. A common concern is that it may be inflationary. Of course, there is a historical connection between wars and inflation. But whether or not that is a necessary connection, there is no such necessary connection between inflation and an enhanced defense effort. The argument here is perfectly simple. What causes inflation is an excessively rapid growth of *total* spending—public and private.

It is worth noting that during the Administrations of Presidents Eisenhower and Kennedy, when defense expenditures were 9 to 10 percent of GNP, there was little inflation. Also, the acceleration of inflation in the 1970s occurred while defense expenditures as a share of GNP were falling to their lowest level in thirty years.

The point is often made that although defense expenditures will not be large relative to *total* GNP, nevertheless demand is concentrated on certain industries, materials and skills, and will be inflationary in those sectors. This is closely connected to another point.

It is said that the effort to increase defense procurement *quickly* will drive prices up and cause waste in other ways, so that the program would be achieved more efficiently if it were pushed more gradually. However, part of the normal and efficient process by which resources are diverted to the sectors in which there is increasing demand is a rise of prices in those sectors relative to the sectors in which demand is not rising or is declining. Prices and wages in the defense sectors may rise relative to prices and wages elsewhere enough to attract the labor and capital needed for the defense effort. But, if overall economic policy is not inflationary, this need not raise the overall price level.

The Committee on the Present Danger recognizes the problems in managing the expansion of the defense program. It will go more efficiently, quickly and economically if it is well managed. Decisions about the Congressional authorization and appropriations should be made promptly and contracts should be let quickly so that contractors can prepare in an orderly way. The Department of Defense should push forward with its program for expanding the list of qualified contractors and informing potential producers of future defense requirements. The Department should have authority to assist in the building of plant capacity that may not otherwise be available.

At a more general level, the effects of the defense expansion on the economy will depend on the monetary and fiscal policy that accompanies it. But of most significance is the fact that the burden of the program proposed by the Committee on the economy need not be excessive.[2]

## IV. THE ADMINISTRATION'S DEFENSE BUDGET

A look at the Administration's recently submitted defense program reveals that:

a) The five-year defense funding program submitted by the Administration represents an average annual real increase in funding of 7.4 percent. Proposed FY '83 funding represents a 13-percent real increase in total obligational authority (TOA) over the Congressionally approved FY '82 level. Proposed outlays for FY '83 will be less than 5 percent above those proposed by the Carter Administration.

b) Although the Administration is proposing TOA growth rates prior to FY '84 in excess of 10 percent, these levels will not approach the level of funding recommended by the Committee on the Present Danger until after FY '84.

c) The Administration's defense budget will lag several years behind the proposals of the Committee on the Present Danger and the Administration's proposed increases are substantially lower than what the Committee believes is essential. Present U.S. defense funding for FY '81 and FY '82 lags behind the recommendations of the Committee by some $68 billion. With the Administration's request for FY '83 included, the lag is approximately $83 billion.

d) The overwhelming majority of defense funding is devoted to conventional programs. Authorizations for spending on strategic forces in FY '83, according to the Administration's request, will account for only 9 percent of the total defense budget. U.S. nuclear forces, especially strategic nuclear forces, will remain vulnerable for most of this decade.

e) The cumulative difference between the proposed Administration budget for the period FY '81-FY '85 and the higher Committee recommendations is over $90 billion. Congressional action could increase the gap further. (The cumulative difference between the Administration's revised September '81 defense budget and the higher Committee recommendations would have been well over $100 billion.)

f) The net result of recent Congressional and Administration defense budget actions is a level of authorizations for FY '82 which is only slightly higher than the level proposed by the previous Administration—a level deemed grossly inadequate by the Committee on the Present Danger.

These proposed levels of funding—following the Soviet takeover of Afghanistan, the destruction of any semblance of national self-determination in Poland, and a rapidly mounting threat to established governments in Central America, backed by the further intrusion of Soviet power into the Western Hemisphere—are clearly inadequate.

This is all the more reason why any budgetary revision by the Congress cutting the projected levels of defense funding or deferring or stretching-out the proposed five-year program, against the will of the President, would give a dangerous signal to the Soviet Union and to our Allies.

## V. RECENT DEFENSE BUDGET PROPOSALS

As the following shows, the Reagan Administration's proposed five-year defense budget falls well short of the 1980 recommendation of the Committee on the Present Danger:

TOA—Billions of Current $
(adjusted to FY '83 deflators)

| | '81 | '82 | FISCAL YEAR '83 | '84 | '85 | DIFFERENCE FROM CPD |
|---|---|---|---|---|---|---|
| CPD | 213.7 | 244.7 | 273.1 | 301.8 | 323.6 | — |
| REAGAN '83 | 176.1 | 214.1 | 258.1 | 285.5 | 331.7 | −91 |
| REAGAN '82 | 178.0 | 222.2 | 254.8 | 289.2 | 326.5 | −86 |
| REAGAN REVISED '82 | — | 214 | 244 | 280 | 326.5 | −111 |
| CARTER '82 | 171.5 | 195.5 | 218.4 | 242.6 | 268.4 | −261 |
| CARTER '81 | 167.6 | 190.2 | 211.2 | 233.1 | 255.6 | −299 |

| CUMULATIVE DIFFERENCE BETWEEN CPD & REAGAN '83 | FY '81 | FROM FY '81-FY '82 | FROM FY '81-FY '83 | FROM FY '81-FY '84 | FROM FY '81-FY '85 |
|---|---|---|---|---|---|
| | 37 | 68 | 83 | 99 | 91 |

CUMULATIVE BUDGET PROPOSALS

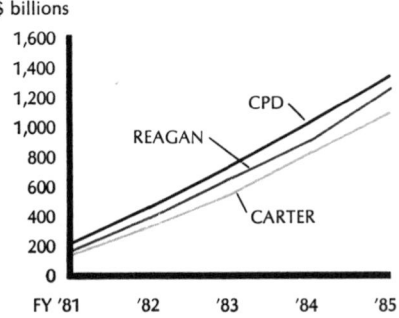

CPD: "Countering the Soviet Threat: U.S. Defense Strategy in the 1980s," 9 May 1980.
Reagan: "DoD Annual Report to Congress for FY '83," February, 1982.
Carter: "DoD Annual Report to Congress for FY '??," January, 1981.

# VI. A COMPARISON OF THE COMMITTEE ON THE PRESENT DANGER'S DEFENSE PROGRAM WITH THE DEFENSE PROGRAM OF THE REAGAN ADMINISTRATION

## Committee Proposals[3]

## *Administration Action*

a) *Strengthening U.S. Nuclear Forces.* For the six-year period, the Committee's program includes strengthening U.S. nuclear forces to overcome near-term and long-term deficiencies. Significant elements provided in the program include:

* Various quick fixes to rectify the rapidly shifting strategic balance within the next few years. These measures include modernization and rebasing of MINUTEMAN III in multiple vertical shelters, improving B-52 survivability by rebasing the bomber force inland and hardening, and re-engining the B-52 bomber for better performance . . .

*FY '82 Action. The Administration has adopted no quick fixes to close the "window of vulnerability." Over the next 5 years, the window will open wider due to the Administration's decisions*

　　*—to retire all B-52Ds during the FY '82-FY '86 time period,*
　　*—to decommission all POLARIS SSBNs before a sufficient number of TRIDENTs become operational,*
　　*—to phase out TITAN ICBMs at the rate of 1 per month beginning in FY '83,*
　　*—not to rebase the B-52 bomber force inland,*
　　*—not to re-engine B-52s,*
　　*—not to restore the survivability of the MINUTEMAN ICBM force by deploying them in the most timely and effective basing mode—multiple, vertical protective shelters.*

*The net result of these actions and inactions will be increased strategic force vulnerability and a decline in total U.S. megatonnage of some 30 percent.*

*FY '83 Proposal. The Administration's FY '83 budget request does not seek adoption of any of the above quick fixes.*

* Construction of 300 MINUTEMAN IV ICBM missiles—to be used in proliferated vertical launching silos. The more expensive MX missile program would be continued at a more modest pace.

*FY '82 Action. No consideration has been given to this option, or to funding a future small ICBM. The MINUTEMAN production line, closed in 1977, remains shut down. The MX program has again been slowed due to deferral of selecting a permanent basing mode.*

## Committee Proposals

## *Administration Action*

*FY '83 Proposal. No consideration has been given to this option.*

- Two additional TRIDENT submarines. In an effort to reduce spending, the TRIDENT submarines are currently being built at a rate so slow that block obsolescence of the current POSEIDON fleet is certain to cause a reduction in U.S. sea-based missile platforms.

*FY '82 Action. Original Administration plans called for 3 TRIDENT SSBNs to be built every 2 years, beginning in FY '85. This was cut back and the Administration is likely to be hard-pressed to keep to its own revised schedule of 1 TRIDENT per year through FY '87. Recent budget cuts of $970 million have impaired the Administration's plan to deliver 1 TRIDENT in FY '82. With the removal of POLARIS submarines from strategic forces, SLBM launchers have decreased from 656 in 1980 to 496.*

*FY '83 Proposal. The Administration has requested $2.8 billion in FY '83 for the procurement of 2 TRIDENT SSBNs. The Administration's five-year defense plan funds 6 more TRIDENT SSBNs (9 were previously authorized) for a total of 15. If the POSEIDON submarines are phased out on schedule and no further TRIDENTs are funded, we would have only 360 SLBM launchers in 1997.*

- The first 100 B-1A long-range combat aircraft capable of penetrating enemy airspace on nuclear or conventional missions. These would subsequently be followed by other B-1 derivatives fitted for carrying cruise missiles, and for other missions.

*FY '82 Action. The decision to produce 100 B-1 derivatives (B-1B) has been made. However, the first squadron will not be ready until 1986, at the earliest. No decision has been made on the production of additional B-1 derivatives, although R & D will be continued on a "stealth" advanced technology bomber for the 1990s.*

*FY '83 Proposal. The Administration has requested $4.8 billion in FY '83 for the B-1B program, up from $2.1 billion in FY '82.*

- Additional air-launched, sea-launched and ground-launched cruise missiles and PERSHING I and PERSHING II tactical ballistic missiles in an overall aggregate of 1300.

*FY '82 Action. The Air Force's ALCM program has suffered delays and the first squadron of ALCM-carrying B-52Gs is expected to reach initial operating capability (IOC) in December 1982. The Navy is proceeding*

## Committee Proposals

## *Administration Action*

*with plans to arm ballistic missile and attack submarines with 200 to 400 nuclear-armed cruise missiles by 1986. No new deployments of PERSHING Is are planned, and the deployment of 108 PERSHING IIs and 464 GLCMs in Europe is scheduled to begin in December 1983.*

*FY '83 Proposal. The Administration has requested $1.9 billion in FY '83 for the accelerated purchase of nuclear and conventionally armed cruise missiles. The Air Force and Navy seek to increase their procurement of cruise missiles above this year's totals.*

• The production and deployment of enhanced radiation warheads to enhance the U.S. nuclear posture at strategic and theater levels.

*FY '82 Action. The decision to produce and stockpile enhanced radiation warheads on U.S. territory has been made. However, the warheads will not be deployed to the appropriate theaters except in times of crisis or conflict.*

*FY '83 Proposal. The Administration has reaffirmed this commitment in its FY '83 budget submission.*

• Expanded civil defense planning and preparations. The current U.S. civil defense program is virtually non-existent. It is predicated on a fundamental belief that nuclear war is too horrible to justify attempts to survive it—a view not shared by the rulers of the Soviet Union.

*FY '82 Action. Civil defense has been given increased emphasis. U.S. strategic defenses are to be upgraded by the addition of new over-the-horizon "backscatter" radars, modernized interceptors, and 6 AWACS surveillance aircraft. R & D for ABM will continue. No decision has yet been made to enhance the survivability of our ICBM force by employing BMD technology. Budget action has forced delays in the upgrading program, particularly in the procurement of F-15 interceptors for CONUS air defense.*

*FY '83 Proposal. The Administration has requested $237 million for civil defense in FY '83. While declaring that current BMD*

## Committee Proposals

## *Administration Action*

*technology is "not adequate" to defend against Soviet missiles, R & D funding for ABM will increase substantially.*

b) *Strengthening U.S. Conventional Forces.* The Committee's proposal for the period 1980–1986 calls for the expansion of U.S. conventional forces in the particulars indicated below.

- Five action Army divisions would be added so as to provide rapidly deployable forces without reducing deterrent strength required for the security of NATO, Japan, South Korea and other Allies.

*FY '82 Action. Instead of adding additional divisions, the Administration has significantly cut the originally planned increase in active Army strength, bringing its planned strength down to 784,000 in FY '82. It will also scale down the active status of the 7th Infantry Division in FY '83 and cut its size from roughly 14,500 to 5,000.*

*FY '83 Proposal. No increases are planned in active Army strength.*

- Nine active tactical air wings (six Air Force, three Navy/Marine) would be added to support ground force increases and to permit the rotational forward deployment of air wings to support stability in the Middle East, the Persian Gulf and other trouble-prone areas.

*FY '82 Action. No new tactical air wings were proposed in FY '82. Recent budget action resulted in the reduction of the A-10 program and the stretch-out of F-15 procurement.*

*FY '83 Proposal. The Administration proposes an increase of 4 Air Force tactical air wings (2 active, 2 Air National Guard and reserve) by FY '86, and 4 more after FY '86. Active Navy tactical air wings will rise from 12 to 14 by FY '87. The Administration also plans purchases of 1,107 F-15s by FY '87, up from the previously planned 729, and has programmed funds in FY '83 to procure 20 A-10s.*

- Ten additional tactical airlift squadrons would be provided to support in-theater movements of U.S. and Allied forces.

*FY '82 Action. No action was taken on this.*

*FY '83 Proposal. This recommendation has yet to be addressed.*

## Committee Proposals

- Current strategic airlift capabilities would be doubled. The use of currently available designs would help accelerate production at minimum cost.

- Additional ships to create a 650-ship navy by 1990—the minimum necessary to provide a three-ocean navy and a permanent Caribbean presence.

## Administration Action

*FY '82 Action. The Pentagon has decided not to procure a new transport plane such as the CX, but rather to buy nearly $11 billion worth of existing transports, including 44 KC-10s and 50 C-5Ns. This is expected to double U.S. airlift capabilities by 1989.*

*FY '83 Proposal. The Administration is requesting $860 million to buy 2 C-5Ns and $829 million for 8 KC-10s in FY '83.*

*FY '82 Action. The Administration's shipbuilding program calls for a 600 "deployable" ship Navy. But, the Administration's shipbuilding program falls well short of the Committee's recommendations, as the following chart indicates:*

| 6-YEAR SHIP CONSTRUCTION | CARTER PROGRAM | *REAGAN* FY '82- FY '87 | COMMITTEE PROGRAM |
|---|---|---|---|
| Submarines | 21 | 25 | 27 |
| Surface Combatants | 49 | 70 | 107 |
| Amphibious Ships | 3 | 11 | 20 |
| Support Ships | 33 | 44 | 79 |
| TOTAL | 106 | 150 | 233 |

*The Administration cut back its FY '82 shipbuilding program from 18 to 15 ships, and its overall shipbuilding program for FY '82- FY '87 by 13 ships. In addition, 18 ships, including 10 in FY '82, will be retired early.*

*To reduce pressure on our naval deployment in the Indian Ocean, only one carrier task force will be on station.*

*FY '83 Proposal. The Administration proposes a 569-ship Navy by FY '83 and a 640-ship Navy by 1990, counting sealift, auxiliary, and reserve mobilization ships. Most of the shipbuilding would take place in the last two years of the five-year plan. Pending that, shipbuilding is barely adequate to sustain current levels, much less provide for growth.*

## Committee Proposals

- Increases in defense manpower levels would be provided as indicated in the following tabulation—with data for 1964 included for comparison (expressed in thousands):

## *Administration Action*

*FY '82 Action. Administration manpower totals do not conform with Committee recommendations. Budgetary actions have slowed the planned manpower buildup. The originally planned buildup in Army strength has been cut significantly, resulting in a planned strength of 784,000 in FY '82. The originally planned buildup in Air Force strength has also been cut, resulting in a planned strength of 581,000 in FY '82. Navy and Marine Corps strength will rise to 745,000.*

*FY '83 Proposal. The Administration plans no change in active Army strength. Modest increases have been requested in planned Air Force and Navy strength. The number of active-duty military personnel is expected to rise to 2,148,000 in FY '83.*

| COMMITTEE MANPOWER PROPOSALS | (1964) | 1980 | 1981 | | 1982 | ACTUAL: *REAGAN* FY '81 | *'82* | 1983 | 1984 | 1985 |
|---|---|---|---|---|---|---|---|---|---|---|
| Army | (972) | 774 | 806 | | 836 | 781 | 784 | 866 | 896 | 926 |
| Navy/Marine | (857) | 713 | 728 | | 743 | 731 | 745 | 758 | 773 | 788 |
| Air Force | (856) | 558 | 573 | | 588 | 570 | 581 | 603 | 618 | 633 |
| | (2685) | 2045 | 2107 | | 2167 | 2082 | 2110 | 2227 | 2287 | 2347 |

## Other Committee Proposals

*Force Readiness and War Reserves.* U.S. military forces should be increased so that they could, if required, resist and overcome military aggression by the Soviets or their client states for a sustained period of time.

## *Administration Action*

*FY '82 Action. Army readiness has shown an improvement since the time 6 of 10 U.S.-based divisions were classified as "unfit for combat." Only one is still rated as unready. This improvement is primarily due to the transfer of non-commissioned officers (NCOs) from overseas bases to U.S.-based divisions. Nevertheless, shortages of spare parts and equipment still plague all of the services, severely impairing their combat readiness. The Navy plans to help combat this by increasing procurement of aircraft spare parts.*

## Other Committee Proposals

### Administration Action

*FY '83 Proposal. The Administration has reiterated its desire to seek necessary improvements in readiness by gradually increasing inventories of war reserves.*

*Equipment Maintenance.* The procurement of modern operational military equipment should be increased to overcome current rates of wear and tear and permit a sizable increase in active force levels over the next five years.

*FY '82 Action. Planned equipment procurement levels have been reduced. The Navy has cut aircraft purchases from the planned 312 in FY '83 to 298, and from 372 in FY '84 to 356. The Air Force will cancel or delay procurement of aircraft or other equipment to comply with recent budget action. It will, however, seek to procure 60 days' supply of missiles and munitions by FY '87 in a move to increase readiness and logistic functions. The Army will increase R & D funding for ballistic missile defense (BMD) and command, control, and communications ($C^3$). Other programs will be cancelled or delayed:*

> *—the ROLAND air defense system will be terminated;*
> *—the planned increase in the production rate of the M-1 tank from 60 to 90 tanks per month will be delayed by one year; the number of tanks procured in FY '82 will drop from 720 to a minimum of 665.*
> *—procurement of 3 fire units and 70 missiles for the PATRIOT missile system will be slowed.*

*FY '83 Proposal. Navy and Air Force aircraft purchases are planned to increase gradually. The Navy plans to buy 288 aircraft in FY '83 and 359 in FY '84. The Navy's five-year aircraft procurement plan calls for 1,917 aircraft over the FY '83–FY '87 period. The Army will seek to procure 776 M-1 tanks in FY '83. The FY '83 budget also calls for procurement of 376 PATRIOT air defense missiles, up from 176 in FY '82.*

*Personnel, Skills and Pay.* The present wage ceilings on military pay have forced U.S. uniformed personnel to absorb a disproportionate share of uncontrolled inflation

*FY '82 Action. The Administration has approved a 10 to 17 percent pay raise for military personnel. While this is not enough to offset the 20 percent disparity between*

## Other Committee Proposals

### *Administration Action*

and devalued dollars abroad. A 20 percent disparity between military and civilian pay scales has been condoned. Inadequacy of pay and allowances is a principal reason for the Services' inability to retain adequate numbers of middle-grade commanders, supervisors and skilled technicians. There should be an immediate and substantial pay increase for military personnel to improve the retention rate of skilled people and to attract more capable volunteers.

*military and civilian pay scales, recruitment and retention rates of skilled military personnel have improved. All military services in FY '81 met the troop strengths authorized by Congress for the first time since the draft ended in 1972. In addition, a record 81 percent of all recruits were high school graduates, up from 68 percent in FY '80. Still, serious manpower problems with the All-Volunteer Force (AVF) remain, and manpower costs are 41 percent of planned FY '83 budget outlays.*

*FY '83 Proposal. The Administration plans to submit a supplemental appropriation for FY '82 to cover the cost of recent pay increases. Military pay is scheduled to rise only 8 percent in FY '83.*

A democratic and equitable Selective Service system should be instituted as changing circumstances require. The call for simple draft registration, without even classification, will do nothing, by itself, to provide and retain skilled personnel necessary for the armed forces. Nothing short of a program to mobilize the nation's human resources can solve the problem.

*FY '82 Action. The Administration has not acted to repeal the Selective Service registration law enacted under the previous Administration. It continues to oppose a draft, preferring to rely on pay and benefit incentives to solve the critical manpower and readiness problems associated with the All-Volunteer Force.*

*FY '83 Proposal. The Administration plans to introduce a new G.I. benefits bill.*

*Industrial Mobilization.* Along with substantially increased defense procurement, the United States should reconstitute its lost capabilities for industrial mobilization, in order to support future military and civil defense requirements.

*FY '82 Action. The increase in U.S. defense funding proposed by the Administration over the FY '82-FY '86 period is planned to increase the growth rate of U.S. defense industrial production. However, problems remain, including those relating to emergency mobilization, because of a continuing decline in essential production capabilities. For example:*

> *—the number of domestic foundries has been steadily declining for 2 decades;*
> *—a critical shortage of strategic materials essential for defense production still exists;*

## Other Committee Proposals

## Administration Action

—long lead-times and production bottlenecks have resulted in increased delays in equipment procurement.

*FY '83 Proposal. Employment in defense-related industries is expected to increase, rising by 347,000 in FY '83 to 2,862,000. The Administration will take steps to encourage defense contractor capital investment, and to develop a production surge capability where economically feasible.*

*Arms Transfers.* The U.S. should resume production and stockpiling of arms suitable for rapid transfer to endangered friends and allies. The U.S. can not afford to draw down its own military inventories as the price for supporting friends.

*FY '82 Action. The Administration proposed creation of a special defense acquisition fund to procure equipment in anticipation of foreign transfers to fulfill requirements of allied and friendly nations, while at the same time minimizing any adverse impact on U.S. force readiness that could result from drawdowns of U.S. service stocks.*

*FY '83 Proposal. The Administration reiterated its goal to improve the acquisition process.*

*Other Administration Proposals. The Administration proposed in its strategic program outlined on 5 October 1981 a comprehensive upgrading and enhancement of U.S. command, control, and communications ($C^3$) capabilities.*

## VII. CONCLUSION

The Administration's defense program is a minimal one. It will not halt the unfavorable trends in the U.S.-Soviet military balance, let alone reverse them.

In the nuclear area, timely programs to restore the survivability of U.S. strategic forces are not included in the Administration's program. The program does seek to bolster U.S. strength in conventional forces, but the levels proposed are, in most cases, well below those put forth by the Committee on the Present Danger two years ago.

Consequently, any reduction in the Administration's proposed defense effort would further erode our national security.

The time for the United States to restore its defenses is fleeting. Failure to close the window of vulnerability could tempt the Soviet Union to exploit its vast military power.

Regretfully, the conclusions reached by the Committee on the Present Danger in its first Statement on 11 November 1976,[4] remain valid today:

> Our country is in a period of danger, and the danger is increasing. Unless decisive steps are taken to alert the nation, and to change the course of its policy, our economic and military capacity will become inadequate to assure peace with security.

*17 March 1982*

## NOTES

1. On 9 May 1980, the Committee on the Present Danger proposed a U.S. Defense Strategy for the 1980s to counter the increasing Soviet threat to American interests. Our current report compares the programs then proposed by the Committee with those of the Reagan Administration and appraises the differences (see Chapter 16).
2. A fuller treatment of Section III, "The Economics of Defense," is contained in the appendix to this report.
3. These proposals are direct quotes from the Committee's 9 May 1980 report: "Countering the Soviet Threat: U.S. Defense Strategy in the 1980s" (Chapter 16).
4. "Common Sense and the Common Danger," 11 November 1976 (Chapter 2).

# APPENDIX

## THE ECONOMICS OF DEFENSE

The most important thing to say about the economics of defense is also the simplest. Defending the country is not free. It has its costs. But so do all other good things—feeding the country, housing the country, and so on. To say that defense, like these other things, has its costs does not imply that those costs are not worthwhile.

The cost of defense is the diversion of productive resources—labor and capital—from other uses. The labor and capital that make military aircraft cannot be used to make video games. The men and women who serve in the armed forces cannot also serve in the police department. But that is true of all other good things. The men and women who raise cattle cannot also run hotels. The question in all these cases is whether the particular use of the resources is more valuable than the alternatives to which they might be put.

People sometimes talk as if there were something special about expenditures for defense in that they yield no product. You cannot eat, drink, wear or ride in what we obtain for our national defense expenditures. But of course there is a product. The product is the national security. That is an extremely valuable product. Without it, most of the other products will not last for long or be worth very much.

It is possible to spend too much or too little on national defense, just as it is possible to spend too much or too little on housing, or on fire departments or on anything else. Even if it is agreed that more spending for defense yields more national security there is a point beyond which the addition to the national security is too small to be worthwhile. Also, even though less spending on national defense would leave more output available for other good purposes, there is some point beyond which reducing spending for defense is obviously too risky. The problem is to find the right point.

During World War II the United States devoted about 50 percent of its national output to the war effort. No one thought that was too much. No one now thinks anything like that is needed today. In the 1920s we spent less than one-half of one percent of our national output for defense. Hardly anyone thinks that would be adequate today. The relevant debate today is about the difference between spending 5½ percent of the GNP for defense and spending 7 percent on defense, despite the fact that the Committee on the Present Danger believes that the defense program proposed by the Administration is inadequate. In fiscal 1981 the United States spent about 5½ percent. The President proposes raising that to about 7 percent by 1985.

The choice between the 5½ percent program and the 7 percent program depends mainly on the assessment of the national security risks and of the contribution which the additional defense spending makes to the national security. (These questions are discussed in our basic paper, "Is the Reagan Defense Program Adequate?") But the choice also depends on the assessment of the cost. This aspect of the choice will be considered here.

The fundamental implication of spending 1½ percent more of the GNP on defense is that we shall have available 1½ percent less of GNP for all other purposes—private consumption, private investment and non-defense expenditures of government. In real terms this means something like this: The Administration estimates that real output will rise by an average annual rate of 3.5 percent between 1981 and 1985. If the defense fraction were held constant, the output available for non-defense purposes would also rise by 3.5 percent per annum. But if the defense program rises as the Administration proposes, real output available for non-defense purposes will rise by an average annual rate of 3.2 percent. The difference between this 3.2 percent annual increase and the 3.5 percent we would have if we kept the defense share constant is the most general measure of the cost of the Administration's defense program.

The Congressional Budget Office makes a lower, and probably more realistic, estimate of the increase in real output in the next several years. But this estimate does not change the picture markedly. According to the CBO estimates, output available for non-defense purposes would rise by 2.7 percent per annum if the defense share was constant and would rise by 2.3 percent per annum with the Administration's defense program.

Even with the CBO estimate of the growth of real output, the output available for non-defense purposes would rise more rapidly between 1981 and 1985 than it did between 1977 and 1981.

There is little doubt that the direct cost of having a defense program equal to 7 percent of GNP rather than 5½ percent of GNP is small. That is, if the additional expenditure makes a significant contribution to the national security it is hard to argue that the diversion of 1½ percent of GNP to that purpose is an excessive burden on the economy.

One must look, however, at possible indirect effects. These effects become most visible when we look at the Federal budget because the process of bringing about the diversion occurs through that budget. It will not be possible to skim 1½ percent of GNP equally off all persons and all uses of output, and the choice of where and how to divert GNP to defense will influence the consequences. That choice will be made through the budget.

For example, suppose that the expenditure of an additional 1½ percent of GNP for defense was financed by a Federal deficit. The main effect would be that the government's borrowing to finance the deficit would crowd out private investment. Roughly speaking, the 1½ percent of additional GNP going into defense would come out of the 6 percent or so of net private savings and net private investment. Thus, what is a small diversion from total output would be a very large diversion from the small but critical part of total output that goes into net private investment.

Financing the expansion of the defense program by borrowing would increase the costs of the expansion. It would repress private investment and the future growth of the economy. When we confront huge defense expenditures for a short period—as in most wars—we typically and properly pay for them in part by borrowing. That is not appropriate for the kind of low-level defense program which we must be prepared to sustain for a long time. But neither is it necessary. It is possible to pay the cost of defense in better ways than running a deficit.

We are talking about financing the difference between a defense program equal to 5.5 percent of GNP and 7.0 percent of GNP—or of financing 1.5 percent of GNP. That is almost exactly the size of the deficit projected for 1985 under the Administration's budget. The tax cuts enacted in 1981 are estimated to reduce the revenue by 4.2 percent of GNP in 1985. Thus, to finance the defense expansion program in 1985 by revenue increase would require an increase equal to about 35 percent of the cut made last year. Non-defense expenditures of government, after the cuts proposed by the Reagan Administration, would be about 14 percent of GNP. Thus, to finance the defense expansion by other expenditure cuts would require a cut of about 10 percent, or, more probably and more reasonably, some combination of revenue increases and expenditure reduction could be used to eliminate the deficit. This can be done without seriously impairing economic incentives or neglecting important functions of government.

It is helpful to look back at the last year when we had a balanced budget and compare it with the Reagan budget for 1985.

| | 1969 ACTUAL | 1985 PROPOSED |
|---|---|---|
| | % of GNP | |
| Total expenditures | 20.2 | 20.9 |
| defense | 8.7 | 7.0 |
| non-defense | 11.4 | 13.8 |
| Total Receipts | 20.5 | 19.1 |
| Surplus | 0.4 | −1.7 |

There is a deficit in prospect now, even though a smaller share of GNP is to be spent for defense because a larger share is being spent for non-defense purposes and a smaller share is being collected in taxes.

To raise the revenue or cut the non-defense expenditures needed to finance the defense expansion will not be pleasant or politically easy. That is only saying in another way what was said at the outset, that defending the country is not costless. But the cost of the proposed program is not basically different from what is suggested by saying that it requires diverting an additional 1½ percent of GNP to defense.

A common concern about the defense expansion is that it may be inflationary. Of course, there is a historical connection between wars and inflations. But whether or not that is a necessary connection, there is no such necessary connection between inflation and a defense program of the kind now proposed by the Administration. The argument here is perfectly simple. What causes inflation is an excessively rapid growth of *total* spending—public and private. If the growth of defense spending is financed in a way that brings about a slowdown in non-defense spending there will be no inflationary pressure of demand. That requires that the increase in defense spending be balanced by increased tax revenue or by a slowdown of non-defense spending or that monetary conditions be maintained which will keep the deficit from being inflationary.

In fact, most economic forecasters inside and outside the government, taking account of the proposed defense increase, predict that the inflation rate will come down during the next five years. That is perfectly consistent with what is expected of overall fiscal and monetary policy.

It is worth noting that during the Administrations of Presidents Eisenhower and Kennedy, when defense expenditures were 9 to 10 percent of GNP, there was little inflation. Also, the acceleration of inflation in the 1970s occurred while defense expenditures as a share of GNP were falling to their lowest level in thirty years.

The point is often made that although defense expenditures will not be large relative to *total* GNP, and can be financed in ways that do not increase the inflationary pressure of *total* demand, nevertheless the defense demand is concentrated on certain industries, materials and skills and will be inflationary in those sectors. This is closely connected to another point. It is said that the effort to increase defense procurement *quickly* will drive prices up and cause waste in other ways, so that the program would be achieved more efficiently if it were pushed more gradually.

There are several things to say about this:

Part of the normal and efficient process by which resources are diverted to the sectors in which there is increasing demand is a rise of prices in those sectors relative to the sectors in which demand is not rising or is declining. We *want* prices and wages in the defense sectors to rise relative to prices and wages elsewhere enough to attract the labor and capital needed for the defense effort. But, if overall economic policy is not inflationary, this need not raise the overall price level. There will be restraint of demand in the non-defense sectors which will slow down price increases there.

Although some shift of relative prices is natural and necessary, this shift will probably not be very great in the next several years. That is because the planned program will not put a great strain on important specialized sectors of the economy. The program does not include many new systems requiring extraordinary absorptions of scientists and engineers in their development. The program begins at a point where defense production is very low. Important parts of the program can be achieved by increasing output up to the level of capacity already existing, and that will reduce rather than increase unit costs. Industrial production in the defense and space industries is a little less now than it was in 1968, whereas total industrial production early in 1980 was 40 percent higher. In 1972 defense procurement absorbed 8.4 percent of the output of the heavy and technological industries, where supply difficulties are most likely to be encountered, insofar as they are encountered at all. By 1977 this ratio had fallen to 6.1 percent. It has since, in 1981, recovered to 7.3 percent. With the President's program it would rise further to 10 percent in 1985. This does not look like a program that will put great strain on many sectors of the American economy.

Of course, there will be points at which slowing down the program will reduce its cost. But it will also be generally true that slowing down the program reduces its value. A plane or a tank delivered ten years from now is not as useful as one delivered five years from now. This has to be taken into consideration, and there is no general principle for answering how much saving is worth how much delay. This has to be decided on a case-by-case basis.

There is a large problem in managing the expansion of the defense program. It will go more efficiently, quickly and economically if it is well-managed. Decisions about the Congressional authorization and appropriations should be made promptly and contracts should be let quickly so that contractors can prepare in an orderly way. The Department of Defense should push forward with its program for expanding the list of qualified contractors and informing potential producers of future defense requirements. The Department should have authority to assist in the building of plant capacity that may not otherwise be available.

At a more general level, the effects of the defense expansion on the economy will depend on the monetary and fiscal policy that accompanies it. But the most significant thing to say is that with reasonably intelligent policy the burden of the program on the economy will not be excessive.

# 18

# HAS AMERICA
# BECOME NUMBER 2?

## The U.S.-Soviet Military Balance and
## American Defense Policies and Programs

"We must provide the defense spending and programs necessary to correct immediate and short-term vulnerabilities and deficiencies. Our nuclear deterrent forces must be made survivable as rapidly as possible to close the window of vulnerability before it opens any wider."

—Ronald Reagan, 20 August 1980

"What are we supposed to do in the meantime—that is, during the period of the 1980s when everybody agrees we shall be in a position of maximum exposure to nuclear war or nuclear blackmail? Under such circumstances the threat of retaliatory attack . . . would lose its credibility and deterrent effect."

—Eugene V. Rostow, SALT II testimony,
6 September 1979

"We are not only facing a period between 1981 to perhaps 1987 in which we are deficient in regional nuclear power, and in conventional power, but, for the first time in post-World War II history, we will be vulnerable and deficient in central strategic nuclear power. . . . The United States has permitted itself to be exposed in this vital area of first-strike vulnerability in the ballistic missile area—fixed silo capability. I think that is an unacceptable position for us to be in."

—Alexander Haig, Confirmation Hearing,
12 January 1981

"The window of vulnerability is really being expanded by (the Administration's strategic) program. . . ."

—Senator Sam Nunn (D-Georgia)
4 November 1981

"A decisive shift in the correlation of forces will be such that come 1985, we will be able to exert our will wherever we need to."

—Soviet President Leonid Brezhnev
in Prague, 1973

## PROLOGUE

In 1978, the Committee on the Present Danger published its analysis of the U.S.-Soviet military balance entitled, "Is America Becoming Number 2: Current Trends in the U.S.-Soviet Military Balance." The Committee's answer then was unequivocal: "Yes, America is becoming Number 2." It is now time to ask: Has America become Number 2? Or has the United States taken the actions necessary to reverse the unfavorable trends in the U.S.-Soviet military balance which our Committee has detailed since its founding?

Since the publication of the Committee's previous report on the military balance, the American public has been exposed to a national debate on SALT II, on Soviet military programs and their implications for U.S. national security, and on alternative means of dealing with the situation. During this period, more and more information has emerged detailing the extent of the Soviet military buildup and the relative decline of U.S. military capabilities.

During the 1980 Presidential campaign, both sides agreed that the trends in the balance had been adverse, and that their cumulative effects necessitated an increased American military effort. The Carter Administration revised upward its planned defense expenditures and argued that its new program would eventually reverse the increasingly adverse trends. Spokesmen for the Reagan campaign countered by arguing that the Carter program would provide too little, too late, and pledged to do more, more expeditiously. In particular, they pointed to a strategic "window of vulnerability," which, under the Carter program, would extend from the early 1980s well into the late 1980s. This window, they contended, must be closed firmly and without delay.

In May, 1980, the Committee on the Present Danger published its own defense program and budget recommendations, summarized in "Countering the Soviet Threat: U.S. Defense Strategy in the 1980s." The report concluded that then current American defense programs were inadequate to preserve the U.S. strategic nuclear deterrent and to restore the fighting capability of U.S. general purpose forces; and it urged a stronger, more timely effort.

Recently, the Committee reviewed its 1980 recommendations and compared them with the current defense plan. The Committee concluded:

> "The Administration's defense program is a minimal one. It will not halt the unfavorable trends in the U.S.-Soviet military balance, let alone reverse them."[1]

The President of the United States has now stated candidly what official analyses have been warning for some time: "The truth of the matter is that on balance the Soviet Union does have a definite margin of superiority—enough so there is risk, and there is what I have called, as you all know several times, a window of vulnerability."[2] And the Secretary of Defense subsequently acknowledged, "Unfortunately, it is true."[3]

Such frank and explicit statements on the part of the President and Secretary of Defense have provoked criticism. Some critics and commentators simply have rejected the statements; others have argued that a margin of Soviet superiority may exist, but that it does not hold military or political significance; and still others have decried the statements as inappropriate, *per se*.

This Committee report updates our previous analysis of the military balance, and examines serious vulnerabilities and deficiencies in U.S. military strength. Its conclusion reinforces the President's statement, and emphasizes that the adverse balance entails both political and military risks. The Committee believes that public understanding of the current situation is the necessary first step to effective remedial action, and that such action is essential to our national well-being.

## THE VIEW FROM THE KREMLIN

Before examining the military balance, it is necessary to understand how the Soviets view the military balance and world politics.

The Soviets view the world in adversarial terms in which the central strategic concept is that of the "correlation of forces." The correlation of forces is a summation of all aspects of relative national power, particularly the relationship between Soviet power and countervailing forces. It encompasses tangibles and intangibles, military and non-military, with the military element paramount. The concept, however, is more than a mere balance sheet; it is also a philosophy of conflict and a guide to action. To the Soviets, the correlation of forces is the major determinant of international relations. An accurate assessment yields correct knowledge of power relationships and trends, permits calculations of the probable cost-risk-benefit of international actions, and determines opportunities and the timing of actions. The task of the Soviet regime is to develop a correlation of forces which advances Soviet interests and achieves Soviet imperialist goals.

The Soviets hold that the military balance is central to the correlation of forces, and that the nuclear balance is central to the military balance; and central to both in the Soviet view is ability to wage war. The ultimate measure of military power, nuclear as well as non-nuclear, is relative capability to wage war. This is also the measure of deterrence. But deterrence, to the Soviets, is not the passive protective concept it is in the West. It is not merely dissuasive; it is also suasive—a direct means of influencing others. It not only undermines the military, or deterrent, power of adversaries, it also bestows a capacity to dictate or influence behavior.

Superiority over the United States in nuclear capability means control over nuclear escalation, which determines the ability to threaten, and influences greatly the decision to use military force of any kind. The Soviets see such an advantage as particularly telling in crises and confrontations.

In considering the military balance, it is essential to keep in mind that the two sides arm for different purposes and regard nuclear arms differently. One of the Committee's founding members has expressed the difference succinctly:

> Our purpose in having nuclear weapons is defensive and deterrent, to prevent aggression against our vital national interests. The Soviet purpose . . . is to serve as the ultimate engine of a process of nuclear blackmail—a process of expansion involving the use of or the credible threat to use propaganda, terrorism, proxy war, subversion, or Soviet troops under the sanction and protection of Soviet nuclear superiority.[4]

Hence, the implications of a nuclear advantage for one side or the other are profoundly different in political, strategic, and moral terms, a fact commonly ignored by advocates of a nuclear freeze (which at present would leave the nuclear, as well as the conventional, advantage with the aggressive rather than the defensive side). Nuclear arms competition is not competition between two sides with the same goal, or the same view of the utility of nuclear weapons. The Soviets do not accept the notion that it is possible to have a surfeit of nuclear weapons in their arsenal. They know that there is all the difference in the world between their capacity to destroy the most important U.S. strategic forces with one-fifth or with four-fifths of their arsenal. In the first case, the Soviet nuclear arm radiates intimidating power throughout the Western world; in the second, the Soviet nuclear threat is checked.

"Détente," to the Soviets, is also inseparable from this chain of logic. They view it as a policy forced upon the West by the changed correlation of forces, and particularly by Soviet strategic superiority. To the Soviets, the essence of détente is that the West will not use military means to oppose further change in the correlation of forces in favor of the Soviet Union. To the West, détente has mistakenly been thought to mean *mutual* restraint and cooperation, particularly to avoid or defuse international incidents that might lead to confrontation and raising the specter of war. But to the Soviets détente has meant that the West, acting prudently in line with the new correlation of forces, would unilaterally avoid such confrontations; i.e., would acquiesce in the expansion of Soviet power and influence.

The Soviets clearly believe that a major shift in the correlation of world forces in their favor has already occurred[5] and will continue unless there is a major change in U.S. defense policies. The foundation of this shift is the change in the military balance in their favor, and the increasing recognition of this change by other governments. It is this change in the military balance that has been assigned the highest priority in Soviet national objectives.

The Soviets now enjoy general military superiority over the West. The Soviets know they do, and they believe the United States also knows it. There are, however, three qualifications as they see it: (1) The edge of superiority is not enough; the Soviets believe that the more superiority the better, and it is only prudent to assume that they intend to continue devoting resources to that objective. (2) Even though the United States recognizes the changed military balance, U.S. leaders do not apparently appreciate its full extent and significance. (3) A truly determined, vigorous U.S. rearmament effort might in time remove Soviet advantages and restore American deterrent power across the spectrum. The Soviets are not convinced that the United States is capable of this, but they know that they must watch carefully. They hope to encourage Western acceptance of the unfavorable balance—resignation to it, in fact. But they fear that should the Americans move decisively to change the balance, the trends can be reversed and the "window of vulnerability" closed. In that event, Soviet leaders might perceive a time-limited window of opportunity, and face difficult decisions as to whether, when and how to seize a fleeting opportunity.

The conclusions to be drawn from this assessment are that the Soviets will continue their military buildup with no diminution of effort or determination; they will seek to further impress the West with the full extent of Soviet power, but they prefer to do so in a way calculated to promote resignation rather than counter-action. The more inadequate the collective Western defense effort, the more confident and assertive the Soviets will become. As relative Soviet power continues to grow, the Soviets expect the U.S. and its allies to move increasingly toward accommodation and appeasement. Already, groups in the U.S. and Western Europe seem fearful over American attempts to reverse the balance, believing that such an effort might provoke the Soviets to exploit the advantages they have already gained.

While the Soviets hope to weaken the West and extend Soviet influence without a major war, Soviet doctrine requires careful, exhaustive preparation for war at any level. Not only is it necessary for the armed forces and the population to be prepared to fight a war, but also the Soviets believe that the side manifestly better prepared for war is most likely to get its way without having to resort to war. Since war may occur, preparations for it can lessen damage and promote victory. Preparation for war most particularly means preparation for nuclear war and for the effective use of nuclear weapons, which the Soviets have skillfully integrated into their military doctrine and operations. To the Soviets the nuclear weapon is not only the most potent instrument of military warfare, it is also one of political warfare. The Soviets understand the political and psychological paralysis that nuclear weapons and the specter of nuclear war can effect in the West, and they seek to promote and exploit that paralysis.

Soviet professional literature—not propaganda written for the West but Russians talking professionally to Russians—makes clear that the Soviets do not share the prevalent view that nuclear war is unthinkable and unwinnable and that the only objective of strategic doctrine must be mutual deterrence. On the contrary, that literature reveals that they look at the world quite differently; that war, even nuclear war, is an extension of politics; that nuclear superiority is politically usable; and that the Soviets must prepare for nuclear war-fighting, war-surviving and war-winning. The goal of their nuclear policy is not necessarily to start a war, but to attain a position of such nuclear superiority as to be able to force Western accommodation to Soviet policy by posing a credible array of unacceptable risks. Yet they also believe that the United States and its allies may well turn and fight when they are driven into the ultimate corner. The Soviets therefore plan on the assumption that war is quite possible, and they are prepared to resort to any means, including nuclear, to win a war.

In the Soviet view, victory will go to the side that is best prepared in equipment, doctrine and morale. Victory is also abetted by surprise, i.e., striking first, and maintaining the initiative. Soviet doctrine emphasizes the importance of a "preemptive" strike on enemy forces, command-control centers, nuclear and conventional reserves, and other military formations, as required. "Preemptive," in this context, means destroying forces of the imminent victims of aggression before they can be used. Consequently, the Soviets have emphasized the development of strong counterforce, offensive capabilities for both intercontinental and theater warfare.

Contrary to U.S. strategic doctrine and planning, Soviet doctrine affirms the utility of defensive operations in the nuclear age. It is the Soviet view that offensive and defensive means operate synergistically, while it is the American tendency to disparage the role and effectiveness of defense against nuclear attacks. The Soviets espouse and implement both active defenses and civil defense, while many Americans believe such defenses to be futile or "destabilizing." As the Secretary of Defense has pointed out:

> While the Soviets have emphasized both offensive and defensive forces, the United States has largely neglected defense preparations. The Soviets have also continued development of and paid increasing attention to civil defense and a wide variety of measures, designed to enhance the prospect of survivability of key elements of their society after the outbreak of a nuclear war.[6]

The Soviets continue to maintain a rich nationwide air defense, while the United States has virtually abandoned such a defense.[7]

The Soviets also sustain an impressive ballistic missile defense development and testing program, with rapidly deployable and current technology systems and systems with future potential. While the United States has deactivated the one ABM site allowed by the SALT I ABM agreement, the Soviets have modernized and enhanced their Moscow ABM site. Clearly, the Soviets agreed to the SALT I ABM Treaty not because they had become converted to the concept of Mutual Assured Destruction (MAD), as American supporters of SALT I argued, but because the United States then enjoyed a significant lead in ABM technology (since lost) and because Soviet strategic goals would have been more difficult to achieve had the United States carried through with its plans to defend its Minuteman ICBM force.

In sum, Soviet military doctrine and programs reflect a determined opponent who sees military force as a means of obtaining political ends, and hence is willing to devote the resources necessary to maintain military superiority.

By contrast, the United States has had an uncertain political and military strategy, and in recent years has appeared to be retreating toward a minimal defense posture inconsistent with its worldwide commitments and interests. This trend has led many to the conclusion that the United States has accepted as inevitable the decline of its power relative to the Soviet Union and, hence, the decline of its role as leader of the Free World.

The Committee on the Present Danger was founded on the belief that such decline is neither acceptable nor inevitable. This is clearly now the view of the American people as well. The question is whether the United States is doing enough to arrest the decline and turn it around in time.[8]

## THE ELEMENTS OF U.S. DEFENSE

### A. Funding

The United States has for a decade and a half grossly underfunded its military forces. This cumulative underfunding has seriously reduced readiness and retarded modernization, in stark contrast to expanding Soviet military capabilities.

Soviet military funding has exceeded that of the United States every year since 1969 with a steady rate of increase that has progressively widened the gap between the two efforts.[9] While the Soviet military budget increased yearly, that of the United States actually declined in real terms nine out of eleven years between FY 1969 and FY 1979.[10] In military investment (arms research, development, procurement, and military construction), the Soviets have outspent the United States by over $400 billion during the past decade.[11] By 1980, annual Soviet military investment was nearly double that of the United States. The important gains in the military balance that have already resulted from the Soviet effort, then, will become even more impressive over the next several years as this differential in investment is reflected in fielded capabilities. That is to say, the force comparisons will continue to worsen before there is any chance for improvement.

As the 1983 Department of Defense Report to Congress concluded, "We have not yet experienced the full consequences of our lagging investments of the 1970s."[12] Secretary of Defense Weinberger recently told the Senate Foreign Relations Committee that the United States now "lacked the requisite military capability for adequate nuclear deterrence as well as conventional defense of our vital objectives and commitments." And, he said, our "military capabilities would become increasingly inadequate to deter aggression."[13]

Underinvestment has prevented the U.S. from keeping pace with Soviet modernization and has brought about deterioration of U.S. military capabilities. In the five years prior to the Reagan Administration, the United States funded only about one-half of the procurement necessary to maintain existing capabilities, without attempting to close the gap with the Soviets.

Meanwhile, the Soviet military buildup proceeds unabated with a steady annual increase in spending that is expected to continue despite predicted problems in the Soviet economy, in Russia's East European satrapies, and elsewhere.

The United States has allies whose forces contribute relatively more to the common defense than do Soviet satellites to Warsaw Pact military capability. Unfortunately, the allies' contributions have lagged at least as much as the American effort (far more in the case of some, such as Japan and Canada) and are rising even more slowly than U.S. expenditures. Coordination with allies, as the Department of Defense points out, can increase "the effectiveness with which our own defense resources are marshaled."[14] Joint efforts are essential, and U.S. allies have much to offer. Important as they are, however, allied contributions do not offset the enormous differences between U.S. and Soviet efforts and capabilities.[15]

The question is often asked whether U.S. allies are contributing their "fair share." The relevant question is whether they, and the United States, are doing enough. The answer is clearly no. Not only are greater and more effective joint efforts necessary, but, as a matter of simple equity, the overall effort of each of our allies should be proportional to that of the United States. Increased joint efforts will further demonstrate Alliance solidarity. Finally, the U.S. and its allies must narrow their differences on appropriate strategy, and on their respective roles and responsibilities, in Europe and elsewhere.

As this report shows, the military balance described by the Committee on the Present Danger in 1978[16] has steadily worsened. Projected trends remain adverse, even given the recently proposed increases in the defense budget. The Committee warned that, in the

GRAPH 1. U.S. Defense Budget as a Percent of Gross National Product, 1940–1981

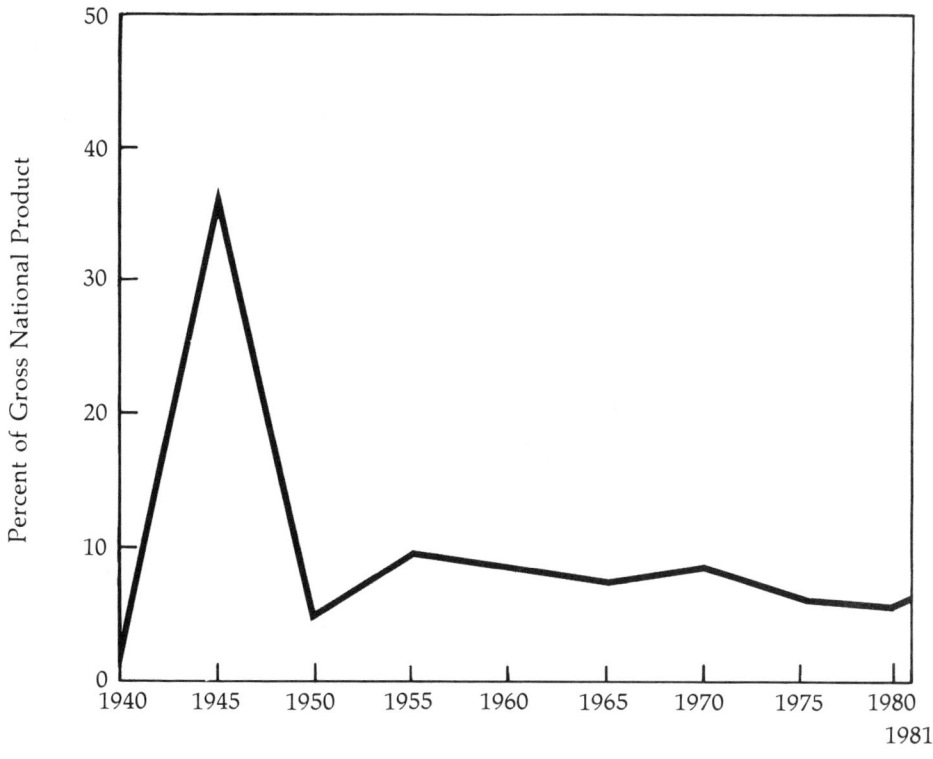

Fiscal Year

*Source:* Secretary of Defense, *Annual Report, FY 1983*, p. I-7.

GRAPH 2. Comparison of US Defense Outlays with Estimated Dollar Cost of Soviet Defense Activities

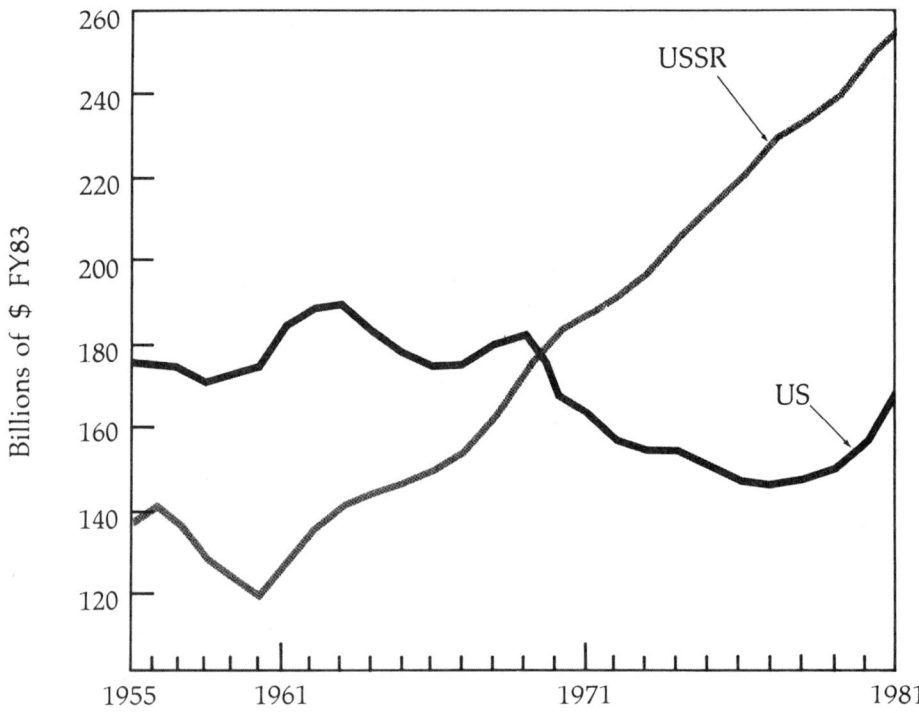

Notes:    U.S. defense outlays include national security programs funded by
          DOD and defense related outlays of Department of Energy, Coast
          Guard, and Selective Service and their Soviet counterparts.

          Excludes retirement, foreign military sales and civil defense.

Source: Adapted from Secretary of Defense, *Annual Report, FY 1983*, p. I-5.

absence of resolute action to reverse the trends in the military balance, the United States
and its allies would face a period of clear Soviet military superiority and increased
international instability. This has come to pass.

A great effort is needed to reverse these trends and to restore U.S. military strength for
meeting the challenges of the 1980s. There should be no misunderstanding about the
magnitude of the task. Increases in defense spending of only a few percent per year will
not halt the growing rate of Soviet advantage. *If Soviet military spending continues to
expand at past and predicted rates, the Administration's proposed defense increases—even
if left intact by Congress—will be clearly inadequate to restore U.S. defenses.*

## Restoring U.S. Strength

The charts on the following page, taken from the Department of Defense report,
"Soviet Military Power," illustrate the magnitude of the task. They show, for example,
that, compared to the 100 or so MX missiles the U.S. proposes to produce over the next
decade, the Soviets produce 200 (comparably sized, or larger) ICBMS *annually,* and have

GRAPH 3. Ratio of Accumulated Military Investments

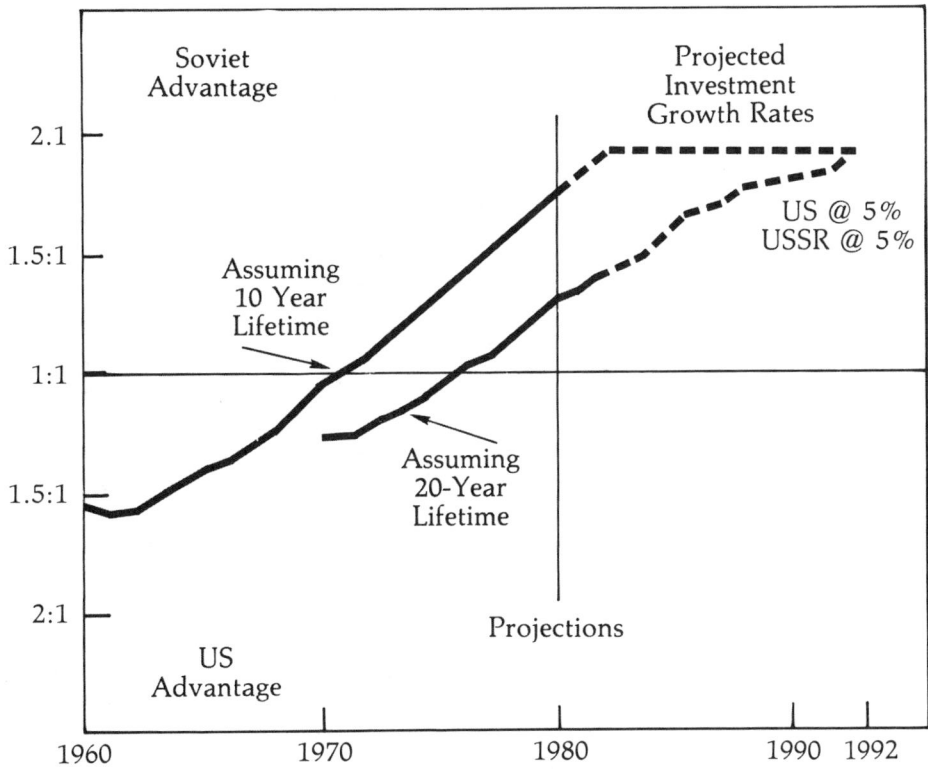

Source: Adapted from Secretary of Defense, *Annual Report, FY 1983*, p. II-8.

GRAPH 4. NATO & Warsaw Pact Military Investment*

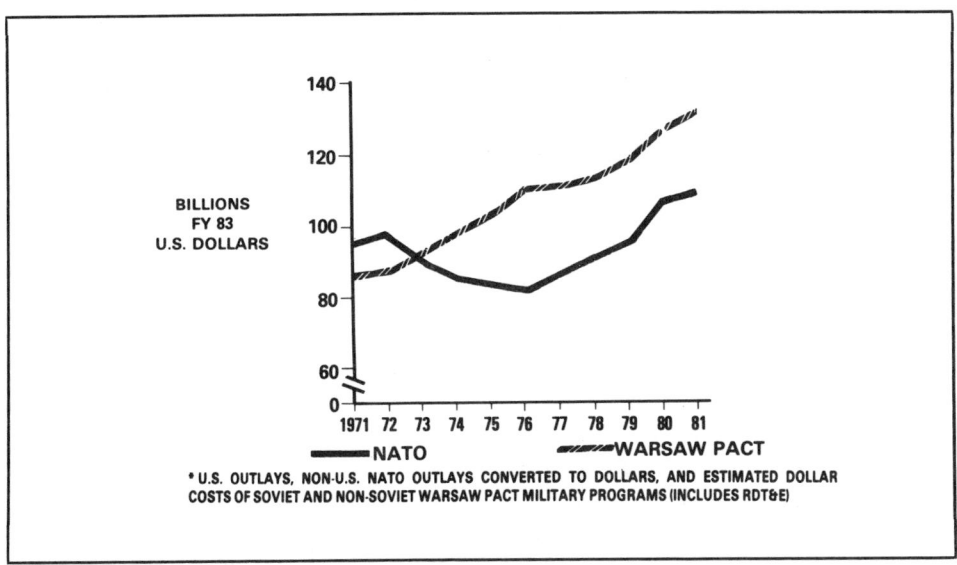

Source: *United States Military Posture for FY 1983*, p. 19.

been doing so for years. Compared to fewer than 400 tanks produced annually in the United States, the Soviets produce 3000. While the United States is just beginning to produce sea-launched cruise missiles, the Soviets have been producing 600–700 per year for several years.[17]

The President was correct earlier this year when he ascribed a margin of military superiority to the Soviets. Awareness of this development resulted during the last half of the 1970s in growing support by the American public of increases in U.S. defense spending.[18] In the 1980 Presidential campaign, both parties, but in particular the Republican Party, endorsed defense increases.

To date, however, the defense increases called for by the Administration remain modest. Instead of demonstrating clearly and immediately U.S. determination to turn the tide, the Administration's initial defense budgetary action was to request only a minimal supplemental to the FY 1981 defense budget of about 4 percent in total obligational authority (TOA) and only .6 percent in actual increased expenditures for that year (which, except for some naval shipbuilding, went for increased operations costs). The FY 1982 defense budget represented real increases in TOA and outlays (expenditures) of about 11 and 5 percent, respectively; and the FY 1983 defense program—the first to be fully produced by this Administration—requests increases of about 13 percent in TOA and 10 percent in outlays, and projects an annual average increase of 7 percent over the five-year defense program period.

The requested 1983 increases, while not trivial, are not enough. Total expenditures are less than 5 percent over the Carter projections for FY 1983 (and the lion's share of this difference is in pay increases). They are significantly below, and two years behind, the expenditures considered necessary by the Committee on the Present Danger back in 1980. Serious under-funding of key weapons programs continues.[19] In light of the long-standing major differences in the U.S. and Soviet efforts, the proposed U.S. defense increases cannot provide the forces needed to meet officially established mission requirements, let alone the challenges of the 1980s. Congressional reduction of the proposed increases would leave an even greater shortfall. Some of the reductions proposed would nearly obliterate differences between the Reagan Administration defense budgets and those projected by the Carter Administration.

There are no effective substitutes for substantially increased defense spending, no inexpensive ways to compensate for the years of U.S. underfunding and massive Soviet spending.[20]

To say this is not to discount allegations of waste and mismanagement in the Department of Defense. All large organizations, public and private, have their share. Nor is it to dismiss the possible existence of ill-advised programs. The point to emphasize is that any such possible savings would be insignificant in comparison with what is required to reduce the imbalance resulting from U.S. negligence and Soviet persistence over the years.

Nevertheless, if defense funds are not spent sensibly and effectively, the case for increased expenditures loses credibility. The necessary increases in defense spending must be applied judiciously; and this requires a clear, agreed strategy to establish consistent priorities and to make prudent choices on expenditures.

*The Committee believes that the most significant defect in American defense policy is the absence of a clear and consistent strategy, with defense programs to support that strategy.*[21]

The United States must develop a comprehensive strategy that can be articulately presented, that reflects the true urgency of the situation, that moves effectively to meet the urgent situation, and that links and justifies the separate defense programs. The FY 1983 Department of Defense *Annual Report to the Congress* is deficient in these respects.

CHART 1.

## Production of Ground Forces Materiel
### USSR and Non-Soviet Warsaw Pact

| | 1976 | | 1977 | | 1978 | | 1979 | | 1980 | |
|---|---|---|---|---|---|---|---|---|---|---|
| | USSR | NSWP | USSR | NSWP | USSR | NSWP | USSR | NSWP | USSR | NSWP |
| Tanks | 2500 | 800 | 2500 | 800 | 2500 | 800 | 3000 | 800 | 3000 | 750 |
| T-55 | 500 | 800 | 500 | 800 | 500 | 800 | 500 | 800 | — | 750 |
| T-64 | 500 | — | 500 | — | 500 | — | 500 | — | 500 | — |
| T-72 | 1500 | — | 1500 | — | 1500 | — | 2000 | — | 2500 | — |
| T-80 | — | — | — | — | — | — | Trial Output | — | Trial Output | — |
| Other Armored Fighting Vehicles | 4500 | 1800 | 4500 | 1900 | 5500 | 1700 | 5500 | 1600 | 5500 | 1200 |
| Towed Field Artillery | 900 | 50 | 1300 | 50 | 1500 | 100 | 1500 | 100 | 1300 | 100 |
| Self-Propelled Field Artillery | 900 | — | 950 | — | 650 | — | 250 | 50 | 150 | 50 |
| Multiple Rocket Launchers | 500 | 250 | 550 | 200 | 550 | 150 | 450 | 150 | 300 | 150 |
| Self-Propelled AA Artillery | 500 | 100 | 500 | 100 | 100 | 50 | 100 | 50 | 100 | 50 |
| Towed-AA Artillery | 500 | 300 | 250 | 250 | 100 | 200 | — | 200 | — | 150 |
| Infantry Weapons | 250,000 | 140,000 | 350,000 | 120,000 | 450,000 | 200,000 | 450,000 | 115,000 | 400,000 | 100,000 |

### Missile Production
#### USSR

| Missile Type | 1976 | 1977 | 1978 | 1979 | 1980 |
|---|---|---|---|---|---|
| ICBMs | 300 | 300 | 200 | 200 | 200 |
| IRBMs | 50 | 100 | 100 | 100 | 100 |
| SRBMs | 100 | 200 | 250 | 300 | 300 |
| SLCMs | 600 | 600 | 600 | 700 | 700 |
| SLBMs | 150 | 175 | 225 | 175 | 175 |
| ASMs | 1,500 | 1,500 | 1,500 | 1,500 | 1,500 |
| SAMs | 40,000 | 50,000 | 50,000 | 50,000 | 50,000 |

### Aircraft Production
#### USSR

| Aircraft Type | 1976 | 1977 | 1978 | 1979 | 1980 |
|---|---|---|---|---|---|
| Bombers | 25 | 30 | 30 | 30 | 30 |
| Fighters/Fighter-Bombers | 1,200 | 1,200 | 1,300 | 1,300 | 1,300 |
| Transports | 450 | 400 | 400 | 400 | 350 |
| Trainers | 50 | 50 | 50 | 25 | 225 |
| ASW | 5 | 10 | 10 | 10 | 10 |
| Helicopters | 1,400 | 900 | 600 | 700 | 750 |
| Utility | 125 | 100 | 100 | 100 | 100 |
| Total | 3,255 | 2,690 | 2,490 | 2,565 | 2,765 |

### Naval Ship Construction
#### USSR

| | 1976 | 1977 | 1978 | 1979 | 1980 |
|---|---|---|---|---|---|
| Submarines | 10 | 13 | 12 | 12 | 11 |
| Major Combatants | 12 | 12 | 12 | 11 | 11 |
| Minor Combatants | 58 | 56 | 52 | 48 | 52 |
| Auxiliaries | 4 | 6 | 4 | 7 | 5 |

Source: Department of Defense, *Soviet Military Power*, pp. 12-13.

The Committee supports defense budget increases beyond those contained in the FY 1983–1987 Five-Year Defense Plan, but it is firmly convinced that improvements in strategy and defense planning are not only possible but indeed essential. A comprehensive military strategy provides meaning and consistency to individual defense programs. With such strategy and planning in place, the need for increased funding will become even clearer. Without them, individual programs will remain vulnerable to Congressional critics.

One of the questions most fundamental to a consistent strategy has to do with the proper balance among types of forces and programs.

## B. Strategic vs. General Purpose Forces?

The United States is faced with two major problems: the erosion and growing vulnerability of the strategic nuclear deterrent and the failure to maintain adequate theater, naval, and general purpose forces (GPF). Bolstering capabilities in both these areas simultaneously is essential. Strengthening one without strengthening the other would result in a perilous situation. The strategic deterrent is directly applicable to a fairly narrow range of threats; it can support but it cannot substitute for the in-theater and mobile forces necessary to meet local and limited challenges. However, the strategic deterrent is the high ground which overshadows all other use of military force, particularly in situations where the Soviet Union is involved. If Soviet dominance of the strategic nuclear level is allowed to persist, Soviet policy-makers may—and almost certainly will—feel freer to use force at lower levels, confident that the United States will shy away from a threat of escalation.

To prevent a continuing succession of hostile initiatives, cumulatively reducing U.S. power, influence, and freedom of action, and to protect allies against coercion, effective forces capable of dealing with various levels of threat are necessary. The U.S. must be prepared in capabilities, as well as in declaratory policy, to fight limited conventional wars on land and at sea, to counter the use or threatened use of nuclear weapons, and to retain the option of responding to naked aggression by employing battlefield or theater nuclear weapons—with confidence in our strategic nuclear capabilities. Relative priority and emphasis between strategic nuclear, theater nuclear, and general purpose forces would be less troublesome if the U.S. devoted the resources necessary to accomplish their respective missions.

There is no greater or more urgent need than to remove the vulnerabilities and deficiencies of U.S. nuclear deterrent forces. The timing is critical since serious vulnerabilities exist today.

In the absence of measures more expeditious and extensive than now planned, U.S. strategic capabilities will remain inadequate to support official strategy and to assure confidence in their deterrent capability—in turn, weakening the deterrent value of other U.S. forces.

In its 1980 report, the Committee on the Present Danger emphasized the overriding importance of this relationship:

"In nuclear weapons, the rapid growth of Soviet strategic and theater capabilities has led to an ominous political and military threat: the threat that beginning in the early 1980s and lasting until at least 1989, when MX is planned to become available in significant quantities,[22] both the survivability and the counter-force capability of U.S. deterrent forces will lack credibility. If this condition is permitted to develop, the use of either conventional or nuclear forces in defense of important U.S. and Allied interests would be rendered imprudent."[23]

President Reagan has also recognized this situation and the necessity to "correct immediate and short term vulnerabilities and deficiencies" in the strategic force posture. He has declared that "our nuclear forces must be made survivable as rapidly as possible to close the window of vulnerability before it opens any wider."[24]

Failure to do this, particularly for the ICBM force, is the most disturbing aspect of the Administration's strategic program. It precludes an effective strategic force modernization program, and presents an insurmountable obstacle to a comprehensive military strategy.

Only 7½ and 9 percent of the FY 1982 and FY 1983 defense budgets, respectively, are devoted to strategic nuclear force programs—an imbalance in effort and priorities.

*Without a major redirected effort, U.S. strategic forces will not meet established require-*
*ments at any time in the 1980s.*

The Committee's emphasis on the strategic nuclear balance does not imply that we believe less attention or less funding for general purpose forces is warranted. Quite the contrary. It is a recognition that a nuclear balance unfavorable to the West tends to magnify the inadequacies of our general purposes forces. This is particularly so since U.S. and allied strategies for deterring or coping with major conventional conflicts are dependent upon a credible threat of nuclear escalation.

General purpose forces, however, are the forces most likely to be used in a variety of contingencies, and their deficiencies have become acute. The lack of adequate readiness and modernization and the erosion of force capability have been documented in recent years. The services have been obliged to sacrifice in some areas in order to maintain minimal standards in others.

The Soviets, in contrast, have funded both quantity and quality—generating large numbers of weapons and continuous programs of modernization. They have increased and improved their massive, offensive-oriented force concentrations in Europe and Asia, and at the same time have developed a considerable power projection capability, threatening American interests in many areas of the world. Major investment in air and naval power has increased the threat of Soviet force projections. All of this greatly complicates the tasks of American military power for the 1980s. The U.S. must protect strategic areas and sea lines of communication, assuring access to supplies. This requires overseas general purpose forces of increased mobility and firepower, along with an improved nuclear balance to insure confident use of such forces.

The defense program recommended in 1980 by the Committee would have provided for broad improvements in force size, readiness, and modernization, without sacrificing one for another. Current and proposed budgets, falling below the Committee's recommendations, leave the services in the predicament of having to choose which essentials to sacrifice. Yet, at the same time, according to suggestions from the Department of Defense, the planning requirements for conventional forces have been substantially expanded—another example of the disparity between force planning objectives and force capabilities.

No strategy has emerged to define the relationship between nuclear and conventional forces, the relative emphases and priorities to be given them, or the nexus between capabilities on the one hand and strategic objectives or force planning factors on the other. To a very large extent, planning appears to be merely more of the same, with hints of a new "conventional emphasis" policy, but also a continuation of nuclear requirements as they have evolved over recent years. The defense budget and program are inadequate to cover these simultaneously. If the military balance is to be effectively, judiciously and promptly corrected, it is as essential to eliminate this confusion as it is to devote the necessary resources.

The Committee urges both.

## THE MILITARY BALANCE

## A. Strategic Nuclear Forces

A steady deterioration in the strategic nuclear balance has taken place. In all indices, save possibly (but doubtfully) numbers of deployed on-line warheads, Soviet superiority, given existing programs, will grow during the next few years. A study conducted in 1978 for an agency of the Department of Defense identified over forty indices of comparison between U.S. and Soviet strategic nuclear forces, and traced these from 1962 to 1982. In 1962, all favored the United States. In 1978, all but a few favored the Soviet Union. It was projected that by 1982 all would favor the Soviets; and this has occurred.[25]

The Chief of Naval Operations, Admiral Thomas Hayward, summarized it starkly during the 1979 SALT II hearings:

> With respect to essential equivalence it is my view that without any question the Soviets will have a first-strike capability over the next few years. If that is not a loss of essential equivalence, I do not know what is, and we have to do something about that to correct it.[26]

Relentless efforts over the past twenty years have moved the Soviet Union from strategic inferiority to strategic superiority over the United States in nuclear capabilities. The Secretary of Defense states: "While our strategic programs have been restrained because of expectations for SALT and detente, the Soviets continually improve the quality of their strategic forces."[27] By 1968 the Soviets were spending twice as much as the United States, and the gap has subsequently widened to a 3.3 to 1 ratio.[28] The cumulative effects of this long-term trend have produced Soviet superiority in strategic nuclear forces.

Superiority, not parity, has been and continues to be the Soviet goal. For twelve years, the Soviets have asserted publicly that nuclear "balance" and "parity" exist between the two sides, while, at the same time, they have produced and deployed weapons systems on a scale and at rates far beyond standards in the West.

Soviet investment in military technology has now permitted the Soviets to shift emphasis from their earlier preoccupation with quantity to advancement of the quality of their strategic nuclear forces. This has produced a greater capability to destroy American strategic deterrent forces before they can be launched, as well as to provide for the survivability and endurance of their own forces. Having made great strides in these areas, it is possible that the Soviets will now place even greater emphasis on the ability to destroy, or negate the effects of, American deterrent forces after being launched. An overwhelming strategic nuclear reserve and secure command and control systems support both capabilities.

## 1. Soviet Programs

Since the Committee's previous assessment of the military balance, Soviet strategic nuclear capabilities have continued to grow. The Soviets produce approximately 200 ICBMs and 200 SLBMs every year, in a variety of modifications and with accurate MIRV warheads.[29] Last year, the Pentagon announced that "certain versions of the SS-18 and SS-19 are among the most accurate ICBMs operational anywhere."[30] Subsequently, the Secretary of Defense stated, "Soviet missiles are now more accurate than ours."[31] More recently, senior Pentagon officials said that the latest version of Soviet ICBM warheads are more accurate than their U.S. counterparts.[32] This has enormous implications for U.S. ICBM survivability. Since the smallest Soviet MIRV warheads are twice as large as the largest U.S. MIRVs, their counterforce potential is far greater. Soviet Backfire bombers continue to be produced, and recent reports of a new Soviet B-1-type strategic bomber, which may well be in operational status before the B-1, have now been officially confirmed.[33]

The Soviet inventory of strategic ballistic missiles materially exceeds the numbers contained in SALT-accountable launchers. In 1980, the Soviets were reported to have staged an exercise that stimulated the reload and refiring of up to 40 SS-18 silo-launchers.[34]

The Joint Chiefs of Staff have summarized the situation:

> According to accumulating evidence, the Strategic Rocket Forces may have plans to reconstitute and reload at least a portion of their silo-based ICBMs during a protracted nuclear conflict. Contingency plans for the reloading and refiring of silos probably have been developed. The cold-launched SS-17 and SS-18 are well suited for refiring. Additional evidence supports the hypothesis that the hot-launch systems also have a reload and refire capability.[35]

In addition, evidence presented in Congressional hearings on SALT II suggested that the Soviet ICBMs might be fired directly from their canisters without being reloaded in silo-launchers.

The number of Soviet strategic ballistic missiles with operational capability is unknown, but it probably greatly exceeds the number of missiles accounted by SALT counting rules; hence, the usually listed inventories of Soviet strategic missiles understate the actual situation.

This point was recently underscored by reports that the Soviets have SS-16 mobile ICBMs deployed at Plesetsk.[36] These missiles are not in the SALT accountable inventory because the Soviets said they had not been deployed, did not include them in the data provided in accordance with SALT II, and specifically promised that they would not be deployed.

Soviet strategic defensive programs complement their offensive programs and "point to a strategic concept of layered, in-depth defense of the homeland."[37] Extensive resources are committed to strategic defensive programs both active (ABM, air defense, anti-satellite, anti-submarine warfare) and passive (civil defense).

As to ABM capabilities, the Soviets have continued to modernize their deployed Moscow ABM system and have vigorously pursued research and development along a variety of lines. In air defense, the Soviets have maintained and modernized a rich bomber defense based upon 10,000 SAM launchers, more than 5,000 radars, and some 2,500 interceptor aircraft. "Soviet air defense systems are unsurpassed and are deployed in great variety and quantities."[38] The civil defense program costs more than the equivalent of $2 billion annually, an effort that has been sustained for a number of years.[39]

## 2. Evaluating U.S. Strategic Forces

Since the essence of American strategic policy is deterrence, and the foremost objective is deterrence of attacks on the United States and its allies, it is essential that our *surviving forces*—i.e., those that can confidently be expected to survive possible enemy attacks—be capable of accomplishing the missions set for them. It is not enough to look at the peacetime inventory of strategic nuclear weapons; one must also assess the adequacy of forces remaining after enemy attacks and countermeasures. Both static (peacetime) comparisons and dynamic (exchange, post-exchange) comparisons are important in assessing the strategic balance.

U.S. strategic forces are expected not only to deter attacks on the U.S. but also to play an important role in "extending deterrence" to allies (i.e., their use in situations where those forces have not themselves been attacked). In peacetime, U.S. strategic forces constitute an essential backdrop for foreign policy; in the event of local confrontations they must provide security against escalation so that other forces may be effective. And, for sound political and military reasons, it has been decided by successive administrations that our strategic forces must have, at a minimum, "essential equivalence" with those of the Soviet Union, in both reality and in the perception of others.

It is essential to evaluate the capabilities of surviving U.S. strategic forces in the event of enemy attack. This varies with differing attack scenarios. Planning for adequate forces following effective strategic warning (i.e., warning that is timely enough, unambiguous enough, and in response to which we do in fact take all necessary actions to increase force survivability) is far different from planning for adequate forces after a surprise attack. If effective strategic warning and effective U.S. responses to that warning (e.g., increasing the alert, dispersal, and operational rates of bomber and submarine forces; upgrading tactical warning, communications, and national command authority responsiveness) could be assumed with high confidence, there would be fewer demands placed on retaliatory forces than if the U.S. continued to plan deterrent forces that could absorb a surprise attack and still be wholly effective. The problem in many analyses of force adequacy is that the attack and response conditions assumed may be imprudently optimistic, elastic, or simply unarticulated. Published analyses by the Department of Defense in recent years have frequently reflected this sort of questionable method in an attempt to make forces and programs appear more satisfactory than they are. For example, even though both the FY 1980 and FY 1981 Department of Defense Reports stipulated that forces must be able to survive "a well-executed surprise attack" and still fulfill all planned missions, both reports reached conclusions as to the adequacy of U.S. forces by assuming (a) strategic warning, (b) Soviet attacks less than "well-executed" and (c) virtually unimpeded access to targets for our surviving forces.

The Committee believes that the standard of a "well-executed surprise attack" should be scrupulously followed in assessing the adequacy of forces. Further, a prudent deterrent must be designed to function in the absence of strategic warning. "Launch-on-warning," when applied to missile forces, is a high-risk, low-confidence option that can and should be avoided by providing for a survivable ICBM force.

Adequacy of forces should be evaluated in terms of the full range of missions that these forces are designed to accomplish. They must meet the objectives and criteria officially established for them. Unfortunately, judgments expressed on the adequacy of these forces often ignore these requirements. Frequently, assertions about the plentitude, or even over abundance, of forces are implicitly based not upon officially established standards but on lesser and more subjective ones, such as "assured destruction" or even "minimum deterrence." In these the full politico-military importance of strategic forces and the full range of objectives they must meet are disparaged or ignored. Former President Carter lent support to this approach when he suggested, in a State of the Union address, that the nuclear force represented by one Poseidon submarine was adequate to destroy 160 Soviet cities—an obvious hyperbole.

Usually implicit, sometimes explicit, is the assumption that U.S. strategic nuclear forces have only one purpose—to target cities. Without addressing all the fallacies of this view, surely a major fallacy is obvious today when *all* official estimates show that the U.S. would suffer far greater damage than would the Soviets by a city-attack exchange. Can such a threat then be made credible against a wide range of possible challenges? The answer is no. In reality, U.S. strategic forces have always had as part of their deterrent mission the option to attack targets other than cities, or, should deterrence fail, to attempt to limit damage. Surely U.S. force capabilities should provide a President with options other than a suicidal attack on cities, and having such options has been official policy for some time.

In the view of this Committee, assessments of strategic force adequacy based upon standards that fall well short of those officially established are inappropriate; hence, it is useful to review those standards contained in official doctrine.

Specific standards and requirements for judging the adequacy of our strategic forces have been officially established for some time. While they have been subject to modification, in essence they have been reaffirmed and reiterated by successive administrations since the Nixon Administration. They are definitely not reducible to minimum deterrence or assured destruction standards.

In 1969, the Nixon Administration added to the assured destruction criterion the need to avoid any major retaliatory force vulnerability in the interests of crisis stability, the need to be substantially equal to the Soviet Union in strategic capability, and the need to be able to limit damage at least against light nuclear attacks. In 1974, several specific requirements were added in the interests of maintaining deterrence, controlling escalation, and denying any Soviet political advantage from the buildup of their strategic forces. U.S. forces, it was declared, must be capable of "riding out even a massive surprise attack" and responding with a variety of controlled, selective, and limited strike options, including options against hardened counterforce targets, while still being able to "withhold an assured destruction reserve for an extended period of time." In addition, it was emphasized that U.S. forces must have visible and measurable capabilities at least equal to those of the Soviet Union, or "essential equivalence."

The annual reports of the Department of Defense under the Carter Administration were not quite as unequivocal. Indeed, they tended to display some uncertainty and ambiguity. Yet, in the final analysis, particularly after "PD-59" officially confirmed the basic tenets of the doctrine inherited from the Nixon and Ford Administrations, official Defense Department statements set forth similarly extensive and demanding standards. These appeared under the rubric of a "Countervailing Strategy" (of which the FY 1981 Report acknowledged, "the name is newer than the strategy"). U.S. forces must be able to "(1) survive a well-executed surprise attack; (2) penetrate any enemy defenses; (3) react with the timing needed, both as to promptness and endurance, to assure the deliberation and control deemed necessary; and (4) destroy their designated targets," in which are specifically included both soft and hard military targets. U.S. strategic forces must be able to control escalation and limit damage to the extent possible, rather than assure escalation and massive destruction by spasm or unlimited responses. A distinction between a "deterrence-only" and a defensive or denial capability was explicitly rejected. ("Our surest deterrent is our capability to deny gain from aggression. . . . There is no contradiction between this attention to the militarily effective targeting . . . and our primary and overriding policy of deterrence.")[40] Assured destruction is not "sufficient in itself as a strategic doctrine," and the U.S. must "have plans for attacks which pose a more credible threat than an all-out attack on Soviet industry and cities . . . while retaining an assured destruction capability in reserve."[41]

It is obvious, then, that official U.S. strategic deterrence doctrine, since at least 1974, has been based upon a need for enduring "war-fighting" capabilities, even for relatively protracted contingencies. The present Administration has only confirmed this. Sensational press reports of a major change in strategy to "war-fighting" and protracted nuclear conflict disguise the fact that such criteria have been officially accepted for some time. Reagan Administration policy, in this regard, reflects continuity, not major change.

Properly evaluated, then, the health and adequacy of our strategic forces must be assessed in that context. Unfortunately, neither today's capabilities nor those programmed for several years fulfill those criteria.

## 3. U.S. Strategic Nuclear Forces

Existing programs in the area of strategic nuclear forces could—depending upon Soviet actions—improve the military situation toward (or, most likely, after) the end of this decade. These long-range improvements, however, leave the U.S. with inadequate forces in the interim years. This has been acknowledged for some time. In the FY 1980 Department of Defense Report, Secretary Brown warned that "our most serious concerns which we need to act now to meet are about the period of early-to-mid-1980s." The FY 1981 report to Congress of the Joint Chiefs of Staff warned that "a period of particular risk is faced in the early 1980s, before U.S. initiatives now programmed can take effect." Since those observations, no steps have been taken to change the situation, and we are now entering the perilous period. This is precisely the period of the window of vulnerability, which is graphically depicted on the facing page.

The graph below is contained in the latest official report to Congress by the Joint Chiefs of Staff.[42] It is based upon "SALT counting rules," which understate the seriousness of the imbalance. For example, Backfire bombers, ICBM reloads, and cruise missiles are excluded from the Soviet force levels depicted. On the other hand, for the United States the curves are improved by optimistic assumptions about B-1, MX and cruise missile deployments. Nevertheless, two facts stand out: The U.S., as President Reagan said, is strategically inferior, and it will remain so as far ahead as projected, twelve years after the election of President Reagan.

GRAPH 5. Strategic Forces:* Pre-Attack Static Ratio Comparison

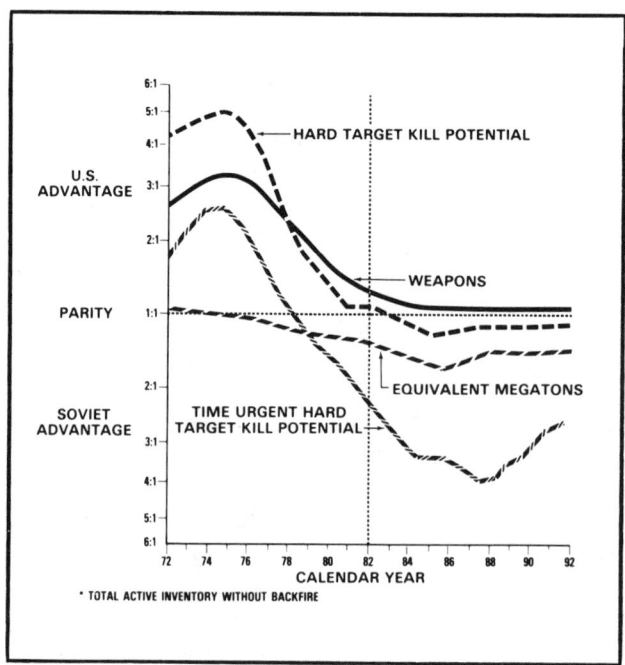

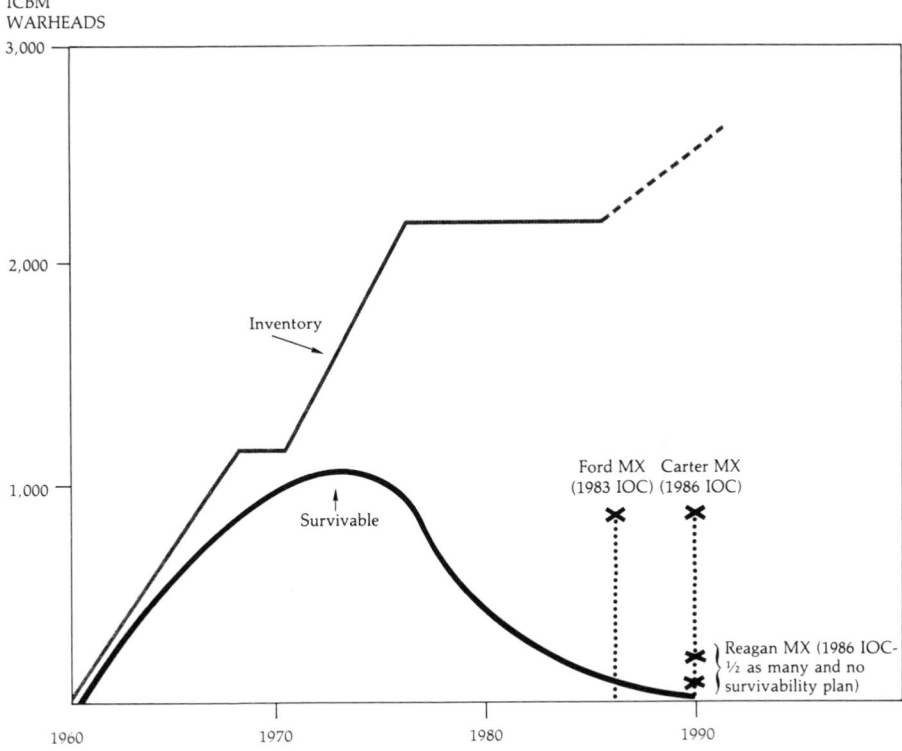

FIGURE 1. The Open Window of Vulnerability

If this chart were then compared with its counterpart, produced in the last year of the Carter Administration, another fact would be clear: The curves have worsened.

U.S. strategic nuclear forces fall short in survivability, target coverage, and endurance. Their vulnerability increases as Soviet programs expand and mature, and as the U.S. fails to take the timely measures necessary to improve its own forces. This combination is moving the United States into an unacceptable strategic posture, one in which U.S. strategic forces could have only a launch-on-warning or preemptive strike alternative to being lost to Soviet attacks. This would not be a launch-on-warning attack *capability,* for the situation would have arisen through neglect rather than a deliberate effort to provide for such capability. The launch-on-warning or preemptive imperative would be the result of a use-them-or-lose-them case of insufficiently survivable or durable forces.

Our ICBMs are already vulnerable to attacks by high-accuracy multiple warheads, which are now in the forces of the Soviet Union. An ICBM disarming attack against our present Minuteman configuration would require a relatively modest fraction of the total Soviet strategic offensive force (only about two thirds of the deployed SS-18s alone, leaving the Soviets 1200 deployed ICBMs).

In the furor over recent statements to this effect by the President and other senior officials, it has apparently been forgotten that this problem was thoroughly acknowledged by the Carter Administration. In 1979, Secretary of Defense Harold Brown told Congress:

The combination of accurate guidance and the large number of warheads expected in the early

1980s will give their ICBM force the ability to destroy our silos with a relatively small fraction of their ICBMs.[43]

Less candidly acknowledged, the bomber force is in equally severe trouble. It is not merely the lack of a timely program for a new strategic bomber; in even more pressing terms, it is the vulnerability and inadequacy of the present bomber force. Repeated cuts in Air Force personnel and O&M budgets have reduced the number of alert bombers to about one-quarter of the active force; and that force is concentrated on too few bases, most of which are too near our coasts. The bombers, then, are increasingly vulnerable to short time-of-flight submarine-launched ballistic missiles. And the penetration to target of bombers that do survive is highly questionable. To cite Secretary Brown again:

"Under some circumstances, SLBMs could pose a significant counterforce threat to our bombers, by barrage attack on our present Strategic Air Command bases. There is also the potential of our bombers being destroyed with ICBM barrage attacks whose larger numbers could compensate for the longer bomber escape time, so that even if the bombers got off the ground, they may not escape the area that is barraged."[44]

The sea-based force appears more survivable at least for those submarines at sea, but information is incomplete, the Soviet ASW program is impressive, and it is most difficult to project the nature of future threats with any confidence. In any case, the communications link remains an Achilles' heel of the sea-based force.

In addition to these vulnerabilities and deficiencies in the TRIAD of offensive forces, there are other major strategic deficiencies that deserve priority attention:

- The overall strategic command, control, communications, and warning capabilities of the U.S. are inadequate for wartime and highly vulnerable to a variety of attacks and disruptions.
- The strategic forces, partly for the reasons already noted, are incapable of carrying out the targeting strategy and strategic objectives assigned to them. In fact, increasingly they can act only as escalatory forces rather than retainable, escalation-dampening forces.
- The strategic posture lacks a defensive component. The proper mix of active and passive defenses, and the most promising techniques for each, should command serious attention. The U.S. needs expanded air defense and civil defense programs; without them "essential equivalence" is far more difficult to attain.

In no other area of military capability is the gap between force objectives, or established force requirements, and capabilities more pronounced than in the strategic nuclear realm. The Reagan Administration has apparently affirmed its commitment to the strategic doctrine and objectives that the Carter Administration grouped under the terms "countervailing strategy" and "essential equivalence," with some modifications. This requires that we have a strategic force capable of surviving well-executed surprise attacks, fulfilling a wide range of missions, and being—in dynamic as well as static comparisons—roughly equal to the strategic forces of the Soviet Union.

*U.S. capabilities fall far short of such standards.* How short is not fully revealed by peacetime inventory comparisons even though these show Soviet superiority in virtually all categories.

*The Committee's analysis of the effect of a hypothetical Soviet surprise attack on American strategic deterrent forces, in the 1984–1985 time frame, suggests that 80 to 90*

GRAPH 6. Strategic Forces* Post Exchange Residuals (Day to Day Alert)

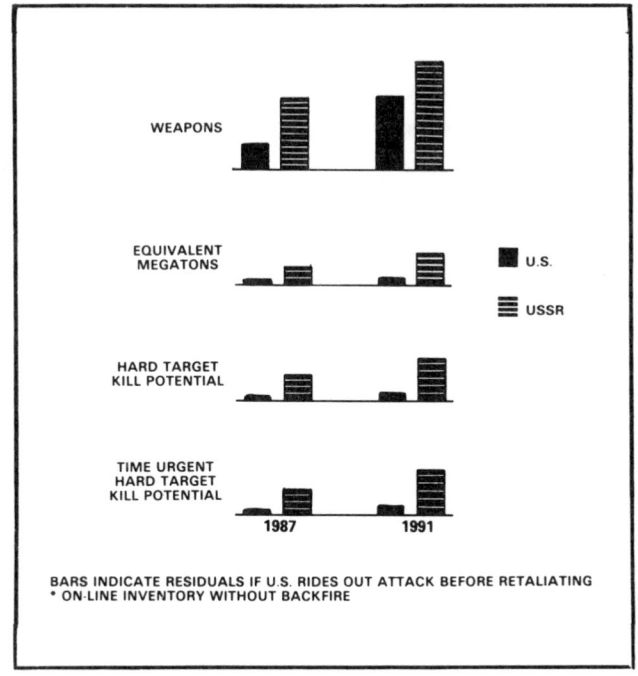

*Source:* Joint Chiefs of Staff, *United States Military Posture for FY 1983,* p. 24. (For numerical comparisons of U.S.-Soviet strategic nuclear forces, see Appendix.)

*percent of U.S. force capabilities could be lost, leaving us with an inadequate and inflexible response capability.*

Official estimates for 1987 and 1991, when much or even all of the force modernization will presumably have been completed, do not look appreciably better:

A Soviet surprise attack would leave the U.S. with a force much closer to former Secretary of Defense McNamara's minimum "assured destruction" force than one that meets today's official doctrine and requirements. Failures in force planning and acquisition may move the U.S. back in actual capabilities toward the minimum deterrence, counter-city doctrine which is neither credible nor effective.

## B. Theater Nuclear Forces

In theater and tactical nuclear forces, Soviet modernization and expansion, compared to that of the United States, have been at least as dramatic as those in the area of strategic forces. The numbers of Soviet tactical and theater weapons for the European theater have steadily increased in recent years. In contrast, the United States has recently withdrawn one thousand warheads from deployment in Europe—a unilateral arms control initiative not reciprocated by the Soviets. Until the production of the new Lance and 8-inch artillery warheads, the United States had introduced only one new theater nuclear system (the Lance) to Europe since the mid-1960s. In contrast, the Soviets have introduced new generations of systems across the board: Not only the well-publicized SS-20, but also the SS-21 (FROG replacement), the SS-X-23 (SCUD B replacement), the

CHART 2. Major Soviet Theater Missiles and Rockets

| SYSTEM | RANGE | REPLACEMENT SYSTEM | RANGE |
|--------|-------|--------------------|-------|
| SS-4 | 2000KM | SS-20 | 5000KM |
| SS-5 | 4100KM | | |
| FROG | 70KM | SS-21 | 120KM |
| SCUD B | 300KM | SS-23 | 500KM |
| SS-12 | 900KM | SS-22 | 900KM |

GRAPH 7. Soviet Long-Range TNF (Longer-Range INF) Ballistic Missile Warheads 1965–1982

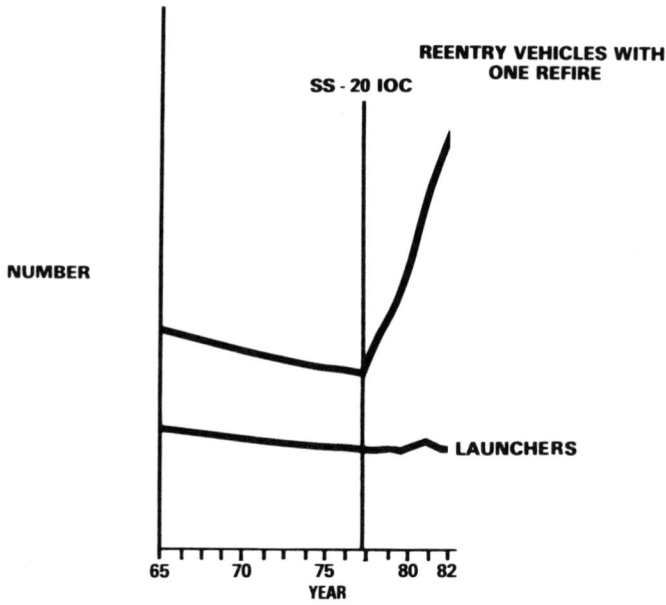

NOTE: THE SYSTEMS INCLUDED IN THIS CHART INCLUDE THE SS-4, SS-5 AND THE SS-20. THE TOTAL NUMBER OF LAUNCHERS HAS REMAINED CONSTANT WITH THE INTRODUCTION OF THE SS-20 DUE TO A DRAW DOWN IN THE NUMBERS OF SS-4s AND SS-5s.

Source: United States Military Posture for FY 1983, pp. 108–109.

SS-22 (SS-12/SCALEBOARD replacement), several new, more capable nuclear strike aircraft and nuclear artillery.

In only the last five years, the number of deployed Soviet IRBM warheads targeted on NATO-Europe and Asia has more than doubled.[45] The Soviets have now deployed in excess of 300 SS-20 IRBM launchers, each having refire capability and refire missiles, each missile carrying 3 highly accurate MIRV warheads. If only one refire missile were assumed per launcher, as the graph above depicts—and it is likely that there are multiple refire missiles for many of the launchers[46]—the Soviets have deployed nearly 2000 SS-20 warheads in recent years.

CHART 3. Currently Deployed Longer-Range INF Missile Systems

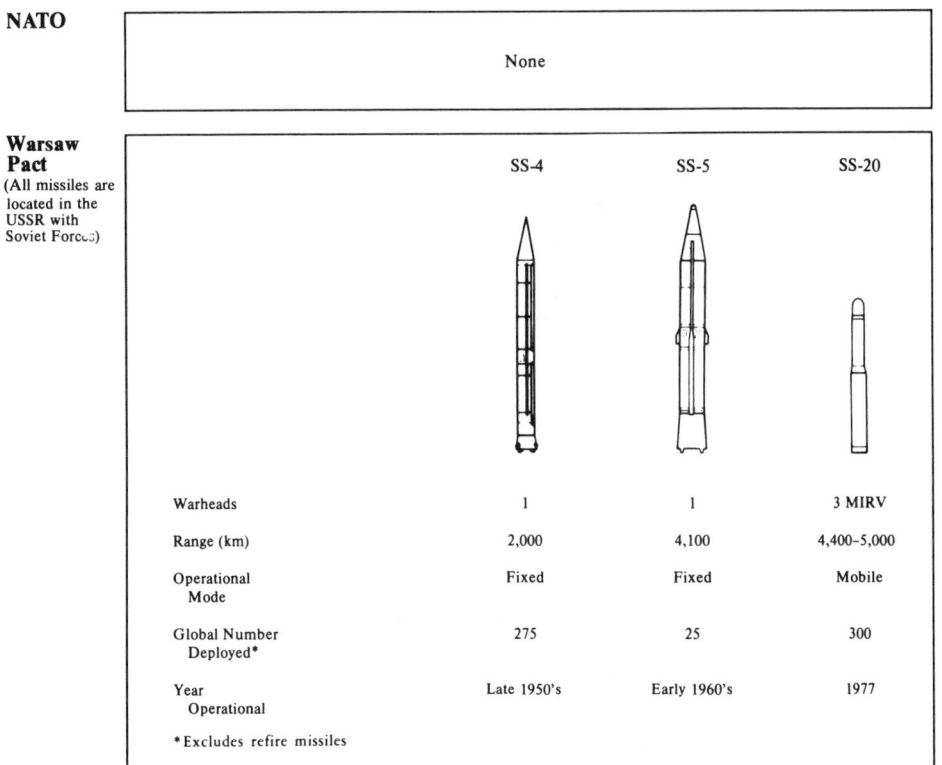

**NATO**

None

**Warsaw Pact**
(All missiles are located in the USSR with Soviet Forces)

| | SS-4 | SS-5 | SS-20 |
|---|---|---|---|
| Warheads | 1 | 1 | 3 MIRV |
| Range (km) | 2,000 | 4,100 | 4,400–5,000 |
| Operational Mode | Fixed | Fixed | Mobile |
| Global Number Deployed* | 275 | 25 | 300 |
| Year Operational | Late 1950's | Early 1960's | 1977 |

*Excludes refire missiles

*Source: NATO and the Warsaw Pact: Force Comparisons, May 1982, p. 49.*

In all, Soviet theater nuclear forces now exceed those of the United States and its NATO allies by 2–6 times in delivery systems, warheads, and megatonnage.

As with the U.S. strategic systems, a major consequence of Soviet actions and relative Western inaction has been the increasing vulnerability of NATO-Europe nuclear forces. NATO's major nuclear assets have become extremely vulnerable to the type of attacks the Soviets are now capable of launching. Theater nuclear forces are concentrated on a few known sites, and lack adequate mobility. The currently planned modifications do not essentially change the situation. The Annual Department of Defense Report this year points out:

> . . . the totality of the improvements in Soviet surface-to-surface missile capabilities appears to have significant implications beyond tactical missions. Soviet range and accuracy improvements significantly enhance the Soviets' ability to support an unreinforced attack because the new systems can launch from peacetime locations, supported by a relatively unstressed logistics system.[47]

The modest deployment of 464 ground-based cruise missiles and 108 Pershing II ballistic missiles tentatively agreed upon in 1979 remains tinged with uncertainty; but, even if carried out fully and on schedule, would hardly restore the balance and do little to correct deficiencies in our theater nuclear capabilities. The decision to produce the enhanced radiation (ER) or reduced blast warhead is welcome, although long overdue.

GRAPH 8. Coverage of Europe from SS-20 Bases East of the Urals

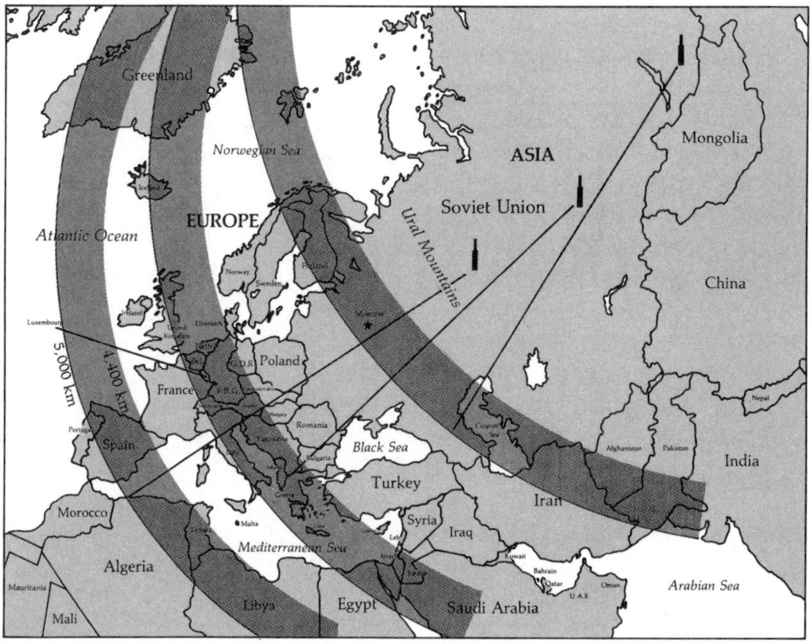

Source: *NATO and the Warsaw Pact: Force Comparisons*, May 1982, p. 53.

(The ER warhead technology has been available, and has been debated, for over twenty years!) It does little, however, to benefit the alliance or U.S. theater capabilities, when retained on U.S. territory.

The increasing imbalance in theater nuclear capabilities has been rationalized in recent years by references to the strategic nuclear umbrella and escalation to strategic war. For example, by former Secretary of Defense Harold Brown: "We do not plan to match the Soviet program system by system or warhead by warhead. . . . Instead, we seek to strengthen the linkage of U.S. strategic forces to the defense of Europe."[48] This, of course, is the NATO strategy of "flexible response"—a strategy not in question here. The foregoing discussion of U.S. strategic force vulnerabilities and Soviet superiority at that level leads to the conclusion that the strategic level cannot make up for imbalances and deficiencies at the theater-tactical nuclear level. The strategic imbalance now magnifies inadequacies at the theater level. Overall, U.S. and NATO-Europe nuclear forces remain ill-suited and inadequate for the roles assigned them in the strategy of flexible response.

There is another paramount problem as well: The failure of the West to formulate a doctrine or to train seriously for tactical nuclear employment leaves it at a disadvantage against an adversary who has formulated such a doctrine and has equipped and extensively trained his forces in accordance with it.

Progress in modernizing theater-tactical nuclear forces and doctrine should be given a higher priority than it has in both NATO and the U.S. Department of Defense. If anything, the focus on questions related to the modest deployment of ground-launched cruise missiles and Pershing II has diverted attention from this more broadly based modernization, and may, in a sense, have impeded it. The Department of Defense today seems more interested in returning to conventional emphasis than in thinking through

GRAPH 9. Target Coverage of Soviet SS-20 and Target Coverage of NATO Pershing II and GLCM

Source: *NATO and the Warsaw Pact: Force Comparisons*, May 1982, p. 57.

and proceeding with theater and tactical nuclear modernization (at sea as well as on land). In this case, the adverse theater nuclear balance seems certain to continue and will, indeed, become worse.

There is another theater element in which the Soviet-Warsaw Pact forces hold tremendous advantage; chemical warfare capabilities. Soviet doctrine employs a combination of conventional, chemical, and nuclear weapons to seize territory with minimal destruction to its assets. "All members of the Warsaw Pact continue to equip and train their forces to operate in chemical and nuclear environments. They also continue to improve their capabilities for the actual use of chemical weapons."[49] The Soviets have large chemical warfare capabilities, both offensive and defensive. Many of their theater delivery systems are believed to possess lethal chemical warheads. The United States, in contrast, has largely neglected chemical defenses and offensive chemical deterrents for its forces while pursuing unenforceable agreements to outlaw chemical weapons in warfare.

## C. General Purpose Forces

In 1978 the Committee stated:

"The Soviets recognize the usefulness of strategic nuclear superiority in enabling them to use superior General Purpose Forces with far diminished risks of escalation."[50]

The Soviet Union's general purpose forces (GPF), the largest and most lavishly equipped of their kind, reflect a cumulative buildup and modernization program covering two decades. All elements of the Soviet GPF have benefited from broad-based upgrading since the early 1960s. Today the Soviets have 135 major military industrial plants in operation, producing more than 150 different types of weapons and awesome amounts of ammunition.[51]

The danger posed to U.S. and allied security has increased proportionately. The net result, according to the Department of Defense, "has been the emergence of Warsaw Pact ground and tactical air forces that are much stronger and better prepared to sustain conventional combat. . . . Pact forces are becoming even better aligned with their military doctrine of defeating NATO quickly and decisively by means of fast-moving, 'blitzkrieg-style' offensive operations." Moreover, the threat posed by this buildup of conventional capabilities is even more serious "precisely because the Atlantic Alliance has lost its compensating advantage in nuclear arms."[52]

As the scope of Soviet geopolitical interests has grown, so has the ability of the Soviet Union to project military power, previously confined to the Eurasian landmass, to more remote areas.

The Soviet Union and its Warsaw Pact satellites, forming a geographical entity, have an advantage afforded by secure internal lines of communication. The United States and its NATO allies have to deal with lengthy—and vulnerable—sea and air communications. Now, through an array of negotiated concessions, the Soviet Union has acquired a formidable infrastructure for projecting military power to a diversity of distant areas. The Soviet military presence thus has become a factor in the Indian Ocean and Southwest and Southeast Asia and the Caribbean—with facilities or access rights in such places as Vietnam, Mozambique, Angola, and Cuba. Meanwhile, the United States has lost basing or access rights in the same regions and has increasingly had to rely upon costly long-range hauls—for which its capabilities have been relatively declining.

Despite the fact that 85 percent or more of U.S. defense expenditure goes for general purpose forces, the combat readiness and sustainability of all four U.S. military services are seriously deficient. Because of long-standing budgetary constraints, the equipment planned for authorized force levels has in many instances not been procured. The typical response to emergencies in the recent past has been to "draw down" equipment and material assigned to U.S.-based active or reserve forces and then, again because of funding constraints, fail to replenish fully. War reserve materiel (ammunition, major and secondary equipment) stocks and procurement are at dangerously low levels, completely inadequate to support any but the shortest wars.[53]

Weapons procurement and modernization for U.S. general purpose forces have been seriously deficient in recent years. Performance in many instances has been insufficient to compensate for peacetime attrition or to prevent gradual atrophy. In comparison with the Soviet Union and Warsaw Pact, U.S. and NATO military investment (R&D, construction, procurement) has lagged alarmingly. Soviet military investment has exceeded that of the United States by some 80–90 percent for several years. Even including the

CHART 4. The Military Manpower Balance 1982

Regular Forces and Reserves
(thousands)

| General Purpose Forces | U.S. | USSR |
|---|---|---|
| Army | 777 | 1,825 |
| Navy | 527 | 443 |
| Air Force | 558 | 1,410* |
| Marines | 188 | 12 |
| Paramilitary-Frontier and Internal Security | 0 | 560 |
| Total GPF | 2,050 | 4,250 |
| Reserves | 851 | 5,000 |
| Grand Total | 2,901 | 9,250 |

*Includes Strategic Rocket Force (SRF) and Air Defense Force (PVO Strany).

Sources: Secretary of Defense, *Annual Report, FY 1983*; *The Military Balance, 1981–1982*, International Institute for Strategic Studies, London, 1981.

GRAPH 10. NATO-Warsaw Pact Force Comparison (in Place in Europe)

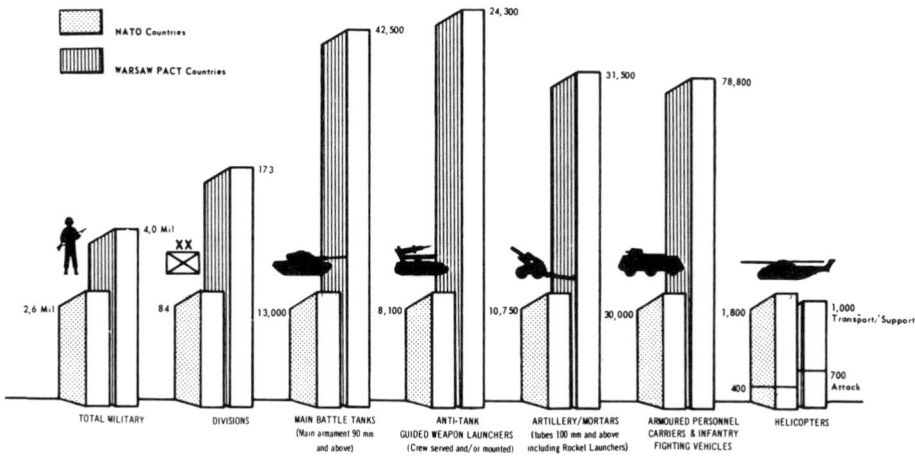

NOTES:  1. WARSAW PACT DIVISIONS NORMALLY CONSIST OF FEWER PERSONNEL THAN MANY NATO DIVISIONS BUT CONTAIN MORE TANKS AND ARTILLERY, THEREBY OBTAINING SIMILAR COMBAT POWER.
2. FORCES IN PLACE IN NATO EUROPE, WARSAW PACT FORCES AS FAR EAST AS BUT EXCLUDING THE 3 WESTERN MILITARY DISTRICTS IN WESTERN RUSSIA (MOSCOW, VOLGA & URAL MILITARY DISTRICTS).

Source: *NATO and the Warsaw Pact: Force Comparisons*, May 1982, p. 11.

GRAPH 11. Medium and Heavy Tanks

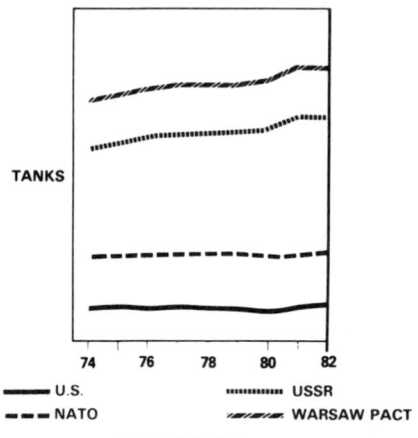

GRAPH 12. Antiaircraft Artillery

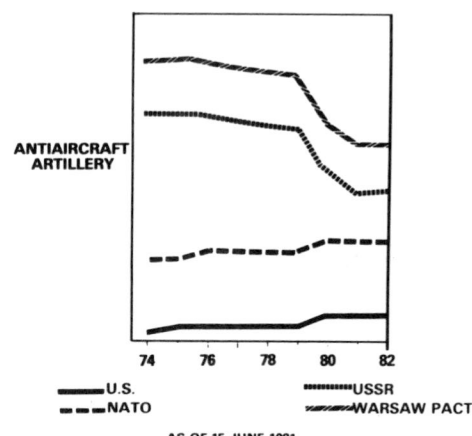

GRAPH 13. Antitank Weapons per Tank

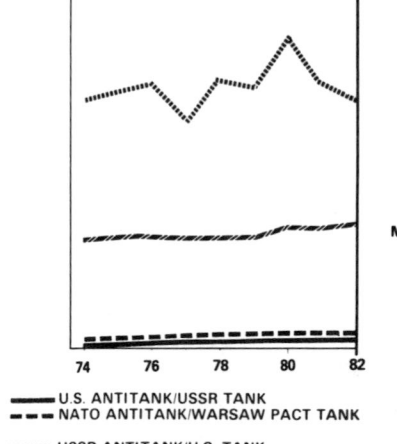

GRAPH 14. Artillery and Multiple Rocket Launchers

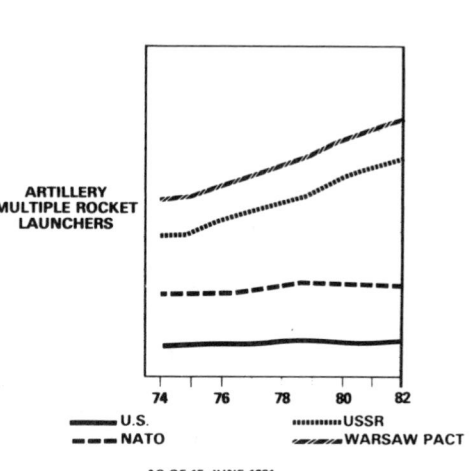

Source: Joint Chiefs of Staff, *Military Posture for FY 1983*, pp. 31–33.

efforts of NATO allies plus Japan, Soviet and Warsaw Pact investment has been greater since 1973—by 35-40 percent in what the Department of Defense terms "effective investment."

Within the limits of the current defense budget, modernization and force expansion will continue to suffer. Secretary Weinberger has said, "Because our first priority is restoring the readiness of forces we already have, the pace of modernization must be slower than would be desirable."[54]

The pre-positioning in Europe of U.S. military equipment—essential to reinforcement of defenses—is below requisite levels. In other critical areas—for example, the Middle

East—such prepositioning scarcely exists. The concept of prepositioning equipment, moreover, depends upon adequate strategic warning, proper and timely response following such warning, and the survivability of pertinent facilities—and on a problematic degree of Soviet nuclear restraint.

The industrial base is of central importance to rapid reconstitution of adequate war reserves as well as to force modernization. As the recently retired Chairman of the Joint Chiefs of Staff, General David Jones, has testified, "The U.S. industrial base cannot influence the first six months of a NATO conflict even if a national emergency is declared."[55] Action by the Administration is imperative to reorient industry toward defense requirements authorized under the Defense Production Act and the National Emergencies Act.

A problem formerly as serious as the readiness and modernization problems, but now being improved, concerns insufficiency of trained, experienced, fully qualified military manpower and of the corresponding civilian support personnel. Skilled technical specialists remain in short supply despite recent increases in pay and incentives. While the enlistment rate is meeting current goals—thanks to major pay increases and high unemployment—the quality of enlistment lags.

The U.S. tactical air combat capability is inadequate to accomplish assigned missions, now expanded to include the Middle East region. The central aspects are relative improvements in quantity, sophistication, and reliability of Soviet air power; lags in U.S. development and procurement rates, which have failed to offset even the normal peacetime attrition; limitations of manpower recruiting and training; and fragility of overseas base and logistics support structures. The Warsaw Pact's more than 7000 combat aircraft in Europe compares to NATO's less than 3000—an imbalance due to become even greater unless U.S. and NATO aircraft purchases increase dramatically. At present, the planned increases are less than dramatic: a 15% expansion for USAF tactical air and 9% for the Navy and Marine Corps.[56] Even those modest expansions are dependent upon future funding.

Before 1970, Soviet tactical aviation was primarily oriented toward the air defense mission for Soviet ground forces. Widespread improvement of high performance surface-to-air missiles and antiaircraft artillery, and incorporation of these in units organic to ground divisions, relieved tactical aviation of much of that mission. This change allowed a refocusing of Soviet tactical aviation to longer-range and heavy-payload ground-attack and fighter-bomber aircraft, capable of theater-wide or deep-strike missions. Consequently, while the numbers have remained about the same, modern offensive capabilities have increased materially. Replacement of older aircraft with modern aircraft has been widespread and rapid.

The Soviet Union's four principal fleets include the world's largest array of naval general purpose surface ships and submarines supported by land-based naval air and on-board offensive and defensive missile capabilities. Soviet surface vessels when within range of land-based aircraft present a particularly formidable threat. New cruise missiles, greatly augmenting the firepower of the fleet, are being introduced. The major threat to U.S. forces, however, is the enormously large and diversified Soviet submarine fleet, richly equipped with cruise missiles as well as torpedoes.

For power projection, the Soviet Union has shifted the emphasis in its surface ship program from short-endurance vessels to much larger, long-endurance vessels with many of the capabilities of U.S. surface fleet operations, including underway replenishment. The 1980s will bring a major increase in Soviet worldwide naval deployments as larger ships of still greater capability are introduced. (See Chart on page 233.)

As pointed out in a 1978 report of the Committee,[57] the Soviet Union exceeded the U.S. in every category of naval ships except aircraft carriers. Although Soviet ship production has declined somewhat in numbers, total tonnage and offensive capability are significantly increasing. The U.S. Navy has suffered in recent years from insufficiency of capital investment, and of funding for training and operations. All U.S. overseas military operations in the contingency of war would be vitally dependent on sea control. The Navy is essential in overseas power projection and has the sole responsibility for the protection of maritime lines of communications. The Navy has simply not enough surface combatant ships to discharge its traditional responsibilities in the Atlantic, the Mediterranean, and the Pacific, while taking on the new major role of controlling the Indian Ocean—and in high probability, the Caribbean—even with a measure of allied support. Naval strength that must be drawn down in one area to meet requirements represents a one-and-a-half ocean capability for a three-plus ocean world.

In order to avoid further reduction of overall fleet capability, a vigorous shipbuilding program, not subject to short-term budget stringencies, is called for.

The current defense program addresses naval shortcomings more fully than it does those of the other services. "The most significant force expansion proposed by the Administration centers on the Navy."[58] The Navy's share of the defense budget is up almost two percentage points for FY 1983, while the other service shares decline. A worthy goal of a 600-ship Navy has been defined, and as the following table shows, the FY 1983–87 Five-Year Defense Plan heads in that direction. The yearly average of ships to be built—29—is deceptive, however, because the accompanying retirement rate will be 10 ships and because the major part of planned shipbuilding is to be postponed to the later years which, by experience, seem never to arrive. (The Navy has actually received less than 50% of the ships contained in the past 15 completed Five-Year Defense Plans.) The 18 ships and 288 aircraft funded for FY 1983 represent an increase, but, even so, the number of ships is at the lower margin of what is needed to maintain current levels, and the number of aircraft is below that required to maintain force levels. Both should be accelerated.

Increased offensive capability foreshadowed for the Navy by the five-year plan is welcome, but a distribution of that capability across a larger number and wider variety of platforms is necessary. To increase the offensive capabilities of the fleet there should be increased production of both the Tomahawk and Harpoon anti-ship cruise missile programs. Additional ships should be used to provide platforms for the Harpoon and the longer-range Tomahawk cruise missiles.

Surface combat ships without an air and submarine complement, and without support ships, cannot constitute an effective fighting force; the insufficiency of numbers in these latter categories must also be remedied. In the presence of Soviet high-altitude surveillance and highly effective anti-ship missile weapons, the surface Navy faces new dimensions of threat not met by present or presently planned defense programs. The strides that have been made, and the further advances likely in maritime surveillance and targeting and weapon delivery at sea, are bringing warfare at sea close to near-perfect efficacy—particularly so if the missile threat is nuclear. The United States Navy must be provided with the capability to defend itself and to respond effectively in kind in event of nuclear combat at sea.

Because of the geographic realities, strategic mobility is an essential element of the U.S. military posture. Currently operational airlift forces are deficient in several respects. Their total capacity is insufficient to deploy and to give early support to U.S. forces in more than one theater. They are dependent upon in-theater and en route bases, which

CHART 5. Soviet Navy Order of Battle

| | | |
|---|---|---|
| **Submarines — Nuclear Powered** | | |
| *SSBN | Ballistic Missile Submarines (YANKEE, DELTA classes) | 62 |
| SSBN | Ballistic Missile Submarines (HOTEL class) | 7 |
| *SSGN | Cruise Missile Submarines | 50 |
| *SSN | Torpedo-Attack Submarines | 60 |
| **Submarines — Diesel-electric Powered** | | |
| SSB | Ballistic Missile Submarines | 18 |
| SSG | Cruise Missile Submarines | 20 |
| *SS | Torpedo-Attack Submarines | 160 |
| **Aircraft Carriers and Aviation Cruisers** | | |
| CVHG | VSTOL Carriers (KIEV class) | 2 |
| CHG | Aviation Cruisers (MOSKVA class) | 2 |
| **Cruisers** | | |
| *CGN | Guided Missile Cruiser (Nuclear) (KIROV class) | 1 |
| *CG | Guided Missile Cruisers (SAM/SSM) | 26 |
| CL | Light Cruisers (SVERDLOV class) | 9 |

| | | |
|---|---|---|
| **Destroyers** | | |
| *DDG | Guided Missile Destroyers (SAM/SSM) | 38 |
| DD | Destroyers | 30 |
| **Frigates (Escorts)** | | |
| *FFG | Guided Missile Frigates (KRIVAK class) | 28 |
| *FF/FFL | Frigates /small frigates | 140 |
| **Small Combatants** | | |
| *Missile Craft | | 145 |
| *Patrol /ASW/ Torpedo Craft | | 395 |
| *Minesweepers | | 395 |
| **Amphibious Ships** | | |
| *LPD | Amphibious Assault Transport Dock (IVAN ROGOV class) | 1 |
| LST | Amphibious Vehicle Landing Ships (ALLIGATOR, ROPUCHA classes) | 25 |
| LSM | Medium Landing Ships (POLNOCNY/MP-4 classes) | 60 |
| **Auxiliary Ships** | | |
| *Mobile Logistics Ships | | 150 |
| *Other Auxiliaries | | 605 |

* Indicates additional units under construction in these categories.

*Source:* Department of Defense, *Soviet Military Power,* p. 40.

may not be available for political reasons and could be vulnerable to enemy attacks. Heavy Army combat equipment (tanks, artillery, and large helicopters) can be accommodated only by the small C-5A fleet, and even then is carried at inefficient rates.

In spite of the fact that the Congressionally Mandated Mobility Study recognized that the USAF was deficient in airlift capability, particularly with regard to the Rapid Deployment Force (RDF), the Air Force has recently announced a decision to cancel funds for the McDonnell-Douglas C-17 military airlifter in favor of purchasing an additional 50 C-5Ns. These 50 aircraft will be added to the 77 already in the fleet. The C-5 program has been plagued with delays and cost overruns. The U.S. should, in addition to purchases of C-5s to enhance present capability, continue R&D on the C-17 with an eye on production by FY 1987, speed the ongoing modernization of the C-141 fleet, and increase purchases of KC-10As.

Enhanced airlift capability, though needed for rapid response, does not match sea lift with respect to potential for forcible entry, sustainability, and operational volume. As the Chief of Naval Operations, Admiral Thomas B. Hayward, testified before the House Armed Services Procurement and Nuclear Systems Subcommittee, there is a "serious shortfall in U.S. strategy mobility."[59] Secretary of Defense Caspar Weinberger notes in his FY 1983 *Annual Report* that "While currently available sealift resources could deliver follow-on forces and resupply, they could not meet the immediate deployment requirements for the initial combat forces and their support."[60] The U.S. presently has available

CHART 6. The Naval Balance 1982

|  | U.S. | USSR |
|---|---|---|
| Aircraft Carriers | 13 | 4 |
| Battleships | 0 | 0 |
| Cruisers/Destroyers | 112 | 104 |
| Nuclear Attack Submarines | 91 | 189 |
| Diesel Attack Submarines | 5 | 198 |
| Amphibious Ships | 65 | 86 |
| Frigates | 86 | 168 |
| Patrol Combatants | 6 | 395 |
| Mine Warfare Ships | 3 | 395 |
| Mobile Logistic Ships | 71 | 150 |
| Combat Support Ships | 23 | 605 |
| Strategic Reserve Ships* | 39 | — |
| TOTAL | 514 | 2,249 |

*Includes appropriate ships from Naval Reserve Force (NRF) and Navy Fleet Auxiliary Force (NFAF).

*Sources:* Secretary of Defense, *Annual Report, FY 1983*, pp. III-19–III-36. Department of Defense, *Soviet Military Power*, p. 40.

24 ships in the Military Sealift Command (MSC), 27 in the Ready Reserve Force, and 167 in the National Defense Reserve Fleet. Although the MSC has the authority to requisition the use of U.S.-owned ships in an emergency, the countries under whose flag the ships fly may not make them available and they therefore cannot be counted on in a crisis. The planned acquisition and conversion of the SL-7 fast (33 knots) sea lift ships will be grossly insufficient (6 in FY 1981 and only 2 in FY 1982), limited to supporting three Marine Amphibious Brigades, or the equivalent of two divisions in combat. The SL-7, being a container ship, requires modern port facilities—not always available in areas where the RDF may be committed.

The Rapid Development Force involves little more than a reassignment of existing forces. Even the modest assignment of forces (1,100 men) to the Sinai multinational peacekeeping force is drawn from the RDF. The RDF, moreover, lacks the appropriate organizational structure; the designated peacetime commander, Army Lieutenant General Robert C. Kingston, has no line of authority over his nominally assigned forces, and the wartime chain of command is left unspecified. Furthermore, the RDF has not been provided with the dedicated equipment and deployment support necessary for its assigned mission. The assignment of dedicated forces and their specialized training are in an embryonic stage.

The most serious barriers to an effective RDF are the lack of overseas bases, staging and support facilities and enough strategic mobility to deploy adequate strength rapidly. In the absence of prepared bases in the immediate vicinity and in view of the serious shortfalls in forward mobility equipment it will not be feasible to support adequately the RDF mission. The RDF as presently planned represents a limited and inadequate capability. It will not be capable of fighting Soviet-supported medium or heavy combat forces. It may acquire the characteristics required to reinforce rapidly U.S. forces which *are* in place and capable of preparing and protecting the off-load terminals, but much remains to be done.

# CONCLUSION

## The Need to Restore U.S. Deterrent Strength

At its founding in 1976, the Committee on the Present Danger stated:

> For more than a decade, the Soviet Union has been enlarging and improving both its strategic and its conventional military forces far more rapidly than the United States and its allies. . . . If we continue to drift, we shall become second best to the Soviet Union in overall military strength.[61]

The drift continued, and the military balance has steadily worsened. The United States has become second best.

In the 1970s, U.S. defense expenditures declined substantially. As a percentage of gross national product, they declined even more substantially, hitting record lows in the first two Carter defense programs. Since 1980, there have been annual increases, but they have been modest. There has been no fundamental change in the deteriorating military situation.

Strategic offensive forces, strategic defensive forces, and theater nuclear weapons have actually been reduced. Modernization of strategic and theater nuclear forces, of Army and Air Force equipment, and of power projection capabilities is not only inadequate but is stretched over too long a period of time. Provision has not been made for the critical survivability and modernization of the ICBM force.

Conventional military force capabilities will be about the same in 1983 as in 1980; so will the numbers of active (and reserve) Army and Marine Corps divisions, of Army and Marine tactical air wings, and of aircraft and ships in the airlift and sealift. There has been an increase of one Navy tactical air wing, and a modest increase in the active fleet. Personnel pay and benefits have been considerably increased and there is a slight improvement in the readiness of some general purpose forces.

Overall, there is no sign of progress adequate to correct the cumulative effects of the many years of highly adverse trends.

Great effort is needed to reverse these trends and to restore U.S. military strength. The modest increases in defense spending since 1980 will not halt the growing rate of Soviet advantage. If Soviet military spending continues to expand at past and predicted rates, the presently proposed U.S. defense increases of about 7% per year—even if left intact by Congress—will be inadequate to restore America's defenses and assure national security in the 1980s.

The pace of modernizing and improving the readiness of our forces must be accelerated. There must be a "quick fix" program to strengthen the U.S. nuclear deterrent. The survivability of U.S. strategic forces is essential to a credible military and foreign policy. Only a survivable U.S. nuclear arsenal will deter Soviet use—or threatened use—of nuclear weapons and enhance the deterrent effect of U.S. conventional forces.

Failure to close the window of vulnerability firmly and rapidly assures the Soviet Union continued strategic superiority and magnifies every other Soviet military advantage.

This report has asked "Has America Become Number 2?" The answer is unequivocally yes. If the United States remains Number 2, it will face increasing Soviet pressures backed by military superiority. U.S. survival would be in jeopardy and the nation would face a series of unacceptable choices between defeat and submission.

As the Committee stated five years ago: "American strength holds the key to our quest for peace and to our survival as a free society in a world friendly to our hopes and ideals."[62]

*29 June 1982*

## NOTES

1. "Is the Reagan Defense Program Adequate?," Committee on the Present Danger, March 1982, Chapter 17.
2. News Conference of 31 March 1982. *New York Times*, 1 April 1982.
3. *Washington Post*, 30 April 1982.
4. Eugene V. Rostow, Statement before a Joint Hearing of the Subcommittees on International Security and Scientific Affairs and on Europe and the Middle East of the Committee on Foreign Affairs, U.S. House of Representatives, 23 February, 1982, in *ACDA Arms Control Bulletin*, 23 February 1982.
5. *Red Star*, 15 January 1980, p. 1.
6. Secretary of Defense, *Annual Report to the Congress*, FY 1983, p. II-11.
7. This strategically significant asymmetry has often been ignored when bombers are addressed in an arms context.
8. For additional discussion of the Soviet view, see two previous Committee publications: "What Is The Soviet Union Up To?" 4 April 1977, and "Is America Becoming Number 2? Current Trends in the U.S.-Soviet Military Balance," 5 October 1978 (Chapters 3 and 7).
9. Secretary of Defense, *Annual Report to the Congress*, FY 1982 and FY 1983; Joint Chiefs of Staff, *U.S. Military Posture*, FY 1982 and FY 1983.
10. Secretary of Defense, *Annual Report, FY 1983*, Table IV.E. 1. Expressed in Total Obligational Authority per fiscal year. (See graphs 1, 2 and 3.)
11. The differences have been weapons procurement (over $230 billion), R & D ($100 billion), construction ($70 billion). Secretary of Defense Weinberger, 21 March 1982. *Soviet Aerospace*, 27 March 1982.
12. Secretary of Defense, *Annual Report, FY 1983*, p. II-5.
13. "Weinberger Calls Forces Insufficient," *New York Times*, 30 April 1982.
14. Secretary of Defense, *Annual Report, FY 1983*, p. 1-36.
15. For allied contributors and a collective comparison, see *NATO and the Warsaw Pact: Force Comparisons*, A NATO Report, May 1982.
16. "Is America Becoming Number 2? Current Trends in the U.S.-Soviet Military Balance," 5 October 1978, Chapter 7.
17. Despite this fact, the media generally, and erroneously, report that the U.S. enjoys a lead in this area.
18. Surveys by American Institute of Public Opinion (Gallup) March 1960–September 1974, January/February 1976, July 1977; Louis Harris and Associates for the Chicago Council on Foreign Relations, December 1974; American Institute of Public Opinion (Gallup) for the Chicago Council on Foreign Relations, 17-26 November 1978.
19. See, e.g., Justin Galere, "The Defense Tradition: The Carter Legacy and the Reagan Challenges," *Armed Forces Journal International*, December 1980.
20. The Committee addressed (Chapter 17) the issue of the adequacy of the defense program and the question of whether the United States can "afford" major increases in "Is the Reagan Defense Program Adequate?" 17 March 1982. It is also useful to recall the following words: "We shall be told that we cannot afford it. We never have doubted, or would doubt, if we were attacked, that the United States could afford to devote whatever resources and manpower might be necessary to preserve itself. Surely, it is folly now to shrink from effort and close our eyes to the crisis of the world struggle." Dean Acheson, *Power and Diplomacy*, Harvard University Press, 1958.

21. It is ironic that, where there have been suggestions of new strategic concepts or goals being formulated in the Department of Defense, they have not been directed toward reducing the gap between strategy and capabilities. To the contrary, suggestions of new guidelines for protracted nuclear conflict and protracted conventional conflict in *several parts of the world at the same time* imply a greater gap between means and ends. Any effective strategy must, at a minimum, address the threat realistically, match means and ends, and be judiciously selective in establishing proper priorities for plans and programs.

22. Since then, the Reagan Administration has canceled the Carter multiple shelter basing concept and cut in half the planned procurement of MX; it has also not decided on an alternative basing mode. The entire MX program is now unclear.

23. "Countering the Soviet Threat: U.S. Defense Strategy In the 1980s," 9 May 1980, Chapter 16.

24. See text of speech to The American Legion National Convention, Boston, Massachusetts, 20 August 1980.

25. *Measures and Trends: U.S. and USSR Strategic Force Effectiveness.* Report for the Defense Nuclear Agency, Santa Fe Corporation, Alexandria, Virginia, 1978.

26. *Military Implications of the Treaty of the Limitation of Strategic Arms and Protocol Thereto,* Hearings, Senate Armed Services Committee, Part I, p. 177. (GPO, 1979) Admiral Hayward was strongly supported by General Richard Ellis, Commander of the Strategic Air Command in 1980, who stated: "An adverse strategic imbalance has developed and will continue for several years to come." See testimony of General Ellis before the Senate Armed Services Committee, 22 February 1980.

27. Secretary of Defense, *Department of Defense Annual Report, FY 1983*, p. II-11.

28. Secretary of Defense, *Department of Defense Annual Report, FY 1981*, p. 73–74.

29. U.S. Department of Defense, *Soviet Military Power*, Washington, D.C., US GPO 1981, p. 12.

30. *Soviet Military Power*, p. 54.

31. *Washington Post*, 16 April 1982, p. A 11. On the following day, the Pentagon's press officer issued a formal statement saying "some of the Soviet missiles are more accurate and some are not." *Washington Post*, 16 April 1982, p. A 11.

32. *Air Force Magazine*, June 1981, p. 25.

33. *Washington Post*, 4 March 1982, p. A1; also see *Defense Daily*, 1 March 1982, p. 3, and *Defense Daily*, 27 May 1982, p. 146.

34. News Release from Congressman Robin Beard, 18 September 1980.

35. *United States Military Posture for FY 1983*, p. 107.

36. Rowland Evans and Robert Novak, "Soviet Freeze Warning," *Washington Post*, 5 April 1982; also, Henry Trewhitt, "Soviet Said to Deploy Long-Range Missiles," *Baltimore Sun*, 6 April 1982.

37. *Soviet Military Power*, p. 64.

38. *Soviet Military Power*, p. 65.

39. *Soviet Military Power*, p. 68.

40. Secretary of Defense, *Annual Report, FY 1981*, p. 67.

41. *Ibid.*, pp. 65–66.

42. *United States Military Posture for FY 1983*, p. 23.

43. *The SALT II Treaty*, Hearings, Senate Foreign Relations Committee, Washington, D.C., GPO, 1979, Part I, pp. 303–304.

44. *The Salt II Treaty*, Hearings, Senate Foreign Relations Committee, Washington, D.C., GPO, 1979.

45. This and other information in this section from Department of Defense *Annual Reports* for FY 1981 through FY 1983; *United States Military Posture for FY 1983*, pp. 27–29, 108; *Soviet Military Power*, pp. 26–277, 30–40; and *NATO and the Warsaw Pact: Force Comparisons.*

46. It should be noted that even if the Soviets froze or curtailed their deployment of SS-20 launchers, they could continue to expand that capability by adding more refire missiles per launcher, a fact the U.S. Government helps obscure by continuing to refer to numbers of SS-20s in terms of launchers, rather than missiles.

47. Secretary of Defense, *Annual Report, FY 1983*, p. 11–12.
48. Secretary of Defense, *Annual Report, FY 1981*, p. 7.
49. Secretary of Defense, *Annual Report, FY 1981*, p. 92.
50. "Is America Becoming Number 2? Current Trends in the U.S.-Soviet Military Balance," p. 24.
51. *Soviet Military Power*, pp. 9–13.
52. Secretary of Defense, *Annual Report, FY 1983*, p. 11–18.
53. In March 1980, the present Secretary of the Navy, John Lehman, testified that the United States had more than a $29 billion shortage of ammunition needed to meet even a thirty-day war reserve level. Secretary Lehman is currently on leave as a Director of the Committee on the Present Danger, pending completion of his public service.
54. Secretary of Defense, *Annual Report, FY 1983*, p. 1–31.
55. Joint Chiefs of Staff, *United States Military Posture for FY 1981*, p. 62.
56. Secretary of Defense, *Annual Report, FY 1983*, p. 1–30.
57. "Is America Becoming Number 2? Current Trends in the U.S.-Soviet Military Balance," 5 October 1978, Chapter 7.
58. Secretary of Defense, *Annual Report, FY 1983*, p. 1–30.
59. See testimony of Admiral Hayward before House Armed Services Committee, 8 February 1982.
60. Secretary of Defense, *Annual Report, FY 1983*, p. 111–91.
61. "Common Sense and the Common Danger," 11 November 1976.
62. "What Is The Soviet Union Up To?," 4 April 1977, p. 14.

# APPENDIX

## SOVIET MISSILE FORCES, 1982

### ICBMs[a]

| TYPE<br>NO. "DEPLOYED" MISSILE LAUNCHERS,<br>1982 (1984) | | SS-11<br>570 (420)<br>MOD 3 | | SS-13<br>60 | SS-16<br>N/A |
|---|---|---|---|---|---|
| Warhead/Missile (no.) | | 1 | 3 | 1 | 1 |
| Yield/Warhead | | 950 KT | 500 KT-1MT | 600 KT | 650 KT |
| Throw-weight/Missile (lbs.) | | 2,200 | 2,500 | 1,500 | 2,000 |
| Aggregate Throw-weight (m.lbs.) | | (both mods - 580) | | 60 | 0-200? |
| Aggregate Warheads (no.) | | (both mods - 1.25) | | 0.9 | 0.40? |
| | | 570* | | 60 | 0-200? |

| SS-17<br>150 (200) | | SS-18<br>308/326 | | | |
|---|---|---|---|---|---|
| MOD 1 | MOD 2 | MOD 1 | MOD 2 | MOD 3 | MOD 4 |
| 4 | 1 | 1 | 8 | 1 | 10/14 |
| 750 KT | 6 MT | 24 MT | 900 KT | 25 MT | 500 KT |
| 6,025 | 6,000 | 16,500 | 16,700 | 16,500 | 16,700 |
| 130 | 20 | | (all mods - 308-313) | | |
| 0.78 | 1.2 | | (all mods - approx. 5.0) | | |
| 520 | 20 | | (approx. 2,500+) | | |

| SS-19<br>300 (400) | | TOTAL | |
|---|---|---|---|
| MOD 1 | MOD 2 | | |
| 6 | 1 | | |
| 550 KT | 10 MT | | |
| 7,525 | 7,000 | | |
| (both mods - approx. 300) | | 1,398# | |
| (both mods - approx. 2.5) | | 9-14 | |
| (approx. 2,000+) | | 6,000 (approx.) | |

Sources: *Soviet Military Power*, U.S. Department of Defense, 1982.

      *U.S.-Soviet Military Balance, Concepts and Capabilities, 1960–1980*. John M. Collins, McGraw-Hill Publications Co., Washington, D.C. 1980.

*The 3 MRVs on the SS-11 Mod 3 count as a single warhead in this chart.

[a] Development of the SS-16 through SS-19 series started in the early 1960s and was completed during the 1969–72 SALT I negotiations. The table does not attempt to forecast the rate of substitution of the next generation of Soviet ICBMs. These are the SFO (small follow-on) to replace the SS-17 and SS-19, and the LFO (large follow-on), to replace the SS-18.

#This figure represents the total number of Soviet SALT-accountable launchers only.

## SLBMs

| TYPE | SS-N-5 | SS-N-6 | | SS-N-8 |
|---|---|---|---|---|
| | | MODS 1 & 2 | MOD 3 | MODS 1 & 2 |
| Range (km.) | 1,400 | 2,400/3,000 | 3,000 | 7,800/9,100 |
| Warheads[b] | 1 | 1 | 2 | 1 |
| Yield/Warhead | 1-2 MT | 1-2 MT | 500 KT-1MT | 1-2 MT |
| Deployment[c] | 57 | (all mods - 400) | | 295 |
| Aggregate Warheads | 57 | (all mods - 400)[a] | | 295 |

| SS-N-17 | SS-N-18 | SS-NX-20 | TOTAL |
|---|---|---|---|
| | ALL MODS | | |
| 3,900 | 6,500/8,000 | 8,300 | |
| 1 | 3/1/7 | 12 | |
| 1 MT | 1-2 MT | ? | |
| 12 | 225 | 20 | 950-1,000[e] (approx.) |
| 12 | 900[d] | 240 | 1,500-2500 (approx.) |

Sources: *Soviet Military Power.*

*U.S.-Soviet Military Balance, Concepts and Capabilities, 1960–1980.*

*Military Balance, 1980–1981.* International Institute for Strategic Studies. London, England, 1981.

[a] The 2 MRVs on the SS-N-6 Mod 3 are counted as a single warhead in this chart.

[b] Over 800 Soviet SLBMs will be fully modernized with multiple warheads by the late 1980s. MIRVs are being deployed on the SS-N-18.

[c] It is assumed that the old G-class and H-class submarines, which carry only 3 missiles (SS-N-4s and SS-N-5s) per boat, will be phased out in the early 1980s. The future mix of missiles is highly uncertain; we have assumed all new deployments (after 1976) to be SS-N-8s, although the arithmetic does not work out exactly: 186 additional missiles can not be deployed in any combination of full-loaded boats that hold 12 (Delta-I) or 16 (Delta-II) missiles per boat.

[d] SS-N-18s variably have 3-7 MIRVs.

[e] This figure represents the total number of SALT-accountable launchers only.

NOTE: Soviet submarine force loadings vary. Therefore, an estimated range is given for the totals.

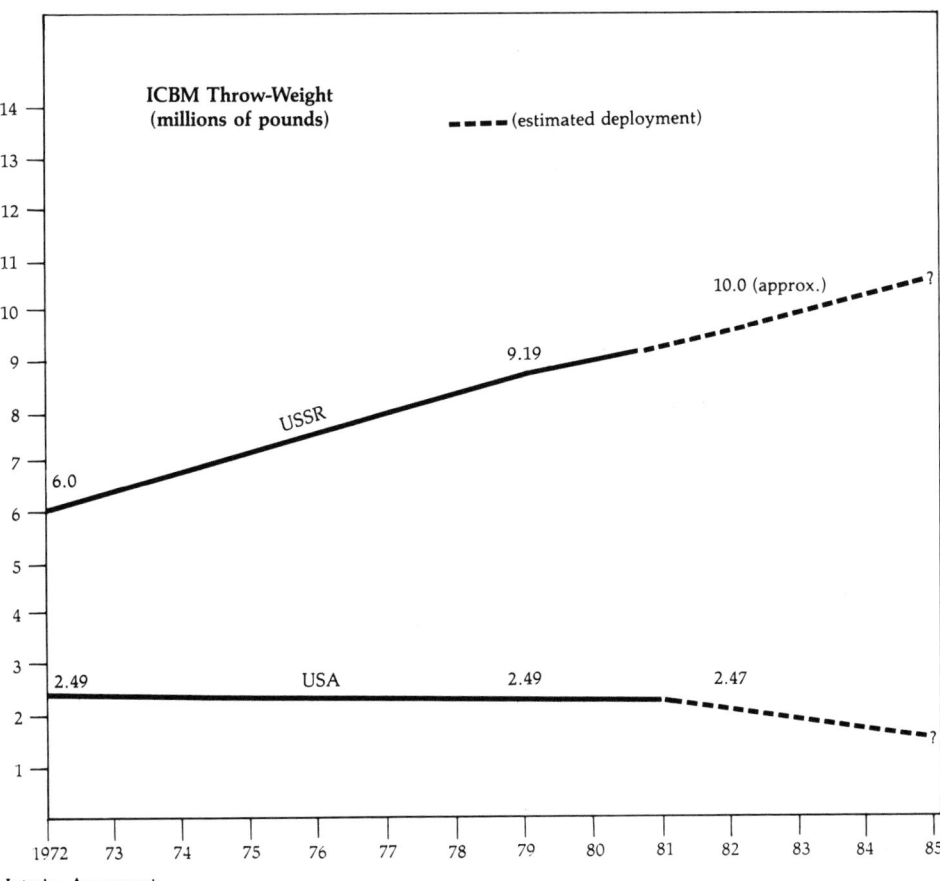

ICBM Throw-Weight
(millions of pounds)     ▬ ▬ ▬ (estimated deployment)

10.0 (approx.)

9.19

USSR

6.0

2.49     USA     2.49     2.47

1972   73   74   75   76   77   78   79   80   81   82   83   84   85

Interim Agreement

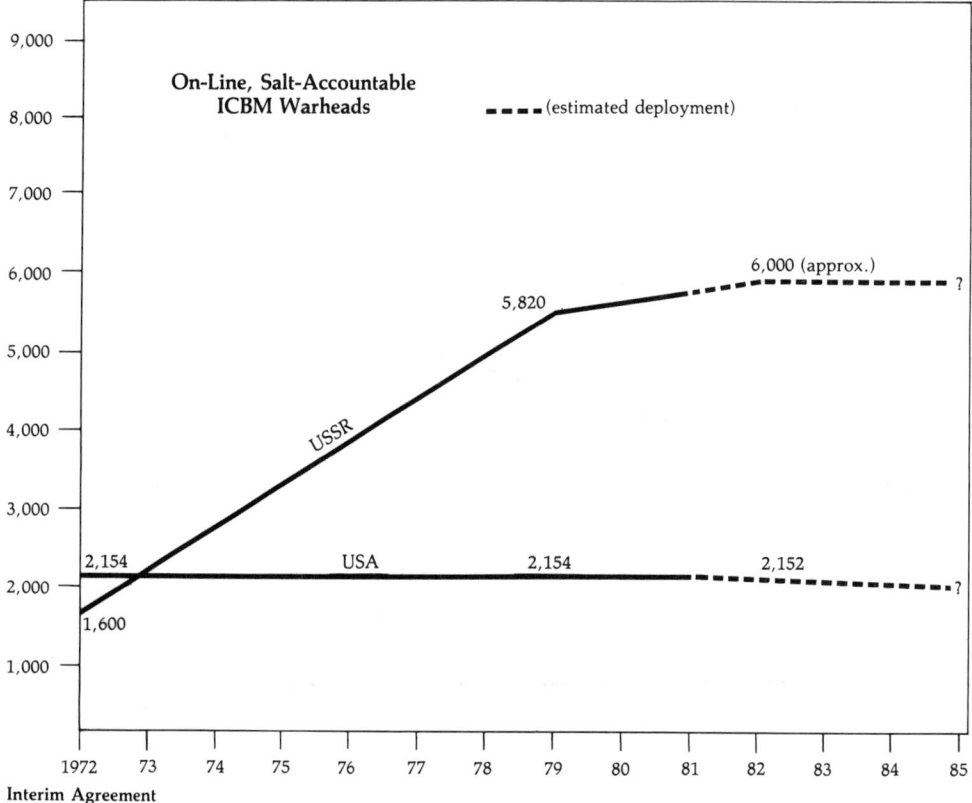

On-Line, Salt-Accountable
ICBM Warheads    ▬ ▬ ▬ (estimated deployment)

USSR

USA

6,000 (approx.)

5,820

2,154    2,154    2,152

2,154

1,600

9,000
8,000
7,000
6,000
5,000
4,000
3,000
2,000
1,000

1972  73  74  75  76  77  78  79  80  81  82  83  84  85

Interim Agreement

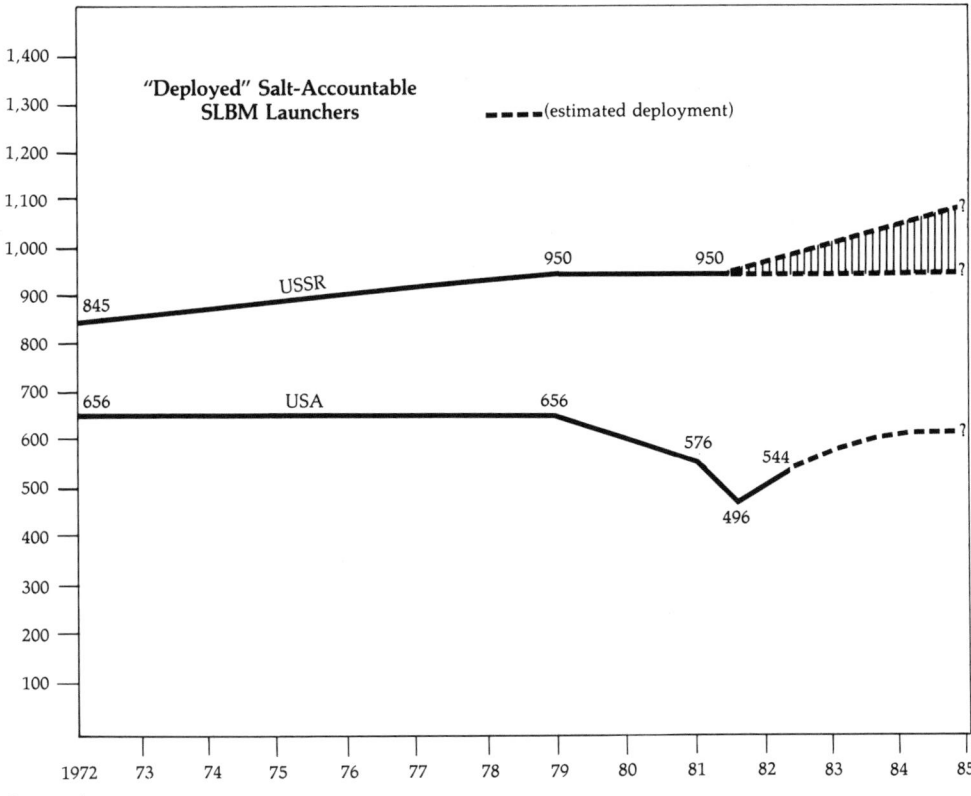

"Deployed" Salt-Accountable
SLBM Launchers        ▬ ▬ ▬(estimated deployment)

Interim Agreement

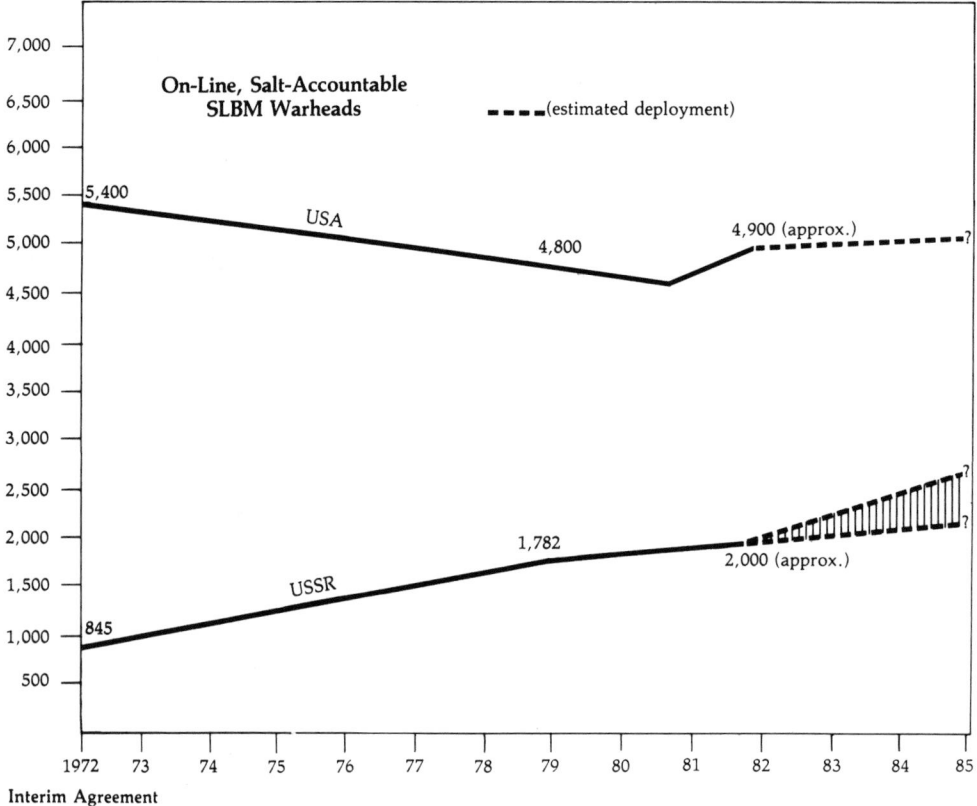

On-Line, Salt-Accountable
SLBM Warheads          ▬ ▬ ▬(estimated deployment)

USA    4,800    4,900 (approx.)    ?

USSR    1,782    2,000 (approx.)    ?

845

5,400

Interim Agreement

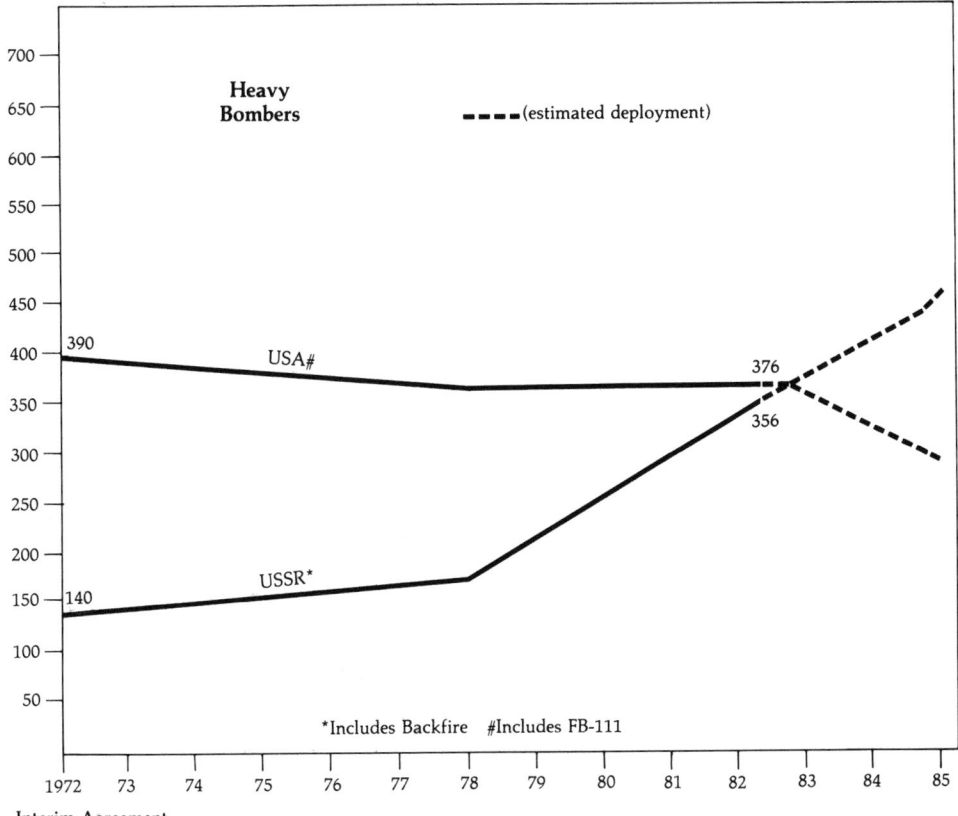

# 19

# U.S. PUBLIC ATTITUDES TOWARD THE NUCLEAR FREEZE AND OTHER NUCLEAR ARMS ISSUES

## The Results of a Nationwide Scientific Poll of American Opinion

The Committee on the Present Danger today [19 April 1984] released the results of a comprehensive, national, in-depth poll on "U.S. Public Attitudes Toward the Nuclear Freeze and Other Nuclear Arms Issues." The poll was conducted for the Committee earlier this month by the independent polling organization of Penn & Schoen Associates.*

The nationwide, scientific sample of 1,000 Americans showed strong opposition to a unilateral nuclear freeze and indeed to any arms control agreement that is not verifiable. It also showed strong public conviction that the Soviets are to blame for the breakdown of the Geneva arms control talks, and that they are violating existing arms control agreements. Further, it revealed that an overwhelming majority of Americans do not believe the Soviet Union is "willing to negotiate a nuclear freeze at equal levels of weapons."

The poll showed that a bilateral nuclear freeze at equal levels is an ideal that a large majority of Americans would like to see achieved through international negotiations. But it also showed that they do not believe this is a realistic expectation.

The poll found that most Americans view the nuclear freeze as "a way to reduce the expense of nuclear arms" rather than as a measure that would reduce the threat of nuclear war. The development of space-based defensive weaponry was also favored, with or without a nuclear freeze.

A substantial majority of Americans, the poll disclosed, support the threatened use of nuclear weapons to deter a Soviet attack against U.S. allies and favor American retaliation in the event of a Soviet attack on the United States, even at the risk of total destruction of both countries.

Among the poll's findings:

---

*Penn & Schoen Associates is a highly respected, independent, national polling organization which has conducted polls for, among others, Senators Edward Kennedy and Paul Tsongas of Massachusetts, Senator Frank Lautenberg of New Jersey, Mayor Edward Koch of New York City and Mayor Marion Barry of the District of Columbia.

—While 64% favor the concept of a nuclear freeze, 63% oppose a unilateral freeze, believing it would threaten U.S. security.

—70% oppose a mutual freeze if Soviet compliance cannot be verified.

—62% believe the Soviets are using the nuclear freeze issue "to try to gain a permanent advantage over the United States."

—By a greater than five-to-one margin, Americans believe the Soviet Union is violating existing nuclear arms control agreements.

—Three out of four Americans support the development of space-based "defensive weapons."

—Two out of three Americans oppose telling the Soviets "that we will not respond with nuclear weapons if they attack our allies."

—63% favor American retaliation in the event of a Soviet attack on the United States "even though it may result in total destruction of both countries."

—70% express confidence in the government "to make the right decisions" regarding American security.

# ANALYSIS OF THE POLL BY PENN & SCHOEN ASSOCIATES

## Summary

The poll of 1,000 U.S. residents conducted between March 31st and April 2nd, 1984, shows that Americans oppose any unilateral nuclear freeze and would oppose any bilateral agreement that did not permit verification of Soviet compliance.

The poll shows that a bilateral nuclear freeze at equal levels is an ideal that Americans would like to see achieved through international negotiations, and overwhelming majorities support such an "ideal" agreement. But at the same time, most Americans see the reality of a nuclear freeze a long way off and believe that any unilateral nuclear freeze would threaten the security of the United States. An overwhelming majority believes that the Soviets would not agree to a nuclear freeze at equal levels and believes, even if they did, they could not be trusted to honor any such agreement.

Surprisingly, Americans see the nuclear freeze as a way to reduce the expense of nuclear arms rather than a measure to reduce the threat of nuclear war. And with or without a nuclear freeze, Americans overwhelmingly favor the establishment of a space-based defensive system.

Suspicions of the Soviet Union are at extremely high levels, as solid majorities believe that the Soviet Union is seeking to expand its territory, is using the freeze to its advantage and is violating international arms accords.

## Overview of the Project

Penn and Schoen was commissioned to undertake an in-depth national poll of 1,000 U.S. residents on the nuclear freeze and related issues. The firm drew a national, random probability sample of U.S. households and conducted the detailed survey by telephone. The questionnaire was designed in conjunction with the Committee on the Present Danger to cover a wide range of areas fully and fairly. All interviewing was done by our professional interviewers out of our offices in New York between March 31st and April 2nd.

The results have an overall statistical accuracy of plus or minus three percentage points at the 95% confidence interval. The exact text of the questions asked and their full results accompany this report.

## Detailed Analysis of the Questions

1. *Attitudes toward the nuclear freeze.* The sample was first asked to describe in their own words what a nuclear freeze means to them. To most of the sample (69%), the term "nuclear freeze" means the stopping of the production of nuclear weapons. Typical responses were:

A nuclear freeze means:

"Not building any more weapons by all nations";

"Freeze production and development of nuclear weapons";

"Stop making nuclear weapons";

"Stopping the spending of money on nuclear arms."

More than 80% of the sample had a response to the open-ended question, showing that the term "nuclear freeze" is known to the overwhelming majority of Americans. And when asked whether they favored the "nuclear freeze," based on their own understanding of it, 64% said they favored it, 27% opposed it and 9% had no opinion.

However, when various alternatives to the nuclear freeze were explained to the public, attitudes on the nuclear freeze changed drastically.

When asked whether they favored "a unilateral halt by the U.S. of all production and all deployment of new nuclear weapons, regardless of whether the Soviets decide to continue building up weapons," only 30% favored it while 63% opposed it. Sixty per cent said that such a unilateral halt to the production of nuclear weapons would "threaten the security of the U.S." rather than just show our peaceful intentions.

There was near universal support for "an agreement between the U.S. and the Soviet Union calling for both nations to freeze their nuclear weapons at current levels." Eighty-one per cent favored such a freeze while 16% opposed it and 4% had no opinion. Such a situation clearly represents an ideal that the American public yearns for.

But support for even a bilateral freeze erodes significantly when it is suggested that such an agreement would leave the Soviet Union with much more nuclear firepower than the U.S. Given these facts, support drops by almost 30 percentage points to a bare majority of 51%.

And if we were unable to verify that the Soviets were living up to their part of the agreement, support for the "freeze" collapses. Only 22% would favor it without verification while 70% would oppose it and 8% had no opinion. In arms negotiations to date, the Soviet Union has steadfastly rejected any plans to allow verification of the results.

When asked how important verification is in any nuclear arms agreement, 76% of the sample answered that verification was "very important."

Thus, while the term "nuclear freeze" is a popular catch-all term for a world without more nuclear weapons, agreement with the concept should not be interpreted as an American desire for a lesser defense or for abandoning nuclear weapons willy nilly.

Americans have an ideal of international cooperation which is their first preference for a world order. In the absence of cooperation from and trust of the Soviet Union, the overwhelming majority believe that it is important to keep American nuclear defenses strong.

2. *Attitudes toward Soviet cooperation.* The American public blames the Soviet Union for the "breakdown in arms-control" negotiations. Fifty-six per cent said the Soviet Union is

to blame while 13% said it is the U.S. government that is at fault.

Since the downing of the Korean airliner, American distrust of the Soviet Union has remained at extraordinary levels. Seventy-one percent believe that the Soviets cannot be trusted to honor an agreement to freeze nuclear weapons at current levels while only 21% say they could be trusted. A majority of all demographic groups—including both men and women—did not trust the Soviets to honor a freeze agreement.

In addition, 70% said they believe that the Soviet Union is "violating existing nuclear arms-control agreements." And 78% think that the Soviets are presently "trying to expand their territory and influence rather than just trying to defend their own territory."

It is this very deep suspicion and mistrust of the Soviets that makes verification a very important issue in determining their attitudes on proposed arms-control agreements. Without verification, Americans see arms-control agreements as tantamount to unilateral arms reductions, which they oppose.

Americans are also highly suspicious of Soviet motives. Most (59%) do not believe that the Soviets are willing to agree to a nuclear freeze at equal levels, and a larger majority (62%) believe that the Soviets are trying to use the nuclear freeze issue "to try to gain a permanent advantage over the U.S."

3. *Americans have high trust in the U.S. government.* In contrast, the sample expressed high confidence in the United States government "to make the right decisions when it comes to protecting the security of the United States." Seventy per cent said they had such trust and confidence in the government while 24% did not have trust in the government.

Trust was highest among men, older people, and the better educated. A majority of all demographic groups, however, expressed trust in the government.

4. *Americans favor nuclear weapons as a deterrent and are willing to retaliate against a nuclear strike.* About two-thirds of the sample said that they opposed telling the Soviets that we will not respond with nuclear weapons if they attack our allies. College-educated respondents were the most opposed to telling the Soviets that we would not use nuclear weapons to defend our allies.

Sixty-three per cent favored retaliation against the Soviet Union after a nuclear attack on the United States, even though such action might result in the destruction of both countries. Interestingly, the college-educated citizens were most opposed to the actual use of nuclear weapons. This same group was the most in favor of keeping up the threat of their use to defend our allies.

5. *Americans favor a space defensive system.* By overwhelming numbers, Americans favor plans "to develop defensive weapons that would operate in space in order to protect the U.S. by destroying any incoming missiles." Seventy-five per cent agreed with that, while 17% opposed it.

Even if a nuclear freeze was negotiated, 54% would still favor continuation of plans for a space defense while 35% would advocate abandoning such plans.

Support for such a defense, even with a nuclear freeze, reinforces the finding that the freeze is seen more as a budget-cutting measure than an answer to the country's defense problems. Only one-third said that a nuclear freeze would reduce the chance of a nuclear war while 55% said it would "only reduce the expense of continuing to develop nuclear weapons."

*19 April 1984*

# THE POLL

1. Based on what you understand a "nuclear freeze" to be, would you favor or oppose the nuclear freeze?

| favor | oppose | don't know |
|-------|--------|------------|
| 64 | 27 | 9 |

2. Here are some different arms control propositions. For each one, tell me whether you favor or oppose it. A UNILATERAL HALT BY THE U.S. OF ALL PRODUCTION AND ALL DEPLOYMENT OF NEW NUCLEAR WEAPONS, REGARDLESS OF WHETHER THE SOVIETS DECIDE TO CONTINUE BUILDING-UP WEAPONS. Do you favor or oppose this?

| favor | oppose | don't know |
|-------|--------|------------|
| 30 | 63 | 7 |

3. An agreement between the U.S. and the Soviet Union calling for both nations to freeze their nuclear weapons at current levels. Do you favor or oppose this?

| favor | oppose | don't know |
|-------|--------|------------|
| 81 | 16 | 4 |

4. Freezing both countries at the present levels of nuclear weapons would leave the Soviets with considerably more nuclear firepower than the United States. Given this fact, do you favor or oppose the proposal to freeze both countries at current levels?

| favor | oppose | don't know |
|-------|--------|------------|
| 51 | 41 | 8 |

5. An agreement between the U.S. and the Soviet Union calling for both nations to freeze their nuclear weapons at an equal but lower level. Do you favor or oppose this?

| favor | oppose | don't know |
|-------|--------|------------|
| 81 | 13 | 5 |

6. Do you think that a nuclear freeze would reduce the chances of a nuclear war or would it only reduce the expense of continuing to develop new nuclear weapons?

| reduce war | reduce expense | don't know |
|------------|----------------|------------|
| 33 | 55 | 12 |

7. Some people have called for a unilateral nuclear freeze, meaning that we would stop producing nuclear weapons no matter what the Soviets do. Do you think that such a move would threaten the security of the U.S. or would it just show our peaceful intentions?

| security | peace intent | don't know |
|----------|--------------|------------|
| 60 | 31 | 9 |

8. How important is verification in any arms control agreement—very important,

somewhat important, or not very important?

| very import | smwht import | not very imp | don't know |
|:---:|:---:|:---:|:---:|
| 76 | 16 | 3 | 4 |

9. If the Soviet side of a nuclear freeze agreement with the U.S. could not be verified, would you favor it or oppose it?

| favor | oppose | don't know |
|:---:|:---:|:---:|
| 22 | 70 | 8 |

10. Do you think the Soviets can be trusted to honor an agreement to freeze nuclear weapons at the current levels?

| trusted | not trusted | don't know |
|:---:|:---:|:---:|
| 21 | 71 | 8 |

11. Do you believe that the Soviet Union is adhering to or violating existing nuclear arms control agreements?

| adhering | violating | don't know |
|:---:|:---:|:---:|
| 13 | 70 | 17 |

12. Where does the fault lie for the breakdown in arms control negotiations—mostly with the Soviet Union or mostly with the United States?

| Soviet Union | United States | don't know |
|:---:|:---:|:---:|
| 56 | 13 | 31 |

13. Do you favor or oppose plans to develop defensive weapons that would operate in space in order to protect the U.S. by destroying any incoming missiles?

| favor | oppose | don't know |
|:---:|:---:|:---:|
| 75 | 17 | 8 |

14. If a nuclear freeze were negotiated, should development of such defensive space weapons continue or should development be abandoned?

| continue | abandon | don't know |
|:---:|:---:|:---:|
| 54 | 35 | 11 |

15. Do you think presently that the Soviets are trying to expand their territory and influence or are they just trying to defend their own territory?

| expand | defend | don't know |
|:---:|:---:|:---:|
| 78 | 16 | 6 |

16. Do you think that the Soviets are willing to negotiate a nuclear freeze at equal levels of weapons or not?

| willing | not willing | don't know |
|:---:|:---:|:---:|
| 29 | 59 | 12 |

17. Do you think that the Soviets are using the nuclear freeze issue to try to gain a permanent advantage over the U.S. or is this not the case?

| gain | not gain | don't know |
|------|----------|------------|
| 62 | 24 | 14 |

18. Do you favor or oppose telling the Soviets that we will not respond with nuclear weapons if they attack our allies?

| favor | oppose | don't know |
|-------|--------|------------|
| 20 | 66 | 14 |

19. In the event of Soviet nuclear attack on the United States, would you favor or oppose American retaliation even though it may result in total destruction of both countries?

| favor | oppose | don't know |
|-------|--------|------------|
| 63 | 22 | 14 |

20. Do you trust the government to make the right decisions when it comes to protecting the security of the United States?

| trust govt | don't trust | don't know |
|------------|-------------|------------|
| 70 | 24 | 6 |

21. What is your age?

| 18–34 | 35–49 | 50–59 | over 60 |
|-------|-------|-------|---------|
| 42 | 25 | 12 | 20 |

22. Into which of the following categories does your family income fall?

| under $7,000 | $7-$15,000 | $15-$25,000 | $25-$35,000 | over $35,000 |
|--------------|------------|-------------|-------------|--------------|
| 9 | 21 | 28 | 20 | 22 |

23. What is the last year of school you have completed?

| below high school | high school | some college | college | above college |
|-------------------|-------------|--------------|---------|---------------|
| 12 | 35 | 27 | 17 | 9 |

24. What is your occupation? (If unemployed, get usual occupation)

| executive | businessman | semi-skilled | skilled | unskilled |
|-----------|-------------|--------------|---------|-----------|
| 25 | 8 | 11 | 13 | 3 |

| homemaker | doesn't work | student | other |
|-----------|--------------|---------|-------|
| 13 | 15 | 8 | 3 |

25. Generally speaking, do you consider yourself as liberal, moderate or conservative?

| liberal | moderate | conservative | don't know |
|---------|----------|--------------|------------|
| 24 | 37 | 34 | 6 |

26. Are you registered to vote in the United States?

(IF YES) Are you registered as a Democrat, Republican or Independent?

| not regis | Democrat | Republican | Independent | don't know |
|-----------|----------|------------|-------------|------------|
| 14 | 41 | 25 | 17 | 3 |

27. Are you or any member of your household a member of a union?

| union | non-union | don't know |
|-------|-----------|------------|
| 27 | 72 | 1 |

28. Code sex

| male | female |
|------|--------|
| 49 | 51 |

29. Region

| northeast | south | midwest | west |
|-----------|-------|---------|------|
| 28 | 29 | 20 | 22 |

# APPENDIX

## DEMOGRAPHICS

NO. 1. Based on what you understand a "nuclear freeze" to be,
would you favor or oppose the nuclear freeze?

|  | FAVOR | OPPOSE | DON'T KNOW |
|---|---|---|---|
| ALL | 64 | 27 | 9 |
| PARTY |  |  |  |
| not regis | 71 | 24 | 5 |
| Democrat | 67 | 24 | 10 |
| Republican | 58 | 33 | 10 |
| Independent | 64 | 30 | 6 |
| IDEOLOGY |  |  |  |
| liberal | 72 | 21 | 7 |
| moderate | 70 | 22 | 7 |
| conservative | 55 | 36 | 9 |
| AGE |  |  |  |
| 18–34 | 68 | 26 | 6 |
| 35–49 | 62 | 31 | 8 |
| 50–59 | 66 | 22 | 13 |
| 60+ | 60 | 27 | 13 |
| INCOME |  |  |  |
| <$7,000 | 60 | 28 | 12 |
| $ 7-$15,000 | 67 | 25 | 8 |
| $15-$25,000 | 66 | 26 | 9 |
| $25-$35,000 | 62 | 28 | 10 |
| $35,000+ | 65 | 29 | 6 |
| EDUCATION |  |  |  |
| <high school | 59 | 27 | 14 |
| high school | 63 | 28 | 10 |
| some college | 66 | 27 | 7 |
| college | 69 | 26 | 5 |
| college+ | 64 | 26 | 10 |
| UNION |  |  |  |
| union | 65 | 26 | 9 |
| non-union | 64 | 28 | 8 |
| SEX |  |  |  |
| male | 64 | 29 | 7 |
| female | 65 | 25 | 10 |
| REGION |  |  |  |
| northeast | 70 | 23 | 6 |
| south | 58 | 32 | 10 |
| midwest | 68 | 21 | 11 |
| west | 62 | 30 | 8 |

NO. 2. Here are some different arms control propositions.
For each one, tell me whether you favor or oppose it.
A UNILATERAL HALT BY THE U.S. OF ALL PRODUCTION AND
ALL DEPLOYMENT OF NEW NUCLEAR WEAPONS, REGARDLESS
OF WHETHER THE SOVIETS DECIDE TO CONTINUE
BUILDING-UP WEAPONS. Do you favor or oppose this?

|  | FAVOR | OPPOSE | DON'T KNOW |
|---|---|---|---|
| ALL | 30 | 63 | 7 |
| PARTY | | | |
| not regis | 33 | 60 | 7 |
| Democrat | 32 | 59 | 8 |
| Republican | 23 | 70 | 7 |
| Independent | 29 | 66 | 5 |
| IDEOLOGY | | | |
| liberal | 39 | 56 | 5 |
| moderate | 31 | 63 | 6 |
| conservative | 22 | 70 | 8 |
| AGE | | | |
| 18–34 | 33 | 63 | 4 |
| 35–49 | 30 | 65 | 5 |
| 50–59 | 25 | 65 | 10 |
| 60+ | 24 | 61 | 15 |
| INCOME | | | |
| <$7,000 | 33 | 52 | 15 |
| $ 7-$15,000 | 29 | 63 | 8 |
| $15-$25,000 | 31 | 60 | 9 |
| $25-$35,000 | 28 | 68 | 4 |
| $35,000+ | 27 | 68 | 5 |
| EDUCATION | | | |
| <high school | 27 | 62 | 11 |
| high school | 29 | 62 | 9 |
| some college | 28 | 68 | 4 |
| college | 31 | 60 | 9 |
| college+ | 32 | 63 | 5 |
| UNION | | | |
| union | 27 | 64 | 8 |
| non-union | 30 | 63 | 7 |
| SEX | | | |
| male | 27 | 69 | 4 |
| female | 32 | 57 | 10 |
| REGION | | | |
| northeast | 39 | 55 | 7 |
| south | 21 | 71 | 7 |
| midwest | 27 | 64 | 8 |
| west | 30 | 64 | 6 |

NO. 3. An agreement between the U.S. and the Soviet Union
calling for both nations to freeze their nuclear weapons at
current levels. Do you favor or oppose this?

|  | FAVOR | OPPOSE | DON'T KNOW |
| --- | --- | --- | --- |
| ALL | 81 | 16 | 4 |
| PARTY | | | |
| not regis | 84 | 12 | 5 |
| Democrat | 83 | 15 | 3 |
| Republican | 77 | 19 | 4 |
| Independent | 81 | 17 | 2 |
| IDEOLOGY | | | |
| liberal | 85 | 13 | 1 |
| moderate | 87 | 10 | 3 |
| conservative | 73 | 23 | 5 |
| AGE | | | |
| 18–34 | 82 | 16 | 2 |
| 35–49 | 77 | 19 | 4 |
| 50–59 | 84 | 13 | 3 |
| 60+ | 80 | 13 | 7 |
| INCOME | | | |
| <$7,000 | 75 | 21 | 4 |
| $ 7-$15,000 | 81 | 15 | 3 |
| $15-$25,000 | 81 | 15 | 4 |
| $25-$35,000 | 85 | 13 | 1 |
| $35,000+ | 80 | 17 | 3 |
| EDUCATION | | | |
| <high school | 77 | 16 | 6 |
| high school | 81 | 16 | 4 |
| some college | 79 | 18 | 3 |
| college | 83 | 16 | 1 |
| college+ | 86 | 9 | 5 |
| UNION | | | |
| union | 82 | 15 | 3 |
| non-union | 80 | 16 | 4 |
| SEX | | | |
| male | 80 | 17 | 2 |
| female | 81 | 14 | 5 |
| REGION | | | |
| northeast | 83 | 12 | 5 |
| south | 76 | 21 | 3 |
| midwest | 87 | 10 | 3 |
| west | 78 | 19 | 3 |

NO. 4. Freezing both countries at the present levels of nuclear weapons would leave the Soviets with considerably more nuclear firepower than the United States. Given this fact, do you favor or oppose the proposal to freeze both countries at current levels?

|  | FAVOR | OPPOSE | DON'T KNOW |
|---|---|---|---|
| ALL | 51 | 41 | 8 |
| PARTY | | | |
| not regis | 52 | 41 | 7 |
| Democrat | 53 | 38 | 9 |
| Republican | 49 | 45 | 7 |
| Independent | 53 | 38 | 9 |
| IDEOLOGY | | | |
| liberal | 61 | 36 | 3 |
| moderate | 54 | 37 | 8 |
| conservative | 44 | 48 | 7 |
| AGE | | | |
| 18–34 | 59 | 38 | 3 |
| 35–49 | 53 | 40 | 7 |
| 50–59 | 51 | 40 | 9 |
| 60+ | 33 | 49 | 17 |
| INCOME | | | |
| <$7,000 | 38 | 47 | 15 |
| $ 7-$15,000 | 46 | 45 | 9 |
| $15-$25,000 | 50 | 41 | 9 |
| $25-$35,000 | 54 | 42 | 4 |
| $35,000+ | 60 | 34 | 6 |
| EDUCATION | | | |
| <high school | 36 | 47 | 17 |
| high school | 47 | 45 | 9 |
| some college | 50 | 44 | 5 |
| college | 63 | 32 | 6 |
| college+ | 71 | 25 | 4 |
| UNION | | | |
| union | 52 | 41 | 7 |
| non-union | 51 | 41 | 8 |
| SEX | | | |
| male | 55 | 40 | 5 |
| female | 48 | 41 | 10 |
| REGION | | | |
| northeast | 54 | 38 | 8 |
| south | 47 | 45 | 8 |
| midwest | 50 | 41 | 8 |
| west | 54 | 39 | 6 |

NO. 5. An agreement between the U.S. and the Soviet Union
calling for both nations to freeze their nuclear weapons
at an equal but lower level. Do you favor or oppose this?

|  | FAVOR | OPPOSE | DON'T KNOW |
|---|---|---|---|
| ALL | 81 | 13 | 5 |
| PARTY |  |  |  |
| not regis | 83 | 12 | 5 |
| Democrat | 82 | 11 | 7 |
| Republican | 80 | 15 | 5 |
| Independent | 82 | 15 | 3 |
| IDEOLOGY |  |  |  |
| liberal | 85 | 10 | 5 |
| moderate | 86 | 10 | 4 |
| conservative | 76 | 18 | 6 |
| AGE |  |  |  |
| 18–34 | 85 | 13 | 2 |
| 35–49 | 78 | 16 | 6 |
| 50–59 | 86 | 8 | 6 |
| 60+ | 77 | 12 | 12 |
| INCOME |  |  |  |
| <$7,000 | 74 | 19 | 7 |
| $ 7-$15,000 | 81 | 13 | 7 |
| $15-$25,000 | 82 | 12 | 5 |
| $25-$35,000 | 87 | 10 | 3 |
| $35,000+ | 80 | 15 | 5 |
| EDUCATION |  |  |  |
| <high school | 77 | 10 | 13 |
| high school | 80 | 14 | 6 |
| some college | 84 | 13 | 3 |
| college | 83 | 14 | 3 |
| college+ | 84 | 11 | 5 |
| UNION |  |  |  |
| union | 86 | 10 | 4 |
| non-union | 80 | 14 | 6 |
| SEX |  |  |  |
| male | 84 | 12 | 4 |
| female | 79 | 14 | 7 |
| REGION |  |  |  |
| northeast | 83 | 11 | 6 |
| south | 84 | 12 | 4 |
| midwest | 81 | 14 | 5 |
| west | 76 | 17 | 7 |

NO. 6. Do you think that a nuclear freeze would reduce the chances of a nuclear war or would it only reduce the expense of continuing to develop new nuclear weapons?

|  | REDUCE WAR | REDUCE EXPENSE | DON'T KNOW |
|---|---|---|---|
| ALL | 33 | 55 | 12 |
| PARTY |  |  |  |
| not regis | 35 | 53 | 12 |
| Democrat | 38 | 49 | 13 |
| Republican | 30 | 60 | 10 |
| Independent | 26 | 62 | 12 |
| IDEOLOGY |  |  |  |
| liberal | 37 | 56 | 6 |
| moderate | 37 | 52 | 12 |
| conservative | 27 | 60 | 12 |
| AGE |  |  |  |
| 18–34 | 33 | 61 | 7 |
| 35–49 | 32 | 59 | 9 |
| 50–59 | 32 | 49 | 18 |
| 60+ | 36 | 42 | 21 |
| INCOME |  |  |  |
| <$7,000 | 36 | 44 | 20 |
| $ 7-$15,000 | 34 | 51 | 15 |
| $15-$25,000 | 33 | 56 | 11 |
| $25-$35,000 | 34 | 57 | 9 |
| $35,000+ | 29 | 61 | 9 |
| EDUCATION |  |  |  |
| <high school | 36 | 39 | 25 |
| high school | 34 | 53 | 13 |
| some college | 32 | 60 | 8 |
| college | 30 | 63 | 8 |
| college+ | 36 | 55 | 8 |
| UNION |  |  |  |
| union | 34 | 55 | 10 |
| non-union | 33 | 55 | 12 |
| SEX |  |  |  |
| male | 33 | 57 | 11 |
| female | 34 | 53 | 13 |
| REGION |  |  |  |
| northeast | 36 | 54 | 10 |
| south | 29 | 58 | 13 |
| midwest | 33 | 52 | 15 |
| west | 36 | 53 | 11 |

NO. 7. Some people have called for a unilateral nuclear freeze, meaning that we would stop producing nuclear weapons no matter what the Soviets do. Do you think that such a move would threaten the security of the U.S. or would it just show our peaceful intentions?

|  | SECURITY | PEACE INTENT | DON'T KNOW |
|---|---|---|---|
| ALL | 60 | 31 | 9 |
| PARTY | | | |
| not regis | 47 | 42 | 11 |
| Democrat | 57 | 31 | 12 |
| Republican | 70 | 24 | 6 |
| Independent | 65 | 30 | 5 |
| IDEOLOGY | | | |
| liberal | 51 | 41 | 8 |
| moderate | 60 | 30 | 10 |
| conservative | 68 | 25 | 7 |
| AGE | | | |
| 18–34 | 55 | 37 | 8 |
| 35–49 | 61 | 32 | 8 |
| 50–59 | 67 | 24 | 9 |
| 60+ | 67 | 21 | 11 |
| INCOME | | | |
| <$7,000 | 46 | 40 | 15 |
| $ 7-$15,000 | 56 | 34 | 11 |
| $15-$25,000 | 64 | 29 | 7 |
| $25-$35,000 | 65 | 29 | 6 |
| $35,000+ | 60 | 29 | 10 |
| EDUCATION | | | |
| <high school | 56 | 34 | 10 |
| high school | 60 | 29 | 11 |
| some college | 62 | 29 | 9 |
| college | 64 | 31 | 6 |
| college+ | 56 | 38 | 6 |
| UNION | | | |
| union | 61 | 31 | 8 |
| non-union | 60 | 31 | 9 |
| SEX | | | |
| male | 62 | 31 | 7 |
| female | 59 | 30 | 11 |
| REGION | | | |
| northeast | 54 | 36 | 10 |
| south | 68 | 25 | 7 |
| midwest | 58 | 30 | 12 |
| west | 63 | 31 | 6 |

NO. 8. How important is verification in any arms control agreement—
very important, somewhat important or not very important?

| | VERY IMPORTANT | SMWHT IMPORT | NOT VERY IMP | DON'T KNOW |
|---|---|---|---|---|
| ALL | 76 | 16 | 3 | 4 |
| PARTY | | | | |
| not regis | 76 | 19 | 3 | 3 |
| Democrat | 74 | 18 | 3 | 5 |
| Republican | 77 | 15 | 4 | 4 |
| Independent | 79 | 16 | 2 | 2 |
| IDEOLOGY | | | | |
| liberal | 76 | 18 | 3 | 3 |
| moderate | 77 | 16 | 3 | 3 |
| conservative | 75 | 17 | 3 | 5 |
| AGE | | | | |
| 18–34 | 75 | 19 | 3 | 3 |
| 35–49 | 75 | 18 | 3 | 4 |
| 50–59 | 82 | 11 | 4 | 3 |
| 60+ | 76 | 12 | 4 | 8 |
| INCOME | | | | |
| <$7,000 | 71 | 21 | 4 | 5 |
| $ 7-$15,000 | 74 | 17 | 2 | 7 |
| $15-$25,000 | 79 | 15 | 2 | 5 |
| $25-$35,000 | 77 | 18 | 4 | 1 |
| $35,000+ | 79 | 15 | 4 | 3 |
| EDUCATION | | | | |
| <high school | 80 | 6 | 5 | 9 |
| high school | 73 | 20 | 3 | 4 |
| some college | 76 | 18 | 3 | 4 |
| college | 79 | 16 | 2 | 4 |
| college+ | 79 | 14 | 5 | 2 |
| UNION | | | | |
| union | 80 | 15 | 3 | 2 |
| non-union | 75 | 17 | 3 | 5 |
| SEX | | | | |
| male | 81 | 13 | 4 | 3 |
| female | 71 | 20 | 3 | 6 |
| REGION | | | | |
| northeast | 74 | 17 | 5 | 4 |
| south | 78 | 15 | 2 | 6 |
| midwest | 75 | 17 | 3 | 5 |
| west | 78 | 18 | 2 | 2 |

NO. 9. If the Soviet side of a nuclear freeze agreement with the U.S. could not be verified, would you favor or oppose it?

|  | FAVOR | OPPOSE | DON'T KNOW |
|---|---|---|---|
| ALL | 22 | 70 | 8 |
| **PARTY** | | | |
| not regis | 25 | 66 | 9 |
| Democrat | 24 | 68 | 8 |
| Republican | 18 | 74 | 8 |
| Independent | 24 | 72 | 5 |
| **IDEOLOGY** | | | |
| liberal | 31 | 65 | 4 |
| moderate | 21 | 72 | 6 |
| conservative | 19 | 72 | 9 |
| **AGE** | | | |
| 18–34 | 29 | 67 | 5 |
| 35–49 | 19 | 74 | 7 |
| 50–59 | 23 | 69 | 8 |
| 60+ | 12 | 73 | 15 |
| **INCOME** | | | |
| <$7,000 | 19 | 63 | 18 |
| $ 7-$15,000 | 20 | 70 | 10 |
| $15-$25,000 | 24 | 69 | 7 |
| $25-$35,000 | 22 | 74 | 4 |
| $35,000+ | 23 | 71 | 6 |
| **EDUCATION** | | | |
| <high school | 15 | 73 | 12 |
| high school | 20 | 69 | 10 |
| some college | 24 | 70 | 6 |
| college | 23 | 73 | 4 |
| college+ | 33 | 62 | 4 |
| **UNION** | | | |
| union | 21 | 73 | 7 |
| non-union | 23 | 69 | 8 |
| **SEX** | | | |
| male | 21 | 74 | 5 |
| female | 24 | 66 | 10 |
| **REGION** | | | |
| northeast | 26 | 64 | 9 |
| south | 19 | 73 | 8 |
| midwest | 23 | 69 | 7 |
| west | 20 | 75 | 5 |

NO. 10. Do you think the Soviets can be trusted to honor
an agreement to freeze nuclear weapons at the current levels?

|  | TRUSTED | NOT TRUSTED | DON'T KNOW |
|---|---|---|---|
| ALL | 21 | 71 | 8 |
| **PARTY** | | | |
| not regis | 24 | 71 | 5 |
| Democrat | 22 | 68 | 10 |
| Republican | 17 | 75 | 8 |
| Independent | 23 | 71 | 6 |
| **IDEOLOGY** | | | |
| liberal | 30 | 63 | 6 |
| moderate | 21 | 69 | 10 |
| conservative | 15 | 80 | 5 |
| **AGE** | | | |
| 18–34 | 27 | 64 | 9 |
| 35–49 | 18 | 75 | 7 |
| 50–59 | 19 | 75 | 6 |
| 60+ | 12 | 77 | 10 |
| **INCOME** | | | |
| <$7,000 | 18 | 70 | 12 |
| $ 7-$15,000 | 18 | 71 | 10 |
| $15-$25,000 | 19 | 73 | 8 |
| $25-$35,000 | 21 | 70 | 9 |
| $35,000+ | 26 | 68 | 6 |
| **EDUCATION** | | | |
| <high school | 15 | 75 | 10 |
| high school | 16 | 74 | 10 |
| some college | 22 | 71 | 6 |
| college | 25 | 66 | 9 |
| college+ | 33 | 60 | 7 |
| **UNION** | | | |
| union | 20 | 72 | 9 |
| non-union | 21 | 71 | 8 |
| **SEX** | | | |
| male | 21 | 71 | 8 |
| female | 20 | 71 | 9 |
| **REGION** | | | |
| northeast | 25 | 67 | 7 |
| south | 17 | 73 | 11 |
| midwest | 18 | 74 | 8 |
| west | 23 | 71 | 7 |

NO. 11. Do you believe that the Soviet Union is adhering to
or violating existing nuclear arms control agreements?

|  | ADHERING | VIOLATING | DON'T KNOW |
|---|---|---|---|
| ALL | 13 | 70 | 17 |
| PARTY |  |  |  |
| not regis | 18 | 62 | 21 |
| Democrat | 13 | 67 | 20 |
| Republican | 9 | 77 | 14 |
| Independent | 16 | 74 | 11 |
| IDEOLOGY |  |  |  |
| liberal | 14 | 69 | 18 |
| moderate | 14 | 70 | 16 |
| conservative | 11 | 75 | 14 |
| AGE |  |  |  |
| 18–34 | 15 | 68 | 18 |
| 35–49 | 14 | 72 | 14 |
| 50–59 | 13 | 67 | 20 |
| 60+ | 7 | 76 | 17 |
| INCOME |  |  |  |
| <$7,000 | 10 | 76 | 14 |
| $ 7-$15,000 | 15 | 65 | 20 |
| $15-$25,000 | 9 | 72 | 18 |
| $25-$35,000 | 10 | 73 | 17 |
| $35,000+ | 19 | 69 | 12 |
| EDUCATION |  |  |  |
| <high school | 11 | 65 | 25 |
| high school | 10 | 72 | 18 |
| some college | 11 | 74 | 15 |
| college | 13 | 72 | 15 |
| college+ | 31 | 59 | 9 |
| UNION |  |  |  |
| union | 13 | 69 | 18 |
| non-union | 12 | 71 | 16 |
| SEX |  |  |  |
| male | 14 | 73 | 13 |
| female | 12 | 68 | 20 |
| REGION |  |  |  |
| northeast | 14 | 67 | 19 |
| south | 11 | 73 | 16 |
| midwest | 13 | 69 | 18 |
| west | 12 | 73 | 15 |

NO. 12. Where does the fault lie for the breakdown in arms control negotiations—mostly with the Soviet Union or mostly with the United States?

| | SOVIET UNION | UNITED STATES | DON'T KNOW |
|---|---|---|---|
| ALL | 56 | 13 | 31 |
| PARTY | | | |
| not regis | 48 | 16 | 35 |
| Democrat | 55 | 14 | 31 |
| Republican | 63 | 10 | 27 |
| Independent | 56 | 11 | 33 |
| IDEOLOGY | | | |
| liberal | 55 | 15 | 30 |
| moderate | 54 | 13 | 33 |
| conservative | 61 | 11 | 29 |
| AGE | | | |
| 18–34 | 59 | 15 | 26 |
| 35–49 | 54 | 12 | 35 |
| 50–59 | 49 | 12 | 39 |
| 60+ | 56 | 10 | 34 |
| INCOME | | | |
| <$7,000 | 49 | 13 | 38 |
| $ 7-$15,000 | 57 | 15 | 29 |
| $15-$25,000 | 59 | 14 | 27 |
| $25-$35,000 | 54 | 10 | 36 |
| $35,000+ | 53 | 13 | 34 |
| EDUCATION | | | |
| <high school | 56 | 15 | 29 |
| high school | 58 | 12 | 30 |
| some college | 55 | 12 | 33 |
| college | 57 | 11 | 32 |
| college+ | 46 | 21 | 34 |
| UNION | | | |
| union | 56 | 13 | 30 |
| non-union | 55 | 13 | 32 |
| SEX | | | |
| male | 55 | 14 | 31 |
| female | 56 | 12 | 31 |
| REGION | | | |
| northeast | 53 | 16 | 31 |
| south | 61 | 12 | 27 |
| midwest | 58 | 11 | 31 |
| west | 53 | 12 | 36 |

NO. 13. Do you favor or oppose plans to develop
defensive weapons that would operate in space in order to
protect the U.S. by destroying any incoming missiles?

|  | FAVOR | OPPOSE | DON'T KNOW |
|---|---|---|---|
| ALL | 75 | 17 | 8 |
| **PARTY** | | | |
| not regis | 76 | 18 | 6 |
| Democrat | 75 | 19 | 7 |
| Republican | 75 | 14 | 10 |
| Independent | 78 | 16 | 6 |
| **IDEOLOGY** | | | |
| liberal | 73 | 23 | 5 |
| moderate | 73 | 19 | 8 |
| conservative | 81 | 11 | 8 |
| **AGE** | | | |
| 18–34 | 78 | 17 | 5 |
| 35–49 | 77 | 19 | 5 |
| 50–59 | 74 | 17 | 9 |
| 60+ | 69 | 15 | 15 |
| **INCOME** | | | |
| <$7,000 | 67 | 19 | 14 |
| $ 7-$15,000 | 75 | 15 | 10 |
| $15-$25,000 | 75 | 17 | 8 |
| $25-$35,000 | 79 | 18 | 4 |
| $35,000+ | 78 | 18 | 4 |
| **EDUCATION** | | | |
| <high school | 77 | 12 | 11 |
| high school | 79 | 12 | 9 |
| some college | 76 | 18 | 6 |
| college | 74 | 21 | 5 |
| college+ | 62 | 33 | 4 |
| **UNION** | | | |
| union | 76 | 19 | 6 |
| non-union | 75 | 17 | 8 |
| **SEX** | | | |
| male | 77 | 17 | 6 |
| female | 74 | 17 | 9 |
| **REGION** | | | |
| northeast | 69 | 23 | 8 |
| south | 82 | 12 | 6 |
| midwest | 70 | 18 | 12 |
| west | 79 | 15 | 6 |

NO. 14. If a nuclear freeze were negotiated, should development of such defensive space weapons continue or should development be abandoned?

|  | CONTINUE | ABANDON | DON'T KNOW |
|---|---|---|---|
| ALL | 54 | 35 | 11 |
| PARTY |  |  |  |
| not regis | 55 | 34 | 11 |
| Democrat | 54 | 35 | 11 |
| Republican | 56 | 31 | 13 |
| Independent | 53 | 41 | 6 |
| IDEOLOGY |  |  |  |
| liberal | 53 | 38 | 9 |
| moderate | 51 | 38 | 11 |
| conservative | 60 | 31 | 9 |
| AGE |  |  |  |
| 18–34 | 59 | 35 | 6 |
| 35–49 | 55 | 35 | 9 |
| 50–59 | 48 | 39 | 12 |
| 60+ | 46 | 31 | 23 |
| INCOME |  |  |  |
| <$7,000 | 46 | 29 | 25 |
| $ 7-$15,000 | 53 | 33 | 13 |
| $15-$25,000 | 55 | 36 | 8 |
| $25-$35,000 | 56 | 36 | 7 |
| $35,000+ | 54 | 37 | 8 |
| EDUCATION |  |  |  |
| <high school | 49 | 26 | 25 |
| high school | 55 | 34 | 11 |
| some college | 57 | 36 | 7 |
| college | 58 | 33 | 9 |
| college+ | 39 | 54 | 7 |
| UNION |  |  |  |
| union | 50 | 39 | 11 |
| non-union | 56 | 34 | 10 |
| SEX |  |  |  |
| male | 56 | 35 | 8 |
| female | 52 | 35 | 13 |
| REGION |  |  |  |
| northeast | 53 | 38 | 10 |
| south | 60 | 29 | 11 |
| midwest | 48 | 38 | 14 |
| west | 56 | 35 | 9 |

NO. 15. Do you think presently that the Soviets are trying
to expand their territory and influence or are they just trying
to defend their own territory?

|  | EXPAND | DEFEND | DON'T KNOW |
|---|---|---|---|
| ALL | 78 | 16 | 6 |
| PARTY | | | |
| not regis | 72 | 22 | 6 |
| Democrat | 75 | 16 | 9 |
| Republican | 85 | 12 | 3 |
| Independent | 80 | 16 | 3 |
| IDEOLOGY | | | |
| liberal | 75 | 18 | 6 |
| moderate | 81 | 14 | 4 |
| conservative | 81 | 14 | 5 |
| AGE | | | |
| 18–34 | 75 | 21 | 4 |
| 35–49 | 81 | 13 | 6 |
| 50–59 | 79 | 14 | 7 |
| 60+ | 82 | 8 | 10 |
| INCOME | | | |
| <$7,000 | 72 | 21 | 7 |
| $ 7-$15,000 | 72 | 19 | 9 |
| $15-$25,000 | 82 | 13 | 5 |
| $25-$35,000 | 78 | 16 | 6 |
| $35,000+ | 83 | 14 | 3 |
| EDUCATION | | | |
| <high school | 67 | 23 | 9 |
| high school | 77 | 16 | 7 |
| some college | 81 | 16 | 3 |
| college | 85 | 11 | 3 |
| college+ | 77 | 13 | 10 |
| UNION | | | |
| union | 81 | 14 | 5 |
| non-union | 78 | 16 | 6 |
| SEX | | | |
| male | 81 | 14 | 6 |
| female | 77 | 17 | 6 |
| REGION | | | |
| northeast | 77 | 16 | 7 |
| south | 76 | 18 | 6 |
| midwest | 79 | 15 | 5 |
| west | 82 | 13 | 5 |

NO. 16. Do you think that the Soviets are willing to negotiate a nuclear freeze at equal levels of weapons or not?

|  | WILLING | NOT WILLING | DON'T KNOW |
|---|---|---|---|
| ALL | 29 | 59 | 12 |
| PARTY | | | |
| not regis | 31 | 59 | 11 |
| Democrat | 30 | 55 | 15 |
| Republican | 22 | 67 | 11 |
| Independent | 33 | 58 | 9 |
| IDEOLOGY | | | |
| liberal | 34 | 57 | 10 |
| moderate | 32 | 55 | 14 |
| conservative | 23 | 66 | 11 |
| AGE | | | |
| 18–34 | 33 | 58 | 9 |
| 35–49 | 32 | 56 | 12 |
| 50–59 | 22 | 64 | 14 |
| 60+ | 21 | 61 | 18 |
| INCOME | | | |
| <$7,000 | 26 | 56 | 18 |
| $ 7-$15,000 | 30 | 56 | 14 |
| $15-$25,000 | 27 | 63 | 10 |
| $25-$35,000 | 28 | 60 | 12 |
| $35,000+ | 33 | 56 | 11 |
| EDUCATION | | | |
| <high school | 26 | 57 | 17 |
| high school | 27 | 63 | 10 |
| some college | 28 | 62 | 10 |
| college | 28 | 57 | 15 |
| college+ | 43 | 43 | 14 |
| UNION | | | |
| union | 32 | 56 | 13 |
| non-union | 28 | 60 | 12 |
| SEX | | | |
| male | 30 | 58 | 12 |
| female | 27 | 60 | 13 |
| REGION | | | |
| northeast | 30 | 56 | 14 |
| south | 26 | 60 | 14 |
| midwest | 28 | 62 | 9 |
| west | 29 | 59 | 12 |

NO. 17. Do you think that the Soviets are using
the nuclear freeze issue to try to gain a permanent advantage
over the U.S. or is this not the case?

|  | GAIN | NOT GAIN | DON'T KNOW |
|---|---|---|---|
| ALL | 62 | 24 | 14 |
| **PARTY** | | | |
| not regis | 57 | 23 | 20 |
| Democrat | 61 | 26 | 13 |
| Republican | 68 | 21 | 11 |
| Independent | 61 | 24 | 15 |
| **IDEOLOGY** | | | |
| liberal | 61 | 30 | 9 |
| moderate | 59 | 26 | 15 |
| conservative | 67 | 20 | 13 |
| **AGE** | | | |
| 18–34 | 58 | 32 | 10 |
| 35–49 | 62 | 25 | 13 |
| 50–59 | 67 | 14 | 19 |
| 60+ | 68 | 14 | 18 |
| **INCOME** | | | |
| <$7,000 | 64 | 14 | 22 |
| $ 7-$15,000 | 56 | 23 | 21 |
| $15-$25,000 | 70 | 20 | 10 |
| $25-$35,000 | 64 | 24 | 11 |
| $35,000+ | 55 | 36 | 10 |
| **EDUCATION** | | | |
| <high school | 63 | 16 | 21 |
| high school | 68 | 15 | 17 |
| some college | 58 | 31 | 11 |
| college | 62 | 29 | 8 |
| college+ | 52 | 40 | 8 |
| **UNION** | | | |
| union | 62 | 25 | 13 |
| non-union | 62 | 24 | 14 |
| **SEX** | | | |
| male | 63 | 25 | 12 |
| female | 61 | 23 | 16 |
| **REGION** | | | |
| northeast | 58 | 29 | 13 |
| south | 69 | 18 | 13 |
| midwest | 61 | 27 | 12 |
| west | 61 | 23 | 16 |

NO. 18. Do you favor or oppose telling the Soviets that we will not respond with nuclear weapons if they attack our allies?

|  | FAVOR | OPPOSE | DON'T KNOW |
|---|---|---|---|
| ALL | 20 | 66 | 14 |
| PARTY |  |  |  |
| not regis | 22 | 57 | 21 |
| Democrat | 22 | 64 | 13 |
| Republican | 18 | 69 | 13 |
| Independent | 20 | 70 | 10 |
| IDEOLOGY |  |  |  |
| liberal | 27 | 61 | 12 |
| moderate | 19 | 65 | 15 |
| conservative | 15 | 73 | 12 |
| AGE |  |  |  |
| 18–34 | 26 | 63 | 10 |
| 35–49 | 15 | 71 | 14 |
| 50–59 | 17 | 69 | 14 |
| 60+ | 17 | 62 | 21 |
| INCOME |  |  |  |
| <$7,000 | 19 | 60 | 21 |
| $ 7-$15,000 | 21 | 65 | 15 |
| $15-$25,000 | 19 | 66 | 15 |
| $25-$35,000 | 22 | 68 | 10 |
| $35,000+ | 19 | 69 | 12 |
| EDUCATION |  |  |  |
| <high school | 18 | 65 | 17 |
| high school | 18 | 64 | 18 |
| some college | 23 | 66 | 11 |
| college | 20 | 68 | 12 |
| college+ | 22 | 71 | 7 |
| UNION |  |  |  |
| union | 20 | 63 | 17 |
| non-union | 20 | 67 | 13 |
| SEX |  |  |  |
| male | 18 | 71 | 11 |
| female | 22 | 61 | 16 |
| REGION |  |  |  |
| northeast | 28 | 57 | 15 |
| south | 15 | 70 | 14 |
| midwest | 20 | 65 | 15 |
| west | 18 | 71 | 11 |

NO. 19. In the event of Soviet nuclear attack on the United States, would you favor or oppose American retaliation even though it may result in total destruction of both countries?

|  | FAVOR | OPPOSE | DON'T KNOW |
|---|---|---|---|
| ALL | 63 | 22 | 14 |
| PARTY | | | |
| not regis | 58 | 28 | 14 |
| Democrat | 62 | 22 | 16 |
| Republican | 69 | 18 | 13 |
| Independent | 64 | 25 | 11 |
| IDEOLOGY | | | |
| liberal | 63 | 26 | 11 |
| moderate | 63 | 21 | 16 |
| conservative | 68 | 20 | 12 |
| AGE | | | |
| 18–34 | 61 | 30 | 10 |
| 35–49 | 67 | 21 | 11 |
| 50–59 | 65 | 14 | 21 |
| 60+ | 63 | 14 | 23 |
| INCOME | | | |
| <$7,000 | 63 | 23 | 15 |
| $ 7-$15,000 | 62 | 24 | 15 |
| $15-$25,000 | 66 | 19 | 15 |
| $25-$35,000 | 64 | 23 | 13 |
| $35,000+ | 65 | 24 | 11 |
| EDUCATION | | | |
| <high school | 64 | 22 | 14 |
| high school | 68 | 18 | 14 |
| some college | 65 | 22 | 12 |
| college | 61 | 27 | 12 |
| college+ | 44 | 30 | 26 |
| UNION | | | |
| union | 63 | 23 | 14 |
| non-union | 64 | 22 | 14 |
| SEX | | | |
| male | 69 | 19 | 12 |
| female | 58 | 26 | 16 |
| REGION | | | |
| northeast | 59 | 25 | 16 |
| south | 65 | 21 | 14 |
| midwest | 65 | 22 | 13 |
| west | 66 | 21 | 13 |

NO. 20. Do you trust the government to make the right decisions
when it comes to protecting the security of the United States?

|  | TRUST GOVT | DON'T TRUST | DON'T KNOW |
|---|---|---|---|
| ALL | 70 | 24 | 6 |
| PARTY | | | |
| not regis | 64 | 29 | 7 |
| Democrat | 69 | 26 | 5 |
| Republican | 78 | 16 | 6 |
| Independent | 63 | 31 | 5 |
| IDEOLOGY | | | |
| liberal | 63 | 32 | 5 |
| moderate | 72 | 23 | 5 |
| conservative | 74 | 19 | 7 |
| AGE | | | |
| 18–34 | 67 | 29 | 4 |
| 35–49 | 66 | 28 | 6 |
| 50–59 | 75 | 18 | 6 |
| 60+ | 77 | 11 | 12 |
| INCOME | | | |
| <$7,000 | 67 | 19 | 15 |
| $ 7-$15,000 | 74 | 19 | 7 |
| $15-$25,000 | 72 | 24 | 4 |
| $25-$35,000 | 66 | 27 | 7 |
| $35,000+ | 67 | 28 | 5 |
| EDUCATION | | | |
| <high school | 70 | 17 | 14 |
| high school | 77 | 17 | 6 |
| some college | 69 | 25 | 6 |
| college | 60 | 36 | 4 |
| college+ | 63 | 32 | 5 |
| UNION | | | |
| union | 69 | 24 | 7 |
| non-union | 70 | 24 | 6 |
| SEX | | | |
| male | 71 | 23 | 6 |
| female | 68 | 25 | 7 |
| REGION | | | |
| northeast | 66 | 29 | 5 |
| south | 75 | 18 | 8 |
| midwest | 67 | 25 | 8 |
| west | 70 | 24 | 5 |

## NO. 21. What is your age?

|  | 18–34 | 35–49 | 50–59 | 60+ |
|---|---|---|---|---|
| ALL | 42 | 25 | 12 | 20 |
| **PARTY** | | | | |
| not regis | 56 | 22 | 11 | 11 |
| Democrat | 39 | 25 | 13 | 23 |
| Republican | 35 | 26 | 14 | 26 |
| Independent | 49 | 29 | 11 | 12 |
| **IDEOLOGY** | | | | |
| liberal | 50 | 24 | 11 | 15 |
| moderate | 43 | 25 | 12 | 20 |
| conservative | 38 | 25 | 15 | 23 |
| **AGE** | | | | |
| 18–34 | 100 | 0 | 0 | 0 |
| 35–49 | 0 | 100 | 0 | 0 |
| 50–59 | 0 | 0 | 100 | 0 |
| 60+ | 0 | 0 | 0 | 100 |
| **INCOME** | | | | |
| <$7,000 | 34 | 12 | 7 | 47 |
| $ 7-$15,000 | 41 | 18 | 11 | 30 |
| $15-$25,000 | 46 | 21 | 14 | 19 |
| $25-$35,000 | 48 | 31 | 10 | 12 |
| $35,000+ | 36 | 37 | 17 | 10 |
| **EDUCATION** | | | | |
| <high school | 27 | 16 | 15 | 41 |
| high school | 37 | 27 | 12 | 24 |
| some college | 54 | 23 | 13 | 10 |
| college | 52 | 25 | 9 | 14 |
| college+ | 26 | 39 | 13 | 22 |
| **UNION** | | | | |
| union | 39 | 31 | 11 | 18 |
| non-union | 43 | 23 | 13 | 21 |
| **SEX** | | | | |
| male | 44 | 25 | 13 | 18 |
| female | 40 | 25 | 12 | 23 |
| **REGION** | | | | |
| northeast | 40 | 25 | 14 | 21 |
| south | 46 | 23 | 13 | 18 |
| midwest | 40 | 26 | 10 | 24 |
| west | 41 | 28 | 12 | 19 |

NO. 22. Into which of the following categories does your family income fall?

| | UNDER $7,000 | $ 7-$15,000 | $15-$25,000 | $25-$35,000 | OVER $35,000 |
|---|---|---|---|---|---|
| ALL | 9 | 21 | 28 | 20 | 22 |
| **PARTY** | | | | | |
| not regis | 19 | 27 | 22 | 20 | 12 |
| Democrat | 7 | 23 | 29 | 20 | 20 |
| Republican | 9 | 17 | 27 | 18 | 29 |
| Independent | 5 | 14 | 32 | 22 | 28 |
| **IDEOLOGY** | | | | | |
| liberal | 9 | 18 | 24 | 30 | 20 |
| moderate | 8 | 19 | 29 | 19 | 24 |
| conservative | 8 | 22 | 30 | 15 | 24 |
| **AGE** | | | | | |
| 18-34 | 7 | 20 | 30 | 23 | 19 |
| 35-49 | 4 | 15 | 23 | 25 | 33 |
| 50-59 | 5 | 18 | 30 | 16 | 31 |
| 60+ | 21 | 30 | 27 | 12 | 11 |
| **INCOME** | | | | | |
| <$7,000 | 100 | 0 | 0 | 0 | 0 |
| $ 7-$15,000 | 0 | 100 | 0 | 0 | 0 |
| $15-$25,000 | 0 | 0 | 100 | 0 | 0 |
| $25-$35,000 | 0 | 0 | 0 | 100 | 0 |
| $35,000+ | 0 | 0 | 0 | 0 | 100 |
| **EDUCATION** | | | | | |
| <high school | 30 | 32 | 19 | 10 | 9 |
| high school | 10 | 27 | 31 | 18 | 14 |
| some college | 5 | 18 | 35 | 22 | 21 |
| college | 3 | 11 | 25 | 26 | 35 |
| college+ | 0 | 9 | 9 | 27 | 54 |
| **UNION** | | | | | |
| union | 7 | 18 | 29 | 24 | 23 |
| non-union | 9 | 22 | 27 | 19 | 22 |
| **SEX** | | | | | |
| male | 6 | 17 | 29 | 21 | 26 |
| female | 11 | 24 | 26 | 19 | 19 |
| **REGION** | | | | | |
| northeast | 10 | 22 | 27 | 21 | 21 |
| south | 8 | 17 | 29 | 21 | 25 |
| midwest | 8 | 24 | 27 | 20 | 21 |
| west | 11 | 21 | 26 | 19 | 23 |

NO. 23. What is the last year of school you have completed?

| | BELOW HIGH SCHOOL | HIGH SCHOOL | SOME COLLEGE | COLLEGE | ABOVE COLLEGE |
|---|---|---|---|---|---|
| ALL | 12 | 35 | 27 | 17 | 9 |
| PARTY | | | | | |
| not regis | 17 | 48 | 20 | 11 | 4 |
| Democrat | 13 | 36 | 27 | 14 | 9 |
| Republican | 10 | 32 | 24 | 24 | 10 |
| Independent | 8 | 26 | 37 | 20 | 10 |
| IDEOLOGY | | | | | |
| liberal | 9 | 34 | 27 | 17 | 12 |
| moderate | 12 | 35 | 29 | 16 | 9 |
| conservative | 10 | 36 | 27 | 20 | 7 |
| AGE | | | | | |
| 18–34 | 8 | 31 | 35 | 21 | 5 |
| 35–49 | 8 | 37 | 25 | 17 | 13 |
| 50–59 | 15 | 35 | 29 | 13 | 9 |
| 60+ | 25 | 41 | 13 | 12 | 9 |
| INCOME | | | | | |
| <$7,000 | 40 | 38 | 17 | 5 | 0 |
| $ 7-$15,000 | 18 | 45 | 23 | 9 | 4 |
| $15-$25,000 | 8 | 39 | 34 | 16 | 3 |
| $25-$35,000 | 6 | 32 | 29 | 22 | 12 |
| $35,000+ | 5 | 23 | 25 | 27 | 21 |
| EDUCATION | | | | | |
| <high school | 100 | 0 | 0 | 0 | 0 |
| high school | 0 | 100 | 0 | 0 | 0 |
| some college | 0 | 0 | 100 | 0 | 0 |
| college | 0 | 0 | 0 | 100 | 0 |
| college+ | 0 | 0 | 0 | 0 | 100 |
| UNION | | | | | |
| union | 12 | 38 | 28 | 10 | 12 |
| non-union | 12 | 34 | 27 | 20 | 7 |
| SEX | | | | | |
| male | 12 | 30 | 29 | 18 | 11 |
| female | 12 | 40 | 25 | 16 | 7 |
| REGION | | | | | |
| northeast | 11 | 39 | 22 | 18 | 10 |
| south | 16 | 31 | 28 | 18 | 7 |
| midwest | 12 | 41 | 27 | 13 | 7 |
| west | 10 | 28 | 33 | 18 | 11 |

NO. 24. What is your occupation? (If unemployed, get usual occupation)

| | EXECUTIVE | BUSINESSMAN | SEMI-SKILLED | SKILLED | UNSKILLED | HOMEMAKER | DOESN'T WORK | STUDENT | OTHER |
|---|---|---|---|---|---|---|---|---|---|
| ALL | 25 | 8 | 11 | 13 | 3 | 13 | 15 | 8 | 3 |
| PARTY | | | | | | | | | |
| not regis | 13 | 8 | 11 | 19 | 7 | 16 | 7 | 17 | 3 |
| Democrat | 24 | 6 | 13 | 13 | 3 | 14 | 18 | 6 | 4 |
| Republican | 28 | 9 | 8 | 11 | 3 | 16 | 19 | 4 | 2 |
| Independent | 33 | 13 | 13 | 13 | 2 | 9 | 6 | 9 | 2 |
| IDEOLOGY | | | | | | | | | |
| liberal | 27 | 7 | 15 | 11 | 2 | 9 | 14 | 11 | 5 |
| moderate | 28 | 6 | 11 | 14 | 4 | 15 | 13 | 7 | 2 |
| conservative | 22 | 13 | 9 | 13 | 3 | 14 | 15 | 7 | 3 |
| AGE | | | | | | | | | |
| 18–34 | 25 | 10 | 12 | 17 | 4 | 11 | 1 | 17 | 4 |
| 35–49 | 37 | 10 | 12 | 14 | 4 | 16 | 1 | 2 | 3 |
| 50–59 | 24 | 8 | 18 | 12 | 3 | 18 | 14 | 0 | 2 |
| 60+ | 10 | 5 | 5 | 6 | 0 | 11 | 60 | 0 | 2 |
| INCOME | | | | | | | | | |
| <$7,000 | 3 | 6 | 7 | 13 | 5 | 12 | 39 | 9 | 7 |
| $ 7-$15,000 | 10 | 7 | 13 | 11 | 5 | 18 | 27 | 7 | 2 |
| $15-$25,000 | 22 | 8 | 15 | 18 | 3 | 11 | 13 | 6 | 4 |
| $25-$35,000 | 31 | 9 | 12 | 16 | 3 | 14 | 6 | 7 | 2 |
| $35,000+ | 46 | 10 | 6 | 9 | 2 | 9 | 5 | 10 | 2 |
| EDUCATION | | | | | | | | | |
| <high school | 4 | 4 | 4 | 14 | 12 | 19 | 32 | 7 | 4 |
| high school | 10 | 7 | 15 | 17 | 5 | 19 | 17 | 6 | 4 |
| some college | 24 | 8 | 13 | 16 | 1 | 10 | 9 | 15 | 3 |
| college | 47 | 14 | 11 | 8 | 0 | 6 | 9 | 4 | 1 |
| college+ | 72 | 7 | 1 | 1 | 0 | 7 | 10 | 1 | 1 |

NO. 24. (Continued)

| | EXECUTIVE | BUSINESSMAN | SEMI-SKILLED | SKILLED | UNSKILLED | HOMEMAKER | DOESN'T WORK | STUDENT | OTHER |
|---|---|---|---|---|---|---|---|---|---|
| UNION | | | | | | | | | |
| union | 28 | 5 | 9 | 19 | 5 | 14 | 12 | 5 | 3 |
| non-union | 24 | 10 | 12 | 11 | 3 | 13 | 16 | 8 | 3 |
| SEX | | | | | | | | | |
| male | 29 | 10 | 6 | 19 | 5 | 3 | 14 | 10 | 3 |
| female | 20 | 7 | 16 | 8 | 2 | 23 | 16 | 6 | 3 |
| REGION | | | | | | | | | |
| northeast | 25 | 7 | 12 | 14 | 3 | 14 | 15 | 7 | 3 |
| south | 24 | 11 | 12 | 11 | 2 | 13 | 15 | 8 | 3 |
| midwest | 22 | 6 | 8 | 16 | 4 | 15 | 17 | 8 | 3 |
| west | 28 | 7 | 14 | 13 | 5 | 9 | 13 | 8 | 4 |

NO. 25. Generally speaking, do you consider yourself as liberal, moderate or conservative?

|  | LIBERAL | MODERATE | CONSERVATIVE | DON'T KNOW |
|---|---|---|---|---|
| ALL | 24 | 37 | 34 | 6 |
| **PARTY** | | | | |
| not regis | 27 | 34 | 31 | 7 |
| Democrat | 30 | 37 | 27 | 7 |
| Republican | 13 | 34 | 51 | 2 |
| Independent | 22 | 43 | 31 | 5 |
| **IDEOLOGY** | | | | |
| liberal | 100 | 0 | 0 | 0 |
| moderate | 0 | 100 | 0 | 0 |
| conservative | 0 | 0 | 100 | 0 |
| **AGE** | | | | |
| 18–34 | 28 | 38 | 31 | 3 |
| 35–49 | 23 | 37 | 33 | 8 |
| 50–59 | 20 | 35 | 40 | 6 |
| 60+ | 18 | 36 | 38 | 9 |
| **INCOME** | | | | |
| <$7,000 | 24 | 32 | 32 | 13 |
| $ 7–$15,000 | 20 | 35 | 36 | 9 |
| $15–$25,000 | 20 | 39 | 37 | 4 |
| $25–$35,000 | 35 | 35 | 26 | 4 |
| $35,000+ | 21 | 40 | 36 | 3 |
| **EDUCATION** | | | | |
| <high school | 19 | 37 | 28 | 16 |
| high school | 23 | 36 | 35 | 6 |
| some college | 24 | 39 | 34 | 3 |
| college | 24 | 34 | 40 | 3 |
| college+ | 32 | 37 | 26 | 4 |
| **UNION** | | | | |
| union | 28 | 36 | 29 | 7 |
| non-union | 22 | 37 | 36 | 5 |
| **SEX** | | | | |
| male | 25 | 35 | 35 | 6 |
| female | 22 | 39 | 33 | 6 |
| **REGION** | | | | |
| northeast | 24 | 38 | 31 | 7 |
| south | 24 | 35 | 34 | 8 |
| midwest | 23 | 35 | 37 | 5 |
| west | 24 | 38 | 36 | 2 |

NO. 26. Are you registered to vote in the United States?
(IF YES) Are you registered as a Democrat, Republican or Independent?

|  | NOT REGIS | DEMOCRAT | REPUBLICAN | INDEPENDENT | DON'T KNOW |
|---|---|---|---|---|---|
| ALL | 14 | 41 | 25 | 17 | 3 |
| PARTY |  |  |  |  |  |
| not regis | 100 | 0 | 0 | 0 | 0 |
| Democrat | 0 | 100 | 0 | 0 | 0 |
| Republican | 0 | 0 | 100 | 0 | 0 |
| Independent | 0 | 0 | 0 | 100 | 0 |
| IDEOLOGY |  |  |  |  |  |
| liberal | 16 | 52 | 14 | 16 | 2 |
| moderate | 13 | 41 | 23 | 20 | 3 |
| conservative | 13 | 32 | 38 | 16 | 1 |
| AGE |  |  |  |  |  |
| 18–34 | 19 | 38 | 21 | 20 | 3 |
| 35–49 | 12 | 40 | 25 | 20 | 3 |
| 50–59 | 12 | 43 | 28 | 15 | 2 |
| 60+ | 8 | 47 | 32 | 10 | 3 |
| INCOME |  |  |  |  |  |
| <$7,000 | 29 | 33 | 26 | 10 | 2 |
| $ 7-$15,000 | 19 | 46 | 21 | 12 | 3 |
| $15-$25,000 | 11 | 43 | 24 | 20 | 2 |
| $25-$35,000 | 14 | 41 | 23 | 19 | 3 |
| $35,000+ | 8 | 37 | 32 | 21 | 2 |
| EDUCATION |  |  |  |  |  |
| <high school | 20 | 45 | 21 | 11 | 3 |
| high school | 19 | 43 | 23 | 13 | 3 |
| some college | 10 | 41 | 22 | 24 | 3 |
| college | 9 | 34 | 36 | 20 | 2 |
| college+ | 6 | 44 | 28 | 20 | 2 |
| UNION |  |  |  |  |  |
| union | 13 | 47 | 21 | 16 | 4 |
| non-union | 14 | 39 | 27 | 18 | 2 |
| SEX |  |  |  |  |  |
| male | 15 | 37 | 23 | 21 | 3 |
| female | 13 | 45 | 27 | 14 | 2 |
| REGION |  |  |  |  |  |
| northeast | 20 | 41 | 22 | 15 | 3 |
| south | 14 | 45 | 23 | 15 | 3 |
| midwest | 10 | 36 | 26 | 25 | 3 |
| west | 11 | 40 | 31 | 16 | 2 |

NO. 27. Are you or any member of your household a member of a union?

|  | UNION | NON-UNION | DON'T KNOW |
|---|---|---|---|
| ALL | 27 | 72 | 1 |
| PARTY | | | |
| not regis | 25 | 73 | 1 |
| Democrat | 30 | 69 | 1 |
| Republican | 22 | 78 | 0 |
| Independent | 24 | 76 | 0 |
| IDEOLOGY | | | |
| liberal | 32 | 67 | 1 |
| moderate | 26 | 74 | 1 |
| conservative | 23 | 77 | 0 |
| AGE | | | |
| 18–34 | 25 | 74 | 1 |
| 35–49 | 33 | 67 | 0 |
| 50–59 | 23 | 77 | 0 |
| 60+ | 24 | 74 | 2 |
| INCOME | | | |
| <$7,000 | 20 | 78 | 2 |
| $ 7-$15,000 | 23 | 77 | 0 |
| $15-$25,000 | 28 | 71 | 1 |
| $25-$35,000 | 32 | 68 | 0 |
| $35,000+ | 27 | 72 | 1 |
| EDUCATION | | | |
| <high school | 26 | 72 | 2 |
| high school | 29 | 70 | 1 |
| some college | 27 | 71 | 1 |
| college | 16 | 84 | 0 |
| college+ | 38 | 62 | 0 |
| UNION | | | |
| union | 100 | 0 | 0 |
| non-union | 0 | 100 | 0 |
| SEX | | | |
| male | 27 | 71 | 1 |
| female | 26 | 73 | 0 |
| REGION | | | |
| northeast | 28 | 71 | 1 |
| south | 18 | 81 | 1 |
| midwest | 34 | 66 | 1 |
| west | 30 | 70 | 0 |

NO. 28. Code sex

|  | MALE | FEMALE |
|---|---|---|
| ALL | 49 | 51 |
| PARTY | | |
| not regis | 52 | 48 |
| Democrat | 45 | 55 |
| Republican | 46 | 54 |
| Independent | 60 | 40 |
| IDEOLOGY | | |
| liberal | 52 | 48 |
| moderate | 46 | 54 |
| conservative | 50 | 50 |
| AGE | | |
| 18–34 | 52 | 48 |
| 35–49 | 49 | 51 |
| 50–59 | 50 | 50 |
| 60+ | 43 | 57 |
| INCOME | | |
| <$7,000 | 36 | 64 |
| $ 7-$15,000 | 41 | 59 |
| $15-$25,000 | 53 | 47 |
| $25-$35,000 | 52 | 48 |
| $35,000+ | 57 | 43 |
| EDUCATION | | |
| <high school | 49 | 51 |
| high school | 42 | 58 |
| some college | 53 | 47 |
| college | 52 | 48 |
| college+ | 61 | 39 |
| UNION | | |
| union | 50 | 50 |
| non-union | 48 | 52 |
| SEX | | |
| male | 100 | 0 |
| female | 0 | 100 |
| REGION | | |
| northeast | 47 | 53 |
| south | 52 | 48 |
| midwest | 47 | 53 |
| west | 50 | 50 |

NO. 29. Region

|  | NORTHEAST | SOUTH | MIDWEST | WEST |
|---|---|---|---|---|
| ALL | 28 | 29 | 20 | 22 |
| **PARTY** | | | | |
| not regis | 39 | 29 | 14 | 18 |
| Democrat | 29 | 32 | 18 | 21 |
| Republican | 25 | 27 | 21 | 27 |
| Independent | 24 | 25 | 30 | 21 |
| **IDEOLOGY** | | | | |
| liberal | 29 | 29 | 19 | 22 |
| moderate | 30 | 28 | 19 | 23 |
| conservative | 26 | 29 | 22 | 23 |
| **AGE** | | | | |
| 18–34 | 27 | 32 | 19 | 21 |
| 35–49 | 28 | 27 | 21 | 24 |
| 50–59 | 31 | 31 | 17 | 21 |
| 60+ | 29 | 26 | 24 | 20 |
| **INCOME** | | | | |
| <$7,000 | 30 | 26 | 17 | 27 |
| $ 7-$15,000 | 30 | 23 | 24 | 23 |
| $15-$25,000 | 28 | 31 | 20 | 21 |
| $25-$35,000 | 29 | 30 | 20 | 21 |
| $35,000+ | 26 | 32 | 19 | 23 |
| **EDUCATION** | | | | |
| <high school | 25 | 38 | 20 | 17 |
| high school | 32 | 26 | 24 | 18 |
| some college | 23 | 30 | 20 | 27 |
| college | 30 | 31 | 16 | 23 |
| college+ | 33 | 25 | 16 | 26 |
| **UNION** | | | | |
| union | 30 | 20 | 26 | 24 |
| non-union | 28 | 33 | 18 | 21 |
| **SEX** | | | | |
| male | 27 | 31 | 19 | 22 |
| female | 29 | 28 | 21 | 21 |
| **REGION** | | | | |
| northeast | 100 | 0 | 0 | 0 |
| south | 0 | 100 | 0 | 0 |
| midwest | 0 | 0 | 100 | 0 |
| west | 0 | 0 | 0 | 100 |

# 20

# U.S. PUBLIC ATTITUDES TOWARD THE DEFENSE EFFORT—PROGRAM, PRIORITIES, AND BUDGET

## The Results of a Nationwide Scientific Poll of American Opinion

The Committee on the Present Danger today [26 April 1984] released the results of a comprehensive, national, in-depth poll on "U.S. Public Attitudes Toward the Defense Effort—Program, Priorities and Budget." The poll was conducted for the Committee earlier this month by the independent polling organization of Penn & Schoen Associates.

The nationwide, scientific sample of 1,000 Americans shows that an overwhelming majority favor continuing defense spending at current or higher levels, despite the fact that they believe current defense expenditures are vastly greater—on average, three times larger—than they actually are.

The poll shows that 61% favor conventional arms expenditures over nuclear arms expenditures. This is in spite of the fact that spending on conventional forces already is over four times greater than spending on nuclear forces. The public believes that spending on nuclear forces is at least twice as much as it actually is.

The public also believes that in the past fifteen years there has been a substantial increase in the number and total destructive power of U.S. nuclear weapons. However, the fact is that there has been a substantial decline in both.

Although the poll shows general public satisfaction with the current state of American defenses, it also shows that a clear majority believes America's military position, compared to the Soviet Union, has not improved or has gotten worse over the past five years. Further, the poll revealed a strong public conviction that the Soviet Union outspends the United States on defense. The poll also shows a strong majority belief that the threat of a nuclear war involving the United States has either remained the same or diminished over the past five years.

Among the poll's specific findings:

—71% support current or greater levels of U.S. defense spending.

—65% support current or higher levels of spending on nuclear forces, even though 62% hold a greatly exaggerated view of the portion of the defense budget allocated to nuclear forces.

—Only 8% recognize that the United States has fewer nuclear weapons than it did 15 years ago, and only 7% are aware that the U.S. nuclear stockpile is less destructive than it was then.

—81% believe the United States devotes far more of its total economic output to defense than is actually the case.

—By a greater than two-to-one margin, Americans believe the Soviet Union is outspending the United States on defense.

—57% think that America's military position compared to the Soviet Union has not improved or has gotten worse in the past five years.

—68% believe that the threat of nuclear war involving the United States is the same or less than it was five years ago.

## ANALYSIS OF THE POLL BY PENN & SCHOEN ASSOCIATES

### Summary

The poll of 1,000 U.S. residents conducted between March 31st and April 2nd 1984, shows that seventy-one per cent favor keeping military spending at current levels or increasing it. Only 27% wanted military spending decreased.

The poll shows that Americans are concerned about defense and foreign policy issues—especially those concerning nuclear weapons.

However, the electorate has been making its decisions on defense-related issues while under serious misconceptions about military spending. Most Americans believe that we spend between 20 and 50 per cent of the national GNP on national defense. They also incorrectly believe that the U.S. has been increasing its stockpile of nuclear weapons and that the U.S. nuclear arsenal has become more destructive. Department of Defense documents show the facts to be quite the opposite.

The public also greatly overestimates the share of the defense budget going to nuclear weapons, as less than one-fifth answered "less than 20%" (the correct answer).

While the poll shows that there is more support for expenditures for conventional weapons rather than nuclear, these sentiments are based on erroneous beliefs about the current state of the country's nuclear defenses and the expenditures being made on it.

Most of the sample registered their satisfaction with American defenses, and though they believe by a margin of 2/1 that we are being outspent by the Soviets, they were divided on which nation has the stronger defense. A majority thinks that our defenses compared to the Soviet Union have not improved or have grown worse during the last five years.

### Overview of the Project

Penn & Schoen was commissioned to undertake an in-depth national poll of 1,000 U.S. residents on defense spending, the public view of the state of our defenses and related issues. The firm drew a national, random probability sample of U.S. households and conducted the detailed survey by telephone. The questionnaire was designed in conjunction with the Committee on the Present Danger to cover a wide range of areas fully and fairly. All interviewing was done by our professional interviewers out of our offices in New York between March 31st and April 2nd.

The results have an overall statistical accuracy of plus or minus three percentage points at the 95% confidence interval. The exact text of the questions asked and their full results accompany this report.

## Detailed Analysis of the Questions

1. *Attitudes toward our defenses.* There is considerable concern about defense, foreign policy issues and nuclear arms. Today, 27% say nuclear arms was one of the most important issues and another 13% name foreign affairs issues such as the Middle East or Central America. Forty-one per cent were concerned about the economy while 16% were concerned about social issues. Such widespread concern for defense-related issues certainly suggests that these will be major topics of importance in the fall election campaign.

2. *Satisfaction with our defenses.* Sixty-seven per cent of the electorate register satisfaction with our current overall defenses and 54% are satisfied with the current state of our nuclear defenses. There was, however, some substantial dissatisfaction, as 29% were dissatisfied with our national defenses and 38% were dissatisfied with the U.S. nuclear defenses. Importantly, very few (13%) people were "very satisfied" with our defenses. This lack of enthusiasm for the strength of the U.S. defense evidences concern about its strength and capacity—doubts which are illustrated in later sections.

3. *Our defenses vs. Soviet defenses.* By 2-1 (56% to 27%), most Americans believe that the Soviets are spending more than the U.S. on their military forces. And when asked who has the stronger military right now, the country split right down the middle: 40% named the U.S. while 41% said it was the Soviet Union. The results were similar on who has the stronger nuclear arsenal: 39% say the U.S. while 38% say the Soviets. Younger people are the most likely to say the Soviets are stronger than the U.S. Interestingly, these figures show a significant group who believe that the U.S. is spending less than the Soviets and still maintaining a stronger military. Nevertheless, about half the sample conceded military superiority to the Soviets.

4. *Misconceptions about defense issues.* The American public is laboring under some basic misconceptions about military spending and our nuclear arsenal. In the first place, most Americans greatly overestimate the amount of our GNP going to defense. When asked what percent of the GNP goes to defense, 9% said over 50%, 14% said 40–50%, 34% said 20–40%, 24% said 10–20% and 6% said less than 10%. In other words 94% did not get the right answer to the question, which is under 10%, according to the Department of Defense's annual report to Congress.

Misconceptions about our nuclear arsenal were even greater. While Defense Department spokesmen say that the U.S. has about 8,000 fewer nuclear weapons today than 15 years ago, 86% of the public believes that it has more. Young and old, Democrat and Republican alike did not get the correct answer to this question. Only 8% said the U.S. has fewer weapons. Generally, those who say the U.S. had more thought the U.S. had a lot more weapons—33% said the U.S. had 1–5,000 more and 23% said it has over 5,000 more weapons. Even the eight per cent who think we have fewer weapons generally underestimate how many fewer weapons the country has.

Similarly, 85% incorrectly believe that the U.S. nuclear weapons stockpile is more destructive than it was 15 years ago. Only 7% believe that it is less destructive. And about half believe that the U.S. nuclear weapons are at least 25% more destructive than they were. Given the real trend of a decrease in arms, most people are overestimating our nuclear destructive power by a factor of five.

The belief about more weapons and greater capacity is linked to misconceptions about military spending. Only 19% believe that less than 20% of the defense budget goes to nuclear weapons. Forty per cent believe that nuclear weapons get 20–40% of the budget and 22% believe that nuclear weapons make up more than 40% of the budget. Of people with an opinion, the median was 32%, over twice the actual figure.

At the same time, most people underestimated the part of the defense budget going to conventional military forces. Of those with an opinion, the median response was about 30%. Only 6% got the right answer—that over 75% of the defense budget goes to conventional military forces.

When asked how much they thought they knew about nuclear arms issues, 8% said they knew a great deal, 54% said "some" and 33% said not much. The responses to these other questions show, however, that the American public is far less-informed on these issues than it believes.

*5. Attitudes toward military spending.* In general, 30% believe that military spending should be increased, 27% believe it should be decreased and 41% believe it should be kept the same. This means that over 70% would be against any reduction in defense spending. There are sharp differences between party members—Democrats are completely divided on what to do with the defense budget—27% would like to see it increased, 35% would like to see it cut while 36% think it should be kept the same. In contrast, Republicans are more likely to favor increases—36% favor increases, only 16% are for reductions and 46% are for keeping expenditures at current levels.

The public is generally more sympathetic to increases in expenditures for conventional weapons than for nuclear ones. When asked whether expenditures for nuclear arms should be increased, decreased or kept the same—20% say increased, 31% decreased and 45% opt for the current level.

When asked about conventional weapons, 43% indicate they thought those expenditures should be increased, 12% say decreased and 42% say kept at the same levels. Thus 85% oppose any reduction in spending on conventional weapons.

This finding is reinforced by a later question which asked whether funding for conventional or nuclear weaponry should receive a higher priority. Sixty-one per cent say that conventional forces should get the highest priority while 25% name nuclear arms.

These figures are not surprising considering the misconceptions that the public has concerning expenditures on nuclear weapons. The public already believes we are spending more on and stockpiling more weapons than is actually the case.

Thirty-five per cent believe that Congress wants to spend too much on defense, 30% say not enough and 27% say the right amount. In contrast, 46% believe Reagan has asked for "too much," 36% say "right amount" and 11% say "not enough."

*6. America's defenses have not improved and the threat of war remains unchanged.* A 57% majority say that America's defenses compared to the Soviet Union have stayed the same or gotten worse in the last five years. Only thirty eight per cent say America's military position compared to the Soviet Union has improved, while 25% say it has gotten worse and 32% say it's the same.

But, given the world situation today, the country is divided on whether the threat of a nuclear war has changed. Thirty per cent believe that the threat of a nuclear war involving the United States has increased in the last five years, 31% say that threat has been reduced and 37% say that there has been no change. Surprisingly, younger people are the most optimistic, with 37% saying the chances of a nuclear war are less today.

*26 April 1984*

# THE POLL

1. Which of these is the most important issue you would like to see your government do something about—general economic policy, issues like abortion and school prayer, foreign policy concerns like the Middle East and Central America or nuclear arms?

| economic pol | social issues | foreign policy | nuclear arms | don't know |
|---|---|---|---|---|
| 41 | 16 | 13 | 27 | 3 |

2. How satisfied are you with the current state of American defenses—very satisfied, somewhat satisfied, somewhat dissatisfied or very dissatisfied?

| very satis | smwht satis | smwht dissatis | very dissatis | don't know |
|---|---|---|---|---|
| 13 | 54 | 20 | 9 | 3 |

3. How satisfied are you with the current state of our nuclear defenses—very satisfied, somewhat satisfied, somewhat dissatisfied, or very dissatisfied?

| very satis | smwht satis | smwht dissatis | very dissatis | don't know |
|---|---|---|---|---|
| 13 | 41 | 23 | 15 | 8 |

4. Who spends more on its military forces today—the United States or the Soviet Union?

| United States | Soviet Union | don't know |
|---|---|---|
| 27 | 56 | 17 |

5. What percentage of this country's total economic output do you think now goes to national defense—under 10%, 10-20%, 20-40%, 40-50% or over 50%?

| less than 10% | 10-20% | 20-40% | 40-50% | over 50% | don't know |
|---|---|---|---|---|---|
| 6 | 24 | 34 | 14 | 9 | 13 |

(The correct answer is: less than 10%.)

6. Who has a stronger military right now—the United States or the Soviet Union?

| United States | Soviet Union | don't know |
|---|---|---|
| 40 | 41 | 19 |

7. Who has the stronger nuclear force—the United States or the Soviet Union?

| United States | Soviet Union | don't know |
|---|---|---|
| 39 | 38 | 23 |

8. Does the United States have more or fewer nuclear weapons today than 15 years ago?

| more | fewer | don't know |
|---|---|---|
| 86 | 8 | 6 |

(The correct answer is: fewer.)

9. IF ANSWERED MORE OR LESS TO QUESTION ABOVE
   How many is it more (or less)?—under 1000, 1000 to 5000, or more than 5000?

   |         | less than 1000 | 1000–5000 | more than 5000 | don't know |
   |---------|----------------|-----------|----------------|------------|
   | MORE:   | 16             | 30        | 21             | 26         |
   | FEWER:  | 3              | 3         | 1              | 1          |

   (The correct answer is: fewer, by more than 5000. Thus, for the entire survey 1% or one out of 100 of the respondents answered correctly.)

10. Is the U.S. nuclear weapons stockpile more or less destructive than it was 15 years ago?

    | more | less | don't know |
    |------|------|------------|
    | 85   | 7    | 8          |

    (The correct answer is: less.)

11. (IF ANSWERED MORE OR LESS TO QUESTION ABOVE)
    By how much is it more (or less)—under 10%, 10 to 25%, 25 to 60% or over 60%?

    |        | under 10% | 10 to 25% | 25 to 60% | over 60% | don't know |
    |--------|-----------|-----------|-----------|----------|------------|
    | MORE:  | 5         | 28        | 24        | 19       | 17         |
    | LESS:  | 2         | 3         | 0.5       | 0.2      | 2          |

    (The correct answer is: less, by over 60%. Thus, for the entire survey 0.2% or one out of 500 respondents answered correctly.)

12. Has America's military position compared to the Soviet Union improved, gotten worse or stayed the same over the past five years?

    | improved | worse | same | don't know |
    |----------|-------|------|------------|
    | 38       | 25    | 32   | 6          |

13. Which do you think should have the higher priority right now, funds for conventional forces or for nuclear forces?

    | conventional | nuclear | don't know |
    |--------------|---------|------------|
    | 61           | 25      | 15         |

14. In general, do you think that spending on defense should be increased, decreased or kept the same?

    | increased | decreased | kept the same | don't know |
    |-----------|-----------|---------------|------------|
    | 30        | 27        | 41            | 2          |

15. Does the Congress want to devote too much money to the military budget, not enough money or the right amount?

    | too much | not enough | right amount | don't know |
    |----------|------------|--------------|------------|
    | 35       | 30         | 27           | 9          |

16. Does President Reagan want to devote too much money to the military budget, not enough money or the right amount?

| too much | not enough | right amount | don't know |
|----------|------------|--------------|------------|
| 46 | 11 | 36 | 7 |

17. How much of the defense budget do you think is spent on nuclear weapons—less than 20%, 20–40%, 41–75% or more than 75%?

| less than 20% | 20–40% | 41–75% | more than 75% | don't know |
|---------------|--------|--------|---------------|------------|
| 19 | 40 | 17 | 5 | 19 |

(The correct answer is: less than 20%.)

18. How much of the defense budget do you think is spent on conventional military forces—less than 20%, 20–40%, 41–75% or more than 75%?

| less than 20% | 20–40% | 41–75% | more than 75% | don't know |
|---------------|--------|--------|---------------|------------|
| 18 | 38 | 19 | 6 | 19 |

(The correct answer is: more than 75%.)

19. Should defense spending on nuclear arms be increased, decreased or kept at its current level?

| increased | decreased | current level | don't know |
|-----------|-----------|---------------|------------|
| 20 | 31 | 45 | 3 |

20. Should defense spending on conventional weaponry like guns, tanks, ships and airplanes be increased, decreased or kept at their current levels?

| increased | decreased | current level | don't know |
|-----------|-----------|---------------|------------|
| 43 | 12 | 42 | 3 |

21. Think for a minute about how things were five years ago; do you think the threat of nuclear war involving the United States was greater than it is now, less than it is now or about the same?

| greater | less | same | don't know |
|---------|------|------|------------|
| 30 | 31 | 37 | 2 |

22. Was the threat of a nuclear war somewhere in the world greater five years ago than it is now, less than it is now or about the same?

| greater | less | same | don't know |
|---------|------|------|------------|
| 29 | 32 | 36 | 2 |

23. How much would you say you know about the issues involving nuclear arms—a great deal, some, not very much or nothing at all?

| great deal | some | not very much | nothing | don't know |
|------------|------|---------------|---------|------------|
| 8 | 54 | 33 | 4 | 1 |

24. What is your age?

| 18–34 | 35–49 | 50–59 | over 60 |
|-------|-------|-------|---------|
| 42 | 25 | 12 | 20 |

25. Into which of the following categories does your family income fall?

| under $7,000 | $7-$15,000 | $15-$25,000 | $25-$35,000 | over $35,000 |
|---|---|---|---|---|
| 9 | 21 | 28 | 20 | 22 |

26. What is the last year of school you have completed?

| below high school | high school | some college | college | above college |
|---|---|---|---|---|
| 12 | 35 | 27 | 17 | 9 |

27. What is your occupation? (If unemployed, get usual occupation)

| executive | businessman | semi-skilled | skilled | unskilled |
|---|---|---|---|---|
| 25 | 8 | 11 | 13 | 3 |

| homemaker | doesn't work | student | other |
|---|---|---|---|
| 13 | 15 | 8 | 3 |

28. Generally speaking, do you consider yourself as liberal, moderate or conservative?

| liberal | moderate | conservative | don't know |
|---|---|---|---|
| 24 | 37 | 34 | 6 |

29. Are you registered to vote in the United States?
(IF YES) Are you registered as a Democrat, Republican or Independent?

| not regis | Democrat | Republican | Independent | don't know |
|---|---|---|---|---|
| 14 | 41 | 25 | 17 | 3 |

30. Are you or any member of your household a member of a union?

| union | non-union | don't know |
|---|---|---|
| 27 | 72 | 1 |

31. Code sex

| male | female |
|---|---|
| 49 | 51 |

32. Region

| northeast | south | midwest | west |
|---|---|---|---|
| 28 | 29 | 20 | 22 |

# APPENDIX

## DEMOGRAPHICS

NO. 1. Which of these is the most important issue you would like to see your government do something about—general economic policy, issues like abortion and school prayer, foreign policy concerns like the Middle East and Central America or nuclear arms?

| | ECONOMIC POL. | SOCIAL ISSUES | FOREIGN POLICY | NUCLEAR ARMS | DON'T KNOW |
|---|---|---|---|---|---|
| ALL | 41 | 16 | 13 | 27 | 3 |
| PARTY | | | | | |
| not regis | 33 | 12 | 9 | 41 | 4 |
| Democrat | 38 | 16 | 14 | 30 | 3 |
| Republican | 51 | 16 | 12 | 17 | 4 |
| Independent | 43 | 14 | 16 | 24 | 4 |
| IDEOLOGY | | | | | |
| liberal | 36 | 13 | 11 | 37 | 2 |
| moderate | 36 | 13 | 13 | 26 | 2 |
| conservative | 41 | 18 | 16 | 21 | 5 |
| AGE | | | | | |
| 18–34 | 35 | 14 | 15 | 35 | 1 |
| 35–49 | 50 | 13 | 10 | 22 | 5 |
| 50–59 | 46 | 20 | 9 | 21 | 4 |
| 60+ | 41 | 19 | 17 | 18 | 4 |
| INCOME | | | | | |
| <$7,000 | 37 | 24 | 14 | 22 | 3 |
| $ 7-$15,000 | 35 | 20 | 11 | 30 | 4 |
| $15-$25,000 | 42 | 17 | 12 | 27 | 3 |
| $25-$35,000 | 43 | 12 | 14 | 27 | 4 |
| $35,000+ | 48 | 9 | 16 | 26 | 1 |
| EDUCATION | | | | | |
| <high school | 29 | 28 | 10 | 27 | 6 |
| high school | 38 | 17 | 14 | 28 | 3 |
| some college | 43 | 14 | 14 | 27 | 2 |
| college | 51 | 11 | 13 | 22 | 4 |
| college+ | 47 | 3 | 15 | 31 | 2 |
| UNION | | | | | |
| union | 42 | 16 | 11 | 29 | 2 |
| non-union | 41 | 15 | 14 | 26 | 4 |
| SEX | | | | | |
| male | 44 | 12 | 15 | 26 | 3 |
| female | 39 | 19 | 11 | 27 | 3 |
| REGION | | | | | |
| northeast | 36 | 14 | 11 | 34 | 4 |
| south | 45 | 19 | 13 | 20 | 4 |
| midwest | 38 | 15 | 16 | 27 | 3 |
| west | 47 | 14 | 14 | 25 | 1 |

NO. 2. How satisfied are you with the current state of American
defenses—very satisfied, somewhat satisfied, somewhat dissatisfied
or very dissatisfied?

|  | VERY SATIS | SMWHT SATIS | SMWHT DISSATIS | VERY DISSATIS | DON'T KNOW |
|---|---|---|---|---|---|
| ALL | 13 | 54 | 20 | 9 | 3 |
| PARTY |  |  |  |  |  |
| not regis | 8 | 58 | 20 | 10 | 4 |
| Democrat | 13 | 49 | 22 | 12 | 4 |
| Republican | 14 | 61 | 17 | 4 | 3 |
| Independent | 15 | 57 | 18 | 8 | 3 |
| IDEOLOGY |  |  |  |  |  |
| liberal | 10 | 49 | 25 | 14 | 2 |
| moderate | 12 | 55 | 21 | 8 | 3 |
| conservative | 16 | 58 | 15 | 7 | 4 |
| AGE |  |  |  |  |  |
| 18–34 | 11 | 59 | 20 | 9 | 1 |
| 35–49 | 15 | 56 | 18 | 8 | 4 |
| 50–59 | 10 | 50 | 22 | 11 | 7 |
| 60+ | 17 | 46 | 22 | 10 | 5 |
| INCOME |  |  |  |  |  |
| <$7,000 | 8 | 55 | 24 | 7 | 6 |
| $ 7-$15,000 | 11 | 52 | 18 | 14 | 4 |
| $15-$25,000 | 13 | 57 | 19 | 9 | 2 |
| $25-$35,000 | 12 | 54 | 24 | 9 | 2 |
| $35,000+ | 18 | 54 | 19 | 7 | 3 |
| EDUCATION |  |  |  |  |  |
| <high school | 14 | 49 | 22 | 11 | 5 |
| high school | 13 | 54 | 21 | 8 | 4 |
| some college | 11 | 58 | 20 | 10 | 2 |
| college | 17 | 55 | 17 | 10 | 1 |
| college+ | 14 | 50 | 23 | 10 | 3 |
| UNION |  |  |  |  |  |
| union | 10 | 58 | 18 | 10 | 3 |
| non-union | 14 | 53 | 20 | 9 | 3 |
| SEX |  |  |  |  |  |
| male | 16 | 59 | 14 | 8 | 3 |
| female | 10 | 50 | 26 | 11 | 4 |
| REGION |  |  |  |  |  |
| northeast | 12 | 52 | 21 | 12 | 3 |
| south | 18 | 53 | 19 | 5 | 5 |
| midwest | 12 | 53 | 21 | 11 | 3 |
| west | 9 | 62 | 18 | 9 | 1 |

NO. 3. How satisfied are you with the current state of our nuclear
defenses—very satisfied, somewhat satisfied, somewhat dissatisfied,
or very dissatisfied?

| | VERY SATIS | SMWHT SATIS | SMWHT DISSATIS | VERY DISSATIS | DON'T KNOW |
|---|---|---|---|---|---|
| ALL | 13 | 41 | 23 | 15 | 8 |
| PARTY | | | | | |
| not regis | 7 | 41 | 26 | 18 | 9 |
| Democrat | 15 | 35 | 25 | 18 | 7 |
| Republican | 13 | 47 | 19 | 11 | 9 |
| Independent | 13 | 46 | 17 | 14 | 9 |
| IDEOLOGY | | | | | |
| liberal | 11 | 34 | 27 | 23 | 5 |
| moderate | 14 | 44 | 21 | 14 | 8 |
| conservative | 15 | 43 | 22 | 10 | 9 |
| AGE | | | | | |
| 18–34 | 11 | 43 | 25 | 18 | 3 |
| 35–49 | 13 | 41 | 24 | 13 | 10 |
| 50–59 | 17 | 36 | 15 | 16 | 14 |
| 60+ | 14 | 39 | 22 | 10 | 15 |
| INCOME | | | | | |
| <$7,000 | 7 | 41 | 23 | 15 | 14 |
| $ 7-$15,000 | 14 | 33 | 24 | 18 | 11 |
| $15-$25,000 | 13 | 47 | 21 | 11 | 8 |
| $25-$35,000 | 12 | 41 | 28 | 15 | 4 |
| $35,000+ | 16 | 39 | 21 | 17 | 7 |
| EDUCATION | | | | | |
| <high school | 17 | 34 | 21 | 13 | 15 |
| high school | 11 | 38 | 28 | 14 | 9 |
| some college | 12 | 48 | 20 | 16 | 5 |
| college | 14 | 42 | 20 | 16 | 7 |
| college+ | 15 | 36 | 18 | 22 | 10 |
| UNION | | | | | |
| union | 11 | 40 | 26 | 15 | 8 |
| non-union | 14 | 41 | 22 | 16 | 8 |
| SEX | | | | | |
| male | 16 | 42 | 22 | 13 | 8 |
| female | 10 | 40 | 24 | 17 | 9 |
| REGION | | | | | |
| northeast | 12 | 34 | 25 | 20 | 9 |
| south | 13 | 43 | 22 | 11 | 10 |
| midwest | 12 | 39 | 23 | 16 | 10 |
| west | 14 | 47 | 20 | 14 | 5 |

NO. 4. Who spends more on its military forces today—the
United States or the Soviet Union?

|  | UNITED STATES | SOVIET UNION | DON'T KNOW |
|---|---|---|---|
| ALL | 27 | 56 | 17 |
| PARTY |  |  |  |
| not regis | 34 | 47 | 19 |
| Democrat | 31 | 51 | 17 |
| Republican | 18 | 68 | 14 |
| Independent | 24 | 59 | 16 |
| IDEOLOGY |  |  |  |
| liberal | 29 | 52 | 18 |
| moderate | 30 | 55 | 15 |
| conservative | 21 | 64 | 15 |
| AGE |  |  |  |
| 18–34 | 27 | 60 | 13 |
| 35–49 | 24 | 58 | 17 |
| 50–59 | 24 | 58 | 18 |
| 60+ | 30 | 46 | 24 |
| INCOME |  |  |  |
| <$7,000 | 35 | 44 | 21 |
| $ 7-$15,000 | 32 | 48 | 20 |
| $15-$25,000 | 25 | 62 | 12 |
| $25-$35,000 | 24 | 58 | 18 |
| $35,000+ | 24 | 60 | 16 |
| EDUCATION |  |  |  |
| <high school | 35 | 47 | 18 |
| high school | 27 | 55 | 18 |
| some college | 27 | 59 | 14 |
| college | 26 | 60 | 15 |
| college+ | 18 | 55 | 27 |
| UNION |  |  |  |
| union | 25 | 52 | 22 |
| non-union | 27 | 58 | 15 |
| SEX |  |  |  |
| male | 25 | 61 | 14 |
| female | 28 | 52 | 20 |
| REGION |  |  |  |
| northeast | 27 | 54 | 20 |
| south | 28 | 56 | 17 |
| midwest | 29 | 56 | 16 |
| west | 23 | 61 | 15 |

NO. 5. What percentage of this country's total economic output do you think now goes to national defense—under 10%, 10-20%, 20-40%, 40-50%, or over 50%?

|  | UNDER 10% | 10-20% | 20-40% | 40-50% | OVER 50% | DON'T KNOW |
|---|---|---|---|---|---|---|
| ALL | 6 | 24 | 34 | 14 | 9 | 13 |
| PARTY |  |  |  |  |  |  |
| not regis | 6 | 20 | 29 | 16 | 14 | 15 |
| Democrat | 5 | 23 | 32 | 15 | 11 | 14 |
| Republican | 8 | 26 | 35 | 11 | 8 | 13 |
| Independent | 9 | 22 | 43 | 11 | 7 | 7 |
| IDEOLOGY |  |  |  |  |  |  |
| liberal | 4 | 23 | 40 | 17 | 8 | 8 |
| moderate | 6 | 24 | 33 | 14 | 11 | 12 |
| conservative | 9 | 27 | 31 | 10 | 8 | 15 |
| AGE |  |  |  |  |  |  |
| 18–34 | 7 | 29 | 35 | 14 | 8 | 6 |
| 35–49 | 6 | 25 | 33 | 12 | 10 | 14 |
| 50–59 | 8 | 16 | 35 | 17 | 9 | 15 |
| 60+ | 5 | 16 | 31 | 14 | 10 | 24 |
| INCOME |  |  |  |  |  |  |
| <$7,000 | 2 | 19 | 18 | 21 | 13 | 26 |
| $ 7-$15,000 | 3 | 21 | 38 | 14 | 10 | 14 |
| $15-$25,000 | 7 | 26 | 31 | 14 | 8 | 12 |
| $25-$35,000 | 8 | 23 | 37 | 12 | 9 | 11 |
| $35,000+ | 9 | 27 | 37 | 12 | 9 | 6 |
| EDUCATION |  |  |  |  |  |  |
| <high school | 5 | 25 | 20 | 14 | 11 | 26 |
| high school | 6 | 20 | 35 | 14 | 12 | 12 |
| some college | 5 | 27 | 37 | 14 | 7 | 10 |
| college | 10 | 23 | 37 | 12 | 9 | 10 |
| college+ | 10 | 30 | 31 | 12 | 7 | 11 |
| UNION |  |  |  |  |  |  |
| union | 5 | 21 | 36 | 14 | 9 | 14 |
| non-union | 7 | 25 | 33 | 13 | 10 | 12 |
| SEX |  |  |  |  |  |  |
| male | 11 | 25 | 35 | 11 | 9 | 10 |
| female | 2 | 23 | 33 | 16 | 10 | 16 |
| REGION |  |  |  |  |  |  |
| northeast | 7 | 25 | 33 | 13 | 11 | 12 |
| south | 6 | 27 | 32 | 13 | 9 | 13 |
| midwest | 5 | 20 | 34 | 16 | 11 | 14 |
| west | 8 | 23 | 37 | 12 | 7 | 13 |

NO. 6. Who has a stronger military right now—the United States or the Soviet Union?

|  | UNITED STATES | SOVIET UNION | DON'T KNOW |
|---|---|---|---|
| ALL | 40 | 41 | 19 |
| PARTY | | | |
| not regis | 37 | 47 | 16 |
| Democrat | 41 | 40 | 19 |
| Republican | 38 | 44 | 18 |
| Independent | 42 | 33 | 25 |
| IDEOLOGY | | | |
| liberal | 38 | 42 | 20 |
| moderate | 41 | 38 | 21 |
| conservative | 39 | 45 | 16 |
| AGE | | | |
| 18–34 | 40 | 46 | 14 |
| 35–49 | 42 | 39 | 20 |
| 50–59 | 34 | 41 | 25 |
| 60+ | 41 | 33 | 26 |
| INCOME | | | |
| <$7,000 | 51 | 32 | 18 |
| $ 7-$15,000 | 45 | 36 | 20 |
| $15-$25,000 | 38 | 44 | 17 |
| $25-$35,000 | 36 | 44 | 20 |
| $35,000+ | 36 | 42 | 22 |
| EDUCATION | | | |
| <high school | 52 | 32 | 16 |
| high school | 38 | 46 | 16 |
| some college | 41 | 39 | 21 |
| college | 36 | 43 | 21 |
| college+ | 39 | 30 | 31 |
| UNION | | | |
| union | 43 | 39 | 18 |
| non-union | 39 | 41 | 20 |
| SEX | | | |
| male | 41 | 39 | 20 |
| female | 39 | 42 | 19 |
| REGION | | | |
| northeast | 38 | 41 | 21 |
| south | 42 | 42 | 16 |
| midwest | 38 | 40 | 22 |
| west | 40 | 41 | 19 |

NO. 7. Who has a stronger nuclear force—the United States or the Soviet Union?

|  | UNITED STATES | SOVIET UNION | DON'T KNOW |
|---|---|---|---|
| ALL | 39 | 38 | 23 |
| PARTY |  |  |  |
| not regis | 37 | 43 | 20 |
| Democrat | 41 | 37 | 22 |
| Republican | 34 | 40 | 26 |
| Independent | 45 | 34 | 21 |
| IDEOLOGY |  |  |  |
| liberal | 45 | 36 | 19 |
| moderate | 40 | 36 | 24 |
| conservative | 35 | 44 | 22 |
| AGE |  |  |  |
| 18–34 | 40 | 43 | 17 |
| 35–49 | 39 | 40 | 21 |
| 50–59 | 35 | 33 | 32 |
| 60+ | 39 | 28 | 32 |
| INCOME |  |  |  |
| <$7,000 | 38 | 35 | 27 |
| $ 7-$15,000 | 40 | 35 | 25 |
| $15-$25,000 | 39 | 42 | 19 |
| $25-$35,000 | 40 | 37 | 23 |
| $35,000+ | 37 | 39 | 24 |
| EDUCATION |  |  |  |
| <high school | 46 | 32 | 22 |
| high school | 34 | 41 | 25 |
| some college | 38 | 41 | 22 |
| college | 42 | 38 | 20 |
| college+ | 50 | 25 | 24 |
| UNION |  |  |  |
| union | 43 | 37 | 20 |
| non-union | 38 | 39 | 24 |
| SEX |  |  |  |
| male | 39 | 39 | 22 |
| female | 40 | 37 | 23 |
| REGION |  |  |  |
| northeast | 41 | 34 | 25 |
| south | 37 | 42 | 21 |
| midwest | 41 | 33 | 25 |
| west | 38 | 43 | 19 |

NO. 8. Does the United States have more or fewer nuclear weapons today
than 15 years ago?

|  | MORE | FEWER | DON'T KNOW |
|---|---|---|---|
| ALL | 86 | 8 | 6 |
| PARTY | | | |
| not regis | 88 | 6 | 5 |
| Democrat | 87 | 6 | 6 |
| Republican | 85 | 8 | 7 |
| Independent | 81 | 12 | 6 |
| IDEOLOGY | | | |
| liberal | 88 | 8 | 4 |
| moderate | 90 | 5 | 5 |
| conservative | 81 | 11 | 8 |
| AGE | | | |
| 18–34 | 88 | 7 | 4 |
| 35–49 | 83 | 12 | 6 |
| 50–59 | 81 | 7 | 12 |
| 60+ | 88 | 5 | 7 |
| INCOME | | | |
| <$7,000 | 86 | 7 | 7 |
| $ 7-$15,000 | 84 | 7 | 9 |
| $15-$25,000 | 85 | 9 | 5 |
| $25-$35,000 | 88 | 7 | 5 |
| $35,000+ | 86 | 8 | 6 |
| EDUCATION | | | |
| <high school | 83 | 7 | 10 |
| high school | 88 | 7 | 5 |
| some college | 87 | 7 | 6 |
| college | 84 | 11 | 5 |
| college+ | 82 | 10 | 8 |
| UNION | | | |
| union | 88 | 6 | 6 |
| non-union | 85 | 9 | 7 |
| SEX | | | |
| male | 83 | 11 | 6 |
| female | 88 | 5 | 6 |
| REGION | | | |
| northeast | 88 | 8 | 4 |
| south | 82 | 10 | 8 |
| midwest | 86 | 9 | 5 |
| west | 86 | 4 | 9 |

NO. 9. How many is it MORE?—under 1000, 100 to 5000, or more than 5000?

|  | UNDER 1000 | 1000-5000 | MORE THAN 5000 | DON'T KNOW |
|---|---|---|---|---|
| MORE | 17 | 33 | 23 | 28 |

(The above numbers do not represent the entire survey. Rather, they represent those who answered this question and said, "More.")

How many is it FEWER?—under 1000, 1000 to 5000, or more than 5000?

|  | UNDER 1000 | 1000-5000 | MORE THAN 5000 | DON'T KNOW |
|---|---|---|---|---|
| FEWER | 36 | 33 | 15 | 16 |

(The above numbers do not represent the entire survey. Rather, they represent those who answered this question and said, "Fewer.")

|  | UNDER 1000 | 1000-5000 | MORE THAN 5000 | DON'T KNOW |
|---|---|---|---|---|
| ALL | 17 | 33 | 23 | 28 |
| PARTY |  |  |  |  |
| not regis | 16 | 34 | 27 | 23 |
| Democrat | 14 | 34 | 24 | 28 |
| Republican | 19 | 32 | 18 | 31 |
| Independent | 21 | 32 | 25 | 22 |
| IDEOLOGY |  |  |  |  |
| liberal | 16 | 32 | 25 | 27 |
| moderate | 18 | 32 | 24 | 27 |
| conservative | 17 | 36 | 22 | 25 |
| AGE |  |  |  |  |
| 18–34 | 20 | 36 | 26 | 17 |
| 35–49 | 18 | 31 | 23 | 28 |
| 50–59 | 10 | 32 | 19 | 38 |
| 60+ | 12 | 28 | 18 | 43 |
| INCOME |  |  |  |  |
| <$7,000 | 15 | 35 | 17 | 33 |
| $ 7-$15,000 | 15 | 33 | 18 | 34 |
| $15-$25,000 | 17 | 37 | 24 | 22 |
| $25-$35,000 | 21 | 25 | 24 | 30 |
| $35,000+ | 13 | 36 | 29 | 23 |
| EDUCATION |  |  |  |  |
| <high school | 10 | 39 | 14 | 36 |
| high school | 19 | 30 | 20 | 31 |
| some college | 16 | 33 | 28 | 22 |
| college | 14 | 33 | 26 | 26 |
| college+ | 20 | 33 | 23 | 24 |
| UNION |  |  |  |  |
| union | 16 | 32 | 24 | 27 |
| non-union | 16 | 33 | 23 | 28 |
| SEX |  |  |  |  |
| male | 16 | 33 | 29 | 22 |
| female | 17 | 33 | 17 | 33 |
| REGION |  |  |  |  |
| northeast | 14 | 27 | 28 | 31 |
| south | 22 | 37 | 17 | 24 |
| midwest | 16 | 35 | 22 | 27 |
| west | 14 | 34 | 23 | 29 |

NO. 9. Does the United States have more or fewer nuclear weapons
today than 15 years ago? (ANSWERED FEWER) How many is it
FEWER?—under 1000, 1000 to 5000, or more than 5000?

| | UNDER 1000 | 1000-5000 | MORE THAN 5000 | DON'T KNOW |
|---|---|---|---|---|
| ALL | 36 | 33 | 15 | 16 |
| **PARTY** | | | | |
| not regis | 54 | 0 | 23 | 23 |
| Democrat | 29 | 46 | 17 | 9 |
| Republican | 40 | 33 | 7 | 21 |
| Independent | 38 | 30 | 15 | 16 |
| **IDEOLOGY** | | | | |
| liberal | 36 | 43 | 21 | 0 |
| moderate | 28 | 33 | 22 | 17 |
| conservative | 36 | 33 | 8 | 23 |
| **AGE** | | | | |
| 18–34 | 35 | 43 | 12 | 10 |
| 35–49 | 35 | 30 | 15 | 20 |
| 50–59 | 43 | 23 | 12 | 22 |
| 60+ | 31 | 25 | 22 | 22 |
| **INCOME** | | | | |
| <$7,000 | 33 | 50 | 0 | 17 |
| $ 7-$15,000 | 32 | 39 | 29 | 0 |
| $15-$25,000 | 46 | 20 | 7 | 27 |
| $25-$35,000 | 36 | 33 | 24 | 7 |
| $35,000+ | 24 | 47 | 12 | 18 |
| **EDUCATION** | | | | |
| <high school | 23 | 34 | 25 | 18 |
| high school | 44 | 25 | 18 | 13 |
| some college | 40 | 35 | 10 | 15 |
| college | 24 | 37 | 11 | 29 |
| college+ | 42 | 46 | 13 | 0 |
| **UNION** | | | | |
| union | 40 | 29 | 22 | 9 |
| non-union | 34 | 35 | 12 | 18 |
| **SEX** | | | | |
| male | 35 | 36 | 14 | 15 |
| female | 37 | 28 | 16 | 18 |
| **REGION** | | | | |
| northeast | 46 | 30 | 8 | 16 |
| south | 32 | 31 | 21 | 16 |
| midwest | 40 | 33 | 9 | 18 |
| west | 13 | 50 | 24 | 12 |

NO. 10. Is the U.S. nuclear weapons stockpile more or less
destructive than it was 15 years ago?

|  | MORE | LESS | DON'T KNOW |
|---|---|---|---|
| ALL | 85 | 7 | 8 |
| **PARTY** | | | |
| not regis | 87 | 5 | 8 |
| Democrat | 84 | 8 | 8 |
| Republican | 85 | 6 | 8 |
| Independent | 86 | 7 | 7 |
| **IDEOLOGY** | | | |
| liberal | 89 | 6 | 5 |
| moderate | 88 | 5 | 7 |
| conservative | 82 | 9 | 9 |
| **AGE** | | | |
| 18–34 | 89 | 7 | 5 |
| 35–49 | 82 | 10 | 8 |
| 50–59 | 82 | 7 | 12 |
| 60+ | 81 | 6 | 13 |
| **INCOME** | | | |
| <$7,000 | 79 | 7 | 14 |
| $ 7-$15,000 | 83 | 7 | 10 |
| $15-$25,000 | 82 | 9 | 9 |
| $25-$35,000 | 89 | 7 | 4 |
| $35,000+ | 89 | 6 | 5 |
| **EDUCATION** | | | |
| <high school | 75 | 10 | 14 |
| high school | 84 | 7 | 9 |
| some college | 86 | 8 | 6 |
| college | 90 | 5 | 5 |
| college+ | 86 | 6 | 8 |
| **UNION** | | | |
| union | 90 | 5 | 5 |
| non-union | 82 | 8 | 9 |
| **SEX** | | | |
| male | 87 | 6 | 7 |
| female | 82 | 8 | 9 |
| **REGION** | | | |
| northeast | 89 | 5 | 6 |
| south | 79 | 13 | 8 |
| midwest | 85 | 7 | 8 |
| west | 86 | 3 | 11 |

NO. 11. By how much MORE is it destructive—under 10%, 10 to 25%,
25 to 60%, or over 60%

|  | UNDER 10% | 10 to 25% | 25 to 60% | OVER 60% | DON'T KNOW |
|---|---|---|---|---|---|
| MORE | 5 | 30 | 26 | 21 | 18 |

(The above numbers do not represent the entire survey. Rather,
they represent those who answered this question and said, "More.")

By how much LESS is it destructive—under 10%, 10 to 25%,
25 to 60%, or over 60%?

|  | UNDER 10% | 10 to 25% | 25 to 60% | OVER 60% | DON'T KNOW |
|---|---|---|---|---|---|
| LESS | 25 | 42 | 6 | 3 | 24 |

(The above numbers do not represent the entire survey. Rather,
they represent those who answered this question and said, "Less.")

NO. 11. Is the U.S. nuclear weapons stockpile more or less destructive
than it was 15 years ago? (ANSWERED MORE) By how much is it
MORE—under 10%, 10 to 25%, 25 to 60%, or over 60%?

| | UNDER 10% | 10 to 25% | 25 to 60% | OVER 60% | DON'T KNOW |
|---|---|---|---|---|---|
| ALL | 5 | 30 | 26 | 21 | 18 |
| **PARTY** | | | | | |
| not regis | 2 | 27 | 32 | 24 | 15 |
| Democrat | 4 | 28 | 28 | 23 | 17 |
| Republican | 6 | 33 | 23 | 16 | 22 |
| Independent | 5 | 29 | 25 | 26 | 15 |
| **IDEOLOGY** | | | | | |
| liberal | 4 | 30 | 30 | 23 | 13 |
| moderate | 5 | 30 | 23 | 22 | 21 |
| conservative | 5 | 29 | 30 | 20 | 16 |
| **AGE** | | | | | |
| 18–34 | 4 | 30 | 28 | 28 | 10 |
| 35–49 | 4 | 30 | 32 | 16 | 18 |
| 50–59 | 8 | 32 | 17 | 20 | 23 |
| 60+ | 4 | 26 | 22 | 13 | 34 |
| **INCOME** | | | | | |
| <$7,000 | 3 | 31 | 29 | 12 | 24 |
| $ 7-$15,000 | 6 | 26 | 28 | 17 | 24 |
| $15-$25,000 | 5 | 31 | 28 | 20 | 15 |
| $25-$35,000 | 4 | 31 | 24 | 28 | 14 |
| $35,000+ | 5 | 27 | 25 | 24 | 19 |
| **EDUCATION** | | | | | |
| <high school | 2 | 35 | 18 | 13 | 31 |
| high school | 3 | 31 | 27 | 21 | 18 |
| some college | 4 | 29 | 32 | 23 | 12 |
| college | 9 | 28 | 20 | 23 | 20 |
| college+ | 6 | 22 | 27 | 22 | 23 |
| **UNION** | | | | | |
| union | 3 | 32 | 26 | 18 | 21 |
| non-union | 5 | 29 | 26 | 23 | 17 |
| **SEX** | | | | | |
| male | 3 | 28 | 28 | 26 | 15 |
| female | 6 | 32 | 24 | 16 | 22 |
| **REGION** | | | | | |
| northeast | 5 | 22 | 28 | 23 | 21 |
| south | 3 | 40 | 23 | 20 | 14 |
| midwest | 6 | 34 | 26 | 17 | 17 |
| west | 5 | 24 | 29 | 23 | 20 |

NO. 11. Is the U.S. nuclear weapons stockpile more or less destructive than
it was 15 years ago? (ANSWERED LESS) By how much is it LESS—
nder 10%, 10 to 25%, 25 to 60%, or over 60%?

|  | UNDER 10% | 10 to 25% | 25 to 60% | OVER 60% | DON'T KNOW |
|---|---|---|---|---|---|
| ALL | 25 | 42 | 6 | 3 | 24 |
| PARTY |  |  |  |  |  |
| not regis | 29 | 28 | 17 | 0 | 27 |
| Democrat | 28 | 52 | 0 | 0 | 21 |
| Republican | 31 | 25 | 13 | 7 | 24 |
| Independent | 15 | 45 | 8 | 0 | 32 |
| IDEOLOGY |  |  |  |  |  |
| liberal | 14 | 57 | 7 | 0 | 21 |
| moderate | 32 | 35 | 11 | 0 | 21 |
| conservative | 27 | 46 | 0 | 4 | 24 |
| AGE |  |  |  |  |  |
| 18–34 | 39 | 41 | 8 | 0 | 12 |
| 35–49 | 20 | 33 | 8 | 0 | 39 |
| 50–59 | 14 | 38 | 0 | 16 | 32 |
| 60+ | 15 | 63 | 0 | 8 | 13 |
| INCOME |  |  |  |  |  |
| <$7,000 | 30 | 38 | 16 | 0 | 15 |
| $ 7-$15,000 | 20 | 45 | 0 | 0 | 35 |
| $15-$25,000 | 32 | 37 | 0 | 10 | 20 |
| $25-$35,000 | 15 | 42 | 9 | 0 | 34 |
| $35,000+ | 36 | 38 | 16 | 0 | 9 |
| EDUCATION |  |  |  |  |  |
| <high school | 58 | 17 | 8 | 0 | 17 |
| high school | 15 | 61 | 0 | 4 | 19 |
| some college | 24 | 33 | 5 | 5 | 33 |
| college | 27 | 48 | 0 | 0 | 26 |
| college+ | 0 | 41 | 40 | 0 | 19 |
| UNION |  |  |  |  |  |
| union | 24 | 37 | 8 | 0 | 31 |
| non-union | 26 | 43 | 5 | 4 | 22 |
| SEX |  |  |  |  |  |
| male | 24 | 44 | 10 | 0 | 22 |
| female | 26 | 40 | 3 | 6 | 25 |
| REGION |  |  |  |  |  |
| northeast | 7 | 50 | 7 | 0 | 35 |
| south | 29 | 37 | 8 | 6 | 20 |
| midwest | 31 | 43 | 0 | 0 | 26 |
| west | 33 | 51 | 0 | 0 | 16 |

NO. 12. Has America's military position compared to the Soviet Union
improved, gotten worse or stayed the same over the past five years?

|  | IMPROVED | WORSE | SAME | DON'T KNOW |
|---|---|---|---|---|
| ALL | 38 | 25 | 32 | 6 |
| **PARTY** |  |  |  |  |
| not regis | 33 | 25 | 37 | 5 |
| Democrat | 33 | 25 | 35 | 7 |
| Republican | 47 | 25 | 24 | 3 |
| Independent | 39 | 22 | 34 | 4 |
| **IDEOLOGY** |  |  |  |  |
| liberal | 31 | 27 | 33 | 9 |
| moderate | 36 | 24 | 35 | 4 |
| conservative | 45 | 23 | 29 | 3 |
| **AGE** |  |  |  |  |
| 18–34 | 37 | 23 | 36 | 3 |
| 35–49 | 39 | 27 | 28 | 6 |
| 50–59 | 38 | 21 | 33 | 7 |
| 60+ | 38 | 25 | 29 | 8 |
| **INCOME** |  |  |  |  |
| <$7,000 | 29 | 26 | 37 | 8 |
| $ 7-$15,000 | 37 | 23 | 34 | 7 |
| $15-$25,000 | 43 | 23 | 31 | 3 |
| $25-$35,000 | 33 | 25 | 34 | 7 |
| $35,000+ | 39 | 28 | 30 | 3 |
| **EDUCATION** |  |  |  |  |
| <high school | 44 | 22 | 28 | 6 |
| high school | 37 | 23 | 34 | 6 |
| some college | 36 | 27 | 33 | 5 |
| college | 43 | 24 | 29 | 4 |
| college+ | 28 | 27 | 38 | 8 |
| **UNION** |  |  |  |  |
| union | 39 | 24 | 30 | 7 |
| non-union | 37 | 24 | 33 | 5 |
| **SEX** |  |  |  |  |
| male | 38 | 27 | 29 | 6 |
| female | 37 | 22 | 35 | 5 |
| **REGION** |  |  |  |  |
| northeast | 34 | 20 | 39 | 7 |
| south | 39 | 23 | 30 | 7 |
| midwest | 39 | 27 | 31 | 3 |
| west | 40 | 29 | 27 | 4 |

NO. 13. Which do you think should have the higher priority right now,
funds for conventional forces or for nuclear forces?

| | CONVENTIONAL | NUCLEAR | DON'T KNOW |
|---|---|---|---|
| ALL | 61 | 25 | 15 |
| PARTY | | | |
| not regis | 64 | 24 | 13 |
| Democrat | 57 | 30 | 13 |
| Republican | 63 | 19 | 17 |
| Independent | 63 | 24 | 13 |
| IDEOLOGY | | | |
| liberal | 66 | 21 | 12 |
| moderate | 64 | 24 | 12 |
| conservative | 56 | 28 | 16 |
| AGE | | | |
| 18–34 | 66 | 25 | 8 |
| 35–49 | 62 | 24 | 14 |
| 50–59 | 54 | 24 | 22 |
| 60+ | 52 | 25 | 23 |
| INCOME | | | |
| <$7,000 | 55 | 19 | 26 |
| $ 7-$15,000 | 61 | 25 | 14 |
| $15-$25,000 | 59 | 31 | 10 |
| $25-$35,000 | 63 | 25 | 12 |
| $35,000+ | 67 | 19 | 15 |
| EDUCATION | | | |
| <high school | 54 | 27 | 19 |
| high school | 57 | 26 | 17 |
| some college | 63 | 26 | 11 |
| college | 65 | 26 | 10 |
| college+ | 70 | 12 | 18 |
| UNION | | | |
| union | 62 | 21 | 18 |
| non-union | 61 | 26 | 13 |
| SEX | | | |
| male | 62 | 24 | 14 |
| female | 60 | 26 | 14 |
| REGION | | | |
| northeast | 63 | 24 | 14 |
| south | 53 | 32 | 15 |
| midwest | 63 | 22 | 15 |
| west | 66 | 19 | 15 |

NO. 14. In general, do you think that spending on defense should be increased, decreased or kept the same?

|  | INCREASED | DECREASED | KEPT THE SAME | DON'T KNOW |
|---|---|---|---|---|
| ALL | 30 | 27 | 41 | 2 |
| PARTY |  |  |  |  |
| not regis | 33 | 24 | 42 | 1 |
| Democrat | 27 | 35 | 36 | 2 |
| Republican | 36 | 16 | 46 | 2 |
| Independent | 23 | 30 | 45 | 1 |
| IDEOLOGY |  |  |  |  |
| liberal | 28 | 35 | 36 | 2 |
| moderate | 28 | 29 | 42 | 2 |
| conservative | 35 | 22 | 43 | 1 |
| AGE |  |  |  |  |
| 18–34 | 30 | 28 | 42 | 1 |
| 35–49 | 33 | 26 | 38 | 2 |
| 50–59 | 34 | 28 | 37 | 2 |
| 60+ | 23 | 27 | 47 | 3 |
| INCOME |  |  |  |  |
| <$7,000 | 34 | 19 | 44 | 3 |
| $ 7-$15,000 | 27 | 27 | 42 | 3 |
| $15-$25,000 | 31 | 26 | 42 | 1 |
| $25-$35,000 | 31 | 31 | 38 | 0 |
| $35,000+ | 28 | 30 | 40 | 2 |
| EDUCATION |  |  |  |  |
| <high school | 34 | 20 | 43 | 3 |
| high school | 34 | 22 | 42 | 2 |
| some college | 27 | 28 | 43 | 2 |
| college | 27 | 33 | 39 | 1 |
| college+ | 20 | 45 | 33 | 2 |
| UNION |  |  |  |  |
| union | 31 | 28 | 39 | 2 |
| non-union | 30 | 27 | 42 | 2 |
| SEX |  |  |  |  |
| male | 28 | 27 | 43 | 1 |
| female | 31 | 27 | 39 | 2 |
| REGION |  |  |  |  |
| northeast | 26 | 33 | 40 | 1 |
| south | 38 | 19 | 41 | 2 |
| midwest | 25 | 28 | 45 | 3 |
| west | 29 | 30 | 41 | 1 |

NO. 15. Does the Congress want to devote too much money to the military budget, not enough money or the right amount?

| | TOO MUCH | NOT ENOUGH | RIGHT AMOUNT | DON'T KNOW |
|---|---|---|---|---|
| ALL | 35 | 30 | 27 | 9 |
| PARTY | | | | |
| not regis | 35 | 31 | 24 | 11 |
| Democrat | 41 | 23 | 26 | 10 |
| Republican | 22 | 42 | 29 | 6 |
| Independent | 37 | 30 | 28 | 6 |
| IDEOLOGY | | | | |
| liberal | 42 | 23 | 26 | 8 |
| moderate | 38 | 28 | 27 | 7 |
| conservative | 26 | 40 | 26 | 8 |
| AGE | | | | |
| 18–34 | 36 | 30 | 27 | 7 |
| 35–49 | 35 | 33 | 23 | 9 |
| 50–59 | 33 | 35 | 23 | 10 |
| 60+ | 32 | 23 | 33 | 12 |
| INCOME | | | | |
| <$7,000 | 33 | 27 | 31 | 9 |
| $ 7-$15,000 | 37 | 26 | 27 | 9 |
| $15-$25,000 | 33 | 31 | 25 | 10 |
| $25-$35,000 | 33 | 29 | 32 | 5 |
| $35,000+ | 36 | 34 | 21 | 9 |
| EDUCATION | | | | |
| <high school | 31 | 28 | 31 | 10 |
| high school | 32 | 30 | 28 | 10 |
| some college | 34 | 32 | 28 | 7 |
| college | 40 | 32 | 21 | 6 |
| college+ | 44 | 20 | 24 | 11 |
| UNION | | | | |
| union | 39 | 24 | 28 | 9 |
| non-union | 33 | 33 | 26 | 8 |
| SEX | | | | |
| male | 31 | 34 | 27 | 7 |
| female | 38 | 26 | 26 | 10 |
| REGION | | | | |
| northeast | 39 | 27 | 25 | 8 |
| south | 26 | 39 | 27 | 9 |
| midwest | 38 | 26 | 27 | 9 |
| west | 37 | 27 | 27 | 9 |

NO. 16. Does President Reagan want to devote too much money to the
military budget, not enough money or the right amount?

|  | TOO MUCH | NOT ENOUGH | RIGHT AMOUNT | DON'T KNOW |
|---|---|---|---|---|
| ALL | 46 | 11 | 36 | 7 |
| PARTY |  |  |  |  |
| not regis | 40 | 18 | 33 | 9 |
| Democrat | 57 | 10 | 25 | 8 |
| Republican | 30 | 10 | 54 | 6 |
| Independent | 49 | 8 | 38 | 5 |
| IDEOLOGY |  |  |  |  |
| liberal | 60 | 14 | 21 | 5 |
| moderate | 50 | 9 | 37 | 5 |
| conservative | 33 | 12 | 47 | 9 |
| AGE |  |  |  |  |
| 18–34 | 46 | 10 | 39 | 5 |
| 35–49 | 47 | 12 | 33 | 7 |
| 50–59 | 43 | 13 | 33 | 12 |
| 60+ | 47 | 8 | 36 | 8 |
| INCOME |  |  |  |  |
| <$7,000 | 38 | 15 | 31 | 15 |
| $ 7-$15,000 | 47 | 10 | 35 | 8 |
| $15-$25,000 | 41 | 12 | 39 | 7 |
| $25-$35,000 | 52 | 12 | 32 | 5 |
| $35,000+ | 51 | 6 | 40 | 4 |
| EDUCATION |  |  |  |  |
| <high school | 39 | 13 | 34 | 14 |
| high school | 40 | 13 | 37 | 10 |
| some college | 47 | 10 | 39 | 5 |
| college | 53 | 10 | 36 | 1 |
| college+ | 67 | 1 | 27 | 5 |
| UNION |  |  |  |  |
| union | 50 | 10 | 31 | 9 |
| non-union | 45 | 11 | 38 | 6 |
| SEX |  |  |  |  |
| male | 46 | 11 | 38 | 5 |
| female | 46 | 10 | 34 | 9 |
| REGION |  |  |  |  |
| northeast | 52 | 11 | 32 | 5 |
| south | 38 | 13 | 40 | 8 |
| midwest | 49 | 11 | 31 | 9 |
| west | 46 | 7 | 41 | 6 |

NO. 17. How much of the defense budget do you think is spent on nuclear weapons—less than 20%, 20-40%, 41-75%, or more than 75%?

|  | LESS THAN 20% | 20-40% | 41-75% | MORE THAN 75% | DON'T KNOW |
|---|---|---|---|---|---|
| ALL | 19 | 40 | 17 | 5 | 19 |
| **PARTY** | | | | | |
| not regis | 9 | 33 | 29 | 9 | 20 |
| Democrat | 18 | 41 | 19 | 5 | 17 |
| Republican | 21 | 44 | 10 | 2 | 23 |
| Independent | 23 | 40 | 17 | 4 | 17 |
| **IDEOLOGY** | | | | | |
| liberal | 21 | 45 | 20 | 4 | 9 |
| moderate | 16 | 43 | 18 | 4 | 19 |
| conservative | 21 | 37 | 14 | 5 | 23 |
| **AGE** | | | | | |
| 18–34 | 21 | 43 | 22 | 6 | 8 |
| 35–49 | 20 | 39 | 13 | 6 | 23 |
| 50–59 | 17 | 42 | 15 | 2 | 23 |
| 60+ | 15 | 35 | 12 | 3 | 36 |
| **INCOME** | | | | | |
| <$7,000 | 8 | 30 | 19 | 10 | 33 |
| $ 7-$15,000 | 14 | 39 | 15 | 8 | 24 |
| $15-$25,000 | 16 | 46 | 18 | 3 | 15 |
| $25-$35,000 | 24 | 44 | 15 | 3 | 14 |
| $35,000+ | 25 | 36 | 18 | 3 | 18 |
| **EDUCATION** | | | | | |
| <high school | 14 | 31 | 19 | 6 | 29 |
| high school | 14 | 39 | 20 | 6 | 22 |
| some college | 19 | 44 | 16 | 6 | 16 |
| college | 24 | 46 | 15 | 1 | 15 |
| college+ | 36 | 36 | 10 | 1 | 17 |
| **UNION** | | | | | |
| union | 15 | 41 | 18 | 4 | 22 |
| non-union | 20 | 40 | 17 | 5 | 18 |
| **SEX** | | | | | |
| male | 25 | 39 | 18 | 3 | 15 |
| female | 12 | 42 | 16 | 6 | 24 |
| **REGION** | | | | | |
| northeast | 18 | 42 | 21 | 5 | 14 |
| south | 19 | 38 | 19 | 6 | 18 |
| midwest | 16 | 40 | 14 | 4 | 25 |
| west | 22 | 41 | 14 | 4 | 20 |

NO. 18. How much of the defense budget do you think is spent on
conventional military forces—less than 20%, 21-40%,
41-75%, or more than 75%?

| | LESS THAN 20% | 20-40% | 41-75% | MORE THAN 75% | DON'T KNOW |
|---|---|---|---|---|---|
| ALL | 18 | 38 | 19 | 6 | 19 |
| PARTY | | | | | |
| not regis | 17 | 38 | 16 | 7 | 21 |
| Democrat | 17 | 45 | 18 | 4 | 16 |
| Republican | 18 | 32 | 22 | 4 | 24 |
| Independent | 23 | 32 | 20 | 7 | 17 |
| IDEOLOGY | | | | | |
| liberal | 22 | 43 | 19 | 7 | 10 |
| moderate | 17 | 38 | 20 | 5 | 20 |
| conservative | 18 | 37 | 19 | 6 | 21 |
| AGE | | | | | |
| 18–34 | 21 | 44 | 20 | 7 | 9 |
| 35–49 | 18 | 33 | 24 | 5 | 21 |
| 50–59 | 15 | 43 | 15 | 4 | 24 |
| 60+ | 13 | 32 | 14 | 5 | 36 |
| INCOME | | | | | |
| <$7,000 | 17 | 35 | 9 | 6 | 33 |
| $ 7-$15,000 | 14 | 36 | 21 | 7 | 22 |
| $15-$25,000 | 18 | 43 | 18 | 5 | 17 |
| $25-$35,000 | 23 | 37 | 21 | 5 | 14 |
| $35,000+ | 16 | 36 | 22 | 6 | 19 |
| EDUCATION | | | | | |
| <high school | 11 | 39 | 13 | 5 | 32 |
| high school | 20 | 40 | 17 | 4 | 19 |
| some college | 19 | 40 | 16 | 8 | 17 |
| college | 17 | 37 | 26 | 5 | 15 |
| college+ | 15 | 29 | 29 | 9 | 18 |
| UNION | | | | | |
| union | 17 | 39 | 19 | 4 | 21 |
| non-union | 18 | 38 | 19 | 6 | 18 |
| SEX | | | | | |
| male | 17 | 39 | 20 | 8 | 16 |
| female | 19 | 38 | 18 | 3 | 22 |
| REGION | | | | | |
| northeast | 14 | 40 | 22 | 6 | 17 |
| south | 20 | 40 | 16 | 6 | 18 |
| midwest | 15 | 39 | 20 | 3 | 23 |
| west | 23 | 33 | 18 | 7 | 19 |

NO. 19. Should defense spending on nuclear arms be increased,
decreased, or kept at its current level?

| | INCREASED | DECREASED | CURRENT LEVEL | DON'T KNOW |
|---|---|---|---|---|
| ALL | 20 | 31 | 45 | 3 |
| PARTY | | | | |
| not regis | 20 | 29 | 49 | 2 |
| Democrat | 18 | 36 | 43 | 3 |
| Republican | 26 | 20 | 51 | 4 |
| Independent | 19 | 41 | 39 | 2 |
| IDEOLOGY | | | | |
| liberal | 17 | 38 | 43 | 2 |
| moderate | 16 | 37 | 45 | 2 |
| conservative | 28 | 22 | 48 | 3 |
| AGE | | | | |
| 18–34 | 19 | 37 | 43 | 1 |
| 35–49 | 21 | 32 | 44 | 3 |
| 50–59 | 25 | 26 | 43 | 6 |
| 60+ | 20 | 21 | 53 | 6 |
| INCOME | | | | |
| <$7,000 | 23 | 19 | 54 | 4 |
| $ 7-$15,000 | 21 | 30 | 45 | 4 |
| $15-$25,000 | 24 | 30 | 43 | 3 |
| $25-$35,000 | 18 | 34 | 45 | 3 |
| $35,000+ | 17 | 37 | 45 | 1 |
| EDUCATION | | | | |
| <high school | 26 | 19 | 49 | 5 |
| high school | 27 | 25 | 45 | 4 |
| some college | 17 | 34 | 47 | 3 |
| college | 17 | 40 | 42 | 1 |
| college+ | 7 | 49 | 40 | 3 |
| UNION | | | | |
| union | 20 | 36 | 42 | 3 |
| non-union | 21 | 30 | 46 | 3 |
| SEX | | | | |
| male | 19 | 32 | 47 | 2 |
| female | 22 | 31 | 43 | 4 |
| REGION | | | | |
| northeast | 14 | 42 | 41 | 3 |
| south | 31 | 19 | 47 | 3 |
| midwest | 19 | 30 | 48 | 4 |
| west | 17 | 33 | 46 | 3 |

NO. 20. Should defense spending on conventional weaponry like guns,
tanks, ships and airplanes be increased, decreased, or,
kept at its current level?

|  | INCREASED | DECREASED | CURRENT LEVEL | DON'T KNOW |
|---|---|---|---|---|
| ALL | 43 | 12 | 42 | 3 |
| PARTY | | | | |
| not regis | 46 | 11 | 40 | 3 |
| Democrat | 41 | 14 | 43 | 3 |
| Republican | 47 | 8 | 41 | 4 |
| Independent | 39 | 16 | 44 | 1 |
| IDEOLOGY | | | | |
| liberal | 41 | 17 | 41 | 2 |
| moderate | 41 | 16 | 40 | 3 |
| conservative | 45 | 6 | 45 | 3 |
| AGE | | | | |
| 18–34 | 46 | 13 | 40 | 1 |
| 35–49 | 48 | 12 | 38 | 3 |
| 50–59 | 34 | 17 | 46 | 4 |
| 60+ | 36 | 8 | 48 | 8 |
| INCOME | | | | |
| <$7,000 | 46 | 9 | 36 | 8 |
| $ 7-$15,000 | 39 | 12 | 45 | 5 |
| $15-$25,000 | 42 | 13 | 43 | 2 |
| $25-$35,000 | 44 | 10 | 43 | 3 |
| $35,000+ | 45 | 16 | 39 | 1 |
| EDUCATION | | | | |
| <high school | 46 | 10 | 36 | 8 |
| high school | 48 | 9 | 40 | 4 |
| some college | 43 | 12 | 44 | 2 |
| college | 36 | 15 | 47 | 1 |
| college+ | 34 | 24 | 39 | 4 |
| UNION | | | | |
| union | 47 | 14 | 37 | 1 |
| non-union | 42 | 12 | 43 | 4 |
| SEX | | | | |
| male | 46 | 10 | 42 | 2 |
| female | 40 | 14 | 42 | 4 |
| REGION | | | | |
| northeast | 41 | 16 | 40 | 4 |
| south | 50 | 10 | 37 | 4 |
| midwest | 36 | 11 | 52 | 2 |
| west | 43 | 12 | 42 | 2 |

NO. 21. Think for a minute about how things were five years ago; do you
think the threat of nuclear war involving the United States was greater
than it is now, less than it is now or about the same?

|  | GREATER | LESS | SAME | DON'T KNOW |
|---|---|---|---|---|
| ALL | 30 | 31 | 37 | 2 |
| PARTY |  |  |  |  |
| not regis | 36 | 29 | 34 | 1 |
| Democrat | 29 | 33 | 35 | 2 |
| Republican | 26 | 26 | 44 | 4 |
| Independent | 30 | 35 | 33 | 1 |
| IDEOLOGY |  |  |  |  |
| liberal | 29 | 36 | 34 | 1 |
| moderate | 28 | 31 | 39 | 2 |
| conservative | 32 | 28 | 39 | 2 |
| AGE |  |  |  |  |
| 18–34 | 29 | 37 | 34 | 0 |
| 35–49 | 31 | 30 | 37 | 2 |
| 50–59 | 29 | 23 | 45 | 3 |
| 60+ | 31 | 26 | 38 | 5 |
| INCOME |  |  |  |  |
| <$7,000 | 30 | 37 | 26 | 7 |
| $ 7-$15,000 | 29 | 27 | 41 | 3 |
| $15-$25,000 | 32 | 25 | 40 | 2 |
| $25-$35,000 | 30 | 35 | 33 | 1 |
| $35,000+ | 27 | 35 | 36 | 1 |
| EDUCATION |  |  |  |  |
| <high school | 38 | 28 | 31 | 3 |
| high school | 27 | 30 | 40 | 3 |
| some college | 29 | 30 | 38 | 2 |
| college | 33 | 36 | 30 | 1 |
| college+ | 27 | 32 | 42 | 0 |
| UNION |  |  |  |  |
| union | 34 | 28 | 37 | 1 |
| non-union | 28 | 33 | 37 | 2 |
| SEX |  |  |  |  |
| male | 27 | 29 | 42 | 1 |
| female | 32 | 33 | 32 | 3 |
| REGION |  |  |  |  |
| northeast | 30 | 32 | 35 | 2 |
| south | 30 | 32 | 36 | 1 |
| midwest | 33 | 29 | 36 | 2 |
| west | 26 | 30 | 42 | 2 |

NO. 22. Was the threat of nuclear war somewhere in the world greater
five years ago than it is now, less than it is now or about the same?

|  | GREATER | LESS | SAME | DON'T KNOW |
|---|---|---|---|---|
| ALL | 29 | 32 | 36 | 2 |
| **PARTY** | | | | |
| not regis | 31 | 31 | 34 | 4 |
| Democrat | 29 | 33 | 37 | 2 |
| Republican | 30 | 29 | 38 | 4 |
| Independent | 29 | 37 | 34 | 0 |
| **IDEOLOGY** | | | | |
| liberal | 29 | 35 | 33 | 3 |
| moderate | 27 | 34 | 38 | 2 |
| conservative | 32 | 30 | 36 | 2 |
| **AGE** | | | | |
| 18–34 | 30 | 36 | 32 | 2 |
| 35–49 | 31 | 32 | 35 | 2 |
| 50–59 | 29 | 28 | 42 | 1 |
| 60+ | 27 | 28 | 39 | 6 |
| **INCOME** | | | | |
| <$7,000 | 24 | 36 | 36 | 3 |
| $ 7-$15,000 | 29 | 28 | 39 | 4 |
| $15-$25,000 | 32 | 32 | 35 | 2 |
| $25-$35,000 | 27 | 37 | 34 | 1 |
| $35,000+ | 29 | 33 | 36 | 2 |
| **EDUCATION** | | | | |
| <high school | 32 | 24 | 42 | 2 |
| high school | 27 | 32 | 37 | 4 |
| some college | 31 | 30 | 37 | 2 |
| college | 30 | 40 | 29 | 1 |
| college+ | 28 | 40 | 31 | 1 |
| **UNION** | | | | |
| union | 32 | 28 | 38 | 2 |
| non-union | 28 | 34 | 35 | 3 |
| **SEX** | | | | |
| male | 29 | 32 | 37 | 2 |
| female | 30 | 33 | 34 | 3 |
| **REGION** | | | | |
| northeast | 31 | 34 | 32 | 3 |
| south | 30 | 33 | 35 | 2 |
| midwest | 27 | 36 | 34 | 2 |
| west | 28 | 27 | 44 | 2 |

NO. 23. How much would you say you know about the issues involving
nuclear arms—a great deal, some, not very much
or nothing at all?

|  | GREAT DEAL | SOME | NOT VERY MUCH | NOTHING | DON'T KNOW |
|---|---|---|---|---|---|
| ALL | 8 | 54 | 33 | 4 | 1 |
| PARTY |  |  |  |  |  |
| not regis | 7 | 44 | 42 | 6 | 1 |
| Democrat | 6 | 55 | 34 | 3 | 1 |
| Republican | 7 | 53 | 34 | 4 | 2 |
| Independent | 10 | 62 | 24 | 3 | 1 |
| IDEOLOGY |  |  |  |  |  |
| liberal | 8 | 58 | 30 | 3 | 1 |
| moderate | 6 | 57 | 32 | 3 | 1 |
| conservative | 9 | 50 | 37 | 4 | 1 |
| AGE |  |  |  |  |  |
| 18–34 | 7 | 61 | 29 | 2 | 1 |
| 35–49 | 8 | 56 | 33 | 3 | 0 |
| 50–59 | 8 | 48 | 38 | 5 | 2 |
| 60+ | 8 | 43 | 39 | 8 | 3 |
| INCOME |  |  |  |  |  |
| <$7,000 | 1 | 46 | 35 | 14 | 3 |
| $ 7-$15,000 | 9 | 42 | 42 | 4 | 2 |
| $15-$25,000 | 6 | 56 | 33 | 3 | 1 |
| $25-$35,000 | 9 | 61 | 27 | 2 | 1 |
| $35,000+ | 9 | 60 | 28 | 2 | 0 |
| EDUCATION |  |  |  |  |  |
| <high school | 3 | 36 | 48 | 11 | 2 |
| high school | 4 | 53 | 37 | 4 | 1 |
| some college | 11 | 58 | 29 | 1 | 1 |
| college | 8 | 60 | 29 | 2 | 1 |
| college+ | 17 | 63 | 17 | 2 | 1 |
| UNION |  |  |  |  |  |
| union | 9 | 54 | 32 | 3 | 2 |
| non-union | 7 | 55 | 33 | 4 | 1 |
| SEX |  |  |  |  |  |
| male | 11 | 54 | 30 | 4 | 1 |
| female | 4 | 55 | 36 | 4 | 2 |
| REGION |  |  |  |  |  |
| northeast | 8 | 54 | 33 | 3 | 2 |
| south | 6 | 55 | 33 | 5 | 0 |
| midwest | 7 | 52 | 35 | 5 | 1 |
| west | 9 | 56 | 31 | 2 | 2 |

NO. 24. What is your age?

|  | 18-34 | 35-49 | 50-59 | 60+ |
|---|---|---|---|---|
| ALL | 42 | 25 | 12 | 20 |
| PARTY |  |  |  |  |
| not regis | 56 | 22 | 11 | 11 |
| Democrat | 39 | 25 | 13 | 23 |
| Republican | 35 | 26 | 14 | 26 |
| Independent | 49 | 29 | 11 | 12 |
| IDEOLOGY |  |  |  |  |
| liberal | 50 | 24 | 11 | 15 |
| moderate | 43 | 25 | 12 | 20 |
| conservative | 38 | 25 | 15 | 23 |
| AGE |  |  |  |  |
| 18–34 | 100 | 0 | 0 | 0 |
| 35–49 | 0 | 100 | 0 | 0 |
| 50–59 | 0 | 0 | 100 | 0 |
| 60+ | 0 | 0 | 0 | 100 |
| INCOME |  |  |  |  |
| <$7,000 | 34 | 12 | 7 | 47 |
| $ 7-$15,000 | 41 | 18 | 11 | 30 |
| $15-$25,000 | 46 | 21 | 14 | 19 |
| $25-$35,000 | 48 | 31 | 10 | 12 |
| $35,000+ | 36 | 37 | 17 | 10 |
| EDUCATION |  |  |  |  |
| <high school | 27 | 16 | 15 | 41 |
| high school | 37 | 27 | 12 | 24 |
| some college | 54 | 23 | 13 | 10 |
| college | 52 | 25 | 9 | 14 |
| college+ | 26 | 39 | 13 | 22 |
| UNION |  |  |  |  |
| union | 39 | 31 | 11 | 18 |
| non-union | 43 | 23 | 13 | 21 |
| SEX |  |  |  |  |
| male | 44 | 25 | 13 | 18 |
| female | 40 | 25 | 12 | 23 |
| REGION |  |  |  |  |
| northeast | 40 | 25 | 14 | 21 |
| south | 46 | 23 | 13 | 18 |
| midwest | 40 | 26 | 10 | 24 |
| west | 41 | 28 | 12 | 19 |

NO. 25. Into which of the following categories does your family income fall?

| | UNDER $7,000 | $7-$15,000 | $15-$25,000 | $25-$35,000 | OVER $35,000 |
|---|---|---|---|---|---|
| ALL | 9 | 21 | 28 | 20 | 22 |
| PARTY | | | | | |
| not regis | 19 | 27 | 22 | 20 | 12 |
| Democrat | 7 | 23 | 29 | 20 | 20 |
| Republican | 9 | 17 | 27 | 18 | 29 |
| Independent | 5 | 14 | 32 | 22 | 28 |
| IDEOLOGY | | | | | |
| liberal | 9 | 18 | 24 | 30 | 20 |
| moderate | 8 | 19 | 29 | 19 | 24 |
| conservative | 8 | 22 | 30 | 15 | 24 |
| AGE | | | | | |
| 18–34 | 7 | 20 | 30 | 23 | 19 |
| 35–49 | 4 | 15 | 23 | 25 | 33 |
| 50–59 | 5 | 18 | 30 | 16 | 31 |
| 60+ | 21 | 30 | 27 | 12 | 11 |
| INCOME | | | | | |
| <$7,000 | 100 | 0 | 0 | 0 | 0 |
| $ 7-$15,000 | 0 | 100 | 0 | 0 | 0 |
| $15-$25,000 | 0 | 0 | 100 | 0 | 0 |
| $25-$35,000 | 0 | 0 | 0 | 100 | 0 |
| $35,000+ | 0 | 0 | 0 | 0 | 100 |
| EDUCATION | | | | | |
| <high school | 30 | 32 | 19 | 10 | 9 |
| high school | 10 | 27 | 31 | 18 | 14 |
| some college | 5 | 18 | 35 | 22 | 21 |
| college | 3 | 11 | 25 | 26 | 35 |
| college+ | 0 | 9 | 9 | 27 | 54 |
| UNION | | | | | |
| union | 7 | 18 | 29 | 24 | 23 |
| non-union | 9 | 22 | 27 | 19 | 22 |
| SEX | | | | | |
| male | 6 | 17 | 29 | 21 | 26 |
| female | 11 | 24 | 26 | 19 | 19 |
| REGION | | | | | |
| northeast | 10 | 22 | 27 | 21 | 21 |
| south | 8 | 17 | 29 | 21 | 25 |
| midwest | 8 | 24 | 27 | 20 | 21 |
| west | 11 | 21 | 26 | 19 | 23 |

NO. 26. What is the last year of school you have completed?

| | BELOW HIGH SCHOOL | HIGH SCHOOL | SOME COLLEGE | COLLEGE | ABOVE COLLEGE |
|---|---|---|---|---|---|
| ALL | 12 | 35 | 27 | 17 | 9 |
| PARTY | | | | | |
| not regis | 17 | 48 | 20 | 11 | 4 |
| Democrat | 13 | 36 | 27 | 14 | 9 |
| Republican | 10 | 32 | 24 | 24 | 10 |
| Independent | 8 | 26 | 37 | 20 | 10 |
| IDEOLOGY | | | | | |
| liberal | 9 | 34 | 27 | 17 | 12 |
| moderate | 12 | 35 | 29 | 16 | 9 |
| conservative | 10 | 36 | 27 | 20 | 7 |
| AGE | | | | | |
| 18–34 | 8 | 31 | 35 | 21 | 5 |
| 35–49 | 8 | 37 | 25 | 17 | 13 |
| 50–59 | 15 | 35 | 29 | 13 | 9 |
| 60+ | 25 | 41 | 13 | 12 | 9 |
| INCOME | | | | | |
| <$7,000 | 40 | 38 | 17 | 5 | 0 |
| $ 7-$15,000 | 18 | 45 | 23 | 9 | 4 |
| $15-$25,000 | 8 | 39 | 34 | 16 | 3 |
| $25-$35,000 | 6 | 32 | 29 | 22 | 12 |
| $35,000+ | 5 | 23 | 25 | 27 | 21 |
| EDUCATION | | | | | |
| <high school | 100 | 0 | 0 | 0 | 0 |
| high school | 0 | 100 | 0 | 0 | 0 |
| some college | 0 | 0 | 100 | 0 | 0 |
| college | 0 | 0 | 0 | 100 | 0 |
| college+ | 0 | 0 | 0 | 0 | 100 |
| UNION | | | | | |
| union | 12 | 38 | 28 | 10 | 12 |
| non-union | 12 | 34 | 27 | 20 | 7 |
| SEX | | | | | |
| male | 12 | 30 | 29 | 18 | 11 |
| female | 12 | 40 | 25 | 16 | 7 |
| REGION | | | | | |
| northeast | 11 | 39 | 22 | 18 | 10 |
| south | 16 | 31 | 28 | 18 | 7 |
| midwest | 12 | 41 | 27 | 13 | 7 |
| west | 10 | 28 | 33 | 18 | 11 |

NO. 27. What is your occupation? (If unemployed, get usual occupation)

| | EXECUTIVE | BUSINESSMAN | SEMI-SKILLED | SKILLED | UNSKILLED |
|---|---|---|---|---|---|
| ALL | 25 | 8 | 11 | 13 | 3 |
| PARTY | | | | | |
| not regis | 13 | 8 | 11 | 19 | 7 |
| Democrat | 24 | 6 | 13 | 13 | 3 |
| Republican | 28 | 9 | 8 | 11 | 3 |
| Independent | 33 | 13 | 13 | 13 | 2 |
| IDEOLOGY | | | | | |
| liberal | 27 | 7 | 15 | 11 | 2 |
| moderate | 28 | 6 | 11 | 14 | 4 |
| conservative | 22 | 13 | 9 | 13 | 3 |
| AGE | | | | | |
| 18–34 | 25 | 10 | 12 | 17 | 4 |
| 35–49 | 37 | 10 | 12 | 14 | 4 |
| 50–59 | 24 | 8 | 18 | 12 | 3 |
| 60+ | 10 | 5 | 5 | 6 | 0 |
| INCOME | | | | | |
| <$7,000 | 3 | 6 | 7 | 13 | 5 |
| $ 7-$15,000 | 10 | 7 | 13 | 11 | 5 |
| $15-$25,000 | 22 | 8 | 15 | 18 | 3 |
| $25-$35,000 | 31 | 9 | 12 | 16 | 3 |
| $35,000+ | 46 | 10 | 6 | 9 | 2 |
| EDUCATION | | | | | |
| <high school | 4 | 4 | 4 | 14 | 12 |
| high school | 10 | 7 | 15 | 17 | 5 |
| some college | 24 | 8 | 13 | 16 | 1 |
| college | 47 | 14 | 11 | 8 | 0 |
| college+ | 72 | 7 | 1 | 1 | 0 |
| UNION | | | | | |
| union | 28 | 5 | 9 | 19 | 5 |
| non-union | 24 | 10 | 12 | 11 | 3 |
| SEX | | | | | |
| male | 29 | 10 | 6 | 19 | 5 |
| female | 20 | 7 | 16 | 8 | 2 |
| REGION | | | | | |
| northeast | 25 | 7 | 12 | 14 | 3 |
| south | 24 | 11 | 12 | 11 | 2 |
| midwest | 22 | 6 | 8 | 16 | 4 |
| west | 28 | 7 | 14 | 13 | 5 |

NO. 27. What is your occupation? (If unemployed, get usual occupation)
(continued)

| | HOMEMAKER | DOESN'T WORK | STUDENT | OTHER |
|---|---|---|---|---|
| ALL | 13 | 15 | 8 | 3 |
| PARTY | | | | |
| not regis | 16 | 7 | 17 | 3 |
| Democrat | 14 | 18 | 6 | 4 |
| Republican | 16 | 19 | 4 | 2 |
| Independent | 9 | 6 | 9 | 2 |
| IDEOLOGY | | | | |
| liberal | 9 | 14 | 11 | 5 |
| moderate | 15 | 13 | 7 | 2 |
| conservative | 14 | 15 | 7 | 3 |
| AGE | | | | |
| 18–34 | 11 | 1 | 17 | 4 |
| 35–49 | 16 | 1 | 2 | 3 |
| 50–59 | 18 | 14 | 0 | 2 |
| 60+ | 11 | 60 | 0 | 2 |
| INCOME | | | | |
| <$7,000 | 12 | 39 | 9 | 7 |
| $ 7-$15,000 | 18 | 27 | 7 | 2 |
| $15-$25,000 | 11 | 13 | 6 | 4 |
| $25-$35,000 | 14 | 6 | 7 | 2 |
| $35,000+ | 9 | 5 | 10 | 2 |
| EDUCATION | | | | |
| <high school | 19 | 32 | 7 | 4 |
| high school | 19 | 17 | 6 | 4 |
| some college | 10 | 9 | 15 | 3 |
| college | 6 | 9 | 4 | 1 |
| college+ | 7 | 10 | 1 | 1 |
| UNION | | | | |
| union | 14 | 12 | 5 | 3 |
| non-union | 13 | 16 | 8 | 3 |
| SEX | | | | |
| male | 3 | 14 | 10 | 3 |
| female | 23 | 16 | 6 | 3 |
| REGION | | | | |
| northeast | 14 | 15 | 7 | 3 |
| south | 13 | 15 | 8 | 3 |
| midwest | 15 | 17 | 8 | 3 |
| west | 9 | 13 | 8 | 4 |

NO. 28. Generally speaking, do you consider yourself as liberal, moderate
or conservative?

|  | LIBERAL | MODERATE | CONSERVATIVE | DON'T KNOW |
|---|---|---|---|---|
| ALL | 24 | 37 | 34 | 6 |
| PARTY |  |  |  |  |
| not regis | 27 | 34 | 31 | 7 |
| Democrat | 30 | 37 | 27 | 7 |
| Republican | 13 | 34 | 51 | 2 |
| Independent | 22 | 43 | 31 | 5 |
| IDEOLOGY |  |  |  |  |
| liberal | 100 | 0 | 0 | 0 |
| moderate | 0 | 100 | 0 | 0 |
| conservative | 0 | 0 | 100 | 0 |
| AGE |  |  |  |  |
| 18–34 | 28 | 38 | 31 | 3 |
| 35–49 | 23 | 37 | 33 | 8 |
| 50–59 | 20 | 35 | 40 | 6 |
| 60+ | 18 | 36 | 38 | 9 |
| INCOME |  |  |  |  |
| <$7,000 | 24 | 32 | 32 | 13 |
| $ 7-$15,000 | 20 | 35 | 36 | 9 |
| $15-$25,000 | 20 | 39 | 37 | 4 |
| $25-$35,000 | 35 | 35 | 26 | 4 |
| $35,000+ | 21 | 40 | 36 | 3 |
| EDUCATION |  |  |  |  |
| <high school | 19 | 37 | 28 | 16 |
| high school | 23 | 36 | 35 | 6 |
| some college | 24 | 39 | 34 | 3 |
| college | 24 | 34 | 40 | 3 |
| college+ | 32 | 37 | 26 | 4 |
| UNION |  |  |  |  |
| union | 28 | 36 | 29 | 7 |
| non-union | 22 | 37 | 36 | 5 |
| SEX |  |  |  |  |
| male | 25 | 35 | 35 | 6 |
| female | 22 | 39 | 33 | 6 |
| REGION |  |  |  |  |
| northeast | 24 | 38 | 31 | 7 |
| south | 24 | 35 | 34 | 8 |
| midwest | 23 | 35 | 37 | 5 |
| west | 24 | 38 | 36 | 2 |

NO. 29. Are you registered to vote in the United States? (IF YES) Are you
registered as a Democrat, Republican or Independent?

|  | NOT REGIS. | DEMOCRAT | REPUBLICAN | INDEPENDENT | DON'T KNOW |
|---|---|---|---|---|---|
| ALL | 14 | 41 | 25 | 17 | 3 |
| **PARTY** | | | | | |
| not regis | 100 | 0 | 0 | 0 | 0 |
| Democrat | 0 | 100 | 0 | 0 | 0 |
| Republican | 0 | 0 | 100 | 0 | 0 |
| Independent | 0 | 0 | 0 | 100 | 0 |
| **IDEOLOGY** | | | | | |
| liberal | 16 | 52 | 14 | 16 | 2 |
| moderate | 13 | 41 | 23 | 20 | 3 |
| conservative | 13 | 32 | 38 | 16 | 1 |
| **AGE** | | | | | |
| 18–34 | 19 | 38 | 21 | 20 | 3 |
| 35–49 | 12 | 40 | 25 | 20 | 3 |
| 50–59 | 12 | 43 | 28 | 15 | 2 |
| 60+ | 8 | 47 | 32 | 10 | 3 |
| **INCOME** | | | | | |
| <$7,000 | 29 | 33 | 26 | 10 | 2 |
| $ 7-$15,000 | 19 | 46 | 21 | 12 | 3 |
| $15-$25,000 | 11 | 43 | 24 | 20 | 2 |
| $25-$35,000 | 14 | 41 | 23 | 19 | 3 |
| $35,000+ | 8 | 37 | 32 | 21 | 2 |
| **EDUCATION** | | | | | |
| <high school | 20 | 45 | 21 | 11 | 3 |
| high school | 19 | 43 | 23 | 13 | 3 |
| some college | 10 | 41 | 22 | 24 | 3 |
| college | 9 | 34 | 36 | 20 | 2 |
| college+ | 6 | 44 | 28 | 20 | 2 |
| **UNION** | | | | | |
| union | 13 | 47 | 21 | 16 | 4 |
| non-union | 14 | 39 | 27 | 18 | 2 |
| **SEX** | | | | | |
| male | 15 | 37 | 23 | 21 | 3 |
| female | 13 | 45 | 27 | 14 | 2 |
| **REGION** | | | | | |
| northeast | 20 | 41 | 22 | 15 | 3 |
| south | 14 | 45 | 23 | 15 | 3 |
| midwest | 10 | 36 | 26 | 25 | 3 |
| west | 11 | 40 | 31 | 16 | 2 |

NO. 30. Are you or any member of your household a member of a union?

|  | UNION | NON-UNION | DON'T KNOW |
|---|---|---|---|
| ALL | 27 | 72 | 1 |
| **PARTY** | | | |
| not regis | 25 | 73 | 1 |
| Democrat | 30 | 69 | 1 |
| Republican | 22 | 78 | 0 |
| Independent | 24 | 76 | 0 |
| **IDEOLOGY** | | | |
| liberal | 32 | 67 | 1 |
| moderate | 26 | 74 | 1 |
| conservative | 23 | 77 | 0 |
| **AGE** | | | |
| 18–34 | 25 | 74 | 1 |
| 35–49 | 33 | 67 | 0 |
| 50–59 | 23 | 77 | 0 |
| 60+ | 24 | 74 | 2 |
| **INCOME** | | | |
| <$7,000 | 20 | 78 | 2 |
| $ 7-$15,000 | 23 | 77 | 0 |
| $15-$25,000 | 28 | 71 | 1 |
| $25-$35,000 | 32 | 68 | 0 |
| $35,000+ | 27 | 72 | 1 |
| **EDUCATION** | | | |
| <high school | 26 | 72 | 2 |
| high school | 29 | 70 | 1 |
| some college | 27 | 71 | 1 |
| college | 16 | 84 | 0 |
| college+ | 38 | 62 | 0 |
| **UNION** | | | |
| union | 100 | 0 | 0 |
| non-union | 0 | 100 | 0 |
| **SEX** | | | |
| male | 27 | 71 | 1 |
| female | 26 | 73 | 0 |
| **REGION** | | | |
| northeast | 28 | 71 | 1 |
| south | 18 | 81 | 1 |
| midwest | 34 | 66 | 1 |
| west | 30 | 70 | 0 |

NO. 31. Code sex.

|  | MALE | FEMALE |
|---|---|---|
| ALL | 49 | 51 |
| **PARTY** | | |
| not regis | 52 | 48 |
| Democrat | 45 | 55 |
| Republican | 46 | 54 |
| Independent | 60 | 40 |
| **IDEOLOGY** | | |
| liberal | 52 | 48 |
| moderate | 46 | 54 |
| conservative | 50 | 50 |
| **AGE** | | |
| 18–34 | 52 | 48 |
| 35–49 | 49 | 51 |
| 50–59 | 50 | 50 |
| 60+ | 43 | 57 |
| **INCOME** | | |
| <$7,000 | 36 | 64 |
| $ 7-$15,000 | 41 | 59 |
| $15-$25,000 | 53 | 47 |
| $25-$35,000 | 52 | 48 |
| $35,000+ | 57 | 43 |
| **EDUCATION** | | |
| <high school | 49 | 51 |
| high school | 42 | 58 |
| some college | 53 | 47 |
| college | 52 | 48 |
| college+ | 61 | 39 |
| **UNION** | | |
| union | 50 | 50 |
| non-union | 48 | 52 |
| **SEX** | | |
| male | 100 | 0 |
| female | 0 | 100 |
| **REGION** | | |
| northeast | 47 | 53 |
| south | 52 | 48 |
| midwest | 47 | 53 |
| west | 50 | 50 |

NO. 32. Region

| | NORTHEAST | SOUTH | MIDWEST | WEST |
|---|---|---|---|---|
| ALL | 28 | 29 | 20 | 22 |
| **PARTY** | | | | |
| not regis | 39 | 29 | 14 | 18 |
| Democrat | 29 | 32 | 18 | 21 |
| Republican | 25 | 27 | 21 | 27 |
| Independent | 24 | 25 | 30 | 21 |
| **IDEOLOGY** | | | | |
| liberal | 29 | 29 | 19 | 22 |
| moderate | 30 | 28 | 19 | 23 |
| conservative | 26 | 29 | 22 | 23 |
| **AGE** | | | | |
| 18–34 | 27 | 32 | 19 | 21 |
| 35–49 | 28 | 27 | 21 | 24 |
| 50–59 | 31 | 31 | 17 | 21 |
| 60+ | 29 | 26 | 24 | 20 |
| **INCOME** | | | | |
| <$7,000 | 30 | 26 | 17 | 27 |
| $ 7-$15,000 | 30 | 23 | 24 | 23 |
| $15-$25,000 | 28 | 31 | 20 | 21 |
| $25-$35,000 | 29 | 30 | 20 | 21 |
| $35,000+ | 26 | 32 | 19 | 23 |
| **EDUCATION** | | | | |
| <high school | 25 | 38 | 20 | 17 |
| high school | 32 | 26 | 24 | 18 |
| some college | 23 | 30 | 20 | 27 |
| college | 30 | 31 | 16 | 23 |
| college+ | 33 | 25 | 16 | 26 |
| **UNION** | | | | |
| union | 30 | 20 | 26 | 24 |
| non-union | 28 | 33 | 18 | 21 |
| **SEX** | | | | |
| male | 27 | 31 | 19 | 22 |
| female | 29 | 28 | 21 | 21 |
| **REGION** | | | | |
| northeast | 100 | 0 | 0 | 0 |
| south | 0 | 100 | 0 | 0 |
| midwest | 0 | 0 | 100 | 0 |
| west | 0 | 0 | 0 | 100 |

# APPENDIX 1

## RONALD REAGAN


November 7, 1980


TO :   MY FELLOW BOARD MEMBERS AND FRIENDS
       OF THE COMMITTEE ON THE PRESENT DANGER:


Four years ago, when the Committee was founded I was pleased
to accept an invitation to join you in your work.  The statements and studies of the Committee have had a wide national
impact, and I benefitted greatly from them.

When, in accordance with Committee policy, I was "furloughed"
last November upon my announcement for the Presidential race,
I accepted my new condition with good grace.  But I was kept
abreast of your work through frequent contact with many of you.

The work of the Committee on the present danger has certainly
helped to shape the national debate on important problems.
Your work will continue, because it is the embodiment of a
truly bipartisan approach to the formulation of national
security policy.

My pledge to develop a broad consensus in this vital field
is one which will have priority status in my Administration.

Since my status as a board member has now been decided
without my participation, I trust that whatever reservoir
of credit is due me will not be rapidly dissipated during
the years of my involuntary leave of absence.


        Sincerely,

RONALD REAGAN

329

Committee on
# THE PRESENT DANGER     1800 Massachusetts Avenue, N.W. • Washington, D.C. 20036 • 202/466-7444

1 June 1982

My dear Mr. President:

We--meaning the Executive Committee of the Committee on the
Present Danger--trust you will be receptive to our thoughts on your
Administration's approach to superpower negotiations on strategic arms.

First, we emphatically commend the primacy placed on reducing
the most destabilizing systems--ballistic missiles--and the corollary
intention to make destructive power itself, the key in computing
strategic ratios. These elements give grounds for hope of breaking free
from the fallacies that subverted SALT. We are with you 100 percent on
these central points.

There will be formidable pressures within this country and beyond
for hurrying along to agreement on any terms whatever as an escape from a
putative arms race. The other side will surely be tenacious of its
strategic edge purposefully built up at great cost to its economy. The
combination is certain to test U.S. resolve to arrive at terms worth having.

The comprehensive agreement to be striven for must--in contrast to
SALT--be so tightly drawn as to prevent the other side from piling up preponderance while professing to comply to the letter of equality. The central essence is equality of destructive power--throwweight, particularly
ICBM throwweight. Whatever the negotiating sequence, no contract--in our
view--should be firmed up without establishing a solution on that score.

We also feel concern about "deployed missiles" as units of account.
One wonders wherein they differ from launchers--the unsatisfactory units of
account in SALT II. In any event, the pertinent figure appears imprudently
low, for within a limit of 850 the other side might actually increase the
ratio of its retained warheads to the diminished number of military targets
in the U.S., thereby bettering its intimidatory first-strike capability.

In our review, which took place last Friday, the members felt
heartened by confidence in your own firm grasp of the basic issues of arms
control. They also asked me to convey to you their unanimous good wishes
for your safety and success in the upcoming mission to Europe.

Respectfully,

*Charls E. Walker*

Charls E. Walker
Chairman, Executive Committee

---

THE WHITE HOUSE

WASHINGTON


July 12, 1982


Dear Charls:

Thank you for your letter of June 1 on the subject
of START.  As we begin the START negotiations, I
greatly appreciate the support of the Committee
on the Present Danger.

I agree with you that our approach contains the
hope of breaking free from the fallacies that subverted SALT.  And, certainly, this will not be an
easy or quick negotiation.   It will test U.S.
resolve.  Because of this, the value of your
Committee's support will become even more essential in buttressing that resolve as time passes.

As you know, we have proposed a phased approach to
the START negotiations.  This approach encompasses
all the significant elements of the strategic
equation -- with significant reductions in ballistic missile warheads, the missiles themselves, and
throw weight in the initial phase and with further
reductions, possible inclusion of other systems,
and equal limits on throw weight, below current
U.S. levels, in the later phase.

Whether the results gained through this approach
will be implemented in a series of agreements or in
a single, comprehensive agreement will be a decision based upon the progress made, and the condition of ongoing negotiations, as the first phase
of the negotiations is completed.  Should we and
the Soviets choose to implement those elements
agreed to in the first phase while we continue to
negotiate other elements, we will certainly do so
in a manner so as not to prejudice other U.S. objectives.  We need not prematurely restrict our flexibility on this issue.

2

Let me take this opportunity to set the record
straight on the issue of throw weight.  Throw
weight is clearly a key indicator of missile
destructive power, and, we, in fact, recognize
and are handling the serious asymmetry in throw
weight.  While we will seek only indirect throw-
weight limits during the initial phase of START
negotiations, we will clearly stand by the principle that we expect the limits on missiles and
missile warheads to result in a very significant
reduction in the total missile throw weight in
the first phase.  Such a significant reduction
will permit us to seek equal throw-weight limits
directly from the Soviets in the later phase.

Turning to the subject of "deployed missiles,"
there is an association between "deployed missiles"
and launchers.  But the problem with SALT II was
that it limited "launchers" and nothing else.
In START, we intend to reduce the number of missiles, and the weapons they carry.  We intend to
cut ballistic missile warheads by roughly one-third,
and to limit ICBM warheads to no more than one-half
of the total number of ballistic missile warheads
permitted.  We also will reduce the number of
"deployed missiles" by roughly one-half.  Certainly,
even at this point, this differs greatly from simply
a launcher limit.  In addition, we intend to take
steps to limit and reduce "non-deployed" missiles,
to the extent that we can, in an effectively verifiable fashion.  It is missiles and the warheads
they carry, not launchers, that we are trying to
reduce.

Finally, I have reviewed the argument that at a
limit of 850 deployed missiles the Soviets may
actually increase the ratio of warheads to military
targets in the U.S., and I find it basically flawed.
First, the actual ratio implied by this argument is
that of weapons to U.S. silos, rather than to all
types of targets.  The argument fails to note that
we are taking action to ensure the survivability of
our ICBM force in the face of multiple attacking
weapons.  While this action does not depend on arms
reduction to be effective, it should complement

3

the reductions we have proposed.  Second, while the number of U.S. fixed silos may be reduced as a result of our proposed reductions, the great majority of military targets in the U.S. (e.g., airfields, $C^3$ facilities, logistics areas, conventional forces) will not be affected.  With fewer overall Soviet missile weapons available, more critical U.S. non-silo installations will thus go unstruck.  If, in fact, the Soviets would concentrate more of their missile weapons on our ICBM force, especially after U.S. ICBM basing has been improved, even more of the critical installations in the U.S. would survive.  Third, the significant reductions in missile throw weight we are seeking in our approach will serve to reduce the Soviet advantage.  Thus, the argument simply misses important aspects of the larger picture.

Once again, I thank you and your Committee for your good wishes.  We are going to have an interesting and challenging period ahead.  I am counting on your valuable support.

Sincerely,

Ronald Reagan

Mr. Charls E. Walker
Chairman, Executive Committee
The Committee on the Present Danger
1800 Massachusetts Avenue, N.W.
Washington, D.C.  20036

Committee on
# THE PRESENT DANGER® 905 Sixteenth Street N.W. • Washington, D.C. 20006 • 202/628-2409

Private

11 January 1984

Dear Mr. President:

Now that the Soviets have stalled the INF and START talks just as we enter a Presidential election year, we anticipate the following:

As the weeks and months pass, there will be increasing pressures within, and particularly outside, the Administration to "moderate" the U.S. negotiating stance, and to demonstrate to the Soviets that we are "serious" about arms control.

In short, there will be pressure on us to negotiate with ourselves while the Soviets look on in silent approval, offering nothing and collecting whatever concessions they can.

As you have long recognized, bad arms control agreements are worse than none at all. Equitable arms control agreements could play a part in insuring U.S. security -- but whether the Soviets are prepared to enter into equitable agreements is subject to doubt. Today, with the military balance precariously tipped against us, America's security is directly dependent on growing strength in our defense forces.

The United States cannot expect to win at a negotiating table what it has lost in the larger arena of political, economic and military influence. Similarly, we or the Soviets would be foolish to relinquish unilaterally at a negotiating table what had been dearly won in the larger arena.

To summarize: Achieving your objective of restoring the U.S.-Soviet military balance is indispensable to a sound U.S. negotiating stance -- calling for genuine equality in arms and rejecting the Soviet drive for what they call "equal security" but which really means Soviet superiority.

This is the only path to prudent arms control agreements and, more importantly, to overall U.S. security.

In this, we support you, publicly and privately, one hundred percent.

Sincerely,

Charls E. Walker
Chairman, Executive Committee

THE WHITE HOUSE

WASHINGTON

February 16, 1984

Dear Mr. Walker:

As we enter this next year, I remain as committed
as ever to pursuing prudent, equitable and
verifiable arms control agreements which would
significantly reduce the nuclear arsenals on both
sides.  The series of initiatives that the U.S.
delegation has placed on the negotiating table in
Geneva over the last three years clearly indicates
to the Soviets that we are serious in that pursuit.
As your letter correctly notes, it was the Soviet
Union, not the United States, that stalled both the
START and INF negotiations.

I agree that as a result of continued Soviet
intransigence, we will face increasing pressures
to make progress in nuclear arms control.  We will
certainly leave no stone unturned in this effort.
However, I believe that we can protect ourselves
from the dangers cited in your letter by keeping
foremost in mind that the purpose of our arms
control policy is to ensure overall U.S. security
even as we seek to enhance stability and to reduce
the risks posed by nuclear forces.

Arms control is an important instrument of U.S.
policy, but it is not an end in itself.  As we
explore ways of pursuing effective arms control,
we will continue to measure each initiative we
consider in light of our fundamental goals of
security and stability.  We will thereby assure
the path to both prudent arms control and overall
U.S. security referred to in your letter.

Thank you for your timely and thoughtful letter and
for the valuable support you and the Committee on
the Present Danger have provided in the past.  We
will count on your invaluable support in the
future.

Sincerely,

*Ronald Reagan*

Mr. Charls E. Walker
Chairman, Executive Committee
Committee on the Present Danger
905 Sixteenth Street, N.W.
Washington, D.C.  20006

# APPENDIX 2

# U.S. MEDIA REACTION TO
# THE COMMITTEE
# ON THE PRESENT DANGER

"The Committee on the Present Danger has emerged as the most widely noticed and quoted of the prospective anti-SALT groups."

Morton Kondracke, *The New Republic*, 17 December 1977.


"The non-partisan Committee on the Present Danger has become an unofficial spokesman for the President's loyal opposition."

*The San Diego Union*, 1978


"In less than two years, the Committee on the Present Danger has had a profound impact on the national security debate in this country."

Stu Cohen, *The Phoenix*, Boston, 1978


"The Committee on the Present Danger has been effective because it has mobilized public opinion behind its arguments."

Sidney Lens, *The Progressive*, 1978


"The CPD has found the glue that can, and has, brought together the best minds from the new right, the old left, big labor, the Democrats, Republicans and independents. . . . You can't put a label on them."

*News World Monthly*, New York, New York, April 1979.

"The Committee on the Present Danger (is a name that)
rapidly becomes more relevant."

Pine Bluff, Arkansas, *Commercial*, 29 April 1979

"One of the private groups that is most influential
at the moment in the debate over national policy is the Committee
on the Present Danger."

St. Petersburg, Florida, *Times*, 23 July 1979

"What the Committee on the Present Danger understands,
whereas Carter apparently does not, is that ideology is
central to the successful exercise of political power. By preserving
its basis in the American version of the social-democratic
experience, by waging a campaign for public support
with undiminished enthusiasm, and by walking the narrow line
between insider and outsider status, the Committee has shown
a political acumen that enables it to maintain influence beyond
the point of its historical glory."

"Resurgent Cold War Ideology: The Case of the Committee
on the Present Danger," Alan Wolfe and Jerry Sanders,
Stanford University Press, 1979, page 75.

". . . the most important organization opposing SALT
(is) the Committee on the Present Danger."

William Sweet, syndicated by Editorial Research Reports, 1979.

"The Committee on the Present Danger (is) unusual and
sophisticated . . . consisting of highly knowledgeable academics
and former government experts who have made powerful critiques
of SALT II and American defense policies."

Saul Friedman, syndicated by Knight-Ridder News Service, 1979.

"If the treaty is defeated, it will be due to the indefatigably and
deeply responsible labors of . . . Paul Nitze and Eugene Rostow
. . . (who) have been the heart and soul of the Committee
on the Present Danger."

John Chamberlain, syndicated columnist, 1979.

"It seems clear that the drumfire of SALT criticism
generated by such commentators as Paul Nitze and the

Committee on the Present Danger had a stiffening effect on
the administration's negotiating position."

James L. Dornan, Jr., Washington Quarterly Magazine, 1979.


". . . The Committee on the Present Danger . . . includes
prominent Democrats and Republicans, old-line liberals, labor
leaders, conservatives, industrialists, and veterans of past
administrations of both parties."

William Ringle, syndicated by Gannett News Service, 1979.


"The Committee could be called the brains behind the opposition
(to SALT II). While it does not lobby, it kindles the fires of those
who do with its detailed analyses of strategic issues."

Congressional Quarterly Weekly Report, 1979.


"The Committee on the Present Danger has done its
work most effectively. The public opinion surveys and the
informed judgment of political professionals agree that the country
is clearly uneasy about the United States' military strength
relative to that of the Soviet Union."

Jack Germond and Jules Witcover,
syndicated by *Washington Star*, 1979.


"The most prominent group against the (SALT II) agreement
is the Committee on the Present Danger, a Washington-based
coalition of former defense officials, high-level government
officers and physicists who are concerned about what they
perceive as declining U.S. strength."

Arnold Abrams, *Newsday*, Long Island, New York, 1979.


"Views voiced only yesterday by the 'alarmists' and
'extremists' of the Committee on the Present Danger have
suddenly acquired respectability."

Walter Laqueur, "Containment for the '80's,"
*Commentary*, p. 33, October 1980.


"Main credit for . . . marshaling evidence to undercut
the Administration's case for SALT II belongs to
the Committee on the Present Danger."

Editorial, "Applause, Please,"
*National Review*, November 28, 1980.

". . . The Committee on the Present Danger (is) a group of
American thinkers who have proven remarkably prescient about
the dangers of Soviet power . . ."

"Message to Moscow," *Pine Bluff Commercial*,
Pine Bluff, Arkansas, December 2, 1980.

"(Mr. Reagan) was already convinced of the military imbalance
through his association with the Committee on the Present
Danger, whose directors and members have had long first-hand
experience in defense, arms control and foreign policy."

Syndicated columnist Roscoe Drummond,
Tulsa, Oklahoma, *World*, December 17, 1980.

"The world view of the Committee on the Present Danger
(a number of whose members now occupy high posts in the
Reagan Administration) now appears to be national policy."

Richard J. Barnet, "A Reporter At Large: The Search for National
Security," p. 103, *The New Yorker*, April 27, 1981.

"Within four years, the Committee fought three major battles with
the pro-detente forces in two Administrations, and in the process
helped to change dramatically the views that Americans held
about the Russians and about themselves."

Richard J. Barnet, "A Reporter at Large: The Search for National
Security," p. 99, *The New Yorker*, April 27, 1981.

"They are developing the new 'grand strategy'
they felt was missing during the Carter Administration."

Curtis Wilkie, Boston, Massachusetts Globe staff,
in Pittsburgh, Pennsylvania, *Press*, May 3, 1981.

"The personnel and perspective of the Committee now are
represented amply on the Reagan foreign-policy team. Reagan
himself belonged to the 150-member committee, and 23 other
members now hold top positions in his Administration. The list
reads like a partial Who's Who of the Reagan Administration."

Robert Scheer, *Los Angeles Times*, September 28, 1981.

"It was the Committee on the Present Danger that took the lead in warning that the Soviets were trying to gain military superiority."

*Chicago Tribune*, January 20, 1982.


"It is a band of learned patriots—a nonprofit, nonpartisan foundation—which for years has evangelized for the nation's common defense."

Holmes Alexander, Frederick, Maryland, *Post*, May 12, 1982.


"(The Committee on the Present Danger is) . . . an influential arms monitoring committee, of which President Reagan was once an active member."

United Press International, June 30, 1982.


"A high-powered organization, of which President Reagan was a founding member in 1976. . . . The Committee, which claimed a sturdy independence throughout the time it berated the Carter administration's military effort, demonstrated its nonpartisan politics in its attack on the Reagan program."

Charles Corddry, *Baltimore Sun*, July 4, 1982.


"(The Committee on the Present Danger is) the galaxy wherein America's chief civilian defense experts gleam."

Dallas *Morning News*, November 11, 1982.


"(The Committee on the Present Danger is) a private organization composed of some of the nation's most respected defense experts, Democrats and Republicans."

Richmond, Virginia, *Times-Dispatch*, November 21, 1982.


"The Committee's main themes . . . all showed up predominantly in the major foreign policy pronouncements of candidates Reagan and Bush, right through their occupancy of the White House and its adjacent Executive Office Building. The origins of Administration policy can be found in the Committee's founding statement."

"With Enough Shovels: Reagan, Bush & Nuclear War," Robert Scheer, Random House, New York, 1982, page 48.

"Founded in 1976 to trumpet a call to arms against the growing military might of the Soviet Union, the Committee on the Present Danger has found a comforting echo in the rhetoric of Ronald Reagan . . . the group's imprint on the Reagan Administration is unmistakeable and probably unprecedented."

"Reagan's Ruling Class," Ronald Brownstein and Nina Easton, The Presidential Accountability Group (Ralph Nader), Washington, D.C., pages 532–33, 1982.

"The Committee on the Present Danger has taken control of American national security policy. A few months after the Reagan Administration took office . . . a member of the National Security Council staff (wrote): 'I might suggest that you consult recent literature of the Committee on the Present Danger for a cogent presentation of the view of our situation that is the basis of the fundamental approach of this Administration.' "

"Russian Roulette: The Superpower Game," Arthur Macy Cox, Times Books, New York, 1982.

"(The Committee on the Present Danger is) a group dedicated to increasing United States military might."

*New York Times*, January 13, 1983.

"The bipartisan organization is committed to strengthening U.S. forces in the face of increased Soviet power."

*Baltimore Sun*, January 14, 1983.

"(The Committee on the Present Danger is) a group of Republicans and Democrats who distrusted the Soviets and questioned whether any arms control treaty would be verifiable."

Providence, Rhode Island, *Bulletin*, January 14, 1983.

"The group has pushed the 'window of vulnerability' argument that U.S. defense spending has been inadequate to preserve this country's strategic nuclear deterrent or to provide adequate general purpose forces."

Seattle, Washington, *Post-Intelligencer,*, January 14, 1983.

"(The Committee on the Present Danger is) a bipartisan group committed to a stronger U.S. defense."

Houston, Texas, *Post*, January 16, 1983.

" 'With Enough Shovels: Reagan, Bush and Nuclear War,' by
Robert Scheer: Scheer pulls no punches in advancing his theory
that the present administration is the puppet of a conspiracy called
the Committee on the Present Danger, which he charges with
'seizure of state power.' "

Book review by Richard Sincere,
*Washington Times*, February 4, 1983.


"The Committee on the Present Danger, . . .
became the best-known and most effective of the groups
campaigning against the SALT II treaty."

*The New Yorker*, February 28, 1983.


"The highly influential and authoritative Committee
on the Present Danger . . ."

*Air Force Magazine*, February 1983.


"Figures fail to tell the complete story of the CPD's influence
on the outcome of the foreign policy debate, however.
Because of the prestige of its membership the Committee had a
catalytic effect on other elite organizations and interest groups
who committed resources of their own to the mobilization
against SALT II, and detente in general."

"Empire at Bay: Containment Strategies and American Politics at
the Crossroads," Jerry W. Saunders, World Policy Paper No. 25,
World Policy Institute, New York, 1983, page 13.

*       *   *   *   *   *   *   *   *   *   *


A Dissenting Note from the John Birch Society:

"More than twenty members of this suspicious group
are now part of the Reagan Administration. The President
himself held membership in Present Danger before
his election. His appointments . . . from its ranks may
mean that the Committee on the Present Danger is itself a
present danger to the United States."

1981

# APPENDIX 3

# FOREIGN PRESS REACTION TO THE COMMITTEE ON THE PRESENT DANGER

"The opposition, led by a coalition of former officials called the Committee on the Present Danger, has certainly scored many points in the past year, winning much support in Congress."

Patrick Brogan, *The Times*, London, England, June 2, 1978.

"One of the most influential groups opposing the (SALT II) treaty—and one which may affect the votes of many Senators when the issue gets to that stage—is the 'Committee on the Present Danger.' "

Nouvelles Atlantiques, Brussels, Belgium, July 11, 1979.

"At its heart there is a body called the Committee on the Present Danger which . . . has produced the best technical analysis of SALT 2's flaw."

David Buchan, *Financial Times*, London and Frankfurt, 1979.

"The Committee exploited this favorable environment with considerable skill . . . it concentrated its energies on shaping the perceptions of American elites in a position to lead opinion and influence executive and legislative decision makers. . . . This activity has generated enough press to fill four separate anthologies of articles that describe the Committee's views. . . . To understand why the 1980's will almost certainly be a decade of major expansion of American military power, one must look at how the issues have been defined and the agenda presented. In this process, without controlling large blocs of votes in the Congress, the Committee has played a very important role."

"The United States and the Present Danger," Samuel F. Wells, Jr., *Journal of Strategic Studies*, London, England, March 1981.

"The Committee . . . has functioned since 1976 as the leading proponent of a stronger military posture for the United States."

"The United States and the Present Danger," p. 60, *The Journal of Strategic Studies*, London, England, Vol. 4, No. 1, March 1981.


"(Mr. Reagan) has gathered into his administration all the best and brightest of the Committee on the Present Danger which so effectively scuppered the SALT 2 treaty in Congress."

*The Economist*, November 28, 1981.


\* \* \* \* \* \* \* \* \* \*


## The View From Moscow . . .


### "Operation 'Undermining' "

Moscow, Nov. 11, 1977, Sovetskaya Rossiya—The lastest lethal brainchild of the U.S. military-industrial complex has the code name "MX."

But why is it necessary to create the MX missiles when the United States already possesses an enormous nuclear missile arsenal? It emerges that the missiles are designed to render the U.S. strategic forces "far less vulnerable." That, in any case, is the explanation given by the Pentagon chief, Defense Secretary H. Brown.

Members of the ultrarightwing "Committee on the Present Danger" to which the most virulent opponents of an improvement in Soviet-U.S. relations belong, also cite this utterly hackneyed "argument." The committee has even distributed a special report on the MX. "The United States must demonstrate that it is adhering firmly to a course of action aimed at defending its strategic interests"—this overtly provocative appeal is contained in the report.

The lobbyists of the U.S. military-industrial complex do not conceal the fact that they are seeking to wreck the Soviet-U.S. talks, at which a definite change for the better has occurred. It is no accident that P. Nitze, one of the leaders of the notorious "Committee on Present Danger," admitted that the creation of the MX missiles could become the "next important problem" in the Soviet-U.S. dialog.

A. Mozgovoy


### "Lying Fantasies and Sober Reflection: What Is Behind the Anti-Soviet Campaign in the United States?

Moscow, March 2, 1978, Za Rubezhom—In the last few months the opponents of the relaxation of international tension, the ending of the arms race and the transition to effective disarmament, have mounted a fierce offensive in the United States aimed, in particular, at wrecking the talks being held between the USSR and the United States on concluding a new strategic arms limitation agreement. Bringing into play the totally false myth of the "growing Soviet military threat," "hawks" of every stripe are making desperate attempts to sow mistrust and hostility toward the Soviet Union, to stir up Americans against the USSR and to make them pay again and again for the arms race in fear of the military threat.

The potential of detente's opponents should not be underestimated. Thus the "Committee on the Present Danger," headed by former Deputy Defense Secretary Paul Nitze, includes former diplomats, prominent lawyers, scientists, high-ranking military men and businessmen. As NEW REPUBLIC notes, this committee has mounted an "offensive against the strategic arms limitation agreement. This offensive is well financed, broad-based, marked by inventiveness and subtlety and often profoundly thought-out."

G. Shiskin

### "Paul Nitze, the War Hawk"

Moscow, March 30, 1978, TASS—TASS commentator Ivan Ablamov writes: An especially annoying voice in the chorus of American "war hawks," who oppose detente in the military field in general and any joint Soviet-American strategic arms limitation measures in particular, is that of Paul Nitze, former U.S. assistant secretary of defense. A few days ago he made a statement again, attacking the very possibility of achieving a new Soviet-American strategic arms limitation agreement. He claims that it would be better for the United States not to have any agreement on SALT than to agree with the outlines of what is emerging in the course of the present talks.

Why is the "war hawk" displeased with these talks? First of all because they rest on the principle of strategic parity, of approximate parity of the forces between the USA and the USSR, while one of the former Pentagon chiefs is dreaming of U.S. "nuclear supremacy" over the Soviet Union.

In P. Nitze's pronouncements one hears nostalgia for the old times which are never to return. His statements reflect the reluctance of certain circles in the USA to reckon with the existing realities. Nitze believes that the United States can do without a strategic arms limitation agreement. And this is passed off as a manifestation of concern for the security of the USA! But who does not know what the breakdown of an agreement on SALT would lead to? It would open the way to new spirals of the arms race, to the growth of arms spending, to the spread of nuclear arms, it would destabilize the strategic situation, worsen political relations and, in the final account, increase the danger of war.

The "war hawk" does not conceal that such a development of events would suit his interests. He sees "future security" of the USA in an accelerated deployment of the Pentagon-suggested systems of such arms as cruise missiles and mobile missiles.

### "In the Trenches of the Cold War"

Moscow, July 28, 1978, Krasnaya Zvezda—"To halt the arms race, insure progress toward the reduction and ultimately the elimination of the threat of a thermonuclear catastrophe—that is the main problem now on the agenda of our life. It is precisely here, on this salient, that the fundamental question is being resolved of how the international situation will develop in the future and it is precisely here that the keenest struggle is now developing." So said Leonid Ilich Brezhnev when he spoke to Pacific Fleet sailors during his tour of Siberia and the Far East.

The strategic arms limitation (SALT) agreement is a very important part of the problem mentioned by L. I. Brezhnev. For several years now it has been the subject of the Soviet-U.S. talks at all levels, including summit level. It is also the subject of an acute struggle between the supporters and opponents of detente in the United States.

While for people of good will in the USSR, the United States and other countries of the world the SALT agreement signifies a breakthrough on the path toward real military detente and ultimately the elimination of the danger of thermonuclear war, for the military-industrial complex the agreement threatens to strike at its most sensitive spot—its millions and billions of income.

That is why the more the distance between the Soviet and U.S. positions on the SALT issue is reduced, the fiercer and more organized the resistance of the agreement's enemies becomes. In recent years U.S. reaction has frequently made attempts to hastily construct a united front of opponents of detente and disarmament. In 1975 the "Citizens for America's Survival" organization was created in Washington.

The notorious "Operation Liberty" organization emerged at the same time but it had no success. A year later a new attempt was made to unite the knights of the arms race. The so-called "Committee on the Present Danger" appeared which included very active and influential reactionaries and numbered 141 members. The "committee" succeeded in rallying around itself many militarist, anti-Soviet and anticommunist organizations which had existed previously. Thus retired General A. Goodpaster, former supreme commander in chief of the NATO allied armed forces in Europe and a member of the "committee," is co-chairman of the national strategy committee of the "U.S. Security Council"—an influential organization which stands guard over the interests of the military-industrial complex. Madam Clare Boothe Luce, widow of the owner of the Time-Life magazine company and former U.S. ambassador to Italy, belongs to the leading organs of the above-mentioned U.S. Security Council and the related "Institute of U.S. Strategy."

The "committee" is linked with many other reactionary organizations, including on the basis of personal contact by eminent members like Generals M. Ridgway and L. Lemnitzer, two former NATO commanders in chief; former Deputy Defense Secretaries P. Nitze and D. Packard; former Secretary of State D. Rusk and his former deputy E. Rostow; L. Kirkland, secretary and treasurer of the AFL-CIO; retired General M. Taylor and others.

The "committee" conducts independent operations against detente and the SALT agreement and coordinates the actions of the organizations which side with it. The "Committee's" members inspire the publication of anti-Soviet articles in newspapers and journals, search out authors of books who are prepared, for a suitable fee, to prove what cannot be proved, organize television debates, and hold pseudo-scientific conferences and mass meetings. All this is to blow up the Soviet "military threat" again and again, to show that in the SALT talks the U.S. side has allegedly embarked on one-sided concessions, and to link the attainment of an agreement with problems which have nothing to do with the disarmament issue ("human rights," the military conflict in the region of the Horn of Africa, and events in Zaire).

B. Karpovich

### "Plot Against Detente"
(Excerpts from 7,000-Word Article)

Moscow, June 1978, SSHA: Ekonomika, Politika, Ideologiya—Since November 1976 a private organization has been operating in the United States, all of the efforts of which have been aimed at a single goal: To impede the improvement of Soviet-American relations and to prevent the further progress of international detente.

Since the organization's members include extremely influential "liberal" politicians and military figures and is backed up by strong business groups, it cannot be regarded as one of the usual anti-Soviet and anti-communist groups which spring up with such frequency in the United States. This is an organization of the so-called "elite," the members of which have for decades had direct access to the State Department, the Pentagon and the National Security Council—that is, to the chief institutions making U.S. foreign policy. As a rule, all of these persons occupied responsible posts in these agencies at one time or another, particularly during the years of the cold war in the Truman and Eisenhower administrations. At the same time, almost all of them have been either directly or indirectly connected for several years with the heads of the overseas military-industrial complex. The organization obviously has sizable financial resources at its disposal and has recently been waging an uninterrupted anti-Soviet campaign in America.

We are referring to the "Committee on the Present Danger" (CPD), established in Washington on 10 November 1976 . . .

Since that time, CPD activities have created such a stir that its real plans are no mystery. This is a real plot against the policy of peaceful coexistence.

We must consider the time and circumstances of this organization's birth. This was a week after the presidential election had been held in the United States and a change of government was coming in Washington. Power would be assumed by new people, some of whom were regarded in anti-Soviet circles as insufficiently militant and, possibly, even supporters of detente. Right wing groups grew alarmed. The creation of the CPD was something like a warning to the White House on their part. The new masters in Washington were unequivocally informed that the opponents of detente were not dozing and would come into sight if necessary.

This happened almost immediately. Although, as we know, there was no real change in the course of American diplomacy, the CPD began to carry out feverish activity. By 12 January 1977 the committee had already issued a dramatic—we could say, hysterical—announcement which stated: "Our nation has entered a time of danger, and this danger is constantly growing. . . . The very survival of our nation might be threatened." Once again the Soviet Union, which favors detente and disarmament, was accused of attempts to "establish world domination from a single center in Moscow" and even of the intention to deliver the "first nuclear strike." The announcement also contained a categorical demand that Washington "change the course of policy reject the 'illusory detente' and increase military expenditures, primarily on 'research and experimental design' "—that is, on the manufacture of the latest types of weapons of mass destruction.

This was the first volley. Later, during all of 1977 and the beginning of this year, the Committee on the Present Danger continued to take advantage of every opportunity and any excuse to interfere in Soviet-American relations and to prevent the convergence of the views of the two great powers on debatable issues. This was done—and is being done—in various ways. The CPD only addresses the general public after everything possible has been done behind the scenes to poison public opinion and throw ruling circles into a panic.

For example, allegedly "documented" data on Soviet weapons are periodically published; these invariably suggest a single conclusion: The United States is becoming weaker than the Soviet Union, a catastrophe lies ahead and the only solution is a substantial increase in Pentagon funds. Some of these "documents" would be the envy of Baron Munchausen.

The logic of the authors of one of these, which was compiled by some kind of secret "Group B," was, for example, so implausible that the Carter Administration rejected its conclusions after a "detailed study" of the material. Nonetheless, the stir caused by the "Group B" report has not died down . . .

Brochures containing the same kind of allegations are also distributed, stating that the purpose of the CPD is to "alert Americans" and "open their eyes" to the Soviet threat. Just as in the 1920's and 1930's, the American citizens are systematically being frightened. Since this time, however, the propaganda is coming directly from former high-level officials, its sting is even most poisonous in some cases.

Another method used by the CPD consists in attempting to torpedo Soviet-American relations by exerting pressure directly on members of Congress. At a specific time, secret information about negotiations is suddenly "leaked." Soon afterward, some press organs begin printing reports alleging that the American Government is making impermissible concessions to the Soviet Union and is even preparing to "surrender" to it. "Information evenings" are immediately organized, at which right-wing figures, "experts on disarmament" and "Sovietology," try to prove the unacceptability of an agreement with the USSR and the need to "talk to the Russians only from a position of strength." Later it is learned that the "secret information" came from top-level officials closely associated with the CPD . . .

Who are the members of the Committee on the Present Danger?

The Americans are being assured that all of its members, 141 persons (most of whom are retired statesmen and still active businessmen), are people with many years of experience and scrupulously honest individuals who only want to warn their nation of the imminent danger. They allegedly know more about the state of affairs than others: Each member once occupied a top-level, key post and each—it goes without saying—spent many years studying Soviet policy at first hand. Motivated, they say, by purely patriotic feelings, these individuals wish to acquaint America and the entire world with the information at their disposal and with the conclusions they have drawn from it. What could be more reasonable or natural?

This is how the rightest press in the United States depicts the founders of the CPD. But do these people represent only themselves? Are they merely retired American officials and nothing more? Or are there definite keys that fit this entire group and its intentions? It would certainly be easy to find the keys that fit.

The head of the CPD executive committee is Eugene Rostow, who was assistant secretary of state in the 1960's. He is not a very well-known man. It is possible, however, that he is the front for an incomparably more influential figure, his brother Walter Rostow. In the Johnson Administration, W. Rostow was the actual head ("executive secretary") of the National Security Council before this he was the head of the State Department planning staff, and before this he worked for the OSS, the American intelligence service succeeded by the CIA. This is a completely well-defined figure . . .

According to reports in the American press, Eugene Rostow worked on the creation of the CPD for 5 months and he was encouraged to do this by none other than former U.S. Secretary of Defense Schlesinger, whose own name, however, was missing from the committee roster (evidently in the expectation of a place in the Carter Administration, which subsequently was offered to him). There is no doubt in Washington that it was precisely Schlesinger who was the "moving spirit" behind the CPD. According to E. Rostow himself, the creation of the committee grew out of conversations with Schlesinger when he was still head of the Pentagon. Schlesinger's extremely anti-Soviet views are no secret to anyone. When he headed the Department of Defense, he did everything to escalate the arms race and subvert the Soviet-American talks . . .

The formal leadership of the committee is in the hands of three men, its chairmen. One of them is former Deputy Secretary of Defense David Packard. . . . Since 1972 David Packard has been retired. But he has not left the scene of the defense business. And he is not the only one. Another CPD co-chairman is Henry H. Fowler, former American secretary of the Treasury. He is also far from a mere statesman.

Fowler is now also retired, but only as a government official. As a banker, with an interest in the arms race—or, in other words, in military superprofits—he is at his post. The fact that Fowler shares the chairmanship of the Committee on the Present Danger with Packard is therefore no coincidence. In one way or another, in one form or another, money, and not merely political views or personal ability, has explained much in the careers of all of these individuals. We can examine the facts from any standpoint but this conclusion is inescapable. Who is Paul Nitze, the leading member of the Committee on the Present Danger and chairman of "policy studies" of the committee? This is a figure from the same circles as the Rostow brothers.

Here again, however, we are not referring only to a top-level government official in retirement . . .

It must be said that this retired American official from the Washington elite has also remained true to himself. At the end of the 1970's he is still thinking in terms of categories of the 1940's and 1950's and evidently cannot and will not change. Detente is apparently more frightening to individuals like these than a third world war.

A dependence on big business magnates with their tremendous military-industrial capital investments actually determines his actions as well . . .

Some mention should also be made of another influential member of the Committee on the Present Danger—L. Kirkland, the third co-chairman of the organization. His name is also missing from the roster of the military-industrial monopolies; he has another sphere of activity. Kirkland is neither a businessman nor a top-level official; he is the secretary and—even more important—the treasurer of the American labor organization, the AFL-CIO, regarded there as second in command to Meany. A right-wing labor boss like Kirkland is apparently needed by figures in the military-industrial complex as a front. In this respect, he is probably just as valuable as Colby to the champions of a new cold war.

Newswoman Clare Luce, who caused quite a sensation during the cold war, is the widow of the man who controlled the largest publishing monopoly, publishing TIME and FORTUNE, and also a member of the CPD. She is necessary to this organization in a different capacity: as an expert on certain propaganda methods.

We have listed some of the civilian representatives of the American military-industrial complex here. We cannot, however, ignore the military figures in this same circle; the former cannot get along without the latter, just as the latter need the former . . .

Four generals were named as CPD members in the American press. Three of them—M. Ridgway, L. Lemnitzer and A. Goodpaster—are alike in one respect. Each was at one time the supreme allied commander of NATO forces in Europe and each persistently demanded a maximum buildup of armaments in this post. Now all of them are retired, but General Ridgway, for example, has become a director of Colt Industries, a company which manufactures costly equipment for missiles in addition to conventional weapons. He also heads the Institute of Industrial Studies founded by the billionaire Mellons . . .

The last of the military men named as members of the CPD, Admiral E. Zumwalt occupied a post in the Pentagon's division for international "security" affairs. As yet, he has not received his share of the profits of the military-industrial complex in the form of an official seat on the board of a particular concern, although Wall Street is already discussing his unofficial ties with this circle. In any case, he is not wasting his time. In June 1977 Admiral Zumwalt went to Peking for some unknown reason: Was he following Schlesinger's example and trying to establish direct contact between the millionaires on the Committee on the Present Danger and the Maoists? . . .

One of the important determining factors in policy for Senator Henry Jackson, just as for the dignitary-businessmen Nitze and Fowler, General Ridgway, Admiral Zumwalt and other leading members of the Committee on the Present Danger, is the superprofits that can be derived from the production of weapons of mass destruction.

Another important fact should also be mentioned. The members of the CPD are not only influential in themselves or because of their influence in the top levels of the bourgeois parties and their contacts with the military-industrial complex; their relations with key political and military agencies in the American Government, particularly the most important of these—the President's National Security Council (NSC)—are of equal importance. All decisions on U.S. domestic and foreign policy are first made by this council and are only later and to some extent submitted to Congress for its approval.

There is every reason to believe that the Committee on the Present Danger has much in common with the staff of the National Security Council. As we mentioned above, banker Fowler was one of its full members in the 1950's, even though he did not occupy any kind of government post at that time. Walt Rostow was the executive secretary of the council and its actual head; Nitze and Generals Taylor, Ridgway, Lemnitzer and Goodpaster were directly associated with it. These old contacts are obviously the reason for the ease with which the CPD now learns Washington's state secrets.

Reports in the American press have indicated that CPD associates and supporters also include some of the members of the Senate and House committees and subcommittees concerned with questions of military policy. Therefore, its ties extend to the executive and legislative branches.

Naturally, not all persons connected with military-industrial corporations should be considered unconditional supporters of a revival of the cold war. They also include stockholders in these corporations who simultaneously have no objection to trade in civilian industrial commodities with the socialist countries and, for this reason, talk about peaceful coexistence. The interests of precisely this group are reflected in the Committee on the Present Danger. This is why any kind of secret coordination of positions by the CPD and the NSC staff on any particular issue might have a genuinely serious effect on U.S. policy.

This is intensified by the fact that the Committee on the Present Danger has influential allies outside the United States. These are not limited to the staff of the State Department, CIA and NATO in Western Europe. The close ties of several members of the CPD to the semisecret international organization, operating under the name of the "Bilderberg Club" and numbering prominent Western European bourgeois politicians and big business magnates among its members, are quite obvious.

The "club" does not conceal the fact that joint policy is discussed at its annual meetings and is then proposed to the governments of the nations concerned. In recent years, the United States has been represented at meetings of the club by such "stars" of the CPD as Nitze, Rusk, Lemnitzer, Goodpaster, Zumwalt and Senator Jackson. The familiarity of these names could hardly be a coincidence. Many say that the Committee on the Present Danger in the United States and the Bilderberg Club in Western Europe are partners working toward the same goal . . .

The Western powers are divided by deep-seated economic and political conflicts. Experience has already shown, however, that this does not prevent forces on the extreme right in these countries from working together against detente. While an entire galaxy of overseas military-industrial corporations can be found behind the screen of the CPD, the outlines of military concerns in the FRG, England, France and other states can be seen just as clearly behind the facade of the Bilderberg Club. Despite existing conflicts, all these groups are united by two motives: anticommunism and the desire to continue the arms race at any cost. This is why accomplices of the American Committee on the Present Danger can now be found in all of the major countries of the capitalist world.

Another fact is also interesting. The announcement of the Committee on the Present Danger of 12 January 1977 contained the following phrase: "If we continue to flow with the current (in the direction of detente—E. G.) . . . the possibility of our convergence with China will disappear." This is quite unequivocal. The same right-wing American circles which categorically object to the improvement of Soviet-American relations are shamelessly advocating a bargain with Maoist China. Apparently, the inspired of the CPD are not traveling to Peking to no purpose. The close ties between these two forces are repeatedly corroborated.

We cannot deny that the American reactionaries' plot against detente has been organized on a broad scale. The conspirators have extensive contacts and tremendous resources at their disposal. Apparently, they themselves are firmly convinced of the success of their maneuvers. We can be confident that they will not miss a single opportunity to undermine detente in the future. The Committee on the Present Danger and the circles backing it up indisputably represent a serious threat to the cause of peace . . .

In recent months, this organization has waged an even more intense campaign against detente. This has apparently been caused by the fear that new practical possibilities for the improvement of Soviet-American relations exist. For example, CPD leaders said at a meeting of the American Foreign Policy Association in March of this year that there was no possibility of military detente between the USSR and the United States. At the same meeting, they demanded that the U.S. Government immediately begin the production of the neutron bomb.

The people backing up the Committee on the Present Danger believe that they are quite strong. As we have already said, they do have resources and contacts, and both of these can even be called abundant. Nonetheless, if we look at the international situation as a whole, the forces supporting detente   are still incomparably stronger than its enemies. Hundreds of millions of people throughout the world now have a clearer understanding than ever before that the desperate game with weapons of mass destruction can lead to the most horrible catastrophe in the history of mankind.

Ernst Henry

". . . the U.S. military-industrial complex and the American hawks who have built their nest in the Committee on the Present Danger (are) the forces that are not fully pleased with the White House and that demand new sacrifices for the sake of the arms race."

Vitali Kobysh,<br>
Novosti, Moscow,<br>
reprinted by the Baltimore Sun, 1978.

Dangerous Blasts Against Detente . . . Drawing of V. Fomichev

"Anti-Soviets from among American retired officials, united in the
so-called 'Committee on the Present Danger,' strenuously spread
the myth about the imaginary Soviet threat."

Cartoon caption,
V. Formichev, *Pravda*,
February 10, 1979.


"Most action is by the so-called 'Committee on the Present
Danger' . . . (which) possesses a pathologically deformed
imagination regarding the Soviet Union's true intentions."

(Leading Moscow Political Journal), 1979.


"The notorious Committee on the Present Danger
launched a vicious campaign to dissuade Senators
from ratifying the (SALT II) treaty."

Radio Moscow, January 13, 1983.


## "ATTENTION, HAWKS!"

Moscow, January 1983, *Kommunist*—Today political "hawks" are in
fashion in Washington. This term usually applies to officials whose
outlook and practical activities are somewhat similar to the militant
representatives of the feathered species. However, it is not merely a
question of individual specimens. Many U.S. political organizations
and institutions claim today that it is precisely they, through their
ideas and representatives, who laid the foundations for and accomplished a most dangerous turn in the international arena from détente
to a new aggravation of tension. However, such organizations and
institutions are clearly overestimating their possibilities and role in
unseemly matters by claiming authorship of the aggressive and militaristic course taken by Washington, which is threatening peace and
security on our planet.

Could anyone be unaware of the fact that the key to major political
decisions is in the hands of big business, which determines its nature
and direction. It was precisely on its instructions that a drastic turn
was taken in U.S. policy at the beginning of the 1980s toward the arms
race and preparations for thermonuclear warfare. As we know, the
American ruling class was then in a difficult situation. Growing economic difficulties and social unrest within the country were added to
the weakened foundations of the political system, which had been so
clearly manifested in the Watergate scandal. In the international arena,
adding to the shameful defeat in Vietnam, factors alarming to Washington developed, such as the growing aspiration of the liberated
countries to reject the path of economic colonialism and the further

strengthening of the positions of world socialism. The inability or, rather, the unwillingness of the power of the rich to find a solution to the situation through the adoption of a sensible approach to present-day realities, triggered adventuristic and hegemonistic aspirations among the most aggressive circles of American imperialism which intended to resolve all its problems through military power.

Such a drastic political turn required an ideological cover, a justification in the eyes of the American and global public of the thoughtless course which led to aggravated confrontation and nuclear catastrophe. This was the objective of an extensive propaganda campaign which was mounted, in which the tone was set by a variety of reactionary organizations which engaged in active efforts by intensifying chauvinistic, conservative and militaristic feelings in the country. Despite all their variety and dissimilarity, the attack mounted on détente, fierce anti-Sovietism and hegemonism became their rallying flag.

One American organization, which seemed to represent the extreme in adventurism, notably stood out on the propaganda field and in the political arena. Its very name was alarming—"The Committee on the Present Danger." It was just about the first in the United States to raise the slogan of pitting the positive trends of the age against the tremendous military machine of American imperialism. The members of the committee became the leading propaganda spokesmen for the forces of reaction and militarism. Finally and decisively, it was precisely the members of the committee, after many years of siege, (that) were able to achieve a mass breakthrough to the peaks of official power in the United States. *The New York Times* wrote, 1 year after the electoral victory of the present Republican administration that "the 'Committee on the Present Danger,' which was created 5 years ago, directed into Reagan's administration 32 of its 182 members in order to achieve a firm position against the Soviet Union. . . . The best known and most influential of the former committee members is, naturally, Ronald Reagan. However, committee members were appointed also to the highest positions in the government. This is literally the equivalent of a seizure of the national security system in the country."

In this context, naturally, the "Committee on the Present Danger" is of particular interest. How was one of the largest "hawkish" nests in the United States created? How were its members trained? What means are they using now in casting a sinister shadow on international relations? The answers to such questions largely help us to understand the origin, nature and direction of activities in the United States of the forces of antidétente most threatening to the cause of peace.

### How They Started

The line from which the United States began to reorganize the forces which had become deeply entrenched in the cold war was the year 1974, when a group which described itself as the "Coalition for a Democratic Society," fired the first volley for effect at détente. It had brought together a handful of American "intellectuals" sharing openly right-wing views (hence their subsequent renaming as "neoconservatives"). They included the journalist N. Podhoretz, R. Perle, an aide to Senator H. Jackson ("the senator from Boeing"), E. Rostow, one of the initiators of the escalation of U.S. aggression in Vietnam, J. Kirkpatrick, Georgetown University professor, and some others. The starting point of the "crusade" against the USSR they preached, was the thesis of "ideological incompatibility." Hence the organizational conclusion of the inexpediency and undesirability of peaceful coexistence with socialism. These were precisely the prerequisites on which the group prepared and published at that time, under Rostow's guidance, a pamphlet entitled "Pursuit of Détente." It was described as an "attack of the very idea that an end to the cold war could be made."

The alliance between the ideologues and theoreticians of anti-détente, on the one hand, and the Pentagon's practitioners of the "hot war" was the next step. A secret conference was held in the underground headquarters of the U.S. Strategic Air Command in Omaha, Nebraska, in 1975. "This was the first time," recalled subsequently one of its participants, "that such a varied and heterogeneous group of experts had met on such a level of secrecy. . . ." What specifically was discussed? "The relative decrease" of the U.S. defense budget during the period of détente was "alarming," for which reason Pentagon appropriations had to be increased urgently and the U.S.-NATO allies had to be urged on. "As we said and reassured ourselves," the participant in the meeting noted, "the U.S. military forces would soon have an excellent new bomber in the B-1; the Pentagon leaders spoke (and soon began to act in that direction) of the accelerated development of the MX missile and the new Trident submarine. We planned the neutron bomb for the European front." It was thus that literally underground a cool planning of a new spiral in the arms race was initiated, aimed at restoring to American imperialism its lost military superiority. The tone at the conference in the concrete-lined bunker was set by P. Nitze, who had held a number of high positions in the Pentagon starting in the 1950s, and had remained in the course of his entire political career an unrepentant, as the American press wrote, "irreconcilable supporter of a hard line" toward the Soviet Union. Once again at the conference Nitze made the threatening statement that eventually the Soviet Union would acquire a "potential which would enable it to win a war." Such was his pretext for rejecting the SALT II treaty, because of which, as a sign of protest, 1 year previously, he had openly resigned his membership in the American SALT talks delegation.

It would have seemed that if Nitze was indeed fearful of Soviet superiority, SALT II, which imposed limitations not only on the United States but the USSR, would have been the best means to prevent a similar situation. The entire point, however, was that the opponents of SALT II in the United States had completely different plans. They were described by R. Molander, who was then a member of the U.S. National Security Council. "One month (after his appointment—the author)," Molander writes, "I met the first of a small but quite influential group of people who fiercely opposed SALT for the single reason that it could prevent America from acquiring the opportunity of dealing a first strike at the Soviet Union. I will never forget the way an Air Force colonel lectured me to the effect that we should have used nuclear bombs on the Soviets at the end of the 1940s before they themselves had acquired that weapon. He told me that if SALT were to fail we would soon gain once again the opportunity to use nuclear bombs against them and that this time we should make use of this opportunity."

It is no accident, therefore, that it was precisely SALT II that the oponents of détente made the main target of their counterattack. This treaty made it harder for the more adventuristic forces in the United States to achieve their cherished objective—to unleash a nuclear war on the socialist world.

### Mobilization of Forces

The troubadours of the new cold war round gradually rallied their ranks more and more tightly. A sufficiently strong, although initially small group of U.S. noted individuals developed, which began to hold meetings on a permanent basis. In addition to Rostow and Nitze, it included J. Schlesinger, who had been dismissed by President Ford as defense secretary, for holding excessively militaristic views, even from the president's viewpoint, Texas banker Ch. Walker, former deputy secretary of the treasury in the Nixon administration, California magnate D. Packard, head of the Hewlett-Packard Company and formerly deputy secretary of defense and, finally, H. Fowler, former secretary of the treasury in the Johnson administration. Urging one another on with talks about the "Soviet threat," and planning a new round in the arms race in the United States, they were promoting the creation of a political organization which could launch a frontal attack on détente.

The "Committee on the Present Danger" was created on the initiative of this group in Washington, in November 1976. It was named after an organization which had been set up at the beginning of the 1950s and which, joining the Truman administration, was exerting pressure with a view to increasing military appropriations and had succeeded in tripling them! The leadership and the members of the reborn committee deserve special consideration. Three of its members became co-chairmen. The first of them, D. Packard, was, in addition to his California interests, closely linked to the main powers on Wall Street. He was a member of the international committee of Rockefeller's Chase Manhattan Bank, and one of the directors of Standard Oil of California and Morgan's U.S. Steel. The second co-chairman, H. Fowler, was a partner in the Wall Street brokerage of Goldman-Sachs and a regent of the Morgan-related Carnegie Foundation. Finally, the third co-chairman was L. Kirkland, the treasurer (and currently the head) of the AF of L-CIO, the American trade unions organization. The character of this so-called "defender of the interests of the American working people," is confirmed by the fact that he was a member of the boards of the Rockefeller and Carnegie foundations. E. Rostow became chairman of the executive committee of the new organization, while P. Nitze headed its political research. Incidentally, the latter had spent more than a decade at work at the Dillon-Reed Wall Street brokerage, and was married to the heiress of one of the founders of Rockefeller's Mobil Oil Company.

The study of the initial committee membership (numbering 141 people) showed that two other factions within the ruling class were quite heavily represented, factions which from the very beginning had pioneered the resumption of the cold war—"neoconservative" ideologues and military practitioners. Members of the "think tanks" working on ideological and political problems were heavily represented precisely by "hawks:" Georgetown University (seven members), Stanford (five) and the American Enterprise Institute. In turn, the generals were represented in the committee by illustrious names including two former commanders in chief of NATO forces in Europe, two deputy defense secretaries, a former chairman of the Joint Chiefs of Staff, the chiefs of staff of the Army and Navy, not to mention less important generals.

Furthermore, there was another striking coincidence which distinguished the committee from many other reactionary organizations which were beginning to appear in the United States and, as proved to be the case later, which played a decisive role in the fact that the majority of American leading circles switched to extreme nationalistic and militaristic positions. From the very beginning, the committee represented the extreme right wing of the most important operational center of the largest transoceanic magnates influencing U.S. foreign policy—the New York Council on Foreign Relations.

In the 1970s, as before, the members of the council, which was supported by the Eastern Seaboard groups of the American financial oligarchy, the Rockefeller, Morgan and Ford groups above all, had remained the backbone of all new political organizations of American business. Thus, the leading organ (the "Policy Formulation Committee"), which was created in 1972 by the "Business Round Table" organization, which rallied the heads of the 200 largest American companies, had half its members come from the Council on Foreign Relations. Sixty percent of the American membership of the so-called Trilateral Commission, which had been established above all through the efforts of the Rockefellers in 1972, were also council members. That is why it is no accident but quite natural that 40 percent of the membership and two-thirds of the leadership of the "Committee on the Present Danger," in 1976, were also its members.

It is true that the "Business Round Table" dealt mainly with American domestic political and economic problems. In a few years the Trilateral Commission became the main instrument of big business in U.S. foreign policy. Adding to the slogan of "cooperation" with the Soviet Union the words "and competition," it gave the impetus for withdrawal from détente. However, under those circumstances, given its open reliance on direct confrontation with the socialist world, the "Committee on the Present Danger" was nevertheless way ahead. At that time, as *The New York Times* said, such a slogan was still a "cry in the wilderness," in terms of the predominant mood of the majority of U.S. ruling circles. Characteristically, the committee was created not "from above"—under the guidance of the Council on Foreign Relations, as had been the case with the Trilateral Commission, but "from below," and included no more than about 3 percent of the council's membership. Nevertheless, the views of the "Committee on the Present Danger" began to metastacize ever more dangerously.

### The Cancer Grows

Having gathered strength, the "Committee on the Present Danger" engaged in tempestuous efforts in inflating the "psychological warfare" against the Soviet Union. Some of its pamphlets (such as "What Is the Soviet Union Up To?") were openly aimed at fanning militaristic hysteria in the United States. Others (such as "Is America Becoming No 2?") aimed at the base nationalistic feelings of the American petit bourgeois. The core of the committee's political program, and its No. 1 target was to undermine the very possibility of the conclusion of the SALT II treaty. In pursuit of nuclear superiority, the "hawks" hoped to blast the main foundation for normalizing relations between the USSR and the United States, thus causing détente irreparable damage.

On the eve of the 1976 presidential elections the "Committee on the Present Danger" opposed President Ford's reelection, considering his program excessively moderate. In a letter to Schlesinger, dated May 1976, Rostow openly counseled pitting Reagan against Ford and drafting for his benefit "the base of a possible speech." However, the hope of promoting Reagan as the official Republican candidate for the presidency was not to be. After Carter's victory a seemingly dark period came for the committee. A committee leadership delegation, which had visited Carter in August 1977, had been "despondent" as the press noted because of the president's arguments that U.S. public opinion would not support increased military expenditures.

At that point the Committee on the Present Danger changed its tactics, converting to an extensive systematic campaign to promote its views, encouraging nationalistic and conservative feelings. It focused particular efforts on changing the very way of thinking in the main foreign policy "brain center" of the U.S. ruling class—the Council on Foreign Relations out of which, strictly speaking, it had come. Nitze, Pipes, Perle, Cline, Zumwalt and other committee members frequently spoke at council meetings mainly on Soviet (or, rather, anti-Soviet) topics. They were joined by previously silent members of the "related" committee of the Center for International and Strategic Studies of Georgetown University—Crocker, Hyland and others.

During the period of détente the strategic concept held by the Council on Foreign Relations was the doctrine of "world order." Its most important component was the idea that the preservation of international peace and security was impossible without a certain cooperation with the Soviet Union. The effort to forecast international events for a 10- to 15-year period ("Project for the '80s"), undertaken by the council in the mid-1970s, on that basis, was also relatively well-weighed. However, common sense and sensible voices became increasingly weak until 1979, when the project was declared "naive" and "insufficiently grounded in political realities." The problems of ideological justification of the new round in the arms race and the hardening of the policy "from a position of strength" found their place on the council's agenda.

Under those circumstances the Committee on the Present Danger became energized even further. In July 1980 a delegation of leading committee members visited Reagan, who had become by then the official Republican party candidate. As the American press wrote, "he was told that the country must engage in extensive military rearmament and undertake to resume the policy of containment of the Soviet Union." After Reagan had won the elections, as an American journalist wrote, "the view of the Committee on the Present Danger on the subject of peace seemed to become national policy." Actually, it did not merely seem that way.

## The Hour Struck

The point was not only that committee member Reagan had become president of the United States. Several dozen committee members showed up in the highest governmental positions. They rapidly became part of the fabric of institutions which made key foreign political decisions and assumed their effective control. A study of the administrative positions they hold indicates that the members of the Committee on the Present Danger assumed control over the basic mechanisms related to the implementation by American imperialism in the international arena of a policy of force and intervention in the internal affairs of other countries and government authorities the domination of which presented them with great opportunities to block within the administration the very possibility of taking steps toward peace, cooperation and disarmament.

The U.S. National Security Council, the Pentagon and the CIA were the main bases of the brigade of fierce anti-Soviets. R. Allen was the first to take over the National Security Council, while R. Pipes became the council's chief expert on problems related to the Soviet Union. G. Kemp, another committee member, was put in charge of handling U.S. Middle East policy.

Members of the Committee on the Present Danger took over equally important positions in the Pentagon. F. Iklé became deputy secretary of defense for planning policy and took as his assistant R. Stilwell, another committee member. R. Perle became deputy secretary of defense for problems of "international security." Committee member J. Lehman became secretary of the navy, while A. Hoeber became assistant secretary of defense for scientific research. Finally, W. Casey, another committee member, became head of the CIA, while eight other members accounted for almost one-half of the consultative authority under the U.S. president on problems of foreign intelligence.

The concentrated takeover by committee members of leading positions related to disarmament talks blocked tightly possibilities of achieving any major progress whatsoever in this area. E. Rostow became director of the Arms Control and Disarmament Agency, while J. Douglas became his deputy. W. Van Cleave was promoted chairman of the committee advising the agency. In turn, Nitze was appointed U.S. representative to the Soviet-American talks on medium-range nuclear missiles in Europe. Even such a newspaper as *The New York Times* was forced to note that "virtually every senior official in the administration, dealing with limiting strategic armaments, is an opponent of the 1979 treaty," i.e., of SALT II. The noted American historian A. Schlesinger, former adviser to President Kennedy, exclaimed on this subject that "allowing Rostow and Nitze to discuss armament control with the Russians—my God! It is like sending someone suffering from typhoid fever to fight the epidemic!" That same Rostow openly stated after his appointment that the main thing for the United States is "the total resumption of the policy of containment," and that limiting armaments in general would play a "secondary role."

Finally, committee members took over the most important international channels whose function, strictly speaking, was to smooth clashes between countries and promote mutual cooperation. J. Kirkpatrick became permanent U.S. delegate to the United Nations, while K. Adelman became her senior deputy. M. Novak became the U.S. representative to the UN Human Rights Commission. M. Kampelman was appointed representative to the Madrid talks on the implementation of the Helsinki accords. Immediately following their appointments, these U.S. officials mounted an unrestrained campaign of slander and a real "witch hunt" directed above all against the USSR and other socialist countries.

The members of the Committee on the Present Danger do not have in the least a monopoly on the initiative of generating cold war waves within the Republican administration. Those around them share their overall spirit. However, even under these circumstances the committee members stand out with their extremist views. Their "personal" contribution to the administration's policy is, specifically, their aspiration to burn all bridges of cooperation between East and West and urge on the United States into a condition of "permanent war" against the Soviet Union.

### Trade as a Club

The advent of the Reagan administration to power marked the triumph of reliance on force not only in foreign policy but in an area in which one might think practical interests of American business would prevail. We are referring to foreign economic relations between the

United States and the socialist countries, the USSR above all. The journal FOREIGN AFFAIRS openly noted at the beginning of 1982 that a "virtually complete turn" had taken place in the U.S. approach to trade with the Soviet Union. Whereas previously, according to the journal, the United States considered such trade "one of the keys if not the main key to reaching a policy of agreement with Moscow," now it is considered as a means for the adoption of "punitive sanctions." As was to be expected, the committee members were among the pioneers and most active participants in promoting this "turn."

Starting in the autumn of 1978 the Council on Foreign Relations set up a special group to study nominally the role of the Soviet Union in world economics. "The reinterpretation of the problem of trade and payments" involving the USSR was the more prosaic topic discussed at one of its meetings. The meaning of the group's activities became clear when one of its participants, R. Vernon, published in the summer of 1979 in the journal FOREIGN AFFAIRS, an article symbolically entitled "Brittle Foundations of East-West Trade." In calling for the breaking of trade relations, the author formulated as a justification the thesis to the effect that the Soviet Union received from such trade "disproportional" benefits, for the "social profit" of the USSR is considerably higher than the "private profit" of the individual American companies which, furthermore, compete against each other, while the USSR can pursue a centralized line. It is easy to note that the Soviet Union was thus "accused" of possessing advantages stemming from its socialist social system and foreign trade monopoly.

Other studies of East-West trade were published in the United States, quite clearly revealing the hopes of American imperialism of using, among others, Soviet imports of American technology for the purpose of undermining the Soviet economy. In their view, Soviet imports of such technology could "be used as crutches on which the patient will become dependent to such an extent that he would be unable to reject them and walk without their help." However, the Soviet Union did not fall into this dangerous trap. This was yet another reason for the conclusion that trade with the Soviet Union had to be ended.

Awareness of their own helplessness triggered increasing anger in the respective U.S. circles, and only after a few months in power the Reagan administration organized the undermining of trade with the Soviet Union on a planned basis. However, its initial attempt to force the U.S. allies as well to convert trade and economic relations with the USSR into a cold war weapon, made at the summit conference of seven Western countries in Ottawa, in July 1981, was unsuccessful. Incidentally, at the meeting held by the U.S. National Security Council, preceding that in Ottawa, the Pentagon suggested that naked pressure be exerted on the allies to make them follow in Washington's fairway. The means suggested were so unceremonious as to embarrass most of those attending the session. The only ones among them who supported the Pentagon line in full were W. Casey and J. Kirkpatrick, i.e., two members of the Committee on the Present Danger.

The Ottawa failure did not disturb the American administration, which undertook to pressure its allies. In January 1982 a special

American delegation was sent to Western Europe with the task of wrecking East-West trade. It was headed by J. Buckley, while F. Iklé was its second most influential member. The Buckley-Iklé delegation made another trip to the Western European capitals in March 1982, this time to promote "possible new economic sanctions" against the Soviet Union. It was actually a question of blocking the laying of the Urengoy-Western Europe gas pipeline and stopping Western credit to the USSR. The shameless overseas pressure and blackmail failed. The Western European countries, interested in the building of the pipeline, rejected the efforts of the American administration. The latter had to backtrack and reluctantly to lift the "sanctions." Washington suffered a major political defeat in this "important strategic problem," as Washington had officially described its subversive action, which was to last for the duration of this century.

The militant anti-Soviet forces within the American administration, however, did not lay down their arms. They are fiercely trying to change the very nature of trade relations between the West and the Soviet Union. Whereas the official slogan of the 1964–1965 World Fair in New York was "Peace Through Trade," the Reagan administration essentially raised the slogan of "Trade-Economic War on the Socialist World."

### A Course of Perpetuating War

A course of "open confrontation" between the United States and the USSR on a global and regional scale became the core of the "new military strategy" of the Reagan administration. However, its structural component is the concept of "active counteraction" with the help of the multivariant use of strategic nuclear weapons. Another one is the concept of "geographic escalation." *The New York Times* notes that the essence of the "geographic" or, as it is also known, "horizontal" escalation concept is the following: "Under the cover of the resurrected nuclear containment weapons, the American armed forces must be ready to fight with conventional weapons in a protracted global conflict." In this respect the strategic doctrine of the Reagan administration is directly indebted to two members of the Committee on the Present Danger holding leading positions in the Pentagon—F. Iklé and J. Lehman. The former was described by *The Washington Post* as the "intellectual sponsor" of the idea of "protracted warfare."

Indeed, as early as the middle of 1980, as adviser to Reagan, the candidate for the presidency, Iklé was the first to formulate the concept that the United States must mandatorily convert the confrontation with the Soviet Union into a "protracted" military conflict, in the course of which it will acquire the possibility and time to organize on a mass basis a war industry output. Iklé emphasized that the United States cannot tolerate a "passive and indifferent attitude toward the political coloring of the world map," but must retain a "superiority in terms of territorial and resource safety" simultaneously "in several parts of the world." Such was the cynical prescription for initiating a power confrontation with the USSR and above all for "bringing order" in the "rear" of American military structures along the entire perimeter of the intended global clash. It was precisely to this effect that the key role, according to Iklé, was to be assumed by the U.S. Navy. It was no accident, therefore, that its new secretary J. Lehman, proclaimed straight off that the United States had to achieve "naval superiority."

The plans of American imperialism for an unrestrained arms race began rapidly to acquire substance. It was proclaimed that the U.S. Navy will be increased by one-third and the number of navy ships raised to 600. In his militaristic excitement Lehman told newsmen that he intended in general to "block the Soviet navy" in order to prevent it from hindering his operations. At the same time, plans were drafted according to which in the first year of war with the Soviet Union the United States ("as in the Korean War") would double or triple its war output and in 3 years ("as in World War II") would increase it by a factor of 8. According to other plans the waging of a "protracted war" on the USSR and world socialism at large would triple the American budget and would channel to this purpose one-half of the country's gross national product.

By the end of 1982 the plan had been divided into three specific stages: "horizontal escalation," "global conflict" and "protracted warfare." According to Pentagon estimates, preparations for its implementation alone required the appropriation of an additional $750 billion to the Reagan administration's already planned unprecedented 5-year military expenditures totaling $1.6 trillion. Such concepts are no longer merely irresponsible. This is not even "teetering on the brink of war." It is an insane gamble on a world war.

### The 'Hawks' Attack

Having made their nest at the peaks of official power in Washington and charted a course of total confrontation with the socialist world, the "hawks" of anti-détente and militarism are zealously seeing to it that with every passing day U.S. policy becomes more aggressive. They are expressing their open discontent at any deviation from this path.

As of the spring of 1981, intensifying their efforts, the members of the Committee on the Present Danger mounted a general offensive within and without the administration for the implementation of their adventuristic plans. R. Perle, for example, openly proclaimed that in relations with the Soviet Union the policy of détente "was a wrong policy and is wrong today and that, in general, this is not our policy." R. Pipes is already calling for practical preparations for nuclear war the likelihood of which, according to him, has reached the 40 percent figure. In addressing a Senate committee, F. Iklé emphasized that increased U.S. defense expenditures must be "considerably greater than is currently proposed by the administration."

The Committee on the Present Danger increased its pressure on the administration from the outside as well. According to E. Rostow, currently the committee's activities are focused not only on keeping the administration along a militaristic course in general, but also to "spank" it "if it deserves it" because of insufficient zeal in this respect. Thus, in March 1982 the committee stated that U.S. military expenditures are barely "minimal," for which reason they should be increased drastically. A decisive step was taken in May. N. Podhoretz published in *The New York Times* a long article entitled "The Torment of Neoconservatives Regarding Reagan's Foreign Policy." It sharply criticized the administration for its failure to succeed in deploying "American ground forces" in the Persian Gulf, had allowed itself to "find itself in a defensive position in Central America" and, above all, for its insufficiently energetic confrontation with the Soviet Union. Proclaiming that the "neoconservatives" find themselves as a result of all this "in a state of virtual political despair," Podhoretz expressed "hope for a miracle"—for the fact that the Reagan administration would "correct" its "errors." Informed of the article, President Reagan personally telephoned the author to assure him that the American policy was not one of détente. Actually, this was merely the beginning of a new, dangerous turn in the course pursued by official Washington under the pressure of extremist forces. In London on 8 June and in the United Nations on 17 June the U.S. President delivered speeches the main line of which was unrestrained anti-Sovietism.

However, even this did not satisfy the hawks. They immediately undertook to exert further pressure on the administration. Secretary of State A. Haig became one of their targets. In the middle of June 1982 G. Will published in *Newsweek* on the need to fight "creeping Haigism." On 18 June a decisive meeting between Haig and representatives of right-wing forces took place in Washington. It was attended not only by leaders of the "neoconservatives" and members of the Committee on the Present Danger (N. Podhoretz, I. Christol, M. Novak) but also by one of the leaders of the extreme right, R. Viguerie. According to press reports, a "unanimous agreement" was reached at the meeting: Haig was to go. He resigned 1 week later. It is noteworthy that he was replaced by Shultz, one of the founders of the Committee on the Present Danger, who appointed as his deputy another committee member, A. Wallis.

However, the facts prove that the committee members themselves are not entirely unanimous on problems of U.S. foreign policy. This was clearly manifested by the resignation of E. Rostow from the position of director of the Disarmament Control Agency, who was one of the main initiators of the creation of the committee.

The current situation, marked by the fact that the power in the United States is in the hands of circles the unrestrained adventurism of which, it would seem, should make inadmissible the very idea of their running the leading capitalist power, is not only dangerous but profoundly unnatural in the nuclear century. For understandable reasons, the ideals of cannibals cannot attract willing supporters. It is becoming increasingly clear to the simple Americans that the only "prospect" offered by the pathological anti-Soviets is the conflagration of an annihilating nuclear conflict. The suicidal juggling with the possibility of unleashing a nuclear war is triggering an opposite effect, creating concern and condemnation among broad American circles. As the noted American observer J. Reston has pointed out, against this back-ground "important discussions" on a national scale have begun in the United States, unlike anything similar during at least the past 50 years.

The essence of the debate which is currently under way in the United States is whether common sense or muscle power, consolidation of peace or nuclear catastrophe will prevail. For the first time in the history of that country, millions of people are participating in the debate. The sympathy of the rank-and-file Americans is not on the side of the members of the administration who are dangling nuclear bombs over their heads and over the entire world.

# INDEX

# ABOUT THE EDITOR

**Charles Tyroler, II** has been Director of the Committee on the Present Danger (CPD) since its founding in 1976. He served in President Truman's Administration as Director of Manpower Supply, Department of Defense, under Secretaries Marshall and Lovett. Mr. Tyroler currently serves as one of three members of the President's Intelligence Oversight Board.

**Ambassador Max M. Kampelman** (who has written the Introduction) has served Presidents Carter and Reagan as Chairman, U.S. Delegation to the Conference on Security and Cooperation in Europe (CSCE) and is a partner in the Washington law firm of Fried, Frank, Haris, Shriver, and Kampelman. Ambassador Kampelman earlier served as Legislative Counsel to Senator Hubert Humphrey and has been the General Counsel and a member of the Board of Directors of the CPD since its founding.